International **Business**

International **Business**

Theory and Practice

Ehud **Menipaz** & Amit **Menipaz**

SAGE www.sagepublications.com
Los Angeles • London • New Delhi • Singapore • Washington DC

Originally published in 2011 by

SAGE www.sagepublications.com
Los Angeles • London • New Delhi • Singapore • Washington DC

This South Asia edition published in 2012 by

SAGE Publications India Pvt Ltd
B1/I-1 Mohan Cooperative Industrial Area
Mathura Road
New Delhi 110 044, India

Published by Vivek Mehra for SAGE Publications India Pvt Ltd and printed at Saurabh Printers Pvt Ltd.

ISBN: 978-81-321-1036-1 (PB)

To our family

CONTENTS

PREFACE

Welcome to the first edition of *International Business: Theory and Practice*. This book is a result of a journey into seminal and current theoretical paradigms and management practices in international business. An effort has been made to present the most current, accessible, and practically oriented book in international business, geared toward the student and the practicing executive alike.

The beginning of the 21st century was marked by global economic adjustments, and has been characterized by an intense interest in the theories of international business as well as the development and enhancement of practices in international and global business management. *International Business: Theory and Practice* brings theoretical thinking to bear on real-world practices by introducing the reader to key international business topics and providing ample examples. Focusing on international, national, and regional environments, and the businesses and organizations within these contexts, *International Business: Theory and Practice* considers all relevant issues, including corporate social responsibility, business ethics, global strategy, international supply chains, entrepreneurship, and digital technology.

To help the reader understand these issues and their relevance to business practices, the book includes insights from global managers and entrepreneurs. The text and the supporting material are written so that they may be used in an introductory course at either the undergraduate or graduate level. The text provides the instructor with the flexibility to complement the material with added readings and case studies to reflect the needs of the intended audience and keep the material current.

The Structure of the Book

The book presents a set of concepts, frameworks, and paradigms that are necessary tools for the student of international business or the executive who operates in the international arena and is interested in learning more about it. The book is based on the premise that an executive may (and should) plan, organize, design, operate, and control a business enterprise with the purpose of succeeding in international business ventures. The concepts contained in the text are appropriate for both large multinational enterprises (MNEs) as well for small- and medium-size enterprises (SMEs).

Part One introduces the reader to the international business environment (Chapter 1), including the multinational enterprise and the important concepts of corporate citizenship, social responsibility, and ethics (Chapter 2).

Part Two focuses on the national and regional business environment, including the cultural context of international business (Chapter 3), the political and legal environments (Chapter 4), and economic systems and international trade (Chapter 5). An understanding of these environments and systems is most important as they define the drivers of international trade in goods and services. It has been scientifically proven that these environments impact on business results and many strategic decisions, such as international alliances, mergers, and acquisitions, must include careful consideration of these issues.

Part Three further explores the issue of international trade, capital investment, and regionalization, including foreign direct investment and the location of regional headquarters (Chapter 6), international trade and regional integration (Chapter 7), and the international financial system (Chapter 8). This latter chapter deals with the global monetary system, foreign exchange markets, and financial instruments.

The next two parts build on the concepts discussed earlier in the book and present a framework for international business strategy and international management.

Part Four presents the essentials of international business strategy, including internal and external environmental assessment, and structuring internationally sound business goals and objectives (Chapter 9). It also covers sustainability and growth strategies in international business, such as global alliances, joint ventures, and mergers and acquisitions (M&As) (Chapter 10).

Part Five deals with international management organizational functions, such as global technology management (Chapter 11), global human resources management (Chapter 12), international financial management (Chapter 13), global operations and supply chain management (Chapter 14), global marketing, sales, and after sale services and support (Chapter 15), and international accounting and taxation (Chapter 16).

It should be noted that the chapters are constructed so as to allow some overlap. The various concepts are presented through examples and business case studies. An effort is made to present decisions in the context of a particular country and industry. The book also recognizes and provides coverage of commercial ventures in growth industries, such as digital products and services, biotechnology, and nanotechnology. Since many businesses today strive for early internationalization, a further feature of the book is the introduction of concepts that are useful for the aspiring global entrepreneur and executive.

It is a basic premise of the book that the reader should be aware of the dynamic and changing environment of international business and, thus, be ready to identify, early on, evolving trends and changes, and be familiar with ways and means to adjust MNEs to these changes.

It is further noted that the world is experiencing a global economic crisis creating innovative, significant, and exciting opportunities. These changes involve business management paradigms and practices on the one hand and, on the other hand, new paradigms for corporate governance, public oversight and scrutiny, organizational transparency, environmental sustainability and accountability, and voluntary professional standards. The book recognizes the world economic crisis and provides paradigms that may survive the crisis.

The ideas contained in the book represent the state of the art and are based on the most current material available. Our goal is to ensure that the executive or business owner who is familiar with the material contained in this book will be able to make informed decisions regarding international business opportunities for both domestic and international enterprises.

Students will benefit from *International Business: Theory and Practice* in several ways. First, the book presents an integrative view of the international business environment and international management functions. It leads the student from the global environmental essentials, through international corporate strategy to international management functions in a structured way. Second, the book is written from an international point of view from the outset and is based on theories and cases drawn from virtually all continents and trade regions. In bringing a truly global approach to bear, the authors have drawn upon scientific writings as well as professional reports and real-life case histories. Third, the theories and paradigms are explained in terms that are geared towards students taking the core academic courses in international business. The delivery is straightforward in order to enhance and simplify the learning process. Fourth, the book presents a current view of international business, in an exciting and challenging way, pointing out opportunities for internationalization in emerging industries, such as digital commerce, biotechnology, and "green" technologies. Fifth, each chapter contains a country focus, providing a comparative overview of national business characteristics.

Executives will benefit from *International Business: Theory and Practice* in a number of ways. First, the book lays out the foundations of international business, rigorously explaining terms and paradigms that are at the basis of international commerce. Second, the book points out new trends and shifting methodologies which are at the forefront of management thinking and reflect the changing management practices resulting from the world economic crisis. Third, the book relates to business cases drawn from a variety of industries and may serve as a benchmark as well as a guide to best practices for the international, or would-be-international, management executive. Fourth, the book maps out the economic and environmental essentials of various countries around the world, providing business executives with the initial information required to decide on the next market to be penetrated, the location for the next regional headquarters to be set up, or the location of the next manufacturing facility to be built. Of particular relevance are the comparative country profiles contained at the end of each chapter. These may assist the executive in identifying the next foreign market to enter or the next country in which to establish an operation.

Lecturers will benefit from *International Business: Theory and Practice* in a number of ways. First, the book provides the current paradigms and theories regarding international business, bringing the reader up to date on the issues that are deemed necessary by most academic institutions. Second, the book provides an overview of international business using ample examples of real international business cases and demonstrating the use of the methodologies described. Third, the book provides insight into topics promoted in curricula developed in business schools around the world, such as social responsibility, the role of technology in international business, and entrepreneurship. Fourth, the book has a companion website, including a lecture resources area, which is continuously kept current. The *lecturer resources area* is password-protected and only lecturers adopting the textbook will have access to the material within it. The lecturer resources area contains material that lecturers may use in order to support their teaching, such as an Instructor's Manual, PowerPoint presentations, and links to relevant academic journals and other websites. *The Instructor's Manual* includes: a general introduction on how to use the book, sample syllabi for courses and seminars, sample answers to the questions or exercises within the book, suggested solutions or approaches to the questions listed at the end of any case studies within the book, small group projects, lists of potential seminar topics for discussion, multiple choice and/or essay questions with sample answers, examination questions with sample answers, recommendations regarding videos, and other relevant information. *PowerPoint presentations* for easy reproduction of each chapter are available. The presentations are structured in such a way that they can guide the lecturer through a lesson. The PowerPoint presentations include bullet points highlighting the main issues, definitions of key terms, charts, and figures. Recommendations on *videos and case studies* are available, as well as updates on some of the material published in the book.

The *student resources* area of the website contains a variety of resources that students can use when preparing for an exam or when writing an essay. This area includes a brief *introduction to the book* and how it can best be used to maximize learning as well as key learning outcomes for each chapter. This section includes a *test bank* to encourage self-study, *online readings* through free electronic access to a selection of articles published in SAGE journals and books. It should be noted that all SAGE companion websites include a *standard study skills* section for students.

Acknowledgments

We are grateful for the support, suggestions, ideas, and reviews provided by many executives, academics, consultants, and students around the world throughout the development of the first edition of *International Business: Theory and Practice*. The resulting manuscript reflects the creative suggestions, innovative pedagogy, and identified needs of students, lecturers, and executives alike.

We are indebted to the dedicated editors and staff of SAGE Publications, who have been supportive and extremely helpful in bringing our manuscript to book form. Special thanks are owed to Delia Martinez Alfonso, Senior Editor; Natalie Aguilera, Commissioning Editor; Kiren Shoman, Associate Director, Books Editorial; Assistant Editors Anne Summers and Clare Wells; Alana Clogan, Editorial Assistant; Vanessa Harwood, Production Editorial Manager; and Ben Sherwood, Marketing Manager.

We are deeply grateful for the support and encouragement of our family who had the patience to endure our commitment of time to this project at the expense of precious quality time with them.

In conclusion, we trust that *International Business: Theory and Practice* reflects the current issues that are of importance to students, lecturers, and practicing and aspiring international executives. It provides a solid introduction to the essential issues in international business and allows for further study of those issues. As in any text of this kind, it draws upon and presents theories, paradigms, and cases that have been developed over several decades by many thought leaders, academics, and executives. Every effort has been made to provide appropriate citations and references. If any omissions or errors are identified by the readers, we will be grateful to have them called to our attention so that they can be duly rectified.

Ehud Menipaz
Amit Menipaz

New York, NY
February 2011

ABOUT THE AUTHORS

Ehud Menipaz

Currently a visiting scholar at the Leonard N. Stern School of Business, New York University, Ehud Menipaz is the Solomon & Abraham Krok Chaired Professor of Entrepreneurial Management and the Founding Chair of the Ira Center for Business, Technology & Society at Ben Gurion University, Israel. He is a former senior partner with Ernst & Young International, engaged with assignments in the private and public sectors. Ehud specializes in international business management and functional derivatives. He holds a BSc in Industrial Engineering and Management, an MSc in Operations Research, an MBA in Finance, and a PhD in Management. His articles have appeared in *The European Journal of Operations Research*, *International Journal of Production Research*, *International Institute of Electrical and Electronic Engineers Transactions*, *Journal of Productivity and Quality*, *International Journal of Computers and Simulation*, *Management Decisions*, *Journal of Global Marketing*, *International Journal of Business Performance Management*. His interest in operational systems has led to several manuscripts in that area, including *Essentials of Production and Operations Management,* published concurrently in the USA, England, Japan, New Zealand, and Singapore by Prentice Hall. He has addressed students, faculty and executives in the USA, Canada, the Far East, Europe, South America, and Africa. He has been involved in conceiving, and has been a member of the organizing committee and chairman of several international scientific conferences, including "The First Regional Conference on Forging Regional Cooperation in the Mediterranean Basin" and "The International Conference of Innovation and Logistics," all resulting in published proceedings. He serves as a referee and an associate editor for a number of international scientific journals, including the *International Journal of Corporate Governance* and he is a national team leader of the Global Entrepreneurship Monitor (GEM) research program. He is a member of the

Strategic Management Society, the Academy of Management, and the Association of International Business. Combining scientific work with community involvement, Ehud sponsors entrepreneurship education programs associated with the Junior Achievement Award worldwide and has served as a director and CEO of several organizations. He is married, has three children and four grandchildren, and enjoys piano playing, downhill skiing, and tennis.

Amit Menipaz

Amit Menipaz has been involved in international business as an entrepreneur, management consultant, and a senior executive for multinational enterprises across North America, China, Europe, and the Middle East. He currently serves as Country Manager for eBay, a leader in global e-commerce. A graduate of the University of Toronto, Canada, in Industrial Engineering and Management, he holds an MBA from INSEAD, Fontainebleau, France. As an entrepreneur, he co-founded a web content management company in North America. As a management consultant he has worked for both Deloitte Touche and A.T. Kearney in North America and Western Europe. In this capacity he worked with multinational enterprises on benchmarking, reengineering, knowledge management, systems selection, and merger and acquisition planning across North America. He oversaw the launch of a number of hi-tech and telecommunication start-ups across Western Europe during the internet boom at the turn of the century. For six years Amit ran a partnership with Hutchison Whampoa of Hong Kong, leveraging Israeli technologies together with European designers and Chinese manufacturers to develop innovative consumer electronics and telecommunications products for markets in Europe and the USA. Having worked at both the headquarters and overseas subsidiaries of multinational enterprises, managing the opening and closing of regional and country headquarters, and launching both consumer and internet products into various geographic markets—Amit brings a unique blend of experience, practical insights, and contemporary examples that help link business theories with the hands-on practice of managing an international business day-to-day. Amit is married, has two children, and enjoys traveling, learning new languages, music, reading, tennis, skiing, and Latin dancing.

GUIDED TOUR

Welcome to the guided tour of *International Business: Theory and Practice*. This tour will take you through the main sections and special features in the text.

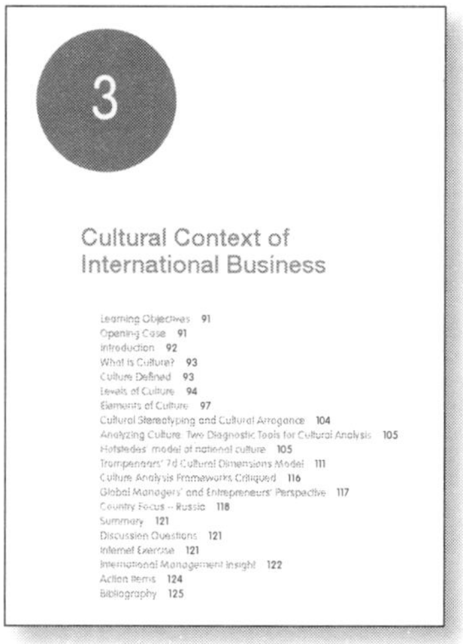

A clear list of contents is provided for each chapter.

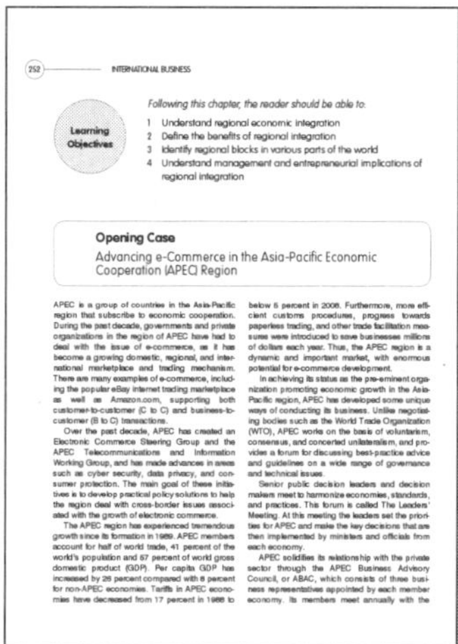

Learning objectives: Readers are given an outline of what they should be able to do by the end of each chapter, and **Opening cases** present the topic for each chapter within a real-life context.

Introduction: The introduction provides the overall framework for each chapter.

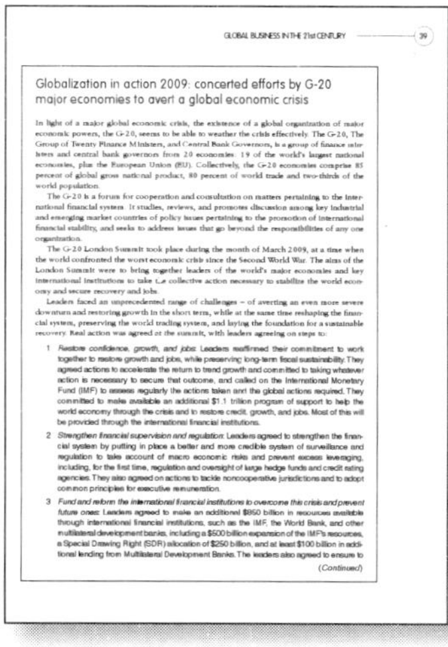
GLOBAL BUSINESS IN THE 21st CENTURY 39

Globalization in action 2009: concerted efforts by G-20 major economies to avert a global economic crisis

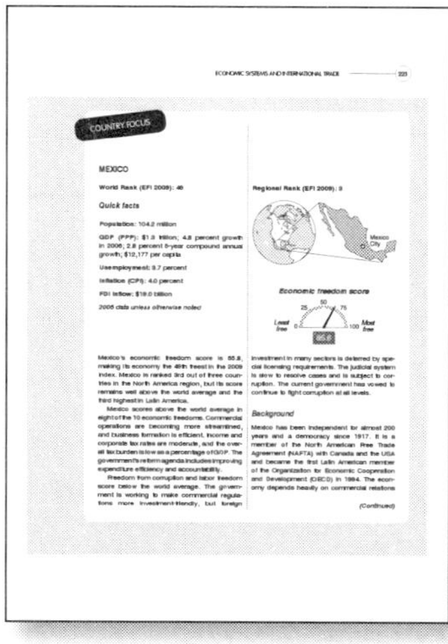
ECONOMIC SYSTEMS AND INTERNATIONAL TRADE

COUNTRY FOCUS

MEXICO

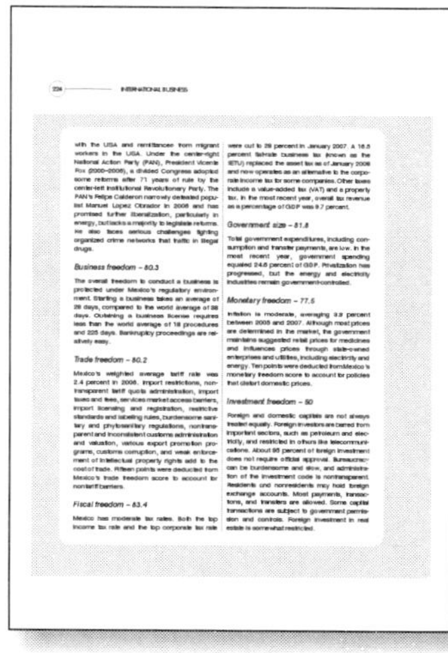

Boxes: Boxes provide further examples of the key themes in international business in action.

Country focus: The economies of different countries are looked at in depth, including trade freedom, government size, and property rights.

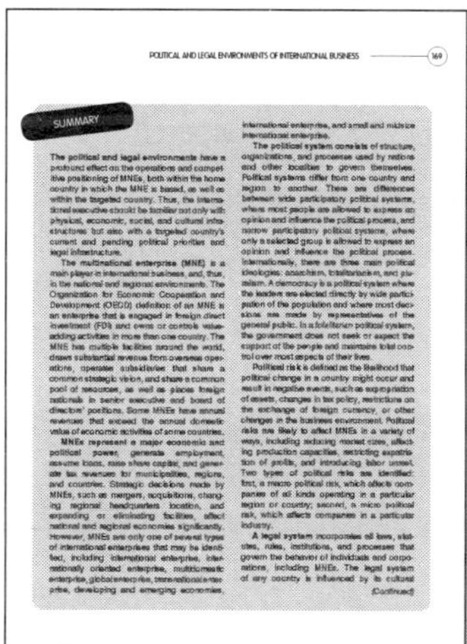
POLITICAL AND LEGAL ENVIRONMENTS OF INTERNATIONAL BUSINESS

SUMMARY

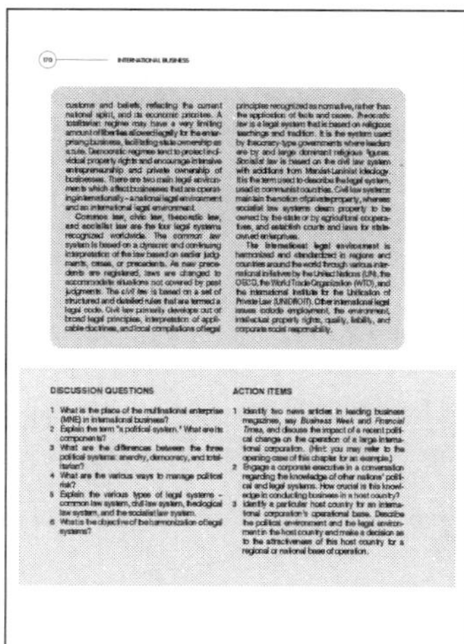
INTERNATIONAL BUSINESS

DISCUSSION QUESTIONS

ACTION ITEMS

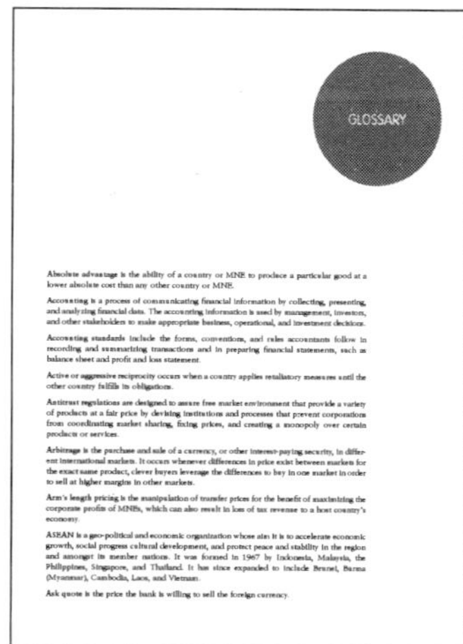
GLOSSARY

Chapter summary: The main concepts and issues in each chapter. Followed by **Discussion questions:** Questions are provided to encourage you to explore what you have learnt, *and* **Action items:** Further activities for students promote more discussion and independent learning.

Glossary: A quick reference of concise definitions and key terms.

COMPANION WEBSITE

Be sure to visit the companion website at http://www.sagepub.co.uk/**menipaz** to find a range of teaching and learning materials for both lecturers and students, including the following:

For lecturers:

- **Instructor's manual**: Contains materials to support lecturer's seminar and class teaching, including teaching notes, sample answers to exercises within the textbook, and seminar topics for discussion.
- **PowerPoint slides**: PowerPoint slides highlighting the main issues in each chapter.

For students:

- **Full-text journal articles**: Full access to selected SAGE journal articles provides students with a deeper understanding of the topics in each chapter.
- **Glossary**: A glossary of key terms and definitions is available online.
- **Links to relevant websites**: Direct links to relevant websites for each chapter are provided.
- **Study Skills:** This bank of downloadable chapters from existing SAGE books is packed with ideas to aid effective study.

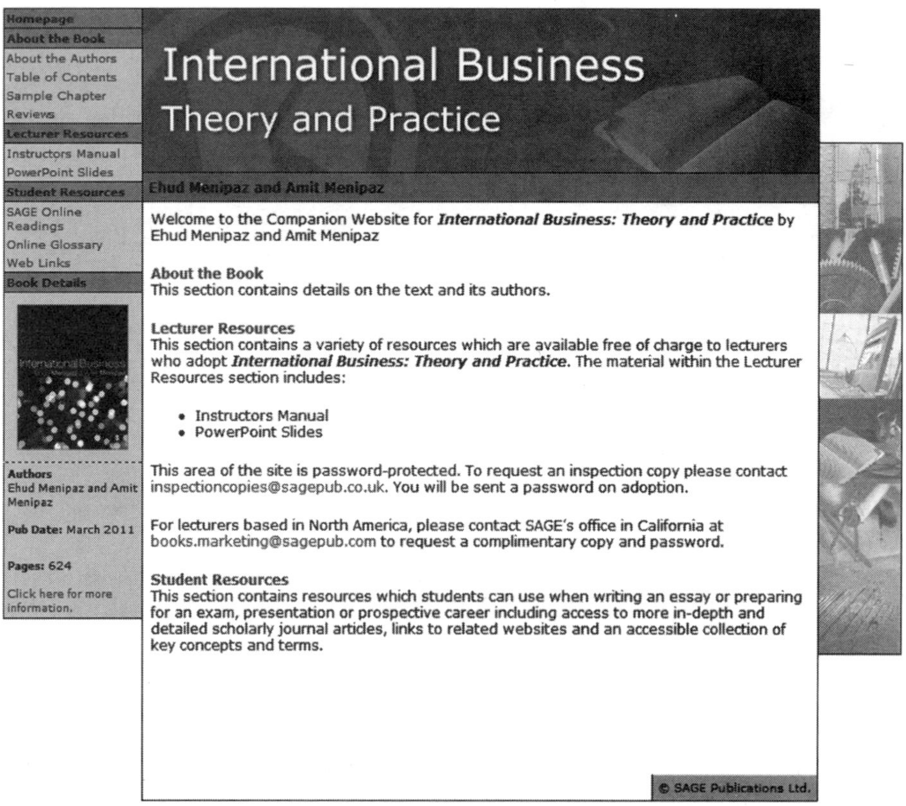

PART 1

Introduction to International Business Environment

1

Global Business in the 21st Century

Learning Objectives

Following this chapter, the reader should be able to:

1. Describe the globalization phenomenon and processes
2. Appreciate its significance to business executives
3. Identify the multinational enterprise and its role
4. Be able to assess and apply frameworks of globalization

Opening Case
The Telecommunication Industry: Success in Global Business

Most if not all the telecommunication companies have gone global. For some of these companies, global operations is a key for success. At the same time, organizing properly to uncover the global business potential is a must. Take for example Nokia Corporation (www.nokia.com). Nokia is a global telecommunications company that during the last 15 years went from a near-bankrupt conglomerate to a global leader in cell phones (mobile telephones), delivering almost 30 percent annual compound growth in revenues during the turn of the century while changing most of its product lines. By the beginning of the 21st century, Nokia had the highest margins in the cell phone industry, a negative debt–equity ratio, the most recognized nonUS brand in the world, Europe's highest market share, a presence in 140 countries, and unique corporate structures, processes and culture that gave it the feel of "a small company soul in a big corporate body." Along with growth in size and diversity, however, came growth in complexity: Nokia had to develop multiple businesses and technologies (all the while facing great technological uncertainties like the convergence of mobile telephony and the Internet and the growing mobile commerce applications), and had to manage a growing network of alliances and a number of acquisitions, mostly in the USA. Clearly, Nokia faced key managerial issues as it considered how to address the current challenges while maintaining unique corporate values and workplace practices that made it possible to execute in a most cost and operationally efficient manner while continuing to innovate.

The old landscape

Nokia is indeed part of the globalized telecommunication industry. This was not the case earlier on. During the last part of the 20th century, telecommunications national markets around the world were highly centralized. In most nations, there was a dominant telecommunications provider – AT&T in the United States, British Telecom in Britain, Deutsche Telekom in Germany, NTT in Japan, and Telebras in Brazil. The provider was often state-owned, and even when it wasn't, its operations were tightly regulated by the state. Cross-border competition between telecommunications providers was nonexistent. Typically, regulations prohibited foreign firms from entering a country's telecommunications market and competing head-to-head with the domestic carrier. Most of the traffic carried by telecommunications firms was voice traffic, almost all of it was carried over copper wires, and most telecommunications firms charged their customers a premium to make long-distance and international calls.

The transformation

By the turn of the century, most telecommunications markets around the world had already been deregulated. This allowed new competitors to emerge and compete with the dominant provider. State-owned monopolies were privatized, including British Telecom and Deutsche Telekom.

Several dominant telecommunications firms, state-owned or otherwise, were broken up into smaller companies. For example, Bell had gone through a breaking up into so-called "Baby Bells," smaller telecommunication providers. In addition, in 1998, Brazil's state-owned telecommunications monopoly, Telebras, was privatized and broken up into 12 smaller companies that were allowed to compete with each other.

The new landscape
New wireless technologies have facilitated the emergence of new competitors, such as Orange and Vodafone in Britain, which now compete head-to-head with British Telecom, the former state monopoly. The Internet caused a major increase in the volume of data traffic (e.g., Web surfing), which is now growing much more rapidly than that of voice traffic. Much of this data traffic is being transmitted over new digital networks that utilize fiber optics, Internet protocols, and digital switches to send data around the world at the speed of light. Telecommunications firms are investing billions in digital networks to handle this traffic. Furthermore, in 1997, the World Trade Organization initiated an agreement among almost 70 countries to open their telecommunications markets to foreign competition and to abide by common rules for fair competition in telecommunications.

The globalized landscape
Most of the world's biggest markets, including the United States, the European Union (EU), and Japan, are by now fully liberalized and open to foreign competition. A global market for telecommunications services is the current reality. Telecommunications companies are starting to penetrate each other's markets. Prices are falling, both in the international market, where prices have long been kept artificially high by a lack of competition, and in the wireless market, which is rapidly becoming price competitive with traditional wire-line telecommunications services.

As competition intensifies, national telecommunications companies are entering into marketing alliances and joint ventures with each other to offer multinational companies a single global telecommunications provider for all their international voice and data needs. For example, AT&T, and British Telecom merged their international operations into a jointly owned company that will have \$10 billion in revenues. The venture focused on serving the global telecommunications needs of multinational corporations, enabling workers in Manhattan to communicate as easily with computer systems in New Delhi, say, as with colleagues in New Jersey. AT&T, and British Telecom estimate the market for providing international communications services to large and medium-sized business customers will expand to \$180 billion in 2007. Other companies that are working together on a global basis include MCI-WorldCom, the number two long-distance carrier in the USA, and Telefonica of Spain, which is also Latin America's biggest telecommunications carrier. The Sprint Corporation, the number three long-distance carrier in the USA, is partly owned by Deutsche Telekom and France Telecom. This trio is positioning itself to compete with the WorldCom/Telefonica and AT&T/BT ventures to gain the business of multinational customers in the brave new world of global telecommunications.

International and Global Business: An Introduction

As the opening case on telecommunication indicates, the effects of internationalization and globalization are all around. These effects pervade our lives as individuals and professionals and materialize in numerous instances. To wit, let us recall a typical morning in many countries these days. We wake up in an IKEA-made bed (www.ikea.com), are clothed with a suit made in Hong Kong (www.samstailor.com), and use briefed upon waking up by the Cable News Network (www.CNN.com) to news editions generated in Atlanta, Hong Kong or London. We visit our e-mail messages or sign on to a Skype voice and data service (www.skype.com), designed and launched in Europe and acquired by North American-based eBay (www.ebay.com), using a computer, assembled in Mexico (in order to reduce tariffs on importing to the USA), with Puerto Rico's Intel-manufactured chips (www.intel.com) and a Centrino chip designed in Israel and equipped with Microsoft software compiled in Israel (www.microsoft.com). Once at the breakfast table, we enjoy citrus juice imported from Spain or Mexico by Chiquita international fruit producer and marketer (www.chiquita.com) and coffee made by the regional Nestlé manufacturing facility (www.nestle.com), a Swiss-based company that spans the globe and touches almost all countries in the world. Table 1.1 lists countries, territories, and continents of the world and indicates the population. One should take account of the differences in population sizes and be cognizant of the fact that population growth rates may vary among countries and continents, contributing to the dynamics of international business. In Table 1.2 the size of economic activity and economic productivity, measured in gross domestic product (GDP) and GDP per capita, are recorded. Again, the variability and change in the GDP should be noted, as it may affect the attractiveness of certain markets. Note also the many countries in which the GDP per capita is below the world's average. Figure 1.1 demonstrates the growth of world exports, which exceeds the growth of GDP. This fact, plus the growth of international trade noted in Figure 1.2, demonstrate the magnitude and increasing importance of international business.

TABLE 1.1 Population of Countries, Territories, Continents, and Subcontinents as of 2010 and 2015 (projected in thousands)

Country/territory	*2010*	*2015*
Afghanistan	29,121	32,579
Albania	3,660	3,765
Algeria	34,586	36,640
American Samoa (US)	66	71
Andorra	85	86
Angola	13,068	14,443
Anguilla (UK)	15	16
Antigua and Barbuda	87	92
Argentina	41,343	43,432
Armenia	2,967	2,984
Aruba (The Netherlands)	105	112
Australia	21,516	22,751
Austria	8,214	8,224
Azerbaijan	8,304	8,681
Bahamas	310	325
Bahrain	738	783
Bangladesh	158,066	168,821
Barbados	286	291

(Continued)

TABLE 1.1 Cont.

Country/territory	*2010*	*2015*
Belarus	9,613	9,439
Belgium	10,423	10,454
Belize	315	347
Benin	9,056	10,449
Bermuda	68	70
Bhutan	700	742
Bolivia	9,947	10,801
Bosnia and Herzegovina	4,622	4,618
Botswana	2,029	2,183
Brazil	201,103	212,346
Brunei	395	430
Bulgaria	7,149	6,867
Burkina Faso	16,242	18,932
Myanmar	53,414	56,320
Burundi	9,863	11,574
Cambodia	14,753	16,148
Cameroon	19,294	21,387
Canada	33,760	35,100
Cape Verde	509	546
Cayman Islands (UK)	50	56
Central African Republic	4,845	5,392
Chad	10,543	11,631
Chile	16,746	17,435
China	1,330,141	1,361,513
Colombia	44,205	46,737
Comoros	773	883
Congo (Brazzaville)	4,126	4,755
Congo (Kinshasa)	70,916	82,657
Cook Islands (NZ)	11	10
Costa Rica	4,516	4,814
Côte d'Ivoire	21,059	23,295
Croatia	4,487	4,465
Cuba	11,477	11,582
Cyprus	1,103	1,189
Czech Republic	10,202	10,130
Denmark	5,516	5,582
Djibouti	741	828
Dominica	73	74
Dominican Republic	9,794	10,521
Ecuador	14,791	15,868
Egypt	80,472	88,487
El Salvador	6,052	6,141
Equatorial Guinea	651	741
Eritrea	5,793	6,528
Estonia	1,291	1,249

TABLE 1.1

Country/territory	*2010*	*2015*
Ethiopia	88,013	103,134
Faroe Islands (Denmark)	49	50
Fiji	958	1,024
Finland	5,255	5,271
France	64,768	66,301
French Polynesia	291	310
Gabon	1,545	1,705
Gambia	1,824	2,063
Georgia	4,601	4,525
Germany	82,283	81,946
Ghana	24,340	26,585
Gibraltar (UK)	29	29
Greece	10,750	10,776
Greenland (Denmark)	58	58
Grenada	108	111
Guam (US)	181	193
Guatemala	13,550	14,919
Guernsey (UK)	66	66
Guinea	10,324	11,780
Guinea-Bissau	1,565	1,726
Guyana	748	739
Haiti	9,203	10,083
Honduras	7,989	8,747
Hong Kong (China)	7,090	7,235
Hungary	9,880	9,747
Iceland	309	319
India	1,173,108	1,251,696
Indonesia	242,968	255,759
Iran	67,038	70,532
Iraq	29,672	33,310
Ireland	4,250	4,476
Isle of Man (UK)	77	79
Israel	7,354	7,935
Italy	58,091	57,689
Jamaica	2,847	2,950
Japan	126,804	124,719
Jersey (UK)	92	93
Jordan	6,407	6,623
Kazakhstan	15,460	15,761
Kenya	40,047	44,753
Kiribati	99	106
North Korea	22,757	23,149
South Korea	48,636	49,115
Kosovo	1,815	1,871

(*Continued*)

TABLE 1.1 Cont.

Country/territory	*2010*	*2015*
Kuwait	2,789	3,279
Kyrgyzstan	5,509	5,913
Laos	6,994	7,811
Latvia	2,218	2,152
Lebanon	4,125	4,151
Lesotho	1,920	1,948
Liberia	3,685	4,196
Libya	6,461	7,132
Liechtenstein	35	36
Lithuania	3,545	3,495
Luxembourg	498	527
Macau (China)	568	593
Macedonia	2,072	2,096
Madagascar	21,282	24,651
Malawi	15,448	17,715
Malaysia	26,160	28,433
Maldives	396	393
Mali	13,796	15,718
Malta	407	414
Marshall Islands	66	72
Mauritania	3,205	3,597
Mauritius	1,294	1,340
Mayotte (France)	231	270
Mexico	112,469	118,689
Federated States of Micronesia	107	105
Moldova	4,317	4,300
Monaco	31	31
Mongolia	3,087	3,318
Montenegro	667	647
Montserrat (UK)	5	5
Morocco	31,627	33,323
Mozambique	22,061	24,166
Namibia	2,128	2,212
Nauru	14	16
Nepal	28,952	31,551
Netherlands	16,783	17,079
Netherlands Antilles	229	236
New Caledonia (France)	230	242
New Zealand	4,252	4,438
Nicaragua	5,996	6,517
Niger	15,878	19,034
Nigeria	152,217	167,271
Northern Mariana Islands (US)	48	44
Norway	4,676	4,754
Oman	2,968	3,287

TABLE 1.1

Country/territory	*2010*	*2015*
Pakistan	177,277	190,752
Palau	21	21
Panama	3,411	3,657
Papua New Guinea	6,065	6,672
Paraguay	6,376	6,783
Peru	29,907	31,631
Philippines	99,900	109,616
Poland	38,464	38,302
Portugal	10,736	10,825
Puerto Rico (US)	3,978	4,025
Qatar	841	874
Romania	22,181	21,961
Russia	139,390	136,010
Rwanda	11,056	12,662
Saint Barthélemy (France)	7	7
Saint Helena (UK)	8	8
Saint Kitts and Nevis	50	52
Saint Lucia	161	164
Saint Martin (France)	30	32
Saint Pierre and Miquelon (France)	6	6
Saint Vincent and the Grenadines	104	103
Samoa	192	198
San Marino	31	33
São Tomé and Príncipe	176	194
Saudi Arabia	29,207	31,551
Senegal	14,086	16,044
Serbia	7,345	7,177
Seychelles	88	92
Sierra Leone	5,246	5,879
Singapore	4,701	4,881
Slovakia	5,470	5,496
Slovenia	2,003	1,983
Solomon Islands	610	680
Somalia	10,112	11,607
South Africa	49,109	48,286
Spain	40,549	40,482
Sri Lanka	21,514	22,383
Sudan	41,980	46,813
Suriname	487	513
Swaziland	1,354	1,436
Sweden	9,074	9,153
Switzerland	7,623	7,698
Syria	22,198	22,879
Taiwan	23,025	23,212
Tajikistan	7,487	8,192

(*Continued*)

TABLE 1.1 Cont.

Country/territory	*2010*	*2015*
Tanzania	41,893	46,123
Thailand	66,405	68,210
Timor-Leste	1,155	1,272
Togo	6,200	7,091
Tonga	123	131
Trinidad and Tobago	1,229	1,222
Tunisia	10,589	11,096
Turkey	77,804	82,523
Turkmenistan	4,941	5,231
Turks and Caicos Islands (UK)	24	26
Tuvalu	10	11
Uganda	33,399	39,941
Ukraine	45,416	44,009
United Arab Emirates	4,976	5,780
United Kingdom	61,285	62,175
United States	310,233	325,540
Uruguay	3,510	3,585
Uzbekistan	27,866	29,200
Vanuatu	222	236
Venezuela	27,223	29,275
Vietnam	89,571	94,349
British Virgin Islands	25	27
United States Virgin Islands	110	109
Wallis and Futuna	15	16
Western Sahara	492	571
Yemen	23,495	26,667
Zambia	12,057	13,017
Zimbabwe	11,652	14,230
World	**6,830,586**	**7,200,009**
Continents and Subcontinents		
Africa	1,013,053	1,130,866
The Americas	935,116	985,971
North America	456,526	479,393
South America	397,720	420,479
Central America	122.699	131,221
Greater Antilles	37,299	39,161
Lesser Antilles	1,742	1,796
Asia	4,119,627	4,321,504
Europe	727,792	724,427
Western Europe	401,985	404,648
Eastern Europe	325,807	319,779
Oceania	34,998	37,241
Soviet Union (Former)	282,925	281,141

Source: Adapted from *Current CIA World Fact Book*.

TABLE 1.2a Countries' Gross Domestic Product (GDP)

Rank	*Country*	*GDP (millions of US$)*
	World	**58,070,000**
	European Union	16,180,000
1	United States	14,430,000
2	Japan	5,108,000
3	People's Republic of China	4,814,000
4	Germany	3,273,000
5	France	2,666,000
6	United Kingdom	2,198,000
7	Italy	2,090,000
8	Brazil	1,499,000
9	Spain	1,466,000
10	Canada	1,335,000
11	Russia	1,232,000
12	India	1,095,000
13	Mexico	1,017,000
14	Australia	930,000
15	South Korea	809,700
16	Netherlands	799,000
17	Turkey	608,400
18	Indonesia	514,900
19	Switzerland	484,100
20	Belgium	461,500
21	Poland	423,000
22	Sweden	397,700
23	Saudi Arabia	384,000
24	Austria	374,400
25	Norway	369,000
26	Republic of China (Taiwan)	361,500
27	Venezuela	353,500
28	Greece	338,300
29	Iran	331,800
30	Denmark	308,300
31	Argentina	301,300
32	South Africa	277,400
33	Thailand	266,400
34	Finland	242,300
35	Colombia	228,600
36	United Arab Emirates	228,600
37	Ireland	226,800
38	Portugal	219,800
39	Israel	215,700
—	Hong Kong	208,800
40	Malaysia	207,400
41	Czech Republic	189,700

(Continued)

TABLE 1.2a Cont.

Rank	*Country*	*GDP (millions of USD$)*
42	Egypt	188,000
43	Pakistan	166,500
44	Nigeria	165,400
45	Singapore	163,100
46	Romania	160,700
47	Philippines	158,700
48	Chile	150,400
49	Algeria	134,800
50	Peru	127,400
51	Hungary	124,200
52	Ukraine	115,700
53	Kuwait	114,900
54	New Zealand	109,600
55	Kazakhstan	107,000
56	Qatar	92,540
57	Bangladesh	92,120
58	Vietnam	91,760
59	Morocco	90,780
60	Slovakia	88,300
61	Iraq	70,100
62	Angola	69,710
63	Croatia	61,720
64	Libya	60,610
65	Ecuador	55,610
66	Cuba	55,430
67	Syria	54,350
68	Sudan	54,290
69	Oman	52,340
70	Slovenia	49,550
71	Belarus	49,040
72	Luxembourg	46,510
73	Bulgaria	44,780
74	Dominican Republic	44,720
75	Azerbaijan	42,510
76	Serbia	42,390[5]
77	Sri Lanka	41,320
78	Tunisia	39,570
79	Guatemala	36,470
80	Lithuania	35,960
81	Ethiopia	33,920
82	Lebanon	32,660
83	Uruguay	31,610
84	Turkmenistan	30,730
85	Uzbekistan	30,320
86	Kenya	30,210

TABLE 1.2a

Rank	Country	GDP (millions of USD$)
87	Costa Rica	29,290
88	North Korea	28,200
89	Burma	26,520
90	Yemen	26,240
91	Panama	24,750
92	Latvia	24,200
93	Cyprus	23,220
94	Trinidad and Tobago	23,000
95	Côte d'Ivoire	22,910
96	Jordan	22,560
97	El Salvador	22,170
98	Tanzania	22,160
99	Cameroon	21,820
—	Macau	21,700
100	Bahrain	19,360
101	Estonia	18,050
102	Bolivia	17,550
103	Bosnia and Herzegovina	16,960
104	Uganda	15,660
105	Ghana	14,760
106	Brunei	14,700
107	Honduras	14,580
108	Paraguay	13,610
109	Afghanistan	13,320
110	Senegal	12,610
111	Nepal	12,470
112	Zambia	12,290
113	Jamaica	11,920
114	Iceland	11,780
115	Albania	11,730
116	Equatorial Guinea	11,180
117	Democratic Republic of the Congo	11,100
118	Georgia	10,980
119	Gabon	10,940
120	Cambodia	10,900
121	Botswana	10,810
122	Mozambique	9,654
123	Mauritius	9,156
124	Namibia	9,039
125	Madagascar	8,974
126	Macedonia	8,825
127	Mali	8,757
128	Armenia	8,683
129	Republic of the Congo	8,632
130	Papua New Guinea	8,200

(*Continued*)

TABLE 1.2a Cont.

Rank	*Country*	*GDP (millions of USD$)*
131	Burkina Faso	7,780
132	Malta	7,714
133	The Bahamas	7,403
134	Chad	6,974
135	Haiti	6,908
—	West Bank and Gaza	6,641
136	Benin	6,401
137	Nicaragua	6,298
—	French Polynesia	6,100
138	Laos	5,721
139	Moldova	5,328[8]
140	Niger	5,323
—	Jersey	5,100
141	Rwanda	5,011
142	Liechtenstein	4,993
143	Malawi	4,909
144	Kyrgyzstan	4,681
145	Tajikistan	4,577
146	Montenegro	4,444
147	Guinea	4,436
148	Mongolia	4,212
149	Barbados	3,595
150	Zimbabwe	3,556[6]
—	New Caledonia	3,300
151	Mauritania	3,241
—	Kosovo	3,237
152	Suriname	3,147
153	Fiji	3,048
154	Swaziland	2,929
—	Guam	2,773
155	Togo	2,771
—	Guernsey	2,742
156	Somalia	2,731
—	Isle of Man	2,719
—	Faroe Islands	2,400
—	Aruba	2,258
—	Cayman Islands	2,250
157	Sierra Leone	2,064
—	Greenland	2,000
158	Central African Republic	1,983
159	Cape Verde	1,755
160	Eritrea	1,694
161	Lesotho	1,624
162	Bhutan	1,493
163	Burundi	1,410
164	Belize	1,407

TABLE 1.2a

Rank	*Country*	*GDP (millions of USD$)*
165	Maldives	1,300
166	Guyana	1,196
167	Antigua and Barbuda	1,180
—	British Virgin Islands	1,095
168	Djibouti	1,089
—	Gibraltar	1,066
169	San Marino	1,048
170	Saint Lucia	991
171	Liberia	868
172	The Gambia	726
173	Grenada	683
174	Solomon Islands	668
175	Seychelles	656
—	Northern Mariana Islands	633.4
176	Saint Vincent and the Grenadines	625
177	East Timor	599
178	Samoa	567
179	Vanuatu	554
180	Saint Kitts and Nevis	547
181	Comoros	525
—	American Samoa	462.2
182	Guinea-Bissau	438
183	Dominica	376
184	Tonga	259
185	Federated States of Micronesia	238.1
—	Turks and Caicos Islands	216
186	São Tomé and Príncipe	189
—	Cook Islands	183.2
187	Palau	164
188	Marshall Islands	161.7
189	Kiribati	114
—	Anguilla	108.9
—	Falkland Islands	105.1
—	Montserrat	29
190	Tuvalu	14.94
—	Niue	10.01
—	Tokelau	1.5

Source: Adapted from *Current CIA World Fact Book*.

TABLE 1.2b Countries' Gross Domestic Product (GDP) Per Capita

Rank	*Country*	*US$*	*Year estimated*
1	Liechtenstein	122,100	2007
2	Qatar	121,700	2009
3	Luxembourg	78,000	2009
—	Bermuda	69,900	2004
4	Norway	58,600	2009
—	Jersey	57,000	2005
5	Kuwait	54,100	2009.
6	Singapore	50,300	2009
7	Brunei	50,100	2009
—	Faroe Islands	48,200	2008
8	United States	46,400	2009
9	Andorra	44,900	2008
—	Guernsey	44,600	2005
—	Cayman Islands	43,800	2004
—	Hong Kong	42,700	2009
10	Ireland	42,200	2009
11	United Arab Emirates	42,000	2009
12	San Marino	41,900	2007
13	Switzerland	41,700	2009
14	Iceland	39,600	2009
15	Austria	39,400	2009
16	Netherlands	39,200	2009
17	Australia	38,800	2009
—	Gibraltar	38,500	2006
—	Virgin Islands, British	38,500	2004
18	Bahrain	38,400	2009
19	Canada	38,400	2009
20	Sweden	36,800	2009
21	Equatorial Guinea	36,600	2009
22	Belgium	36,600	2009
23	Denmark	36,000	2009
—	Greenland	35,400	2007
—	Falkland Islands	35,400	2002
24	United Kingdom	35,200	2009
—	Isle of Man	35,000	2005
25	Finland	34,900	2009
26	Germany	34,100	2009
27	Spain	33,700	2009
—	Macau	33,000	2009
28	France	32,800	2009
29	Japan	32,600	2009
—	European Union	32,600	2009
30	Greece	32,100	2009

TABLE 1.2b

Rank	*Country*	*US$*	*Year estimated*
31	Italy	30,300	2009
32	Monaco	30,000	2006
33	Bahamas, The	29,800	2009
34	Taiwan (Republic of China)	29,800	2009
35	Israel	28,400	2009
36	South Korea,	28,000	2009
37	Slovenia	27,900	2009
38	New Zealand	27,300	2009
39	Czech Republic	25,100	2009
40	Oman	23,900	2009
41	Malta	23,800	2009
42	Trinidad and Tobago	23,100	2009
43	Portugal	21,800	2009
—	Aruba	21,800	2004
44	Slovakia	21,200	2009
45	Cyprus	21,200	2009
46	Saudi Arabia	20,400	2009
47	Seychelles	19,400	2009
48	Estonia	18,700	2009
49	Hungary	18,600	2009
50	Barbados	18,500	2009
51	Antigua and Barbuda	18,100	2009
52	Saint Vincent and the Grenadines	18,100	2009
—	French Polynesia	18,000	2004
53	Poland	17,900	2009
54	Croatia	17,600	2009
—	Puerto Rico	17,200	2009
—	Netherlands Antilles	16,000	2004
55	Lithuania	15,400	2009
56	Libya	15,200	2009
57	Saint Kitts and Nevis	15,200	2009
58	Russia	15,100	2009
—	Guam	15,000	2005
—	New Caledonia	15,000	2003
59	Malaysia	14,800	2009
60	Chile	14,700	2009
61	Latvia	14,500	2009
—	Virgin Islands (US)	14,500	2004
62	Gabon	13,900	2009
63	Argentina	13,800	2009
64	Mexico	13,500	2009
65	Lebanon	13,100	2009
66	Botswana	13,100	2009

(Continued)

TABLE 1.2b Cont.

Rank	*Country*	*US$*	*Year estimated*
67	Venezuela	13,100	2009
68	Iran	12,900	2009
69	Uruguay	12,700	2009
70	Bulgaria	12,600	2009
—	Northern Mariana Islands	12,500	2000
71	Mauritius	12,400	2009
—	Anguilla	12,200	2008
72	Panama	11,900	2009
73	Kazakhstan	11,800	2009
74	Belarus	11,600	2009
75	Romania	11,500	2009
—	Turks and Caicos Islands	11,500	2002
76	Turkey	11,200	2009
77	Saint Lucia	10,900	2009
78	Costa Rica	10,900	2009
79	Grenada	10,800	2009
—	**World**	**10,500**	**2009**
80	Azerbaijan	10,400	2009
81	Serbia	10,400	2009
82	Brazil	10,200	2009
83	Dominica	10,200	2009
84	South Africa	10,100	2009
85	Montenegro	9,800	2009
86	Cuba	9,700	2009
87	Colombia	9,200	2009
—	Cook Islands	9,100	2005
88	Suriname	9,000	2009
89	Republic of Macedonia	9,000	2009
90	Angola	8,900	2009
91	Peru	8,600	2009
92	Dominican Republic	8,300	2009
93	Jamaica	8,200	2009
94	Palau	8,100	2008
95	Thailand	8,100	2009
96	Belize	8,100	2009
97	Tunisia	8,000	2009
—	American Samoa	8,000	2007
98	Ecuador	7,400	2009
99	El Salvador	7,100	2009
100	Algeria	7,000	2009
—	Saint Pierre and Miquelon	7,000	2001
101	Turkmenistan	6,900	2009
102	People's Republic of China	6,600	2009

TABLE 1.2b

Rank	*Country*	*US$*	*Year estimated*
103	Namibia	6,400	2009
104	Ukraine	6,400	2009
105	Albania	6,300	2009
106	Bosnia and Herzegovina	6,300	2009
107	Kiribati	6,100	2009
108	Egypt	6,000	2009
109	Armenia	5,900	2009
—	Niue	5,800	2003
110	Samoa	5,400	2009
111	Bhutan	5,400	2009
112	Jordan	5,300	2009
113	Guatemala	5,200	2009
114	Nauru	5,000	2005
—	Mayotte	4,900	2005
115	Vanuatu	4,800	2009
116	Bolivia	4,600	2009
117	Morocco	4,600	2009
118	Tonga	4,600	2009
119	Syria	4,600	2009
120	Sri Lanka	4,500	2009
121	Swaziland	4,400	2009
122	Georgia	4,400	2009
123	Honduras	4,200	2009
124	Maldives	4,200	2009
125	Paraguay	4,100	2009
126	Republic of the Congo,	4,100	2009
127	Indonesia	4,000	2009
128	Fiji	3,900	2009
129	Guyana	3,800	2009
—	Wallis and Futuna	3,800	2004
130	Iraq	3,600	2009
131	Cape Verde	3,400	2009
—	Montserrat	3,400	2002
132	Philippines	3,300	2009
133	Mongolia	3,200	2009
134	India	3,100	2009
135	Vietnam	2,900	2009
—	West Bank and Gaza	2,900	2008
136	Djibouti	2,800	2009
137	Nicaragua	2,800	2009
138	Uzbekistan	2,800	2009
139	Pakistan	2,600	2009
140	Solomon Islands	2,600	2009

(*Continued*)

TABLE 1.2b Cont.

Rank	*Country*	*US$*	*Year estimated*
141	Kosovo	2,500	2007
142	Marshall Islands	2,500	2008
143	Yemen	2,500	2009
—	Saint Helena, Ascension and Tristan da Cunha	2,500	1998
—	Western Sahara	2,500	2007
144	Papua New Guinea	2,400	2009
145	Nigeria	2,400	2009
146	Timor-Leste	2,400	2009
147	Cameroon	2,300	2009
148	Sudan	2,300	2009
149	Moldova	2,300	2009
150	Federated States of Micronesia	2,200	2008
151	Kyrgyzstan	2,100	2009
152	Laos	2,100	2009
153	Mauritania	2,100	2009
154	North Korea	1,900	2009
155	Cambodia	1,900	2009
156	Tajikistan	1,800	2009
157	São Tomé and Príncipe	1,700	2009
158	Lesotho	1,700	2009
159	Côte d'Ivoire	1,700	2009
160	Chad	1,600	2009
161	Bangladesh	1,600	2009
162	Kenya	1,600	2009
163	Tuvalu	1,600	2002
164	Senegal	1,600	2009
165	Benin	1,500	2009
166	Ghana	1,500	2009
167	Zambia	1,500	2009
168	The Gambia	1,400	2009
169	Tanzania	1,400	2009
170	Haiti	1,300	2009
171	Uganda	1,300	2009
172	Mali	1,200	2009
173	Burkina Faso	1,200	2009
174	Nepal	1,200	2009
175	Burma	1,100	2009
176	Comoros	1,000	2009
177	Madagascar	1,000	2009
178	Guinea	1,000	2009
—	Tokelau	1,000	1993
179	Ethiopia	900	2009
180	Malawi	900	2009

TABLE 1.2b

Rank	*Country*	*US$*	*Year estimated*
181	Mozambique	900	2009
182	Sierra Leone	900	2009
183	Togo	900	2009
184	Rwanda	900	2009
185	Afghanistan	800	2009
186	Central African Republic	700	2009
187	Eritrea	700	2009
188	Niger	700	2009
189	Guinea-Bissau	600	2009
190	Somalia	600	2009
191	Liberia	500	2009
192	Burundi	300	2009
193	Congo, Democratic Republic of the	300	2009
194	Zimbabwe	<100	2009

Source: Adapted from *Current CIA World Fact book*.

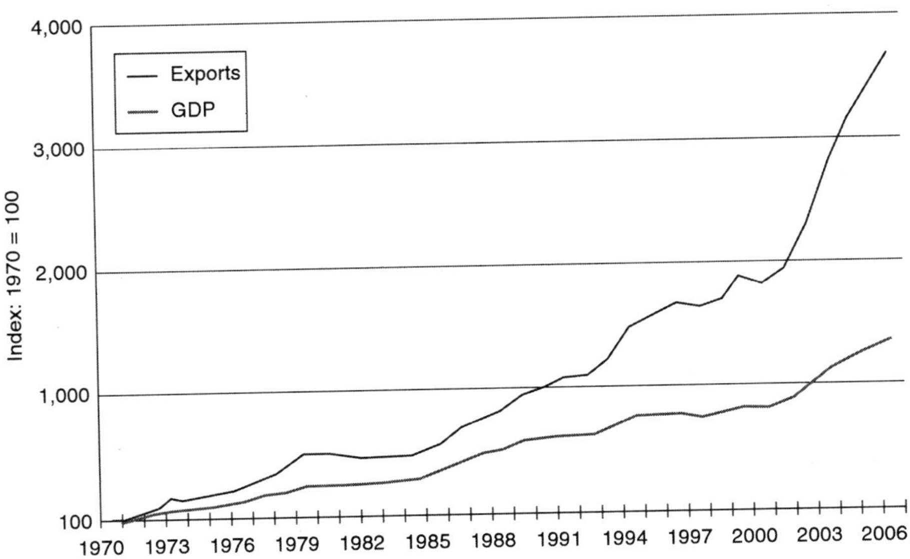

FIGURE 1.1 Comparing the growth rates of world's GDP and world's exports (Adapted from Current CIA World Fact Book)

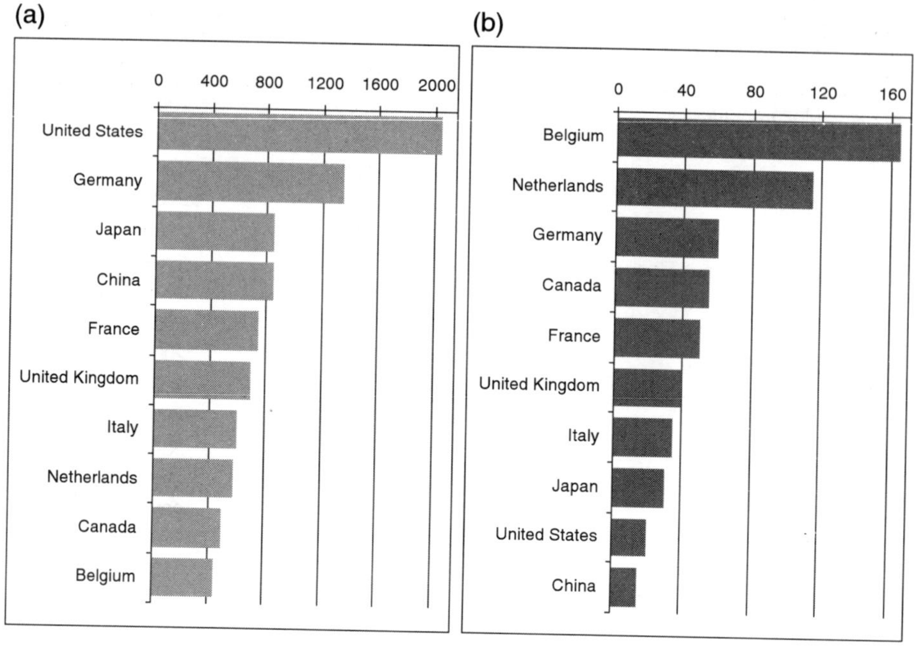

FIGURE 1.2 Leading countries in international merchandise trade. (a) Total annual value of products trade (exports + imports) in billions of US dollars. World Trade Organization (www.wto.org). (b) Total annual value of products trade (exports + imports) as a percentage of nation's GDP

International Business

International business is defined as all business activities, including the creation and transfer of resources, goods, services, know-how, skills, and information, which transcend national boundaries. The resources may be raw materials, energy, technological know-how and patents, capital, and organizational skills. Goods include manufactured parts, sub-assemblies, and assemblies. Services may include accounting, financial, legal, consulting, import and export, health care, and transportation. Know-how may include product and process technological innovations, copyrights, trademarks, and brands. Skills may include organizational and managerial skills. Information includes databases as well as information networks.

One may look at the economic activity of an organization and describe it as a set of consecutive business activities, each adding value to the product or service created. These activities are described in terms of the value added by each one of the activities. As such, all products and services that are brought into or shipped away from a certain country involve value-generating activities, such as design, development, production, delivery, and after-sale service and support activities. It is the proportion of the value-added activities that are performed across country lines that fall under the definition of international business. Take, for example, IKEA (IKEA.com), the producer of household furniture and fixtures. IKEA may purchase wood, kilned and dried in Norway. It then produces furniture parts and assemblies in Sweden, which may have been designed in Denmark. Following shipping to the USA, it is put on display in the stores, to be purchased and assembled by customers. Each of these activities adds value to the final piece of furniture by IKEA and constitutes part of international trade when it crosses international boundaries. The total values of goods and services involved in these activities and business transactions worldwide are upwards from $16 trillion (oecd.org), well over the sales volume of some of the largest corporations and larger than some countries' gross national product (GNP). The prevalence of the value of internationally shipped and transferred services is demonstrated in Table 1.3, which lists the services that are internationalized quickly.

As more services and goods are transferred and traded around the world, commercial, currency, country, and cross-cultural risks grow, as shown in Figure 1.3. The 2008 global financial crisis made clear the implicit currency and financial risk of international business.

TABLE 1.3 Leading Companies in International Services Trade

Industry	*Representative activities*	*Representative companies*
Architectural, construction, and engineering	Construction, electric power utilities, design engineering services for airports, hospitals, dams	ABB, Bechtel Group, Halliburton, Kajima, Philip Holzman, Skanska AB
Banking, finance, and insurance	Banks, insurance, risk evaluation, management	Citigroup, CIGNA, Barclays, HSBC, Ernst & Young
Education, training, and publishing	Management training, technical training, English language training	Berlitz, Kumon Math & Reading Centers, NOVA, Pearson, Elsevier
Entertainment	Movies, recorded music, Internet-based entertainment	Time Warner, Sony, Virgin, MGM
Information services	E-commerce, e-mail, funds transfer, data interchange, data processing, network services, professional computer services	Infosys, EDI, Hitachi, Qualcomm, Cisco
Professional business services	Accounting, advertising, legal, management consulting	Leo Burnett, EYLaw, McKinsey, AT. Kearney, Booz Allen Hamilton, Cap Gemini
Transportation	Aviation, ocean shipping, railroads, trucking, airports	Maersk, Sante Fe, Port Authority of New Jersey, SNCF (French railroads)
Travel and tourism	Transportation, lodging, food and beverage, recreation, travel on aircraft, ocean carriers, and railways	Carlson Wagonlit, Marriott, British Airways

Source: World Trade Organization (www.wto.org).

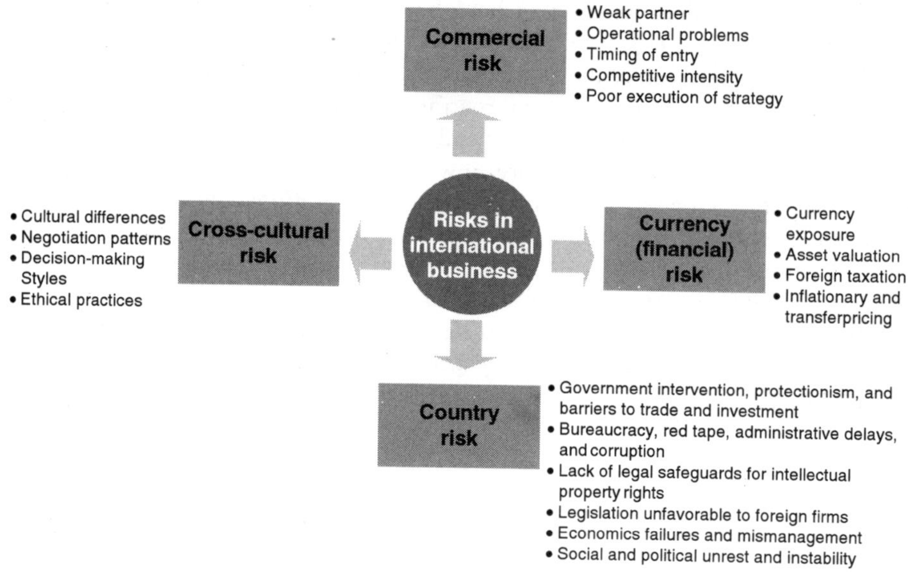

FIGURE 1.3 The four risks of international business

The entities involved in international business may be individuals, nongovernmental organizations (NGOs), government organizations, and international bodies, such as the United Nations, the World Trade organization (WTO), the World Bank, or the International Monetary Fund (IMF). However, the main entity involved in international business is the multinational enterprise (MNE). The definitions of an MNE vary. Several representative terms are used to describe multinational organizations. A multi-domestic firm is an enterprise with multiple international subsidiaries that are relatively independent from headquarters. The global firm consists of closely integrated international subsidiaries controlled and coordinated from central headquarters. The transnational firm consists of subsidiaries that may fulfill strategic and central roles, typically reserved for headquarters in global firms. The MNE is defined by the Organization for Economic Cooperation and Development (OECD) as an enterprise that engages in foreign direct investment (FDI) and owns or controls value-adding activities in more than one country. In many cases, the MNE has "multiple" facilities around the globe, owns a majority stake in plants in North America, Europe, and the Pacific Rim, derives a "substantial" portion of revenues from foreign operations, operates subsidiaries that share a common strategic vision, draws from a common pool of resources, and places foreign nationals or expatriates at the board level and/or in senior management posts. Sometimes, the MNE is known as a multinational corporation (MNC) or a global corporation (GC).

Most MNEs are based in the USA, Japan, Germany, Britain, and France, as noted in Table 1.4.

The corporations that fall under the MNE, MNC, and GC definition are indeed the main participants in the international business. They are engaged in

TABLE 1.4 Geographic Location and Revenues of Multinational Enterprises (MNEs)

Country	*Number of MNEs*	*Revenues of MNEs (in Billions of US dollars)*
US	170	6,645
Japan	70	2,334
Germany	35	1,648
France	38	1,612
United Kingdom	38	1,528
Netherlands	14	773
China	20	570
Switzerland	12	481
Italy	10	427
South Korea	12	404
Canada	14	285
Spain	9	264
Australia	8	175
Russia	5	158
Mexico	5	147
Belgium	4	133
India	6	122
Sweden	6	118
Brazil	4	115

international transactions: namely, transactions that involve more than one country. The economic activity of these organizations make up the bulk of international trade, and the funds invested in them very often are funds available through international investment.

As suggested, the MNEs are the main drivers and beneficiaries of international business. Many of the large global corporations and professional service firms are defined as MNEs. For example, Intel employs over 140,000 employees in hundreds of facilities in tens of countries around the globe. It controls and owns facilities in a variety of countries; each is part of Intel's value-added chain. Ernst & Young, a global accounting and professional firm, employs about 120,000 people in more than 100 countries, operating as an international network of wholly owned and associated professional firms. Both Intel and Ernst & Young enjoy international presence that leads to global brand recognition in major markets, such as the USA and the EU, may recruit highly skilled employees, from India and France, raise capital in efficient capital markets, such as the USA, Germany, and the UK, and create manufacturing and service facilities in low labor-rate countries such as Vietnam and Indonesia. In many instances, these organizations transfer capital, information, services, and products from one country to another and, thus, create the global business ecosystem.

There are other types of international organizations that should be identified. The early multinational enterprise (EME) is an enterprise that at the very start-up phase decides to go international and enjoy the benefits, as well as rise up to the challenges, of having international operations. Numerous so-called high technology enterprises fall into this category. Take for example VKB (vkb-tech.com). VKB was founded in 2000 with the mission of creating a standard for high-performance, low-cost virtual interface solutions across a wide range of products in the communications, computing, and entertainment markets. It has developed proprietary electro-optic technology and has applied for patent protection (both in the USA as well as numerous other markets it expected to do business in around the world), and very early on was seeking to develop international business relationships to capitalize on the commercial opportunity presented by the current and planned products. These relationships include the servicing of highly-targeted OEM prospects in Europe, the Middle East, North America, and Asia and identifying strategic financial and operational partners. Another distinct type of MNEs are small and midsize enterprises that are engaged in international business activities without any facilities that are owned overseas they are called small and midsize international enterprises (SMIEs).

Domestic and international business

Businesses that have started as domestic businesses may grow to become international by intent: for example, Procter & Gamble, McDonalds, and Starbucks were founded in the USA and operated as domestic businesses, but now may be defined as MNEs, conducting their business internationally. In the same manner, the French corporation of Danone started as a domestic bottle and glass manufacture in 1966, and changed first into a pan-European entity and then into a fully fledged MNE by the beginning of the 21st century, with operations in Europe, the USA, Africa, Latin America, and Asia.

Sometimes the internationalization of firms happens early in its life and at times firms seem to operate with no home base at all. Some international entrepreneurs operate by running virtual start-up sites, bringing together a network of business partners, managerial skills, and technological know-how, and using outsourcing bases. These virtual operating businesses may have headquarters in a certain country, but most or all of their activities occur outside its headquarters' country and elsewhere in the world. As an example, one well-known online poker company that recently did an initial public offering (IPO) of its shares is based on a Caribbean island for tax and legal reasons but its customers/players are mostly from the USA and Western Europe.

Domestic business and international business work in different environments and have different operating practices. Unlike domestic business, international business is performed in foreign countries, each with its own national and business culture, and its own economic conditions and legal environment. Political risks as well as economic risks apply in operating an international business. Executives need to be familiar with currency and monetary policies, which are different in every country. Inflation rates, currency exchange fluctuations, and changes in laws on repatriation of profits may affect the profitability of businesses with facilities located overseas, which also requires knowledge and understanding on the part of the executive. As an example, if a US-based corporation conducts business in Europe, fluctuations in exchange rates affect business results. If the US dollar goes down relative to the Euro – the European Union currency – then products being shipped from the USA to Europe command higher profit margins (assuming that production costs stay the same). Consequently, the internationally oriented manager should put more effort in promoting sales in Europe during this period to take advantage of the higher profit. Operating practices are also different for international businesses, as national cultural differences as well as business culture differences are present. Differences in culture become an issue and may affect communication, control mechanisms, productivity, incentive scheme bases, management practices, and quality procedure. For example, as Nestlé took over a major ownership stake of Osem Foods International in Israel, Nestlé's worldwide operational and reporting systems had to be carefully introduced, taking into account the local reporting practices based on national and business cultures. In a similar manner, when the Japanese-based Kao Corporation took over Didak, the Canadian memory device manufacturer, care had to be taken in introducing Japanese management practices into the manufacturing facilities in Kanata in the province of Ontario, Canada.

The drivers to expand internationally

Businesses vie to operate internationally because of four reasons: first, expanding markets; second, improving economic gains; third, positioning themselves strategically to face future threats or exploit future opportunities; and fourth, addressing randomly "discovered opportunities."

Expanding market share is a main driver for international operations. Take, for example, the Danone Group, the French-based producer of fresh dairy products, beverages, biscuit, and cereal products, and infant foods. Whereas it started as a domestic producer, today, nearly 31 percent of Danone sales are on emerging markets. This brings Danone close to its marketing target, which is to have 40 percent of business on emerging markets and 60 percent in developed countries – a balanced presence that means the Danone Group benefits from both the high potential of developing economies and the steady demand of more mature markets. In recent years, Danone has built up strong positions on emerging markets to take the number-one place in each of its three core businesses.

As to the economic driver to go international, Danone's successful international expansion rewards a strategy focusing on a limited number of countries, selected for their growth potential, where Danone has the size to achieve significant economies of scale. These economies of scale help provide the same products and the same services with lower costs, enabling a larger profit margins or allowing flexibility in setting prices at a level appropriate for local conditions in the target country or region.

At times, companies may go international because of strategic positioning needs. In the case of Danone, going international was a strategic decision. Danone decided to provide products within the reach of most consumers in target countries, with high-profile brands, and using an effective, wide-ranging distribution system for sales close to consumers. Danone decided on profitable growth in emerging markets, stressing affordability, awareness, and availability. Strategically, in Western Europe, Danone planned for a continued, steady growth, building on strengths that include well-established positions in each of its core businesses. In each of Danones' business lines it vies to be a world leader, which gives it a clear competitive advantage in terms of marketing expertise, industrial efficiency, breadth of product ranges, and targeted R&D. In each case, world leadership is built on strong number one positions in local markets, enabling Danone to forge close ties to consumers through an unrivalled familiarity with local tastes, balanced long-term relationships with major retailers, and a recognized capacity for effective innovation. Danone's worldwide strategic core values are a strong health and well-being positioning, at the heart of concerns of consumers and new consumption opportunities (times or places), combined with the dynamism of the growth of emerging countries.

Many MNEs seem to be expanding into China for sound strategic reasons: marketing, economic, and strategic. China presents the potential for a huge market, as well as a relatively inexpensive place for manufacturing resources, including labor. At the same time, MNEs seem to establish themselves in China simply in order to be there before their competitor. Consumer goods, chemical derivatives producers, electronic and electric supplies, toy manufacturers, and other manufacturers and distributors are all present or considering how to start up a base of operation (BOO) or a regional headquarters (RHQ) in China. In fact, a booming economy coupled with a maturity in Chinese consumer tastes and spending power is leading to a seemingly insatiable appetite for luxury goods in China, translating into enormous potential for global luxury retailers and consumer products manufacturers. Strategically, as more regions define themselves as economic entities, creating rules and regulations that reduce customs and tariffs on cross-border trade within a region, companies set up shop within these regions in order to exploit the opportunities ahead. For that reason, North American, Asian, and Latin American companies in a variety of industries have created a base of operations, manufacturing plants and regional headquarters within EU country members, in order to do business freely. As of 2010, there are 27 member states in the EU (Austria, Belgium, Bulgaria, Cyprus, Czech Republic, Denmark, Estonia, Finland, France, Germany, Greece, Hungary, Ireland, Italy, Latvia, Lithuania, Luxemburg, Malta, Poland, Portugal, Romania, Slovakia, Slovenia, Spain, Sweden, The Netherlands, United Kingdom). There are also some candidate countries to be admitted into the EU, including Croatia, Iceland, and Turkey. This leaves only 11 European countries that are not yet members or candidate members to be included in the EU. All the more reason, strategically to start operations within the EU.

Sometimes, a chance event makes the company go international. For example, a key corporate executive may travel on vacation and may decide that the destination might be a good place to do business. Alternatively, a local friend points to a local opportunity that should not be missed. These events may explain why and how numerous small and midsize enterprises, with less than 100 employees, go international.

A Quick Review

1. International business is defined as all business activities, including the creation and transfer of resources, goods, services, know-how, skills, and information, which transcend national boundaries.
2. MNEs are the main drivers and beneficiaries of international business.
3. Domestic firms expand internationally because of four reasons: expanding markets, improving economic gains, strategic positioning, and randomly "discovered opportunities."

The Globalization Phenomena

Side by side with the accelerated increase in the sheer size of international business and trade in the 21st century, globalization as a process and as a state of affairs has become a focus of attention for executives and managers as well as for business management educators and scientists. Globalization may be defined as the increasing of worldwide integration of markets for goods, services, and capital concurrent with the increased role for MNEs in the world economy and an increased intervention into domestic and regional policies and affairs by international institutions such as the IMF, the WTO, the World Bank, and the United Nations. The question is what globalization means for the business executives and others involved in the world economy.

Over the last three decades political, economic, and cultural trends have been marked by the use of the term "globalization" as one of the most fashionable buzzwords of contemporary business, political, and academic debate. In many cases, globalization has been used as a synonym for one of the following phenomena:

- The pursuit of classical "free market" policies in the world economy (otherwise known as a "liberal economy").
- The growing dominance of Western or American forms of political, economic, and cultural life.
- The proliferation of new information technologies (the "Internet Revolution").
- The notion that the world community is facing the creation of one single unified community in which major sources of conflict have vanished ("global integration").

Social scientists seem to agree that globalization means a fundamental change in the understanding of space and time by human beings. As geographical distances seem to be reduced by new communication infrastructures, globalization promises far-reaching implications for all.

These far-reaching implications are exemplified by the following experience of an Ethiopian goat farmer. Discovering the potential in the use of selling through the Internet, the farmer offers – over the Internet – to provide goats to Ethiopian families located nearby. The goats are purchased and paid for by Ethiopian immigrants residing in New York City and London through the Internet using credit cards. The Ethiopian farmer sells the merchandise internationally and earns US dollars or Euros, even though he has never left the village. Globalization causes time and distances as well as national boundaries to be compressed and vanish, as evidenced by this example. Another example, yet, are call centers that are based in Scotland or India supporting a customer in Hong Kong who needs help with his printer. The customer is reaching the support desk by dialing a local number, without knowing where the call has been routed to.

The chronology of globalization

The term globalization has only become commonplace in the past three decades. However, as indicated in Table 1.5, it has evolved during the past two centuries.

Nineteenth and twentieth-century philosophy, literature, and social research include references to the changing experiences of distance and time that are transformed by the introduction of high-speed forms of transportation, such as air travel and communication such as the Internet and cell phones. Distance, in geographic terms, has lost relevance, as noted in Table 1.6. This, in turn, significantly increases possibilities for human interaction across existing geographical and political borders.

During the turn of the 20th century, it has been argued that economic and technological trends of that time implied the emergence of a "new world" and that the invention of the steam engine, electricity, and the telephone offered major challenges to relatively static and homogeneous forms of local community life that had long represented the main arena for most human activity. At about the same time economic activity increasingly transcended the borders of local communities while the steamship, railroad, automobile, and air travel considerably intensified rates of geographical mobility. Some argued that the compression of distance posed fundamental questions for democracy. It has been observed that increasingly dense networks of social ties across national borders rendered local forms of self-government ineffective. New high-speed technologies attributed a shifting and unstable character to social life, as demonstrated by the increased rates of change and turnover in the economy. This lack of stability raised questions regarding democracy and governance in constantly moving and changing communities, countries, and regions.

Globalization and society

As of the beginning of the 21st century, the determinants of globalization become clear. First, globalization is associated with deterritorialization, since a growing variety of social and economic activities take place irrespective of the geographical location of participants due to advances in telecommunication, digital computers,

TABLE 1.5 Phases of Globalization Since the Early 1800s

Phase of globalization	*Approximate period*	*Triggers*	*Key characteristics*
First phase	19th century	Introduction of railroads and ocean transportation	Growth of manufacturing: increase in cross-border trade of commodities and products
Second phase	1900 to 1930	Use of electricity; the development of transportation and communication infrastructure	Emergence of multinational enterprises (MNEs)
Third phase	1945 to 1980	Post World War II reconstruction of Europe; formation of General Agreement on Tariff and Trade (GATT)	Reduction of barriers to trade; an increase in the number and size of MNEs; the development of global capital markets; an increase in cross-border flow of money
Fourth phase	1980s to 2000	Growth of speed and vehicles of telecommunication; increased efficiencies of manufacturing; the effective provision of consulting and other services; the privatization of state-owned enterprises; the dominance of emerging markets	Growth in cross-border trade of products, services and capital; the rise of small and medium enterprises (SMEs) and international entrepreneurship; the formation of trade regions
Fifth phase	2000 onwards	Realization of a global, interconnected world; the immense power of global enterprises	Increased focus on sustainability and social responsibility of MNEs; decreasing role of national governments; emergence of voluntary international organizations that monitor international business and trade

TABLE 1.6 The Demise of Distance

In this time period...	*Fastest transportation was via...*	*At a speed of...*
1500–1840s	■ Human-powered ships and horse-drawn carriages	10 miles/h
1850–1900	■ Steamships ■ Steam locomotive trains	36 miles/h 65 miles/h
Early 1900s–today	■ Motor vehicles ■ Propeller airplanes ■ Jet aircraft	75 miles/h 300–400 miles/h 500–700 miles/h

Source: Adapted from Dicken (1992). *Global Shift.* New York: Guilford, p. 104.

and video-conferencing. Second, globalization is associated with social interconnectedness across existing geographical and political boundaries. This interconnectedness is important as it affects not only distant events but also impacts local and regional events. As an example, the United Nations might be making decisions based on facts and figures collected globally, which then affect events in a particular community, country, or region. Third, globalization relates to the speed or velocity of activities. The networking and expanding of activities across national borders is based on fast flows and movements of human resources, information, capital, goods and services. Fourth, while globalization may describe a state of affairs at any one time, it should be considered also as a process whereby the rate of change in the degree of deterritorialization, the measure of interconnectedness, and the velocity rate of activities is constantly on the rise, leading to the current degree of globalization. For example, the advent of mobile commerce – the execution of commercial transactions over the internet using cell phones – increased the rate and efficiency of commercial transaction processes. All four of the above determinants affect both the rate of change and the degree of globalization.

The challenges of globalization

The obvious wide-ranging impact of globalization on social, economic, and business affairs calls for public debate and thought leadership by executives and researchers alike. This book addresses the first imperative of globalization which is that business executives and public decision makers in the West should pay closer attention to the cultures and traditions of peoples in overseas and developing countries. Western social and political scientists have traditionally assumed the existence of territorially bound communities, whose borders can be clearly delineated from those of other communities. Based on this assumption, one may conclude by extension that relations between national and sovereign states are not governed by any law. Since the achievement of justice or democracy assumes an effective political sovereign, and since it may not exist at the global level, then justice and democracy may not be unattainable at the global level.

The very existence of the globalization phenomenon raises a number of challenging questions regarding world order. It is questionable whether nation-states are self-sufficient forms of communities that cater to all needs of human beings. Intense deterritorialization and the intensification of social, economic, and business relations across borders renders even the most powerful and privileged political, national, and economic units with limited control and make them part of a network of social relations that transcends national borders completely. As an example, deregulated and global financial markets, telecommunication, and transportation industries imply a profound quantitative increase in and intensification of new industries and social networks. As a result the distinction between what is foreign and what is domestic becomes unclear, and the traditional tendency to think of the domestic arena as a privileged site for the realization of normative ideals and principles becomes obsolete. This means that core ideals of justice and democracy should be addressed on a global level and that globally chartered bodies should be created and empowered to provide for same. Furthermore, it seems that in a globalizing world, the lack of democracy or justice at the global level impacts the pursuit of justice or democracy at the national or regional level and vice versa. To wit, growing inequality which results from economic globalization is related to growing domestic inequality in the Western democracies. Similarly, the ongoing destruction of the ozone layer by countries like the USA, Japan, and Australia impacts most other countries and calls for transnational cooperation and regulation to control ozone layer destruction. Acting irresponsibly at a global level regarding the ozone layer means that people of all nations, regardless of the national degree of pollution, are future victims of a polluted environment.

In G-8 international meetings (forums of the group of eight industrialized nations), as well as in high-powered world economic forums like the Davos, Switzerland meeting, world leaders debate and consider the implications of the globalizing world. Supporters of globalization stress the moral obligations towards the residents of third world countries with whom the developed countries share little in the way of language, custom, or culture. At the same meetings, supporters of globalization argue for the universality and necessity of democratic values, justice, and social and economic equality. The supporters of globalization defend significant legal and political reforms as a necessity to address the inequities of a world in which millions of people die of starvation each year. In contrast, opponents of globalization dispute the importance, urgency and necessity to do same and are of the opinion that the world community has not achieved a sufficiently articulated sense of a common fate such that far-reaching attempts to achieve greater global justice could prove successful.

Related to the arguments for and against globalization is the issue of the creation and empowerment of world bodies such as the WTO, the IMF, the World Bank, the United Nations, and the International Court of Law in the Hague. In addition, one should consider the prospects of democratic institutions at the global level. Some argue that globalization requires the empowerment of democratic institutions to the transnational level. Nation-state-based democracy is not equipped to deal with present-day globalization such as ozone depletion or growing economic inequality. In addition, a growing transnational form of activity by MNEs and NGOs calls out for transnational modes of democratic decision-making. A case in point is the European Union, which was conceived as a supranational democracy. If the EU is to help succeed in supporting the principle of sovereignty in a borderless world, it needs to strengthen its elected representative institutions and guarantee the political, civil, social, and economic rights of all Europeans. Recently, both France and the Netherlands rejected far-reaching proposals to strengthen the EU constitution, supporting the contrarian views. The contrarian underscores the utopian character of such proposals, arguing that democratic politics is based on deep feelings of trust, commitment, and belonging that remain uncommon at the global level. Since commonalities of belief, history, and custom compose necessary preconditions of any viable democracy, and since these commonalities are missing beyond the nation-state, global, or cosmopolitan democracy is doomed to fail.

Globalization and business

While world leaders and scientists argue the merits and pitfalls of globalization, its manifestations are found all around us, underlying the understanding that the business ecosystem today consists of global markets, global resources, global production, global supply chains, and global management skills. Table 1.7 details the factors contributing to and the implications of the globalization of business.

The consumer may buy food and consumer products of any kind with global brand names such as Coca Cola drinks, McDonald hamburgers, Huggies baby diapers, Starbucks coffee, Levy jeans, MTV music channel, and United Parcel Service (UPS). No matter which country you are a citizen of, your friends and colleagues are able to identify the global brands and attest to their quality. The value of all goods and services exported and imported around the world is on the rise and affects even the relatively strong local enterprises. These local enterprises should soon find a way to join strategic international partners, if only to defend their domestic market share.

TABLE 1.7 The Factors and Implications of Market Globalization

Factors contributing to business globalization	*Impact of business globalization*	*Social implications of business globalization*	*Corporate implications of business globalization*
• Reduction of barriers to trade • Increase of international capital transfer and investment • Transition to market-based economies • Privatization of state-owned enterprises in former Soviet Union countries • Adoption of free trade in China • Industrialization, economic development, and modernization • Technology advancements • Integration of world financial markets	• The formation of regional economic and trade blocs • Interdependence of national economies • Growth of foreign direct and portfolio investments • The emergence of global supply chains of multinational corporations • Convergence of worldwide consumer expectations and preferences	• Loss of national identity and sovereignty • Increase in outsourcing, causing loss of jobs • Increase of the gaps between rich and poor • Increased impact on sustainability and the environment • Increase influence of globalization on local culture and heritage	• New business opportunities • Emerging implications of global supply chains (alternative sources of supply, etc.) • New corporate competitive environment – global and interconnected • Higher exposure to economic, political, and business risks • More discerning consumer communities • More sourcing and outsourcing opportunities

Implications of globalization

In the eyes of the consumer, globalization means lower prices because of increased competition, better selection, and improved service. It also means that the origin of products and location of many MNEs' headquarters become unknown and irrelevant to the consumer. How many Europeans are aware of the fact that the Procter & Gamble Corporation is based in Cincinnati, Ohio, or that the global news network CNN is headquartered in Atlanta, Georgia, along with the headquarters of the Coca Cola Company. In this manner, how many users of the software firewall company Check Point are familiar with its origins in Israel? Globalization also means the diffusion of new services which have been introduced by MNEs. Take for example the proliferation of HSBC (Hong Kong and Shanghai Banking Corporation) local branches with connectivity to branches around North America and the world. This proliferation means that if one takes a loan from an HSBC branch in the Boston area, the dollars are actually originated from deposits made in England or Singapore. The connectivity and globalization of financial markets contributed to if not caused the 2008 world financial crisis. In the same manner if you are the owner of an American car what do you know about the many foreign, based part manufacturers that end up in the car?

In the eyes of the producer or provider of goods and services, globalization means that the facilities involved may be based anywhere in the world and the location may be selected based on least cost and highest quality of workmanship available. The term used to describe the network of suppliers dispersed across continents is a global supply chain. Most industries, such as the car industry, the consumer electronics products industry and the biotechnology industry, use global supply chains.

In the eyes of investment funds managers, as well as corporate executives, globalization means that capital required for investment and operations may be raised in a number of stock markets that compete for their business and, thus, reduce the registration, bureaucracy, and reporting requirements on the one hand and allow corporations and funds to acquire ownership and hold portfolio investments in countries overseas on the other.

As indicated in Tables 1.8–1.10 and Figure 1.4, worldwide value chain activities of corporations are prevalent and manifest themselves in all sectors of the economy. As opposed to the almost endless opportunities made available by globalization to the consumer, producer and corporate executives, the case for workers is somewhat less clear. Some argue that labor is globalization's missing link. The flow of workers across borders is heavily controlled, leaving the global market for labor far more distorted than those for capital and raw materials. The world price of capital may be set in the USA, and that of crude oil set in Saudi Arabia, but there is no such thing as a world price of labor. Wages can differ by a factor of 10 or more, depending only on the passport of the wage-earner. Relaxing the movement of labor even a little may generate large efficiency gains. Harvard University researches calculate that letting poor workers into rich countries, in modest numbers (equivalent to 3 percent of the hosts' labor force) for a limited period, could

TABLE 1.8 The Internationalization of the MNEs Value Chain Activities

MNEs value chain activities	*Research & development*	*Procurement (sourcing)*	*Manufacturing*	*Marketing*	*Distribution*	*After sale service and support*
MNEs examples regarding value chain activities	e-Bay, the Internet merchandise and re-seller service provider, executes its development work in Israel, California, and India. Monsanto, the biotechnology and agriculture MNE, has R&D locations in the USA and leading corporate centers elsewhere, constantly searching the world over for new products	Alcatel-Lucent, the French telecommunication equipment maker is outsourcing its information technology globally. Dell, the PC supplier, as well as other consumer goods and services, performs order processing in India	Whirlpool Corp, the white goods manufacturer and owner of Maytag and Amana, has plants in the USA, Mexico, and China	HSBC, the global financial giant, operates branches in most urban centers to be close to the customers, including London, New York, Paris, Tel Aviv, and Hong Kong	Florsheim, the maker of footwear, is using an international network of corporate-owned and franchised stores to reach its customers in Australia, USA, Canada, South America, and Europe	Schneider Electric is an MNE based in Europe and specializes in energy management with operations in more than 100 countries, including after sale service and support centers

TABLE 1.9 Involvement of Intermediaries and Institutions in Various International Value Chain Activities

Value chain activities	*Institutions*	*Intermediaries*
International market research	• Marketing consultants • Market research firms • Legal/business advisors	
Research & development (R&D)	• Academic institutions/ universities • Research & development facilities	• Scientific and academic conferences
Purchasing: sourcing and outsourcing	• Financial institutions • Logistics and transportation service provider • Insurance and custom brokers	• Trading companies • Brokers • Import/export agents
Manufacturing and operations	• National standards institutes • Industry voluntary standards institutes • Financial institutions	• Maintenance services providers • Manufacturing service suppliers
International marketing	• Consultant • Market research firm	• Import/export agents • Marketing agents and distribution facilities
International distribution	• Logistics, warehousing, transportation service providers • Freight forwarder • Insurance company • Customs broker	• Export management companies • Trading companies • Sales representatives • Distributors • Brokers • Importers • Retailers
After sale service and support	• After sale service and support company • Consumer groups advocates	• Retail outlets • Service consultants

reap benefits to the developing world worth $200 billion a year. With numbers like that one has to question why so much energy is spent freeing trade and capital, and so little expended freeing labor. The United Nations has recently called for more temporary migration from poor countries to rich ones, even though guest-worker programs rarely work in the long run. The Gastarbeiter program in Germany – which invited Turks, Yugoslavs and others needed at the time to fill the factory jobs created by the country's post-war economic miracle – failed. Many of Germany's "guests" never left, and their families soon arrived. The bracero program in America – which, from 1942 to 1964, recruited Mexican field hands to pick cotton and sugar beets in Texas and California – fared no better. The entry of hundreds of thousands of farm workers provided camouflage for a substantial flow of undocumented labor.

TABLE 1.10 Rank of Market Values of Multinational Enterprises (By Industry Sector Size)

Sector	*2005 market value (US$ billions)*	*Percentage of world total*	*Representative firms*
Financials	5,832	24.3	Capital One, Danske Bank, Royal Bank of Scotland
Consumer discretionary	2,667	11.1	Coach, Adidas, Salomon, Matsushita Electric
Information technology	2,635	11.0	Microsoft, Oracle, Hoya, Taiwan Semiconductor Manufacturing
Industrials	2,431	10.1	Landstar Systems, Shenzhen Expressway, Haldex
Energy	2,316	9.7	Mobil, Total, China Oilfield Services
Health care	2,274	9.5	GlaxoSmithKline, Novartis, Baxter International
Consumer staples	2,134	8.9	Procter & Gamble, Unilever, China Mengniu Dairy, Honda
Telecom services	1,394	5.8	AT & T, China Mobile, Royal KPN
Materials	1,316	5.5	Dow Chemical, Alcan, Vitro SA
Utilities	956	4.0	Duke Energy, Empresa Nacional de Electricidad SA, Hong Kong, and China Gas, Ltd.
Total	**23,955**	**100.0**	

Source: Business Week Global 1200, www.businessweek.com.

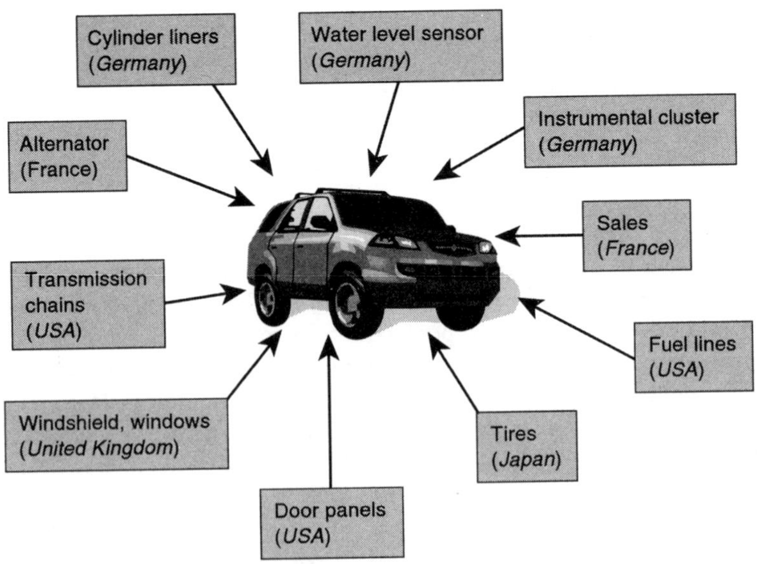

FIGURE 1.4 Countries where suppliers of components for the Chevrolet Tahoe are located

Globalization in action 2009: concerted efforts by G-20 major economies to avert a global economic crisis

In light of a major global economic crisis, the existence of a global organization of major economic powers, the G-20, seems to be able to weather the crisis effectively. The G-20, The Group of Twenty Finance Ministers, and Central Bank Governors, is a group of finance ministers and central bank governors from 20 economies: 19 of the world's largest national economies, plus the European Union (EU). Collectively, the G-20 economies comprise 85 percent of global gross national product, 80 percent of world trade and two-thirds of the world population.

The G-20 is a forum for cooperation and consultation on matters pertaining to the international financial system. It studies, reviews, and promotes discussion among key industrial and emerging market countries of policy issues pertaining to the promotion of international financial stability, and seeks to address issues that go beyond the responsibilities of any one organization.

The G-20 London Summit took place during the month of March 2009, at a time when the world confronted the worst economic crisis since the Second World War. The aims of the London Summit were to bring together leaders of the world's major economies and key international institutions to take the collective action necessary to stabilize the world economy and secure recovery and jobs.

Leaders faced an unprecedented range of challenges – of averting an even more severe downturn and restoring growth in the short term, while at the same time reshaping the financial system, preserving the world trading system, and laying the foundation for a sustainable recovery. Real action was agreed at the summit, with leaders agreeing on steps to:

1. *Restore confidence, growth, and jobs*: Leaders reaffirmed their commitment to work together to restore growth and jobs, while preserving long-term fiscal sustainability. They agreed actions to accelerate the return to trend growth and committed to taking whatever action is necessary to secure that outcome, and called on the International Monetary Fund (IMF) to assess regularly the actions taken and the global actions required. They committed to make available an additional $1.1 trillion program of support to help the world economy through the crisis and to restore credit, growth, and jobs. Most of this will be provided through the international financial institutions.
2. *Strengthen financial supervision and regulation*: Leaders agreed to strengthen the financial system by putting in place a better and more credible system of surveillance and regulation to take account of macro economic risks and prevent excess leveraging, including, for the first time, regulation and oversight of large hedge funds and credit rating agencies. They also agreed on actions to tackle noncooperative jurisdictions and to adopt common principles for executive remuneration.
3. *Fund and reform the international financial institutions to overcome this crisis and prevent future ones*: Leaders agreed to make an additional $850 billion in resources available through international financial institutions, such as the IMF, the World Bank, and other multilateral development banks, including a $500 billion expansion of the IMF's resources, a Special Drawing Right (SDR) allocation of $250 billion, and at least $100 billion in additional lending from Multilateral Development Banks. The leaders also agreed to ensure to

(*Continued*)

they have the facilities needed to meet the needs of emerging markets and developing countries and speed up reform of international financial institutions to ensure national representation is in line with the changing balance of the world economy.

4 *Promote global trade and investment and reject protectionism, to assure prosperity*: Leaders committed not to resort to protectionism, direct or indirect, and put in place a transparent monitoring mechanism; and to take measures which promote trade, including a commitment to make available $250 billion to halt the slow-down in trade finance, which facilitates up to 90 percent of world trade.

5 *Build an inclusive, green, and sustainable recovery*: Leaders reaffirmed their commitment to meeting the Millennium Development Goals and to delivering on development aid pledges; made $50 billion available to low-income countries, including through the proceeds of agreed IMF gold sales; agreed that the IMF would further support low-income countries; and called on the United Nations (UN) to establish an effective mechanism to monitor the impact of the crisis on the poorest and most vulnerable regions and countries.

A Quick Review

1 Globalization may be defined as the increase in worldwide integration of markets for goods, services, and capital concurrent with the increased role for multinational enterprises (MNEs) in the world economy and an increased intervention into domestic and regional policies and affairs by international institutions such as the International Monetary Fund (IMF), the World Trade Organization (WTO), the World Bank, and the United Nations.

2 For the consumer, globalization means lower prices, better selection, improved service, and blurred origin of goods and services. For the producer, globalization presents the opportunity to create a global supply chain. Globalization allows MNEs to raise capital on better terms. However, the flow of workers across borders is still highly controlled locally, limiting the opportunity for economic efficiency.

Globalization measurement

A useful tool to measure the degree of globalization was devised and is continuously reported by A.T. Kearney, an international professional firm. A globalization index (Globalization Index) tracks and assesses changes in key components of global integration, such as trade and investment flows, movement of people across borders, volumes of international telephone traffic, Internet usage, and participation in international organizations. In fact this index tracks globalization intensity by measurements relating to four main categories:

- ***economic integration***, combining data on trade and foreign direct investment (FDI) inflows and outflows;

- ***personal contact***, tracking international travel and tourism, international telephone traffic, and cross-border remittances and personal transfers (including worker remittances, compensation to employees, and other person-to-person and nongovernmental transfers);
- ***technological connectivity***, counting the number of Internet users, Internet hosts, and secure servers through which encrypted transactions are carried out;
- ***political engagement***, including each country's memberships in a variety of representative international organizations, personnel and financial contribuions to UN peacekeeping missions, ratification of selected multilateral treaties and amounts of governmental transfer payments and receipts.

During 2005, the 62 countries that are ranked account for 96 percent of the world's GDP and 85 percent of the world's population. Major regions of the world, including developed and developing countries, are covered to provide a comprehensive and comparative view of global integration. The data for the full sample of 62 countries is collected from international organizations that include the World Bank, International Monetary Fund, the United Nations, and International Telecommunications Union.

The degree of globalization changes from country to country and is changing from year to year. To be exact, many countries are becoming more and more "global," while other countries, because of local political and social changes, are actually going backwards with regards to globalization. In Figure 1.5 the globalization index of various countries is noted.

During the period between 2002 and 2005, there were changes in countries' rankings. In 2005, the USA got into the top five group for the first time in the annual ranking of the world's most globalized nations, rising to fourth place from its previous 12th. Singapore and Ireland are ahead on the strength of their increased political engagement and foreign trade ties. Despite weaker connections with the rest of the world in the political and economic realms, the USA rose due to its technological strength. The USA ranked first in both the number of Internet users and secure servers. Russia dropped eight spots between 2002 and 2005 to 52nd of the 62 nations in the index as its oil-dependent economy saw a continued decline in trade as a share of GDP. Iran, finished last, which has been the case for past five years.

Measuring the impact of globalization

Measuring the degree of globalization shows a positive relationship between public spending on education and globalization, especially in developing countries (see Figure 1.6). Governments put a lot of effort into rethinking the spending on education. For example, what President Fox of Mexico initiated during the turn of this century. While resources alone do not guarantee a more educated population, assigning more resources to education creates possibilities of more schools and teachers.

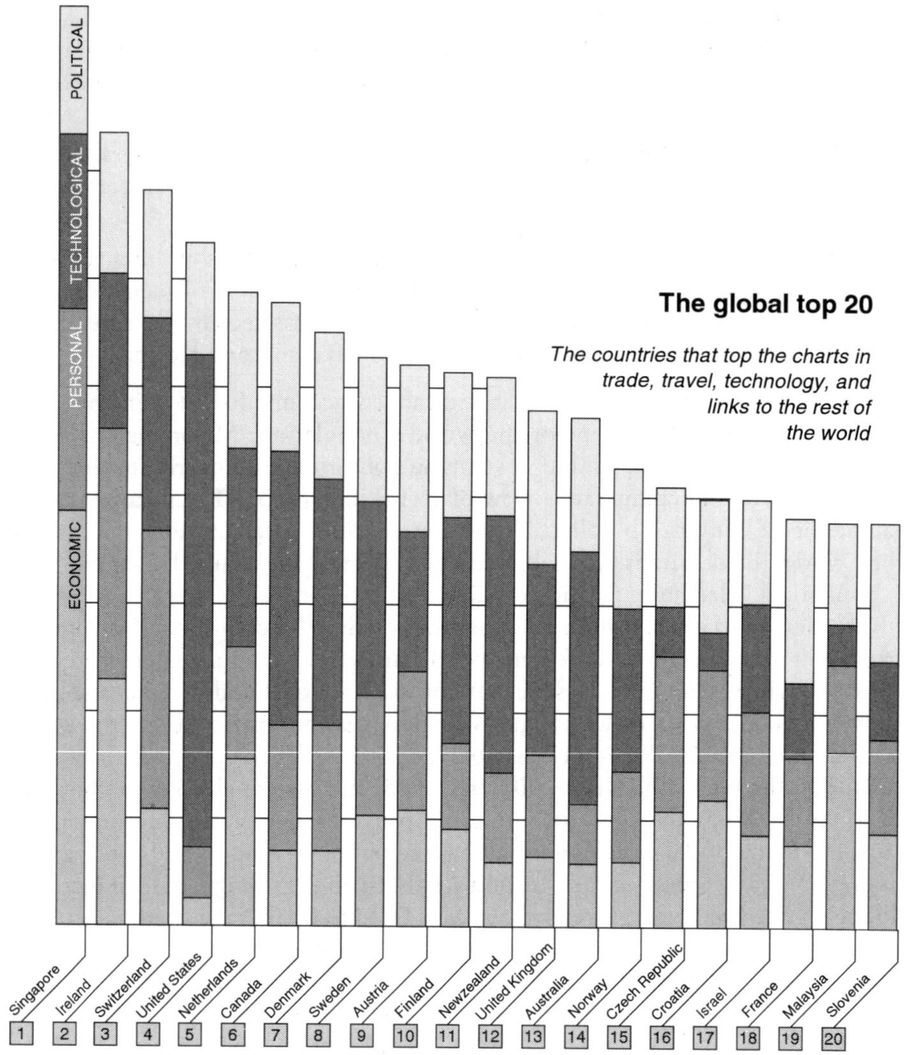

FIGURE 1.5 Measuring globalization (Adapted from A.T. Kearney, Measuring globalization at http://www.atkearney.com/shared_res/pdf/2004G-index.pdf)

Another interesting observation is that there is a positive relationship between globalization and political freedom, political rights and civil liberties and a negative relationship with perceived levels of corruption (Figure 1.7).

In light of recent terrorists attacks and the arguments for and against fighting terrorism and the effect of fighting terrorism on aggravating terrorism, it is interesting to find out how terrorism is fed on globalization. Some have theorized

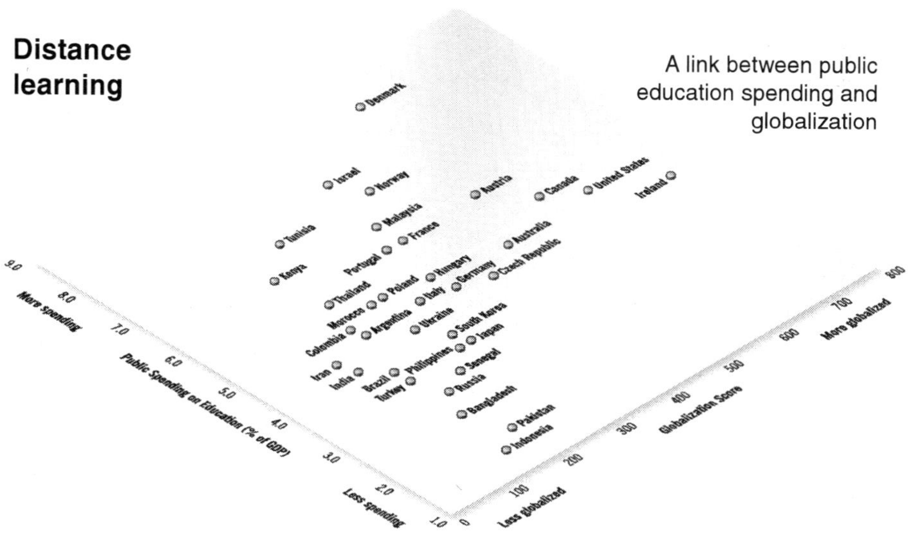

FIGURE 1.6 Globalization and education (Adapted from A.T. Kearney, Measuring globalization)

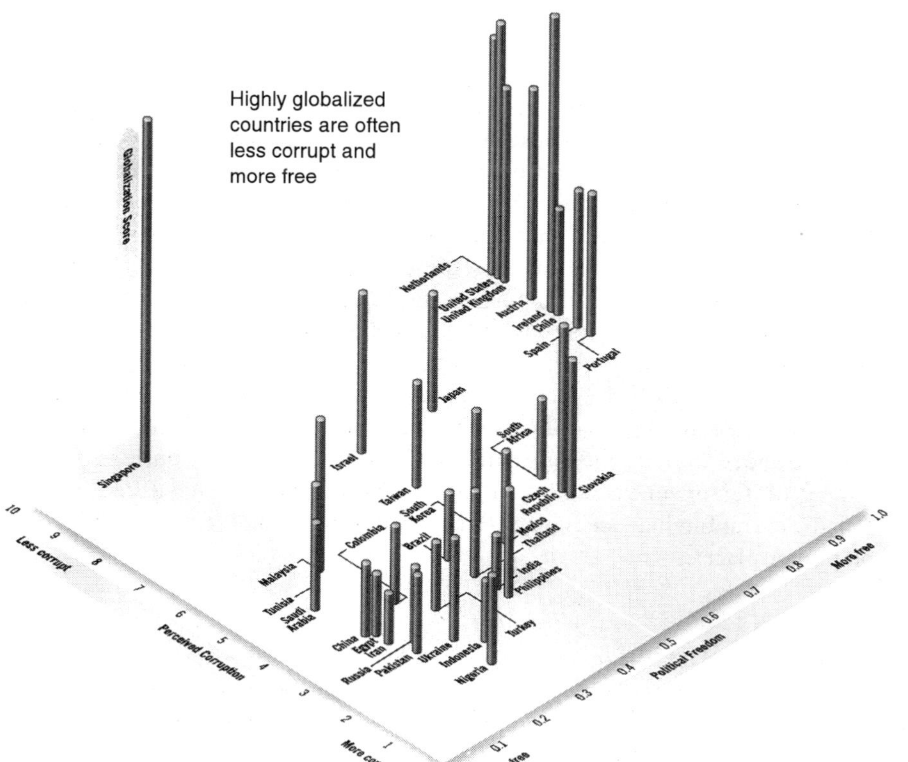

FIGURE 1.7 Globalization and democracy (Adapted from A.T. Kearney, Measuring globalization)

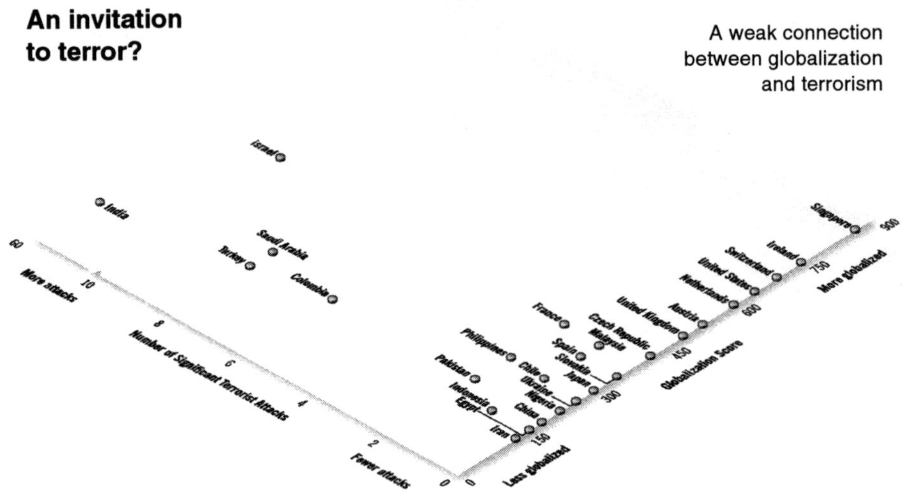

FIGURE 1.8 Globalization and terror (Adapted from A.T. Kearney, Measuring globalization)

that the more global a country is, the more susceptible it is to terror attacks. Open physical borders of countries and with close contact with the outside world may allow terrorists to enter and operate freely. Furthermore, angered with the unequal distribution of globalization's benefits, terrorists may target more globalized societies. It is also argued that the more technologically advanced countries are more susceptible to terror, as was the case with the September 11 attacks where the terrorists used e-mail, Internet, and cell phones in planning the attacks. This is not the case. In fact, there is little correlation between a country's level of global integration and the number of significant international terrorist attacks (see Figure 1.8). In fact, globalized countries may be more capable of combating terrorism, since they join international security and intelligence networks. India, for example, decided to ratify the International Convention for the Suppression of the Financing of Terrorism in 2003. The city of New York has established its own so-called Central Intelligence Agency (CIA) with offices in Israel, Iraq, and Jordan, among other places.

Globalization: on balance

It seems that globalization is here to stay, affecting the international business environment as it affects each one of us. Thus, it is best to acknowledge its contribution to human kind and find the best ways to extend its benefits to the largest number of people, regions, and countries. As the share of developing countries in world trade and population increases, they become not only the largest producers but also the largest consumers of goods and services. In this case, globalization acts as a catalyst, increasing international investment and trade and enables the transfer of technologies into developing countries.

Labor rates of workers in foreign subsidiaries of MNEs in developing countries are better than average local rates, along with appropriate benefits such as health, education, and transportation allowances. Furthermore, globalization presents opportunities for higher mobility to foreign nationals. In addition, globalization allows for the voluntary adoption of Western accounting and operational reporting standards and practices. Adhering to these standards and practices makes it possible for domestic businesses based in developing countries to offer their stock in various world stock exchanges. As an example, Infosys, the Indian-based computer giant, has offered its stock in New York's NASDAQ, following the voluntary adoption of Generally Accepted Auditing Standards (GAAS) and Generally Accepted Accounting Practices (GAAP).

Concurrent with increased globalization, the power of MNEs grows more marked. This perceived power increase is being met by expectations that MNEs will take a more active and responsible role in social issues and act in an environmentally responsible manner. As an example, as the United Nations celebrates its 60 years of existence, calls are being made for MNEs to be more involved in helping to promote peace and human rights around the world. These expectations are not unreasonable. As a matter of fact, some MNEs have annual sales Figures that are larger than some countries, attesting to their power and possible influence on world affairs. However, the power and influence of MNEs should not be overstated, since small and medium-size enterprises in many economies still contribute more than 50 percent of GDP.

A worldwide benchmarking and competitive analysis of various business-related phenomena is also part of globalization. For example, one should note the important measure of the Index of Economic Freedom (IEF) published by The Heritage Foundation, as marked in Figure 1.9.

Other significant measures are The Ease of Doing Business measure published by the World Bank and the International Financial Corporation, as in Table 1.11, and the Global Entrepreneurship Index, generated by the Global Entrepreneurship Monitor (GEM) Consortium, which compares and contrast the intensity of entrepreneurship and innovation worldwide, as indicated in Table 1.12.

Lastly, as globalization takes hold in various countries and its influence becomes more marked, it seems that there is a growing need for a globalization infrastructure. This infrastructure includes a network of bilateral and multilateral trade agreements, associations and memberships in international bodies such as the IMF, the World Bank, the WTO; some may even suggest an associate membership role in various bodies of the United Nations. As this book explores the area of international business, one should be aware that globalization should be balanced against strong and viable domestic factors as executives make various business decisions. As globalization involves greater interaction between different national and business cultures, it is imperative that executives be aware of decisions that best exploit opportunities in the international arena.

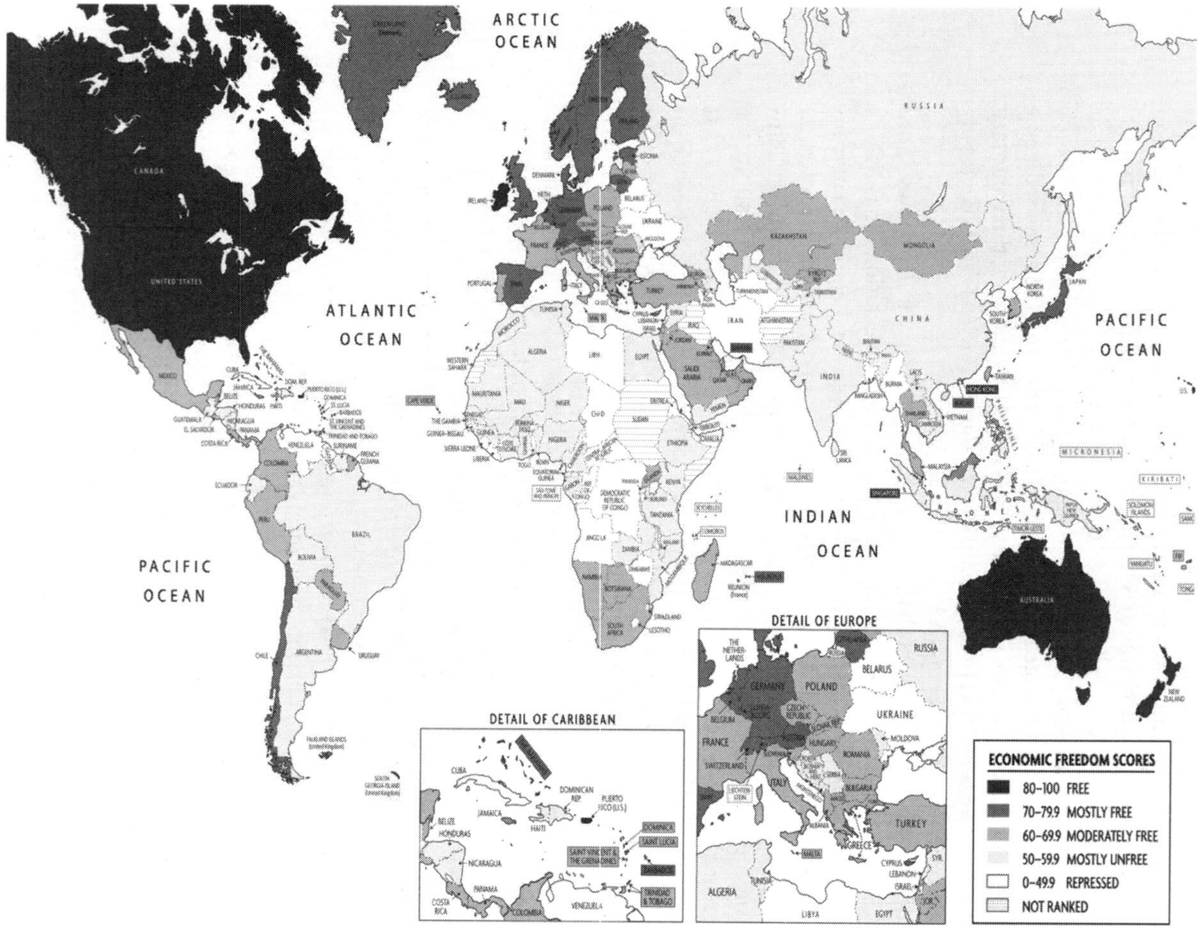

FIGURE 1.9 Distribution of economic freedom (Adapted from Miller T. Holmes, K. R. (2009) Index of economic freedom. Washington DC, The Heritage Foundation and Dow Jones & Company, Inc., 2009)

TABLE 1.11 Top 30 Countries on the Ease of Doing Business

1. Singapore	11. Iceland	21. Switzerland
2. New Zealand	12. Japan	22. Estonia
3. United States	13. Thailand	23. Korea
4. Hong Kong, China	14. Finland	24. Mauritius
5. Denmark	15. Georgia	25. Germany
6. United Kingdom	16. Saudi Arabia	26. Netherlands
7. Ireland	17. Sweden	27. Austria
8. Canada	18. Bahrain	28. Lithuania
9. Australia	19. Belgium	29. Latvia
10. Norway	20. Malaysia	30. Israel

Source: World Bank and the International Finance Corporation (2009). *Doing Business 2009.* Washington, DC: the World Bank.

TABLE 1.12 The Rank of the Countries in Terms of the Global Entrepreneurship Index

Rank	*Country*	*Gross domestic product adjustment for purchasing power (GDPPP)*	*Rank*	*Country*	*Gross domestic product adjustment for purchasing power (GDPPP)*
1.	New Zealand	25320	23.	France	31458
2.	Iceland	39603	24.	Czech Republic	22077
3.	Denmark	36903	25.	Spain	29951
4.	United States	44384	26.	United Arab Emirates	35661
5.	Australia	33947	27.	Portugal	21555
6.	Sweden	33799	28.	Italy	30777
7.	Ireland	46587	29.	Malaysia	13251
8.	Norway	45206	30.	Germany	31855
9.	Canada	35776	31.	Peru	6617
10.	Finland	34654	32.	Jordan	4287
11.	Switzerland	35106	33.	Latvia	15781
12.	Israel	30578	34.	Japan	33014
13.	Hong Kong	38227	35.	Croatia	14040
14.	Netherlands	34059	36.	Colombia	8631
15.	Chile	13494	37.	Poland	13615
16.	Slovenia	24172	38.	China	8242
17.	Belgium	34580	39.	Uruguay	11028
18.	Singapore	31652	40.	South Africa	14159
19.	United Kingdom	34075	41.	Argentina	15437
20.	Korea	25574	42.	Hungary	19451
21.	Puerto Rico	20223	43.	Dominican Republic	8760
22.	Austria	36445	44.	Turkey	9307
45.	Egypt	5388	55.	Philippines	5207
46.	Macedonia	8822	56.	Bolivia	4453
47.	Thailand	9435	57.	Venezuela	7315
48.	Greece	26483	58.	Brazil	9176
49.	Kazakhstan	9841	59.	Bosnia and Herzegovina	7048

(*Continued*)

TABLE 1.12 Cont.

Rank	*Country*	*Gross domestic product adjustment for purchasing power (GDPPP)*	*Rank*	*Country*	*Gross domestic product adjustment for purchasing power (GDPPP)*
50.	Romania	10206	60.	Mexico	10963
51.	Jamaica	4503	61.	Ecuador	7456
52.	India	3789	62.	Uganda	1648
53.	Serbia	5351	63.	Iran	3456
54.	Russia	12595			

Source: Permission to use GEM 2009 summary has been kindly granted by the copyright holders. Our thanks go to the authors, national teams, researchers, funding bodies, and other contributors who have made this possible.

Global Focus – The Growth of SMEs

Small and medium-size enterprises have gone global using an aggressive approach in producing and marketing both traditional and high-technology products. As an example, Diesel Company of Italy extended globally from a humble beginning in 1978.

Diesel

For the global youth culture, Diesel's fashions are highly preferred to other brands. Founded in Italy in 1978, Diesel started out as an SME, and eventually grew to achieve annual sales of more than US$1 billion, 85 percent of which comes from abroad. Diesel produces unusual but popular men's and women's casual wear. Competing with Donna Karan and Tommy Hilfiger, Diesel wear is futuristic. Its jeans come in exotic shades and styles. Diesel management sees the world as a single, borderless macro-culture, and Diesel staff includes an assortment of personalities from all parts of the globe who create an unpredictable, dynamic vitality, and energy. The firm focuses on design and marketing, leaving the production of jeans to subcontractors.

Diesel is Europe's hottest blue jeans brand, and has expanded its distribution to over 80 countries through department stores and specialty retailers, as well as some 200 Diesel-owned stores from Paris to Miami to Tokyo. At over $100 a pair, Diesel jeans are expensive for many, but controversial advertising has propelled the company to huge international success. The company's advertising has featured sumo wrestlers kissing, a row of chimpanzees giving the fascist salute, and inflatable naked dolls in a board meeting with a hugely overweight CEO. Its ads poke fun at death, obesity, murder, and do-gooders. Some people in the USA see the prankish campaigns as politically incorrect. For instance, under pressure from activists, Diesel withdrew ads that applauded smoking and gun ownership with slogans such as "145 cigarettes a day will give you that sexy voice and win new friends." Another ad featured nuns in blue jeans below the copy: "Pure, virginal 100 percent cotton. Soft and yet miraculously strong."

If Starbucks can charge several dollars for coffee, then Diesel executives believe they can persuade consumers to pay $108 for its jeans. Diesel was one of the first companies to have a major Internet presence (www.diesel.com). Selling jeans via an online virtual store, Diesel's web advertising is hip, with a powerful, market-friendly message that drives its popularity to youth worldwide. The firm introduces some 1,500 new designs every 6 months, and employs a multicultural team of young designers who travel the globe for inspiration and weave their impressions into the next collection.

Diesel is a classic success story in international business by a smaller firm. Its strategy is instructive for other marketers of jeans such as Kitson, Lucky Brand, Mavi Jeans, and 7 For All Mankind.

Sources: Diesel's online website at www.diesel.com; Edmondson, Gail (2003). Diesel is smoking but can its provocative ads keep sales growth hot?, *Business Week,* February 10, p. 64; Hoover's online website for Whirlpool Corporation, www.hoovers.com; Helliker, Kevin (1998). "Teen retailing: the underground taste makers – is Diesel apparel a bit too trendy for its own good?", *Wall Street Journal,* December 9, p. B 1; OECD (1997). *Globalization and Small and Medium Enterprises (SMEs).* Paris: OECD; Sansoni, Sylvia (1996). "Full steam ahead for Diesel; will its pricey jeans and outrageous ads succeed in the *U.S.?" Business Week,* April 29, pp. 58–60.

COUNTRY FOCUS

CHINA

World Rank (EFI 2009): 132

Regional Rank (EFI 2009): 28

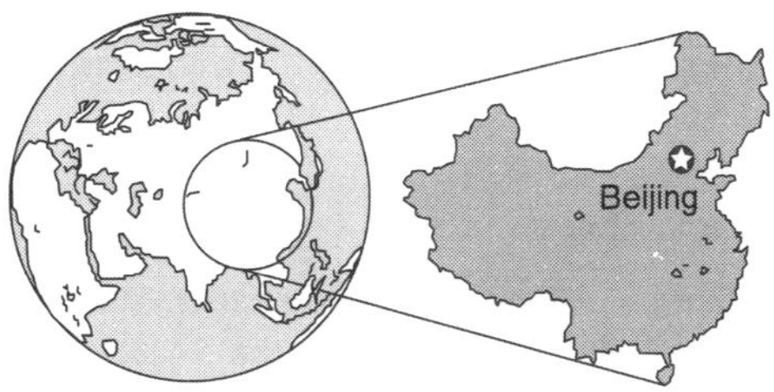

Quick facts

Population: 1.3 billion

GDP (PPP): $6.1 trillion; 11.1 percent growth in 2006; 10.1 percent 5-year compound annual growth; $4.644 per capita

Unemployment: 4.0 percent

Inflation (CPI): 4.8 percent

FDI inflow: $69.5 billion

2006 data unless otherwise noted

Economic freedom score

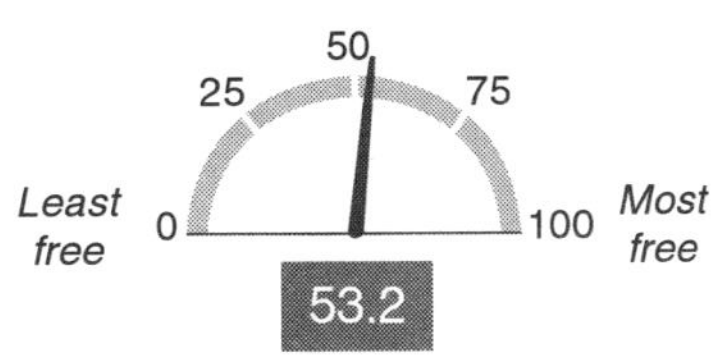

(Continued)

China's economic freedom score is 53.2, making its economy the 132nd freest in the 2009 Index. China is ranked 28th out of 41 countries in the Asia-Pacific region, and its overall score is slightly lower than the global and regional averages.

China scores relatively well in trade freedom, mainly because of lower tariff rates. Despite heavy nontariff barriers, it has benefited from global trade and investment for three decades and is an emerging economic power. Rapid development of coastal cities has resulted in increasing disparities in economic freedom and wealth across the country. Efforts to embrace more market principles have been made, although progress has been limited. Along with its new labor law, China implemented an antimonopoly law in 2008 that largely exempts state enterprises.

The state still guides and directs much economic activity and, while allowing some response to market forces by enterprises and individuals, the Communist Party still maintains ultimate authority over economic decisions. Investment freedom, financial freedom, and property rights are very weak. Foreign investment is controlled and regulated, and the judicial system is highly politicized. The state maintains tight control of the financial sector and directly or indirectly owns all banks. Urbanization and the corresponding need for more job growth have driven overall economic policy.

Background

China is an authoritarian state that has liberalized its economy markedly since the early 1980s. However, the ruling Communist Party maintains tight control of political expression, speech, assembly, and religion. China joined the WTO in 2001. Since then, the economy has grown rapidly, and China's industrial and manufacturing sector is now second only to that of the USA. Corruption and a weak rule of law remain serious problems. The government is struggling to manage social unrest, environmental degradation and the world's largest-ever migration from rural to urban areas.

Business freedom – 51.6

The overall freedom to start, operate, and close a business is constrained by China's regulatory environment. Starting a business takes about the world average of 38 days, but obtaining a business license requires more than the world average of 18 procedures and 225 days. China lacks legal and regulatory transparency.

Trade freedom – 71.4

China's weighted average tariff rate was 4.3 percent in 2006. Despite lower nontariff barriers pursuant to WTO requirements, import and export bans and restrictions, import and export licensing, nontransparent tariff classifications, complex regulations and standards, subsidies, state trading in certain goods, services market restrictions, issues involving the protection of intellectual property rights, and inconsistent and corruption-prone customs administration add to the cost of trade. Twenty points were deducted from China's trade freedom score to account for nontariff barriers.

Fiscal freedom – 70.6

China has a high income tax rate and a moderate corporate tax rate. The top income tax rate is 45 percent. As of January 2008, the tax systems for foreign and domestic enterprises were merged, and the top corporate tax was reduced to 25 percent. Other taxes include a value-added tax (VAT) and a real estate tax. In the most recent year, overall tax revenue as a percentage of GDP was 17.0 percent.

Government size – 88.9

Government expenditures, including consumption and transfer payments, are relatively low.

In the most recent year, central government spending equaled 19.2 percent of GDP. Consolidated government spending (including local governments and social security) is estimated to be more than 30 percent of GDP.

Monetary freedom – 72.9

Inflation is moderate, averaging 3.7 percent between 2005 and 2007. The market determines the prices of most traded products, but the government maintains prices for petroleum, electricity, pharmaceuticals, coal, agricultural products and other "essential" goods. Subsidies allow state-owned enterprises to produce and sell goods to wholesalers and retailers at artificially low prices. Fifteen points were deducted from China's monetary freedom score to adjust for measures that distort domestic prices.

Investment freedom – 30

China's Foreign Investment Catalogue delineates sectors in which foreign investment is encouraged, permitted, restricted and prohibited, as well as such specific restrictions as caps on foreign ownership and permissible types of investment. Investors face regulatory nontransparency, inconsistently enforced laws, and regulations, weak International Property Rights (IPR) protection, corruption, industrial policies protecting local firms, and a legal system that cannot guarantee the sanctity of contracts. Foreign investors may access foreign exchange for current account transactions like repatriating profits, but capital account transactions are tightly regulated.

Financial freedom – 30

China's complex financial system is tightly controlled by the government. The China Banking Regulatory Commission supervised roughly 8,900 financial institutions in 2007. China has two private banks, but four state-owned banks account for over 50 percent of total assets. The state directs the allocation of credit, and the big four state-owned banks lend primarily to state-owned enterprises. Numerous foreign banks have opened branches but face burdensome regulations. Foreign participation in capital markets is limited. Expanding access to financial services remains a challenge.

Property rights – 20

China's judicial system is weak, and many companies resort to arbitration. Even when courts try to enforce decisions, local officials can ignore them with impunity. All land is state-owned, but individuals and firms may own and transfer long-term leases, subject to many restrictions, as well as structures and personal property. The Property Law allows automatic renewal of residential property rights; commercial and industrial grants are renewed absent a conflicting public interest. Intellectual property rights are not enforced effectively. Copyrights, patents, brand-names, trademarks, and trade secrets are routinely stolen.

Freedom from corruption – 35

Corruption is perceived as widespread. China ranks 72nd out of 179 countries in Transparency International's Corruption Perceptions Index for 2007. Corruption limits foreign direct investment and affects banking, finance, government procurement, and construction most severely, and there is a lack of independent investigative bodies and courts.

Labor freedom – 61.8

China's labor regulations hinder overall employment and productivity growth. The nonsalary cost of employing a worker is high. Dismissing a redundant employee can be relatively costly and may require prior consultation with the local

(Continued)

bureau of labor union. The ability to terminate employment varies according to the location and size of the enterprise. A new employment law aimed at providing greater protection and benefits for more workers became effective January 1, 2008.

Source: Adapted from Terry Miller and Kim R. Holmes, *2009 Index of Economic Freedom* (Washington, DC: The Heritage Foundation and Dow Jones & Company, Inc., 2009), at www.heritage.org/index.

SUMMARY

Globalization. Globalization materializes in many ways and affects consumers, producers, executives, workers, and other participants in the world economy. It brings along great promise for the future but presents considerable risks. In light of globalization, executives are required to balance forces of standardization, coordination and centralization against adherence to local adaptation and decentralization.

International business. International business is all business activities, including the creation and transfer of resources, goods, services, know-how, skills and information, and transcends national boundaries.

Multinational enterprise (MNE). An enterprise that engages in foreign direct investment and owns or controls value-adding activities in more than one country.

Other terms used to describe international business entities. Multidomestic firm, global firm, transnational firm, early multinational enterprise, and small and midsize international enterprise.

The drivers to expand internationally are to find new markets, to improve economic gains, to position the corporation strategically to exploit future opportunities and to respond to "discovered opportunities."

The A.T. Kearney-devised measure of globalization is based on measuring economic integration, personal contact, technology connectivity, and political engagement.

Social scientists see in globalization a fundamental change in the understanding of space and time by human beings.

Global supply chain. Global supply chain is the term describing the network of suppliers dispersed across continents and deployed by most industries, including the car industry, the consumer electronics products industry, and the biotechnology industry.

The changing nature of international business environment. It is a basic premise of the book that business executives should be aware of the changing nature of the international business environment and be able to respond in a timely, efficient, and effective manner. This chapter and the following chapters aim to describe and demonstrate a set of decision-making frameworks, managerial tools, and data sources that assist the business executive to operate in the dynamic environment of international business.

DISCUSSION QUESTIONS

1 What is the definition of international business?
2 Can you identify globalization effects in your country as well in another country?
3 Identify a company that has gone global and explain what of the four reasons (or a combination of them) motivated the move?
4 What is the effect of globalization on education, democracy, and terror?

INTERNET EXERCISE

Franchise Opportunities at McDonald's

One of the best-known franchise operations in the world is McDonald's; and in recent years the company has been working to expand its international presence. Why? Because the US market is becoming saturated and the major growth opportunities lie in the international arena. Visit the McDonald's website (www.mcdonalds.com) and find out what is going on in the company. Begin by perusing their latest annual report and see how well they are doing both domestically and internationally. Then turn to the franchise information that is provided and find out how much it would cost to set up a franchise in the following countries: Belgium, Brazil, South Korea, Mexico, Slovenia, and Turkey. Which seems like the most attractive international investment? In addition to this group, in what other countries is the firm seeking franchisees? Would any of these seem particularly attractive to you as investor? Which ones? Why?

Then, based on this assignment and the chapter material, answer the following questions:

1 Will the fact the euro has become the standard currency in the EU help or hinder a new McDonald's franchisee in Europe?
2 If there are exciting worldwide opportunities, why does McDonald's not exploit these itself instead of looking for franchisees?
3 What is the logic in McDonald's expansion strategy?

ACTION ITEMS

1 Identify two news articles from the *Wall Street Journal* (www.wsj.com), the *Financial Times* (www.ft.com), *Business Week* (www.businessweek.com), or *The Economist* (www.economist.com) and discuss how globalization affect the decisions made by NMEs both small (SMEs) and large.
2 Initiate a discussion with an executive of a local business. Discuss and summarize how knowledge of the international business environment may enhance the profitability and competitive position of his domestic company.
3 Sign on an Internet site (http://geography.about.com/library/maps/blrindex.htm) which provides a comprehensive set of maps. Identify three developed countries and three developing countries in various continents. What kind of information relevant to international business can be identified from this Internet site?

A Case

Carrefour, Tesco, and Wal-Mart: The Globalization Pains of the Retailing Industry

What the world needs now?

"This is still today a local industry," says Sir Terry Leahy, boss of Tesco. On April 12, his British supermarket chain said that underlying group pre-tax profit in the year to February 26 rose by 21 percent to £2 billion (US$3.8 billion). With sales up by 12 percent to £37 billion, Tesco confirmed its place as the world's third-largest retailer, after America's Wal-Mart and France's Carrefour. Now Sir Terry is pushing Tesco's international expansion even harder – a risky business for all retailers.

"Despite globalization, local differences still hold sway over mass retailing," says Sir Terry. "What works well in one country does not necessarily work in another." What this means, he cautions, is that building a global retailing business could take "decades of work." The pitfalls are numerous, as many of his rivals already know to their cost.

Wal-Mart, which dwarfs everyone, with US$285 billion of worldwide sales last year, is also expanding overseas. It is doing well against Tesco in Britain through the Asda chain, which it bought in 1999. But in Germany Wal-Mart is struggling against even more aggressive discounters, such as Aldi. In Japan, Wal-Mart has a controlling stake in the Seiyu retail chain, but losses there have been growing. Wal-Mart's policy of "everyday low prices" is proving hard to sell to the Japanese, who often associate low prices with poor quality. With operations in some 30 countries, Carrefour is the most international of the supermarket chains. Last month, it announced a 15 percent fall in net profits in 2004, to €1.4 billion ($1.8 billion). This was partly because of a charge it took on selling its stores in Japan, which it has decided to quit after four years of struggle. Carrefour is also selling 29 hypermarkets in Mexico after troubles there. Jose Luis Duran, the firm's former finance director who became chief executive in February after controlling shareholders forced a boardroom reshuffle, says it is likely that Carrefour will quit any overseas market in which it cannot become one of the top-three retailers. Tesco has also had a few problems overseas: for instance, facing strong competition from discount chains in some central European markets. Even so, Tesco's total international sales grew by 13 percent to, £7.6 billion in 2004. Some 60 percent of its overseas investments are in Thailand, South Korea, Ireland, and Hungary, generating together a return on investment of over 15 percent. Last year it bought a 50 percent stake in a Chinese supermarket chain to extend its presence in what many retailers see as Asia's most promising market. Its biggest challenge abroad is to expand beyond hypermarkets into smaller convenience stores, as it has done to great effect at home. When retailers achieve a dominant position at home, the appeal of growing overseas can seem strong – not least because they may face a domestic backlash against their size. Tesco, with almost 30 percent of Britain's grocery market, has recently found itself having to defend itself against criticism, just as Wal-Mart is doing in America. To continue growing at home, Wal-Mart is trying to expand into some areas where it is less welcome, such as unionized states and places (such as New York City) that dislike giant superstores. In America (but not always overseas), Wal-Mart is a nonunion firm. This week, a union filed a complaint with the government urging an investigation into allegations – disputed by Wal-Mart – that Thomas Coughlin, a former Wal-Mart executive and friend of the firm's late, legendary founder, Sam Walton, violated federal labor law by financing antiunion activities.

With such headaches at home, it is hardly surprising that even the world's biggest retailer finds it hard to deal with the many local difficulties that beset shopkeepers who venture abroad.

Discussion issues

1 In the face of globalization, what are the various responses used by the retailing industry?
2 How does the international business environment impact on the effectiveness of these responses?

Bibliography

Batra, R. (1993). *The Myth of Free Trade*. New York: Touchstone Books.

Bhagwati, J. (1989). *Protectionism*. Cambridge, MA: MIT Press.

Business Week Global 1200 (n.d.). Breaking it down by industry. www.businessweek.com.

Caves, R. E. (1993). Japanese investment in the US: Lessons for the economic analysis of foreign investment. *The World Economy*, 16, 279–300.

Dicken, P. (1992). *Global Shift*. New York: Guilford, p. 104.

Ernst & Young (2005). *China: The New Lap of Luxury*.

Friedman, Thomas (2005). *The World is Flat*. New York: Farrar, Straus, and Giroux.

International Monetary Fund (April 2006). World Economic Outlook database, www.imf.org.

Goldsmith, J. (1996). The winners and the losers. In J. Mander and E. Goldsmith (eds) *The Case Against the Global Economy*. San Francisco, CA: The Sierra Book Club.

Gottschalk, P., et al. (1997). Cross-national comparisons of earnings and income inequality. *Journal of Economic Literature*, 35, June.

Greider, W. (1997). *One World, Ready or Not: The Manic Logic of Global Capitalism*. New York: Simon and Schuster.

Kearney, A. T. (2005). Globalization at work. *Foreign Policy Magazine*, May/June.

Knickerbocker, F. T. (1973). *Oligopolistic Reaction and Multinational Enterprise*. Boston, MA: Harvard Business School Press.

Krugman, P. (1996). *Pop Internationalism*. Cambridge, MA: MIT Press.

Lashinsky, A. (2004). Where Dell is going next. *Fortune*, October 18, 115–20.

Levitt, T. (1983). The globalization of markets. *Harvard Business Review*, May–June, 92–102.

Ohmae, K. (1995). Putting global logic first. *Harvard Business Review*, (January–February) 119–25.

Radrik, D. (1997). *Has Globalization Gone too Far?* Washington, DC: Institution for International Economics.

Reich, R. B. (1991). *The Work of Nations*. New York: A. A. Knopf.

Scheuerman, W. (2002). Globalization. In E. N. Zalta (ed.), *The Stanford Encyclopedia of Philosophy*. Stanford University and the Texas A & M.

Servan-Schreiber, J. J. (1968). *The American Challenge*. New York: Atheneum.

Stewart, A. (1997). Easier access to world markets. *Financial Times, 8*, December 3.

United Nations Conference on Trade and Development. (2005). *World Investment Report 2005*. Geneva, Switzerland: United Nations.

Vesosco, S. /5W Infographic (July 24, 2007). Fortune Global 500 (www.money.cnn.com/fortune). *FORTUNE*, from "Tale of 229 Cities," pp. 96–97.

Williams, F. W. (1994). Trade round like this may never be seen again. *Financial Times, 8*, April 15.

World Trade Organization (2005). *International Trade Trends and Statistics*. Geneva, Switzerland: World Trade Organization.

World Trade Organization (2006). Geneva, Switzerland: World Trade Organization.

2

Corporate Citizenship, Social Responsibility, and Ethics

Learning Objectives

Following this chapter, the reader should be able to:

1. Describe the main ethical and social responsibility issues confronted by multinational enterprises (MNEs) around the world and in countries in which they operate
2. Explain the ways in which host countries, and nongovernmental, and international organizations attempt to regulate foreign investments and business practices
3. Identify the efforts to make MNEs more responsive to social agendas and become part of the communities in which they operate

Opening Case

HSBC Corporate Social Responsibility

Source: Adapted from various HSBC reports, www.hsbc.com/.../hsbc-goes-carbon-neutral-three-months-early.

The Hong Kong and Shanghai Banking Corporation (HSBC) termed the world's local bank, is a world leader in financial services, and makes a point of managing shareholders' investment and customers' money responsibly; it has set precedents for other banks to follow and continues to develop self-imposed ethical principles. A few of the ways in which the bank treats employees, customers, and global issues with respect are discussed below.

Responsible lending
The lending policies are fair, with a clear assessment of risk and, for larger projects, environmental and social impact. Criteria for investing of funds are stringent, while satisfying the shareholders by making excellent returns. The bank is prepared to decline business that fails to meet these standards.

Social responsibility
As part of the corporate social responsibility outreach, HSBC has particular commitment to local communities, focusing on educational and environmental projects that will enhance the quality of life and protect natural resources across the globe.

HSBC encourages its employees, to contribute some of their work time to local communities through one of our many environmental and educational projects.

Environmental focus
In December 2004, HSBC made a commitment to be the first major bank in the world to become carbon neutral across all of its worldwide operations by 2006. HSBC is reducing its energy consumption and contributing to conservation projects to compensate for the inevitable impact the bank has upon the planet.

The linchpin of HSBC worldwide support for the environment is its "Investing in Nature" program, in partnership with the World Wildlife Fund (WWF), Earthwatch, and Botanic Gardens Conservation International (BGCI). Through HSBC work with BGCI, it aims to protect 20,000 plant species from extinction; with the WWF, HSBC is working to breathe new life into three of the world's major rivers, the Yangtze, Amazon, and Rio Grande; and with Earthwatch, HSBC employees can become involved in a huge variety of field-based conservation projects across the globe.

Educational focus

Recent educational projects to which HSBC employees have given their time and expertise include:

- An HSBC Volunteer Action program in Brazil which, since it was set up in 2000, has seen more than 1,500 staff help over 10,000 children. Activities range from computer classes to collecting clothes and gifts for the children.
- Members of staff raised funds for Water Aid to provide piped water, sanitation, and hygiene programs to communities in Malawi, Ghana, and Mozambique.
- Helping to combat illiteracy in Malta by running story-telling sessions for local children.
- Mentoring underprivileged children in Australia through HSBCKids, an innovative partnership with children's charity Barnardo's.
- The Helping Hands Staff Volunteer Program, which was launched in Mumbai in 2001, and has since been extended to four other cities in India. HSBC employees assist nongovernmental organization (NGOs) and other charities to offer services such as training in book-keeping, teaching English, and education to children who have not had the chance to go to school.
- The HSBC Financial Literacy Program partners with Students in Free Enterprise to promote financial literacy, with an emphasis on young people and female entrepreneurs. It is currently active in 28 countries.

HSBC goes carbon neutral three months early

Source: www.hsbc.com/.../hsbc-goes-carbon-neutral-three-months-early

HSBC has become the first major bank to go "carbon neutral". It has reduced its carbon dioxide (CO_2) emissions to zero by reducing energy use, buying green electricity, and then offsetting the remaining CO_2 emissions by investing in carbon projects. The bank made the announcement on the final day (6 October) of a UK government-sponsored conference, "Climate Change: The Business Forecast." In 2004, HSBC made public its intention to go carbon neutral by January 2006 and has achieved its objective three months ahead of schedule. Based on last year's data, HSBC estimated the company's CO_2 emissions for the last three months of 2005 will be around 170,000 tons and so in order to compensate for these emissions, at least 170,000 tons of carbon credits need to be bought. Through a competitive tender process the bank has received details of around 100 offset projects from dozens of countries.

To ensure these credits are credible, genuinely incremental and cost-effective, HSBC has enlisted the help of environmental partners, the Climate Group and ICF Consulting. Following exhaustive investigation, a final portfolio of projects has been assembled with four carbon offset suppliers. These projects are located in New Zealand, Australia, India, and Germany, at a total cost of US$750,000, or US$4.43 per ton. Sir John Bond, HSBC Group Chairman, said:

> HSBC is constantly looking at ways to increase energy efficiency and reduce its output of environmentally damaging waste. As part of this plan the bank has pledged to cut its net emissions to zero and will embark on a carbon neutral 'dry run' for the last quarter of 2005, to ensure it is fully prepared ahead of the previously announced January 2006 deadline.

Dr Steve Howard, CEO of the Climate Group commented,

> This is the first time that a major bank has been able to reduce their new carbon dioxide emissions to zero. We congratulate HSBC for reducing its energy use, announcing targets for the future and now setting a trend of carbon neutrality for other major companies to follow.

HSBC's commitment to carbon neutrality is part of a package of environmental measures announced in December 2004 by the bank to help tackle climate change. In July 2005, HSBC also announced company-wide three-year environmental targets to reduce energy and water use, waste production, and cut CO_2 emissions by 5 percent.

Earlier this year HSBC was ranked by the Carbon Disclosure Project among the top 60 companies globally in terms of climate leadership.

Introduction

The opening case of this chapter illustrates the importance and convergence of corporate social responsibility and ethical behavior standards and practices by organizations that are involved internationally. The HSBC case indicates the affirmative action that is taken by better society. Following Iraq's invasion of Kuwait in August 1990, a United Nations Oil-for-Food Program was instituted in December 1996. The program was intended to relieve the extended suffering of Iraqi civilians as a result of the comprehensive sanctions on Iraq from the United Nations, most of Iraq's 26 million people were solely dependent on rations from the oil-for-food plan. The program suffered from widespread corruption and abuse. The program was continuously dogged by accusations that some of its profits were unlawfully diverted to the government of Iraq and to UN officials. These accusations were made in many countries, including the US and Norway. The United Nations program raises the issue of ethical behavior and demonstrates that what is considered unethical behavior in some countries, say in the USA, may be an acceptable behavior in others, like Iraq before the 2003 occupation. These country-to-country perceived differences in ethical behavior converge in an accelerated manner and must be carefully considered by the international executives of MNEs and other organizations as they make business decisions.

It is apparent that never before have MNEs been under such critical scrutiny of the way in which they conduct business. There has been a significant increase in the expectations of a wide range of stakeholders – international consumers, employees, investors, communities, governments, and NGOs – regarding MNEs' commitment to socially responsible business practices. Senior corporate decision makers continuously find themselves faced with conflicting demands on their attention, time, and resources. As a result, corporate social responsibility is becoming a progressively more important component of good business practice. It is not only a question of what not to do and how not to act. It is a question of what to initiate, actively or proactively, to practice and demonstrate good corporate citizenship in countries in which the MNEs operate. The relatively new dimension of management, corporate social responsibility (CSR), poses several challenges. First and foremost is how to formulate powerful CSR investments strategies, while maximizing and capturing both the social and economic values from CSR investments.

Corporate Social Responsibility of MNEs

MNEs aim to achieve superior strategic CSR as well as enhancing firm value. *CSR aims to provide senior corporate executives, in a variety of industries, with the knowledge and practical tools and frameworks for integrating social responsibility as part of the corporate strategy*. This chapter explores how CSR can significantly improve business performance, how to incorporate it into the company strategy, and how to drive it throughout the organization. Executives should deepen their understanding of the political consequences of their business decisions in order to manage risks more effectively and to interact more constructively with external constituencies.

With the new skills and knowledge provided by the CSR awareness, executives are able to improve the manner in which they conduct business and enable firms to achieve higher levels of economic and social performance – positively driving the bottom line, while also significantly contributing to the betterment of society.

Figure 2.1 describes the processes entailed in CSR. Starting with the business opportunity, the enterprise takes into account stakeholders' expectations side by side with financial, social, and environmental considerations.

Leading corporations around the world have already realized that CSR is much more than random actions. It is a complete set of policies, practices, and plans integrated in the business activities and in the decision-making processes. To encourage the corporation's staff to promote CSR issues, top management should reward such behavior. MNEs around the world that have adopted CSR include Shell, Chase Bank, HSBC, the Cooperative Bank, McDonald's, Body Shop, Motorola, Nike, Novo Nordisk, and Novartis.

CSR means making decisions that contribute to the business' success and at the same time honoring ethical values and respecting people, communities, and the natural environment. The belief is that only through integrating social, environmental, and economical considerations, termed triple bottom line, can the MNE succeed in the long run. This kind of integration can be effectively applied only when the MNE holds an open and sincere dialogue with its stakeholders. Novo Nordisk, a Danish pharmaceutical group, provides a pretty good picture of who are its stakeholders. A mapping of all Novo Group's stakeholders appears in Figure 2.2, while the environmental impact of the Novo Nordisk Corporation is shown in Figure 2.3.

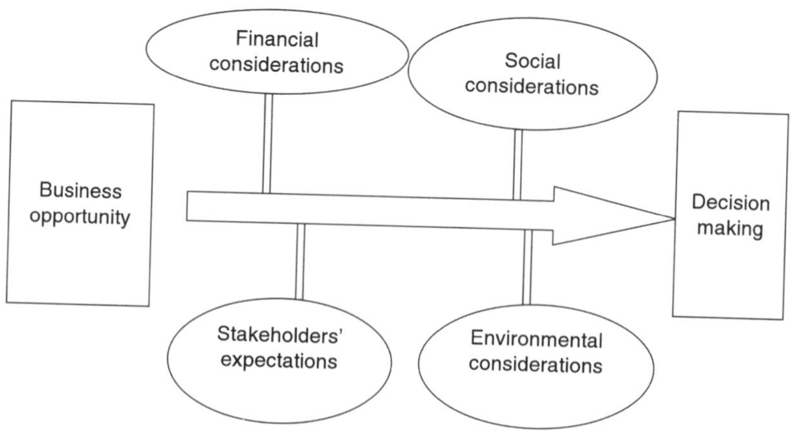

FIGURE 2.1 Corporate social responsibility (CSR)

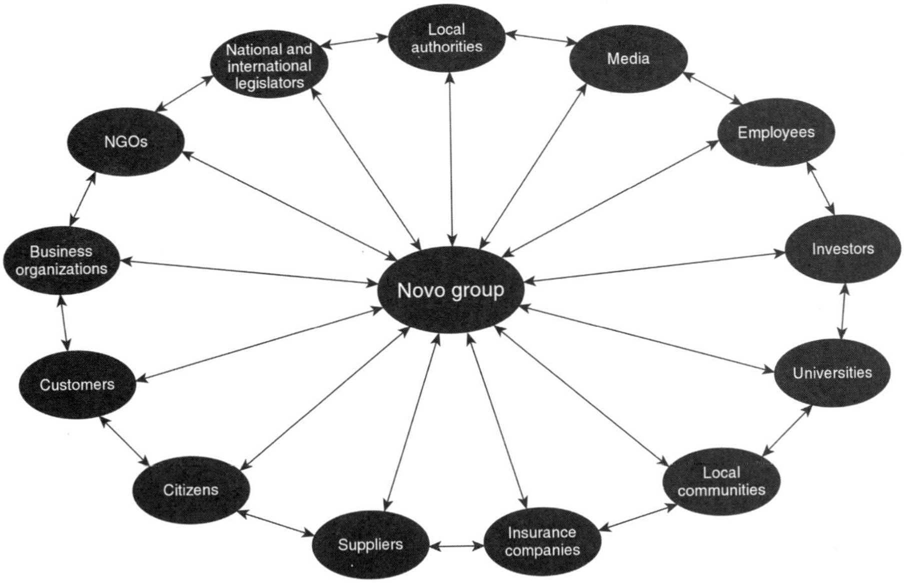

FIGURE 2.2 The Novo group's stakeholders (*Source*: The Novo Group Environmental and Social Report 2000)

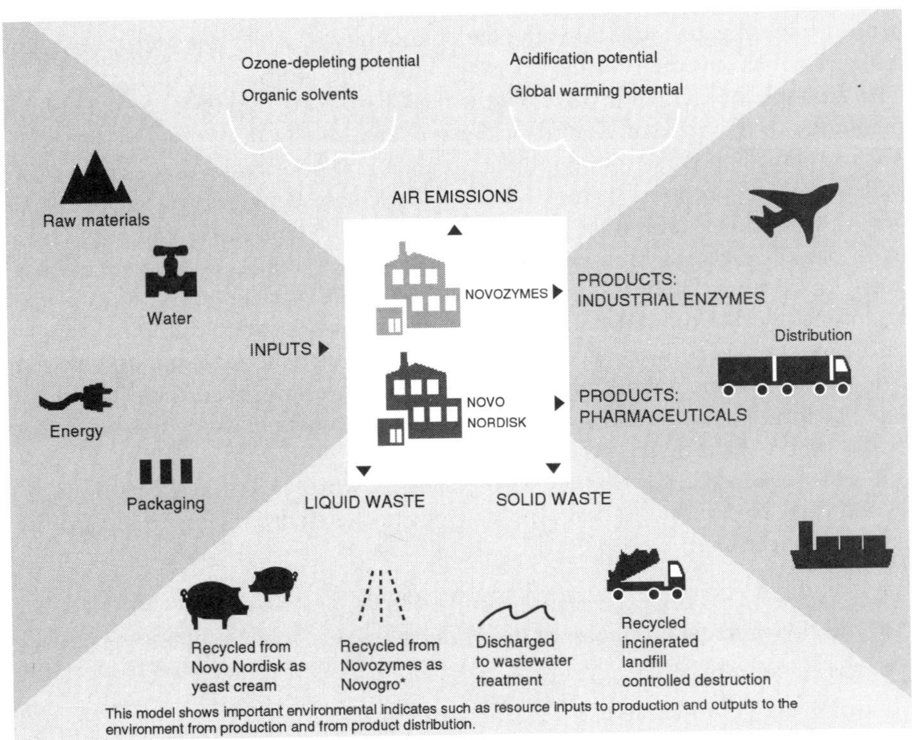

FIGURE 2.3 The environmental impact of Novo Nordisk Corporation (*Source*: Novo Nordisk A/S Triple Bottom Line Report 2001)

CSR relates to different issues that vary by businesses, by size, by sector, and even by geographic region. However, it usually includes marketplace issues, extended across a wide range of business activities that define a corporate relationship with its customers, such as the following: (1) integrity of product manufacturing and quality; (2) disclosure, labeling, and packaging; (3) marketing and advertising; (4) selling practices; (5) pricing; and (6) distribution and access.

Along with CSR comes the notion of corporate accountability, which requires the firm to be accountable to all of its stakeholders regarding its social, environmental, and economic impacts on them. This comes with the duty to report to all stakeholders about these impacts, good and bad, and what the corporation does to enhance the positive impacts and minimize the negative impacts.

Academic research around the world has established that, by being accountable to their stakeholders, corporations can gain a high reputation, consumer's and employees' loyalty and community support, all of which can translate into tangible financial benefits.

One of the most common and apparent fields of CSR is involvement in the community. At times, community involvement is as paramount as a corporate social activity that it is wrongly considered as the only activity that makes the corporation socially responsible. The degree of the involvement in the community varies. However, a true involvement requires much more than random donations in cash or cash equivalents. International corporations, aware of their significant part in promoting and strengthening the community in which they operate, build strategies which suit their businesses as well the community.

An example of such an involvement is the Chase Bank initiative in the Harlem community in the State of New York. By and large, banks didn't see the financial benefits they could gain from building a branch in a poor and socioeconomically challenged neighborhood such as Harlem. The Chase Bank recognized the need for ATM machines and other financial services in the Harlem community. Thus, Chase Bank decided to found a branch in Harlem. By doing so, Chase Bank has gained much more than just financial benefit. Once the Harlem branch was operating, businesses all around it started to prosper. Businesses like restaurants, maintenance services, and delivery services were now needed by the bank and its workers. Residents of Harlem found jobs within the bank and improved their chance of employability. Thus, the bank contributed to the sustainability of the neighborhood as well as gaining financial benefits.

Another case of CSR is that of Novo Nordic. A world leader in the pharmacology industry, Novo Nordic has taken account of the environmental impact of its activities concerning:

- the use of resources (water, energy, packaging material, raw material);
- the environmental impacts of its products (enzymes and medicines);
- gas emissions;
- solid and liquid waste and ways used to recycle.

As part of its CSR program, Citigroup financial group has increased the amount of business it conducts with women and minority group by 20 percent. The group has launched a project that encourages suppliers' diversity and includes professional training and seminars.

Countries around the world have initiated national guidelines and laws that govern CSR issues by publicly traded corporations. In 2002, the French Parliament published the requirements of the "new economic regulations" law that requires all nationally listed corporations in France to report their social and environmental performance. This includes reports regarding, the environment, employees, the local community, and international labor issues. In May 2002, a Minister on Sustainable Development was appointed. As of March 2000, the United Kingdom announced the appointment of a Minister of Corporate Social Responsibility and as of July 2000 all UK pension funds were required to disclose how they take into account social, ethical, and environmental considerations in their investment decisions. The same requirement of pension funds has been in existence in Belgium since 2001. The Australian law requirement regarding CSR has been in effect since March 2003. The purpose of the Australian law is to provide investors with information on how the investment policies of investment corporations comply with their corporate values and goals.

Ethics and Global Management

The ethical behavior of business has become a major issue in the USA, Europe, and elsewhere. Concerned citizen's groups, such as Citizen United in Washington, DC, as well as the media, increase the public's concerns regarding ethics in international business and international organizations. Ethics is the study of morality, standards and practices of good conduct. Many MNEs have developed codes of ethics to guide their behavior and ensure that corporate decisions worldwide conform to these standards. Consider the ERi Lilly pharmaceutical corporation. Lilly provides low-cost antibiotics, training for international medical personnel and technology to enable the manufacture of products for treatment in 143 countries. As of 2006, Lilly employed 44,415 workers, out of which 20,507 were working overseas. The company claims that developing a new drug takes 10–15 years and requires an investment in research and development of US$800 millions to US$1 billion. This mammoth effort, which entails sizable resources, lengthy and complex processes, and major executive decisions along the way, requires an appropriate ethical behavior. Lilly has developed a code of business conduct that reads as follows (2009 Eli Lilly Code of Conduct):

> We maintain a code of conduct (known as The Red Book: Code of Business Conduct) that applies to all employees worldwide, requiring them to display proper business conduct, avoid conflicts of interest, comply with laws, and protect company assets. Because we are a U.S.-based company, our business conduct policies often reflect a blend of the requirements of United States law and those of other countries in which we operate. Activities conducted and employees working in various countries around the world must comply at all times with applicable laws, even if those laws are more

stringent than those established by The Red Book and our global policies. Conversely, employees throughout the world must comply with our global policies, even if they are more stringent than local laws.

All employees are required to read and understand The Red Book and to report suspected violations of law or company policies, unless a country-specific law indicates otherwise. A hotline number is published in The Red Book to enable employees to report suspected violations anonymously. Discrimination or retaliation is prohibited against employees who report suspected violations in good faith. Our chief executive officer and all members of financial management must also sign the Code of Ethical Conduct for Lilly Financial Management, a supplemental code that recognizes the unique responsibilities of these individuals in ensuring proper financial reporting and internal controls.

Bribery and Conflicts of Interest

We do not tolerate bribery on any level within our company. If any employee is found guilty of accepting or offering a bribe, disciplinary action will be taken, which may include discharge from our company. Employees may use the hotline or other channels to report any suspicious activity.

Employees are responsible for reporting any possible conflicts of interest that may arise during their employment. Included in these conflicts of interest is the case where an employee owns a significant interest in any other business that is associated, aims to be associated, or competes with Lilly. Doing business with any relative or family member is considered a conflict of interest, as is employment with any other firm related to or in competition with Lilly.

Political Lobbying and Contributions

Our employees must comply with The Red Book: Code of Business Conduct section on "Dealing with Government Officials and Political Parties." This section details appropriate employee conduct as it relates to the following topics: political financial support, payments to officials or employees of a government or public international organization, and interaction with government officials (initiated by company employees or vice versa). Lilly corporate political donations are made based on a budget for such contributions. This budget is determined annually. Throughout the year, members of the company's government affairs organization bring forward specific recommendations for company contributions. The chief financial officer and general counsel of the company must approve corporate contributions made in the United States. The general counsel for international operations approves financial support given outside the United States.

AntiTrust and Competition Laws

Antitrust and competition laws and regulations vary by country, but regulations similar to those that apply in the U.S. regulate business carried out in most foreign countries. The U.S. Foreign Corrupt Practices Act also applies to activities outside the U.S. Violations of such laws can have severe consequences to both individuals and the company. In The Red Book, we outline several situations that may arise pertaining to anti-trust and competition laws so employees are able to recognize these situations and refrain from engaging in them. Employees are encouraged to consult with a company attorney about any questionable situations.

Ethics seem to be getting different interpretations in different regions and countries in the world. The following is a description of some ethical issues in selected countries.

Ethics in Japan

With defect cover-ups, kickbacks, price-rigging, and bribery scandals making headlines almost daily, Japan's shoddy business ethics are back in the spotlight. In a well-publicized case, public prosecutors in Tokyo indicted Mitsubishi Motors and four of its top executives for covering up defects affecting thousands of vehicles. Mitsubishi Motors admitted systematically concealing customer complaints in Japan for more than 20 years, maintaining two sets of records on customer complaints: one set for public audit and one for company use only. This eventually resulted in a recall of 600,000 cars domestically and 200,000 cars internationally. Over the past years, Bridgestone, Mitsubishi Electric, and Sanyo Electric have also been caught hiding defects in tires, television sets, and solar-cell systems, respectively. In another case, members of the Japanese yakuza have speculated with property on proposed routes leading to the Kansai Airport, under development. In addition, they substituted industrial waste for the uncontaminated landfill required for the airport construction.

Accusations of sexual harassment were also brought to the public eye, even though there is no specific law against sexual harassment resulting in charges based on general civil law. As well, court actions result in a few thousand dollars to the accusers. Equal opportunity issues also haunt Japanese firms. There is a general tendency not to hire and not to promote women into management ranks. This tendency is related to the traditional roles Japanese society set for women, and hiring of women is by and large for secretarial or manual jobs. Another area of concern is the intensive Japanese lobbying in the USA and elsewhere. While lobbying is an acceptable activity, some feel that Japanese business interests at times are at odds with local business interests, and it is inappropriate for prominent local personalities to agree to represent Japanese interests.

Ethics in China

Reform in China, initiated a quarter of a century ago, has led to transformation from a centrally planned economy to a market economy, resulting in some fundamental changes in China's society and precipitating major social as well as economic changes. New goals for industrial and economic productivity required an overhaul of the entire system of incentives and focus has shifted towards material rewards to improve workforce motivation and enterprise performance. The supremacy and importance of economic freedom and individual wealth have replaced Confucian and Maoist values. More and more attention is paid to economic gain, while maintaining high ethics ground has become less important.

As about half of industrial output and of retail sales are from state-owned enterprises, we are witnessing a shift, with state-owned enterprises becoming independent. The Chinese state's control is shifting from direct ownership and control to indirect control through economic policy and regulatory overseeing.

At the same time, government is still a significant stakeholder in China. State-owned enterprises are essentially small societies on their own. The state is responsible for all of its members, from housing and medical care to retirement benefits. The Chinese government is very powerful and interferes in business enterprises either through direct ownership or through stringent policies and regulations. The Chinese government imposes very strict control on dissemination of information, and freedom of speech is severely limited. Thus, good relations with local and national government are essential to a company's successful performance in China.

Ethics and social responsibility seem to take a back seat in China. With government, stockholders, and personal wealth driving Chinese corporations, social responsibility appears to be diminishing. When compared to American counterparts, consciousness of environmental issues is much lower in China. Pollution is significant in China, as noted by – among other phenomena – the smog hovering over Beijing, and other industrial zones. Deterioration of the environment, notably air pollution, soil erosion and the steady fall of the water table, pose threats to China.

Poor professional and business ethics reflect on consumers in China. Consumers are considered a neglected stakeholder by some Chinese corporations, since China has fairly limited and often not enforced product safety regulations. Punishment for safety violations is usually minimal – often only compensatory damages. Punitive damages do not apply in product safety cases. In recent years, there has been an increased awareness of unethical consumer practices. Bootlegged copies of software, music, and movies are commonplace in Chinese markets, where aggressive counterfeiting takes place. China's legal system leaves a lot to be desired. In most of the world, counterfeiting, unauthorized production and sale of exact copies of original goods is dealt with by enacting comprehensive anti–counterfeiting criminal laws. However, in China there is no clear definition of counterfeiting; the laws governing this phenomenon are vague and enforcement is sparse. Few offenders are ever charged and sent to prison.

Other neglected stakeholders in Chinese corporations are the employees, who are often forced to work in intense, low-paid, unsafe jobs. The first labor law was issued in China towards the end of the last century, but it is not strictly enforced. Government officials are ready to put up with foreign investment with disregard for the labor force. Many Western companies, such as Ann Taylor, and Liz Claiborne, are taking advantage of China's inexpensive labor. Wages are extremely low, for close to 96 hours per week, without overtime pay. While labor rates represent a sustainable competitive advantage for the Chinese economy, they also punish Chinese workers, who cannot fully enjoy the fruits of their labor. Many American companies are supporting lowering standards in China by withdrawing their companies and production orders in northern China and relocating to southern Chinese territories. Both Wal-Mart and J.C. Penny have withdrawn northern orders, which were rerouted to the south. Revenue incentives for this withdrawal are numerous, including decreased wages and benefits, undermining social safety nets, subcontracting, and excessive overtime. The ethical cost to the Chinese southern workers are also equally excessive, most of which include systematic denial of fundamental worker and human rights. This is accomplished since few regulation laws exist in the southern cities of China such as Jiangsu and Zhejiang, near the port of Shanghai, and Guangdong, right above Hong Kong. The result is that the majority of factory managers in the south deny employees their legal work contracts, which allows upper-level management leverage the use of widespread arbitrary firings. Management enjoys these "dictatorial" privileges since many of the workers are young uneducated women from the countryside. Unfortunately, this attribute leaves these female workers unaware of their legal rights. Most of these women are not aware of the US Corporate Codes of Conduct that they are granted working under American corporations. The economic dichotomy that exists between northern and southern China is the driving force that persuades large American conglomerates to relocate. In the north, companies are publicly owned and must pay their employees a minimum wage of 50 cents per hour, as contrasted by the southern privately owned companies that can pay as low as 13 cents per hour. Workers within northern territories are granted health and social security benefits, workman's compensation, child-care, sick days, continuing education, and pension insurance. Workers within the private sectors are not exposed to these benefits. In state-owned enterprises in the north, excessive overtime is a legal offense, whereas companies of the private sector are exempt. In the north overtime is reimbursed, whereas the south views overtime as part of a workers' expected norm. In northern China, subcontracting and part- time work is prohibited. Southern China is mostly a vast subcontracting network, where workers are hired on a contingency basis. This means that when there is work, the workers get paid; but when there is no work, payment is also withheld. In the south, living conditions are poor and there is less concern for health and safety protections. Northern factories are highly regulated by the government, whereas southern providences along the coast above Hong Kong are mostly without regulation. As a final incentive, worker and corporate taxes are also reduced. All of these factors have led to a noticeable cost difference between northern and southern sections of China.

In addition to the ethics issues mentioned above, Chinese-backed industry and business spying present a problem for MNEs operating in China and elsewhere. For example, Amgen, a publicly traded international biotechnology firm, found that there was a Chinese attempt to steal a cell culture for an anemia drug, named Epogen. Kimberly-Clark, producing feminine-care pads in the province of Hebei, in northeast China, found that their proprietary technology was stolen and used in a competing plant nearby to produce the same products, managed by Kimberley-Clark's own plant manager.

Women managers in China, confront a "glass ceiling," preventing them from reaching management positions. In particular, women's retirement age is 60, whereas men's retirement age is 65, preventing women from reaching the upper management levels. In addition, women are not well represented in the Communist Party, which seems to help in reaching managerial prominence.

There has been also a concern about possible compromising ethical practices in Hong Kong, which coincided with the 1997 transfer of sovereignty to China. Hong Kong has a very sound economy and a free market system. There are indications that managers of industrial organizations in Hong Kong are focused on long-term company profit and they should not be concerned with social responsibility and ethics issues. Additionally, studies found that pressure to protect the organization at all costs exists in Hong Kong. It seems that CSR and ethics in Hong Kong seem to closely imitate those of the Chinese.

All of the above cause growing concern within MNEs about doing business in China and repeated calls for action. Recent efforts by the Chinese government to deal with the aforementioned issues are welcomed by MNEs and international NGOs such as the World Trade Organization (WTO).

Corruption and International Business

In the context of a business transaction, domestic or international, the issue of corruption occupies a prominent place. Actually, not all corruption may be regarded as illegal. The literature offers various definitions of corruption. The definition used in this book is that corruption is an exchange between two parties which (a) has an influence on the allocation of business resources either immediately or in the future; and (b) involves the use or abuse of public or collective responsibility for private needs and wants. Although measuring corruption is difficult, it has been estimated that in developed economies the "underground economy," the portion of the economic activity that is not reported in public accounts, accounts for about a quarter of the gross national product (GNP). One can estimate the magnitude of this issue for economies such as France, with a GNP of $1,762 billion. It is obvious that some industries, such as the infrastructure industry, are more prone to corruption than others. Large procurement initiatives and mega projects in aerospace, communications, infrastructure, energy, and transportation are part of the infrastructure industry. It is estimated that payments of 10–20 percent of the value of the procurement or project may be paid to officials that are involved or influence the closing of the deal.

Causes and consequences of corruption

Corruption may be found anywhere, as it is related to transactions of any kind, including business transactions. However, corruption tends to be more paramount in developing and transitional economies, such as Russia during the transition period from a centrally planned economy to a free market economy. During that period Russia, as other economies in transition, lacked appropriate legal frameworks and legal controls. According to the organization called Transparency International, factors supporting corruption include low public sector pay, immunity of public officials, secrecy in government, media restrictions, accelerated privatization, financial liberalization, increase in foreign direct investment (FDI), and international trade. Another factor contributing to corruption is a high level of government involvement in the regulation of economic activity. In some cases, like Nigeria, high government involvement in business, coupled with a lack of transparency, lack of appropriate financial reporting standards and practices, weak legal infrastructure and a socially acceptable norm of direct payments to officials, leads to corruption.

It has been scientifically proven that culture may contribute to corruption. Specifically, it was found that a culture profiled as high on uncertainty avoidance, masculinity, and power distance would be more susceptible to corruption. High uncertainty avoidance is associated with corruption, because corruption reduces uncertainty; masculinity is associated with corruption, since corruption enhances ownership of material things; power distance is associated with corruption, since corruption permits arbitrary judgment.

It is a well-accepted understanding of international executives and public decision makers in many countries that corruption impedes growth and progress. Corruption has been known to expose the firm to court actions, public humiliation, and significant and unexpected business risks. From a public point of view, corruption alters appropriation of resources without due course, it instills a sense of unfairness and uncertainty among civil servants and the general public, and it deters potential investors and international economic organizations.

Corruption measurement

As explained above, corruption is a major phenomenon related to international business. Executives who operate worldwide should determine a place to conduct their business based on several factors; one of them being the level of corruption. At the same time, international bodies engaged in regulating and harmonizing international trade should monitor the level and the dynamics of corruption. To this end, a corruption measurement scheme was devised by an organization called Transparency International (TI). TI publishes the *Corruption Perception Index (CPI)*, a measure of corruption that is calculated from multiple survey responses in a variety of countries. The TI Corruption Perceptions Index is a composite survey, that reflects the perceptions of business people and country analysts, both resident and nonresident. It draws on 16 different polls from 10 independent institutions. For a country to be included, it must feature in at least three polls. As a result, a number of countries, including some which could be among the most corrupt, are missing because not enough survey data are available.

Table 2.1 lists the 2005 scores for 159 countries for which data are available. TI notes that more than two-thirds of the nations surveyed scored less than 5 out of a best score of 10, indicating serious levels of corruption in a majority of the countries surveyed. TI concludes that corruption continues to threaten development and that poverty and corruption go hand in hand in the world's least developed countries. Despite progress on many fronts, including the imminent entry into force of the United Nations Convention against Corruption, 70 countries – nearly half of those included in the Index – scored less than 3 on the CPI,

TABLE 2.1 Corruption Perception Index (2005), as compiled by Transparency International

Country rank	*Country*	*2005 CPI score**	*Confidence range***	*Surveys used****
1	Iceland	9.7	9.5–9.7	8
2	Finland	9.6	9.5–9.7	9
	New Zealand	9.6	9.5–9.7	9
3	Denmark	9.5	9.3–9.6	10
4	Singapore	9.4	9.3–9.5	12
5	Sweden	9.2	9.0–9.3	10
6	Switzerland	9.1	8.9–9.2	9
7	Norway	8.9	8.5–9.1	9
8	Australia	8.8	8.4–9.1	13
9	Austria	8.7	8.4–9.0	9
10	Netherlands	8.6	8.3–8.9	9
	United Kingdom	8.6	8.3–8.8	11
11	Luxembourg	8.5	8.1–8.9	8
12	Canada	8.4	7.9–8.8	11
13	Hong Kong	8.3	7.7–8.7	12
14	Germany	8.2	7.9–8.5	10
15	USA	7.6	7.0–8.0	12
16	France	7.5	7.0–7.8	11
17	Belgium	7.4	6.9–7.9	9
	Ireland	7.4	6.9–7.9	10
18	Chile	7.3	6.8–7.7	10
	Japan	7.3	6.7–7.8	14
19	Spain	7.0	6.6–7.4	10
20	Barbados	6.9	5.7–7.3	3
21	Malta	6.6	5.4–7.7	5
22	Portugal	6.5	5.9–7.1	9
23	Estonia	6.4	6.0–7.0	11
24	Israel	6.3	5.7–6.9	10
	Oman	6.3	5.2–7.3	5
25	United Arab Emirates	6.2	5.3–7.1	6
26	Slovenia	6.1	5.7–6.8	11
27	Botswana	5.9	5.1–6.7	8
	Qatar	5.9	5.6–6.4	5
	Taiwan	5.9	5.4–6.3	14
	Uruguay	5.9	5.6–6.4	6
28	Bahrain	5.8	5.3–6.3	6
29	Cyprus	5.7	5.3–6.0	5
	Jordan	5.7	5.1–6.1	10
30	Malaysia	5.1	4.6–5.6	14
31	Hungary	5.0	4.7–5.2	11
	Italy	5.0	4.6–5.4	9
	South Korea	5.0	4.6–5.3	12
32	Tunisia	4.9	4.4–5.6	7
33	Lithuania	4.8	4.5–5.1	8
34	Kuwait	4.7	4.0–5.2	6
35	South Africa	4.5	4.2–4.8	11
36	Czech Republic	4.3	3.7–5.1	10
	Greece	4.3	3.9–4.7	9
	Namibia	4.3	3.8–4.9	8
	Slovakia	4.3	3.8–4.8	10

TABLE 2.1

Country rank	*Country*	*2005 CPI score**	*Confidence range***	*Surveys used****
37	Costa Rica	4.2	3.7–4.7	7
	El Salvador	4.2	3.5–4.8	6
	Latvia	4.2	3.8–4.6	7
	Mauritius	4.2	3.4–5.0	6
38	Bulgaria	4.0	3.4–4.6	8
	Colombia	4.0	3.6–4.4	9
	Fiji	4.0	3.4–4.6	3
	Seychelles	4.0	3.5–4.2	3
39	Cuba	3.8	2.3–4.7	4
	Thailand	3,8	3.5–4.1	13
	Trinidad and Tobago	3,8	3.3–4.5	6
40	Belize	3.7	3.4–4.1	3
	Brazil	3,7	3.5–3.9	10
41	Jamaica	3.6	3.4–3.8	6
42	Ghana	3.5	3.2–4.0	8
	Mexico	3.5	3.3–3.7	10
	Panama	3.5	3.1–4.1	7
	Peru	3.5	3.1–3.8	7
	Turkey	3.5	3.1–4.0	11
43	Burkina Faso	3.4	2.7–3.9	3
	Croatia	3.4	3.2–3.7	7
	Egypt	3.4	3.0–3.9	9
	Lesotho	3.4	2.6–3.9	3
	Poland	3.4	3.0–3.9	11
	Saudi Arabia	3.4	2.7–4.1	5
	Syria	3.4	2.8–4.2	5
44	Laos	3.3	2.1–4.4	3
45	China	3.2	2.9–3.5	14
	Morocco	3.2	2.8–3.6	8
	Senegal	3.2	2.8–3.6	6
	Sri Lanka	3.2	2.7–3.6	7
	Suriname	3.2	2.2–3.6	3
46	Lebanon	3.1	2.7–3.3	4
	Rwanda	3.1	2.1–4.1	3
47	Dominican Republic	3.0	2.5–3.6	6
	Mongolia	3.0	2.4–3.6	4
	Romania	3.0	2.6–3.5	11
48	Armenia	2.9	2.5–3.2	4
	Benin	2.9	2.1–4.0	5
	Bosnia and Herzegovina	2.9	2.7–3.1	6
	Gabon	2.9	2.1–3.6	4
	India	2.9	2.7–3.1	14
	Iran	2.9	2.3–3.3	5
	Mali	2.9	2.3–3.6	8
	Moldova	2.9	2.3–3.7	5
	Tanzania	2.9	2.6–3.1	8

(*Continued*)

TABLE 2.1 Cont.

Country rank	*Country*	*2005 CPI score**	*Confidence range***	*Surveys used****
49	Algeria	2.8	2.5–3.3	7
	Argentina	2.8	2.5–3.1	10
	Madagascar	2.8	1.9–3.7	5
	Malawi	2.8	2.3–3.4	7
	Mozambique	2.8	2.4–3.1	8
	Serbia and Montenegro	2.8	2.5–3.3	7
50	Gambia	2.7	2.3–3.1	7
	Macedonia	2.7	2.4–3.2	7
	Swaziland	2.7	2.0–3.1	3
	Yemen	2.7	2.4–3.2	5
51	Belarus	2.6	1.9–3.8	5
	Eritrea	2.6	1.7–3.5	3
	Honduras	2.6	2.2–3.0	7
	Kazakhstan	2.6	2.2–3.2	6
	Nicaragua	2.6	2.4–2.8	7
	Palestine	2.6	2.1–2.8	3
	Ukraine	2.6	2.4–2.8	8
	Vietnam	2.6	2.3–2.9	10
	Zambia	2.6	2.3–2.9	7
	Zimbabwe	2.6	2.1–3.0	7
52	Afghanistan	2.5	1.6–3.2	3
	Bolivia	2.5	2.3–2.9	6
	Ecuador	2.5	2.2–2.9	6
	Guatemala	2.5	2.1–2.8	7
	Guyana	2.5	2.0–2.7	3
	Libya	2.5	2.0–3.0	4
	Nepal	2.5	1.9–3.0	4
	Philippines	2.5	2.3–2.8	13
	Uganda	2.5	2.2–2.8	8
53	Albania	2.4	2.1–2.7	3
	Niger	2.4	2.2–2.6	4
	Russia	2.4	2.3–2.6	12
	Sierra Leone	2.4	2.1–2.7	3
54	Burundi	2.3	2.1–2.5	3
	Cambodia	2.3	1.9–2.5	4
	Congo, Republic of	2.3	2.1–2.6	4
	Georgia	2.3	2.0–2.6	6
	Kyrgyzstan	2.3	2.1–2.5	5
	Papua New Guinea	2.3	1.9–2.6	4
	Venezuela	2.3	2.2 -2.4	10
55	Azerbaijan	2.2	1.9–2.5	6
	Cameroon	2.2	2.0–2.5	6
	Ethiopia	2.2	2.0–2.5	8
	Indonesia	2.2	2.1–2.5	13
	Iraq	2.2	1.5–2.9	4
	Liberia	2.2	2.1–2.3	3
	Uzbekistan	2.2	2.1–2.4	5

TABLE 2.1

Country rank	*Country*	*2005 CPI score**	*Confidence range***	*Surveys used****
	Congo, Democratic Republic	2.1	1.8–2.3	4
	Kenya	2.1	1.8–2.4	8
56	Pakistan	2.1	1.7–2.6	7
	Paraguay	2.1	1.9–2.3	7
	Somalia	2.1	1.6–2.2	3
	Sudan	2.1	1.9–2.2	5
	Tajikistan	2.1	1.9–2.4	5
57	Angola	2.0	1.8–2.1	5
	Cote d'Ivoire	1.9	1.7–2.1	4
58	Equatorial Guinea	1.9	1.6–2.1	3
	Nigeria	1.9	1.7–2.0	9
	Haiti	1.8	1.5–2.1	4
59	Myanmar	1.8	1.7–2.0	4
	Turkmenistan	1.8	1.7–2.0	4
	Bangladesh	1.7	1.4–2.0	7
60	Chad	1.7	1.3–2.1	6

2005 Corruption Perception Index, 2005. Transparency International.

* The Corruption Perception Index (CPI) score relates to perceptions of the degree of corruption as seen by business people and country analysts, and ranges from 10 (highly clean) to 0 (highly corrupt).

** The confidence range provides a range of possible values of the CPI score. This parameter reflects how a country's score may vary, depending on measurement precision. Nominally, with 5 percent probability the score is above this range and with another 5 percent it is below. However, particularly when only few sources (n) are available an unbiased estimate of the mean coverage probability is lower than the nominal value of 90 percent.

*** The surveys used refer to the number of surveys that assessed a country's performance: 16 surveys and expert assessments were used and at least three were required for a country to be included in the CPI.

indicating a severe corruption problem. Among the countries included in the index, corruption is perceived as most rampant in Chad, Bangladesh, Turkmenistan, Myanmar, and Haiti, which are also among the poorest countries in the world. The United Nations has set a goal to halve extreme poverty by 2015. Corruption hampers achievement of the Millennium Development Goals (MDGs) by undermining the economic growth and sustainable development that would free millions from the poverty trap. TI asserts that fighting corruption must be central to plans to increase resources to achieve the goals, whether via donor aid or in-country domestic action. Moreover, extensive research shows that foreign investment is lower in countries perceived to be corrupt, which further thwarts their chance to prosper. When countries improve governance and reduce corruption, they reap a "development dividend" that, according to the World Bank Institute (WBI), can include improved child mortality rates, higher per capita income and greater literacy.

Nineteen of the world's poorest countries have been granted debt service relief under the Heavily Indebted Poor Countries (HIPC) initiative, testifying to their economic reform achievements. Not one of these countries, however, scored above 4 on the CPI, indicating serious to severe levels of corruption. These countries still face the grave risk that money freed from debt payments now entering national budgets will be forfeited to greed, waste or mismanagement. The commitment and resources devoted to qualifying for HIPC must also be applied to winning the fight against corruption. Stamping out corruption and implementing recipient-led reforms are critical to making aid more effective, and to realizing the crucial human and economic development goals that have been set by the international community.

As to the dynamics of corruption, according to TI, an increase in perceived corruption from 2004 to 2005 is measured in countries such as Costa Rica, Gabon, Nepal, Papua New Guinea, Russia, Seychelles, Sri Lanka, Suriname, Trinidad, and Tobago, and Uruguay. Conversely, a number of countries and territories show noteworthy improvements – a decline in perceptions of corruption – over the past year, including Estonia, France, Hong Kong, Japan, Jordan, Kazakhstan, Nigeria, Qatar, Taiwan, and Turkey.

The recent ratification of the UN Convention against Corruption established a global legal framework for sustainable progress against corruption. The Convention, which entered into force in December 2005, is expected to accelerate the retrieval of stolen funds, push financial institutions to take action against money laundering, allow nations to pursue foreign companies and individuals that have committed corrupt acts on their soil, and prohibit bribery of foreign public officials. Low-income countries that embrace and implement the UN Convention against Corruption will have a head start in the race for foreign investment and economic growth.

TI found that wealth is not a prerequisite for successful control of corrupion. To wit, the perception of corruption has decreased significantly in lower-income countries such as Estonia, Colombia, and Bulgaria over the past decade.

In the case of higher-income countries such as Canada and Ireland, however, there has been a marked increase in the perception of corruption over the past 10 years, showing that even wealthy, high-scoring countries must work to maintain a climate of integrity. Similarly, the responsibility in the fight against corruption does not fall solely on lower-income countries. Wealthier countries, apart from facing numerous corruption cases within their own borders, must share the burden by ensuring that their companies are not involved in corrupt practices abroad. Offenders must be prosecuted and debarred from public bidding. The opportunity for ensuring sustainable progress also lies in the hands of the WTO which needs to actively promote transparency and anti-corruption in global trade. The lessons are clear: risk factors such as government secrecy, inappropriate influence of elite groups, and distorted political finance apply to both wealthy and poorer countries, and no rich country is immune to the scourge of corruption. Transparency International ends its report with a number of recommendations for actions:

- by lower-income countries – increase resources and political will for anti-corruption efforts; enable greater public access to information about budgets, revenue, and expenditure;

- by higher-income countries – combine increased aid with support for recipient-led reforms; reduce tied aid, which limits local opportunities and ownership of aid programs;
- by all countries – promote strong coordination among governments, the private sector and civil society to increase efficiency and sustainability in anti-corruption and good governance efforts; ratify, implement, and monitor existing anti-corruption conventions in all countries to establish international norms, including the UN Convention against Corruption, the OECD Anti-bribery Convention, and the regional conventions of the African Union and the Organization of American States.

Corrupt practices

There are various forms of corrupt practices. Some of the most common ones are listed below.

Smuggling is the illegal trade and movement of goods across international borders, so as to avoid paying custom duties and tariffs and break quota rules. Smuggling of goods such as drugs, liquor, cigarettes, pharmaceuticals, and guns (were prohibited) is common because of local demand for these products in selected regions. Smuggling of illegal immigrants has become common: for example, between France and the UK, North Africa and the European Union, Mexico and the USA, and Cuba and the USA.

Money laundering involves concealing the source of funds by channeling them into legitimate business activities and depositing the funds in banks in other countries. Money laundering has been fueled by drug trade and privatization in the former Soviet Union and elsewhere. Electronic clearance of funds around the world makes money laundering possible and accessible. The G-7 Financial Action Task Force lists 15 countries as centers for money laundering, comprising the Bahamas, the Cayman Islands, Panama, Dominican Republic, St Kitts and Nevis, St. Vincent and the Grenadines, the Cook Islands, the Marshall Islands, Nauru, Niue, Israel, Lebanon, Liechtenstein, Russia, and the Philippines. The task force work is of particular importance in light of the fact that terrorist activities in the USA, Spain, and elsewhere are aided by money laundering. The task force has developed a monitoring system and retaliates against countries that do not limit money laundering activities.

Piracy means using illegal and unauthorized means to obtain goods, such as copying software. *Counterfeiting* involves both using illegal means to obtain goods as well as attempting to pass the copied products as an original, such as producing and selling a fake copy of Microsoft Office software, a pair of Levi's jeans, a spare part for a GM car, etc. Both phenomena have been growing rapidly and represent a substantial threat to intellectual property to international manufacturers.

Bribery may be defined as payment made in the context of international business to enhance goodwill by foreign authorities and personalities. Hundreds of millions of dollars are being paid worldwide by MNEs in order to enhance the chances of winning contracts or business deals. The bribes are made to foreign government officials and foreign politicians.

Corruption: National and Global Response

The Foreign Corrupt Practices Act (FCPA)

The response to corruption prevention and eradication is carried out at various levels – municipal, national, regional, and global. Many developed countries have initiated processes that may, in time, reduce and eliminate corruption. Among these countries are the USA, Canada, and the EU countries. However, developing countries have also established independent commissions against corruption. Among these countries are Thailand, Zimbabwe, Poland, and China's Special Administrative Region (SAR) of Hong Kong. Of particular significance and relevance is the US government initiative of the late 1970s, termed the Foreign Corrupt Practices Act (FCPA), which was amended in 1998. The act was a result of admissions by more than 400 corporations of making questionable or illegal payments. The companies, most of them voluntarily, have reported paying out well in excess of $300 million in corporate funds to foreign government officials, politicians, and political parties. These corporations have included some of the largest and most widely held public companies in the USA; over 117 of them rank in the top Fortune 500 industries. The abuses disclosed run the gamut from bribery of high foreign officials in order to secure some type of favorable action by a foreign government to so-called facilitating payments that allegedly were made to ensure that government functionaries discharge certain ministerial or clerical duties. Sectors of industry typically involved are drugs and health care; oil and gas production and services; food products; aerospace, airlines and air services; and chemicals.

The payment of bribes to influence the acts or decisions of foreign officials, foreign political parties, or candidates for foreign political office was deemed unethical. It is counter to the moral expectations and values of the American public: not only is it unethical, but also it is bad business. It erodes public confidence in the integrity of the free market system. It short-circuits the marketplace by directing business to those companies too inefficient to compete in terms of price, quality or service, or too lazy to engage in honest salesmanship, or too intent upon unloading marginal products. In brief, it rewards corruption instead of efficiency and puts pressure on ethical enterprises to lower their standards or risk losing business. Bribery of foreign officials by some American companies casts a shadow on all US companies. The exposure of such activity can damage a company's image, lead to costly lawsuits, cause the cancellation of contracts, and result in the appropriation of valuable assets overseas. Corporate bribery is also unnecessary. The Secretary of Treasury testified before the Subcommittee on Consumer Protection and Finance: "Paying bribes. . . are simply not necessary to the successful conduct of business in the United States or overseas. My own experience as

Chairman of the Bendix Corp. was that it was not necessary to pay bribes to have a successful export sales program."

Corporate bribery also creates severe foreign policy problems for the USA. The revelation of improper payments invariably tends to embarrass friendly governments, lower the esteem for the USA among the citizens of foreign nations, and lend credence to the suspicions sown by foreign opponents of the USA that American enterprises exert a corrupting influence on the political processes of their nations. For example, in 1976, the Lockheed scandal shook the Government of Japan to its political foundation and gave opponents of close ties between the USA and Japan an effective weapon with which to drive a wedge between the two nations. In another instance, Prince Bernhardt of the Netherlands was forced to resign from his official position as a result of an inquiry into allegations that he received $1 million in pay-offs from Lockheed. In Italy, alleged payments by Lockheed, Exxon, Mobil Oil, and other corporations to officials of the Italian Government eroded public support for that government and jeopardized US foreign policy, not only with respect to Italy and the Mediterranean area, but also with respect to the entire NATO alliance. Finally, a strong anti-bribery statute would actually help US corporations resist corrupt demands. According to former Gulf Oil Chairman Bob Dorsey:

> A US committee considered two possible approaches for curbing the type of bribery payments. One approach is to require that these payments be publicly disclosed and criminal penalties imposed for failure to disclose. The other approach, which the committee adopted eventually, is to outlaw the payoffs with criminal sanctions. There emerged a clear consensus that foreign bribery is a reprehensible activity and that action must be taken to proscribe it. After carefully considering all the testimony adduced, the committee concluded that bribery will be outlawed rather than legalized through disclosure.
>
> The committee also found that criminalization is no more difficult to enforce than disclosure. Both approaches involve proving beyond a reasonable doubt the same factual and legal elements. Most importantly, though, criminalization is far less burdensome on business. Most disclosure proposals would require US corporations doing business abroad to report all foreign payments including perfectly legal payments such as for promotional purposes and for sales commissions.
>
> A disclosure scheme, unlike outright prohibition, would require US corporations to contend not only with an additional bureaucratic overlay but also with massive paperwork requirements. Subject to the FCPA are not only the US firms but also wholly owned US subsidiaries and other US entities controlled by foreign corporations, including their directors, employees, and agents. Actions taken abroad by US citizens, nationals, or residents are covered under the FCPA even if conducted for a foreign corporation. The FCPA also prohibits indirect foreign payments, which can be interpreted as covering the foreign subsidiaries of US corporations as well. Violations of the FCPA can result in fines of up to $2 million to firms and $100,000, plus imprisonment for up to five years for individuals. Both firms and individuals are also liable to a civil fine if they violate the anti-bribery provisions.
>
> The FCPA also required issuers of securities to meet accounting, record-keeping, and corporate control standards. The Justice Department of the US government is responsible for criminal and civil enforcement of the anti-bribery provisions with

respect to domestic concerns. The Securities and Exchange Commission (SEC) is responsible for civil enforcement of the anti-bribery provisions with respect to issuers, be it domestic or foreign.

Corruption: the United Nations response

Although the FCPA was a credible response to corruption, it has been just a local, national response. Extensions to other regions were required as well as a concerted effort worldwide. An important initiative has been the United Nations' efforts to improve international cooperation in crime prevention and criminal justice. (The following is largely based on a UN document appearing at www.unodc.org and www.unis.unvienna.org.)

The United Nations asserts that corruption is a complex social, political, and economic phenomenon that impacts every aspect of society. It causes reduced investments or even disinvestment, with many long-term effects, including social polarization, lack of respect for the rule of law and human rights, undemocratic practices, and diversion of funds intended for development and essential services. The United Nations Office on Drugs and Crime (UNODC) is leading the global efforts to improve international cooperation in crime prevention and criminal justice. Fighting corruption is part of the overall work of UNODC and aims to create the foundations for democracy, sustainable development and the rule of law. To further pursue these goals and build on long-term efforts, UNODC launched a Global Program against Corruption (GPAC) in 1999. The activities of UNODC and technical cooperation projects undertaken by this program assist member states in building integrity, as well as preventing and controlling corruption through: advancing knowledge and expertise on anti-corruption measures and tools; providing technical assistance to build and strengthen national capacities to prevent and control corruption; and enhancing coordination and cooperation among organizations active internationally in anti-corruption policy and advocacy. To date, 180 countries have ratified the program. The United Nations provides guidance and technical assistance to member states upon request. In providing these services, UNODC follows an integrated approach to corruption: namely, one that is fact-based, transparent, non-partisan, inclusive, comprehensive, impact-oriented, and flexible. Its various elements incorporate activities that can be executed both individually and in packages at the international, national, and subnational (e.g., municipal) levels. It takes into consideration that corruption is a complex phenomenon; its character differs from country to country depending on the prevailing social, economic, and cultural conditions and, particularly, the legal context. The GPAC is composed of three main components: action learning, technical cooperation, and evaluation.

The UN initiative maintains judicial integrity in the following manner. Since 2000 the program supports chief justices from common and civil law countries in identifying and applying best practices in strengthening judicial integrity and capacity. The outcome of this process has been: a list of key objectives for judicial reform; a set of measurable performance indicators; a comprehensive assessment methodology for judicial integrity and capacity; a draft Universal Declaration on Judicial Conduct; and a "safe" and productive learning environment for chief justices in which they can be exposed to best practices regarding judicial reform, management of change and the strengthening of the rule of law.

The United Nations takes a lead in interagency coordination

In December 2001, UNODC was requested by the Office of the United Nations Deputy Secretary General to enhance coordination and cooperation across all organizations internationally active in anti-corruption policy, advocacy, and operations. This effort was undertaken to avoid duplication and to assure effective and efficient use of existing resources. As a result, UNODC has taken the lead in establishing an Interagency Anti-Corruption Mechanism that will assure better synergy across the United Nations and other agencies active in the field of anti-corruption work and is supporting the United Nations Office for Internal Oversight Services (OIOS) in developing an Organizational Integrity Initiative aimed at mainstreaming ethics throughout the United Nations, system. By 2005, the program managed 15–20 technical assistance projects supporting member states in preventing and controlling corruption. At present, projects are being implemented in Hungary, Lebanon, Nigeria, South Africa, Colombia, Indonesia, Romania, the Islamic Republic of Iran, and Uganda. GPAC also works to improve coordination among donors and to identify and promote best practices. Technical cooperation reflects a modular approach of comprehensive anti-corruption measures, or tools, which may be implemented in different stages at the international, national, and local levels. This maximizes the flexibility of such measures to fit the needs and context of each country or subregion.

The UN initiative resulted in the creation of a set of useful tools required to prevent and combat corruption

Manuals are considered as both policy guidelines and a practical set of "tools" to promote a common understanding of policies and enhance governments' capacities to build integrity to fight national and transnational corruption. The United Nations Anti-Corruption Toolkit is a set of tools and case studies designed to help "fix" corruption problems of all kinds. The Manual on Anti-Corruption Policy intends to guide policymakers, and the United Nations Compendium of International Legal Instruments against Corruption is a comprehensive guide to existing legal instruments. The Handbook on Anti-Corruption Measures for Prosecutors and Investigators has been developed in close collaboration with the US Department of Justice and Combating Bribery of Foreign Officials in International Business Act (CBFOIF) with the required collaboration, dissemination, and support. The United Nations, an organization with universal membership and a global mandate, claims to be ideally positioned to deal with global challenges. Member states have accepted the fact that corruption is a global phenomenon and mandated UNODC through the General Assembly to support the negotiation of the United Nations Convention against Corruption. The Convention serves as the centerpiece for efforts against corruption, and UNODC will assist member states in ratifying it and implementing its provisions. More specifically, UNODC will provide advisory services, including training, to help close the gap between existing law and what is being called for or codified as standards in the new Convention.

The OECD convention

The Organization for Economic Cooperation and Development (OECD) groups 30 member states sharing a commitment to democratic government and the market economy. With active relationships with some 70 other countries and NGOs, it has a global reach. It is best known for its publications and its statistics, and its work covers economic and social issues from macroeconomics to trade, education, development, and science and innovation. The OECD is an organization of economically developed countries, supporting democracy and free markets, and as such was quick to follow the US government initiative of FCPA. On June 27, 2000, the OECD issued guidelines for MNEs which integrated the OECD's Combating Bribery of Foreign Officials in International Business Act (CBFOIF). The guidelines include a major section on corruption. In this section, it is stated that domestic or multinational enterprises should not offer, nor give in to demands, to pay public officials or the employees of business partners any portion of a contract payment. They should not use subcontractors, purchase orders, or consulting agreements as means of channeling payments to public officials, to employees of business partners or to their relatives or business associates. Enterprises should ensure that remuneration of agents is appropriate and for legitimate services only. Where relevant, a list of agent employed in connection with transactions with public bodies and state-owned enterprises should be kept and made available to competent authorities. MNEs should enhance the transparency of their activities in the fight against bribery and extortion and disclose the management systems that the company had adopted in order to honor these commitments. The enterprise should also foster openness and dialogue with the public so as to promote its awareness of and cooperation with the fight against bribery and extortion. The guidelines further indicate that MNEs should promote employee awareness of and compliance with company policies against bribery and extortion through appropriate dissemination of these policies and through training programs and disciplinary procedures. The guidelines call on MNEs to adopt management control systems that discourage bribery and corrupt practices and adopt financial and tax accounting and auditing practices that prevent the establishment of "off the books" or secret accounts or the creation of documents which do not properly and fairly record the transactions to which they relate. Lastly, the guidelines request that MNEs should not make illegal contributions to candidates for public office or to political organizations and that contributions should fully comply with public disclosure requirements and should be reported to senior management.

While the OECD guidelines were ratified by many countries, as was indicated earlier by the findings of Transparency International, corruption is still very much a part of international business and is still a concern. Thus, it is too early to determine if the guidelines have had the effect of curbing corruption in international business transactions among the signatory countries even with the threat of country audits that might be initiated by the OECD.

Corruption: other global responses

The Commonwealth countries, encompassing a population of approximately 1.8 billion people and making up about 30 percent of the world's total, supported the OECD initiatives regarding corruption. In addition, member states of the *Organization of American States (OAS)* signed the Inter-American Convention against Corruption (IACAC). The IACAC requires each signatory country to make bribery of foreign officials a crime and an extraditable offense. Signatories must update their domestic legislation to criminalize a set of specific corrupt acts related to bribery and illicitly obtained benefits. Cooperation among signatories is strengthened on extradition, mutual legal assistance, and asset forfeiture for corruption-related crimes. The work by OAS is continuing and as late as October 14, 2005 amended the convention with a Follow-Up Mechanism for IACAC, requesting greater access to information contained in the reports issued by the OAS on country performance and increased involvement of civil society in related efforts. The amendments were approved by the Committee of Experts responsible for reviewing the implementation of the IACAC by countries in the southern hemisphere. The IACAC was toted as the most clear-cut tool available to countries of the Americas in developing a sound anti-corruption platform in the southern hemisphere.

The World Bank views good governance and anti-corruption as central to its poverty alleviation mission. Nowadays, hundreds of governance and anti-corruption activities are taking place throughout the World Bank Group. They focus on internal organizational integrity, minimizing corruption on World Bank-funded projects, and assisting countries in improving governance and controlling corruption.

Combining participatory action-oriented learning, capacity-building, tools and the power of data, the WBI, in collaboration with many units in the World Bank Group, supports countries in improving governance and controlling corruption. Using a strategic and multidisciplinary approach, the Bank applies action-learning methods to link empirical surveys, their practical application, collective action, and prevention. Concrete results on the ground are emphasized in the World Bank educational programs. This integrated approach is supported by a comprehensive governance database. Companies determined by the Bank to have engaged in corrupt or fraudulent practice are blacklisted from participation in Bank-financed contracts, either indefinitely or for a limited amount of time. The *International Monetary Fund* (IMF) has taken similar steps. Each September, the Board of Governors of the World Bank and the IMF meet to discuss their role, work, and strategy to reduce poverty and preserve global financial stability. The discussions in 2005 centered on the MDGs to encourage developing countries to increase efforts toward poverty eradication. Everybody wants a world without extreme poverty, and policies in both rich and poor countries should advance that goal. However, some argue that the MDGs proposed at the UN Millennium Summit do not work to eradicate extreme poverty. Instead, they focus almost exclusively on redistributing wealth from rich to poor countries – a practice that promotes corruption and inefficiency – as opposed to encouraging poor countries to generate their own wealth.

Notwithstanding the debate regarding international aid versus national economic development, efforts are being made by all the aforementioned international organizations as well as by the WTO to eradicate corruption.

Bribe payments: tax treatment

In most developed countries, such as the USA, tax laws state that payments made to a foreign government official that are unlawful under the FCPA, cannot be deducted as a business expense. However, in Germany, Greece, Luxemburg, Belgium, and France, foreign bribe payments were tax deductible in whole or part, as late as 2004. The OECD recommends that those member countries which do not disallow the deductibility of bribes to foreign public officials reexamine such treatment with the intention of denying this deductibility. Such action may be facilitated by the trend to treat bribes to foreign public officials as illegal. The OECD further instructs its own Committee on Fiscal Affairs, in cooperation with the Committee on International Investment and MNEs, to monitor the implementation of this recommendation, to promote the recommendation in the context of contacts with nonmember countries and to report to the OECD Council as appropriate.

SMEs Ethics and Social Responsibility

Small and medium-sized enterprises (SMEs) should be as concerned about issues of ethics and corporate social responsibility as large MNEs. The Enron Corporation scandal seemed to indicate that nonethical behavior typifies larger corporations; the economic impact of SMEs is so significant (more than 50 percent of the GNP of many Western countries is created by SMEs) that it cannot be disregarded in the context of this chapter. This is the opinion of academics, ethics experts, and UN officials who are currently constructing a global anti-corruption treaty intended to cover both public and private sectors.

The lack of codes of ethics at SMEs is because they have fewer resources and because entrepreneurs often assume their businesses can do without a code of ethics. In fact, these are the reasons that make international small-business owners and employees even more open to the temptation of business practices and to lack of regard to social responsibility obligations than larger MNEs. A study conducted by DePaul University's John Olsen and Marc Schniederjans, of the University of Nebraska at Lincoln, indicated cases of bribery, general dishonesty, shady dealings with corrupt officials, and payoffs to local mobsters by international SMEs. They were also found to contribute illicit cash or manpower at the request of host governments, who wanted unions busted or favors for influential ethnic and religious groups.

The argument is that some of the questionable practices were a result of the fact that business schools do not offer an integrated and robust program on the subjects of ethics and social responsibility: to be able to articulate and respond to an ethical challenge, like taking kickbacks or hiring of relatives, appropriate training is essential. Without such training, wrong executive decisions hurt the bottom line, reduce revenues, and may cause the demise of an international SME.

The intimacy involving international SMEs requires further attention to the creation of a code of ethics and the adoption of acceptable ethical standards and practices, including appropriate controls. It is prudent that SMEs adopt the following practices:

1. Have an unbiased third party appraise the corporate ethics, or, for lack of resources, self-audit, by checking level of oversight and identifying vulnerable areas.
2. Draft a code of conduct, review it annually and use employee suggestions to improve it.
3. Train the workers and managers by using hypothetical but relevant examples.
4. Solicit feedback by using a hotline and by establishing a direct link to senior management.
5. The senior management should provide ethical leadership and network on these issues with other business leaders.

COUNTRY FOCUS

INDIA

World Rank (EFI 2009): 132

Regional Rank (EFI 2009): 28

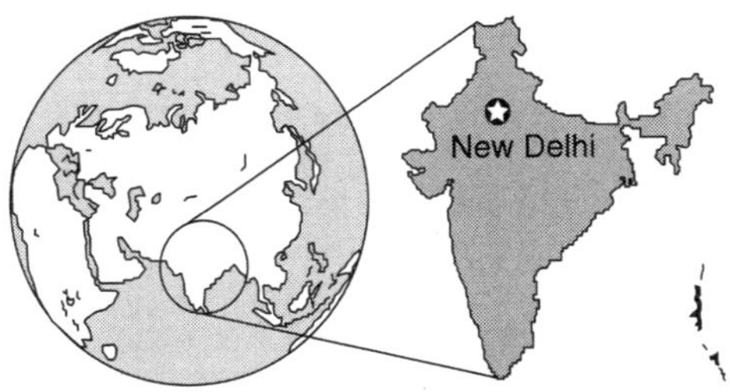

Quick facts

Population: 1.1 billion

GDP (PPP): $2.7 trillion 9.7 percent growth in 2006; 7.6 percent 5-year compound annual growth; $2,469 per capita

Unemployment: 7.2 percent

Inflation (CPI): 6.4 percent

FDI inflow: $16.9 billion

2006 data unless otherwise noted

Economic freedom score

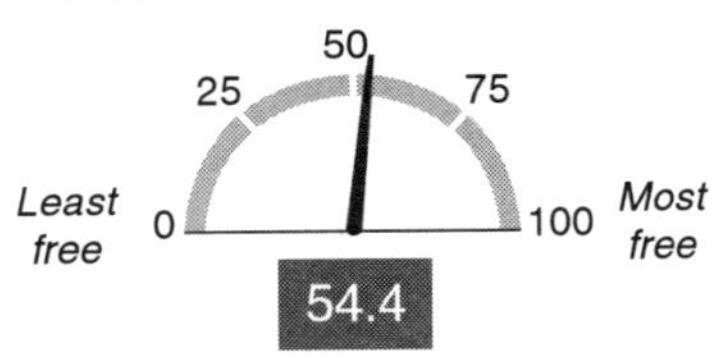

(Continued)

India's economic freedom score is 54.4, making its economy the 123rd freest in the 2009 Index. India is ranked 25th out of 41 countries in the Asia-Pacific region, and its overall score is below the world average.

Renouncing its previous insistence on central planning, India continues to move forward slowly with market-oriented economic reforms. Achieving average growth of about 8 percent over the past five years, the economy has emerged as a leader in information technology and other business process sectors. However, progress in strengthening institutional capacity and enhancing overall economic freedom and prosperity has been rather slow and marginal. India has no notably strong economic institutions, and the few areas that score better than the world average are government size, labor freedom, and property rights.

India could improve in business freedom, trade freedom, financial freedom, investment freedom, and freedom from corruption. The average tariff rate is high, and nontariff barriers further impede trade. Foreign investment is overly regulated, and the judicial system remains clogged by a large case backlog. Public debt is high, and the general government fiscal deficit continues to grow.

Background

India is the world's most populous democracy and one of Asia's fastest-growing economies. Its 1991 "big bang" liberalization shed decades of cumbersome regulations and trade protectionism. Since then, the economy has grown rapidly, first in services and recently in manufacturing. On a national level, the ruling Congress Party-led coalition has not accomplished much in the way of economic liberalization, restrained by its dependence on leftist parties. State-led economic reform has been far more successful. India still suffers from weak property rights and widespread corruption.

Business freedom – 54.4

The overall freedom to start, operate, and close a business remains restricted by India's regulatory environment. Starting a business takes an average of 30 days, compared to the world average of 38 days. Obtaining a business license requires about the world average of 18 procedures and 225 days. Bankruptcy is difficult.

Trade freedom – 51

India's weighted average tariff rate was 14.5 percent in 2005. Large differences between bound and applied tariff rates, import and export restrictions, services market access restrictions, import taxes and fees, complex and nontransparent regulation, onerous standards and certifications, discriminatory sanitary and phytosanitary measures, restrictive licensing, domestic bias in government procurement, problematic enforcement of intellectual property rights, export subsidies, inadequate infrastructure, counter-trade policies, and complex and nontransparent customs add to the cost of trade. Twenty points were deducted from India's trade freedom score to account for nontariff barriers.

Fiscal freedom – 73.8

India's tax rates are high. The top income and corporate tax rates are 33.99 percent (30 percent plus a 10 percent surcharge and a 3 percent education tax on that total). Other taxes include a value-added tax (VAT), a dividend tax, and a tax on insurance contracts. In the most recent year, overall tax revenue as a percentage of gross domestic product (GDP) was 17.7 percent.

Government size – 77.8

Total government expenditures, including consumption and transfer payments, are moderate. In the most recent year, government spending equaled 27.2 percent of GDP. The state still plays a major role in over 200 public sector enterprises.

Monetary freedom – 69.3

Inflation is moderately high, averaging 6.1 percent between 2005 and 2007. The government subsidizes agricultural, gas, and kerosene production; applies factory, wholesale and retail price controls on "essential" commodities, 25 crops, services, electricity, water, some petroleum products, and certain types of coal; and controls the prices of 74 bulk drugs that cover 40 percent of the market. Another 354 drugs are to be brought under controls by a new pharmaceutical policy. Domestic price and marketing arrangements apply to commodities like sugar and certain cereals. Fifteen points were deducted from India's monetary freedom score to account for policies that distort domestic prices.

Investment freedom – 30

Foreign direct investment is limited by law. Foreign investment is prohibited in most real estate, retailing, legal services, agriculture, security services, and the railways. Procedures do not discriminate against foreign companies in sectors where licensing is required, but certain industries are subject to export obligations and local content requirements. Bureaucracy is nontransparent, potentially corrupt, and burdensome. Residents need central bank approval to open foreign currency accounts domestically or abroad. Nonresidents may hold conditional foreign exchange and domestic currency accounts. Capital transactions and some credit operations are subject to restrictions and requirements.

Financial freedom – 40

India's financial sector includes 28 state-owned banks (which control about 71 percent of commercial banking), 29 private banks, and 31 foreign banks. Access to financial services varies sharply around the country. High credit costs and scarce access to financing still impede development of the private sector. Foreign banks account for about 8 percent of total commercial bank assets. Along with other restrictions, foreign banks operating in India may not directly or indirectly retain more than a 5 percent equity stake in a domestic private bank. The insurance sector is partially liberalized. Capital markets are relatively well developed; the stock market is one of Asia's largest, but foreign participation remains limited.

Property rights – 50

Because of large backlogs, courts take years to reach decisions, and foreign corporations often resort to international arbitration. Protection of property for local investors is weak, and protection of intellectual property rights is problematic. Proprietary test results and other data about patented products submitted to the government by foreign pharmaceutical companies have been used by domestic companies without any legal penalties.

Freedom from corruption – 35

Corruption is perceived as significant. India ranks 72nd out of 179 countries in Transparency International's Corruption Perceptions Index for 2007. Corruption continues to be a major concern, especially in government procurement of telecommunications, power, and defense contracts.

Labor freedom – 62.3

India's informal economy remains a large, important source of employment. The nonsalary cost of employing a worker is moderate, but dismissing a redundant employee is costly. The difficulty of laying-off a worker creates a disincentive for job creation.

Source: Adapted from Terry Miller and Kim R. Holmes, *2009 Index of Economic Freedom* (Washington, DC: The Heritage Foundation and Dow Jones & Company, Inc., 2009), at www.heritage.org/index.

SUMMARY

The chapter examines some of the **corporate social responsibility** and ethical issues involved in international business, and describe the ways in which business, governments, and international organizations regulate corporate appropriate conduct.

There is considerable convergence of corporate social responsibility and ethical behavior standards and practices by organizations that are involved internationally.

MNEs are critically scrutinized for the way in which they conduct business by a variety of domestic and international stakeholders.

Corporate social responsibility (CSR) is aimed to provide senior corporate executives, in a variety of industries, with the knowledge and practical tools and frameworks for integrating social responsibility as part of the corporate strategy.

Corruption is an exchange between two parties which (a) has an influence on the allocation of business resources either immediately or in the future; and (b) involves the use or abuse of public or collective responsibility for private needs and wants.

Ethics is the study of morality, standards, and practices of good conduct.

A Corruption Perception Index (CPI) is a measure of corruption that is calculated from multiple survey responses in a variety of countries and ranks these countries accordingly.

Money laundering involves concealing the source of funds by channeling them into legitimate business activities and depositing the funds in banks in other countries.

Bribery may be defined as payment made in the context of international business to enhance good will by foreign authorities and personalities.

The global response to corruption is aided by, among others, initiatives of governments, the OECD, the Commonwealth, the United Nations, The World Bank, The International Monetary Fund, and the World Trade Organization.

DISCUSSION QUESTIONS

1. What are the main issues that an international executive faces regarding corporate social responsibility?
2. What are the main ethical issues alluded to in the chapter? Can you relate these issues to a particular location?
3. What are the essential elements of the Foreign Corrupt Practices Act (FCPA)?

INTERNET EXERCISE

Mitsubishi's Philanthropy

In this chapter some of the social responsibility problems that Mitsubishi (MNC) has had in recent years were discussed.

However, on the other side of the coin, the huge Japanese MNC has been trying very hard to improve its image and to address its social responsibility shortcomings. Visit the company's website at www.mitsubishi.com and learn some of the latest social-type of activities in which the firm has been engaged.

In particular, look closely at the "philanthropy" and "environment" sections of the website. Then answer these questions: (l) What are some of the most recent things that Mitsubishi is doing in terms of philanthropy? Do you think these actions represent sincere concern for the community or do you think that Mitsubishi is simply trying to create a positive image for itself to offset past bad coverage by the press? (2) What steps is the MNC taking in its environmental efforts and of what value are these actions? (3) Based on your responses to these questions, what conclusions can you draw regarding the current social responsibility stance of Mitsubishi?

ACTION ITEMS

1. Assuming that you are planning to establish a base of operations in Nigeria. Which rules of conduct should you adopt and use?
2. Initiate a meeting with an executive in your neighborhood. Inquire about his knowledge of the various rules of conduct, compacts and agreements that govern corruption handling and acceptable business practices.

Bibliography

Abadisky, H. (2002). *Organized Crime*. New York: Wadsworth.

Albanese, J. (2004). *Organized Crime in Our Times*. Cincinnati, OH: Anderson.

Beare, M. (ed.). (2004). *Critical Reflections on Transnational Organized Crime, Money Laundering, and Corruption*. Toronto: University of Toronto Press.

Black, J. A. (2003). *Organized Crime*. Broomall, PA: Mason Crest.

Chow, D. C. K. (2002). *A Primer on Foreign Investment Enterprises and Protection of Intellectual Property in China*. The Hague: Kluwer.

Criminal Intelligence Service Canada. (1997–2004). *Annual Reports on Organized Crime in Canada*. Ottawa: Criminal Intelligence Service Canada.

Edwards, P., Michel A. (2004). *The Encyclopedia of Canadian Organized Crime: From Captain Kidd to Mom Boucher*. Toronto: McClelland & Stewart.

European Union. (2004). *European Union Organised Crime Situation Report, 2004*. Luxembourg: Office for Official Publications of the European Communities.

Global Corruption Report 2005 (2005). Transparency International.

Grennan, S., et al. (2000). *Gangs: An International Approach*. Upper Saddle River, NJ: Prentice-Hall.

Heidenheimer, A. J. Johnston, M., LeVine, V. T. (1987). *Political Corruption: A Handbook*. New Brunswick, NJ: Transaction.

Husted, B.W. (1999). Culture and corruption. *Journal of International Business Studies*. 30(2).

Husted, B.W. (1999). Wealth, culture and corruption. *Journal of International Business Studies*, 30(2).

Kelly, R. J. (2000). *Encyclopedia of Organized Crime in the United States: From Capone's Chicago to the New Urban Underworld*. Westport, CT: Greenwood.

Kenney, D. J., Finckenauer, J. O. (1995). *Organized Crime in America*. Belmont, CA: Wadsworth.

Liddick, D. (2004). *The Global Underworld: Transnational Crime and the United States*. Westport, CT: Praeger.

Lunde, P. (2004). *Organized Crime: An Inside Guide to the World's Most Successful Industry*. New York: D.K. Publishing.

Macrae, J. (1982). Wealth, culture and corruption. In Husted, B. W. (ed.) *Journal of International Business Studies*, 30 (2), 340.

Mahan, S. (ed.) (1998). *Beyond the Mafia: Organized Crime in the Americas*. Thousand Oaks, CA: Sage.

Mauro, P. (1995). Corruption and growth. *Quarterly Journal of Economics*, 110 (3), 681–712.

Nash, J. R. (1993). *World Encyclopaedia of Organized Crime*. New York: De Capo Press.

National Criminal Intelligence Service (2000–2003). UK *Threat Assessments*. London: National Criminal Intelligence Service.

Nicaso, A., Lamothe, L. (1995). *Global Mafia: The New World Order of Organized Crime*. Toronto: Macmillan Canada.

Rugman, A. M., Hodgetts, R. M. (2000). *International Business*, 2nd edn. London: Pearson.

Schleifer, A., Vishny, R. (1993). Corruption. *Quarterly Journal of Economics*, Autumn.

Van Duyne, P. C. et al. (2004). *Threats and Phantoms of Organized Crime, Corruption and Terrorism: Critical European Perspectives*. Netherlands: Wolf Legal Publishers.

Vittell, S. J., Nwachukwo, S. L., Barnes, J. H. (1993). The effects of culture on ethical decision-making: an application of Hoftstede's typology. *Journal of Business Ethics*, 12, 753–60.

Xiaohe, L. (1997). Business ethics in China. *Journal of Business Ethics*, October, 1509–18.

PART 2

International Business Environment

3

Cultural Context of International Business

Learning Objectives

Following this chapter, the reader should be able to:

1 Define culture and be able to explain the importance of national cultures
2 Define determinants of culture and their impact upon international business activities
3 Describe cultural change and the interaction between companies and culture
4 Describe and apply frameworks of culture classification

Opening Case
International Students at the University of Canterbury

The following paragraphs are taken from a website that is designed as a cultural guide for international students at the University of Canterbury. What are the key elements of culture that international students attending the program at the University of Canterbury in New Zealand face? Could the same be said about your university as well?

Adjusting to living in New Zealand
Learning to live in a new culture is a little like learning to ride a bicycle for the first time. To begin with you feel uncertain, perhaps unsafe, and certainly very self-conscious. Your first few efforts may involve an accident or two. However, it is not long before you are riding well and making good progress down the road. Fairly soon you begin to think of the bicycle as an extension to yourself and you find it hard to imagine that you ever had any difficulties riding!

How can you learn to ride the bicycle of New Zealand? Be prepared! There are three things you can do:

1 Know as much as possible about New Zealand.
2 Expect to find differences.
3 Expect to feel "culture shock" but know it does not last long.

Know as much as possible about New Zealand
Go to your library, surf the Internet, ask your friends. Find as much out as you can about New Zealand. Who are the Maori? Who are the All Blacks? What is the Prime Minister's name? Who is the mayor of Christchurch? What is the geography and climate like? How do New Zealanders greet each other? Who are the world famous New Zealanders? Where are the Southern Alps? etc.

Expect to find differences
Of course, there will be many differences between where you live now and living in Christchurch. Perhaps you have thought of some already. Moving country can be a bit like a journey into the unknown (and we should know, all the international student advisers have made such a journey).

Source: Adapted from the University of Canterbury website.

Introduction

International business is markedly different from domestic business, since it involves transactions between different countries. Thus, awareness regarding cultural differences is a key success factor in international business. Specifically, national differences regarding political, economic, and legal issues influence the revenues, costs, profits, and risks associated with doing business in different countries and regions. This chapter explores the different cultures across and within regions and countries and their effect on international business. There are four main factors regarding culture in international business: cross-cultural literacy; cultural adjustments; cultural effect on profitability of international ventures; and cultural change over time.

Cross-cultural literacy is defined as an understanding of how cultural differences across and within regions and countries can affect the way business is practiced. While globalization seems to translate to sameness in business communication, business standards, and business practices, there are major differences that significantly affect the conduct of business. Western business people assume that since people in other countries adopt Western dress codes, Western food habits, and Western music, the conduct of business is the same. Not necessarily so. Chinese businessmen are highly influenced by a 5,000-year-old ideology, for example, that values relationships backed by reciprocal obligations. Furthermore, the Communist regime insists that foreign multinationals interested in pursuing ventures in China support socialist causes at the community or provincial level. Another Chinese cultural tradition that requires attention is the practice of "guanxiwang," freely translated as "relationship network" which means favors need to be paid back or reciprocated.

Cultural adjustments refer to the care that must be taken in translating cultural knowledge into cultural practice. For example, in reference to the Chinese "guanxiwang," the reciprocity may not be construed as bribery, which is largely deemed illegal by Western legal codes. In the United States, the Foreign Corrupt Practices Act (FCPA) bans a US corporation from bribing government officials to gain business in a foreign country, while the German legal code may allow this as an expense.

Culture effect on profitability is also noted in different countries or regions. To wit, in countries or regions that value organized labor disputes, more working days are lost due to these disputes. Some European countries such as England and France, as well as Canada, lose more working days due to these disputes than Japan. Religious civic holidays may also add to the costs of doing business in a given country or region. The Ramadan, a Muslim holiday, lasts for one month and involves a daily fasting routine, which may significantly affect labor productivity, which in turn may affect business profitability.

It is customary to identify various types of risk involved in international business – commercial risk, country risk, currency risk, and cross-cultural risk – as noted in Figure 3.1. The latter refers to the risk entailed from operating a business in a different culture from the home-base culture.

Cultural issues may be subjected to change over time. Countries and regions adopt, different cultural patterns at times slowly.

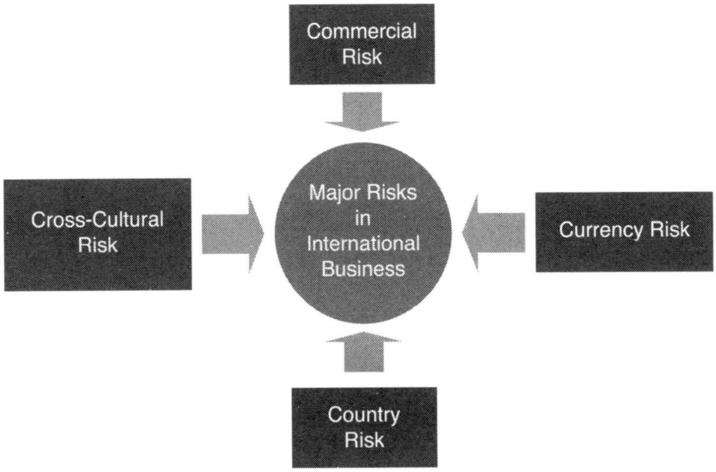

FIGURE 3.1 The four major risks in international business

The chapter starts off with a definition of culture, followed by a discussion of levels of culture. Next, the highlights of elements of culture are presented, including language, religion, values and attitudes, social structures, aesthetics, stereotypes, and cultural arrogance. We conclude with a description of two diagnostic tools for analyzing culture.

We discuss the implications of culture for business practice, including the effect of culture on international mergers and acquisitions throughout the chapter.

What is Culture?

The following paragraphs provide a definition of culture and discuss levels of culture as well as elements and models of culture. These issues provide both the theoretical basis and the application implications relevant to international business.

Culture Defined

Culture is commonly defined as the predominating attitudes and behavior that characterize the functioning of a group, a community, an organization, or a nation. It is the manifestation of a set of values, beliefs, rules, and institutions held by such a group and expressed by the individual actions and reactions of each member.

Consider when traveling how different groups in different cultures treat similar situations differently due to the local culture and its underlying values, beliefs, and rules. For example, a cow walking down the street in a small town in India is considered sacred and left more or less to do as it pleases. In North America, it might be considered a great excuse for a barbecue. In contrast, a dog walking down the street of a small town in the United States might be considered a family pet or a stray dog, but the same dog in Vietnam could be considered a great excuse for a barbecue there. Which one of the conflicting reactions or interpretations is correct?

The answer depends on what your cultural norms, beliefs, values, and attitudes are about each case. If you are part of a culture that holds cows to be sacred or views dogs as loving pets (almost part of the family), then killing and eating the creatures would be considered wrong somehow. However, if you are part of a culture that views these creatures as an acceptable food source, then killing and eating them would seem to be a natural thing to do.

To understand culture more in depth, it is important to learn to become sensitive to various elements of culture and the associated assumptions, rules, and behavior they engender. However, before describing some of these elements of culture, it must first be recognized that there are different levels of culture.

Levels of Culture

It is said that from a great enough distance all human beings look the same. However, if you look more closely at different groups, many differences, both physical and otherwise, become more and more obvious the closer you are.

A similar phenomenon is true regarding culture. For almost every cultural group, if you look carefully and closely enough, you can identify distinct subgroups within the whole. Subcultures can be defined as a shared set of norms, beliefs, values, customs, experiences, and symbols that reflect a subset of the larger group or within the cultural framework guard unique opinions which are not shared throughout the group as a whole.

For example, among the worldwide religious group of Christians, there is a shared belief in Jesus Christ as the son of God, in Sunday as the day of rest and in the Holy Bible. However, while Catholics (a subculture of the entire Christian population) feel that Christian priests should be fully committed to "Mother Church" and guiding their community and are therefore forbidden to marry and have a family, Protestants (another subculture of the general Christian population) feel that priests should be allowed to marry and have a family.

National culture reflects the dominant culture within a particular political and geographic boundary of a nation-state. The dominant culture is usually determined by a shared group that represents the majority of the population, or has the most economic or political power within the nation-state. Typically, the education, business and political systems that evolve adopt the dominant culture's language, priorities, rules, and norms as those of the nation-state as a whole.

However, political and geographic boundaries do not necessarily reflect cultural boundaries. For example, two distinct and formal cultures thrive within the nation-state of Canada (an English-speaking and a Francophone one). Alternatively, there is a culturally distinct group of Kurdish people living in a region which is shared by both Iraq and Turkey (some living as a minority culture in each country).

Most business is performed within the political boundaries of a nation-state and as such, is subject to the dominant national culture's influence on language, laws, norms, values, symbols, and so forth.

In addition, all major social institutions – religion, education, family, politics, and law – are intimately influenced by the national culture. Furthermore, these social institutions (e.g., the family) are integral to the transmission of the commonly shared values and beliefs of a culture from generation to generation.

It is very common in any national culture to find many subcultures defined either by their common historical background (e.g., immigrants), religious beliefs (e.g., Greek Orthodox), or community focus (e.g., a "family town" vs a "football town").

Business culture

Managers responsible for any function of international business are primarily concerned with the norms, values, and rules of the local business culture. These norms are always a subset or guided by the general norms of the local culture. For example, a local culture's attitudes towards time could dictate business discipline about arriving at and starting business meetings on time. Local culture norms regarding the role of women could influence the openness of senior managers to working with women (even if from a different culture) as equals.

The implications of these differences go far beyond simply understanding the local business etiquette: they dictate to people what are the "acceptable ways" of doing business in a society. It is not just a guide to the appropriate way to dress for a meeting or how to exchange business cards, or how to address a colleague or a superior. These acceptable business practices direct all aspects of the business, from employer–employee relations and organizational structure decisions, to negotiation strategies and marketing plans.

Intel Prepares Staffers for Culture Shock

(Hermoni, O., *Globes*, July 11, 2004)

Israelis love to ask questions, argue, and get straight to the point. These are some of the pearls of wisdom global chip giant Intel offers American staffers before they visit Israel, where it has several sites, including key research and development (R&D) centers.

As part of a course for staff in America, Intel workers are enlightened about the culture shock that awaits them when they visit the country. Some of the points made at Intel's "Working with Israelis" session are:

- Don't raise politics in conversation. Better stick to topics like tourism or sports – especially football, basketball, and swimming. If politics comes up, listen, be attentive, and avoid confrontation.
- Be aware and sensitive to the fact that many Israelis have suffered personal tragedies in the political-security conflict.

(Continued)

- Present your ideas clearly and get directly to the point. Prepare to be interrupted and cut to pieces in the course of your presentation.
- Israelis like to argue and enjoy discussing every topic enthusiastically. Visitors may be startled by this fervor, but in most cases don't mistake passionate argument for anger, but just a different culture of expression.
- It is acceptable to talk generally about one's personal life and a polite inquiry about an Israeli colleague's family will be warmly received.
- If you are making a presentation, be armed with plenty of supporting facts, and keep the slide show shorter than usual to allow for questions. Israelis prefer to ask questions immediately and not wait for the end of the presentation. Be prepared.

Intel said its handouts on working in Israel were prepared for the company by external consultants.

Intel has operated in Israel for 30 years and employs 5,400 workers in Haifa, Jerusalem, Kiryat Gat, Petah Tikva, and Yakum. Over this period Intel's local branches have produced products worth over $10 billion, and the company's R&D centers here are behind the company's latest Centrino mobile technology.

To the international business professional, taking the time to understand and learn about the local business culture can often make the difference between a successful venture and a failed experiment into different international markets.

Organizational and occupational culture

Before describing some of the elements of culture, there are two other distinct cultural subgroups of which international managers must be aware.

Organizational culture reflects the norms and values within a specific organization. For example, in the automotive sector, a company such as Ferrari considers itself a leader in style, speed, power, and status, while a company like Volvo prides itself on safety, reliability, and family values. Each of the organizations creates within it a particular organizational culture by actively promoting its beliefs, values, and norms through rewarding behavior that is consistent with those norms and punishing (or simply not rewarding) other behavior.

Similarly, occupational cultures reflect the common values, beliefs, and norms within a particular profession such as a law office, a medical clinic, and so forth. Each of these occupations abides by similar norms which are developed during studies, but reinforced at work through the organizational structure, the advancement system, the interactions between colleagues, clients and superiors, and the various symbols of status, power, control, or success displayed by the individuals within the occupation.

Occupational cultures can also be interpreted as subcultures within an organizational culture that manifest in different functional departments. For example, the norms and behaviors in any given situation in the R&D department would not normally be expected to be similar to those in the Quality Assurance Department or the Finance Department.

<table>
<tr><td rowspan="2">Visible Cultural Makeup (Culture)</td><td colspan="2">Fine Arts</td><td>Literature</td></tr>
<tr><td colspan="2">Drama</td><td>Classical Music</td></tr>
<tr><td rowspan="4">Noticeable Cultural Makeup (Folk Culture)</td><td>Humor</td><td>Religion</td><td>Folk Dancing</td></tr>
<tr><td>Popular Music</td><td>Cooking</td><td>Rites of Passage</td></tr>
<tr><td>Courtship Practice</td><td>Dress Diet</td><td></td></tr>
<tr><td colspan="3">Language</td></tr>
<tr><td rowspan="5">Undercurrents of Cultural Makeup (Fundamental Culture)</td><td>Family Relationships</td><td>Nonverbal Communications</td><td>Gender Roles</td></tr>
<tr><td colspan="2">Superior–Subordinate Relationship</td><td>Conversational Patterns</td></tr>
<tr><td colspan="2">Preference of Cooperation vs Competition</td><td>Eye Behavior</td></tr>
<tr><td colspan="2">Decision–Making Patterns</td><td>Concept of Beauty</td></tr>
<tr><td colspan="2">Methods of Problem–Solving</td><td>Conversational Patterns</td></tr>
</table>

FIGURE 3.2 Elements of culture (www.changingminds.org)

Elements of Culture

Understanding and describing a national or community culture is not always a straightforward exercise. A group's beliefs, habits, values, and assumptions about what is right or beautiful or appropriate manifests itself in hundreds or thousands of little ways in the course of everyday life.

The elements of culture are shown in Figure 3.2, organized into three categories: visible cultural makeup; noticeable cultural makeup; and undercurrents of cultural makeup (or fundamental, culture).

In order to establish a general understanding and appreciation of different expressions of cultures before applying analytical tools targeting business priorities, we provide a brief overview of some of the major elements that together help to distinguish one culture from another.

Language

As a primary means of communication, language is at once one of the most obvious expressions of a different culture, as well as an element that can provide some of the deepest insights into it, should you choose to analyze it closely. Language consists both of spoken communications as well as unspoken communications (i.e., body language). Each of these conveys meaning both in form and in content that reflects on the culture with which you are interacting.

Upon arriving in a foreign country, one of the first things you notice is that people are speaking in a different language or in some cases the same language, but with a different accent or different local jargon. Exploring further, it is possible to identify concepts in any language which are more important in a particular culture by considering the ideas for which there are many subtly different words: for example, the 50 different ways Inuit describe snow or the 30 different ways desert tribes can describe sand.

Also, the manner people phrase ideas and address one another says a great deal about the local cultural norms regarding gender, workplace hierarchy, treatment of elders, etc. This includes whether an introductory discussion is typically formal or intimate, what topics are considered impolite in certain circumstances, and so forth.

Another strong reflection of cultural norms relates to body language. How close together people stand when conversing, how much they use their hands as visual aids, or whether or not physical touch is common or avoided can tell you a lot about how formal or informal relationships are meant to be in different professional and social settings or how people relate to concepts such as "personal space," "hierarchy," and "active listening."

Table 3.1 indicates the most common primary languages of the world.

Figure 3.3 lists language-related blunders in advertising campaigns for various products.

Religion

Many values and beliefs that define various communities are based in religious beliefs. Views ranging from appropriate dress, dietary habits, or premarital sex to the definition of a business workweek, the role of women in the business community or a set of taboos that should not be used in marketing campaigns are often greatly influenced by the dominant religion of a particular nation-state or close-knit local community.

TABLE 3.1 The Most Common Primary Languages in the World

Rank	*Language*	*Approximate number of native speakers (millions)*	*Countries with a substantial number of native speakers*
1	Mandarin Chinese	874	China, Singapore
2	Hindi	365	India
3	English	341	United States, United Kingdom
4	Spanish	322	Argentina, Mexico, Spain
5	Bengali	207	Bangladesh, India
6	Arabic	198	Algeria, Egypt, Saudi Arabia
7	Portuguese	176	Brazil, Portugal
8	Russian	167	Russian Federation, Ukraine
9	Japanese	125	Japan
10	German	100	Germany, Austria
11	Korean	78	South Korea, North Korea
12	French	77	France, Belgium, Quebec (Canada)
13	Turkish	75	Turkey, Central Asia, Eastern Europe

Source: Adapted from the database of *Ethnologue: Languages of the World*, 14th edn.

- Pepsi's "Come alive with the Pepsi Generation" translated into "Pepsi brings your ancestors back from the grave," in Chinese.
- An American T-shirt maker in Miami printed shirts for the Spanish market which promoted the Pope's visit. Instead of "I saw the Pope" (el Papa), the shirts read "I saw the potato" (la papa).
- The American slogan for Salem cigarettes, "Salem-Feeling Free", was translated into the Japanese market as "When smoking Salem, you will feel so refreshed that your mind seems to be free and empty".
- When Parker Pen marketed a ball-point pen in Mexico, its ads were supposed to have read, "it won't leak in your pocket and embarrass you". Instead, the company thought that the word "embarazar" (to impregnate) meant to embarrass, so the ad read: "It won't leak in your pocket and make you pregnant".
- Coors put its slogan, "Turn it loose," into Spanish, where it was read as "Suffer from diarrhea".
- Clairol introduced the "Mist Stick," a curling iron, into German only to find out that "mist" is slang for manure. Not too many people had use for the "manure stick".
- When Gerber started selling baby food in Africa, they used the same packaging as in the USA, with a beautiful baby on the label. Later they learned that in Africa, companies routinely put pictures on the label of what's inside, since most people can't read.
- Scandinavian vacuum manufacturer Electrolux used the following in an American campaign: "Nothing sucks like an Electrolux".
- In Italy, a campaign for Schweppes Tonic Water translated the name into "Schweppes Toilet Water".

FIGURE 3.3 Blunders in international advertising (From www.english-zone.com)

A wide range of different religions are practiced around the world and many of them have their own subgroups that each practice variations of the main religion through differing interpretations or traditions based on local custom. The following are some examples of religions and their subgroups around the globe:

- Christian – Roman Catholic, Eastern, Protestant, Greek Orthodox, etc.
- Muslim – Sunni, Shiah, etc.
- Buddhist – Lamaist, Southern, etc.
- Jewish – Ashkenaz, Sephardic, Orthodox, Conservative, etc.
- Hindu – Sikh Buddhist, Christian, etc.
- Japanese – Buddhist, Shintoist.
- Chinese – Buddhist, Taoist, Confucian.

The dominant religion in any potential market has a profound effect on the acceptable norms of the local community and can often present unique advantages for those who are aware of them. For example, in predominately Christian countries, the November–December time frame is the biggest retail season of the year and can account for 40–60 percent of annual sales of many consumer goods (e.g., digital cameras, tennis rackets, or Sony Play Stations). However, in China, this phenomenon occurs around end of January or beginning of February, relating more to the Chinese New Year.

Even religious communities within a dominant culture of a nation-state can often represent a targeted business opportunity for those who understand their specific needs. For example, the Muslim and Jewish communities in many countries are not allowed by their religion to eat pork or food with pork additives (e.g., lard as a preservative). They are therefore often willing to pay a premium for food products that possess halal (Muslim) or kosher (Jewish) certification.

Values and attitudes

Values reflect the ideas, beliefs, and customs to which people have an emotional attachment. They include things like respect for one's elders, marital fidelity, honesty, and integrity or material wealth.

Values influence how people balance their work and personal lives, how focused they are on accumulating material wealth or how comfortable they feel about smoking, drinking, and drugs. In some countries hard work, success, and material wealth are appreciated (e.g., Singapore and the United States). In others, a life of culture or leisure is more valued, and work is regarded as a means to secure these pursuits (e.g., France or Greece). In some countries values dictate how tolerant a society will be to certain vices such as drinking or smoking. In many Muslim countries, the use of alcohol or drugs is strictly forbidden and severely punished.

Attitudes are positive or negative views, judgments, opinions, or feelings that individuals have towards certain objects, concepts, or situations around them. These often reflect underlying values. For example, a Westerner observing the Kumbh Mela bathing ritual in the Ganges River in India (which is held every few years), where hundreds of thousands of people bathe in the holy river together – many of them naked – might say: "I don't like this ritual as it seems dirty and uncivilized given how people are displaying themselves in public." This attitude to a religious ritual in India could reflect strong beliefs or values regarding cleanliness or public exposure of the human body.

Values and attitudes are both learned from role models in a community such as parents, teachers or religious leaders. They vary from country to country, however: whereas values tend to be rigid and resistant to change, attitudes tend to be more flexible and quick to adapt to changing circumstances. Values are generally related to very important fundamental issues in society, whereas attitudes can be found regarding both important and unimportant aspects of daily life.

Attitudes towards advances in technology, the family unit, sex, and education can each strongly influence the local reaction to a particular advertising campaign or consumer product. Understanding the local values and attitudes of a community is a critical step in considering the possible reactions or interpretations of a given marketing message and will determine the success or failure of such an initiative.

Three other common aspects of life, which are worth mentioning as they often have a direct impact on common practices in the workplace, are attitudes towards time, personal space, and work and achievement.

Time

There are many stereotypes regarding different people from different cultures and how they manage time, schedules, and meetings. For example, it is commonly understood that Germans are always punctual, arrive at meetings on time, and expect to complete the meeting on time. The Japanese, who are also known for their precision and punctuality, actually assume meetings will always begin two minutes later than the appointed time, but end on schedule. The stereotypical Italian is generally more focused on relationship management than time management and is notorious for starting meetings late and ending them flexibly. Of course, these are generalizations; however, it is true that in every culture (whether national, communal, or organizational) you can observe that people have very distinct and consistent attitudes towards time and note to what extent they relate to it as an absolute measure or as a broad guideline for scheduling their activities throughout the day. Clearly, two individuals with vastly different attitudes in this regard can quickly interpret one another's actions as disrespectful. For example, if one of them always arrives on time and expects to finish the meeting at the appointed hour, and the other arrives casually 20 minutes into the meeting, the punctual individual might be personally insulted at the other's disrespect for the scheduled time of the meeting. It might be interpreted as a sign that the latecomer does not consider the discussion or colleague important enough to arrive on time.

Personal space

Different cultures have different attitudes about the "appropriate" distance people should stand from each other during a conversation. This distance can be interpreted as comfortable, aggressive engaged, or disdainful. For example,

> a Hispanic community leader in Los Angeles and an Anglo-American businessman fell into conversation at charity event. As the former moved closer, the latter backed away. It took nearly 30 minutes of waltzing around the room for the community leader to realize that "Anglos" were not comfortable standing in such close physical proximity. (Earley and Mosakowski, 2004)

When interacting with individuals from different cultures, being aware and sensitive of attitudes regarding personal space is critical if you are trying to have a constructive discussion or build a trusting relationship with the other person.

Work and achievement

Attitudes towards work and achievement are obviously related to business practices, as they can often lead to mistaken assumptions regarding a work colleague's commitment to the company, dedication to their work or, in some cases, even their abilities. For example, there is a saying among the French that "The French work to live, and the Americans live to work." The implication by the French is that while French people see work as a means to an end (i.e., a certain quality of life to be enjoyed), the American attitude towards work is that it represents the end in itself. That is why it is considered rude to discuss business during meals in France, whereas, in the USA this would be considered an efficient use of time.

The attitudes towards achievement have similar implications. For example, in Hong Kong, material wealth is highly valued and can be seen as a sign of status within the community. In the USA, individual achievement is highly valued and is often rewarded not just financially, but in status symbols such as a private office. In Japan, however, loyalty, dedication, and contribution to the team are more highly valued than individual achievement, and this is manifested in open-plan offices (where the manager sits in the center of the room among the staff), no individual ownership of intellectual property by company engineers or scientists (though this is now beginning to change) and a strong expectation of spending both the whole workday as well as much of your social life with your work colleagues as a sign of dedication. In such a community, longevity, and rank are appreciated above all else.

Manners and customs

Understanding a local culture's manners and customs is an important element of building a trusting and productive business relationship with fellow colleagues, potential customers, or important suppliers. At worst, it helps avoid embarrassing mistakes or unintended slights. At best, a real understanding can help to create more open communications and a deeper relationship.

Manners

There are certain typical ways of behaving, dressing, speaking, or listening considered to be appropriate or polite in every culture. These norms differ and can sometimes even seem completely foreign and incomprehensible to someone who has never experienced them. For example, it is common among the French for a male colleague to greet a female colleague at the office with a light kiss to each cheek. The same action in the USA could be considered grounds for a sexual harassment lawsuit. When exchanging business cards in many Asian countries, it is polite to receive the card in both hands, read the card carefully and have it in front of you during the entire meeting in order of the rank of the people in the meeting. This is because in Asia, your business card is considered to be an extension of yourself and should be treated with respect. In North America or Western Europe it is usually considered to be a document with some contact information to be kept in your bag for use after the meeting rather than an integral part of the encounter.

Customs

When habits or behaviors in certain situations are practiced from one generation to the next, they become local customs or traditions. In North America, it is a custom at the end of high school for students to celebrate graduation with a formal party know as a "prom." In France, it is a custom to bring a gift of a bottle of wine when invited for dinner at someone's home. In many cultures there are traditional folk dances that are part of local customs and that are danced on special occasions such as weddings or other community celebrations.

Gift-giving is often a complex custom that arises in business scenarios, where different cultures have very different expectations, rules, and policies. For example, in Asia, small gifts to a business colleague are common and also obligate the receiver to reciprocate in the future, but do not necessarily imply anything regarding the business negotiations. In contrast, gifts to US business associates could be regarded with suspicion and sometimes even considered a form of bribery.

Social structure

Different cultures have different views towards the organization of their community, groups, and institutions. The system of social and political relationships is often dictated by traditional roles of various people or groups in the community and can often be very hard to overcome.

Three common "classifications" in a society are gender, caste, and class.

Gender

The role of women in society and especially in business is very different in Fundamentalist Islamic Arab states than it is in the Netherlands or Canada. In Japan, senior women executives are rare, even though at home the woman is considered to be the head of the household and manages all the family finances.

Caste

A caste system is one in which individuals are born into a specific social group (or caste) with very little opportunity of breaking out of this group. Most marriages, career opportunities or business relationships are limited to the group into which they have been born. This is a very common phenomenon in India among the hundreds of different ethnic and religious groups.

Class

A class system is one in which the social stratification is more closely related to personal ability and actions than the group into which you are born. However, opportunities may vary greatly depending on which class you start in and can influence your eventual potential. For example, in the USA and much of Western Europe there are well-known poor, middle class, and wealthy social groups. It is clearly more challenging for someone born into a poor social group to achieve the same accomplishments as a person from a wealthy group, given the advantages the wealthy have in terms of education, resources, network of contacts, and role models.

Aesthetics

"Beauty is in the eye of the beholder" is a well-known phrase that expresses clearly a warning to patrons of the arts that any work of art may be appreciated by one person, while dismissed by others. Much of the decision is based on a subjective opinion of what is "beautiful."

Different cultures have different opinions on colors, shapes, textures, structures, and functional vs aesthetic priorities. For example, red in North America is often used as a warning or is the color of stop signs. In China, it is considered good luck and small red packets are handed out to friends and family during Chinese New Year. In France, purple is considered to be a royal color, while in Spain it is used for funerals and is associated with death.

These differences are critically important when designing a local marketing and promotion strategy or designing a website for international use, given those choices of form and color can convey serious and unintended messages to different audiences depending on their aesthetic norms.

Cultural Stereotyping and Cultural Arrogance

Cultural stereotyping

Although it is valuable to begin any international interaction with some understanding of the general norms, values, and customs of the local culture, it is important to carefully account for the differences among individual members of that culture or subculture. Assuming that all people from a certain culture feel, believe, and behave identically is referred to as stereotyping and can often lead to wrong and destructive conclusions.

As a starting point, research on a local culture can heighten managers' awareness of potential differences, cause them to be more sensitive to their own assumptions about certain situations and be more patient with circumstances they do not always fully understand. However, stereotypes should be treated as hypotheses to be proved or disproved on a case-by-case basis, rather than as a broadly true assumption that applies to all individuals in a given community. Understanding the difference between a hypothesis about an individual and your assumptions about the individual is an essential part of developing appropriate responses to culturally different circumstances.

Cultural arrogance

Another dangerous aspect of cultural interaction is when one or both of the individuals in question consider their own culture to be the authority on what is right and wrong. This type of arrogant and egoistical attitude may seem unlikely in its extreme form, even among managers with limited international experience, but in fact it often expresses itself in subtle actions of disapproval, disdain or even hostile attitudes towards some of the local ways of doing business, hosting guests or negotiating agreements. Bribery is an obvious example, but it is often the more subtle ways of how different cultures regard taking responsibility for one's own actions, how much an individual is expected to sacrifice for the sake of the group or the importance of deadlines in meetings or project deliverables. Poorly applied assumptions may label certain individuals as lazy or irresponsible even though they may simply be behaving according to the local norms and delivering good results.

Analyzing Culture: Two Diagnostic Tools for Cultural Analysis

We are now familiar with the definitions, levels, and some of the major elements of culture, as well as the dangers of overly relying on general stereotypes at the cost of understanding an individual person and their motivations.

We are now ready to explore diagnostic cultural analysis tools used in the study and practice of international management. These diagnostic tools are of practical value to the international business person. The two models we will describe here are Hofstede's Model of National Culture and Trompenaars' 7d Culture Model.

Hofstedes' model of national culture

Gert Hofstede introduced the first model of cultural characterization based primarily on differing values and beliefs with regard to work, providing a clear link between the national and business cultures of a location. This made it a particularly useful model for international managers, as it highlights differences which have a direct impact on cross-cultural negotiations, multinational management of a global network of offices, and cross-cultural management issues for expatriate managers in new and unfamiliar settings.

Hofstede identified five cultural value dimensions with which he would characterize different cultures. The first four dimensions he identified through a study of 39 IBM subsidiaries and 110,000 people throughout the world (Hofstede, 1980). Later research by Hofstede and others added more countries and introduced the fifth dimension of "long-term orientation" (Hofstede, 1991; Hofstede and Bond, 1998). The first four dimensions were researched through a survey developed by Hofstede, as a Western researcher investigating other cultures. The fifth dimension was based on a survey and questions developed with Asian researchers and, reflects Confucian values.

The following are the five dimensions of national cultural values identified by Hofstede:

1. *Power distance* – expectations regarding equality among people.
2. *Uncertainty avoidance* – typical reactions to situations considered different and dangerous.
3. *Individualism* – the relationship between the individual and the group in society.
4. *Masculinity* – expectations regarding gender roles.
5. *Long-term orientation* – a basic orientation towards time.

Power distance

This dimension is concerned with how a particular culture views the idea of inequality. It focuses on how superiors and subordinates in an organization interact and what assumptions and behaviors about each group are considered to be "the norm."

The values that are generally associated with high power distance cultures are:

- inequality is fundamentally good,
- everyone has a place – some are high, some are low,
- most people should be dependent on a leader,
- the powerful are entitled to privileges,
- the powerful should not hide their power.

Organizations in countries that demonstrate high power distance generally demonstrate a high degree of hierarchy and management control of employees. An underlying assumption tends to be that people dislike work and try to avoid it, and therefore management and processes are meant to monitor and control to ensure compliance and effort. Employee training generally emphasizes compliance (follow orders) and trustworthiness. Decision making is typically centralized and top-down, and the hierarchical organizational structure generally creates many levels of management and supervisors.

Uncertainty avoidance

This dimension relates to the behaviors and beliefs of people in the face of uncertainty or ambiguity. Higher uncertainty avoidance cultures seek to structure social systems where rules and regulations dominate, and order and predictability are valued. In these cultures risky situations create stress and upset people.

The following are the values generally associated with high uncertainty avoidance cultures:

- conflict should be avoided,
- deviant people and ideas should not be tolerated,
- laws are very important and should be followed,
- experts and authorities are usually correct,
- consensus is important.

Organizations with a high uncertainty avoidance culture tend to value loyalty and seniority over performance and ability, both when hiring and compensating staff. They tend to have very strict processes and procedures, are very task focused and tend towards large organizations. Employees are usually more concerned with job security and avoiding competition or confrontation. These tend to be people who are extremely risk averse.

Individualism/collectivism

This dimension highlights two opposing beliefs: (1) people are unique and can be valued in terms of their own achievements, status, and other unique characteristics; or (2) people are defined in terms of the groups to which they belong, and their role in the group and obligations to it take precedence over the individual.

The following are the values generally associated with cultures that demonstrate high individualism:

- people are responsible for themselves,
- individual achievement is ideal,
- people need not be emotionally dependent on organizations or groups.

The values that are generally associated with cultures that demonstrate high collectivism are:

- individual identity is based on group membership,
- group decision making is best,
- groups protect individuals in exchange for their loyalty to the group.

In collectivist cultures, organizations tend to select managers who belong to the family, friends or extended family (e.g., China). Being a relative or known by the owners becomes more important than the individual's personal qualifications. In contrast, in cultures with high individualism (e.g., United States) favoritism toward family and friends is considered unfair and at times illegal, as in these cultures the belief is that all people should be evaluated against the same objective criteria regardless of the personal relationship to key individuals. The cultural belief is that open competition allows the most qualified individual to get the job.

People in collectivist organizations tend to be promoted primarily on the basis of seniority and learn to expect that the major reward for working is to be taken care of by the organization. Managers tend to be motivated by a "call to duty" to work for the good of the group.

Decision making in collectivist cultures is generally done by the older senior managers (especially in high power distance cultures), but in many cases can also involve a lot of consensus building and group decision making, particularly if many of the people are related or represent a close-knit social group. In such cases, the needs and feelings of the group members become part of the decision-making process, which also tends to make it longer.

Masculinity

This dimension refers to the overall tendency of a culture to support or encourage the traditional masculine orientation: that is, that the business culture of a society takes on traditional masculine values such as an emphasis on advancement and earnings. However, within each culture there still remains gender differences in values and attitudes.

The following values are generally associated with a high masculinity culture:

- gender roles should be clearly distinguished;
- men are assertive and dominant;
- machismo or exaggerated maleness in men is good;
- people – especially men – should be decisive;
- work takes priority over other duties such as family;
- advancement, success, and money are important.

In highly masculine societies, jobs are clearly defined by gender (i.e., male-type jobs and female-type jobs) and work tends to be central and important to people, particularly men. Recognition on the job is considered a prime motivator. People work long hours, more than five days a week, take short vacations and often trade off family priorities to work pressures. In low masculinity cultures, people are generally more concerned with their quality of life. Work must be balanced with family life, and they tend to take more time off and have longer vacations.

In masculine culture, managers are expected to act decisively, avoid intuitive decision making, and prefer to work in large organizations focused on performance and growth.

Long-term (Confucian) orientation

Organizations with long-term oriented cultures tend to be more sensitive to social relationships, synthesizing conflicting viewpoints, seeking practical solutions, and managing internal social relationships. Organizations with short-term oriented cultures tend to be focused on usable skills, logical analysis, and approach to organizational decisions that respond to immediate needs and changes.

Hiring in short-term oriented cultures is focused on the immediate skills, experience, and abilities a candidate has to contribute immediately to the organization, as he is not expected to be there long and training investments would not necessarily provide a return on investment for the company. In long-term oriented cultures, skills have less importance than a "personal fit" of the individual with the company staff and culture, as it is assumed that training and job experience will erase any initial "weaknesses" the candidate may have in terms of experience and abilities in time.

Typical American companies (i.e., short-term orientation) tend to focus on short-term financial objectives, motivate staff with quick promotions and pay raises and react to market changes by hiring and firing people as necessary to ensure the financial health of the company. Patience is often considered a sign of weakness or indecisiveness. Typical Chinese companies (i.e., long-term orientation) place less importance on financial objectives, but prioritize constant growth and long-term paybacks, allowing for more experimentation and development of long-term "game plans" over time – not letting immediate changes in the marketplace disrupt their plans without very strong evidence. Patience is often considered a sign of strength, reliability, and leadership.

Using the Hofstede framework for analysis of cultures

The analysis of Hofstede is summarized below. Figure 3.4 displays the position of various countries with regard to power distance and individualism. Figure 3.5 shows the position of the countries with regard to power distance and uncertainty avoidance.

In Figure 3.4, various countries have been plotted on a chart contrasting power distance with individualism/collectivism. The upper right quadrant (labeled 1) shows a grouping consisting of countries predominantly from Asia, Africa, Central and South America, and the Middle East, which typically scored relatively high on power distance, and also tended to score high on collectivism. By comparison,

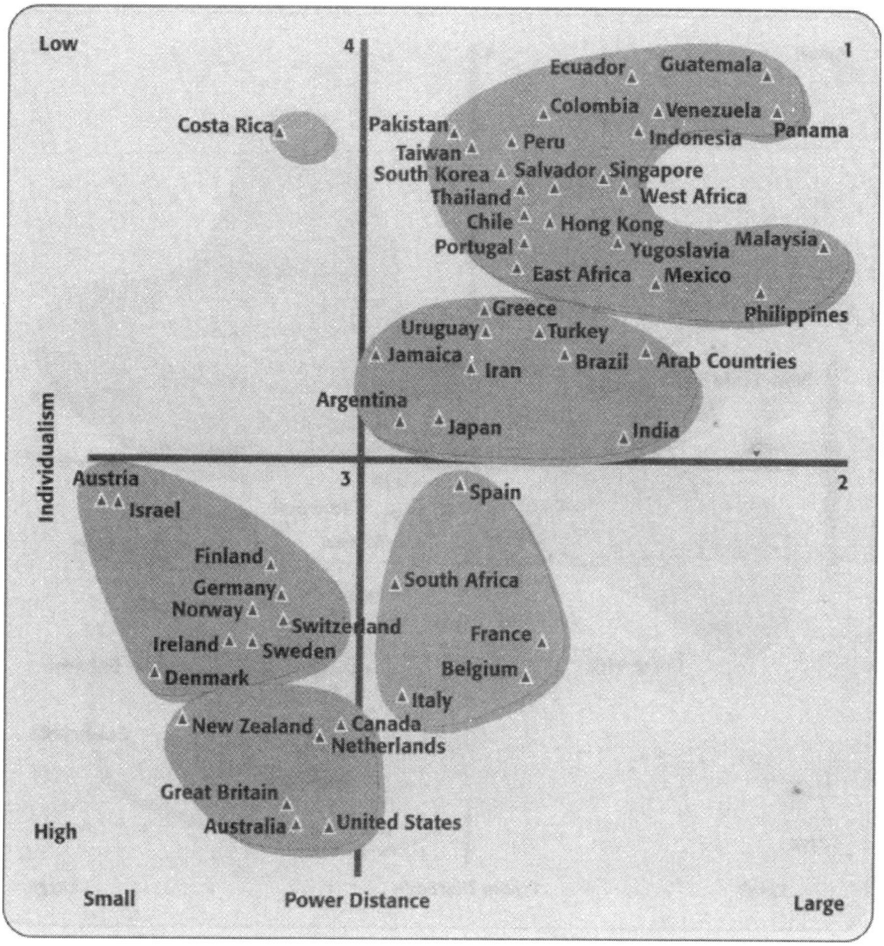

FIGURE 3.4 Power distance and individualism vs collectivism (From http://www.clearlycultural.com/geert-hofstede-cultural-dimensions/)

the lower left quadrant (labeled 3) reflects clusters of countries predominantly from North America, Western Europe, and Australia that tend to score low on power distance and high on individualism (i.e., low on collectivism). This suggests certain relationships among the various dimensions that seem to encourage certain attitudes and behaviors in the various cultures.

Figure 3.5 charts various countries on the two dimensions of power distance and uncertainty avoidance. Again, though less clearly, there appears to be a distinct grouping in quadrant 4 of North America, Western Europe (predominantly northern countries), Australia, and Jamaica – all cultures low on both power distance and uncertainty avoidance. The opposite cluster in quadrant 2 includes many Asian, Central and South American, and Middle Eastern cultures, typically high on both power distance and uncertainty avoidance.

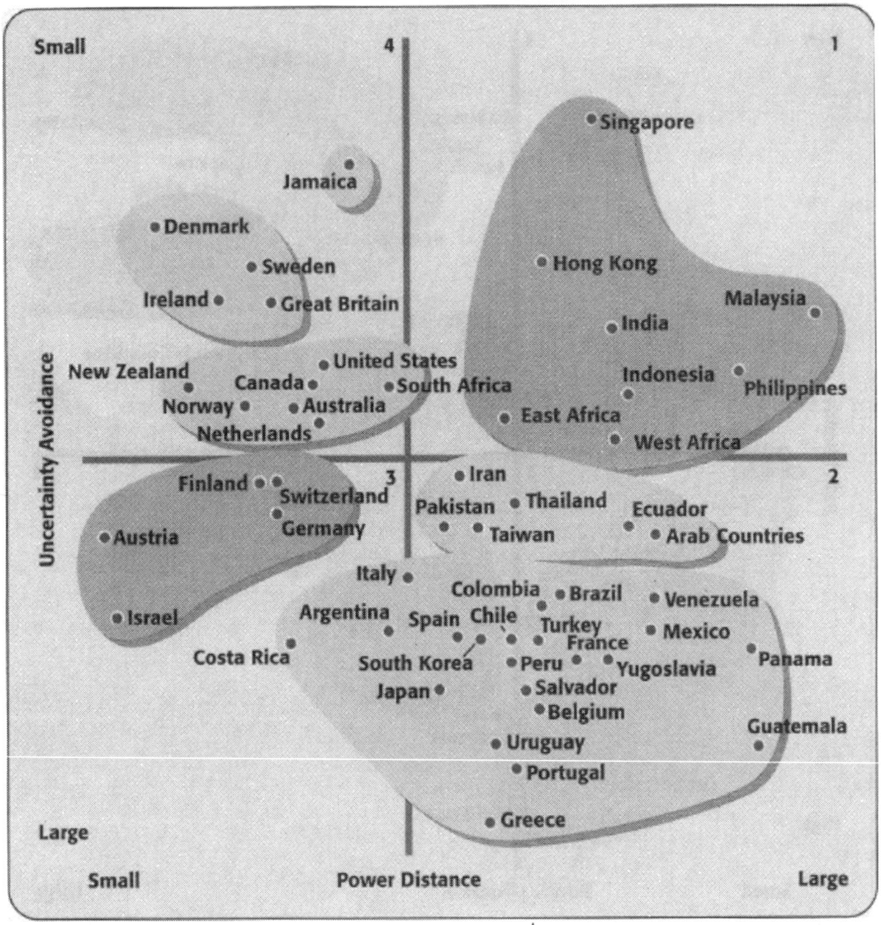

FIGURE 3.5 Power distance and uncertainty avoidance (From http://www.clearlycultural.com/geert-hofstede-cultural-dimensions/)

If you locate your country on one of these charts, would you consider the indicated placement on the chart to be consistent with your own personal knowledge of the national culture? Do you think that new managers that come to your country would benefit from recognizing many of these differences in order to best adapt their personal styles or formal efforts to the business challenges of the local community?

Geographic clusters

Based on the research by Hofstede and others, Ronen and Shenkar (1985) developed eight clusters of countries which are grouped according to the similarities of employee attitudes towards: the importance of work goals, need fulfillment and job satisfaction, managerial, and organizational variables and work role and interpersonal orientation. The country characteristics and dimensions are outlined in Tables 3.2 and 3.3.

Trompenaars' 7d cultural dimensions model

This model, created by Fons Trompenaars, approaches the study of different cultures from an anthropological perspective. The study encompassed a 10-year period, involving 15,000 managers from 28 countries, and represented 47 national cultures. It considered three categories of dimensions: relationships with people; perspective on time; and relationships with the environment. The basic thesis is that every culture is defined by the approach that groups of people take to deal with the basic problems of survival.

TABLE 3.2 Country Cultural Characteristics

	Hofstede's dimensions				
Region/ country	*Individualism–collectivism*	*Power distance*	*Uncertainty avoidance*	*Masculinity–femininity*	*Other dimensions*
North America	Individualism	Low	Medium	Masculine	
Japan	Collectivism	High and low	High	Masculine and feminine	Authority is respected; superior must be a warm leader
Europe: Anglo	Individualism	Low/ medium	Low/ medium	Masculine	
Europe: Germanic	Medium	Low	Medium/ high	Masculine	
Near Eastern	Collectivism	High	High	Masculine	
Nordic	Medium/high individualism	Low	Low/ medium	Feminine	
Latin Europe	Medium/high individualism	High	High	Medium masculine	
China	Collectivism	Low	Low	Masculine and feminine	Emphasis on tradition, Marxism
Africa	Collectivism	High	High	Feminine	
Latin America	Collectivism	High	High	Masculine	Extroverted

Source: From http://www.clearlycultural.com/geert-hofstede-cultural-dimensions/.

TABLE 3.3 Country Cultural Clusters Based on Attitudes

Country cluster	*Countries*
Nordic	Finland, Norway, Denmark, Sweden
Germanic	Austria, Germany, Switzerland
Anglo	United States, Australia, Canada, New Zealand, United Kingdom, Ireland, South Africa
Latin European	France, Belgium, Italy, Spain, Portugal
Latin American	Argentina, Venezuela, Chile, Mexico, Peru, Colombia
Far Eastern	Malaysia, Singapore, Hong Kong, Philippines, South Vietnam, Indonesia, Taiwan, Thailand
Arab	Bahrain, Abu-Dhabi, United Arab Emirates, Kuwait, Oman, Saudi Arabia
Eastern Mediterranean	Turkey, Iran, Greece
Independent	Brazil, Japan, India, Israel

Table 3.4 summarizes the seven dimensions of the model alongside a critical question illustrating the intended meaning.

Trompenaars sought to characterize each of the communities' cultural preference somewhere on the spectrum between the two extremes described above. We will now define each of the dimensions separately and consider how they relate to management issues.

Universalism vs particularism

In a "universalistic" culture people believe in abstract principles which define the rules, laws, religion or general norms which should be applied without exception to all individuals. Therefore, people look to rules or acceptable norms to guide their decisions in any given situation to ensure that they are "doing the right thing."

In a "particularistic" culture, people treat rules as only a general guide to life situations and focus much more on the unique situation, the individuals involved and their own relationship with those individuals in order to come to a decision. In particularistic societies there are generally rules in place; however, it is expected that exceptions to these rules will be made for family relations, close friends or special circumstances. Thus, although guided by rules to some extent, people take personal relationships and extraordinary circumstances into account when making a decision in order to ensure that they are "doing the right thing."

In exploring people's tendencies towards one of these two extremes, Trompenaars used dilemmas in order to provoke people into indicating their biases. As an example, Trompenaar used the following story:

> A motorist hits a pedestrian while going 35 miles per hour in a 20 mile-per-hour zone. The driver's lawyer notes that if a witness says the driver was only going 20 mph, the

TABLE 3.4 Seven Dimensions of Trompenaars' Cultural Dimensions Model

Cultural dimension	*Critical question*
Relationships with people	
Universalism vs particularism	Do we consider rules or relationships more important?
Individualism vs collectivism	Do we act mostly as individuals or groups?
Specific vs diffuse	How extensively are we involved with the lives of other people?
Neutral vs affective	Are we free to express our emotions or are we restrained?
Achievement vs ascription	Do we achieve status through accomplishment or is it part of our situation in life (e.g., gender, age, social class)?
Perspective on time	
Sequential vs synchronic	Do we perform tasks in sequence or several tasks at once?
Relationship with the environment	
Internal vs external control	Do we control the environment or does it control us?

Source: Adapted from Trompenaars' and Hampden-Turner (1997).

judge will be lenient. The question is: should a friend who is a witness expect to feel obligated to testify to the lower speed? In universalistic cultures like the United States or Switzerland, the answer tends to be a clear no (over 93% voted no). In particularistic cultures, like South Korea, the answer is far from clear. Over 40% voted yes suggesting that friendship should supersede the law.

Although no culture is purely universalistic or pluralistic, in every culture there is strong pull in one direction. For example, in more universalistic cultures the basis for commercial or partnership agreements are contracts and the law. Once a contract is signed by both parties, abiding by the terms becomes a matter of integrity and obligation. However, in a pluralistic culture the relationships between the buyers, suppliers, or partners is more important than any contract in making a decision at any given moment. The changing circumstances and trusting relationship are meant to dictate the appropriate decision rather than any legal obligation or contract that reflected the best judgment of all parties at some time in the past.

The challenge for a "universalistic manager" to do business in a "pluralistic culture" is dealing with this ambiguity. Conversely, the challenge for a "pluralistic manager" to do business in a "universalistic culture" is understanding that the emphasis on the legal and contractual aspects of an agreement does not indicate a lack of trust in the person, the relationship or the business opportunity but a "way of doing things."

Individualism vs collectivism

In the preceding section, we studied the Hofstede view of individualism vs collectivism which described a collective culture as one in which people associate themselves strongly with a group (personal or professional) and that the majority of compensation, accountability, and planning are group based rather than individual based. The 7d model applies a similar definition, although some of the country rankings do not match with those in the Hofstede model. This could be either because the research was done more recently or because Trompenaars used a more refined methodology that may have uncovered more subtle nuances from the participants on this dimension.

For example, a question Trompenaars used to study this dimension asked about the typical organizations in each country. One choice represented organizations where individual work and individual credit were common practice. The other choice represented group work and group credit. In more collectivist societies such as India and Mexico, less than 45 percent of the workers said that their jobs involved individual work with individual credit. Surprisingly, the findings showed some of the former Eastern Bloc countries such as the Czech Republic, Russia, Hungary, and Bulgaria were the most individualistic in their organizations – even more so than the USA.

Neutral vs affective

The neutral vs affective dimension of the 7d model concerns the acceptability of expressing emotions. In cultures with a more neutral orientation, people expect interactions to be objective and detached. The focus is more on the task and less on the emotional nature of the interaction. People emphasize achieving objectives without messy interference of emotions. In contrast, in cultures with a more affective orientation, all forms of emotion are appropriate in almost every situation. Expressions of anger, laughter, and gesturing, and a range of emotional outbursts are considered normal and acceptable. The natural and preferred way is to find an immediate outlet for emotions (Trompenaars, 1994; Trompenaars and Hampden-Turner, 1998).

For example, imagine a negotiation between two individuals. One of them has prepared a proposal for the other to consider, but upon receiving it the receiver responds by stating that the proposal is insane, which offends the person who wrote it. What would be the appropriate reaction to such an extreme and insulting response? To react expressively and let the other person know that their behavior was insulting and "put them in their place" or, to ignore the feelings of insult and focus on the terms in order to avoid "showing any weaknesses."

Specific vs diffuse

This dimension brings to mind a problem constantly facing most working people: balancing work and home life. The "right answer" to that equation depends on the tendency in each culture to either specific or diffuse relationships at work.

In a specific-oriented culture, business life is completely segregated from home life. A person interacts with work colleagues (whether subordinate, peer, or superior) for the purposes of accomplishing business objectives, and knowledge of colleagues is generally limited to information required to do so.

In a diffuse-oriented culture, business relationships are expected to be more involved, personal, and encompassing. "Getting to know the person" is as important as accomplishing the task at hand, and in some cases more so, if the goal is building trusting partnerships. It is expected that work colleagues will interact with one another both at work and out of work in a natural way.

For example, imagine that your boss comes to your office one day and asks you to come over on the weekend and help him paint his house. In specific cultures the employee would feel no obligation to help with anything outside of his job description. In diffuse cultures the employee would feel an obligation to help his boss in any way possible, although it is beyond the requirements of the job.

Achievement vs ascription

The dimension identified as achievement vs ascription addresses how a particular society accords or grants status. In achievement-oriented cultures, people earn status by their performance and accomplishments. In contrast, when a culture bases status on ascription, a person's inherent characteristics or associations define status. For example, ascription-oriented societies often assign people status based on schools or universities attended or a person's age. Ascribed status does not require any justification. It simply exists. In such cultures, titles and their frequent usage play a large part in interactions (Trompenaars, 1994; Trompenaars and Hampden-Turner, 1998).

Time orientation

A shared understanding of time is critical for a group of businesses or managers to coordinate among themselves and with their partners. Differences in the way cultures deal with the past, present, and future become very apparent during business transactions and partnerships.

In future-oriented societies, such as the USA, organizational change is considered necessary and beneficial. A static organization is a dying one. For both people and organizations, the assumption is that competition stimulates higher performance. It is assumed that individuals can influence the future. Both managers and workers assume that hard work now can lead to future success.

In past-oriented societies, people often assume that life follows a preordained path based on traditions and/or the will of God. As such, strategic planning for the organization has little importance. A changing organization is suspicious to both employees and society. Stability is revered. Within these organizations, it is thought that senior people make the best decisions, because they have the authority and wisdom to know what is right. Symbols and rituals dominate the organizational culture.

Another important aspect is the time horizon. The way cultures deal with the past, present, future, and the boundaries between them. For example, the Mexicans and the Chinese have long-time horizons and distinct boundaries among the time zones (Trompenaars and Hampden-Turner, 1997).

Internal vs external control

This dimension concerns belief regarding control over fate. It is best expressed in the way people interact with nature. Do we dominate nature or does nature dominate us?

To measure this dimension, Trompenaars and his colleagues presented managers with the following options: "It is worthwhile trying to control important natural forces, like the weather" and "Nature should take its course and we just have to accept it the way it comes and do the best we can" (Trompenaars and Hampden-Turner, 1997). Arab countries such as Bahrain, Egypt, and Kuwait are the most fatalistic, with less than 20 percent of managers choosing the control over nature option. This contrasts with over 50 percent of the managers from Spain and Cuba, who chose the control over nature option.

Differences in the cultural values regarding relationships with nature can affect how organizations and managers approach strategic and operational problems. In cultures where it is believed that nature dominates people, managers are likely to be fatalistic. They believe that situations must be accepted and reacted to rather than changed. In such cultures, people do not emphasize planning and scheduling. Work schedules must adjust to other priorities such as family.

In contrast, where cultural values support the notion that people dominate nature, managers tend to be proactive. They believe that situations can be changed. Strategic plans and operations reflect the belief that obstacles can be overcome. What works is what is important. Organizations focus on using concrete data that suggest the best way to solve problems.

So what?

When working in other countries and with people from overseas, first research their national culture along these seven dimensions, assume the people use these and, when talking with national groups, take account of these dimensions.

Culture Analysis Frameworks Critiqued

Hofstede, as well as Trompenaars and Hampden-Turner, derive their data from questionnaires that were distributed among professionals. Hofstede collected the data among employees of IBM (11,000), and Trompenaars and Hampden-Turner collected their data among executives from different organizations.

Hofstede's work is based on a questionnaire originally designed to evaluate work values and is focused towards that end. Trompenaars and Hampden-Turner's questionnaires, in contrast, asked respondents for preferred behavior in a number of both work and leisure situations. What both studies have in common is that in both questionnaires the focus is on the ultimate goal stated by the individual and that the underlying values are derived from a series of questions about outer layers of the culture "onion."

Both approaches have a very practical flavor. Yet at the same time, the underlying value claims are frequently the result of very little data, or are derived from a limited number of questions. At the very least, this has the potential to lead to questions regarding the statistical validity of the results. It may also not consider that certain dimensions, or values, may be wrongly derived. Examples of this would include the notion that when looking at Hofstede's data, Italy is portrayed as an individualistic culture, or that French respondents show a preference for universalism in one answer in Trompenaars and Hampden-Turner's questionnaire and for particularism in all the other answers. Such contradicting findings clearly suggest the influence of other (intervening) variables.

Global Managers' and Entrepreneurs' Perspective

Developing cultural profiles

Managers and entrepreneurs should gather information on cultural determinants from the media, relevant research, and conversations regarding the culture in a specific region or country. From these cultural determinants, managers and entrepreneurs can develop cultural profiles, including people's attitudes, behavioral norms, and working environments. These cultural profiles help plan for differences between origin country and destination country in motivation, ethics, communication, loyalty, and productivity.

Ethnocentric and polycentric approach

As globalization draws more companies into the international arena, the understanding of local cultures becomes a necessary competitive tool. In fact, the understanding of local cultures may change corporations from being ethnocentric, operating under the belief that self-ethnic culture is superior to that of others, to polycentric, appreciating and being responsive to local cultures in which the company operates. Becoming polycentric means improving culture literacy and appreciating the local cultural dimensions. Improved cultural literacy and better understanding of the local cultures lead to more effective use of resources, better relationships with the local stakeholders, and more robust marketing practices.

Expatriates

The international activities of individuals and corporations call for more personnel relocation from country of origin to foreign countries. The placement of managers from an origin country (expatriates) into a new country calls for culture literacy and may call for a difficult adjustment. Managers who come from a country where power distance is not common may feel much less comfortable in countries where power distance is accentuated. The customs and manners of the new environment should be studied and respected while operating as an expatriate in a new, foreign country. For example, when a Japanese corporation entered Canada, its newly relocated Japanese executives found themselves with the task of adjusting to an environment with less team decision making and a more individual system of responsibility and authority.

Work attitudes

It has been observed that cultural literacy leads to the creation of better wage and compensation schemes by international companies, as different cultures hold different attitudes towards work. North American employees tend to work harder and longer hours if they can secure a higher compensation based on efforts or results. Some European countries may value more free or leisure time and may be less responsive to monetary gains associated with longer hours and greater effort.

COUNTRY FOCUS

RUSSIA

World Rank (EFI 2009): 146

Regional Rank (EFI 2009): 41

Quick facts

Population: 142.5 million

GDP (PPP): $1.9 trillion; 7.4 percent growth in 2006; 6.6 percent 5-year compound annual growth; $13,116 per capita

Unemployment: 6.2 percent

Inflation (CPI): 9.0 percent

FDI inflow: $28.7 billion

2006 data unless otherwise noted

Economic freedom score

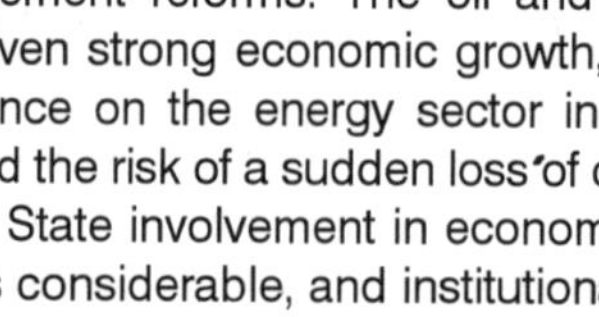

Russia's economic freedom score is 50.8, making its economy the 146th freest in the 2009 Index. Russia is ranked 41st out of 43 countries in the Europe region, and its overall score is below the world average.

Russia scores above the world average only in fiscal freedom and government size, partly because of earlier taxation and budgetary management reforms. The oil and gas sector has driven strong economic growth, but overdependence on the energy sector increases volatility and the risk of a sudden loss of competitiveness.

State involvement in economic activity remains considerable, and institutional constraints on economic freedom are severe. Nontariff barriers add significantly to the cost of trade. Inflation is high, and prices are heavily controlled and influenced by the government. Virtually all foreign investment faces official and unofficial hurdles, including bureaucratic inconsistency, corruption, and outright restrictions in lucrative sectors like energy. Corruption weakens the rule of law and increases the fragility of property rights and the arbitrariness of law enforcement.

Background

The Russian Federation was formed in 1992 after the dissolution of the Union of Soviet Socialist Republics. President Boris Yeltsin's erratic rule (1991–1999) was replaced by a more authoritarian "sovereign democracy" under President Vladimir Putin (2000–2008). Dmitry Medvedev, Putin's protégé, was elected president in March 2008, but Putin remains as prime minister. After chaotic privatization in the 1990s, the state has reasserted its role in extractive industries and some other sectors and depends heavily on sales of natural resources, especially oil and natural gas. A growing consumer economy is bolstered by an emerging middle class. Russia, in partnership with China, is a founding member of the Shanghai Cooperation Organization. Accession to the World Trade Organization has stalled.

Business freedom – 54

The overall freedom to conduct a business is limited by Russia's regulatory environment. Bureaucratic obstacles are a particular problem for small businesses. Obtaining a business license takes much more than the world average of 18 procedures and 225 days. Bankruptcy proceedings can be lengthy and difficult.

Trade freedom – 60.8

Russia's weighted average tariff rate was 9.6 percent in 2005. Adding to the cost of trade are the following: prohibitive tariffs, quotas, and services market access barriers; import and export restrictions; discriminatory import and export taxes, charges, and fees; nontransparent regulations and standards; discriminatory licensing, registration, and certification; complex and non-transparent customs valuation; customs fees; inefficient and arbitrary customs administration; subsidies; corruption; and weak enforcement of intellectual property rights. Twenty points were deducted from Russia's trade freedom score to account for nontariff barriers.

Fiscal freedom – 78.9

Russia has a low income tax rate and a moderate corporate tax rate. The individual income tax rate is a flat 13 percent, and the top corporate tax rate is 24 percent. Other taxes include a value-added tax (VAT) and a property tax. In the most recent year, overall tax revenue as a percentage of GDP was 36.9 percent.

Government size – 70.6

Total government expenditures, including consumption and transfer payments, are moderate. In the most recent year, government spending equaled 31.3 percent of GDP. The state maintains a strong presence in such key sectors as energy and mining. The reform agenda includes a new framework for saving and distributing oil revenues, as well as measures to address anticipated spending increases for public welfare and social projects.

Monetary freedom – 65.5

Inflation is high, averaging 9.5 percent between 2005 and 2007. The government influences prices through regulation, extensive subsidies, and numerous state-owned enterprises and utilities. Fifteen points were deducted from

(Continued)

Russia's monetary freedom score to account for policies that distort domestic prices.

Investment freedom – 30

Foreign and domestic investments are treated equally under the law, although the government tends to prefer joint ventures with foreign companies as a minority shareholder, especially in strategic sectors. Investment is restricted in many areas. Government approval is required for all investments over 50 million rubles (about $2 million), investment ventures in which the foreign share exceeds 50 percent, or investments in housing and construction projects. Inconsistent and burdensome government regulation, unreliable contract enforcement, inadequate infrastructure, and corruption deter investment. Residents and nonresidents may hold foreign exchange accounts, subject to restrictions. Capital payments and transfers are also subject to restrictions. Foreign ownership of nonagricultural land that is not located near international borders is permitted.

Financial freedom – 40

Russia's financial sector is not fully developed and is subject to government influence. Supervision and transparency are insufficient, although regulations improved in 2006. More than 1,000 licensed and registered banks are small and undercapitalized, but consolidation is underway. The Central Bank of Russia regulates the banking sector, which is dominated by two state-owned banks. Foreign banks may establish subsidiaries, but the government has not permitted foreign banks to set up branches in Russia. As of 2007, there were 857 insurance companies, 27 of which are foreign-controlled. Capital markets are relatively small but growing and are dominated by energy companies.

Property rights – 25

Protection of private property is weak. The judicial system is unpredictable, corrupt, and unable to handle technically sophisticated cases. Contracts are difficult to enforce, and an ancient antipathy to them continues to impede Russian integration into the West. Mortgage lending is in its initial stages. Violations of intellectual property rights continue to be a serious problem.

Freedom from corruption – 23

Corruption is perceived as pervasive. Russia ranks 143rd out of 179 countries in Transparency International's Corruption Perceptions Index for 2007. Corruption remains all-encompassing, both in the number of instances and in the size of bribes sought. Manifestations include misuse of budgetary resources, theft of government property, kickbacks in the procurement process, extortion, and official collusion in criminal acts. Customs officials are extremely inconsistent in their application of the law.

Labor freedom – 60

Russia's relatively rigid labor regulations discourage overall employment and productivity growth. The nonsalary cost of employing a worker is high, and the difficulty of firing a worker creates a disincentive for additional hiring. Regulations related to the number of work hours are rigid.

Source: Adapted from Terry Miller and Kim R. Holmes, 2009 Index of Economic Freedom (Washington, DC: The Heritage Foundation and Dow Jones & Company, Inc., 2009), at www.heritage.org/index.

SUMMARY

What is culture? Culture is commonly defined as the predominating attitudes and behavior that characterize the functioning of a group, community, organization, or nation. It is the manifestation of a set of values, beliefs, rules, and institutions held by such a group and expressed by the individual actions and reactions of each member.

Levels of culture. For almost every cultural group, if you look carefully and in more closely, one can identify distinct subgroups within the whole. Subcultures can be defined as a shared set of norms, beliefs, values, customs, experiences, and symbols that reflect a subset of the larger group or within the cultural framework guard unique opinions which are not shared throughout the group as a whole. For example, national culture and business culture may be regarded as different kinds of subcultures.

Elements of culture. Elements that together help distinguish one culture from another include language, religion, values and attitudes, manners and customs, and aesthetics. Each of these elements affects the business strategies, practices, and standards in each of the localities in which business is conducted. For example, attitudes towards time should be considered when negotiating a binational contract. A hasty approach to conclude the terms of an agreement may be considered offensive in some cultures. Commitments to deadlines may also be considered in light of the local attitude towards the time element.

Warning against stereotyping. Assuming that all people from a certain culture feel, believe, and behave identically is referred to as stereotyping and can often lead to wrong and destructive conclusions.

Analysis tools: Hofstede and 7d model. There are two accepted frameworks for studying cultural differences. The Hofstede framework suggests five value dimensions (such as individualism vs collectivism). Understanding these dimensions may help multinational enterprises be more successful internationally. Trompenaars and Hampden-Turner suggested a seven-dimension framework, including relationships with people (universalism vs particularism, individualism vs collectivism, specific vs diffuse, neutral vs affective, achievement vs ascription), perspective on time (sequential vs synchronic), and relationship with the environment (internal vs external control). These frameworks help corporations understand people's culture, including innovation, human resources practices, and risk-taking.

DISCUSSION QUESTIONS

1 What is the definition of culture?
2 Can you identify cultural elements in your country as well in another country?
3 What are the dimensions of culture according to Hofstede?
4 What are the risks associated with cultural stereotyping?

INTERNET EXERCISE

BMW Goes National and International

BMW is an internationally known auto firm. However, in recent years the company has been finding that its success in Europe does not necessarily translate into the American market, the largest, richest target for overseas sales. Visit the BMW site at www.bmw.com and look at what the big automaker is doing in both Europe and the USA. Compare and

(Continued)

contrast both the similarities and the differences in these markets. Then answer these three questions: (1) How do you think cultural differences affect the way the firm operates in Europe vis-à-vis the USA? (2) In what way is culture a factor in auto sales? (3) Is it possible for a car company to transcend national culture and produce a global automobile that is accepted by people in every culture? Why or why not?

Sony's Approach

Sony is a multinational corporation (MNC) that sells a wide variety of goods in the international marketplace. These range from electronics to online games to music, and the Japanese MNC is even in the entertainment business (Sony Pictures Entertainment), producing offerings for both the big screen as well as for television. Visit Song's website at www.sony.com and read about some of the latest developments in which the company is engaged. Pay close attention to its new offerings in the areas of electronics, television shows, movies, music, and online games. Then answer these three questions: (1) What type of cultural challenges does Sony face when it attempts to market its products worldwide? Is demand universal for all of these offerings or is there a "national responsiveness/globalization" challenge, as discussed in the chapter, that must be addressed? (2) Investigate the Sony credit card that the company is now offering online. Is this a product that will have worldwide appeal, or is it more likely to be restricted to more economically advanced countries? (3) In managing its far-flung enterprise, what are two cultural challenges that the company is likely to face and what will it need to do to respond to these?

Searching Online for Excellence

This chapter focused on human resource management (HRM) approaches that are used by MNCs to develop their international workforce as well as to better prepare their home-office personnel to meet the international challenge. Two of the firms that are particularly interested in developing effective HRM programs and practices are PepsiCo and Honeywell: visit the websites of these companies at www.pepsico.com and www.honeywell.com, respectively. In each case, look carefully at the firm's current operations and international expansion activities. In most cases the organization's current annual report will provide you with much of this information, but also look at special product lines and new developments that are taking place. Then tie your findings to the chapter material by answering these four questions: (1) In what areas of the world is each firm beginning to focus more of its attention? (2) What types of training and development programs do you believe will be of value to each company in these efforts? Be specific and describe the tools and techniques that you would expect the firms to use. (3) What challenges do you think each will face in creating these programs and what are some steps that will be of value in minimizing these challenges? (4) Do you think a global leadership program such as the one discussed at the end of this chapter and used by General Electric would have value to any of these three firms in developing their leadership programs? Why or why not?

INTERNATIONAL MANAGEMENT INSIGHT

A Jumping-Off Place

A successful, medium-sized US manufacturing firm in Ohio has decided to open a plant near Madrid, Spain. The company was attracted to this location for three reasons. First, the firm's current licensing agreement with a German firm is scheduled to come to an end within 6 months, and the US manufacturer feels that it can do a better job of building and selling heavy machinery in the European Union (EU) than the German firm. Second, the US manufacturer has invested almost US$300 million in R&D over the last three years. The result is a host of new patents and other technological breakthroughs that now make this company a worldwide leader in the production of specialized heavy equipment. Third, the labor costs in Spain are lower than in most other EU countries, and the company feels that this will prove extremely helpful in its efforts to capture market share in Greater Europe.

Because this is the manufacturer's first direct venture into the EU, it has decided to take on a

Spanish partner. The letter will provide much of the on-site support, such as local contracts, personnel hiring, legal assistance, and governmental negotiations. In turn, the US manufacturer will provide the capital for renovating the manufacturing plant, the R&D technology, and the technical training.

If the venture works out as planned, the partners will expand operations into Italy and use this location as a jumping-off point for tapping the Central and Eastern European markets. Additionally, because the cultures of Spain and Italy are similar, the US manufacturer feels that staying within the Latin European cultural cluster can be synergistic. Plans for later in the decade call for establishing operations in Northern France, which will serve as a jumping-off point for both Northern Europe and other major EU countries, such as Germany, the Netherlands, and Belgium. However, the company first wants to establish a foothold in Spain and get this operation working successfully; then it will look into expansion plans.

Questions

1 In what way will the culture of Spain be different from that of the United States? In answering this question, refer to Figures 3.4 and 3.5 and Tables 3.2 and 3.3.
2 If the company expands operations into Italy, will its experience in Spain be valuable, or will the culture be so different that the manufacturer will have to begin anew in determining how to address cultural challenges and opportunities? Explain.
3 If the firm expands into France, will its previous experience in Spain and Italy be valuable in helping the company address cultural challenges? Be complete in your answer.

Beijing, Here We Come!

A large toy company located in Canada is considering a business arrangement in the People's Republic of China (PRC). Although company representatives have not yet visited the PRC, the president of the firm recently met with their representatives in Ottawa and discussed the business proposition. The Canadian CEO learned that the PRC government would be quite happy to study the proposal, and the company's plan would be given a final decision within 90 days of receipt. The toy company is now putting together a detailed proposal and scheduling an on-site visit.

The Canadian firm would like to have the mainland Chinese manufacturer produce a wide variety of toys for sale in Asia as well as in Europe and North America. Production of the toys requires a large amount of labor time, and because the PRC is reputed to have one of the largest and least expensive workforces in the world, the company believes that it can maximize profits by having the work done there. For the past 5 years, the company has had its toys produced in Taiwan. Costs there have been escalating recently, however, and because 45 percent of the production expense goes for labor, the company is convinced that it will soon be priced out of the market if it does not find another source.

The company president and three officers plan on going to Beijing next month to talk with government officials. They would like to sign a five-year agreement, with a price that will not increase by more than 2 percent annually. Production operations will then be turned over to the mainland Chinese, who will have a free hand in manufacturing the goods.

The contract with the Taiwanese firm runs out in 90 days. The company already has contracted this firm, and the latter understands that its Canadian partner plans to terminate the agreement. One major problem is that if the toy company cannot find another supplier soon, it will have to go back to the Taiwanese firm for at least 2 more years. The contract stipulates that the agreement can be extended for another 24 months if the Canadian firm makes such request; however, this must be done within 30 days of expiration of the contract. This is not an alternative that appeals to the Canadians, but they feel they will have to take it if they cannot reach an agreement with the mainland Chinese.

Questions

1 What is the likelihood that the Canadians will be able to reach an agreement with the mainland Chinese and not have to go back to their Taiwanese supplier?

(Continued)

2 Are the Canadians making a strategically wise decision in letting the Chinese from the PRC handle all the manufacturing, or should they insist on getting more actively involved in the production process? Defend your answer.
3 What specific cultural suggestions would you make to the Canadians regarding how to do business with the mainland Chinese?

A Southern Expansion

A small but rapidly growing US irrigation equipment company is thinking about expanding its operation into the South American market. Founded eight years ago, the firm has annual sales of $25 million and is growing at a 25 percent annually compounded rate. Most of these sales are in the United States, although the company has been trying to penetrate the Indian market and had sales of $1 million there last year.

The company sells a patented piece of irrigation equipment that has proven performance capabilities. The biggest problem for the firm is that many buyers prefer better-known companies' products, so it has to compete vigorously based on price. Thus, the board of directors is considering entering markets that are not competitive. "There is a very little irrigation equipment selling in South America," the chair of the board recently told top management. "Why don't we look into this market and see if we can develop a foothold. Admittedly, the agriculture community down there won't be as knowledgeable as they are in the states, but we could end up getting in on the ground floor."

Following up this suggestion, the company sent three representatives to South America to investigate the market. These individuals all agreed that there is a large, untapped potential in the region that could be the base for the very profitable foreign venture. As a result, the company has drafted a preliminary plan of action for doing business in Venezuela, Brazil, Chile, and Peru. If sales are sufficient in these four countries, the firm will then expand to other South American locations. The company wants to enter into a business arrangement with foreign partners whereby the firm provides the equipment and the partners handle the selling activities. Each country would have a central sales office that would serve as the link between the firm and its local foreign-run outlets. The head of this seals office would be a US citizen appointed by company headquarters' senior management. This individual would be responsible for providing assistance to the local outlets and keeping headquarters' senior management informed about developments in the region. The sales office head would have a small staff consisting of two expatriates and three locals.

Initial plans call for setting up the first unit in each country within the next 18 months and, if things go according to plan, expanding coverage to an average of three outlets per country within the first 3 years. In each case, the company will set up the initial units in the country's agricultural centers and then slowly expand into other areas.

Questions

1 What type of training do you recommend for the expatriate managers?
2 Would you recommend the use of cultural assimilators? If not, why not? If yes, for whom?
3 If there are operating problems, would it be possible to use organization development techniques to resolve them?

ACTION ITEMS

1 Identify two news articles from the *Wall Street Journal* (www.wsj.com), the *Financial Times* (www.ft.com), *Business Week* (www.businessweek.com), or *The Economist* (www.economist.com) and discuss how cultural issues are raised in the context of national or international business. Identify the main elements of culture that are referred to in the articles.
2 Initiate a discussion with an executive of a local business. Discuss and summarize how international culture literacy may enhance profitability and competitive position.
3 Sign on an internet site http://www.isabellemori.homestead.com/tests.html which details gestures in different cultures. Can you identify those you are not familiar with? As well, take the test "What is in the name?" How well did you do?

Bibliography

Abecasis-Phillips, J. A. S. (1992). *Doing Business with the Japanese*. Lincolnwood, IL: NTC Publishing.

Adler, N. J. (1986). *International Dimensions of Organizational Behavior*. Belmont, CA: Wadsworth.

Althen, G. (1988). *American Ways: A Guide for Foreigners in the United States*. Yarmouth, MA: Intercultural Press.

Axtell, R. E. (1990). *Do's and Taboos around the World*. New York: John Wiley and Sons.

Axtell, R. (1991). *Gestures: The Do's and Taboos of Body Language around the World*. New York: John Wiley and Sons.

Banks, J. A., & McGee, C. A. (1989). *Multicultural Education*. Needham Heights, MA: Allyn & Bacon.

Barsoux, J. L., Lawrence, P. (1990). *Management in France*. London: Cassell.

Bedi, H. (1991). *Understanding the Asian Manager*. North Sydney, Australia: Allen & Unwin.

Black, J. S., Gregerson, H. B., Mendenhail, M. E. (1992). *Global Assignments – Successfully Expatriating and Repatriating International Managers*. San Francisco, CA: Jossey-Bass.

Braganti, L., Devine, E. (1988). *The Traveler's Guide to Latin American Customs and Manners*. New York: St. Martin's Press.

Braganti, L., Devine, E. (1988). *The Traveler's Guide to European Customs and Manners*. New York: St. Martin's Press.

Braganti, L., Devine, E. (1988). *The Traveler's Guide to Asian Customs and Manners*. New York: St. Martin's Press.

Brislin, R. W., Cushner, K. (1986). *Intercultural Interactions: A Practical Guide*. Newbury Park, CA: Sage.

Casse, P. (1981). *Training for the Cross-Cultural Mind*. Washington, DC: SIETAR International.

Casse, P., Deol, S. (1985). *Managing Intercultural Negotiations*. Washington, DC: SIETAR International.

Cavusgil, S. T., et al. (2008). *International Business*. Upper Saddle River, NJ: Prentice Hall, p. 145.

Condon, J. C. (1984). *With Respect to the Japanese: A Guide for Americans*. Yarmouth, MA: Intercultural Press.

Cooper, R. (1992). *Thais mean Business: The Foreign Businessman's Guide to Doing Business in Thailand*. Singapore: Times Books International.

Copeland, L., Griggs, L. (1985). *Going International: How to Make Friends and Deal Effectively in the Global Marketplace*. New York: Plume.

DeMente, B. (1986). *Japanese Etiquette and Ethics in Business*. Lincolnwood, IL: Passport Books/National Textbook.

Diamond, J. (1999). *Guns, Germs, and Steel: The Fates of Human Societies*. New York: W. W. Norton & Company.

Earley, P. C., Mosakowsky, E. (2004). Cultural intelligence. *Harvard Business Review*, October, 142–8.

Elashmawi, F., Harris, P. R. (1993). *Multicultural Management: New Skills for Global Success*. Houston; TX: Gulf Publishing.

Ethnologue. (n.d.). *Database of Languages of the World*, 14th edn. www.ethnologue.com.

Fernandez, J. P. (1991). *Managing a Diverse Work Force*. Lexington, MA: D. C. Heath.

Hall, E. T. (1982). *The Hidden Dimension*. New York: Doubleday.

Hall, E. T., Hall, M. R. (1990). *Understanding Cultural Differences: Germans, French, and Americans*. Yarmouth, MA: Intercultural Press.

Hall, E. T., et al. (1985). *Hidden Differences: Studies in International Communication*. Garden City: Anchor Press.

Hall, E. T., et al. (1987). *Hidden Differences: Doing Business with the Japanese*. Garden City, NJ: Anchor Press/Doubleday.

Hampton-Turner, C., Trompenaars, A. (1993). *The Seven Cultures of Capitalism*. New York: Doubleday.

Hampton-Turner, C., Trompenaars, A. (1997). *Riding the Waves of Culture*. New York: Doubleday.

Harris, P. R., Moran, R. T. (1991). *Managing Cultural Differences: High Performance Strategies for a New World of Business*. Houston, TX: Gulf Publishing.

Hijirida, K., Yoshikawa, M. (1987). *Japanese Language and Culture for Business and Travel*. Honolulu, Hawaii: University of Hawaii Press.

Hill, C. W. L. (2004). *Global Business Today*. Boston, MA: McGraw-Hill/Irwin.

Hofstede, G. (1991). *Cultures and Organizations: Software of the Mind*. New York: McGraw-Hill.

Hofstede, G. , Bond M. H. (1998). *Confucius connection: From cultural roots to economic growth, Organizational Dynamics*. 16(4): 5–21.

Huntington, S. P. (1996). *The Clash of Civilizations and the Remaking of World Order*. New York: Simon & Schuster.

Johnson, M., Moran, R. T. (1992). *Cultural Guide to Doing Business in Europe*. Oxford, UK: Butterworth-Heinmann.

Joynt, P., Warner, M. (1985). *Managing in Different Cultures*. New York: Columbia University Press.

Kalb, R., Welch, P. (1992). *Moving Your Family Overseas*. Yarmouth, MA: Intercultural Press.

Kohls, L. R. (1981). *Developing Intercultural Awareness*. Washington, DC: SIETAR International.

Kolde, E-J. (1985). *Environment of International Business*. Boston, MA: Kent Publishing.

Kras, E. (1989). *Management in Two Cultures – Bridging the Gap between US and Mexican Managers*. Yarmouth, MA: Intercultural Press.

Lee, E. (1980). *The American in Saudi Arabia*. Yarmouth, MA: Intercultural Press.

Leppert, P. (1990). *Doing Business with the Chinese: A Taiwan Handbook for Executives*. Sebastopol, CA: Patton Pacific.

Locke, D. C. (1992). *Multicultural Understanding – A Comprehensive Model*. Newbury Park, CA: Sage.

Mann, R. (1989). *Expats in Malaysia: A Guide to Business, Working and Living Conditions*. Toronto, Canada: Gateway.

Meyers, S., Lambert, J. (1991). *Managing Cultural Diversity – A Trainer's Guide*. Solana Beach, CA: Intercultural Development, Inc.

Moran, R. T., Stripp, W. G. (1991). *Successful International Business Negotiations*. Houston, TX: Gulf Publishing.

Nydell, M. K. (1987). *Understanding Arabs – A Guide for Westerners*. Yarmouth, MA: Intercultural Press.

Richmond, Y. (1992). *From Nyet to Da – Understanding the Russians*. Yarmouth, MA: Intercultural Press.

Ronen, S., Shenkar, O. (1985). Clustering countries on attitudinal dimensions: a review and synthesis. *Academy of Management Review*. 10(3), 435–54.

Rossman, M. L. (1986). *The International Businesswoman: A Guide to Success in the Global Marketplace*. Westport, CT: Praeger.

Rowland, D. (1993). *Japanese Business Etiquette*. New York: Warner Communications.

Simons, G. F., Vazquez, C., Harris, P. R. (1993). *Transcultural Leadership*. Houston, TX: Gulf Publishing.

Tan, R. (1992). *Indian and Malay Etiquette: A Matter of Course*. Singapore: Landmark Books.

Trompenaars, F. (1994). Riding the Waves of Culture: Understanding Cultural Diversity in Business. Chicago: Irwin.

Trompenaars, F., Hampden-Turner, C. (1998). Riding the waves of culture: Understanding cultural diversity in global business. New York: McGraw Hill.

Walmsley, J. (1987). *Brit-think, Ameri-think: A Transatlantic Survival Guide*. New York: Penguin.

Weber, Y., Menipaz, E., (2003). Measuring cultural fit in mergers and acquisitions. *International Journal of Business Performance Management*, 5(1), 54–72.

Wenzhong, H., Grove, C. L. (1991). *Encountering the Chinese – A Guide for Americans*. Yarmouth, MA: Intercultural Press.

Zimmerman, M. (1985). *How to Do Business with the Japanese: A Strategy for Success*. New York: Random House.

4

Political and Legal Environments of International Business

Learning Objectives

Following this chapter, the reader should be able to:

1. Identify the ways in which politics affects international business, trade and investments, as well as qualify political risks
2. Identify the legal systems of various countries, and find ways to manage the MNEs' affairs in other environments
3. Understand the way in which both the political and legal environments affect the MNEs' operations and competitive environments

Opening Case
West China, The New Frontier

Over the past two decades, China has gone through a major development phase, especially along the coast and urban centers in Eastern China. The Shanghai World Exposition in 2010 has demonstrated the formidable capability of China to embark on major development projects and complete them within time and to specification. However, with growth slowing in the crowded and costly coastal centers, Beijing is urging business into the hinterlands. Multinational Enterprises (MNEs), including Boeing (BA), Caterpillar (CAT), Goodyear (GT), Alcoa (AA), Unisys (UIS), and Microsoft (MSFT), are wooed by western provinces of China, such as Sichuan. Situated 2,000 km from Beijing, Sichuan is eager to get new investment away from the coastal cities and become a preferred place for regional plants and headquarters for MNEs. The western provinces, such as Sichuan, have much to offer in this context. A manufacturing worker in this part of China earns approximately half of what he or she might make in Guangzhou or Shanghai. The local infrastructure is very good, including abundant energy, brand new highways and power grids, and a large market.

The central government of China declared a priority to develop China's hinterlands and launched a "Develop the West" policy. Anxious about a rising tide of industrial and farmer protests in central and western China, Beijing is giving top priority to narrowing the income gap between rich coastal cities and the rest of the country and has started a program to attract MNEs to China's west. Billions of dollars have been spent on bridges, expressways, and power plants to boost the economies of inland China. The western provinces arrange for delegations that come to visit Beijing, Shanghai, and Guangzhou to get MNEs interested in relocating or opening new facilities in China's west. After years of aggressive expansion, coastal China, and particularly the Pearl River and Yangtze River deltas, is facing growing pains. Labor and land costs are rising fast in Shanghai, and industrial space is hardly available. Labor costs are inching up in Guangdong too, but the bigger problem is finding any workers at all for its huge manufacturing sector. Foreign direct investment (FDI) in central and western China has been increasing, while MNEs, including Honda (HMC), Intel (INTC), General Motors (GM), and Motorola (MOT), now run operations in interior China and the western provinces of China. There is no shortage of skilled labor – and increasingly growing consumer markets. Other growing regions are in Xinjiang, whose capital Urumqi is 2,500 km from Beijing, as well as Inner Mongolia and Yunnan, which borders Vietnam.

Introduction

Large MNEs have revenues that frequently exceed those of many countries. They can and have a powerful influence on global politics, given their large economic influence in politicians' representative districts, as well as their extensive financial resources available for public relations and political lobbying. Given the MNEs' international reach and mobility, regions within countries, and countries themselves, compete with other countries for MNEs to locate their facilities and regional headquarters. Once an MNE establishes a base of operations in a particular municipality, region or country, significant personal and corporate tax revenues, employment, and economic activity accrue. To compete, countries and regional political districts often offer incentives to MNEs, such as tax breaks, pledges of governmental assistance, improved infrastructure, and lax environmental, safety, and labor standards.

The political and legal environment has a profound effect on the operations and competitive positioning of MNEs, both within the home country in which the MNE is based as well as within the targeted country. As the opening case indicates, operations and competitive positioning of Western MNEs depend not only on physical, economic, social, and cultural infrastructure, as has been explained in the last chapter, but also on the targeted country's political priorities and legal infrastructure. The international executive is faced with stakeholders based in the home country and in the targeted country, all of whom should be supportive of the MNE's activities, and at times may be aggravated and at odds with each other. It is imperative that executives of MNEs are able to respond to multinational stakeholders, as well as planning proactively, identifying, and responding to the various stakeholders' expectations. It is clear from the opening case that China's recent economic expansion follows a sudden expansion of international and domestic markets. The central regime in China, as well as being on the end of political pressure from the western provinces in China, are betting on the massive infrastructure build-up to offset the relative disadvantage of the western Chinese provinces. However, apart from the physical infrastructure, there is a more difficult infrastructure to be developed – in the legal and social frameworks that can adapt and prevail in the process of globalization. In the past, the western inner regions of China were less friendly to free-market competition, and corruption was more prevalent. Opening up to MNEs and foreign investment is expected to help stimulate the necessary legal and social infrastructure changes. These changes will make the western provinces more cosmopolitan and help attract MNEs and foreign investments.

The political environment determines the main participants in the environment, determines the relationships among them, and the rules of the game that govern the political processes. The political environment also determines and has an influence on the legal environment, since it is the governing bodies in each society that are charged with the authority and the responsibility to create and impose rules and regulations, codes of behavior, standards, and practices. In the case of the western Chinese territories, it is the mayors and the provincial rulers who exert political pressure on the central government to allow MNEs the freedom of operation, the appropriate ownership rules, and the necessary development of appropriate supporting infrastructure for such ventures to prosper in their territories. In the following paragraphs the MNE, a major business entity that operates internationally, is going to be identified and described.

The MNE as a Player in National and Regional Environments

The main player in international business, and, thus, in the national and regional environments is the multinational enterprise (MNE), alongside governments and labor. The MNE is the entity that is most frequently dealt with in this book. It affects, and is affected, by international environments, including the national and regional political and legal environments. The next several paragraphs are devoted to the MNE as a main constituent in these environments.

Let us first deal with the terms used to describe international enterprises. In Table 4.1 there is a short taxonomy, a categorization, of the various forms of the international enterprise. Of particular relevance is the term multinational enterprise, the MNE. The Organization for Economic Cooperation and Development (OECD), definition of an MNE is an enterprise that is engaged in foreign direct investment (FDI) and owns or controls value-adding activities in more than one country. The MNE has, in most cases, multiple facilities around the world (in North America, Europe, South America, and South East Asia), draws a substantial revenue from overseas operations, operates subsidiaries that share a common strategic vision, and share a common pool of resources, as well as places foreign nationals in senior executive and board of directors positions.

Some of the corporations that are considered MNEs and have almost all of the characteristics described by OECD above are Apple Computer, AOL, AT&T, Bombardier, BP, Coca-Cola, Dell, The Walt Disney Company, Exxon, Fiat, Ford, Google, General Electric, General Motors, Halliburton, Hearst Corporation, Honda, HSBC, Hutchison Whampoa Limited, IBM, McDonald's, Microsoft, Nestlé, Nike Inc. Nintendo, Nissan, Nortel Networks, Nokia, Monsanto, Pfizer, Schlumberger, Shell, Sony, Toshiba, Toyota, Wal-Mart Stores, and Yahoo.

MNE and international business

There are several reasons why MNEs are affecting, and being affected, by the political and legal environments. First, MNEs command a formidable international network for trade in resources, supplies, finished products, and services. In order to understand this network and its importance, one may gauge the level of MNE internationalization. The level of internationalization is measured by the Transnationality Index (TNI) which has been devised by the United Nations Conference on Trade and Development (UNCTAD). This index is calculated

TABLE 4.1 Taxonomy of International Enterprises

	International joint venture with no complete coverage of Asia, Europe or the Americas	*International sales and no international joint venture or ownership*	*Multiple international subsidiaries loosely controlled by headquarters*	*Subsidiaries are centrally integrated by headquarters*	*Subsidiaries partially controlled by headquarters*	*Control value–added activities overseas*	*MNEs based in an emerging economy*	*Engaged in international business with no direct foreign investment*
International enterprise (IE)	×							
Internationally oriented enterprise (IOE)		×						
Multidomestic enterprise (MDE)			×					
Global enterprise (GE)				×				
Transnational enterprise (TE)					×			
Multi national enterprise (MNE)						×		
Developing & emerging economies MNE (DMNE)							×	
Small & midsize international enterprise (SMIE)								×

as the average of three ratios: foreign assets to total assets; foreign sales to total sales; and foreign employment to total employment. The MNEs are ranked by foreign assets in 2003 (see Table 4.2). Included in this ranking are, among others, General Electric of the USA, Vodafone Group of the UK, Hutchison Whampoa of Hong Kong, and Vivendi Universal. Only six out of the top 10 non-financial MNEs, ranked by foreign assets, are based in North America. Internationalization of MNEs not necesseraly increase profitability. There are several reasons for the reduced profitability. First, the intensely globalized firms lack core competencies to allow them to compete successfully in all countries; second, they have to invest heavily in corporate coordination; and, third, there are financial difficulties involved in controlling liquidity and leverage for growth of global operations.

MNE evolution

The current prominence of MNEs is a result of a long evolution of international business and trade. Large multinational enterprises were always in existence. As far back as the Greek and Roman empires, the multinationals had value-added activities within the home country and other countries, and produced and marketed goods and services through operations charged with local and foreign capital, raw material, and employees. They developed organizations that dealt with both local and foreign political and legal environments.

The first modern era multinational, founded March 20, 1602, was the Dutch East India Company (Vereenigde Oostindische Compagnie or VOC in Dutch means "United East Indies Company"). It was established when the Estates-General of the Netherlands granted it a monopoly to carry out colonial activities in Asia. It was the first MNE to issue stocks. The VOC consisted of six Chambers (Kamers) in Amsterdam, Middelburg (for Zeeland), Enkhuizen, Delft, Hoorn, and Rotterdam.

The company established its headquarters in Batavia on Java (now known as Jakarta, Indonesia). Other colonial outposts were also established in the East Indies, which later became Indonesia. One such outpost was the Spice Islands (Moluccas), which include the Banda Islands, where the VOC forcibly maintained a monopoly over nutmeg and mace. Methods used to maintain the monopoly included the violent suppression of the native population, including extortion and mass murder. The VOC traded throughout Asia. Ships coming into Batavia from the Netherlands carried silver from Spanish mines in Peru and supplies for VOC settlements in Asia. Silver, combined with copper from Japan, was used to trade with India and China for textiles. These textile products, such as cotton and silk, as well as ceramics, were either traded within Asia for the coveted spices or brought back to Europe. The VOC was also instrumental in introducing European ideas and technology to Asia. The Company supported Christian missionaries and traded modern technology with China and Japan. A VOC trading post on Dejima, an artificial island in Nagasaki Bay, was for a long time the only place where Europeans could trade with Japan.

TABLE 4.2 The World's Top 100 Nonfinancial MNEs, Ranked by Foreign Assets, 2003

Ranking by						Assets		Sales		Employment			No. of affiliates		
Foreign assets	TNI[b]	11[c]	Corporation	Home economy	Industry[d]	Foreign	Total	Foreign[e]	Total	Foreign	Total	TNI[b] (Percent)	Foreign	Total	II[c]
1	77	37	General Electric	United States	Electrical & electronic equipment	258 900	647 483	54 086	134 187	150 000	305 000	43.2	1068	1398	76.39
2	7	95	Vodafone Group Pic	United Kingdom	Telecommunications	243 839[f]	262 581	50 070	59 893	47 473	60 109	85.1	71	201	35.32
3	72	12	Ford Motor Company	United States	Motor vehicles	173 882[f]	304 594	60 761	164 196	138 663[p]	327 531	45.5	524	623	84.11
4	90	65	General Motors	United States	Motor vehicles	154 466[f]	448 507	51 627	185 524	104 000	294 000	32.5	177	297	59.60
5	10	76	British Petroleum Company Pic	United Kingdom	Petroleum expl./ref./distr.	141 551	177 572	192 875	232 571	86 650	103 700	82.1	60	117	51.28
6	31	41	Exxonmobil Corporation	United States	Petroleum expl./ref./distr.	116 853[f]	174 278	166 926	237 054	53 748[p]	88 300	66.1	218	294	74.15
7	22	80	Royal Dutch/Shell Group	United Kingdom/Netherlands	Petroleum expl./ref./distr.	112 587[f]	168 091	129 864	201 728	100 000[p]	119 000	71.8	454	929	48.87
8	68	94	Toyota Motor Corporation	Japan	Motor vehicles	94 164[f]	189 503	87 363	149 179	69 314	264 410	47.3	124	330	37.58
9	16	48	Total	France	Petroleum expl./ref./distr.	87 840[f]	100 989	94 710	116 117	60 931	110 783	74.1	419	602	69.60
10	62	68	France Telecom	France	Telecommunications	81 370[f]	126 083	21 574	52 202	86 626	218 523	48.8	118	211	55.92
11	14	58	Suez	France	Electricity, gas and water	74 147[f]	88 343	33 715	44 720	111 445	172 291	74.7	605	947	63.89
12	89	34	Electricite De France	France	Electricity, gas and water	67 069	185 527	16 062	50 699	51 847[i]	167 309	32.9	204	264	77.27
13	80	63	E.On	Germany	Electricity, gas and water	64 033[f]	141 260	18 659	52 330	29 651	69 383	41.2	478	790	60.51
14	85	74	Deutsche Telekom AG	Germany	Telecommunications	62 624	146 601	23 868	63 023	75 241[p]	248 519	37.0	97	178	54.49
15	59	67	RWE Group	Germany	Electricity, gas and water	60 345	98 592	23 729	49 061	53 554[p]	127 028	50.6	377	650	58.00
16	23	23	Hutchison Whampoa Limited	Hong Kong, China	Diversified	59 141	80 340	10 800	18 699	104 529	126 250	71.4	1900	2350	80.85
17	32	40	Siemens AG	Germany	Electrical & electronic equipment	58 463[f]	98 011	64 484	83 784	247 000	417 000	65.3	753	1011	74.48
18	53	46	Volkswagen Group	Germany	Motor vehicles	57 853[f]	150 462	71 190	98 367	160 299	334 873	52.9	203	283	71.73
19	21	35	Honda Motor Co Ltd	Japan	Motor vehicles	53 113[f]	77 766	54 199	70 408	93 006[p]	131 600	72.0	102	133	76.69
20	34	89	Vivendi Universal	France	Diversified	52 421[f]	69 360	15 764	28 761	32 348[j]	49 617	65.2	108	238	44.54
21	42	83	ChevronTexaco Corp.	United States	Petroleum expl./ref /distr.	50 806	81 470	72 227	120 032	33 843	61 532	59.2	93	201	46.27
22	3	30	News Corporation	Australia	Media	50 803	55 317	17 772	19 086	35 604[j]	38 500	92.5	213	269	79.18

(Continued)

TABLE 4.2 Cont.

Ranking by						Assets		Sales		Employment			No. of affiliates		
Foreign assets	TN[b]	11[c]	Corporation	Home economy	Industry[d]	Foreign	Total	Foreign[e]	Total	Foreign	Total	TN[b] (Percent)	Foreign	Total	II[c]
23	65	29	Pfizer Inc	United States	Pharmaceuticals	48 960[f]	116 775	18 344	45 188	73 200[p]	122 000	47.5	73	92	79.35
24	93	85	Telecom Italia Spa	Italy	Telecommunications	46 047	101 172	6 816	34 819	14 910	93 187	27.0	33	73	45.21
25	50	18	BMWAG	Germany	Motor vehicles	44 948	71 958	35 014	47 000	26 086	104 342	54.0	129	157	82.17
26	60	53	Eni Group	Italy	Petroleum expl./ref./ distr.	43 967[f]	85 042	29 341	58 112	36 658	76 521	50.0	154	226	68.14
27	4	9	Roche Group (Umoe AS)	Switzerland	Pharmaceuticals	42 926	48 089	22 790	23 183	57 317[p]	65 357	91.8	139	159	87.42
28	95	79	DaimlerChrysler AG	German/ American	Motor vehicles	41 696[f]	225 143	55 195	153 992	76 993	362 063	25 2	261	558	50.36
29	44	32	Fiat Spa	Italy	Motor vehicles	41 552	79 160	36 078	53 353	88 684	162 237	58.3	339	436	77.75
30	5	3	Nestle SA	Switzerland	Food and beverages	41 078[f]	72 402	44 308	65 329	247 506	253 000	74.1	471	501	94.01
31	55	5	IBM	United States	Electrical & electronic equipment	40 987[f]	10 4457	55 369	89 131	180 515[p]	319 273	52 6	315	342	92.11
32	83	47	ConocoPhillips	United States	Petroleum expl./ref./ distr.	36 510[f]	82 402	29 428	90 491	14 932[j]	39 000	38.4	103	147	70.07
33	46	31	Sony Corporation	Japan	Electrical & electronic equipment	35 257[f]	84 880	44 366	64 661	96 400	162 000	56.6	236	299	78.93
34	96	71	Carrefour SA	France	Retail	34 323[f]	49 335	39 368	79 780	138 283	419 040	50.6	128	231	55.41
35	96	24	Wal-Mart Stores	United States	Retail	34 018	104 912	47 572	256 329	361 765	1500 000	25.0	67	83	80.72
36	69	54	Telefonica SA	Spain	Telecommunications	33 466[n]	66 825	10 508	32 054	85 765[p]	148 288	46.9	133	199	66.83
37	36	70	Veolia Environnement SA	France	Water Supply	33 399[f]	49 154	17 578	32 283	205 694	309 563	62.9	424	760	55.79
38	43	21	Procter & Gamble	United Stales	Diversified	33 361	57 048	27 719	51 407	68 694[p]	110 000	58.3	174	215	80 93
39	41	10	Sanofi-Aventis	France	Pharmaceuticals	33 024[f]	44 484	12 291	22 247	36 576	75 567	59.3	335	385	87 01
40	57	16	Hewlett-Packard	United States	Electrical & electronic equipment	32 144[f]	74 708	43 843	73 061	73 158[j]	142 000	51 5	179	215	83.26
41	92	77	Mitsubishi Corporation	Japan	Wholesale trade	31 258[f]	78 342	20 054	130 912	14 765[j]	49 219	28.4	170	314	54.14
42	87	13	Deutsche Post AG	Germany	Transport and storage	29 524	195 748	19 714	45 166	175 775	383 173	34.9	341	406	83.99
43	35	62	Unilever[h]	United Kingdom/ Netherlands	Diversified	28 654[f]	47 952	27 635	48 186	179 000	234 000	64.5	316	522	60.54
44	6	49	Philips Electronics	Netherlands	Electrical & electronic equipment	28 524	36 626	31 594	32 773	136 750	164 438	85.8	263	378	69.58
45	63	91	Nissan Motor Co Ltd	Japan	Motor vehicles	28 517	73 386	42 002	64 082	50 836[q]	123 748	48.5	58	146	39.73
46	11	27	Lalarge SA	France	Mon-melalic prodicts	28 127	31 365	13 117	15 415	50 524	75 338	80.6	389	489	79 55

47	66	56	Repsol YPF SA	Spain	Petroleum expl./ret./ distr.	27 933	48 034	14 515	40 710	14 824	30 644	47.5	81	124	65.32
48	48	28	BASFAG	Germany	Chemicals	27 099	42 437	21 999	37 653	37 054	87 159	54.9	206	259	79.54
49	25	33	Compagnle De Saint-Gobain SA	France	Non-metallic mineral products	27 056	38 008	23 834	33 967	122 696	172 811	70.8	612	791	77.37
50	45	6	Novartls	Switzerland	Pharmaceuticals	26 748[f]	49 317	16 078	24 864	41 031	78 541	57.0	232	256	90.63
51	84	75	Milsui 1 Co Ltd	Japan	Wholesale trade	26 262[f]	52 709	47 508	105 938	10 826[p]	39 735	38.0	198	364	54.40
52	86	14	Altri a Group Inc	United States	Tobacco	25 711[f]	96 175	34 371	60 704	40 557[p]	165 000	36.0	196	234	83.76
53	78	81	Endesa	Spain	Electric services	25 468	58 155	6 228	18 328	12 939	26 777	42.0	85	177	48.02
54	8	4	Alcan Inc.	Canada	Metal and metal products	25 275[f]	31 957	13 172	13 640	38 000	49 000	844	306	326	93.29
55	26	90	BHP Billlton Group	Australia	Mining & quarrying	24 254	36 675	17 673	24 943	25 294	35 070	69,7	42	98	42.86
56	28	50	Glaxosmihkllne Pic	United Kingdom	Pharmaceuticals	23 893	42 813	32 296	35 006	56 360[p]	100 919	68.0	158	229	69.00
57	82	55	Renault SA	France	Motor vehicles	22 342[f]	71 283	27 330	42 353	34 921[p]	130 740	40.9	136	207	65.70
58	37	93	Anglo American	United Kingdom	Mining & quarrying	21 623	43 105	10 872	18 562	151 000	193 000	62.3	197	524	37.60
59	19	87	Koninkline Ahold	Netherlands	Retail	20 884	29 552	47 744	63 262	189 945[f]	257 140	733	74	164	45.12
60	20	64	AES Corporation	United States	Electricity, gas and water	20 871[f]	29 904	6 257	8 415	216 22[j]	30 000	72.1	56	93	60.22
61	54	22	Dow Chemical Company	United States	Chemicals	20 039	41 891	19 810	32 623	22 964[p]	46 400	52.7	216	267	80 90
62	18	43	Volvo AB	Sweden	Motor vehicles	19 451	31 787	23 160	24 023	47 603	75 740	73.5	233	319	73.04
63	47	57	Pinaull-Prlntemps Redoule SA	France	Wholesale trade	19 254[f]	30 649	16 828	30 767	51 847	100 779	56.3	287	449	63.92
64	74	42	Bayer AG	Germany	Pharmaceuticals' chemicals	18 892	47 020	17 033	32 334	48 700	115 400	45.0	236	320	73.75
65	1	1	Thomson Corporation	Canada	Media	18 418	18 732	7 943	8 159	38 350	39 000	98.0	300	310	96.77
66	33	36	Singlsl Ltd	Singapore	Telecommunications	17 911	21 668	4 872	6 884	8 642[l]	19 061	65.3	23	30	76.67
67	30	52	British American Tobacco Pic[g]	United Kingdom	Tobacco	17 871[f]	33 891	27 972[i]	41 832	68 702	86 941	66.2	248	363	68.32
68	81	99	National Grid Transco	United Kingdom	Energy	17 663	41 780	7 673	15 848	9 029	27 308	41.2	42	244	17.21
69	24	2	Nokia	Finland	Telecommunications	17 050[f]	29 273	36 763	37 202	28 979	51 359	71.2	98	103	95.15
70	99	84	Hitachi Ltd	Japan	Electrical & electronic equipment	16 296	89 545	21 177	80 602	80 226	326 344	23.0	309	670	46.12
71	49	20	United Technologies Corporation	United States	Transport equipment	16 212	34 648	14 257	31 034	143 000	203 300	54.4	345	422	81.75

(Continued)

TABLE 4.2 Cont.

Ranking by: Foreign assets	TN[b]	11[c]	Corporation	Home economy	Industry[d]	Assets: Foreign	Assets: Total	Sales: Foreign[e]	Sales: Total	Employment: Foreign	Employment: Total	TN[b] (Percent)	No. of affiliates: Foreign	No. of affiliates: Total	II[c]
72	94	88	Petronas - Petroliam Nasional Bhd[l]	Malaysia	Petroleum expl./ref./distr	16 114	53 457	8 981	25 661	3 625	30 634	25.7	234	411	56.93
73	38	92	McDonald's Corporation	United States	Retail	15 913	25 525	11 101	17 140	240 142	4w18 000	61 5	26	67	38.81
74	27	25	Slora Enso OYJ	Finland	Paper	15 910	22 646	10 382	15 373	29 156	42 814	68.6	229	285	80.35
75	61	44	Du Pont (El.) De Nemours	United States	Chemicals	15 840[f]	37 039	14 888	26 996	39 657[j]	61 000	49.0	115	158	72.78
76	12	82	Rio Tinto Pic	United Kingdom	Mining & quarrying	15 419	24 015	9 773	10 009	26 000	36 016	78.0	68	145	46.90
77	98	86	Duke Energy Corporation	United States	Electricity, gas and water	15 414[f]	56 203	5 537	22 529	46 521	23 600	23.6	33	73	45.21
78	40	38	Lvmh Moet-Hennessy Louis Vuitlon SA	France	Textile and leather	15 386[h]	24 356	8 285	15 063	35 360	56 241	60.4	296	390	75.90
79	73	66	Thyssenkrupp AG	Germany	Metal and metal products	15 237[f]	36 841	20 074	45 641	92 179	184 358	45.2	389	668	58.23
80	67	15	Abbott Laboratories	United States	Pharmaceuticals	15 214	26 715	7 703	19 661	33 1661	72 181	47.3	103	123	83 74
81	70	76	Matsushita Electric Industrial Co., Ltd.	Japan	Electrical & electronic equipment	14 739[f]	69 449	42 025	69 839	170 965	290 493	46.8	274	504	54.37
82	100	100	Verizon Communications	United States	Telecommunications	13 831[f]	165 968	2 449	67 752	17 269	203 100	6.8	13	219	5.94
83	76	88	Metro AG	Germany	Retail	13 600[f]	33 571	32 104	67 690	107 210	242 010	44.1	245	549	44.63
84	28	39	Norsk Hydro Asa	Norway	Diversified	13 429	32 729	23 158	25 716	30 866	44 602	66.8	254	335	75.82
85	52	97	Christian Dior SA	France	Textiles	13 368	31895	8 461	15 745	36 391	56 815	53.3	10	35	28.57
86	2	8	CRH Pic	Ireland	Lumber and other building materials dealers	13 184[f]	13 976	13 070	13 608	51 694	54 239	95.2	421	476	88.45
87	64	61	Scottish Power	United Kingdom	Electric Utilities	12 991	24 665	4 753	10 352	6 663	14 339	48.4	71	115	61.74
88	71	72	Alcoa	United States	Metal and metal products	12 931[f]	31 711	8 319	21 504	70 700	120 000	46.1	104	188	55.32
89	9	11	Publicis Groupe SA	France	Business services	12919[f]	13 400	4 367	4 679	21 451	35 166	823	295	342	86 26
90	97	73	Marubeni Corporation	Japan	Wholesale trade	12 814[f]	39 722	25 175	73 815	17 231[j]	24 417	24.5	161	293	54.95
91	13	60	Holcim AG	Switzerland	Non-metallic mineral products	12 808[g]	20 091	6 596	10 187	46 948	48 200	75.3	105	170	61 76

92	5	17	Cadbury Schweppes Pic	United Kingdom	Food & beverages	12 804	14 209	8 862	10 525	48 390	55 799	87.0	94	113	83.19
93	79	26	Wyeth	United States	Pharmaceuticals	12 776	29 727	6 269	15 851	21 617[i]	52 385	41.3	67	84	79.76
94	88	96	Statoil Asa	Norway	Petroleum expl./ret./ distr.	12 721	33 174	9 664	37 239	7 491	19 326	34.4	35	112	31.25
95	17	98	BAE Systems Pic	United Kingdom	Transport equipment	12 695	16 832	17 530	22 450	48 900	72 300	73.8	57	248	22.98
96	56	19	Robert Bosch GmbH	Germany	Machinery and equipment	12 683[m]	40 410	32 761[m]	45 919	123 000	232 000	51.9	210	256	82.03
97	51	45	Motorola Inc	United States	Telecommunications	12 618	32 098	17 983	27 058	48 400[j]	88 000	53 6	79	109	72 48
98	39	51	Bertelsmann	Germany	Media	12 498[j]	25 466	14 694	21 219	46 157	73 221	605	320	468	66.38
99	75	7	Samsung Electronics Co., Ltd.	Republic of Korea	Electrical & electronic equipment	12 387[b]	56 524	41 362	54 349	19 026[j]	55 397	44.1	80	69	89.69
100	91	59	International Paper Company	United Stales	Paper	12 088	35 525	6 992	25 179	28 980	82 800	32.3	93	148	62.84

[a] All data are based on the companies' annual reports unless otherwise stated,

[b] TNI is the abbreviation tor "Transnationaiity Index' The Transnationlity Index is calculated as the average of the following three ratios foreign assets to total assets, foreign sales to total sales and Foreign employment to total employment.

[c] It is the abbreviation for "internationlaization Index' The Index is calculated as the number of foreign affiliates divided by number of all affiliates (Note: Affiliates counted in this table refer to only majority-owned affiliates)

[d] Industry classification for companies follows the United States Standard Industrial Classification as used by the United States Securities and Exchange Commission (SEC).

[e] Foreign sales are based on the origin of the sales unless otherwise stated.

[f] In a number of cases companies reported only partial foreign assets. In these cases, the ratio of the partial foreign assets to the partial (total) assets was applied to total assets to calculate the total foreign assets. In all cases, the resulting figures have been sent for confirmation to the companies

[g] Data for outside Europe.

[h] Foreign assets data are calculated *by* applying the share of both foreign sales in total sales and foreign employment in total employment to total assets

[i] Data were obtained from the company as a response to an UNCTAD survey.

[j] Foreign employment data are calculated by applying the share of both foreign assets in total assets and foreign sales in total sales to total employment

[k] In a number of cases companies reported only partial region-specified sales In these cases, the ratio of the partial foreign sales to the partial (total) sales was applied to total sales to calculate the total foreign sales In all cases, the resulting figures have been sent for confirmation to the companies

[l] Foreign sales are based on customer location

[m] Data for outside Western Europe

[n] Foreign assets data are calculated by applying the share of foreign assets In total assets of the previous year to total assets this year

[o] Foreign employment data are calculated by applying the share of foreign employment in total employment of Philip Morris in the previous year to total employment of Altrta Group this year

[p] Foreign employment data are calculated by applying the share of foreign employment in total employment of the previous year to total employment this year.

[q] Foreign employment data are calculated by applying the average of the shares of foreign employment in total employment of all companies in the same industry (left out the extremes) to total employment

Note. The list includes non-financial TNCs only. In some companies, foreign investors may hold a minority share of more than 10 per cenl.
Source: Adapted from United Nations' organization UNCTAD at http://www.unctad.org/sections/dite dir/docs/wir2005topl00 en.pdf UNCTAD/Erasmus University database.

By 1669, the VOC was the richest privately held MNE in the world, with over 150 merchant ships, 40 warships, 50,000 employees, a private army of 10,000 soldiers, and a dividend payment of 40 percent.

Since then MNEs have grown by number and revenues. Comparing the gross domestic product (GDP) of selected countries with the revenues of the world's largest MNEs, it seems that some MNEs have annual revenues that exceed the annual domestic value of economic activities of countries such as Austria, Turkey, Denmark, Greece, Finland, Thailand, and Singapore. Time Warner Corporation, the last MNE on the Global Fortune 100 list, with annual revenues of almost $43 billion approximates the GDP of Morroco.

MNEs are recognized as major players in political and legal environments for a number of reasons. They represent a major economic and political power, generate employment, garner loans, raise share capital, and generate tax revenues for municipalities, regions, and countries. Strategic decisions made by MNEs, such as mergers and acquisitions, changing location of regional headquarters, or expanding or eliminating facilities, affect economies significantly. Consider the information on foreign direct investment worldwide in Figure 4.1. The amount of money involved in FDIs that are indicated for both developed and developing countries are very significant by world standards.

MNEs may be found in almost all types of industries today. However, most current-day MNEs are in the electrical and consumer electronics and equipment, automotive, chemicals, pharmaceuticals, and petroleum exploration and distribution industries. Of particular interest are the global food and beverage MNEs, which include the production and distribution of products with a fairly short shelf life. Food giants like Nestlé and Danone are obvious members of the global MNE

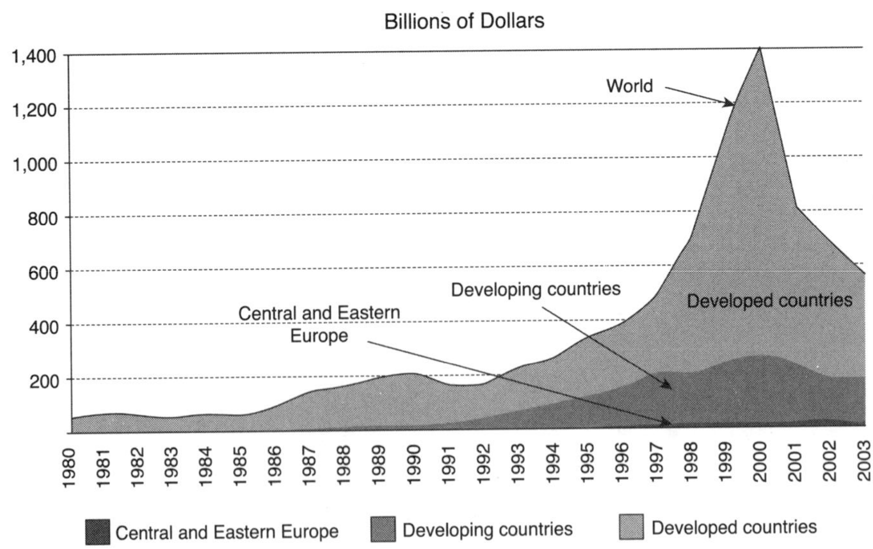

FIGURE 4.1 FDI inflows, global and by group of countries, 1980–2003. (Adapted from the 2004 UNCTAD database)

food industry. However, one may also find small and medium international enterprises (SMIEs) such as New York Style Brand, whose New York Style Bagel Crisps are produced in Bulgaria, and distributed outside the USA by Manassen Foods of Australia and Hutchinson of New Zealand.

It is apparent that hundreds of billions of dollars, and in some years over $1 trillion, are involved in strategic decisions made by MNEs. To wit, information supplied by UNCTAD indicates that as of 2005, MNEs are expected to strategically relocate their regional headquarters (20 percent), their R&D functions (22 percent), logistics/support services (60 percent), distribution/sales (62 percent), and production (70 percent). Furthermore, it has been observed that over three-quarters of the global industrial output is generated by the top 1,000 MNEs and about one-third to one-half of world trade is based on internal MNEs' trade. The list of MNEs referred to earlier should be augmented by financial institutions which are active internationally, such as Citigroup (USA), Mizuho Financial Group (Japan), HSBC Holdings (UK), and Wells Fargo (USA). These financial institutions play a major role in international business, just like all the nonfinancial MNEs. The formation of behemoth financial groups around the world is expected to continue through mergers, acquisitions, and strategic alliances and affect other industries as well. This trend has been further induced by the global financial crisis of 2008–2010.

Another important trend in the context of MNEs is the growth of service MNEs, especially in professional services, media, air travel, tourism, and education. This growth is fueled by the growth of the service sectors in Western economies which venture into new international markets to exploit expertise, skills, and economies of scale. The growth in service MNEs is also enhanced by the globalization, harmonization, and deregulation of the regulatory standards and practices. For example, the adoption of accounting standards and practices by many countries allowed North American-based accounting and consulting firms to practice abroad. The passing of laws governing large store openings in Eastern Europe and the Far East allowed companies like Office Depot and Toys 'R' Us to operate the large-scale retail operations they have come to master in the United States. The development of information and telecommunication technologies, such as Internet, cell phones, electronic commerce (E-commerce), and mobile commerce (M-commerce), helped to further the growth of service MNEs, whose services are time-specific and knowledge-intensive.

The arguments for and against MNEs vary by the country, the state of economic development of the country, by industry, by market orientation, and by the constituency affected: namely, labor, regional government, national government, etc.

Whatever the case may be, MNEs, home country and host country governments are engaged in an interdependent relationship. The MNE's advanced technology, managerial knowledge, capital resources, and global distribution network are essential to local economies. At the same time, MNEs need the support of local governments for infrastructure, as in the case of the western Chinese provinces, favorable and credible business standards and practices, appropriate education and professional training and appropriate telecommunication systems and financial organizations. The MNEs and various levels of government are in a continuous negotiating position, and at times are at odds on issues such as safety, environment, or labor issues. The continuous give-and-take relationships between local governments and MNEs are an attestation to the fact that MNEs cannot be all together borderless. But this local identity should not necessarily be a liability. At times, an MNE's local identity is an asset, such as in the case of selected foods made in France in regions of repute, such as Champagne or Cognac.

The Political Environment

The national and international political environment has a major impact on MNEs' decisions and operations. As municipal, regional, and national governments change their policies, MNEs have to change their strategies, decisions, and practices. The beginning of the 21st century seems to be presenting a higher degree of political instability and, as such, has caused MNEs to operate with a higher degree of risk. To understand more clearly how politics and business interact at many different levels, and develop the corporate skills required to manage the risk involved in international operations, some definitions and descriptions of politics are necessary:

1. *Politics is defined as the science of government or governing, especially the governing of a political entity, such as a nation, and the administration and control of its internal and external affairs.* The word "politics" is derived from the Greek word for city-state, *polis*. Corporate, religious, academic, and every other organization, especially those constrained by limited resources, contain dominance hierarchy and therefore politics. Politics is most well known in relation to the administration of governments.
2. The oldest form of government was a tribal organization that was characterized by elders, rule. This form of government was replaced by a system of feudalism and monarchy where a single family dominated the political affairs of a community, defining and delegating all forms power, authority and titles.
3. The following terms are used in regard to politics:
   - *Power* is the ability to impose one's will on another, including by force and violence.
   - There are two forms of power: incentive power, the power to reward, and coercive power, the power to punish.
   - Legitimate power, the power of the policeman or the referee, is the power given to an individual by a recognized authority to enforce standards of behavior. *Legitimate power* is similar to coercive power in that unacceptable behavior is punished by fine or penalty.
   - *Referent power* is granted to individuals by virtue of accomplishment or attitude.
   - *Expert power* comes from education or experience.

- *Authority* is the power to enforce laws, to request obedience, to command, and to judge.
- *Legitimacy* is an attribute of government gained through the acquisition and application of power in accordance with recognized or accepted standards or principles, say, by being elected.

There is an expectation that MNEs behave in a political manner with regards to their host and home countries: that is, the MNE is expected to acquire, develop, secure, and use its own political influence and power in relation to other entities, such as governments, unions, interest groups, the general public, and international nongovernmental organizations (NGOs), among others. The expectation to work in a political savvy manner is not different from what is expected from corporations operating domestically, it is just that the issues seem to be much more complex when it comes to operating internationally, like in the case of MNEs.

One may view political processes as an added expense that the MNE should bear as part and parcel of taking operations internationally. For example, Japanese firms are known to create well-positioned and highly paid lobbying groups in Washington to help pursue their interests, such as removing import quotas, lowering import tariffs, and granting export licences for selected technologies. Local firms may create lobbying groups to help maintain import tariffs, maintain import quotas, and limit the exportation of proprietary technologies.

Political systems and ideologies

Political systems include the organizations and the processes that constitute them. Political systems differ from one country and region to another, and are influenced by the local history, geography, tradition, and culture. There are differences between wide participatory political systems, where most people are allowed and exercise the right to voice an opinion and influence the results, and narrow participatory political systems, where only a selected group is allowed to express an opinion and influence the results. Worldwide, there are three main political ideologies. Anarchism is a political system that promotes personal liberties and deems public government unnecessary. Totalitarianism is a political system that promotes total control by the public government (e.g., communism, fascism) and effectiveness, and presents no concern for personal liberties whatsoever. Pluralism is a political system that is based on the belief that all groups, private and public, should participate in political organizations and processes, like democracies and constitutional monarchies.

A democracy is a political system where the leaders are elected directly by wide participation of the population and where most decisions are made by representatives of the general public. In representative democracies, the governing body represents various groups that participate in passing laws and enforcing them. Representative democracies are touted worldwide as the best political systems to promote transparency, integrity, effectiveness, and efficiency of governments. They are based on freedom of expression, periodic elections, complete civil, and property rights, equal treatment of minority groups and professional (nonpolitical) bureaucracy. The organizations, the processes, and operational practices of democracies vary. For example, some countries follow a parliamentary democracy, where various regions in the country select representatives.

International business and democracy

Political savvy by MNEs means that executives and corporate decision makers should understand the essential elements of democracies and the various kinds of democracies. Democracies entail various kinds of freedom as well as specific limits on freedoms. The justification for these limits is that they are necessary to guarantee the existence of democracy, or the existence of the freedom themselves. According to this argument, allowing free speech for the opponents of free speech logically undermines free speech. In Europe, this has become a political issue with the rise of Islamist political argument, which often does explicitly reject such liberal freedoms. Opinion is divided on how far democracy can extend, to include the enemies of democracy in the democratic process.

There is a list of items that fall under the freedom category – freedom of expression, including speech, assembly, and protest. There are various legal limitations, like copyright and defamation; more general restrictions may include curbs on antidemocratic speech, on attempts to undermine human rights, on the promotion or justification of terrorism, and in some cases on "anti-Western" ideas. In the US more than in Europe, during the Cold War, such restrictions generally applied to Communists; now they are mainly applied to Islamists. Freedom of the press and access to alternative information sources is considered a characteristic of a liberal democracy. For certain groups, however, this freedom may be limited: Islamist media now face restrictions in many democracies, including censorship of satellite broadcasting in France, and proposed bans on Islamist websites in several countries. Freedom of association is also restricted in democracies, for groups considered a threat to the state or to society. Most democracies have procedures to ban organizations – on suspicion of terrorism, for instance – and usually without a prior judicial procedure. The European Union (EU) has an official list of banned organizations, overriding the freedom of association in the European Convention on Human Rights and the national constitutions. Equality before the law and due process under the rule of law is considered a characteristic of a liberal democracy, but the United States held certain categories of prisoners in Guantanamo Bay, and possibly in other secret prisons, without trial, and without any specific grounds in domestic or international law. If relatively small numbers of people, seen as mortal enemies by the majority of the population, are excluded from legal protections, a country may still be seen as a liberal democracy: it is not qualitatively different from repressive autocracy, but quantitatively different.

The election processes in democracies and representation differs among democracies

For example, some electoral systems, such as the various forms of proportional representation, attempt to ensure that all political groups (including minority groups that vote for minor parties), are represented in the nation's legislative bodies, according to the proportion of total votes they cast; rather than the proportion of electorates in which they can achieve a regional majority (termed majority representation).

This proportional vs majority approach is not just a theoretical problem, as both forms of electoral system are common around the world, and each creates a very different kind of government. One of the main points in this context is having someone who directly represents a little region in a country vs having everyone's vote count the same, regardless of where in the country one happens to live. Some countries such as Germany and New Zealand have a large proportion of representatives elected from constituencies and then share out compensating mandates so that parties are represented proportionally. This way they get the best of both worlds. This system is commonly called mixed member proportional.

There are various kinds of democracies

A nonliberal democracy is a political system where democratic elections exist, and the government is elected by a democratic majority, but it might encroach on the liberty of individuals, or minorities. This may be due to a lack of constitutional limitations on the power of the elected executive, or violations of the existing legal limitations. The experience in some post-Soviet states is of this sort. Some critics of nonliberal regimes now suggest that the rule of law should take precedence over democracy. A social democracy is considered a spin-off of socialist and communist ideas, in a nonviolent and pro-democratic setting. Many social democratic parties in the world are evolutions of revolutionary parties that, for ideological or pragmatic reasons, renounced violence as a means of promoting their ideas. In North America and Western Europe, most parties calling themselves Socialist or Communist are actually social democratic. Social democracies are characterized by market regulation, social security (known as the welfare state), subsidized or government-owned education systems and health services, progressive taxation, environmental awareness, multiculturalism, and secular education. Examples of social democracies that are liberal democracies are the Scandinavian countries, with their intensive welfare systems and progressive taxation regimes.

Although there are many virtues to democracies, there are disadvantages and ongoing issues that should be addressed:

1 Democratic regimes explicitly state that power belongs to the people. This raises the issue of whether immigrants should be allowed to vote. The issue remains controversial in Germany, and in other countries where naturalization of immigrants and their children is a disputed topic. The European Union requires that resident EU migrants are given a vote, at least in the European Parliament elections. In some EU member states, they are allowed to vote in local and regional elections as well. An immigrant who is still a citizen in another country has the right to vote in his home country, in the government elections. The principle is that one person should not have two votes. In most European countries an immigrant worker has the right to vote

in local elections and in European parliament elections, but one can only have one vote, not two votes.

2 Democracy, and especially liberal democracy, assumes a sense of shared values. For historical reasons, many countries lack the cultural and ethnic unity of the ideal nation-state. There may be sharp ethnic, linguistic, religious, and cultural divisions. In fact, some groups may be actively hostile to each other. A democracy, which by definition allows mass participation in decision making, also allows the use of the political process against the "other side." That is especially visible during democratization, if a previous nondemocratic government suppressed internal rivalry. The collapse of the Soviet Union and the democratization of Soviet bloc states led to wars and civil war in the former Yugoslavia, in the Caucasus, and in Moldova. Wars have also continued in Africa and other parts of the Third World. Nevertheless, supporters of democracy claim that statistical research shows that the fall of Communism and the increase in the number of democratic states were accompanied by a dramatic decline in total warfare, interstate wars, ethnic wars, revolutionary wars, and in the number of refugees and displaced persons.

3 At times, democracy encourages the elected representatives to change the law and introduce many new laws without necessity. A legal system where any common citizen may be breaking a law in ignorance most of the time is an invitation for law enforcement personnel to misuse power.

4 Democracies have been accused of slowness and complexity in their decision making and short-term focus. Modern liberal democracies, by definition, allow for regular changes of government. That has led to a common criticism of democracies' short-term focus. In four or five years the government faces a new election, and it must think of how it will win that election. That may encourage a preference for policies that will bring short-term benefits to the electorate before the next election, rather than unpopular policies with longer-term benefits.

5 Public choice theory is a branch of economics that studies the decision-making behavior of voters, politicians, and government officials from the perspective of economic theory. A problem studied in public choice theory is that each voter has little influence and may therefore have a rational ignorance regarding political issues. This may allow special interest groups to gain subsidies and regulations beneficial to them but harmful to society.

6 The cost of political campaigning in representative democracies means that the system favors the rich, who are only a very small minority of the voters. It may encourage candidates to make deals with wealthy supporters, offering favorable legislation if the candidate is elected.

7 A major criticism of democracy is the fear that it will become a "tyranny of the majority." It may therefore be argued that one minority tyrannizes another minority in the name of the majority. This politically active and dominant group might decide that a certain minority (religion, political

belief, etc.) should be criminalized (either directly or indirectly). This undermines the idea of democracy as an empowerment of the electorate as a whole. For example, several European countries have introduced bans on personal religious symbols, aimed at those considered symbolic of Islamism – the hijab or "Islamic headscarf." In France, they are banned in public schools under the law on secularity and conspicuous religious symbols. Opponents see this as a violation of rights to freedom of religion. In the name of what is termed by some the tyranny of the majority, democracies prohibit pornography, limit or forbid abortion, limit recreational drug use, tax the rich, criminalize homosexuality, and disadvantage ethnic minorities. Some might say that the initial abandonment of impoverished ethnic minority residents in New Orleans after Hurricane Katrina in 2005 illustrates the degree to which a minority underclass can be isolated in a democracy.

Several safeguards are in place to help counteract the weaknesses of democracies:

1 The presence of a constitution in many democratic countries acts as a safeguard. Generally, changes in these constitutions require the agreement of an overwhelming majority of elected representatives, or require a referendum. These requirements are often combined.
2 Democracies practice separation of powers into legislative, executive, and judicial branches, thus making it more difficult for a small majority to impose their will. Members of a majority may limit oppression of a minority, since in the future they may well be in a minority themselves.
3 Majority rule is preferable to other systems, and the tyranny of the majority is preferrable to the tyranny of a minority.

Empirical statistical evidence shows that more democracy leads to less internal violence. In a democracy the people can remove the government without changing the legal basis for government, which reduces political uncertainty and instability, and assures citizens who disagree with present policies that they are given a regular chance to change those who are in power or the policies with which they disagree. This is preferable to a system where political change takes place through violence. At times, democracies may have an overextended political stability, when the government in power remains the same for a long period of time. This materializes when power is shared by only two parties, alternating the roles of government and opposition. Democracy could be a disadvantage for a country in wartime, when a fast and unified response is necessary, as power in democracy is not concentrated. Monarchies and dictatorships can act immediately and forcefully. However, it is a fact that most democratic countries succeed in maintaining their security. Research indicates that democracies are more likely to win wars than nondemocracies. In addition, while there are exceptions, political institutions of a democracy, parliamentary system, political stability, and freedom of the press are all associated with lower corruption. Democracies generally enjoy a higher GDP and do not declare war on other democracies. However, at the beginning of the 21st century, the link between economic development and what is generally called liberal democracy is actually quite weak and may even be getting weaker... the growing number of affluent authoritarian states suggests that greater wealth alone does not automatically lead to greater political freedom.

Conducting business in democratic countries

Democratic countries usually provide for a stable business environment. There are a number of reasons for that. Chances are that there is less risk of a military takeover, as the government is voted in by the people regularly. In addition, transparency, laws that govern tax laws, ownership, profit repatriation, and other democratic institutions and processes contribute to an environment that allows free competition. There are exceptions. Nondemocratic nations like some of the Gulf Sheikdoms as well as Singapore, Hong Kong, South Korea, and Taiwan, have enjoyed significant economic growth, while India, a democratic country, has had a relatively slow economic growth over the same period. A company should be familiar with the democratic institutions and the processes. MNEs executives should be involved in lobbying the political parties and the government to help create an appropriate and favorable business environment. As an example, during the first decade of the 21st century, Intel got Chinese government incentive of US$2 billion to set up a new fabrication plant. Also, tax incentives are offered in the new especially designated areas in mainland China.

International business and totalitarian systems

In a totalitarian political system, the government does not seek or necessarily expect the support of the people and maintains total control over most aspects of people's lives. At the beginning of the 21st century, Iraq is going through a transformation from a totalitarian political system to a democratic political system. Other countries such as North Korea and China are still running totalitarian governments. There are number of characteristics of a totalitarian system:

1. Leaders must impose authority, as the regime does not get approval by the people and thus maintains power by military force or by holding fraudulent elections.
2. Political rights that refer to people's ability to vote and run for public office and as elected officials and to vote on public policies are denied.
3. Civil liberties, which include people's freedom to develop views, institutions, and personal autonomy, are denied.

There are two types of totalitarian political systems – theocratic and secular. In a theocratic totalitarian political system the religious leaders are also the political leaders, ruling according to religious beliefs and laws. A secular totalitarian political system is of various forms – communist, right wing, and tribal. North Korea is a secular totalitarian country; Iran is a theocratic totalitarian country. A special case of a totalitarian political system is a communist totalitarian political system, like Cuba, where the communist party holds political and economic powers, and runs the country according to the belief that social and economic equality is achieved when the government owns and controls all types of economic activity. In communist countries, the government maintains ownership of the means of production (resources, land, and plants) and decides on production and prices. A tribal totalitarian political system, where a particular tribe seizes control of a country or a region, is commonplace in some African countries like Rwanda. Right-wing totalitarian political systems, where governments allow far-reaching economic rights, are found in Brazil, Argentina, Paraguay, and Argentina, where the government allows for private rights and supports economic growth; however, these governments limit political freedoms and oppose left-wing organizations of any form. The case of China is that economic rights are granted gradually and the state is transferring ownership of plants to private hands, while maintaining complete control over political organizations and allowing no political rights.

Conducting business in totalitarian countries

Totalitarian countries make for a risky environment for business. The main risk stems from the arbitrary nature of decisions made in totalitarian countries. While no opposition is staged to MNEs' activities in a host country due to the central nature of the government, business laws may be nonexistent, incomplete or changed arbitrarily without due and transparent process. Furthermore, senior government bureaucrats may interpret the law as they please. Another risk entailed in doing business in a totalitarian country is the fact that MNEs are blamed for helping local government to exploit the local population.

Because of the inherent risk of conducting business in totalitarian countries, business executives should consider carefully the decision to establish shop in such countries, and if indeed a base of operation or regional headquarters is established, the executive should become familiar with the government organizations, the senior leaders and with the host country's relevant processes. As to the advantages and disadvantages trade-off, the risk involved should be assessed in light of the currently exercised civic and political liberties in a host country and how these affect the expected business results and the fulfillment of stakeholders' expectations.

Typically, in these types of environments, personal relationships and connections (in China this is known as "Guangxi") to the various government officials, wealthy and powerful locals, and/or important business partners are even more critical to the business executive. At times, these personal relationships are the only means through which an executive can gain any political visibility regarding regulatory changes.

Political leadership and economic growth

The international business environment is in a constant state of change. The political leadership affects the business environment in a variety of ways. Research is helping to get an insight into the relationship between a country's political leadership and economic growth rate. A paper by Jones and Olken (2005) that tracks economic growth within countries found that it varied sharply across decades. They examined economic growth of countries and showed that randomly-timed leadership transitions were associated with shifts in country growth rates. There is evidence that leaders matter, particularly in autocratic settings. Autocrats affect growth directly, through fiscal and monetary policy, and also through influence on political institutions that, in turn, appear to affect growth. In particular, it is found that small movements toward democracy following the death of an autocrat appear to improve growth, whereas dramatic democratizations are associated with reductions in growth. The results suggest that individual leaders can play crucial roles in shaping the growth of nations.

MNEs and countries: the winds of change

MNEs and countries continue to be the dominant units of international trade and commerce, but economic globalization and the dispersion of technologies, especially information technologies, place strains on governments. Country regimes that were described above and have managed the challenges of the 1990s may be overwhelmed by those of 2020. Totalitarian regimes face new pressures to democratize, but new democracies may lack the adaptive capacity to survive and develop into democratic maturity. Immigration is increasing around the world: from North Africa and the Middle East into Europe, from Latin America and the Caribbean into the USA, and from Southeast Asia into Europe and the Americas. As a result, more countries are multiethnic and multireligious and face the challenge of integrating immigrants into their societies while maintaining their own ethnic and religious identities. Global economic growth has the potential to enhance democratization. In fact, by 2020 democratization may be partially reversed among the states of the former Soviet Union and in Southeast Asia, some of which never really embraced democracy. Russia and most of the Central Asian regimes appear to be slipping back toward totalitarian regimes, and global economic growth probably will not reverse such a trend on its own. The development of more diversified economies in these countries is crucial to foster the growth of a middle class, which in turn would spur democratization. Central Asian countries are suffering severe economic inequalities and leaders must deal with large youth populations that lack economic opportunities. Central Asian governments are likely to suppress dissent and revert to totalitarian regimes to maintain order, risking growing insurgencies. Chinese leaders face a dilemma over how much to accommodate pluralistic pressure and relax political controls or risk a popular backlash if they do not. Beijing should move towards political reform if China wants to be a major global player. Younger Chinese leaders who are already exerting influence as mayors and regional officials have been trained in Western-style universities and have a good understanding of international standards of governance. Thus, China may pursue an "Asian way" of democracy that might involve elections at the local level and a consultative mechanism on the national level, perhaps with the Communist Party retaining control over the central government.

The Middle East countries have, thus far, been excluded from the democratization process by repressive regimes. Major leading efforts by the USA and other countries in establishing a working democracy in Iraq and Afghanistan – and democratic consolidation in Indonesia – set an example for other Muslim and Arab states, creating pressures for change.

A Freedom House study shows an expanding gap in the levels of freedom and democracy between Islamic countries and the rest of the world: see, for example, the map of freedom as depicted in Figure 4.2. Some studies relate the lack of economic growth in the Middle East, besides the energy sector, to the slow pace. The current and continuing high oil prices allow regimes in the Middle East to put off economic and fiscal reforms, while radical Islamic parties may try to gain political power through democratic elections.

The use of computing and networking technology with high capacity, speed, affordability, and mobility has significant political implications. Empowered individuals and small groups can connect with one another and plan, mobilize, and accomplish tasks with more satisfying and efficient results than their governments can provide. This affects individuals' relationships with their governments and puts pressure on governments for more responsiveness. The UK mobilized a responsive government program, initiated by the then Prime Minister Tony Blair, based on intensive use of Internet technology. China has experienced the fastest rate of increase of Internet and cell phone users in the world and leads the market for broadband communication. Middle Eastern governments are also developing

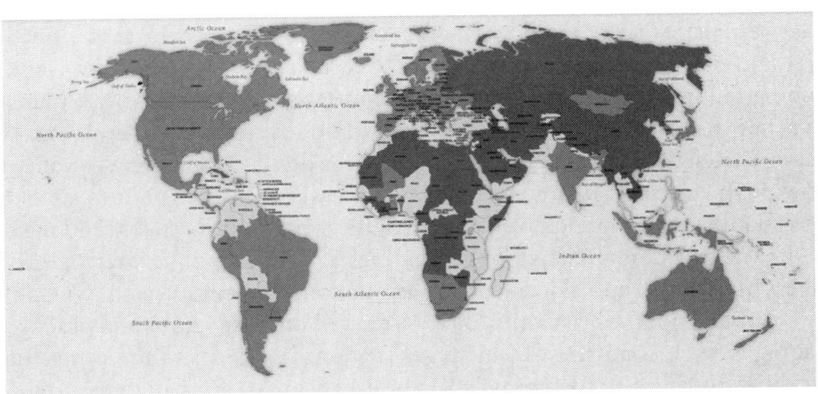

FIGURE 4.2 A map of religious freedom of countries around the world (Adapted from P. Marshall, (ed.) (2000). Religious Freedom in the World: A Global Survey of Freedom and Prosecution. Washington, DC: Freedom House)

high-speed information infrastructures, although they are not yet widely available to the population and thus do not help the spread of democracy. Some countries seek to control the Internet and its contents, but they face increasing challenges as new networks offer a variety of ways of communicating. An interesting political consequence of technology is that technology-enabled immigrant communities communicating in native languages lead to the preservation of language and culture in the face of widespread emigration and cultural change, as well as the generation of political and economic power. Global terror organizations with domestic cells, are spreading around the globe, and are already using telecommunications to form groups, some political, to garner power and coordinate activities.

World climate changes are being met with an increase in legislation on environmental issues by governments and international organizations. This impacts MNEs' political environments. However, the impact on political environments differs from country to country. For example, the USA, the EU, China, Russia, Japan, and India account for about two-thirds of the carbon dioxide emissions into the atmosphere. These countries, to varying degrees, require MNEs to control operations regarding damaging emissions with resulting economic impact. MNEs should be familiar with changing regulations, being fully aware that any weather-related event, such as a major tsunami in the Indian Ocean or a devastating hurricane in the Gulf of Mexico, may initiate intensified calls for harsher legislation regarding environmental issues, affecting MNEs' operations, cost structure, and profitability.

Other changes that affect the political environment for MNEs are failures of leading social groups to adapt to the demands of free markets and democracy. This, in turn, drives indigenous movements that seek change largely through democratic means to consider more drastic means to get their share of political power and economic wealth. This is the case of some Latin American countries. Rising nationalism and a trend towards populism also present a challenge to governments in Asia. Countries such as Laos, Cambodia, and Burma are currently unable to deliver on growing popular demands of free markets and democracy and risk becoming failures in their drive towards democracy. A further evolving phenomenon is new forms of identity politics centered on religious convictions and ethnic affiliation. Religious identity is likely to become an increasingly important factor in how people define themselves. The trend toward identity politics is linked to increased mobility, growing diversity of hostile groups within states, and the diffusion of modern communications technologies. Trends point towards growing numbers of converts and a deepening religious commitment by many religious followers. For example, Christianity, Buddhism, and other religions and practices are spreading in such countries as China as Marxism declines, and the proportion of evangelical converts in the heavily Catholic Latin America countries is rising. By 2020, China and Nigeria will have some of the largest Christian communities in the world, a shift that will reshape the traditionally Western-based Christian institutions, giving them more of an African or Asian identity. Western Europe is not showing a growing global religious trend, except for the migrant communities from Africa and the Middle East. Many religious followers, such as Hindu nationalists, Christian evangelicals in Latin America, Jewish fundamentalists in Israel, or Muslim radicals – are becoming activists. While there are some differences, all these groups share a global view that advocates change of society, and a religious belief that connects local conflicts to some other wider and significant struggle. Related to religious conviction as a political issue is the spread of radical Islam outside of the Middle East and Africa, which has had a significant global impact. It creates an authority that transcends national boundaries and calls for a return by Muslims to the era when Islamic civilization was at the forefront of global change and controlled a major portion of the civilized world. Radical Islam continues to make inroads, with Muslim migrants in France, the Netherlands, and Germany, among others. The phenomenon of radical Islam may develop into a major national, regional, and international crisis. On the other hand, a Hamas majority government of the Palestinian Authority may encourage other radical Muslim groups to look for a democratic means to achieve their political ends. Similarly, a Shia-dominated Iraq is likely to encourage greater political activism by Shia minorities in other Middle Eastern nations, such as Saudi Arabia and Pakistan.

To summarize, all around the world a growing quest for democratization and political freedom of expression and activism can be seen. MNEs' executives must be aware of fundamental changes in people's values and attitudes regarding political systems in various countries and regions. Executives who are considering conducting business in Latin America should be aware that since state-owned companies are sold and privatized, nationwide resentment leads to sentiments against democracy. At the same time in China, a favorite target country for many MNEs, an increase in economic freedom is not met with a change in the communist political regime at the national level. However, selected provinces in China, like Guangdong, are holding democratic elections at the regional and local level. More political changes are bound to happen in China and South East Asia that will change the business environment.

Political Risk

Political risk is defined as the likelihood that political change in a country occurs and will result in negative events, such as expropriation of assets, changes in tax policy, restrictions on the exchange of foreign currency, or other changes in the business environment.

Political risk is one of the four risks entailed in international business (commercial risk, cross-cultural risk, currency risk, and political risk), as shown in Figure 4.3.

Political risks are likely to affect MNEs in a variety of ways, reducing market sizes, affecting production capacities, restricting expatriation of profits, introducing labor unrest, etc. One may identify two types of risks: a macro political risk, which affects companies of all kinds operating in a particular region or country, and a micro political risk, which affect companies in a particular industry. Political risks may be caused by corrupt political leadership, frequent government changes, political involvement by religious and military leaders, national or regional ethnic

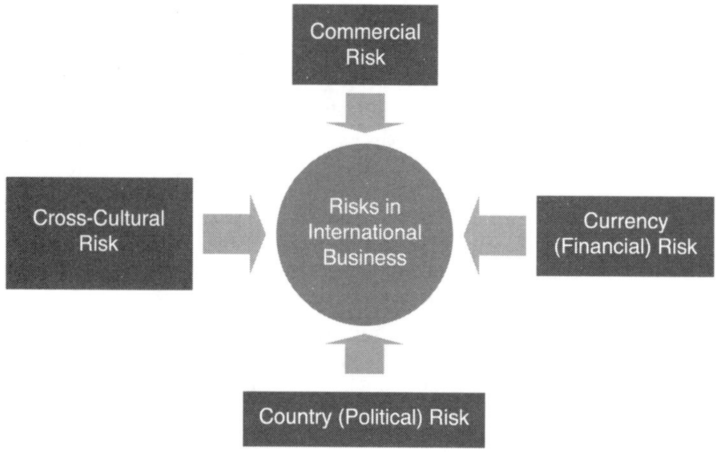

FIGURE 4.3 Political risk as one of four major risks in international business

conflicts, and unstable relations with other countries. Political risks may arise from regional violence which discourages investment by MNEs and affects negatively the ability of the company to produce and distribute products, recruit employees, or raise capital. MNEs are cognizant of the fact that revolutions or wars may result in violence that would affect business activities, increasing business risk. For example, oil production was halted during the Second Gulf War. Other reasons for violence may be a result of racial or ethnic conflicts, like the one that has occurred in Bosnia during the 1990s, involving Serb citizens. Political risk may materialize through terrorism, the effects of which are being felt increasingly during the first decade of the 21st century. In fact, one may observe the presence of "global terrorism," whereby Al-Qaida seem to have created an international network of local terrorist cells that may spring into action at short notice, using identical operating practices across the cells. Kidnapping is another risk that MNEs are exposed to. Executives operating in high-risk areas are acutely aware of the possibility that they or their relatives might be kidnapped for ransom. Some South American countries as well as parts of Eastern Europe are more prone to kidnapping than other parts of the world. Another political risk is property seizure, where governments seize assets of MNEs through confiscation (seizure of assets with no compensation), expropriation (seizure of assets with compensation), or nationalization (seizure of assets of an entire industry). A government's frequent policy changes pose a political risk in that the rules of investment, ex-appropriation of profits, and other terms of reference may change and thus will require an adjustment by MNEs working in a particular locality. Another political risk is the introduction of laws that dictate the amount of goods or services that may be supplied by a local supplier, termed "local content requirements." These requirements may be dictated by the trade agreements that a host country has with other countries, and may have negative effects on an MNE, especially if local suppliers or materials are not competitive.

Managing political risk

MNEs have to be aware of political risks and their causes, as well as to be able to manage the political risks involved in their international operations. Following major political unrest and terrorist attacks during the first decade of the 21st century, the importance of geopolitics has become apparent. Differences among countries and regions that were disappearing in part during the latter part of the past century have become of importance again. Thus, the political risks involved in international operations become paramount. These risks affect production, marketing, and operations. It is important to analyze political risks and manage them by dealing with a number of key questions:

- What are the political events that are likely to occur?
- What are the financial losses expected as a result?
- How can the expected losses be minimized?
- What changes should the MNE take today to hedge against these possible outcomes of a political change?

There are generally several types of political risks, classified by the main causes of risks: war and acts of violence; terrorism; kidnapping; property confiscation; and changing domestic business regulations.

War and acts of violence may discourage investments by international companies, since they restrict the MNE's operations in a host country, including personnel recruitment, production, distribution, marketing, sales, and after sale service and support. War and violence may cause destruction of assets and harm MNEs' employees. As an example, during the First and Second Gulf Wars, production and distribution of oil and gas in Kuwait and Iraq had ceased. The oil wells were set on fire by the Iraqi regime as part of the conflict. The beginning of the 21st century is haunted by disputes between ethnic, racial, and religious groups in a number of localities around the world, including Indonesia, which is composed of hundreds of ethnic groups, the Middle East, and areas of the former Soviet Union.

Global terrorism has become a major world phenomenon. Most countries around the world are targets for global terrorism, including Spain, Italy, the USA, Britain, Indonesia, and Turkey. The September 11, 2001 terror attacks on the New York World Trade Center, the Pentagon and, unsuccessfully on the White House in Washington, DC, serve as a landmark. Following these events, major disruption was created in business transactions and financial market operations. The need to create back-up systems and crisis management centers in order to manage the risks involved has become apparent.

In some South American countries, kidnapping is used to pursue political goals. Small militant groups dissatisfied with current governments may resort to kidnapping. At times, it may be used to fund a terrorist group's activities. In Iraq, kidnapping and killing of foreign nationals was used to make a political statement. Some MNEs purchase kidnapping insurance and train their executives to avoid trouble.

Another major political risk is property seizure by a government, where assets of MNEs that are doing business within a particular country are taken without compensation. This type of property seizure is termed confiscation. Alternatively, assets, real estate, and machinery may be expropriated: namely, taken away with some limited compensation. Nationalization is a general term used to describe the taking over of entire industries. Nationalized industries are usually those that are important for the security or economic viability of a country. Nationalization may occur because governments would like to gain control over the cash flow generated by the industry, for ideological reasons, in an effort to turn around nonprofitable businesses and save jobs, and to help initiate large-scale projects, like hydroelectric power generation facilities, major desalination facilities, and toll highways. Nationalization has been practiced by Cuba, North Korea, Vietnam, USA, Canada, France, Brazil, Mexico, Poland, and India and poses a political risk that needs to be dealt with.

Business regulations of a particular country may be changed by a newly formed government or by a newly created political party. The changes in business regulations may include limiting foreign ownership of local corporations and encouraging the use of local raw material or personnel (local content requirements). Some of these changes may be affected immediately, and may have an immediate impact on corporate strategies. Figure 4.4 indicates political risk in selected countries.

Measures used to manage political risk

MNEs must monitor and detect pending changes in the political environment, as well as try to manage political risks. There are several ways to manage political risk. The MNE may simply avoid investing in a country, which might be missing an opportunity. The MNE may decide to adapt, which is to augment the risk, by using locally generated funds, by catering to the local taste, culture and tradition, by providing local development assistance in the development of the region, and enhancing quality of life, by selecting a relevant partner, and by arranging for appropriate insurance.

MNEs are taking measures to manage local risks in a number of ways. First, they are using local employees, including local current and former politicians, to gain an understanding of local political events, may use agencies that specialize in assessing political risks. In addition, they may try to influence local politicians and employ lobby groups to promote their causes. Lobbying is the hiring of people to represent an MNE's views on political matters and secure appropriate legislation.

The relationship between political freedom and economic freedom is depicted in Figure 4.5 and substantiates the significant role that political freedom plays in facilitating economic growth.

The Legal Environment

Every country has a legal system that incorporates all laws, statutes, rules, institutions, and processes that govern the behavior of individuals and corporations, including MNEs. By its very nature, the legal system of any country is influenced

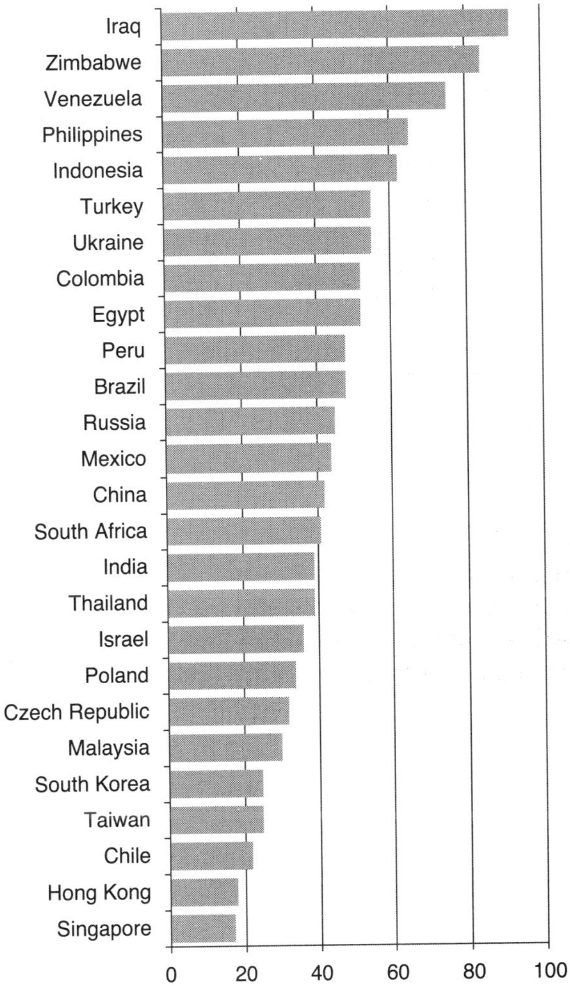

FIGURE 4.4 Political risk in selected countries. On a scale of 0 to 100, the rankings combine measures of political risk (such as the threat of war) and economic risk (such as the size of fiscal deficits). They also include measures that affect a country's liquidity and solvency (e.g., its debt structure and foreign-exchange reserves)

by its cultural customs and beliefs, and reflects the current national spirit and economic priorities. A totalitarian regime may allow few liberties for the enterprising business, facilitating state ownership as a rule. Democratic regimes tend to protect individual property rights and encourage intensive entrepreneurship and private ownership of businesses. As has been explained earlier, one of the political risks for MNEs is to have a country that is nationalizing businesses. The nationalization is indeed sanctioned by the legal system, which, apparently, is influenced by the national mood of the people. There are a number of examples of nationalizations that were initiated because of a strong nationalistic mood and the need for

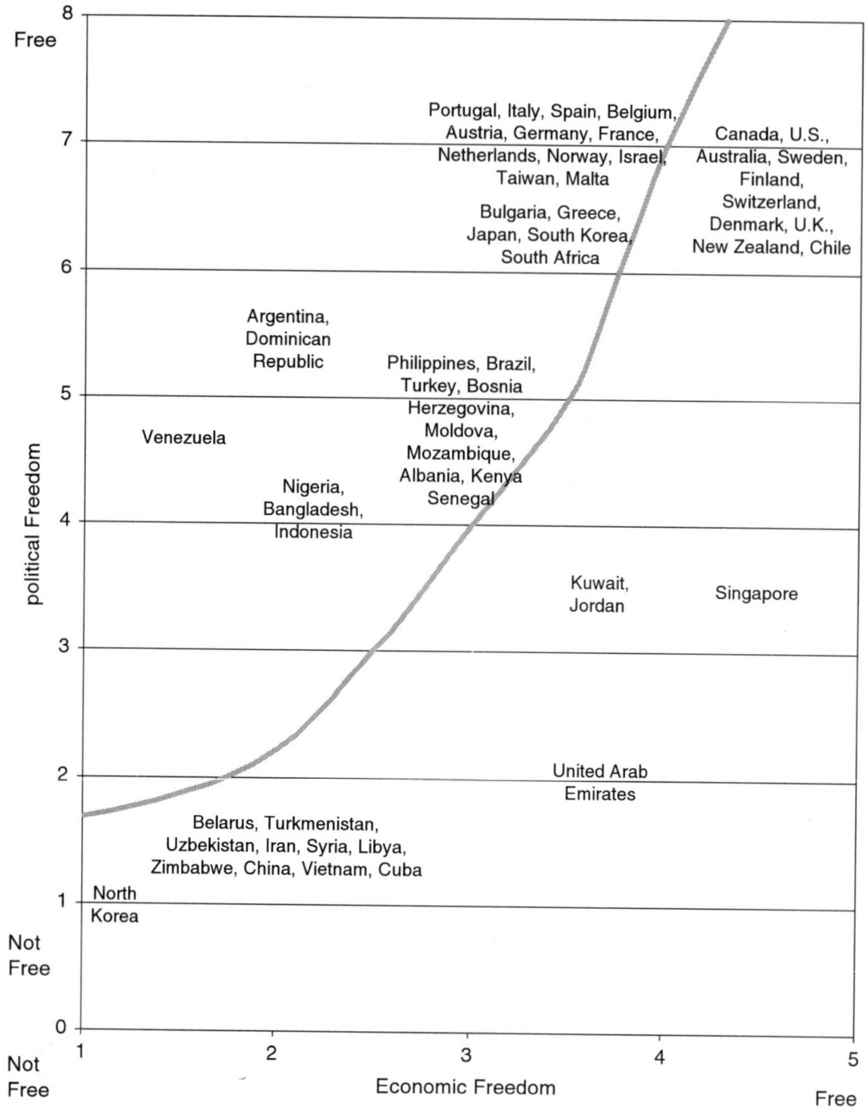

FIGURE 4.5 Relationship between political freedom and economic freedom for a sample of countries (Freedom House. Accessed at www.freedomhouse.org)

countries to protect themselves from perceived calamities, or from compromising national interests.

For example, the Conservative government of Edward Heath nationalized the aero-engine part of the bankrupt Rolls-Royce plc, since it was deemed to be of strategic importance to the UK. In Canada, the Canadian National Railways was created from several systems nationwide following their bankruptcy during and after the World War I. Also in Canada, following the quiet revolution in the

Province of Quebec, the Lesage provincial government nationalized electricity production to create Hydro-Québec. All US railroads were nationalized under the United States Railroad Administration during World War I as a wartime measure, but were returned to their private owers almost immediately after the war. Nationalization of the oil industry has taken place in many countries, including Libya, Kuwait, Mexico, Saudi Arabia, and Venezuela. As early as 1948, the new Romanian communist regime nationalized, by decree, all the existing private companies and their assests in Romania, leading to the transformation of the Romanian economy from a free market economy to a centralized one. Under a presidential decree of July 26, 1956, the Egyptian President Gamal Abdel Nasser nationalized the Suez Canal Company. This led England, France, and Israel to launch a combined attack on Egypt that was stopped by the USA and the former Soviet Union.

In all of these cases, the legal system aligned itself with and supported government actions that have had major effects on the national and regional business environments. In most cases, major MNEs had to change their business and functional strategies, resulting in significant long-term consequences.

Legal systems

Two main legal environments which affect businesses that are operating internationally – a *national legal environment* and an *international legal environment*. While the national legal environment consists of legal systems, legal organizations, and legal processes, the international legal environment consists of comparable components that transcend international boundaries completely. Nations, or countries, around the world are using one of four national legal systems: common law, civic law, theocratic law, and socialist law. In the following paragraphs, each is discussed in detail.

The *common law* system is based on a dynamic and continuing interpretation of the law based on earlier judgments, cases, or precedents. As new precedents are registered, laws are changed to accommodate situations not covered by past judgments. The common law constitutes the basis of the legal systems of England and Wales, the Republic of Ireland, all the states of the United States, except Louisiana, all the provinces of Canada, except Quebec (which follows the civil law), Australia, New Zealand, South Africa, India, Sri Lanka, Malaysia, Brunei, Pakistan, Singapore, Hong Kong, and other Commonwealth and English-speaking countries. Every country which has been colonized at some time by Britain uses common law, except those that had been colonized by other nations, such as Quebec (which follows French law to some extent) and South Africa (which follows Roman Dutch law), where the prior civil law system was retained to respect the civil rights of the local colonists. India's system of common law is a mixture of English law and the local Hindu law. The criminal law (part of the common law system) is largely governed by the common law in England, and has been entirely codified in many US states. Codification is the process whereby a statute, or law, is passed with the intention of restating the common law position in a single document to limit new interpretation. There are several major works that summarize the common law.

Among them is *Commentaries on the Laws of England*, written by Sir William Blackstone and first published in 1765–1769. Today, it has been superseded in the English part of the United Kingdom by *Halsbury's Laws of England*, which covers both common and statutory English law. The US Supreme Court judge Oliver Wendell Holmes Jr also published a volume called *The Common Law* which remains a classic in the field. In the United States, the *Corpus Juris Secundum* is a compendium of the common law and its variations throughout the various state jurisdictions. The American Law Institute publishes *Restatements of the Common Law*, which are often cited by American courts and lawyers when they need to invoke uncodified common law doctrines. Since the common law is based on precedents, business agreements should consider all possible eventualities, are lengthy and entail intensive work by lawyers. It is also noted that the common law system is more flexible than others, since it does not rely on a uniform code of law.

The *civil law* is based on a set of strucured and detailed rules that are termed as legal code. Civil law is primarily developed out of broad legal principles, interpretation of applicable doctrines, and local compilations of legal principles recognized as normative, rather than the application of facts and cases. Thus, the difference between civil law and common law is in the methodological approach to codes and statutes. *Civil* or *civilian* law is the most used legal system in the world. It was first used during the fifth century BC in Rome, and is practiced today in continental Europe, in the Province of Quebec (Canada), in the State of Louisiana (USA), Japan, Latin America, and in former colonies of continental European countries. With the development of nationalism in the 17th century and around the time of the French Revolution, the generally accepted civil law became fractured into separate national systems. This led to the development of several distinct national codes, including the most influential French Napoleonic Code, and the German and Swiss codes. The German civil code has been the basis for the legal systems of Japan and South Korea, since Germany was a rising power in the late 19th century when many Asian nations were introducing civil law. In China, the German Civil Code was introduced in the later years of the Qing Dynasty and formed the basis of the law of the Republic of China which remains in force in Taiwan after the Peoples Republic of China was formed in October 1949. Even though in most countries one distinct legal system is employed, there are also mixed systems, such as the laws of Scotland, Namibia, and South Africa. In so far as the implications of applying the civil law are concerned, common law opinions are much longer and contain elaborate reasoning, whereas legal opinions in civil law countries are usually very short and formal in nature. Also, business agreements in countries which follow the civil law system tend to be shorter than in the case of common law countries. Other implications involving the civil law systems noted include the selection and appointment of judges. Civil law judges are usually trained and promoted separately from attorneys, whereas common law judges are usually selected from accomplished and reputable attorneys. Three main groups of civil law countries are identified:

- French civil law – France, the Benelux countries, Spain and former colonies of those countries.

- German civil law – Germany, Austria, Switzerland, Greece, Japan, South Korea, Republic of China (Taiwan).
- Scandinavian civil law – Denmark, Sweden, Finland, Norway, Iceland.

It has been argued that civil law countries tend to emphasize social stability, whereas common law countries focus on the rights of an individual, affecting the economic development of each group differently. Consequently, one should expect to note a difference in the economic development of American, British, and Australian economies compared to the German and Italian economies, an argument that is not necessarily substantiated. The civil law has also served as the foundation for socialist law used in Communist countries, incorporating civil law with Marxist-Leninist ideas.

Theocratic law is a legal system based on religious teachings and tradition. It is the system used by theocracy-type governments where leaders are, by and large, dominant religious figures. The term theocracy (in Greek, the "rule by god") is a form of government in which religion plays a dominant role. In a theocracy, the administrative hierarchy of the government is identical with the administrative hierarchy of the religion. Some attribute the concept of theocracy as the characteristic government for Jews. Currently, the nations that may be considered as theocracies are Vatican City, partially Iran (defined as Islamic Republic), and Saudi Arabia (even though the kings have absolute power). Also, elements of theocracy may be found in Afghanistan and Algeria. Generally, theocratic law systems may be primarily of three types: Islamic, Hindu, and Jewish. The Islamic theocracy, being the most prevalent, restricts business transactions in a variety of ways, including a ban on interest on deposits. An alternative to interest payments and charges is devised, including profit sharing. A further ban on alcohol restricts MNEs operating in these countries from selling alcoholic goods. Strict adherence to dress codes by women is among other restrictions. MNEs operating in these countries should be sensitive to the local customs and practices, as well as to the letter of the law.

Socialist law is based on the civil law system, with additions from Marxist-Leninist ideology. It is the term used to describe the legal system used in communist states. Civil law systems maintain the notion of private property, whereas socialist law systems deem property to be owned by the state or by agricultural cooperatives, and establish courts and laws for state-owned enterprises. The demise of communism around the world also indicated the demise of socialist law. Even the People's Republic of China has revised its laws allowing for land rights by local committees which own the land and contract the right to use this land to individuals.

Table 4.3 indicates the main legal systems in various countries, while Table 4.4 presents examples of the differences between common law and civil law systems.

International Legal Issues

As has been explained earlier, companies and others corporations operating internationally are subject to both national legal systems, within home and host

TABLE 4.3 Main Legal Systems in Various Countries

Common law	*Civil law*	*Religious law*	*Socialist law*	*Mixed systems*
Australia Ireland New Zealand United Kingdom Canada United States India Pakistan Ghana Nigeria Zimbabwe Malaysia	Much of western Europe and Latin America Turkey Japan Mexico	Middle East, North Africa, and a few countries in Asia	Russia China Cuba North Korea Kazakhstan Uzbekistan Ukraine Azerbaijan Moldova Tajikistan Kyrgyzstan	Much of Eastern Europe, Philippines Puerto Rico South Africa Thailand Sri Lanka Ethiopia Hong Kong Bahrain Qatar Singapore Morocco Tunisia Vietnam Egypt

TABLE 4.4 Examples of Differences Between Common Law and Civil Law

Legal issues	*Civil law*	*Common law*
Ownership of intellectual property	Determined by registration	Determined by prior use
Enforcing agreements	Commercial agreements become enforceable only if properly notarized or registered	Proof of agreement is sufficient for enforcing contracts
Specificity of contracts	Contracts tend to be brief because many potential problems are already covered in the civil code	Contracts tend to be very detailed, with all possible contingencies spelled out. Usually more costly to draft a contract
Compliance with contracts	Noncompliance is extended to include unforeseeable human acts such as labor strikes and riots	Acts of God (floods, lightning, hurricanes, etc.) are the only justifiable excuses for noncompliance with the provisions of contracts

countries, as well as to international legal systems. The international legal system articulates several issues that are relevant to international operations of corporations and other organizations. Some of these issues are of an ethical nature more than of a legal nature, such as employment, environment, intellectual property rights, quality, liability, and corporate social responsibility.

Harmonization

In recent years a major effort has been made to harmonize legal systems: namely, to make national legal systems more standardized and compatible so that a legal expert who is knowledgeable about one national system will be able to function effectively in other national systems. For that reason and in order to facilitate international business and trade transactions, bilateral, and multilateral treaties and agreements have been initiated regarding intellectual property rights, taxation, arbitration, and industrial standards. In addition, international organizations have helped with the harmonization process: in particular, the United Nations (UN), the Organization for Economic Cooperation and Development (OECD), the World Trade Organization (WTO), and the International Institute for the Unification of Private Law (UNIDROIT), which studies needs and methods for modernizing, harmonizing, and coordinating private and, in particular, commercial law between nations and between groups of nations. The harmonization of legal systems helps reduce the need to hire local legal experts for all and any international transactions. For example, countries belonging to the EU standardize legal systems to help and ease pan-European trade.

International harmonization of legal systems

The standardization and harmonization of legal systems is crucial for international business transactions and operations. To this end, the League of Nations conceived the UNIDROIT Statute in 1926, and reaffirmed it in 1940. The UNIDROIT Institute, an organization associated with the United Nations, is based on member countries. UNIDROIT's 59 member countries are drawn from five continents and represent a variety of different legal, economic and political systems, as well as different cultural backgrounds. Among the members of Unidroit are Argentina, Australia, Austria, Belgium, Bolivia, Brazil, Bulgaria, Canada, China, Greece, Iran, Iraq, Ireland, Israel, Italy, Japan, Luxembourg, Malta, Mexico, Netherlands, Nicaragua, Nigeria, Norway, South Africa, Spain, Sweden, Switzerland, Tunisia, Turkey, UK, USA, Uruguay, and Venezuela. UNIDROIT's objective is to prepare current, harmonized, and uniform rules of laws that govern business transactions. However, at times, this leads to the raising of issues of public law, since transactional law and regulatory law are intertwined. If at all possible UNIDROIT structures uniform laws.

During the last several decades, new technologies, new business models, new environmental standards, and new business practices have called for new solutions, and where transactions tend to be international, these solutions should be harmonized, and be widely accepted. The eligibility of a business issue for harmonization or unification is to a large extent conditional upon the will of countries to change domestic legal codes in favor of a new international solution on that issue. When an international legal code should be devised, it takes the form of an international convention. These conventions may indicate terms of reference or general principles that may help countries design their own domestic laws.

International intellectual property rights

Intellectual property rights establish ownership over designs, software, chemical formulas and the like, which results in a patent, a trademark or a copyright. The ownership entails rights over income generated based on the intellectual property in the form of license fees or royalties. Nations vary regarding their treatment of infringements of intellectual rights. Some countries are more lax in regard to protecting intellectual property rights. As a result, the Business Software Alliance (BSA), which oversees the rights of software developers, initiated an international public call to report the use of illegally copied software packages and initiate revenue protection, as well as legal actions. The following is a discussion of the various forms of intellectual property laws.

A copyright may be applied in creative and artistic works such as books, software, and music, giving a copyright holder the exclusive right to control reproduction of such works for a period of time equal to the life of the author or the creator of the work plus 50 years. A patent is granted regarding an invention, giving the patent holder an exclusive right to commercially exploit the invention for a certain period of time (which is typically 17 years from the filing date of a patent application). A trademark is a distinctive sign or symbol that is used to distinguish the products or services from all other similar products and services. Coca Cola is an example of a trademarked sign. An industrial design right establishes the property rights of the designer over the appearance and design of an industrial part or product. A trade secret is a subject of confidential information concerning the proprietary knowledge of a business. Industrial property is a general term describing patents, trademarks, designs, and inventions. In all cases the protection of intellectual property is governed by laws and conventions that have been devised over hundreds of years. The copyright was devised side by side with the development of the printing press. An international copyrights convention was struck through the *Berne Convention of Literary and Artistic Work*, devised late in the 19th century. The Berne Convention automatically extends protection of a copyright holder in one signatory country to all others, so that the copyright needs to be registered in only one office of a signatory country.

Legal jurisdiction and MNEs

Legal jurisdiction represents the authority of a court to hear and decide in a case. The court must have both *subject matter jurisdiction*, the power to hear the type of case in question, which may be granted by the government, and *personal jurisdiction*, the power to make a decision affecting the parties involved, which the court gets as a result of the parties' consent. As an example, in the USA the state courts may have jurisdiction to deal with criminal and civil cases but not patent or immigration cases. The term jurisdiction may also be used to define the amount of money a court has the power to award. For example, a small claims court may have jurisdiction only to hear cases up to a relatively low monetary amount.

International business cases present difficulties when it comes to the definition of jurisdiction, as MNEs are subject to several countries' legal jurisdictions. At a minimum, MNEs are subject to host and home countries' legal systems. As an example for the multiple jurisdiction issue, take the case of a US bank operating in the UK, which, following a review of its business strategy, decided to reduce its staff in the UK from about 850 to 650. At the beginning of the calendar year around 90 employees were dismissed, 49 of whom were asked to leave the bank within two days on the grounds that they were employed in an area which had sensitive commercial implications and their function ceased immediately. The British Department of Employment was notified, as per British law, more than 90 days in advance of these redundancies; the Department treats this notification as confidential until the redundancies occur. Under the law, employers must also inform the representatives of independent recognized trade unions about the redundancies. The Banking, Insurance and Finance Union (BIFU), while claiming to have members among the staff, was not recognized by the bank; therefore, the company was not obliged, under national legislation, to notify the union and did not do so. Each employee made redundant was given a written explanation of the method of selection for redundancy. Web and Internet-type products and services make it even more difficult to determine jurisdictions, since these are dependent on the location of production, distribution, and marketing of the products and services.

As can be seen, MNEs are subject to several jurisdiction levels: an international level, regional level, national level, and state or province level. At the *international level*, a firm is subject to international law and to a growing body of international regulations regarding business transactions and operations. The international law is difficult to enforce. However, if both parties agree, cases may be brought before the International Court of Justice in The Hague in the Netherlands. In addition, if both parties agree to an arbitration, cases may be brought before the International Court of Arbitration, the Inter-American Commercial Arbitration Commission, the Canadian–American Commercial Arbitration Commission or, in cases involving international investments, the International Center for Settlement of Investment Disputes.

Recently, the regional, meta-national, jurisdiction has become more paramount. The EU, the Association of Southeast Asian Nations (ASEAN), and other regional jurisdictions harmonize and unify their national legal systems and develop a regional legal system to enforce the law. MNEs should also comply with both national and state, or province, legal systems. Specifically, both the home and the host country's national legal systems should be respected by an MNE.

Corporate-related international legal issues

The international legal environment presents other important issues that MNEs should be aware of and be ready to deal with. For example, *human rights*, including employment practices, humanitarian intervention, and self-determination, have a major impact on corporate strategies and operations. Even though international laws pertain mostly to international human rights law, which dates from World War II and its aftermath, the UN Charter, signed June 26, 1945, sought to acknowledge the importance of human rights and established it as a matter of international concern. Thus, MNEs with major manufacturing operations overseas should consider the implications of the UN Charter to its operations as well as local, domestic laws. Because MNEs' manufacturing operations are mostly based in Third World countries, where employment legal codes do not exist or are not enforced, employment issues such as compensation, continuity of employment, social benefits, and labor conditions become more of an ethical issue than a legal issue.

Competition laws involve both *antitrust regulations*, otherwise known as antitrust laws, and *subsidies*. Antitrust regulations are designed to assure a free market environment that provides a variety of products at a fair price. *Antitrust laws* allow for the institutions and processes that prevent corporations from coordinating market sharing, fixing prices, and creating a monopoly over certain products or services. As in the case for product liability laws, the USA and the EU lead in their antitrust regulations, whereas the developing countries' antitrust laws are yet to be further developed. In addition, Japan does not enforce antitrust laws. Since the number of international mergers and acquisitions made by expanding MNEs is used increasingly, both host and home country antitrust and takeovers legal provisions are important. The USA has recently undertaken a major effort to adopt a global approach to regulation and enforcement, and proposed the establishment of an international agency to oversee international mergers and acquisitions – alternatively, possibly operating as part of the WTO. National laws regarding *subsidies* are at odds with some international regulations devised by the WTO. A subsidy is assistance provided to local businesses by the local government, giving a local company an unfair advantage over international competitors.

The protection of *corporate and individual property* is of importance to MNEs. In many countries, there are rules limiting foreign 100 percent ownership of assets. In the USA, a controlling majority of shares of airlines, and radio and television companies is not allowed, mainly because these kinds of businesses are considered to be of strategic importance. In international business, the issue of *product origin* is important for determining custom duties and tariffs. The product origin determination is based on the amount of the product value that is added domestically. As an example, the EU defines a product as European made if 60 percent of value is added in Europe. An Indian law of origin requires that literally all of the value of cars made by MNEs in India be added locally, to qualify for the "Made in India" marks on cars.

National *marketing, distribution, advertising, and promotion laws* are of paramount importance. These rules govern, among other issues, the content and spirit of commercials that appear in various media, the use of local distribution channels, local distribution levies and taxes, pricing strategies, and product packaging and product safety and liability. *Product liability* defines the responsibility of manufacturers, distributors, executives, and public organizations towards the customers regarding product faults that may cause damage or injury. The legal codes in the USA regarding product liability are very well developed and very strict; the comparable European codes are less severe and developing countries have very weak or nonexisting legal codes regarding product liability. MNEs operating internationally should be aware of the implications of product liability to their operations in various geographical areas. There are a number of competition laws that are of relevance to MNEs. Laws regarding *recycling and waste management, trade, transportation, and personal and corporate taxes*, are also part of the legal environment that affects corporations in various localities and in international transactions.

Treaties and Conventions

Treaties are agreements of two or more countries. When ratified by many countries, a treaty may become an internationally acceptable agreement, a convention, enforced by an international body acceptable to all parties. There are many treaties in place on a variety of business-related issues, including treaties on trade, navigation, and tax harmonization. Among the treaties regarding protection of intellectual property rights is the Paris Convention for the Protection of Intellectual Property, the Berne Convention, the Madrid Trademark Convention, and the Universal Copyright Convention. Other international treaties deal with patent protection, including the Paris Convention for the Protection of Industrial Property. The Paris Convention sets a one-year grace period from the time of application for a patent in one country during which the patent's filer has priority in registering the patent in other countries. Another international treaty governing patent protection is the *Patent Cooperation Treaty*, which permits a one-stop application for patents in all participating countries.

Treaties and conventions are key to assuring stable business environments. The EU and other regions around the world have facilitated the free movement of goods, services, and citizens of member nations across members' borders.

The United Nations

A unique and important international organization that is part of the international political and legal business environment is the *United Nations* (UN) (www.un.org). As the economic activity of MNEs become larger than a number of countries, the UN becomes even more central to international business. The UN was founded after the Second World War to foster peace and political stability around the world. The UN created agencies that provide food and medical supplies, educational training, and financial resources to member nations in need. The member states provide funding to the UN, with each contribution determined by the member state gross national product (GNP). Most nations in the world are UN members. The UN Secretary General is elected by all members and serves for a five-year term. The Secretary General heads the UN. All member states have an equal vote in the *General Assembly*, which is the main statutory body of the UN that discusses and recommends any action and approves the UN budget and the make-up of the other organizations. The *Security Council* consists of 15 members. Five state members (China, France, the UK, Russia, and the USA) are permanent and 10 other member states are elected by the General Assembly for two-year terms. The Council is responsible for ensuring international peace and security. The *Economic and Social Council* is responsible for economics, human rights, and social matters. The *International Court of Justice* consists of 15 judges elected by the General Assembly and Security Council. It can hear disputes only between nations, not cases brought against individuals or corporations. It has no compulsory jurisdiction, and thus, its judgments are basically disregarded. The *Secretariat* administers the operations of the UN and is headed by the Secretary General. As an example, the Oil-for-Food program which was administered during the crisis in Iraq, was overseen by the UN Secretariat.

The United Nations Conference on Trade and Development (UNCTAD) is part of the UN Economic and Social Council. UNCTAD has a broad mandate in international trade and economic development, which has a direct effect on MNEs' international business environments.

COUNTRY FOCUS

THE PHILIPPINES

World Rank (EFI 2009): 104

Quick facts

Population: 86.3 million

GDP (PPP): $272.0 billion; 5.4 percent growth in 2006; 5.2 percent 5-year compound annual growth; $3,153 per capita

Unemployment: 7.3 percent

Inflation (CPI): 2.8 percent

FDI inflow: $2.3 billion

2006 data unless otherwise noted

Regional Rank (EFI 2009): 20

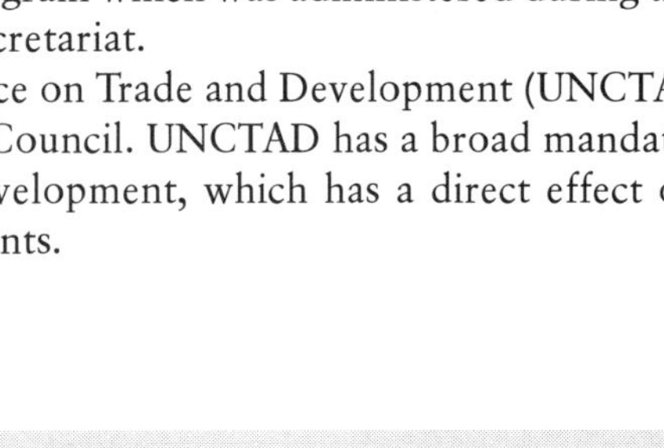

Economic freedom score

The Philippines has an economic freedom score of 56.8, making its economy the 104th freest in the 2009 Index. The Philippines is ranked 20th out of 41 countries in the Asia-Pacific region, and its overall score is slightly below the world average.

The Philippines has pursued a series of structural reform measures to develop a more vibrant private sector, generate more job opportunities, and enhance business competitiveness. Overall progress has been mixed, and the Philippines still relies heavily on remittances from abroad. The economy scores above the world average in four of the 10 economic freedoms. Fiscal freedom is only slightly above average because income and corporate tax rates are burdensome. The top corporate tax rate, however, is set to be reduced as of January 1, 2009. The average tariff rate is low, but nontariff barriers remain significant. Government expenditures are relatively low.

The Philippines is weak in business freedom, investment freedom, property rights, and freedom from corruption. The government imposes both formal and nonformal barriers to foreign investment. Contracts can be hard to enforce. Inflation is moderate, but the government subsidizes the prices of several basic goods. The judicial system is weak and vulnerable to extensive political influence.

Background

The Philippines returned to democracy in 1986 after two decades of autocratic rule. President Gloria Arroyo took office in 2001 and since then has weathered multiple impeachment attempts. The government has done little to liberalize the Philippines' economy or quell domestic insurgencies, thereby setting back efforts to attract much-needed foreign investment in basic industries and infrastructure. About one-third of the Philippines' annual GDP is derived from overseas remittances.

Business freedom – 49.3

The overall freedom to conduct a business is limited by the Philippines' regulatory environment. Starting a business takes an average of 58 days, compared to the world average of 38 days. Obtaining a business license takes less than the world average of 225 days. Closing a business can be a difficult and lengthy process.

Trade freedom – 78.6

The Philippines' weighted average tariff rate was 3.2 percent in 2006. Import and export restrictions, quotas, services market access barriers, import and export taxes, import licensing requirements, restrictive and nontransparent standards, labeling and other regulations, domestic bias in government procurement, inconsistent and nontransparent customs valuation and administration, export subsidies, widespread corruption, and weak protection of intellectual property rights add to the cost of trade. Fifteen points were deducted from the Philippines' trade freedom score to account for nontariff barriers.

Fiscal freedom – 75.4

The Philippines has burdensome tax rates. The top income tax rate is 32 percent. The top corporate tax rate is 35 percent but is scheduled to be reduced to 30 percent as of January 1, 2009. Other taxes include a value-added tax (VAT), a real property tax, and an inheritance tax. In the most recent year, overall tax revenue as a percentage of GDP was 14.4 percent.

Government size – 90.8

Total government expenditures, including consumption and transfer payments, are low. In the most recent year, government spending equaled 17.5 percent of GDP. Progress in privatization, VAT reform, and fiscal prudence has helped to reduce the public debt. Over 40 percent of the power sector is privately owned.

Monetary freedom – 77.2

Inflation is moderate, averaging 4.1 percent between 2005 and 2007. The government

(Continued)

influences prices through state-owned enterprises and utilities and controls the prices of electricity distribution, water, telecommunications, and most transportation services. Price ceilings are usually imposed on basic commodities only in emergencies, and presidential authority to impose controls to check inflation or ease social tension is rarely exercised. Ten points were deducted from the Philippines' monetary freedom score to account for policies that distort domestic prices.

Investment freedom – 40

Foreign investment is restricted in a number of sectors. All foreign investment is screened and must be registered with the government. Foreign investors receiving incentives may be subject to performance and local sourcing requirements. Other impediments include regulatory inconsistency and lack of transparency, corruption, and inadequate infrastructure. Dispute resolution can be cumbersome and complex, and the enforcement of contracts is weak. Residents and nonresidents may hold foreign exchange accounts subject to some restrictions. Payments, capital transactions, and transfers are subject to some restrictions, controls, quantitative limits, and authorizations. Foreign investors may lease but not own land.

Financial freedom – 50

Banking dominates the growing financial sector, handling more than 90 percent of financial activity. In general, the financial system welcomes foreign competition, and capital standards and oversight have improved. Consolidation has progressed, and nonperforming loans have gradually declined to about 5 percent of total loans. The five largest banks provide a full range of financial services and represent about 50 percent of the total assets of all commercial lenders. Two large banks are state-owned, and another is partly state-owned. A small government Islamic bank serves Muslim citizens in the south. Credit is generally available at market terms, but banks must lend specified portions of their funds to preferred sectors. Foreign firms may fully own insurers and set up local subsidiaries. Capital markets are centered on the Philippine Stock Exchange.

Property rights – 30

The judicial system is weak. Judges are nominally independent, but some have been appointed strictly for political reasons and are corrupt. Organized crime is a strong impediment to the administration of justice, and delays and uncertainty concern investors. Despite some progress, enforcement of intellectual property rights remains problematic.

Freedom from corruption – 25

Corruption is perceived as pervasive. The Philippines ranks 131st out of 179 countries in Transparency International's Corruption Perceptions Index for 2007. A culture of corruption is long-standing. Enforcement of anti-corruption laws is inconsistent, and the public perception of judicial, executive, and legislative corruption remains high.

Labor freedom – 51.4

The Philippines' inflexible labor regulations hinder overall productivity and employment growth. The nonsalary cost of employing a worker is low, but the difficulty of firing a worker creates a disincentive for additional hiring.

Source: Adapted from Terry Miller and Kim R. Holmes, *2009 Index of Economic Freedom* (Washington, DC: The Heritage Foundation and Dow Jones & Company, Inc., 2009), at www.heritage.org/index.

SUMMARY

The political and legal environments have a profound effect on the operations and competitive positioning of MNEs, both within the home country in which the MNE is based, as well as within the targeted country. Thus, the international executive should be familiar not only with physical, economic, social, and cultural infrastructures but also with a targeted country's current and pending political priorities and legal infrastructure.

The multinational enterprise (MNE) is a main player in international business, and, thus, in the national and regional environments. The Organization for Economic Cooperation and Development (OECD) definition of an MNE is an enterprise that is engaged in foreign direct investment (FDI) and owns or controls value-adding activities in more than one country. The MNE has multiple facilities around the world, draws substantial revenue from overseas operations, operates subsidiaries that share a common strategic vision, and share a common pool of resources, as well as places foreign nationals in senior executive and board of directors' positions. Some MNEs have annual revenues that exceed the annual domestic value of economic activities of some countries.

MNEs represent a major economic and political power, generate employment, assume loans, raise share capital, and generate tax revenues for municipalities, regions, and countries. Strategic decisions made by MNEs, such as mergers, acquisitions, changing regional headquarters location, and expanding or eliminating facilities, affect national and regional economies significantly. However, MNEs are only one of several types of international enterprises that may be identified, including international enterprise, internationally oriented enterprise, multidomestic enterprise, global enterprise, transnational enterprise, developing and emerging economies, international enterprise, and small and midsize international enterprise.

The political system consists of structure, organizations, and processes used by nations and other localities to govern themselves. Political systems differ from one country and region to another. There are differences between wide participatory political systems, where most people are allowed to express an opinion and influence the political process, and narrow participatory political systems, where only a selected group is allowed to express an opinion and influence the political process. Internationally, there are three main political ideologies: anarchism, totalitarianism, and pluralism. A *democracy* is a political system where the leaders are elected directly by wide participation of the population and where most decisions are made by representatives of the general public. In a *totalitarian* political system, the government does not seek or expect the support of the people and maintains total control over most aspects of their lives.

Political risk is defined as the likelihood that political change in a country might occur and result in negative events, such as expropriation of assets, changes in tax policy, restrictions on the exchange of foreign currency, or other changes in the business environment. Political risks are likely to affect MNEs in a variety of ways, including reducing market sizes, affecting production capacities, restricting expatriation of profits, and introducing labor unrest. Two types of political risks are identified: first, a macro political risk, which affects companies of all kinds operating in a particular region or country; second, a micro political risk, which affects companies in a particular industry.

A legal system incorporates all laws, statutes, rules, institutions, and processes that govern the behavior of individuals and corporations, including MNEs. The legal system of any country is influenced by its cultural

(Continued)

customs and beliefs, reflecting the current national spirit, and its economic priorities. A totalitarian regime may have a very limiting amount of liberties allowed legally for the enterprising business, facilitating state ownership as a rule. Democratic regimes tend to protect individual property rights and encourage intensive entrepreneurship and private ownership of businesses. There are two main legal environments which affect businesses that are operating internationally – a national legal environment and an international legal environment.

Common law, civic law, theocratic law, and socialist law are the four legal systems recognized worldwide. The *common law* system is based on a dynamic and continuing interpretation of the law based on earlier judgments, cases, or precedents. As new precedents are registered, laws are changed to accommodate situations not covered by past judgments. The *civil law* is based on a set of structured and detailed rules that are termed a legal code. Civil law primarily develops out of broad legal principles, interpretation of applicable doctrines, and local compilations of legal principles recognized as normative, rather than the application of facts and cases. *Theocratic law* is a legal system that is based on religious teachings and tradition. It is the system used by theocracy-type governments where leaders are by and large dominant religious figures. *Socialist law* is based on the civil law system with additions from Marxist-Leninist ideology. It is the term used to describe the legal system, used in communist countries. Civil law systems maintain the notion of private property, whereas socialist law systems deem property to be owned by the state or by agricultural cooperatives, and establish courts and laws for state-owned enterprises.

The international legal environment is harmonized and standardized in regions and countries around the world through various international initiatives by the United Nations (UN), the OECD, the World Trade Organization (WTO), and the International Institute for the Unification of Private Law (UNIDROIT). Other international legal issues include employment, the environment, intellectual property rights, quality, liability, and corporate social responsibility.

DISCUSSION QUESTIONS

1. What is the place of the multinational enterprise (MNE) in international business?
2. Explain the term "a political system." What are its components?
3. What are the differences between the three political systems: anarchy, democracy, and totalitarian?
4. What are the various ways to manage political risk?
5. Explain the various types of legal systems – common law system, civil law system, theological law system, and the socialist law system.
6. What is the objective of the harmonization of legal systems?

ACTION ITEMS

1. Identify two news articles in leading business magazines, say *Business Week* and *Financial Times*, and discuss the impact of a recent political change on the operation of a large international corporation. (Hint: you may refer to the opening case of this chapter for an example.)
2. Engage a corporate executive in a conversation regarding the knowledge of other nations' political and legal systems. How crucial is this knowledge in conducting business in a host country?
3. Identify a particular host country for an international corporation's operational base. Describe the political environment and the legal environment in the host country and make a decision as to the attractiveness of this host country for a regional or national base of operation.

Bibliography

Acs, Z., Yeing, B. (eds) (1999). *Small and Medium-Size Enterprises in the Global Economy*. Ann Arbor, MI: The University of Michigan Press.

Banejri, K., Sambharya, R. (1996). Vertical keiretsu and international market entry: The case of the Japanese automobile ancillary industry. *Journal of International Business Studies*, 27 (1), 89–113.

Bartlett, C. A., Ghoshal, S. (1989). *Managing Across Borders: The Transnational Solution*. Cambridge, MA: Harvard Business School Press.

Behrman, J. N., Boddewyn, J. J., Kapoor, A. (1975). *International Business–Government Communications*. Lexington: MA: Lexington Books.

Boddewyn, J. J. (1998). Political aspects of MNE theory. *Journal of International Business Studies*, Fall, 341–63.

Boddewyn, J. J., Brewer, T. L. (1994). International business political behavior: new theoretical directions. *Academy of Management Review*, 19, 119–43.

Braithwaite, J., Drahos, P. (2000). *Global Business Regulation*. Cambridge, UK: Cambridge University Press.

Brewer, T. L. (1993). Government policies, market imperfections, and foreign direct investment. *Journal of International Business Studies*, 1, 101–20.

Brush, C. A. (1995). *International Entrepreneurship: The Effect of Firm Age on Motives for Internationalization*. New York: Garland.

Buckley, P., et al. (1997). *International Technology Transfer by Small and Medium-size Enterprises: Country Studies*. New York: St. Martin's Press.

Caves, R. E. (1996). *Multinational Enterprise and Economic Analysis*. Cambridge, UK: Cambridge University Press.

Craig, C. S., Douglas, S. P. (1997). Managing the transnational value chain – strategies for firms from emerging markets. *Journal of International Marketing*, 3, 71–84.

Doz, Y. L. (1980). How MNEs cope with host government intervention. *Harvard Business Review*, March–April, 149–57.

Fujita, M. (1998). *The Transnational Activities of Small and Medium-Size Enterprises*. Boston, MA: Kluwer.

Jones, B. F., Olken, B.A. (2005). Do leaders matter? National leadership and growth since WWII, *Quarterly Journal of Economics*, 120 (3), 835–64.

Keim, G. D., Zeithaml, C. P. (1986). Corporate political strategy and legislative decision making: a review and contingency approach. *Academy of Management Review*, 11 (4), 828–43.

Kim, W. C. (1988). The effects of competition and corporate social responsiveness on multinational bargaining power. *Strategic Management Journal*, 9, 289–95.

Klassen, E., Whyback, C. (1994). Barriers to the management of international operations. *Journal of Operations Management*, 11, 385–97.

Makhija, M. V. (1993). Government intervention in the Venezuelan petroleum industry: an empirical investigation of political risk. *Journal of International Business Studies*, 3, 531–55.

Marshall, P. (ed.) (2000). *Religious Freedom in the World: A Global Survey of Freedom and Prosecution*. Washington, DC: Freedom House.

Menipaz, E., Ben-Yair, A. (2002). Strategic hierarchical harmonization model for complex holding corporations. *Communication in Dependability and Quality Management: an International Journal*, 5 (2), 37–53.

Menipaz, E., Ben-Yair, A. (2003). Heuristic optimization model to maximize product's marketability and corporate sustainability. *Communication in Dependability and Quality Management: an International Journal*, 6 (2), 120–33.

Menipaz, E., Lowengart, O. (2002). On the marketing of nations: a gap analysis of managers' perceptions. *Journal of Global Marketing*, 15 (3/4), 65–94.

Moore, K., Lewis, D. (2000). *Birth of the Multinational*. Copenhagen. Denmark: Copenhagen Business School Press.

Müller, H., Wolff, J. (2004). Dyadic democratic peace strikes back: reconstructing the social constructivist approach after the monadic renaissance. Paper presented at the 5th Pan-European International Relations Conference, The Hague, September, 9–11.

Rolfe, R. J., Ricks, D. A., Pointer, M. M., McCarthy. (1993). Determinants of FDI incentive preferences of MNEs. *Journal of International Business Studies*, 3, 335–5.

Silver, R. (2005). *Broken Promises: The United Nations at 60*. A film. Washington, DC: A Citizens United Foundation and Peace River Company.

Tallman, S. B. (1988). Home country political risk and foreign direct investment in the United States. *Journal of International Business Studies*, Summer.

Weber, Y., Menipaz, E. (2003). Measuring cultural fit in mergers and acquisitions. *International Journal* of *Business Performance Management*, 5 (1), 54–72.

Wells, L. T. (1998). Multinationals and the developing countries. *Journal of International Business Studies*, 29 (1), 101–14.

World Competitiveness Yearbook (2005). Lausanne, Switzerland: International Institute of Management Development (IMD).

World Investment Report (2005). United Nations Conference on Trade and Development (UNCTAD).

Yeung, H. W. C. (1994). Transnational corporations from Asian developing countries: their characteristics and competitive edge. *Journal of Asian Business*, 10 (40), 17–58.

5

Economic Systems and International Trade

Learning Objectives

Following this chapter, the reader should be able to:

1. Recognize the main economic systems used by countries around the world, their relative importance and significance, and their characteristics
2. Be aware of the various international trade theories which are used to explain, describe, and predict trade transactions and govern many of the MNEs' business affairs
3. Understand the way in which economic systems and trade theories are used in the context of international business
4. Understand how and why governments limit or enhance trade with other countries

Opening Case
The Internet Enabled Economy

The Internet has, in a short space of time, become fundamental to the global economy. More than a billion people worldwide, just about 15 percent of the world population uses it, both at work and in their social lives. Over the past three decades it has grown from an experimental research network and currently underpins a range of new economic activities, as well as activities and infrastructures that support mostly Western economies, from financial markets and health services to energy and transport.

Major changes are taking place in how one accesses the Internet and how one makes use of it. As a result, the Internet's reach, capabilities, and potential achievements are high on the social and political agenda of many countries.

The Internet offers access to a host of activities through both wired and wireless technologies. It provides a platform for innovation, for new communication technologies, the provision of new products and services, and access to an unparalleled wealth of information. But this also raises concerns, mostly in the area of reliability, scalability, security, and openness of access.

If *global supply-chain management* depends on the Internet, then a breakdown or security breach could cause major economic damage. If people's *personal data are compromised online*, it may breach their privacy or affect many other aspects of their lives.

Looking forward, the Internet is poised to connect an ever-greater number of users, objects, and information infrastructures. This means that the legal and social framework governing its use and development also needs to be adaptable, carefully crafted, and coordinated across political domains, international borders, and multiple stakeholder communities. It seems that the economy has become an Internet economy.

Enhancing economic activity

The Internet is making economic activity more efficient, faster, and cheaper, and is extending social interaction in unparalleled ways. Increasingly, the largest productivity gains for businesses come from using online networks in some form. The multinational food giant Nestlé, for example, now receives all of its orders directly from supermarkets over the Internet. The global shipping company UPS uses online networks to optimize its delivery routes, and saved 3 million gallons of fuel in 2006 from nearly 100,000 trucks employed.

The Internet has also brought unprecedented user and consumer empowerment as well as opportunities for new innovative and social activities. Individuals have greater access to information, which facilitates comparisons and creates downward pressure on prices. Internet users are extremely active, creating new content themselves, and interacting in new ways.

The Internet is quickly permeating all economic and social domains, and most public policy areas. For instance, e-government has become the prime tool for supporting government functions and interaction with citizens and businesses.

Healthcare systems are increasingly making use of the Internet and online networks to increase affordability, quality and efficiency, through electronic patient record systems, remote patient monitoring and healthcare delivery, along with improved diagnostics and imaging technologies.

Educational performance is found to be correlated with home access to, and use of, computers – all other things being equal. Moreover, environment friendly technologies based on the Internet in buildings and transport systems and alternative power-generating systems can help address climate change and improve energy efficiency.

The influence of the "network of networks" is inherently global. It helps to forge closer integration of world economies and societies. Moreover, as the Internet expands even further, it can help the economic and social development of people of all countries. Whereas there have been remarkable developments in recent years, much remains to be done. To wit, about one-fifth of the world's population uses the Internet, but over 5 billion people still lack access to it.

The technological evolution

Before the rapid development of the Internet, separate systems – telephone, television and video, individual computer systems – stored and transmitted voice, video, and data. Today, these systems are converging onto the Internet. In addition to convergence of network platforms, convergence is also taking place at several other levels:

1 At the content level, with video on demand (VOD) and television over Internet Protocol networks (IPTV).
2 At the business level, with companies offering combined television, Internet, and telephone services to subscribers.
3 At the device level, with multipurpose devices that can combine e-mail, telephone, and Internet.

Converged media

We are in the era of converged media. Users upload some 10 hours of video per minute alone to the video-sharing site YouTube. Towards the end of the first decade of the 21st century, nearly 400 million people are registered to use free VOIP (voice over Internet Protocol) software, Skype, enabling them to make phone calls worldwide at little or no extra cost via their existing Internet access. Converged media are also increasingly becoming mobile, with the expansion of wireless broadband networks.

As convergence takes place and investment in next generation networks (NGN) begins, the role of very fast optical fiber networks "to the home" becomes increasingly important, given that emerging applications, such as high-definition television and VOD, require increasing amounts of bandwidth.

The regulatory challenges associated with convergence are significant. With migration to Internet Protocol (IP) based networks, one network can handle many types of converged services. This means that governments face a fundamental shift in the way they regulate broadcasting and telecommunication services. The issue for the future of the Internet economy is how best to stimulate a competitive environment as technologies and markets evolve, to ensure that the Internet can meet growing expectations, especially as high-speed networks, both fiber and wireless, develop. For this, insight is needed into the impact of convergence on competition, the regulatory and policy issues of network infrastructure and services, the promise of multiplatform competition, and the implications for greater connectivity, pricing, sustainable competition, investment, and innovation.

As communication platforms converge towards using the Internet Protocol (IP), IP addresses are crucial to the scalability of the Internet and thus to the continued growth of the Internet economy, as all devices connected to the Internet need IP addresses to communicate.

Internet, information, and communication (IIC) technologies
IIC technologies are changing how research and creative activity are undertaken: for example, by facilitating distributed research, simulation, or virtual worlds. They are also changing the organization of science, research, and innovation, by linking the creativity of individuals and allowing organizations to collaborate, pool distributed computing power, and exploit new ways of disseminating information. The global nature of the Internet is further spurring the pace and scope of research and innovation, and encouraging new kinds of entrepreneurial activity. Digital technology and the Internet are also transforming platforms for delivering news, entertainment and other information. Participative networks enable users to contribute to developing, rating, collaborating, and distributing Internet content and customizing Internet applications, driving a range of new social and economic opportunities alongside new models of production. In Korea, for example, more than 40 percent of Internet users have their own blog. In several emerging markets and countries, the challenge is to encourage innovation, growth and change, and develop appropriate governance that does not stifle creativity or affect the openness of the Internet as a dynamic platform for innovation.

Emerging business models
Because the marginal costs of exchanging and reproducing information and digital content are very low, another challenge is to facilitate access to and use of digital content and develop new business models while preventing unauthorized use. Many new business models are emerging around the provision of content, and this area is evolving rapidly. The music and video industries, for example, are still grappling with these issues as they seek to develop new, more effective, and popular ways to commercialize their products online, while protecting the revenue generation and intellectual property rights.

Productivity and economic growth
Another pressing need is to better understand the role and contribution of the Internet and other information and communications technology in driving productivity and economic growth, and as a platform for innovation, increased collaboration, and shared creation. There is also a need to analyze the economic, social, and cultural impacts of emerging Internet technologies, applications and services, including virtual worlds, sensor-based networks, and social networking platforms.

In addition, more should be done to promote more open and competitive markets for goods and services, and to meet the challenges of transforming government and the public sector so that they are more efficient, transparent, and accountable.

Source: Adapted from www.oecd.org/FutureInternet.

Introduction

International business involves transactions taking place within and between economic systems through local, regional, and international trade. Economic systems create, govern and maintain the structure within which citizens earn a living, create wealth and sustain the poor, the disadvantaged, the retired, and the elders. It is within economic systems that most nations commercialize technologies in the quest to advance their economic well-being and standard of living. Whereas all economic systems are real, an interesting phenomenon of the 21st century is the emergence of Internet-based economic systems and communities based on the Internet technology which transcend international boundaries completely. The e-Bay market place facilitates buying and selling of goods just like in market places, creating virtual economic systems. The trades may be local or international, transcending international boundaries. However, the shopping experience is virtual, aided by graphical presentations of items for sale, listing of product characteristics, bidding mechanism and built-in quality and service checks and balances.

Whether real or virtual, economic systems are different from one country or region to another and are influenced by factors of production, such as availability of raw materials, labor skill level and energy, and by local cultures. The Global Entrepreneurship Monitor (GEM), an intensive, longitudinal, international research project, substantiates the fact that a country which values individualism rewards entrepreneurs, and new venture creators with high economic returns and other incentives.

In recent history one identifies periods of high economic activity as well as periods of low economic activity. The turn of the 20th century was marked with intense economic activity and saw the successful commercialization of significant technologies, which created significant wealth and contributed to the economic well-being of the Western world. On the other hand, during the first decade of the last century, a major economic downturn caused a slowdown and a shrinking of the world economy. This chapter describes the various economic systems used by countries around the world and the relationships between economic systems, national cultures, and political environments. In addition, recent changes in economic systems are described, including the market-based economic reforms and changes that are being implemented in China and Eastern European countries. Following the description of economic systems around the world, the relationships between economies are explored, including international trade frameworks and practices. The activities of multinational enterprises (MNEs) and other international organizations influence and being influenced by national economies as well as by international trade.

Economic Systems

Economic systems consist of national structures and processes that allocate the use of resources and govern the conduct of business activities. Economic systems reflect the local culture and tradition. Some tend to have an individual orientation, and some have a group orientation. Most economic systems may be described on a continuum from the market economy (focused and promotes the individualistic point of view in structure, processes, and rewards) to the centrally planned economy (focused and promotes the social well-being of the community). In between is the mixed economy. Thus, economies of countries around the world may be categorized into three types: market economy, centrally planned economy, and mixed economy.

The market economy

A *market economy* is an economy in which goods and services are freely traded, at a price which is determined by matching sellers' supply and buyers' demand.

Supply is the quantity of a good or service that producers or sellers are willing to provide at a specific selling price. *Demand* is the quantity of a good or service that buyers are willing to purchase at a specific selling price. In a market economy most of a country's economic sources such as land, manufacturing plants, and investment capital, are owned, for the most part, by individuals or companies and not by the government.

In a market economy potential buyers bid up to, but not more, than they are willing to pay for a specific good or service and potential sellers offer to lower the price down to the price in which they are willing to sell a good or service. When these prices match, a trade is made at the set price. Both bid prices and ask prices are influenced by competition among buyers and sellers, respectively. Supply, demand, and prices make up a market economy. Many variables affect the price and volume of goods or services that are sold and bought. For example, the price of oil changes in direct relationship with changing production rates and political behavior of the oil-producing countries on the supply side and the introduction of cars that are using alternative forms of energy on the demand side. When the amount of oil available for sale around the world decreases – namely, the amount of supply is low – the same amount of customers are competing for a smaller amount of oil. As a result, the bid prices increase, resulting in a higher price per barrel of oil. When the amount of oil available around the world increases – namely, the amount of supply is high – the asking price is lowered, resulting in a lower price per barrel of oil.

In a market economy, entrepreneurship, which is the initiation of ventures based on a business opportunity and an intention to make a profit and accumulate assets and wealth, is encouraged and rewarded.

A market economy in its purest form with no, or only little, government intervention is called a *free market*. It largely cannot be found. The economic crisis of 2008–2009 made it very clear that a fairly significant government control is necessary, at times, in order to navigate even the most robust economy.

Market economy evolution

It is argued that a free market is a natural form of social organization and social activity that emerged in early-modern Europe. By the 19th century, with the emergence of liberalism, the market economy had received political support. However, it is not clear if the political support preceded the emergence of the market economy, or followed it. Many economists have studied the market economy as it has evolved since the 19th century. The well-known economic philosopher Karl Marx argued that the market economy is a long-term transition from feudalism to capitalism. He found the market economic system to be unfair and developed an alternative economic and political system in the form of communism. Other economists assumed that most individuals and countries are interested in growing their own wealth, and studied the relationship between market economy and economic wealth, and between economic freedom and wealth. According to the economist Kenneth Arrow, a system of free trade leads to the best distribution of wealth among members in societies. Other economists, like Milton Friedman, argued that there is a direct relationship between economic freedom and economic growth, a relationship that has not been fully substantiated, but is constantly monitored by the Index of Economic Freedom (IEF) of the Heritage Foundation (see below). Whereas no market economies are pure free markets, the understanding gained into such economies helps explain the behavior, appeal, growth, and sustainability of Internet-based economies, such as e-Bay, as well as the black market and underground economies that exist in various societies.

Market economy and degree of market freedom

A market economy strives in democratic countries, and, despite economic downturns, seems to contribute consistently to the wealth of countries. In 1986 the Heritage Foundation, a nongovernment research organization, identified the key factors that may be used to measure the degree of freedom of an economy of countries. Based on 50 variables, an Index of Economic Freedom was constructed. The IEF does not define a free market but is used to assess the degree of market freedom, or the degree to which the government let the economy govern itself. The 50 variables are grouped into the following main categories: trade policy, fiscal burden of government, government intervention in the economy, monetary policy, capital flows and foreign investment, banking and finance, wages and prices, property rights, regulation, and informal market activity. Each category is assigned a number between 1 and 5 and the IEF is calculated as the arithmetic mean of the values assigned to each category.

Table 5.1 indicates the distribution of economic freedom as determined by the IEF, as of 2009, while Table 5.2 provides the corresponding country rankings during the period 1995–2009. It should be noted that only a minority of the world countries provide a market economy environment.

Characteristics of a market economy

An important basic idea in a market economy, such as North America, is that governments neither control local and international trade, nor own most of the country assets. In particular, a market economy is supported by a democratic form of government as well as a culture that supports individualism and entrepreneurship. Market economies are based on *free choice*: that is, a consumer is free to select from broad offerings of products or services. In a market economy the customers enjoy *price flexibility*: that is, the price paid for products and services is freely adjusted according to the supply and demand. Market economies also allow the *free choice for business activity*: that is, individuals and corporations are free to decide on what business they would like to pursue, decide freely on introduction of new products and services, and define the territory in which they will pursue the business and provide after sale service and support.

Needless to say, a market economy, while being driven by market forces of supply and demand, still requires government involvement. In particular, governments are charged with the responsibility of providing a stable political and economic environment, securing a fair and equitable competition, and protecting individual property rights. Governments in a market economy are charged with the responsibility of enacting anti-trust laws that encourage the development of business areas with as many competitors as the market may sustain. The anti-trust

TABLE 5.1 The Distribution of Economic Freedom Based on the Index of Economic Freedom

World rank	*Country*	*Overall score*	*Change from 2008*	*Business freedom*	*Trade freedom*	*Fiscal freedom*	*Government size*	*Monetary freedom*	*Investment freedom*	*Financial freedom*	*Property rights*	*Freedom from corruption*	*Labor freedom*
1	Hong Kong	90.0	0.3	92.7	95	93.4	93.1	86.2	90	90	90	83	86.3
2	Singapore	87.1	–0.2	98.3	90	91.1	93.8	86.8	80	50	90	93	98.1
3	Australia	82.6	0.4	90.5	84.8	61.4	64.3	84.7	80	90	90	86	94.7
4	Ireland	82.2	–0.3	93.0	85.8	69.2	64.9	84.3	90	90	90	75	79.7
5	New Zealand	82.0	1.2	99.9	84.6	62.5	49.6	84.6	80	80	95	94	89.6
6	United States	80.7	–0.3	91.9	86.8	67.5	59.6	84	80	80	90	72	95.1
7	Canada	80.5	0.3	96.5	88.2	76.6	53.7	80.8	70	80	90	87	81.9
8	Denmark	79.6	0.4	99.9	85.8	35.4	20.4	86.6	90	90	95	94	99.4
9	Switzerland	79.4	–0.1	82.9	85.4	67.5	65.3	83.9	70	80	90	90	79.2
10	United Kingdom	79.0	–0.5	89.8	85.8	61.0	40.3	80.4	90	90	90	84	78.5
11	Chile	78.3	–0.3	66.3	85.8	78.2	90.1	77.3	80	70	90	70	75.0
12	Netherlands	77.0	–0.4	86.5	85.8	50.9	36.2	87.0	90	90	90	90	63.3
13	Estonia	76.4	–1.5	75.9	85.8	81.5	67.3	79.7	90	80	90	65	48.5
14	Iceland	75.9	0.1	93.6	88	76.2	44.0	75.3	70	70	90	92	59.9
15	Luxembourg	75.2	0.5	76.2	85.8	66.3	54.4	80.2	90	80	90	84	45.1
16	Bahrain	74.8	2.6	79.6	80	99.9	79.4	74.0	60	80	60	50	85.1
17	Finland	74.5	–0.1	95.1	85.8	64.3	28.6	87.4	70	80	95	94	44.8
18	Mauritius	74.3	1.7	83.3	86.8	92.2	80.8	71.1	80	70	60	47	71.5
19	Japan	72.8	–0.2	85.8	82	67.5	61.1	93.6	60	50	70	75	82.5
20	Belgium	72.1	0.5	93.2	85.8	41.5	28.3	81.0	90	80	80	71	70.5
21	Macau	72.0	n/a	60.0	90	79.3	93.3	80.3	70	70	60	57	60.0
22	Barbados	71.5	0.2	90.0	64.6	70.9	66.3	74.5	50	60	90	69	80.0
23	Austria	71.2	–0.2	78.6	85.8	49.9	27.1	80.9	70	70	90	81	78.7
24	Cyprus	70.8	–0.5	70.0	80.8	76.6	42.2	85.7	70	70	90	53	70.0
25	Germany	70.5	–0.1	90.3	85.8	58.5	38.2	80.8	80	60	90	78	43.4
26	Sweden	70.5	–0.4	95.9	85.8	35.0	7.3	82.1	80	80	90	93	55.5
27	The Bahamas	70.3	–0.8	74.7	56	96.5	84.4	75.5	40	70	75	50	80.4
28	Norway	70.2	1.6	88.1	89.2	50.3	50.5	78.1	60	60	90	87	48.6
29	Spain	70.1	1.0	76.8	85.8	58.6	55.3	78.9	80	80	70	67	48.3

30	Lithuania	70.0	–1.0	82.4	85.8	87.6	65.3	75.8	70	80	50	48	54.6
31	Armenia	69.9	0.0	83.7	86.4	90.0	89.7	77.8	70	70	35	30	66.3
32	Georgia	69.8	0.5	86.6	80.6	86.8	74.6	70.9	70	60	35	34	99.4
33	El Salvador	69.8	1.3	67.3	81.8	85.7	87.9	77.4	70	70	50	40	67.5
34	Botswana	69.7	1.5	71.2	69	75.1	70.6	71.8	70	70	75	54	70.0
35	Taiwan	69.5	–0.7	69.5	85.2	76.2	89.4	82.1	70	50	70	57	45.7
36	Slovak Republic	69.4	–0.6	73.4	85.8	84.1	57.4	78.7	70	70	50	49	75.3
37	Czech Republic	69.4	1.2	65.1	85.8	80.2	43.0	79.7	70	80	70	52	67.8
38	Uruguay	69.1	1.2	65.6	83.4	82.2	76.5	72.8	70	30	70	67	73.7
39	Saint Lucia	68.8	n/a	87.7	72	74.0	68.5	85.1	40	40	70	68	82.8
40	South Korea	68.1	–0.5	90.4	70.2	70.4	72.5	80.0	70	60	70	51	46.4
41	Trinidad and Tobago	68.0	–1.6	60.1	79.8	79.7	75.6	72.2	70	70	60	34	78.3
42	Israel	67.6	1.3	67.8	86	57.1	35.1	83.7	80	70	70	61	64.9
43	Oman	67.0	–0.3	63.3	83.6	98.5	61.1	71.4	60	60	50	47	75.0
44	Hungary	66.8	–0.8	77.4	85.8	70.6	19.2	73.8	80	70	70	53	68.4
45	Latvia	66.6	–1.7	73.8	85.8	82.3	58.5	71.1	70	60	55	48	61.6
46	Costa Rica	66.4	2.2	60.3	81.8	82.8	88.4	69.7	70	50	50	50	61.2
47	Malta	66.1	0.1	70.0	85.8	63.1	41.7	82.7	50	60	90	58	60.0
48	Qatar	65.8	3.6	75.7	81.6	99.9	69.1	67.3	40	50	50	60	64.7
49	Mexico	65.8	–0.3	80.3	80.2	83.4	81.8	77.5	50	60	50	35	59.8
50	Kuwait	65.6	–2.5	67.4	81	99.9	63.7	71.7	50	50	50	43	79.3
51	Jordan	65.4	1.3	68.9	78.8	83.0	56.9	80.3	50	60	55	47	74.1
52	Jamaica	65.2	–0.5	87.8	70.6	75.3	62.2	75.4	80	50	50	33	67.4
53	Portugal	64.9	1.0	81.1	85.8	61.6	35.4	79.9	70	60	70	65	40.3
54	United Arab Emirates	64.7	2.2	574	80.8	99.9	86.3	69.8	30	50	40	57	76.2
55	Panama	64.7	0.0	74.5	76.2	82.6	89.8	77.9	70	70	30	32	44.1
56	Bulgaria	64.6	0.9	73.5	85.8	86.2	58.7	72.8	60	60	30	41	78.4
57	Peru	64.6	0.9	65.1	79.4	79.7	91.8	86.5	60	60	40	35	48.7
58	Malaysia	646	0.7	70.8	78.2	83.0	81.4	79.9	40	40	50	51	71.5
59	Saudi Arabia	64.3	1.8	79.6	81.8	99.6	73.4	68.4	40	50	40	34	76.4
60	Saint Vincent and the Grenadines	64.3	n/a	78.2	73.6	64.7	60.9	75.6	40	40	70	61	78.5
61	South Africa	63.8	0.4	74.6	74.8	689	77.6	74.3	50	60	50	51	56.8

(Continued)

TABLE 5.1 Cont.

World rank	*Country*	*Overall score*	*Change from 2008*	*Business freedom*	*Trade freedom*	*Fiscal freedom*	*Government size*	*Monetary freedom*	*Investment freedom*	*Financial freedom*	*Property rights*	*Freedom from corruption*	*Labor freedom*
62	Albania	63.7	1.3	67.0	75.8	92.8	75.6	79.6	70	70	30	29	47.2
63	Uganda	63.5	–0.3	58.7	75.2	80.4	86.9	78.4	50	60	30	28	87.9
64	France	63.3	–1.4	87.4	80.8	50.9	145	71.7	60	70	70	73	54.5
65	Romania	63.2	1.5	74.9	85.8	87.0	70.0	75.0	60	50	35	37	57.1
66	Belize	63.0	0.0	75.5	69.6	68.8	77.6	78.4	50	50	50	30	806
67	Thailand	63.0	0.7	71.1	75.6	74.4	90.6	69	30	60	50	33	76.5
68	Slovenia	62.9	2.7	84.5	85.8	62.9	38.4	78.6	60	50	60	66	42.8
69	Mongolia	62.8	–0.8	71.0	81.2	81.3	699	76.7	60	60	30	30	67.7
70	Dominica	62.6	n/a	76.4	74.2	67.4	52.2	79.8	60	30	60	56	70.0
71	Namibia	62.4	1.0	74.4	88.4	67.2	69.7	74.6	40	50	30	45	85.0
72	Colombia	62.3	0.2	77.4	72.4	72.9	65.9	70.6	60	60	40	38	66.0
73	Madagascar	62.2	–0.2	60.5	72.6	80.9	86.3	73.9	70	50	50	32	46.0
74	Kyrgyz Republic	61.8	0.7	75.3	876	93.4	74.9	71.5	50	50	25	21	69.5
75	Turkey	61.6	1.6	69.9	86.6	73.2	83.4	71.1	50	50	50	41	40.3
76	Italy	61.4	–1.2	78.7	80.8	55.8	24.7	80.8	70	60	50	52	61.3
77	Cape Verde	613	3.4	57.1	65.4	65.5	62.2	76.9	60	60	70	49	46.9
78	Macedonia	61.2	0.2	58.2	81.6	89.4	65.1	85.4	50	60	30	33	59.8
79	Paraguay	61.0	1.0	61.7	83.6	96.6	90.4	76.7	60	60	30	24	27.0
80	Fiji	61.0	–0.8	66.0	69.6	76.0	76.0	77.3	30	60	30	40	84.8
81	Greece	60.8	0.2	78.7	80.8	66.5	46.3	78.8	50	50	50	46	61.2
82	Poland	60.3	0.0	53.7	85.8	69.0	42.2	80.8	60	60	50	42	59.8
83	Kazakhstan	60.1	–1.0	579	86.2	82.8	87.5	70.0	30	60	25	21	80.5
84	Nicaragua	59.8	–1.0	57.6	79.2	78.8	71.0	69.5	70	50	25	26	70.6
85	Burkina Faso	59.5	3.8	58.7	70.4	80.7	83.7	83.7	40	50	30	29	69.0
86	Samoa	59.5	n/a	61.5	70	86.2	56.2	75.7	30	30	60	45	80.2
87	Guatemala	59.4	–0.4	54.1	78.4	79.4	93.5	73.3	50	50	30	28	57.3
88	Dominican Republic	59.2	1.5	63.7	73	85.3	91.1	74.1	50	40	30	30	55.1
89	Swaziland	59.1	0.6	68.6	71.6	64.3	70.6	73.1	50	40	50	33	69.6
90	Kenya	58.7	–0.6	66.9	71.8	78.6	81.5	74.0	50	50	30	21	63.1

91	Honduras	58.7	−0.2	64.4	78	85.1	79.7	73.5	50	60	30	25	40.9
92	Vanuatu	58.4	n/a	69.0	63	95.3	84.0	78.7	30	40	40	31	52.6
93	Tanzania	58.3	1.8	48.1	75.6	80.6	83.4	73.4	60	50	30	32	49.9
94	Montenegro	58.2	n/a	68.7	80.2	89.1	45.3	78.9	40	50	40	33	57.2
95	Lebanon	58.1	−1.9	60.0	80.8	91.7	64.1	77.3	30	60	30	30	57.4
96	Ghana	58.1	1.0	56.7	63	83.2	65.7	69.6	50	60	50	37	45.3
97	Egypt	58.0	−0.5	64.7	63.4	89.5	66.1	65.9	50	50	40	29	61.3
98	Tunisia	58.0	−2.1	81.6	53	76.5	78.3	78.4	30	30	50	42	60.1
99	Azerbaijan	58.0	2.6	74.6	78.4	79.7	77.5	66.3	30	40	25	21	87.0
100	Bhutan	57.7	n/a	61.7	42	83.6	58.3	75.9	30	30	60	50	85.8
101	Morocco	57.7	2.1	76.2	68	65.1	76.5	80.5	60	50	35	35	30.8
102	Pakistan	57.0	1.4	72.5	65.6	80.4	90.7	72.2	40	40	30	24	54.5
103	Yemen	56.9	3.1	74.9	76.2	83.2	57.1	66.5	50	30	30	25	75.8
104	The Philippines	56.8	0.8	49.3	78.6	75.4	90.8	77.2	40	50	30	25	51.4
105	Brazil	56.7	0.5	54.4	71.6	65.8	50.3	77.2	50	50	50	35	62.7
106	Cambodia	56.6	0.8	42.7	63.4	91.4	94.5	80.0	50	50	30	20	44.5
107	Algeria	56.6	0.4	72.5	68.6	77.2	74.1	78.6	50	30	30	30	55.5
108	Zambia	56.6	0.4	68.8	71.2	72.9	82.1	64.1	50	50	30	26	51.0
109	Serbia	56.6	n/a	56.0	78	85.9	46.3	65.8	40	50	40	34	70.0
110	Senegal	56.3	−2.0	65.0	71.2	65.1	77.0	76.5	40	40	50	36	42.5
111	Sri Lanka	56.0	−2.4	73.7	71	73.2	80.5	59.4	20	40	40	32	70.8
112	The Gambia	55.8	−11	59.9	59.6	71.9	74.4	71.9	50	50	30	23	67.0
113	Mozambique	55.7	0.2	54.2	73.4	77.7	76.5	75.9	50	50	30	28	41.1
114	Mali	55.6	0.1	42.2	73	69.4	81.4	79.6	50	40	30	27	63.8
115	Benin	55.4	0.1	43.8	67.4	67.2	88.5	79.6	40	60	30	27	50.3
116	Croatia	55.1	1.0	59.9	87.6	68.7	31.7	79.0	50	60	30	41	43.4
117	Nigeria	55.1	0.0	55.1	61.8	84.4	64.3	77.9	30	40	30	22	85.8
118	Gabon	55.0	0.9	59.9	57	61.7	84.8	73.8	40	40	40	33	60.0
119	Côte d'Ivoire	55.0	1.0	45.8	70.4	58.1	87.6	79.1	40	60	30	21	57.8
120	Moldova	54.9	−3.0	70.1	81.6	85.3	51.3	67.6	30	50	40	28	45.1
121	Papua New Guinea	54.8	n/a	60.1	87.2	67.4	71.0	81.4	30	30	20	20	81.1
122	Tajikistan	54.6	0.2	45.1	82.6	89.3	85.9	63.2	30	40	30	21	58.7

(Continued)

TABLE 5.1 Cont.

World rank	Country	Overall score	Change from 2008	Business freedom	Trade freedom	Fiscal freedom	Government size	Monetary freedom	Investment freedom	Financial freedom	Property rights	Freedom from corruption	Labor freedom
123	India	54.4	0.3	54.4	51	73.8	77.8	69.3	30	40	50	35	62.3
124	Rwanda	54.2	0.0	58.9	61.2	76.8	76.8	70.8	40	40	30	28	59.5
125	Suriname	54.1	–0,2	41.5	64.2	67.7	75.5	72.2	30	30	40	35	84.8
126	Tonga	54.1	n/a	79.0	56	82.5	58.0	68.9	40	20	20	17	99.4
127	Mauritania	53.9	–1.2	53.6	75.6	75.4	65.9	77.7	50	40	25	26	502
128	Niger	53.8	1.0	36.9	70.4	66.3	88.8	89.5	50	40	30	26	40.6
129	Malawi	53.7	11	45.2	68.8	70.7	48.6	69.8	50	50	50	27	57.2
130	Bolivia	53.6	0.5	58.5	81.8	84.8	71.9	67.9	20	60	20	29	41.9
131	Indonesia	53.4	0.2	46.7	76.4	77.5	88.0	71.6	30	40	30	23	50.9
132	China	53.2	0.1	51.6	71.4	70.6	88.9	72.9	30	30	20	35	61.8
133	Nepal	53.2	–0.9	60.5	63.2	86.3	91.0	78.7	20	30	30	25	46.9
134	Bosnia and Herzegorine Herzegovina	53.1	–0.8	59.9	77.2	71.8	37.6	79.0	50	60	10	33	52.1
135	Ethiopia	53.0	0.5	62.6	68.6	77.4	82.7	65.5	40	20	30	24	59.4
136	Cameroon	53.0	–1.3	39.3	56	69.6	93.6	76.0	40	50	30	24	51.5
137	Ecuador	52.5	–2.8	54.0	72.6	85.8	83.1	75.0	30	40	25	21	38.3
138	Argentina	52.3	–1.8	62.1	70	70.3	75.6	60.6	50	40	20	29	45.6
139	Micronesia	51.7	n/a	59.8	81	97.4	0.0	76.7	30	30	30	30	82.3
140	Djibouti	51.3	0.1	38.1	31.8	80.8	59.4	76.6	50	60	30	29	57.9
141	Syria	51.3	4.2	61.4	54	87.0	74.9	67.2	40	20	30	24	54.9
142	Equatorial Guinea	51.3	–0.3	45.7	59.4	75.5	86.3	81.4	30	40	30	19	46.1
143	Maldives	51.3	n/a	83.2	44	95.8	0.0	76.5	30	30	30	33	90.1
144	Guinea	510	–1.8	45.2	59.6	711	91.9	57.4	40	40	20	19	66.3
145	Vietnam	51.0	0.6	61.7	63.4	74.3	77.3	67	30	30	10	26	70.0
146	Russia	50.8	1.0	54.0	608	78.9	706	65.5	30	40	25	23	60.0
147	Haiti	50.5	1.5	37.7	79.4	77.9	93.8	69.0	30	30	10	16	61.2
148	Uzbekistan	50.5	–l.4	68.4	65.4	88.3	68.1	62.6	30	20	20	17	64.9
149	Timor–Leste	50.5	n/a	47.0	73	64.7	84.0	74.1	30	20	20	26	66.0
150	Laos	50.4	0.1	59.5	66.4	70.6	89.7	75.4	30	20	10	19	63.5
151	Lesotho	49.7	–2.5	61.7	57	63.1	36.2	73.1	30	40	40	33	62.7

152	Ukraine	48.8	−2.2	40.5	84	77.0	39.0	68.1	30	40	30	27	52.4
153	Burundi	48.8	2.6	34.4	63	72.5	55.8	72.7	40	30	30	25	64.3
154	Togo	48.7	−0.2	36.6	70.6	53.7	86.6	81.5	30	30	30	23	44.7
155	Guyana	48.4	−0.4	60.9	72.6	66.5	3.2	69.6	40	40	40	26	65.2
156	Central African Republic	48.3	−0.3	39.5	50.4	65.4	94.0	75.0	40	30	20	20	48.7
157	Liberia	48.1	n/a	40.2	53.8	73.8	97.2	70.1	30	20	25	21	49.8
158	Sierra Leone	47.8	−0.5	57.0	66	80.9	86.3	73.8	30	20	10	21	33.4
159	Seychelles	47.8	n/a	65.5	28.4	73.8	0.0	78.1	50	30	50	45	57.1
160	Bangladesh	47.5	3.3	62.9	40.2	72.8	94.2	67.3	20	20	25	20	52.3
161	Chad	47.5	−0.4	35.7	58.4	50.5	90.8	78.6	40	40	20	18	42.6
162	Angola	47.0	0.1	43.6	72	85.2	62.2	61.8	20	40	20	22	43.5
163	Solomon Islands	46.0	n/a	67.2	66.4	68.9	0.0	73.5	20	30	30	28	76.3
164	Kiribati	45.7	n/a	62.5	55	42.2	0.0	88.7	30	30	30	33	85.6
165	Guinea–Bissau	45.4	1.1	24.2	66.8	88.4	49.1	73.5	30	30	20	22	50.5
166	Republic of Congo	45.4	0.0	50.1	55.4	60.2	77.6	73.9	30	30	10	21	45.6
167	Belarus	45.0	−0.4	63.7	67.2	79.4	30.9	66.8	20	10	20	21	70.8
168	Iran	44.6	−0.4	60.6	57.4	810	79.7	60.1	10	10	10	25	52.4
169	Turkmenistan	44.2	0.8	30.0	79.2	90.9	93.6	68	10	10	10	20	30.0
170	Sao Tome and Principe	43.8	n/a	45.1	60	75.0	22.0	61.4	40	30	30	27	48.0
171	Libya	43.5	4.8	20.0	90	81.7	68.1	70.3	30	20	10	25	20.0
172	Comoros	43.3	n/a	46.5	27.2	64.6	88.1	78.9	20	20	30	26	31.8
173	Democratic Republic of Congo	42.8	n/a	34.3	62.2	73.3	85.3	59.5	30	20	10	19	34.5
174	Venezuela	39.9	−4.8	50.8	59.6	70.6	69.3	53.7	10	30	5	20	30.1
175	Eritrea	38.5	n/a	18.3	69.2	86.4	9.9	59.0	10	20	10	28	73.9
176	Burma	37.7	−18	20.0	72.2	81.8	98.5	45.3	10	10	5	14	20.0
177	Cuba	27.9	0.4	10.0	64.4	45.9	0.0	67.0	10	10	10	42	20.0
178	Zimbabwe	22.7	−6.7	30.8	50.4	44.1	4.6	0	10	10	5	21	51.2
179	North Korea	2.0	−1.0	0.0	00	0.0	0.0	0.0	10	0	5	5	0.0
n/a	Afghanistan	n/a	n/a	n/a	n/a	n/a	n/a	n/a	n/a	n/a	n/a	n/a	n/a
n/a	Iraq	n/a	n/a	n/a	n/a	n/a	n/a	n/a	n/a	n/a	n/a	n/a	n/a
n/a	Liechtenstein	n/a	n/a	n/a	n/a	n/a	n/a	n/a	n/a	n/a	n/a	n/a	n/a
n/a	Sudan	n/a	n/a	n/a	n/a	n/a	n/a	n/a	n/a	n/a	n/a	n/a	n/a

Source: Adapted from Terry Miller and Kim R. Holmes, ***2009 Index of Economic*** Freedom (Washington, DC: The Heritage Foundation and Dow Jones & Company, Inc., 2009), at www.heritage.org/index.

TABLE 5.2 The Country Ranking According to the Index of Economic Freedom, 1995–2009

Country	*1995*	*1996*	*1997*	*1998*	*1999*	*2000*	*2001*	*2002*	*2003*	*2004*	*2005*	*2006*	*2007*	*2008*	*2009*
Afghanistan	n/a	n/a	n/a	n/a	n/a	n/a	n/a	n/a	n/a	n/a	n/a	n/a	n/a	n/a	n/a
Albania	49.7	53.8	54.8	53.9	53.4	53.6	56.6	56.8	56.8	58.5	57.8	60.3	61.4	62.4	63.7
Algeria	55.7	54.5	54.9	55.8	57.2	56.8	57.3	61.0	57.7	58.1	53.2	55.7	55.4	56.2	56.6
Angola	27.4	24.4	24.2	24.9	23.7	24.3	n/a	n/a	n/a	n/a	n/a	43.5	44.7	46.9	47.0
Argentina	68.0	74.7	73.3	70.9	70.6	70.0	68.6	65.7	56.3	53.9	51.7	53.4	54.0	54.2	52.3
Armenia	n/a	42.2	46.7	49.6	56.4	63.0	66.4	68.0	67.3	70.3	69.8	70.6	68.6	69.9	69.9
Australia	74.1	74.0	75.5	75.6	76.4	77.1	77.4	77.3	77.4	77.9	79.0	79.9	81.1	82.2	82.6
Austria	70.0	68.9	65.2	65.4	64.0	68.4	68.1	67.4	67.6	67.6	68.8	71.1	71.6	71.4	71.2
Azerbaijan	n/a	30.0	34.0	43.1	47.4	49.8	50.3	53.3	54.1	53.4	54.4	53.2	54.6	55.3	58.0
Bahamas	71.8	74.0	74.5	74.5	74.7	73.9	74.8	74.4	73.5	72.1	72.6	72.3	72.0	71.1	70.3
Bahrain	76.2	76.4	76.1	75.6	75.2	75.7	75.9	75.6	76.3	75.1	71.2	71.6	71.2	72.2	74.8
Bangladesh	38.7	51.1	49.9	52.0	50.0	48.9	51.2	51.9	49.3	50.0	47.5	52.9	46.7	44.2	47.5
Barbados	n/a	62.3	64.5	67.9	66.7	69.5	71.5	73.6	71.3	69.4	70.1	71.9	70.0	71.3	71.5
Belarus	40.4	38.7	39.8	38.0	35.4	41.3	38.0	39.0	39.7	43.1	46.7	47.5	47.0	45.3	45.0
Belgium	n/a	66.0	64.6	64.7	62.9	63.5	63.8	67.6	68.1	68.7	69.0	71.8	72.5	71.7	72.1
Belize	62.9	61.6	64.3	59.1	60.7	63.3	65.9	65.6	63.5	62.8	64.5	64.7	63.3	63.0	63.0
Benin	n/a	54.5	61.3	61.7	60.6	61.5	60.1	57.3	54.9	54.6	52.3	54.0	55.1	55.2	55.4
Bhutan	n/a	n/a	n/a	n/a	n/a	n/a	n/a	n/a	n/a	n/a	n/a	n/a	n/a	n/a	57.7
Bolivia	56.8	65.2	65.1	68.8	65.6	65.0	68.0	65.1	64.3	64.5	58.4	57.8	54.2	53.1	53.6
Bosnia and Herzegovina	n/a	n/a	n/a	29.4	29.4	45.1	36.6	37.4	40.6	44.7	48.8	55.6	54.4	53.9	53.1
Botswana	56.8	61.6	59.1	62.8	62.9	65.8	66.8	66.2	68.6	69.9	69.3	68.8	68.1	68.2	69.7
Brazil	51.4	48.1	52.6	52.3	61.3	61.1	61.9	61.5	63.4	62.0	61.7	60.9	56.2	56.2	56.7
Bulgaria	50.0	48.6	47.6	45.7	46.2	47.3	51.9	57.1	57.0	59.2	62.3	64.1	62.7	63.7	64.6
Burkina Faso	n/a	49.4	54.0	54.5	55.0	55.7	56.7	58.8	58.9	58.0	56.6	55.8	55.1	55.7	59.5
Burma	n/a	45.1	45.4	45.7	46.4	47.9	46.1	45.5	44.9	43.6	40.5	40.0	41.0	39.5	37.7
Burundi	n/a	n/a	45.4	44.7	41.1	42.6	n/a	n/a	n/a	n/a	n/a	48.7	46.9	46.2	48.8
Cambodia	n/a	n/a	52.8	59.8	59.9	59.3	59.6	60.7	63.7	61.1	60.0	56.7	55.9	55.9	56.6
Cameroon	51.3	45.7	44.6	48.0	50.3	49.9	53.3	52.8	52.7	52.3	53.0	54.6	55.6	54.3	53.0
Canada	69.4	70.3	67.9	68.5	69.3	70.5	71.2	74.6	74.8	75.3	75.8	77.4	78.0	80.2	80.5
Cape Verde	n/a	49.7	47.7	48.0	50.7	51.9	56.3	57.6	56.1	58.1	57.8	58.6	56.5	57.9	61.3

Central African Republic	n/a	n/a	n/a	n/a	n/a	n/a	n/a	59.8	60.0	57.5	56.5	54.2	50.6	48.6	48.3
Chad	n/a	n/a	45.1	46.6	47.2	46.8	46.4	49.2	52.6	53.1	52.1	50.0	50.1	47.8	47.5
Chile	71.2	72.6	75.9	74.9	74.1	74.7	75.1	77.8	76.0	76.9	77.8	78.0	77.7	78.6	78.3
China	52.0	51.3	51.7	53.1	54.8	56.4	52.6	52.8	52.6	52.5	53.7	53.6	52.0	53.1	53.2
Colombia	64.5	64.3	66.4	65.5	65.3	63.3	65.6	64.2	64.2	61.2	59.6	60.4	59.9	62.2	62.3
Comoros	n/a	n/a	n/a	n/a	n/a	n/a	n/a	n/a	n/a	n/a	n/a	n/a	n/a	n/a	43.3
Congo, Demo. Republic of	41.4	39.5	39.5	40.6	34.0	34.8	n/a	n/a	n/a	n/a	n/a	n/a	n/a	n/a	42.8
Congo, Republic of	n/a	40.3	42.2	33.8	41.6	40.6	44.3	45.3	47.7	45.9	46.2	43.8	44.4	45.3	45.4
Costa Rica	68.0	66.4	65.6	65.6	67.4	68.4	67.6	67.5	67.0	66.4	66.1	65.9	64.0	64.2	66.4
Cote d'Ivoire	53.4	49.9	50.5	51.3	51.7	50.2	54.8	57.3	56.7	57.8	56.6	56.2	54.9	53.9	55.0
Croatia	n/a	48.0	46.7	51.7	53.1	53.6	50.7	51.1	53.3	53.1	51.9	53.6	53.4	54.1	55.1
Cuba	27.8	27.8	27.8	28.2	29.7	31.3	31.6	32.4	35.1	34.4	35.5	29.3	28.6	27.5	27.9
Cyprus	n/a	67.7	67.9	68.2	67.8	67.2	71.0	73.0	73.3	74.1	71.9	71.8	71.7	71.3	70.8
Czech Republic	67.8	68.1	68.8	68.4	69.7	68.6	70.2	66.5	67.5	67.0	64.6	66.4	67.4	68.1	69.4
Denmark	n/a	67.3	67.5	67.5	68.1	68.3	68.3	71.1	73.2	72.4	75.3	75.4	77.0	79.2	79.6
Djibouti	n/a	n/a	54.5	55.9	57.1	55.1	58.3	57.8	55.7	55.6	55.2	53.2	52.4	51.2	51.3
Dominica	n/a	n/a	n/a	n/a	n/a	n/a	n/a	n/a	n/a	n/a	n/a	n/a	n/a	n/a	62.6
Dominican Republic	55.8	58.1	53.5	58.1	58.1	59.0	59.1	58.6	57.8	54.6	55.1	56.3	56.8	57.7	59.2
Ecuador	57.7	60.1	61.0	62.8	62.9	59.8	55.1	53.1	54.1	54.4	52.9	54.6	55.3	55.2	52.5
Egypt	45.7	52.0	54.5	55.8	58.0	517	51.5	54.1	55.3	55.5	55.8	53.2	54.4	58.5	58.0
El Salvador	69.1	70.1	70.5	70.2	75.1	76.3	73.0	73.0	71.5	71.2	71.5	69.6	68.9	68.5	69.8
Equatorial Guinea	n/a	n/a	n/a	n/a	45.1	45.6	47.9	46.4	53.1	53.3	53.3	51.5	53.2	51.6	51.3
Eritrea	n/a	n/a	n/a	n/a	n/a	n/a	n/a	n/a	n/a	n/a	n/a	n/a	n/a	n/a	38.5
Estonia	65.2	65.4	69.1	72.5	73.8	69.9	76.1	77.6	77.7	77.4	75.2	74.9	78.0	77.9	76.4
Ethiopia	42.6	45.9	48.1	49.2	46.7	50.2	48.9	49.8	48.8	54.5	51.1	50.9	53.6	52.5	53.0
Fiji	54.7	57.4	58.0	58.2	58.4	57.8	53.7	53.9	54.7	58.0	58.2	58.4	60.8	61.8	61.0
Finland	n/a	63.7	65.2	63.5	63.9	64.3	69.7	73.6	73.7	73.4	71.0	72.9	74.0	74.6	74.5
France	64.4	63.7	59.1	58.9	59.1	57.4	58.0	58.0	59.2	60.9	60.5	61.1	62.1	64.7	63.3
Gabon	57.5	55.7	58.8	59.2	60.5	58.2	55.0	58.0	58.7	57.1	54.8	56.1	54.8	54.2	55.0
The Gambia	n/a	n/a	52.9	53.4	52.1	52.7	56.6	577	56.3	55.3	56.5	57.3	577	56.9	55.8
Georgia	n/a	44.1	46.5	47.9	52.5	54.3	58.3	56.7	58.6	58.9	57.1	64.5	69.3	69.2	69.8
Germany	69.8	69.1	67.5	64.3	65.6	65.7	69.5	70.4	69.7	69.5	68.1	70.8	70.8	70.6	70.5

(Continued)

TABLE 5.2 Cont.

Country	*1995*	*1996*	*1997*	*1998*	*1999*	*2000*	*2001*	*2002*	*2003*	*2004*	*2005*	*2006*	*2007*	*2008*	*2009*
Ghana	55.6	577	56.7	57.0	59.4	58.1	58.0	57.2	58.2	59.1	56.5	55.6	57.6	57.0	58.1
Greece	61.2	60.5	59.6	60.6	61.0	61.0	63.4	59.1	58.8	59.1	59.0	60.1	58.7	60.6	60.8
Guatemala	62.0	63.7	65.7	65.8	66.2	64.3	65.1	62.3	62.3	59.6	59.5	59.1	60.5	59.8	59.4
Guinea	59.4	58.5	52.9	61.0	59.4	58.2	58.4	52.9	54.6	56.1	57.4	52.8	54.5	52.8	51.0
Guinea-Bissau	n/a	n/a	n/a	n/a	33.5	34.7	42.5	42.3	43.1	42.6	46.0	46.5	46.1	44.4	45.4
Guyana	45.7	50.1	53.2	52.7	53.3	52.4	53.3	54.3	50.3	53.0	56.5	56.6	53.7	48.8	48.4
Haiti	43.0	41.0	45.8	45.7	45.9	45.7	47.1	47.9	50.6	51.2	48.4	49.2	51.4	49.0	50.5
Honduras	57.0	56.6	56.0	56.2	56.7	57.6	57.0	58.7	60.4	55.3	55.3	57.4	59.1	58.9	58.7
Hong Kong	88.6	90.5	88.6	88.0	88.5	89.5	89.9	89.4	89.8	90.0	89.5	88.6	89.9	89.7	90.0
Hungary	55.2	56.8	55.3	56.9	59.6	64.4	65.6	64.5	63.0	62.7	63.5	65.0	64.8	67.6	66.8
Iceland	n/a	n/a	70.5	71.2	71.4	74.0	73.4	73.1	73.5	72.1	76.6	75.8	76.0	75.8	75.9
India	45.1	47.4	49.7	49.7	50.2	47.4	49.0	51.2	51.2	51.5	54.2	52.2	53.9	54.1	54.4
Indonesia	54.9	61.0	62.0	63.4	61.5	55.2	52.5	54.8	55.8	52.1	52.9	51.9	53.2	53.2	53.4
Iran	n/a	36.1	34.5	36.0	36.8	36.1	35.9	36.4	43.2	42.8	50.5	45.0	45.0	45.0	44.6
Iraq	n/a	17.2	17.2	17.2	17.2	17.2	17.2	15.6	n/a	n/a	n/a	n/a	n/a	n/a	n/a
Ireland	68.5	68.5	72.6	73.7	74.6	76.1	81.2	80.5	80.9	80.3	80.8	82.2	82.6	82.5	82.2
Israel	61.5	62.0	62.7	68.0	68.3	65.5	66.1	66.9	62.7	61.4	62.6	64.4	64.8	66.3	67.6
Italy	61.2	60.8	58.1	59.1	61.6	61.9	63.0	63.6	64.3	64.2	64.9	62.0	62.8	62.6	61.4
Jamaica	64.4	66.7	67.7	67.1	64.7	65.5	63.7	61.7	67.0	66.7	67.0	66.4	65.5	65.7	65.2
Japan	75.0	72.6	70.3	70.2	69.1	70.7	70.9	66.7	67.6	64.3	67.3	73.3	72.7	73.0	72.8
Jordan	62.7	60.8	63.6	66.8	67.4	67.5	68.3	66.2	65.3	66.1	66.7	63.7	64.5	64.1	65.4
Kazakhstan	n/a	n/a	n/a	41.7	47.3	50.4	51.8	52.4	52.3	49.7	53.9	60.2	59.6	61.1	60.1
Kenya	54.5	56.4	60.1	58.4	58.2	59.7	57.6	58.2	58.6	57.7	57.9	59.7	59.6	59.3	58.7
Kiribati	n/a	n/a	n/a	n/a	n/a	n/a	n/a	n/a	n/a	n/a	n/a	n/a	n/a	n/a	45.7
Korea, North	8.9	8.9	8.9	8.9	8.9	8.9	8.9	8.9	8.9	8.9	8.0	4.0	3.0	3.0	2.0
Korea, South	72.0	73.0	69.8	73.3	69.7	69.7	69.1	69.5	68.3	67.8	66.4	67.5	67.8	68.6	68.1
Kuwait	n/a	66.1	64.8	66.3	69.5	69.7	68.2	65.4	66.7	63.6	64.6	66.5	66.4	68.1	65.6
Kyrgyz Republic	n/a	n/a	n/a	51.8	54.8	55.7	53.7	51.7	56.8	58.0	56.6	61.0	60.2	61.1	61.8
Laos	n/a	38.5	35.1	35.2	35.2	36.8	33.5	36.8	41.0	42.0	44.4	47.5	50.3	50.3	50.4
Latvia	n/a	55.0	62.4	63.4	64.2	63.4	66.4	65.0	66.0	67.4	66.3	66.9	67.9	68.3	66.6
Lebanon	n/a	63.2	63.9	59.0	59.1	56.1	61.0	57.1	56.7	56.9	57.2	57.5	60.4	60.0	58.1

Lesotho	n/a	47.0	47.2	48.4	48.2	48.4	50.6	48.9	52.0	50.3	53.9	54.7	53.2	52.1	49.7
Liberia	n/a	n/a	n/a	n/a	n/a	n/a	n/a	n/a	n/a	n/a	n/a	n/a	n/a	n/a	48.1
Libya	n/a	31.7	28.9	32.0	32.3	34.7	34.0	35.4	34.6	31.5	32.8	33.2	37.0	38.7	43.5
Liechtenstein	n/a	n/a	n/a	n/a	n/a	n/a	n/a	n/a	n/a	n/a	n/a	n/a	n/a	n/a	n/a
Lithuania	n/a	49.7	57.3	59.4	61.5	61.9	65.5	66.1	69.7	72.4	70.5	71.8	71.5	70.9	70.0
Luxembourg	n/a	72.5	72.8	72.7	72.4	76.4	80.1	79.4	79.9	78.9	76.3	75.3	74.6	74.7	75.2
Macau	n/a	n/a	n/a	n/a	n/a	n/a	n/a	n/a	n/a	n/a	n/a	n/a	n/a	n/a	72.0
Macedonia	n/a	n/a	n/a	n/a	n/a	n/a	n/a	58.0	60.1	56.8	56.1	59.2	60.6	61.1	61.2
Madagascar	51.6	52.2	53.8	51.8	52.8	54.4	53.9	56.8	62.8	60.9	63.1	61.0	61.1	62.4	62.2
Malawi	54.7	56.2	53.4	54.1	54.0	57.4	56.2	56.9	53.2	53.6	53.6	55.4	52.9	52.7	53.7
Malaysia	71.9	69.9	66.8	68.2	68.9	66.0	60.2	60.1	61.1	59.9	61.9	61.6	63.8	63.9	64.6
Maldives	n/a	n/a	n/a	n/a	n/a	n/a	n/a	n/a	n/a	n/a	n/a	n/a	n/a	n/a	51.3
Mali	52.4	57.0	56.4	57.3	58.4	60.3	60.1	61.1	58.6	56.6	57.3	54.1	54.7	55.6	55.6
Malta	56.3	55.8	57.9	61.2	59.3	58.3	62.9	62.2	61.1	63.3	68.9	67.3	66.1	66.0	66.1
Mauritania	n/a	45.5	47.0	43.7	42.8	46.0	48.5	52.5	59.0	61.8	59.4	55.7	53.6	55.2	53.9
Mauritius	n/a	n/a	n/a	n/a	68.5	67.2	66.4	67.7	64.4	64.3	67.2	67.4	69.4	72.6	74.3
Mexico	63.1	61.2	57.1	57.9	58.5	59.3	60.6	63.0	65.3	66.0	65.2	64.7	66.0	66.2	65.8
Micronesia	n/a	n/a	n/a	n/a	n/a	n/a	n/a	n/a	n/a	n/a	n/a	n/a	n/a	n/a	51.7
Moldova	33.0	52.5	48.9	53.5	56.1	59.6	54.9	57.4	60.0	57.1	57.4	58.0	58.7	57.9	54.9
Mongolia	47.8	47.4	52.9	57.3	58.6	58.5	56.0	56.7	57.7	56.5	59.7	62.4	60.3	63.6	62.8
Montenegro	n/a	n/a	n/a	n/a	n/a	n/a	n/a	46.6*	43.5*	n/a	n/a	n/a	n/a	n/a	58.2
Morocco	62.8	64.3	64.7	61.1	63.8	63.2	63.9	59.0	57.8	56.7	52.2	51.5	56.4	55.6	57.7
Mozambique	45.5	48.4	44.0	43.0	48.9	52.2	59.2	57.7	58.6	57.2	54.6	51.9	54.7	55.4	55.7
Namibia	n/a	n/a	61.6	66.1	66.1	66.7	64.8	65.1	67.3	62.4	61.4	60.7	63.5	61.4	62.4
Nepal	n/a	50.3	53.6	53.5	53.1	51.3	51.6	52.3	51.5	51.2	51.4	53.7	54.4	54.1	53.2
Netherlands	n/a	69.7	70.4	69.2	63.6	70.4	73.0	75.1	74.6	74.5	72.9	75.4	75.5	77.4	77.0
New Zealand	n/a	78.1	79.0	79.2	81.7	80.9	811	80.7	811	81.5	82.3	82.0	81.4	78.6	82.0
Nicaragua	42.5	54.1	53.3	53.8	54.0	56.9	58.0	61.1	62.6	61.4	62.5	63.8	62.7	60.8	59.8
Niger	n/a	45.8	46.6	47.5	48.6	45.9	48.9	48.2	54.2	54.6	54.1	52.5	53.2	52.9	53.8
Nigeria	47.3	47.4	52.8	52.3	55.7	53.1	49.6	50.9	49.5	49.2	48.4	48.7	55.6	55.1	55.1
Norway	n/a	65.4	65.1	68.0	68.6	70.1	67.1	67.4	67.2	66.2	64.5	67.9	67.9	68.6	70.2
Oman	70.2	65.4	64.5	64.9	64.9	64.1	67.7	64.0	64.6	66.9	66.5	63.7	65.8	67.3	67.0

(Continued)

TABLE 5.2 Cont.

Country	*1995*	*1996*	*1997*	*1998*	*1999*	*2000*	*2001*	*2002*	*2003*	*2004*	*2005*	*2006*	*2007*	*2008*	*2009*
Pakistan	57.6	58.4	56.0	53.2	53.0	56.4	56.0	55.8	55.0	54.9	53.3	57.9	57.2	55.6	57.0
Panama	71.6	71.8	72.4	72.6	72.6	71.6	70.6	68.5	68.4	65.3	64.3	65.6	64.6	64.7	64.7
Papua New Guinea	n/a	58.6	56.7	55.2	56.3	55.8	57.2	n/a	n/a	n/a	n/a	n/a	n/a	n/a	54.8
Paraguay	659	67.1	67.3	65.2	63.7	64.0	60.3	59.6	58.2	56.7	53.4	55.6	58.3	60.0	61.0
Peru	56.9	62.5	63.8	65.0	69.2	68.7	69.6	64.8	64.6	64.7	61.3	60.5	62.7	63.8	64.6
The Philippines	55.0	60.2	62.2	62.8	61.9	62.5	60.9	60.7	61.3	59.1	54.7	56.3	56.0	56.0	56.8
Poland	50.7	57.8	56.8	59.2	59.6	60.0	61.8	65.0	61.8	58.7	59.6	59.3	58.1	60.3	60.3
Portugal	62.4	64.5	63.6	65.0	65.6	65.5	66.0	65.4	64.9	64.9	62.4	62.9	64.0	63.9	64.9
Qatar	n/a	n/a	n/a	n/a	62.0	62.0	60.0	61.9	65.9	66.5	63.5	62.4	62.9	62.2	65.8
Romania	42.9	46.2	50.8	54.4	50.1	52.1	50.0	48.7	50.6	50.0	52.1	58.2	61.2	61.7	63.2
Russia	51.1	51.6	48.6	52.8	54.5	51.8	49.8	48.7	50.8	52.8	51.3	52.4	52.2	49.8	50.8
Rwanda	n/a	n/a	38.3	39.1	39.8	42.3	45.4	50.4	47.8	53.3	51.7	52.8	52.4	54.2	54.2
Saint Lucia	n/a	n/a	n/a	n/a	n/a	n/a	n/a	n/a	n/a	n/a	n/a	n/a	n/a	n/a	68.8
Saint Vincent and the Grenadines	n/a	n/a	n/a	n/a	n/a	n/a	n/a	n/a	n/a	n/a	n/a	n/a	n/a	n/a	64.3
Samoa	n/a	47.6	51.5	49.9	58.7	60.8	63.1	n/a	n/a	n/a	n/a	n/a	n/a	n/a	59.5
Sao Tome and Principe	n/a	n/a	n/a	n/a	n/a	n/a	n/a	n/a	n/a	n/a	n/a	n/a	n/a	n/a	43.8
Saudi Arabia	n/a	68.3	68.7	69.3	65.5	66.5	62.2	65.3	63.2	60.4	63.0	63.0	60.9	62.5	64.3
Senegal	n/a	58.2	58.1	59.7	60.6	58.9	58.7	58.6	58.1	58.9	57.9	56.2	58.1	58.3	56.3
Serbia	n/a	n/a	n/a	n/a	n/a	n/a	n/a	46.6*	43.5*	n/a	n/a	n/a	n/a	n/a	56.6
Seychelles	n/a	n/a	n/a	n/a	n/a	n/a	n/a	n/a	n/a	n/a	n/a	n/a	n/a	n/a	47.8
Sierra Leone	49.8	52.3	45.0	47.7	47.2	44.2	n/a	n/a	42.2	43.6	44.8	45.2	47.0	48.3	47.8
Singapore	86.3	86.5	87.3	87.0	86.9	87.7	87.8	87.4	88.2	88.9	88.6	88.0	87.1	87.3	87.1
Slovak Republic	60.4	57.6	55.5	57.5	54.2	53.8	58.5	59.8	59.0	64.6	66.8	69.8	69.6	70.0	69.4
Slovenia	n/a	50.4	55.6	60.7	61.3	58.3	61.8	57.8	57.7	59.2	59.6	61.9	59.6	60.2	62.9
Solomon Islands	n/a	n/a	n/a	n/a	n/a	n/a	n/a	n/a	n/a	n/a	n/a	n/a	n/a	n/a	46.0
South Africa	60.7	62.5	63.2	64.3	63.3	63.7	63.8	64.0	67.1	66.3	62.9	63.7	63.5	63.4	63.8
Spain	62.8	59.6	59.6	62.6	65.1	65.9	68.1	68.8	68.8	68.9	67.0	68.2	69.2	69.1	70.1
Sri Lanka	60.6	62.5	65.5	64.6	64.0	63.2	66.0	64.0	62.5	61.6	61.0	58.7	59.4	58.4	56.0
Sudan	39.4	39.2	39.9	38.3	39.6	47.2	n/a	n/a	n/a	n/a	n/a	n/a	n/a	n/a	n/a

Suriname	n/a	36.7	35.9	39.9	40.1	45.8	44.3	48.0	46.9	47.9	51.9	55.1	54.8	54.3	54.1
Swaziland	63.3	58.6	59.4	62.0	62.1	62.6	63.6	60.9	59.6	58.6	59.4	61.4	60.1	58.4	59.1
Sweden	61.4	61.8	63.3	64.0	64.2	65.1	66.6	70.8	70.0	70.1	69.8	70.9	69.3	70.8	70.5
Switzerland	n/a	76.8	786	79.0	79.1	76.8	76.0	79.3	79.0	79.5	79.3	78.9	78.0	79.5	79.4
Syria	n/a	42.3	43.0	42.2	39.0	37.2	36.6	36.3	41.3	40.6	46.3	51.2	48.3	47.2	51.3
Taiwan	74.2	74.1	70.0	70.4	71.5	72.5	72.8	71.3	71.7	69.6	71.3	69.7	69.4	70.3	69.5
Tajikistan	n/a	n/a	n/a	41.1	41.2	44.8	46.8	47.3	46.5	48.7	50.4	52.6	53.6	54.4	54.6
Tanzania	57.3	57.5	59.3	59.6	60.0	56.0	54.9	58.3	56.9	60.1	56.3	58.5	56.8	56.5	58.3
Thailand	71.3	71.0	66.1	67.3	66.9	66.6	68.9	69.1	65.8	63.7	62.5	63.3	63.5	62.3	63.0
Timor-Leste	n/a	n/a	n/a	n/a	n/a	n/a	n/a	n/a	n/a	n/a	n/a	n/a	n/a	n/a	50.5
Togo	n/a	n/a	n/a	n/a	48.2	46.4	45.3	45.2	46.8	47.0	48.2	47.3	49.7	48.9	48.7
Tonga	n/a	n/a	n/a	n/a	n/a	n/a	n/a	n/a	n/a	n/a	n/a	n/a	n/a	n/a	54.1
Trinidad and Tobago	n/a	69.2	71.3	72.0	72.4	74.5	71.8	70.1	68.8	71.3	71.5	70.4	70.6	69.5	68.0
Tunisia	63.4	63.9	63.8	63.9	61.1	61.3	60.8	60.2	58.1	58.4	55.4	57.5	60.3	60.1	58.0
Turkey	58.4	56.7	60.8	60.9	59.2	63.4	60.6	54.2	51.9	52.8	50.6	57.0	57.4	59.9	61.6
Turkmenistan	n/a	n/a	n/a	35.0	36.1	37.6	41.8	43.2	51.3	50.7	47.6	43.8	43.0	43.4	44.2
Uganda	62.9	66.2	66.6	64.7	64.8	58.2	60.4	61.0	60.1	64.1	62.9	63.9	63.1	63.8	63.5
Ukraine	39.9	40.6	43.5	40.4	43.7	47.8	48.5	48.2	51.1	53.7	55.8	54.4	51.5	51.0	48.8
United Arab Emirates	n/a	71.6	71.9	72.2	71.5	74.2	74.9	73.6	73.4	67.2	65.2	62.2	626	62.6	64.7
United Kingdom	77.9	76.4	76.4	76.5	76.2	77.3	77.6	78.5	77.5	77.7	79.2	80.4	79.9	79.4	79.0
United States	76.7	76.7	75.6	75.4	75.5	76.4	79.1	78.4	78.2	78.7	79.9	81.2	81.2	81.0	80.7
Uruguay	62.5	63.7	67.S	68.6	68.5	69.3	70.7	68.7	69.8	66.7	66.9	65.3	68.4	67.9	69.1
Uzbekistan	n/a	n/a	n/a	31.5	33.8	38.1	38.2	38.5	38.3	39.1	45.8	48.7	51.5	51.9	50.5
Vanuatu	n/a	n/a	n/a	n/a	n/a	n/a	n/a	n/a	n/a	n/a	n/a	n/a	n/a	n/a	58.4
Venezuela	59.8	54.5	52.8	54.0	56.1	57.4	54.6	54.7	54.8	46.7	45.2	44.6	47.9	44.7	39.9
Vietnam	41.7	40.2	38.6	40.4	42.7	43.7	44.3	45.6	46.2	46.1	48.1	50.5	49.8	50.4	51.0
Yemen	49.8	49.6	48.4	46.1	43.3	44.5	44.3	48.6	50.3	50.5	53.8	52.6	54.1	53.8	56.9
Zambia	55.1	59.6	62.1	62.7	64.2	62.8	59.5	59.6	55.3	54.9	55.0	56.8	56.2	56.2	56.6
Zimbabwe	48.5	46.7	48.0	44.6	47.2	48.7	38.8	36.7	36.7	34.4	35.2	33.5	32.0	29.5	22.7

*Note: Scores for "Serbia and Montenegro".

Source: Adapted from Terry Miller and Kim R. Holmes, *2009 Index of Economic Freedom* (Washington, DC: The Heritage Foundation and Dow Jones & Company, Inc., 2009), at www.heritage.org/index.

laws help maintain free competition and thus cause prices to be low to the benefit of the consumer. In short, governments in market economies try to prevent the creation of a *monopoly*, where one company controls the level of product or services supply, and thus controls prices. The anti-trust laws are enforced by government institutions, such as the Federal Trade Commission (FTC) in the USA or the Office of Fair Trading (OFT) in the UK.

The important role of governments in a market economy has become apparent during the global economic crisis. As the economic crisis deepened, calls for a greater control over capital markets' operations and over the compensations of senior executives that manage investment firms were voiced. As an example, the US government set an upper limit on the salary of executives of financial firms. In addition, governments are expected to protect personal property rights, including real assets such as land, and intellectual property. By securing personal property rights, the free market economy helps promote entrepreneurship, as the entrepreneur is sure to enjoy the fruits of the entrepreneurial initiatives.

Centrally planned economy

The centrally planned economy is prevalent in such countries as China, North Korea, and Cuba, and to a lesser degree in India. France, Brazil, the UK, and Canada may be positioned somewhere in the middle of a continuum between pure market economy and pure centrally planned economy. A centrally planned economic system consists of institutions and processes that allow the government to centrally allocate resources and conduct business activities. In a centrally planned economy the government owns all the land and other resources. All the decisions related to prices of raw materials, products and services, and allocation of capital are made by the government. A major assumption in a centrally planned economy is that the welfare of the group or the nation is more important than the welfare of the individual. The goal of these economic systems is to achieve specific social, economic, and political objectives through the government's complete control over the economic system, including production and distribution decisions. The central economic systems were adopted as an economic, social, and political solution to many problems that were haunting Europe around the turn of the 20th century. Revolutions that occurred in Russia, in 1917, in China and North Korea during the late 1940s and in Cuba in 1959 established totalitarian political systems along with centrally planned economic systems. By the late 1970s central planning was instituted in Albania, Bulgaria, Czechoslovakia, East Germany, Hungary, Poland, Romania, Yugoslavia, Cambodia, China, North Korea, Vietnam, Angola, Mozambique, Cuba, and Nicaragua.

From centrally planned economy to market economy

Major changes occurred in centrally planned economies towards the end of the last century, as market-based economies took hold in many of the former communist countries. There were several reasons for these changes. First, market economies had not delivered goods of sufficient value added and quality. Second, productivity of most stakeholders, citizens, workers, and scientists was generally lower in these countries, because of lack of financial incentives and entrepreneurial rewards. Lower productivity was prevalent in most of the manufacturing industries, resulting from backward production facilities, and leading to lower innovation rates and subsequently, a lower standard of living in communist countries such as Cuba, North Korea, and China. Third, emerging economies did achieve accelerated growth when private ownership and entrepreneurial initiatives were allowed, as has been the case for Singapore, Hong Kong, South Korea, and Taiwan.

The China case

China adopted the communist political system and a centrally planned economy in 1949. However, China's problems with a centrally planned economy were prevalent towards the end of the past century. China's population was poor, victims of economic failures, and structural conservatism. Towards the end of the last century, China decided to adopt capitalist modes of investment and competition. It has recognized the importance of science and technology as a foundation for national competitiveness and internalized the importance of nongovernmental international organizations such as the World Trade Organization (WTO), which it joined in 2008.

As of the first decade of the 21st century, Chinese economy has grown significantly from production of steel, automobiles, toys, textiles, and household appliances. By its own official accounts, the average growth of gross domestic product (GDP) is at an impressive average at 8.7 percent, and is bound to double every eight years. Some argue that the real growth rates are higher. However, this growth has many problems.

China has 1.3 billion people, out of which 300 million enjoy an acceptable standard of living, while about one billion Chinese citizens live in rural areas and are very poor. Corruption is widespread in provincial governments and in state-owned industries, within the Communist Party. The banking system seems to be close to collapse. Poverty is not confined to the countryside. It is also prevalent in Beijing. Pollution is pervasive, environmental issues are neglected, lakes are polluted, and smog in Beijing, Shanghai, and other cities reduces visibility most summer days. Unemployment is paramount. Migrated workers left the farms and are moving from city to city looking for manufacturing and construction work. The hardships of farmers in the countryside and the migrant workers in the urban centers cause social unrest. Social discontent is paramount, and thousands of civilian protests occur every year.

Another major problem is energy. As for the beginning of the 21st century, China is second to the USA in energy use. While domestic oil or natural-gas supplies are negligible, China has abundant reserves of coal, of which it is the largest global consumer, mining and burning a quarter of the world's yearly output, and contributing to the environmental deterioration.

The case of China contrasts with most common knowledge about the relationship between a free economy and democracy. As opposed to the Anglo-American system of laissez-faire capitalism, which leads to democratic reforms, the Chinese capitalism is under state control. The Chinese steel industry, the automotive industry, and other industries were created by the centralized government and goals are still set centrally, in five-year plans.

The current Communist Party leaders are well educated and young. However, they do not adopt laissez-faire policies, and do not accept the correlation between economic growth and democracy. While economic reforms become paramount in China and private entrepreneurship is allowed and encouraged, a gradual relaxation of controls over press and television reporting has been reversed, including severe, government-initiated content censorship. The changes in the Chinese economy are also marked with the one-country, two-systems policy that is applied regarding Hong Kong and the island of Macao, which were handed over to China from the UK and the Portuguese governments, respectively. In both territories, the Chinese are maintaining the free market economy. Taiwan is watching very closely the easing of these two territories into the Chinese system.

Mixed economy

In a mixed economy, national resources such as manufacturing facilities, natural resources, and land are equally split between government and private ownership. In mixed economies, the government maintains control over industries and resources that are of strategic importance to the national security or long-term sustainability and stability of the country. Typically, the industries controlled by the government in a mixed economy are steel, energy, and military equipment. At times, industries that employ a large proportion of the population in a given economy are also owned by the governments, such as the car and ship building industries. In mixed economies, such as Canada, Denmark, France, Germany, Norway, Spain, Sweden, India, Indonesia, Malaysia, Pakistan, Sri Lanka, Argentina, and South Africa, governments provide comprehensive welfare and health systems. In a mixed economy, the government affects economic activities through a system of incentives and subsidies that are provided to industries on a selective basis. Mixed economies hold the view that efficiency and entrepreneurship should be balanced against society's need for low unemployment, appropriate wealth distribution, and economic growth. Many countries that practice mixed economies face enormous problems with their social welfare systems. Thus, it has been argued that these systems should be modernized and improved, such as the case of the UK, Austria, the Netherlands, and Sweden. At the same time, mixed economies are moving continuously towards market economies. The changes towards market economy are mostly induced by efforts to improve productivity and efficiency, eliminate waste, improve innovations, improve accountability and responsibility, reduce costs, and enhance economic growth. As a result, most mixed economy countries are in the process of massive *privatization*: that is, the selling of government-owned corporate entities and other resources to private investors. Privatization increases the productivity of these companies and resources, facilitates removal of subsidies, and improves management and executive personnel. Privatization also improves the competitiveness of economic entities, as private businesses have to compete for resources on the open market. In turn, the national economy improves in competitiveness, and prices of products and services are reduced as a result of privatization. Another benefit of privatization is the monies paid to the government in return for the assets and the improvement in the national budget deficit situation. It seems that in mixed economy countries, citizens prefer high unemployment, and higher social benefits to lower unemployment, and lower social benefits like in the USA.

National economic development and economic transition

Nations around the world compete for the attention of MNEs and their executives.

Furthermore, in a world that allows for effortless mobility by personnel of a variety of skills, the economic well-being of a country become a source of sustainable competitiveness and growth. There are acceptable measures of *economic development* that have been designed to indicate the economic well-being of a country vs other countries. These measures include a nation's economic output, such as agricultural and industrial production, infrastructure, such as power and transportation facilities, and people's physical health and level of education. The basic premise is that cultural, political, legal, and economic differences between nations can be measured and compared.

One of the commonly used measures of economic development is the *gross national product*, otherwise known as GNP. The GNP is the value of all goods and services produced annually in a particular country. This measure includes all income generated within the country or internationally. If export, import, and international operations by domestic corporations from the GNP are subtracted, one gets the gross domestic product, otherwise termed GDP. Dividing these measures by the country's population size will make these figures per capita, for each of the country's residents. Table 5.3 lists the income of the 10 largest world economies. Using the GNP figures, MNEs may decide whether it is possible for the local residents to buy a particular product or be offered a particular service. Customers in a country that have a lower GNP may be offered basic daily products, whereas customers in countries that have a higher GNP may be offered expensive products.

As GNPs are used to assess a country's economic sustainability, it should be noted that not all the country's economic transactions are accounted for. Economic transactions that are not registered are third-sector activities, not-for-profit organizations' work, household work by spouses, illegal gambling and cash transactions.

TABLE 5.3 The Ten Largest Economies in the World, by GDP

Rank	*Country*	*GDP (US$ millions)*
1	United States	12,912,889
2	Japan	4,976,464
3	Germany	2,875,640
4	United Kingdom	2,272,716
5	China	2,269,745
6	France	2,169,169
7	Italy	1,772,942
8	Spain	1,095,876
9	Canada	1,052,563
10	India	804,967

Source: International Monetary Fund, World Economic Outlook Database – 2009.

In some countries, such as those that were formerly part of the USSR, the official GNP figures reflect no more than 50 percent of the total GNP. Part of the reason is the intensive use of unreported cash transactions, as well as the use of *barter* transactions. A *barter* transaction is the payment for goods and services with an exchange of goods and services. In the USA alone, there are 350,000 businesses that are involved in barter exchange activities.

GNP figures should be used with caution for a number of reasons. First, GNP figures are a current snapshot of a country's economic state, and should also be analyzed for trends, as the rate of change is of importance for determining the economic potential of countries. Second, GNP per capita figures are indeed averages and should be used with care. As an example, out of about 1.3 billion residents in China, across 56 of China's provinces, roughly 300 million residents enjoy a high GNP per capita, comparable to the GNP of some well-developed Western countries. This is true especially around the Chinese eastern seaboard, where luxury items such as Lexus cars are sold in large numbers. Third, the GNP should be corrected through the purchasing power parity (PPP), which is discussed elsewhere in the book. The PPP indicates how much a unit of local currency can one buy in the home country. For comparing income between countries, purchasing power differences must be taken into account.

Another measure of economic development is the *Human Development Index*, which is a measure of the extent to which a country satisfies the needs of its residents. These needs are measured by life expectancy, education, and standard of living. The Human Development Index complements the measures of wealth of countries. As national income allows for investments and budgeting for health, education, welfare and scientific development, the Human Development Index measures the attractiveness of a country to individuals that may stay and contribute to national economies. Thus, it is a very important determinant of sustainable national competitiveness.

Table 5.4 presents country rankings based on the Human Development Index. It is clear that countries are ranked differently over the years and reflect the efforts of all countries to be an attractive place for residents and MNEs.

The Human Development Index helps classify countries into *developing countries, newly industrialized countries,* and *developed countries. Developing countries* or *less developed countries* are countries with a very weak or nonexistent infrastructure and lowest GNP per capita. These countries rely heavily on one main economic activity such as mining, agriculture, or oil production. Many of these countries may be found in Africa, Asia, and the Middle East. *Newly industrialized countries* or *emerging markets* are countries where a significant portion of their GNP and exports are derived from industrial manufacturing. Newly industrialized countries may be found in Asia (China, Hong Kong, South Korea, Singapore, Taiwan, Thailand, Malaysia, and India), Latin America (Brazil, Mexico), and South Africa. *Developed countries* are industrialized, have a strong service economic sector and enjoy the best quality of life. The residents of the industrialized countries enjoy good educational systems, excellent healthcare systems, and the most developed welfare systems. Countries included in this category are the USA, the UK, Canada, Australia, Japan, France, Italy, Spain, Germany, Greece, and New Zealand.

TABLE 5.4 2008 Human Development Index by Countries (Adjusted for Purchasing Power Parity-PPP)

1	Iceland	0.968
2	Norway	0.968
3	Canada	0.967
4	Australia	0.965
5	Ireland	0.960
6	Netherlands	0.958
7	Sweden	0.958
8	Japan	0.956
9	Luxembourg	0.956
10	Switzerland	0.955
11	France	0.955
12	Finland	0.954
13	Denmark	0.952
14	Austria	0.951
15	United States	0.950
16	Spain	0.949
17	Belgium	0.948
18	Greece	0.947
19	Italy	0.945
20	New Zealand	0.944
21	United Kingdom	0.942
22	Hong Kong	0.942
23	Germany	0.940
24	Israel	0.930
25	South Korea	0.928
26	Slovenia	0.923
27	Brunei	0.919
28	Singapore	0.918
29	Kuwait	0.912
30	Cyprus	0.912

Source: International Monetary Fund, World Economic Outlook Database – 2009.

During the first decade of the 21st century, countries have seemed to go through an economic transition, changing economic systems, organization and processes, and moving closer to a market economy. The economic changes in most cases have involved the following:

- legalizing private ownership of assets and enterprises;
- privatizing of state-owned facilities and enterprises;
- reducing of national deficits;
- removing price and other government controls;

- removing trade barriers;
- allowing the expatriation of profits by MNEs;
- maintaining and enhancing a welfare system.

The economic transition towards a market economy entails several problems: (1) a lack of managerial expertise to exploit opportunities in a free market environment; (2) a shortage of capital to get a free market going; (3) double-digit unemployment, like in former Soviet Union countries; (4) public expectations from the economic transition that are not readily fulfilled and cause social unrest; and (5) intensive industrialization and lack of appropriate environmental laws and enforcement cause environmental problems, as in China, where pollution and safety standards are neither well developed nor enforced.

One of the most current cases of an economic system in transition is the case of Russia. In the 1980s the Soviet Union entered a period of freedom and economic restructuring. However, only wealthy, well-connected, and former executives of state-owned enterprises as well as criminals were positioned to considerably enhance their wealth. Some resorted to extortion and other criminal offences in order to get ahead economically. The first two decades of the 21st century will be marked with uncertainties regarding the free market environment and a major effort by the government to maintain an appropriate balance between economic development and social equity.

Economic change and international business

The adoption of a market economy by former centrally planned and mixed economy countries has a significant effect on international business. MNEs are seizing the opportunities to locate manufacturing plants in low-wage and high-growth markets countries, and in the process using the grants, tax concessions, and other benefits provided by national, regional, local, and municipal government agencies. Global capital markets, including the availability of stock exchanges in newly industrialized countries, provide more options for raising capital than ever before, and make it easier for MNEs to set up facilities offshore. The level of workmanship in emerging markets improves as the education systems are enhanced, leading to world-class manufacturing and service skills and performance. As has been pointed out earlier in the chapter, newly industrialized countries make for a sizable middle class with a significant purchasing power. To wit, the middle class in China and India has about 300 million residents each, which is about double the US population. These populations make for a huge market for products and services and, thus, attract the attention of MNEs, international entrepreneurs, and international small and medium-sized businesses.

International Trade

International trade definition and theories

International trade involves two or more economic systems in an exchange of goods and services which transcend international boundaries. Some of the goods exchanged are of low added value, such as agricultural products, and some are high value added, like high-tech consumer goods (iPods, PCs, etc.). The various theories of international trade explain the mechanisms of trade and help predict their behavior over time.

The mercantile theory

Emerging in England in the mid-16th century, the mercantile theory is the first (or preclassical) theory of international trade. The doctrine placed great faith in the ability of a government to improve the well-being of its residents using a system of centralized controls. Under mercantilism, the government had two goals in foreign economic policy. The first goal was to increase the wealth of the nation by acquiring gold. Mercantilists identified national wealth with the size of a nation's reserves of precious metals (which could then be used to hire mercenary armies). The second policy goal was to extract trade gains from foreigners through regulations and controls, so as to achieve a surplus in the balance of trade through maximizing exports (e.g., subsidies) and minimizing imports (e.g., tariffs and quotas).

In a modern economy, however, gold reserves are merely potential claims against real goods on foreigners. In addition, as demonstrated by David Hume in 1752, an influx of gold would increase the domestic price level and boost the price of exports. Hence, the country holding the gold would lose the competitive edge in price that had enabled it to acquire the gold earlier by exporting more than it imported. In contrast, the loss of gold in the foreign nation would reduce prices there and reinforce its exports. Today, gold reserves represent a minor portion of national foreign exchange reserves. Governments use such reserves to intervene in foreign exchange markets (e.g., selling some of these reserves in exchange for local currencies) so as to influence foreign exchange rates.

Mercantilism also overlooked other sources of a country's wealth accumulation such as the quantity of its capital, the skill of its work force, and the strength of other production inputs such as land and natural resources. The new era indicates that a country's wealth today is accumulated mainly through superior competitiveness, which is in turn is determined not only by the abundance of resources but also by national policies, industrial structure, firm efficiency, and individual productivity.

Liberalism and absolute advantage theory

In the 1776 seminal work, *An Inquiry into the Nature and Causes of the Wealth of Nations,* Adam Smith introduced the concept of *laissez-faire* to international trade. Laissez-faire means "freedom of enterprise and freedom of commerce." Elimination of the ubiquitous regulations was the keystone of 19th century liberalism. Smith argued that all nations would benefit from unregulated free trade, which would permit individual countries to specialize in goods they were best suited to produce because of natural and acquired advantages.

Smith's theory of trade has come to be known as the "absolute advantage theory." This theory states that a nation's imports should consist of goods made more efficiently abroad while exports should consist of goods made more efficiently at home. According to this theory, Caribbean countries should export bananas (which has an absolute advantage at home) and import apples from Okanagan Valley in Alberta, Canada (which has an absolute advantage in Canada).

The absolute advantage theory holds that the market would reach an efficient end by itself. Government intervention in the economic life of a nation and in trade relations among nations (e.g., in the form of tariffs) is counterproductive. A nation would benefit from free trade simply because imports would cost less than domestic products it otherwise had to produce. Unlike the mercantilist doctrine that a nation could only gain from trade if the trading partner lost (i.e., zero-sum game), the absolute advantage theory argued that both countries would gain from the efficient allocation of national resources globally.

Table 5.5 provides a simple illustration of how a country gains from free trade. It shows that the Caribbean has an absolute advantage in producing bananas, whereas Canada has an absolute advantage in producing apples. It takes two labor hours to produce a unit of bananas in the Caribbean, whereas it takes 10 hours to produce a unit of apples in Canada. Therefore, the Caribbean should specialize in the production of bananas. Similarly, it takes eight hours to produce a unit of apples in the Caribbean and two hours to produce a unit of apples in Canada. Therefore, Canada should specialize in the production of apples. Smith argued that in a situation such as this, both countries benefit from specialization and trade. World production would increase if both countries specialized in the production of the good in which they have an absolute advantage and then traded to obtain the other goods in which they have an absolute disadvantage.

Comparative advantage theory

The absolute advantage theory could not explain a situation where, for example, one country is more efficient than another in producing *all* goods. Would it still pay for both countries to trade if one country were more efficient than the other in production of all goods? David Ricardo, a 19th century English economist, answered this question in his 1817 landmark book *Principles of Political Economy and Taxation*. He stated that both countries would gain from trade even if one was more efficient in all goods. Thus, it was the *comparative advantage* of a nation in producing a good relative to the other nation that determined international trade flows.

Using the concept of opportunity cost, the amounts of goods given up in order to produce alternative goods, a country has a comparative advantage in producing a good if the opportunity cost for producing the good is lower at home than in the

TABLE 5.5 Labor Hours Required to Produce One Unit of a Good

	Bananas (1 unit)	*Apples (1 unit)*
The Caribbean	2	8
Canada	10	2

other country. So long as the opportunity costs for the same goods differ between countries, open trade will result in gains for each country through specialization in producing goods in which a country has comparative advantage vis-à-vis its trading partner.

The *sources* of comparative advantages are important for international business. The immediate source of trade is a difference in the price of the same goods or commodity between different countries: thus, the difference in opportunity costs, which is determined by the interaction of supply and demand. Therefore, a price differential derives from differences in demand conditions, supply conditions, or both.

In today's world economy, comparative advantage is explained by differences in *comparative production cost,* which depends on the goods production process (especially the state of technology) and on the prices of *production factors*, such as labor, land, capital, and natural resources. Factor prices, in turn, are related to the availability of those factors in the national economy. Economists refer to inputs to the production process as production factors. In the global economy, quality levels of production factors (e.g., knowledge and productivity of workers, patents and intellectual property or service, and efficiency of a banking sector) become most significant for improving a country's exports or attracting foreign direct investment (FDI). While in today's international business environment, factor endowment includes the quality of production factors, in the 19th century, intercountry differences in technology were relatively minor so international variations in comparative advantage were attributed primarily to different national endowments in terms of availability and cost. This was the basis for the *Heckscher–Ohlin theorem*.

Heckscher–Ohlin Theorem

The Heckscher–Ohlin (or H–O) theorem, named after two Swedish economists, explained the link between national factor endowments and comparative advantage of nations. The theorem states that a country has a comparative advantage in commodities whose production is intensive in its relatively abundant factor and, thus, will export those commodities. Meanwhile, a country would import commodities whose production is intensive in the country's relatively scarce factor of production. Thus, differences in comparative advantage are attributed to the differences in the structure of the economy. A country is relatively more efficient in those activities that are better suited to its economic structure and does best with what it has most of. If, for example, the USA is more abundant in capital relative to labor than other countries, it will export such commodities (e.g., motor vehicles) whose production requires a greater use of capital than other products do, and will import labor-intensive commodities (e.g., clothing).

Four assumptions underlie the H–O theorem. First, it is assumed that countries vary in the availability of various factors of production. Second, while each commodity is assumed to have its own specific production function, the production function is assumed to be identical anywhere in the world. *Production function* shows the amount of output that can be produced by using a given quantity of capital and labor. In other words, this theorem assumes that the same amount of the same input will produce the same output in any country. Third, the theorem holds that technology is constant in all trading countries and that the same technology is used in all those countries. Fourth, it assumes that the conditions of demand for production factors are the same in all countries. With identical demand conditions, differences in the relative supply of a factor of production will lead to differences in the relative price of that factor between the two countries.

The implications of the H–O theorem for world trade are significant to world trade and may be summarized as follows:

1 Trade as well as trade gains should be greatest between countries with the greatest differences in economic structure.
2 Trade should cause countries to specialize more in producing and exporting goods that are distinctly different from their imports.
3 Trade policy should take the form of trade restrictions rather than trade stimulation.
4 Countries should export goods that make intensive use of their relatively abundant factors.
5 Free trade should equalize factor prices between countries with fairly similar relative factor endowments but not between countries with markedly different endowments.
6 Factor prices should be nearly equal between countries with more liberal mutual trade.
7 International investment should be stimulated by differences in factor endowments, and international trade and international investment should be negatively correlated.

The Leontief paradox

The central notion of the H–O theorem is that a country exports goods that make intensive use of the country's abundant factor and imports goods that make intensive use of the country's scarce factor. However, this notion was refuted by Wassily Leontief, who attempted, in 1953, to test this proposition for the USA. Using input–output tables covering 200 industries and 1947 trade figures, he found that US exports were apparently labor-intensive and its imports capital-intensive. Since this result contradicts the predictions of the H–O theorem, it has become known as the *Leontief paradox*. The Leontief study motivated further empirical research. The empirical evidence accumulated since then shows many paradoxical results and contains serious challenges to the general applicability of a factor-endowments explanation in other countries such as Germany, India, Canada, and Japan.

The Leontief paradox stimulated a search for explanations for such a paradox. The explanations are summarized below:

1 The US demand for capital-intensive goods is so strong that it reverses the US comparative cost advantage in such goods.

2. US labor-intensive imports were reduced by trade barriers (e.g., tariffs and quotas) imposed to protect and save American jobs.
3. Leontief considered only capital and labor inputs, leaving out natural resource inputs. Because natural resources and capital are often used together in production, a country that imports capital-intensive goods may be actually importing natural resource-intensive goods. For example, the USA imports crude oil, which is capital-intensive.
4. A *factor-intensity reversal* occurs when the relative prices of labor and capital change over time, which changes the relative mix of capital and labor in the production process of a good or commodity from being capital-intensive to labor-intensive (or vice versa).

Human skills and technology-based explanations

Searching for better explanations of the sources of comparative advantage, several scholars challenged the conventional theory of trade which assumed technology and human skills' equivalence among different nations. Rather than a separate theory, the human skills and technology explanations added two new factors of production – namely, *human skills* and *technology gaps* – to the explanation of comparative advantage sources.

Human skill theorists explained the source of comparative advantage in terms of the comparative abundance of professional skills and other high-level human skills, including such as those of (1) scientists and engineers, (2) technicians and draftsmen, (3) managers, (4) other professionals, and (5) skilled manual workers. The argument is that US export industries employ a higher proportion of highly skilled labor than do import-competing industries. Thus, the US exports more skill-intensive manufacturing goods than do other countries. Studies treating professional and skilled human resources as capital reversed the Leontief paradox and found that US exports were actually capital-intensive. The relative abundance of professional and other highly skilled labor in the USA is thus a major source of its comparative advantage in manufacturing products.

Technology theorists argued that certain countries have a special advantage as innovators of new products. They also postulated that there was an *imitation lag* that prevents other countries from immediately duplicating the new products of the innovating country. These two conditions gave rise to technology gaps in those products that afford the innovating country an export monopoly during the period of imitation lag. In other words, for the duration of the imitation gap, the innovator is the only exporter on world markets. Similarly, when a firm discovers a different and more advanced production process or production technology, it enjoys a cost advantage and dominates the world market for a while. For example, it was found, in a particular period, that transportation, electrical machinery, instruments, chemicals, and nonelectrical machinery were the five strongest industries in the USA in terms of R&D, which also accounted for most of US exports of manufactures in the same period. As long as technological progress is being made, the technology gap serves as a major source of comparative advantage. As such, technology, like human skills, is an added and separate factor of production whose relative abundance or scarcity in a country determines comparative advantage or disadvantage in technology-intensive products. This explanation of international trade is at the core of many governments' national economic development agendas.

The product life-cycle model

Related to the technology gap view is the *product life-cycle model*, proposed in the mid-1960s. Developed by Raymond Vernon, it explores the imitation lag and technology gap approach, otherwise noted as imitation-gap approach. It is suggested that changes occur in the input requirements of a new product as it becomes established in a market and standardized in production. As the product cycle develops, the cost advantage will change accordingly, and a comparative advantage in innovative capacity may be offset by a cost disadvantage. To explain the behavior of US exports of manufactures, Vernon developed a four-stage model assuming that the export effects of product innovation are undermined by technological diffusion and lower costs abroad. This life-cycle model includes the following four stages: (1) the USA has an export monopoly in a new product; (2) foreign production of this product begins; (3) foreign production of this product becomes competitive in export markets; (4) the USA becomes an importer of this no-longer-new product.

Figure 5.1 graphically presents the product cycle model of international trade for the innovating country (e.g., the USA) and an imitating country (e.g., Japan or Mexico), respectively. As Figure 5.1 shows, the innovating country starts production of the new product at time 0, but it does not export that product until time A when production exceeds domestic consumption. At time B, foreign production begins to compete against the innovating country's exports, which, in turn, begin to fall. Exports come to an end at time C as the innovating country becomes an importer of this no-longer-new product.

Figure 5.2 shows that an imitating country starts to import the new product from the innovating country at time A'. If this imitating country is a high-income, advanced country (e.g., Japan), then time A' most likely coincides with time A in Figure 5.1. If, however, it is a low-income, developing country (e.g., Mexico), then time A' will come after time A. Local production begins at time B' when the local market grows to sufficient size and cost conditions favor production against imports. If the imitating country is an advanced country, then B' will coincide with B in Figure 5.1. If it is a developing country, B' will come after time B. At time C', when production begins to exceed consumption, the imitating country begins to export, and may export first to third countries and later to the innovating country.

Vernon's theory also suggests that the product cycle model of international trade is associated with the life-cycle stage of the product itself. As the product moves through its life cycle, the life cycle of international trade will change. The *new product stage* is associated with the first production of the product in the innovating country (O–A) and the early portion of the export monopoly stage (A–B). During this stage, production functions are unstable and techniques used in

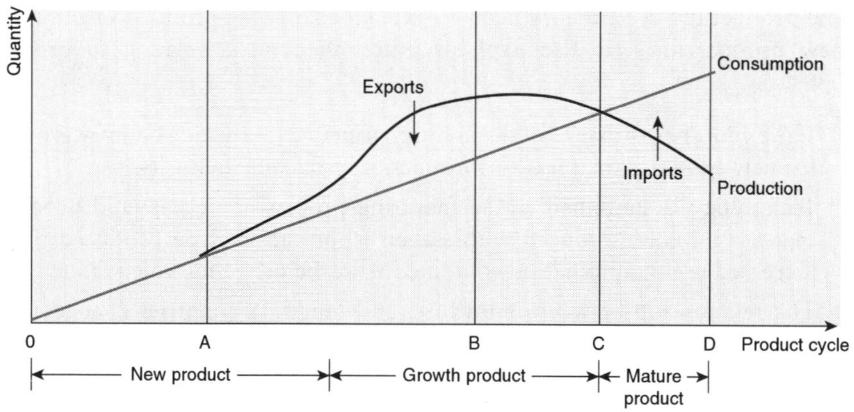

FIGURE 5.1 Product cycle model of international trade – innovating country (Based on Buzzel.com)

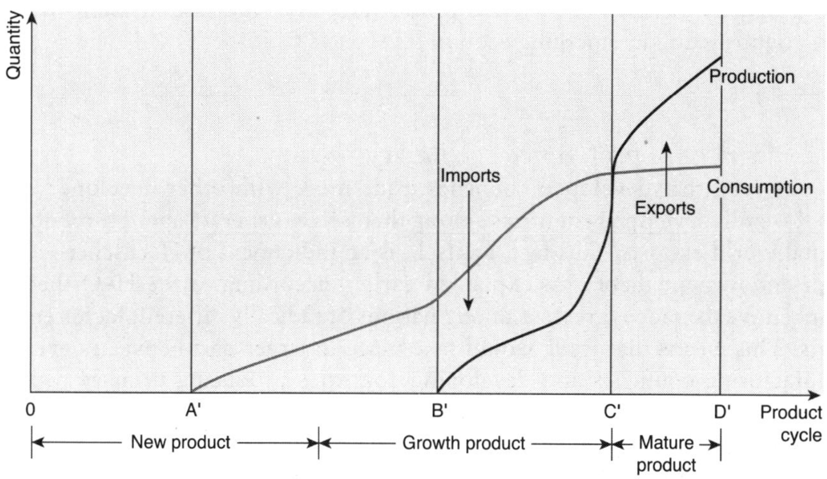

FIGURE 5.2 Product cycle model of international trade – imitating country (Based on Buzzel.com)

production are rapidly changing. No economy of scale is reached. This phase is also characterized by a small number of firms and no close substitute products. The *growth product stage* is associated with the later portion of the export monopoly (A–B) and the start of foreign production (C). During this stage, mass production methods are used to exploit expanding markets, and therefore high returns are achieved from economy of scale and market growth. Finally, the *mature product stage* is associated with the third and fourth stages of the product cycle model of international trade (C–D). This last stage is characterized by production of standardized products with stable techniques and intense price competition.

The product life-cycle theory helps to explain changes in production and trade in new product lines. It also explains other phenomena relating to product cycles:

1 The export performance of the mature, principal innovating country is better for new products than it is for products approaching maturity.
2 Technology is simplified as the maturing process continues, and products that are initially produced with skilled labor can later be produced by an increased use of automation combined with the use of unskilled labor.
3 The relationship between innovating and imitating countries changes over time. Countries that were once the principal innovators might fall into relative decline. The USA, for example, was the first country to build commercial aircrafts. Later, France and Britain adapted new production technology, and developed successful aircraft and space industries.
4 International trade may increase in the later stages of the product cycle. As a consumer good matures and income rises, products once seen as luxury (e.g., cell phones) become a necessity. General growth of per capita incomes broadens the market for mass production, as is the case in many Western countries and in emerging economies such as China.

Linder's income-preference similarity theory

It is observed that developed countries trade more with other developed countries. Overall, developed countries among themselves generate about three-fourths of total world exports. This fact, by itself, is an indictment of Heckscher–Ohlin's factor-endowment theory. As explained earlier, according to the H–O theorem, the incentive to trade is greatest among nations of radically different factor endowments. This means that trade would take place in larger part between developed manufacturing countries and developing countries producing primary products (i.e., natural resource commodities such as oil and petroleum) and labor-intensive goods, such as the case between the USA and Canada.

Staffan B. Linder, a Swedish economist, divided international trade into two different categories: primary products (natural resource products) and manufactures. Linder asserted that differences in factor endowments explain trade in natural resource-intensive products but not in manufactures.

Linder argued that, the more similar the demand preferences for manufactured goods in two countries (e.g., the USA and Canada), the more intensive is the potential trade in manufactures between them. If two countries have the same or similar demand structures, then their consumers and investors will demand the same goods with similar degrees of quality and sophistication, a phenomenon known as *preference similarity.* This similarity boosts trade between the two industrialized countries. To explain the determinants of the demand structure, Linder argues that average *per capita* income is the most important one. Countries with high *per capita* income will demand high-quality "luxury" consumer goods (e.g., motor vehicles) and sophisticated capital goods (e.g., telecommunications equipment and machinery), while low *per capita* income countries will demand low-quality, "necessity" consumer goods (e.g., bicycles), and less sophisticated capital goods (e.g., food processing machinery).

The new trade theory

The set of ideas sometimes referred to as the *new trade theory* was originally expounded in a series of papers by Dixit and Norman, Lancaster, Krugman, Helpman, and Ethier. These theorists argued that countries do not necessarily specialize and trade solely in order to take advantage of their differences; they also trade because of *increasing returns*, which makes specialization advantageous per se. Although this theory is not totally "new," it makes several contributions to the understanding of international trade.

First, the new trade theorists introduce an industrial organization view into trade theory, and include real-life imperfect competition in international trade. They argue that because of economies of scale, there are increasing returns to specialization in many industries. *Economy of scale* is reduction of manufacturing cost per unit as a result of increased production quantity during a given time period. For instance, manufacturing the 100,000th car is much cheaper than making the first. Because of the presence of substantial scale economies, world demand will actually support only a few firms in an industry (e.g., only Boeing and Airbus remain as makers of large passenger jets).

Second, the new trade theory suggests that *interindustry trade* (international trade between different industries in different nations) continues to be determined by H–O theory. In contrast, *intraindustry trade* (international trade involving the same industry) is largely driven by increasing returns resulting from specialization within the industry. This suggests that comparative advantage from factor-endowment differences and increasing returns from economy of scale can coexist because they differ in the application of inter vs intraindustry trade.

Finally, the new trade theory realizes the importance of externality in international specialization and trade. *Externality* occurs when the actions of one agent directly affect the environment of another agent. For example, firms that cause pollution or noise would have an adverse impact on local residents. In international trade, externalities include government policies, political relations between two countries, history of the importing or exporting country, consumption differences between different cultures, accident and luck (e.g., first entrant of the industry), among others. The new trade theorists contend that these externalities could be the alternatives to comparative advantage as the factors influencing actual patterns of international trade.

The new trade theory has a number of implications. First, it helps explain the Leontief paradox by bringing in the economies-of-scale concept. The theory argues that firms engage in trade because they expect increasing returns from larger economies of scale; such economies may not necessarily be associated with factor endowment differences between importing and exporting countries. Scale economies will likely lead countries to specialize and trade with a similar country in terms of income level or consumption preference. Second, this theory helps explain intraindustry trade, which is a substantial two-way trade (i.e., import and export) that takes place with goods that belong to the same industry. Trade is intended to realize economies of scale and may not be correlated with differences in factor endowments. Finally, this theory helps explain intrafirm trade, which occurs when import and export activities take place between the subsidiaries of the same MNE. Driven by the prospect of increasing returns, MNEs see intrafirm trade as a facilitator of global integration of upstream and downstream activities.

Theories overview

Although none of the theories is capable of explaining the entire range of motives for international trade, they collectively provide invaluable insights into why international trade occurs. With reference to the sources of comparative advantage, differences in factor endowments (i.e., Heckscher–Ohlin theorem) survive as the most general explanation of the pattern of "old" trade (e.g., labor-intensive products). The comparative advantage theory, despite its diminishing power in explaining today's international trade, is still capable of explaining international trade in natural resource products. Extending the factor endowments, the H–O theorem (by including skilled labors and technologies) explains current import and export activities between developed and developing countries.

The technological gap (i.e., human skills and technology-based views) and the product life-cycle theories are powerful explanations of trade in "new" products (i.e., manufactures made by a skilled workforce using technologies). These skills and technologies are the key stimulus to improving a country's terms of trade, the major concern of both developed and developing countries today. The *terms of trade* is the relative price of exports: that is, the unit price of exports divided by the unit price of imports. The terms of trade improve if the country exports more goods that are associated with advanced human skills and technologies. In this case, the contribution of foreign trade to the nation's economic growth will be stronger. Although the product life-cycle model is less applicable today than at the time of its inception, it still explains key patterns in the evolution of international trade. A nation's import and export structures change over time. Similarly, every new product has its life stages in the global marketplace.

The Leontief paradox and Linder's income-preference similarity theory provide insights on the triggers of international trade for sophisticated manufacturing products and on trade between regions with similar income levels and consumption preferences. These theories view market demand (income levels and demand structure) as important parameters of international trade. Indeed, international trade today is driven not only by national differences in factor endowments but also by national differences in market demand. Intra-regional trade still accounts for a high proportion of world trade because of similarities in income levels and demand structures, as well as efficiencies arising from reduced uncertainty and transaction costs. The limitation of these theories is that they did not explain how trade activities would take place between two nations sharing similar income levels but with different consumption preferences. Because of this weakness, they seem unable to explain the increasing trade between developed countries and newly industrialized countries (e.g., Singapore, South Korea, Taiwan, and Hong Kong) or emerging markets (e.g., China, Brazil, India, Russia, and Mexico). These countries are not in the same region, nor do they share similar consumption preference with the Western world. Increasing income and elevated purchasing power seem to be the key driver of this trade phenomenon.

The new trade theory enriches our understanding of intraindustry and intrafirm trade. It links national factor endowments with firm behavior and firm incentives in explaining international trade. This link is important because firms rather than countries conduct international trade and investment. The efficiency of international trade is maximized if both national factor endowment differences and economies-of-scale advantages of firms are combined and realized simultaneously. Since the MNE's role in international trade and investment is highly visible, the new trade theory has attracted more attention in recent years. The limitation of this theory, however, is that it overlooks other incentives beyond increasing returns from economy of scale. MNEs seek geographical diversification and accumulate knowledge about the target market from international trade. Chapter 4 articulates these issues in more detail.

Further explanations of international trade are theories that are based on the assessment of country capabilities (or competitiveness as opposed to country competitive advantage). Factor endowment conditions (including human resources, technology, and information) are a critical aspect of country competitiveness, and factor endowment differences between two nations remain an important foundation for international trade. However, other aspects of country capabilities also shape international trade. For example, an importing country's macroeconomic soundness, demand conditions, local competition, government policies, support of related industries (e.g., banking service and foreign exchange hedging systems), as well as culture are expected to affect trade activities. At the same time, an exporting country's infrastructure, business rivalry, openness, and innovation are important factors influencing the volume of, and gains from, export activities. A nation generally gains more from international trade if its competitiveness in the world market is higher than that of other countries. Japan, for instance, is not rich in terms of factor endowments, but its competitiveness in innovation, adaptability, and business management has made it a major player in international trade.

International Trade Patterns

International trade volume and growth

Despite the 2008–2009 subprime mortgage crisis in the industrialized nations, the global financial markets crisis, the food crisis, the climbing cost of oil, concerns about inflation, and worries about a global economic slowdown, global merchandise exports for the year increased by 14.4 percent, which included a 15.2 percent increase for developing countries. Worldwide services exports climbed by 18.1 percent in 2007, with the services exports of developing countries increasing by a similar 18.1 percent. According to the United Nations Conference on Trade and Development (UNCTAD), there is a continued long-term trend towards concentration of exports. Whereas developing countries sold many products and services overseas, an increasing amount of the value of these exports came from a limited number of goods. For several countries, such as Haiti and Nepal, income from citizens working overseas exceeded those countries' exports of goods and services in 2007. As of the first decade of the 21st century, industrialized nations continued to dominate global economic activity and international trade. They accounted for 71 percent of global GDP in 2007, although they had only 15 percent of the world's population. They were responsible for 58.6 percent of the value of merchandise exports for the year, and for 71.9 percent of services exports. On the other hand, the rate of growth of exports of goods and services in 2007 was slightly higher for developing countries than for developed countries.

Figure 5.3 shows the growth in international merchandise trade: the increase in merchandise trade has been paramount in all sectors of the economy, including manufactures, mining and agricultural products, and in most regions.

Service trade

Trade in services has become a major part of global trade, mostly by developed countries. *Service trade* includes the import and export of financial services, information services, the provision of education and training, transportation, tourism, healthcare, accounting, and consulting services.

Developed countries tend to push aggressively for removal of barriers to trade in services. Part of this effort is to ease up work permit regulations in various destination markets.

Trade partners

Canada is the USA's largest trade partner, followed by the European Union (EU), Mexico, and Japan. The reason is that, with the exception of Mexico, three of the USA's four major trading partners are developed economies, which supports

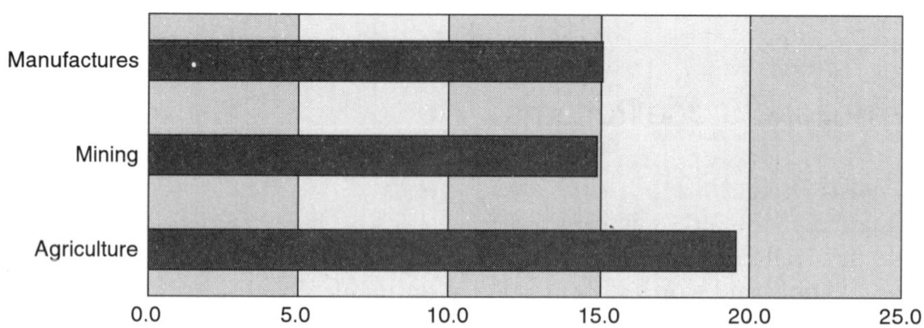

FIGURE 5.3 Value growth of world merchandise trade by sector, 2007 (percentage change) (WTO International Trade Statistics, 2008)

Linder's income-preference similarity theory. Canada, the major partner of the USA has additional advantages in terms of trade with the USA: geographic proximity, relative cultural similarity, and North American Free Trade Agreement (NAFTA) membership. More than 100,000 US companies export to Canada, more than double the number to Mexico, the second-ranked destination. Mexico, the only emerging economy among the four major partners, also benefits from its proximity to the USA and from NAFTA membership. Since NAFTA's establishment in 1994, Mexico's exports have grown threefold, with the USA and Canada accounting for much of the growth. As of 2010, USA's major partners outside the Americas are China, an emerging economy (for imports) and Japan and South Korea (for exports).

With increased globalization, more and more exported products contain a collection of inputs from other countries, including those that end up importing the final product. As an example, information technology exports out of the Philippines, Malaysia, and Thailand represent a value added of no more than 20 percent, given the importation of semiconductors and other manufacturing inputs that go into the exported products. Likewise, exports from China to the USA include manufacturing goods which are made by firms from developed economies, including the USA, Japan and the EU, and use China as an export country.

As explained, the new trade theory suggests that while interindustry trade is governed by the H–O theorem (trade between countries with different factor endowments), intraindustry trade is not. As an example, US textile imports for 2000 come from the EU, Canada, China, Mexico, and India. Thus, although textiles are a labor-intensive product, the imports come from developed as well as developing economies. But the products that come in are different, with those from developed countries being of higher price and quality.

As for the Leontief paradox, the USA exports labor-intensive products when it has no advantage in labor rates. The reason is labor migration. Rather than moving south of the border, US carpet manufacturers rely on Mexican migration to the state of Georgia in order to lower labor costs and remain competitive. While labor costs are still higher in the USA relative to Mexican plants, transportation costs to US customers from Georgia are much lower, making domestic production cost-effective. In this case, wage differentials are not the only factor determining the location of production.

Trade balance

The *balance of trade* is calculated as exports minus imports of goods and services. The United States has the largest trade deficit of any country, though as a percentage of GDP its deficit is much lower than that of many other nations. The US deficit in merchandise trade has persisted since the early 1980s, and has been especially pronounced in trade with Japan during the 1980s and early 1990s and with China in the early 2000s. This deficit has caused great concern about US competitiveness.

In contrast to its deficit in merchandise trade, the USA enjoys substantial surplus in services. For example, the USA has been a major proponent of "open skies" agreements that liberalize the markets for commercial aviation and has fought hard for China to open its market for financial services. In addition, India has become a center for software export. This success played a role in the Indian government's decision to open up its own market to realize the benefits of free trade.

In the new global environment, knowledge is often the most valuable contribution toward a competitive advantage in services. This can be seen clearly in the distribution of US service exports. The USA exports intellectual property and legal services to Europe, while the USA sells mostly education and engineering services in the Asia Pacific region. US freight services are sold mainly in the Asia Pacific and Africa/Middle East regions, and US exports in advertising, insurance, communications, and travel services target Latin America.

Opposition to Free Trade and Globalization

Trade theories show the benefits to be derived from international trade but do not expand on its drawbacks. This is particularly true for the theories of absolute and comparative advantage, which point out that trade allows for the efficient deployment of national resources from which everyone benefits. At the same time, opponents of free trade have been against free trade and most recently against its globalization. Most countries have taken the position that international trade needs first and foremost to protect the interest of their citizens. For example, the US Foreign Trade Act permits price-fixing agreements among exporters if neither US consumers nor US competitors are harmed.

Opinion surveys show that the American public is divided on the benefits of free trade. About half of the US public believes that foreign trade is bad for the US economy. There are several reasons for this view.

1. Although trade may be good for the overall national economy, its impact varies across regional, occupational, and other lines.
2. Surveys show that unskilled workers are much less likely to support free trade, because they are threatened by a shift of their jobs to lower-cost locals, countries, and regions. In contrast, skilled and highly educated people are more likely to benefit from trade, at least in the short term, and hence tend to support free trade.
3. Studies confirm that people with lower income tend to be more negatively disposed toward trade. This is not justified because poor people are more adversely affected by protectionism because it increases the price of consumer goods.
4. The schism between social groups regarding trade may in itself trigger opposition to trade on the part of governments that are worried about its economic, social, and political impact.

To deal with the uneven impact of trade, governments provide trade adjustment assistance in the form of extended unemployment benefits and retraining funds for workers who lose their jobs to overseas competition. Other measures include the provision of wage insurance for workers who lose their jobs as a result of foreign competition.

Another source of opposition to trade is the potential threat it represents to *national sovereignty*. According to this argument, the shift in production to the most efficient location deprives a country of the base it needs to be a viable economic entity. In turn, this will make a country too dependent on nations that may challenge its national interests. This argument is particularly salient in industries considered key to national security, either directly (e.g., the arms industry) or indirectly (e.g., airlines). The USA, like many other countries, prohibits non-US firms from acquiring a majority stake in a US airline on the pretext that the aircraft may need to be mobilized should an emergency occur. For similar reasons, countries sometimes curb the exports of certain products to designated countries.

Free trade sometimes is opposed as a threat to *national culture and institutions*. Some countries, notably France and Canada, impose restrictions on the introduction of foreign media under the pretext that open importation would endanger their culture and language. Countries may establish particularly high tariffs on products that they see as essential to their way of life (e.g., rice in Japan). A major argument against free trade is the adverse consequences for the environment, safety, and workforce exploitation. This is the "lowest denominator" argument, whereby manufacturing shifts to nations with the least protection and employment regulation since they offer the lowest cost base, but eventually, the world at large will end up paying for the adverse impact in the form of environmental degradation, global warming, and further exploitation of the workforce in developing countries.

Trade reciprocity is part of the free trade and globalization phenomena. *Trade reciprocity* occurs when countries open their borders on a bilateral basis for a free flow of goods and services.

Although trade theories assume benefits even when a country opens its borders to free trade unilaterally, economic, political, and social benefits can be gained from trade reciprocity. Consumer groups and exporters alike react positively to trade reciprocity as opposed to a unilateral opening of national borders to trade.

It has been argued that there are two kinds of reciprocity: passive and active. *Passive reciprocity* occurs when a country refuses to lower or eliminate its barriers to trade until the other party does the same. *Active or aggressive reciprocity* occurs when a country applies retaliatory measures until the other party fulfills its obligations.

Reciprocity and retaliation are manifested in international trade through countervailing duties and subsidies applied by various countries. Duties may be set in order to curtail demand for selected products and services produced elsewhere. Subsidies may be used in order to support local producers and service providers in face of foreign competition.

Tariff and Nontariff Trade Barriers

There are two types of barriers to trade – tariff and nontariff barriers. *Tariff barriers* are official constraints on importing of certain goods and services in the form of a total or a partial limitation or in the form of a special monetary levy. *Nontariff barriers* are indirect measures that discriminate against foreign manufacturers or service providers in the domestic market. Whereas tariff barriers have been significantly reduced during the several decades of the General Agreement on Tariffs and Trade (GATT) regime, debate continues on whether similar progress has been made in nontariff barriers.

Although some nontariff barriers like monetary incentives to selected industries, have been targeted by the WTO and eliminated, others have emerged in their place. Sometimes, both tariff and nontariff barriers are applied simultaneously. Various countries may prohibit foreign firms from bidding on strategic defense projects or prevent those firms from winning less-sensitive bids by publicizing the bids in obscure local outlets unlikely to be scrutinized by foreign firms, which are a nontariff barrier.

Both tariff and nontariff regulation-based barriers pose a serious obstacle to international trade, alongside the lack of information, cost, financing, qualified employees, language, and cultural issues.

Tariff trade barriers

Tariff trade barriers include mainly tariffs, quotas, export controls, and anti-dumping laws.

Tariffs

Tariffs are charges that an importer pays above and beyond taxes levied on domestic goods and services. Tariffs are transparent (listed in the Harmonized Tariff Schedule) and are typically based on the value of the product or service. Tariffs were used widely in the 19th century but were incrementally reduced over time, in the USA and in other nations around the world to a level under 10 percent for most products.

Because high tariffs inhibit free trade and economic growth, they have been on the agenda of virtually all rounds of trade negotiations through GATT, the predecessor of WTO, and progress has been made toward their elimination or reduction. Nevertheless, an occasional hike in tariff is applied as a punitive measure to retaliate or obtain reciprocity. Multinational enterprises (MNEs) have been investing efforts to avoid tariffs.

Generally, tariff rates are relatively low today, especially among developed countries. Figure 5.4 shows average import tariff rates among several nations in North and South America.

In the USA, Japan, Canada, and the EU, as of the beginning of the 21st century, about 10 percent of the tariffs exceed the level of 12 percent rates – effectively applied rates for imports from developing countries – protecting the local producers and service providers. These countries exhibit an extremely large variation of tariff rates, with tariff peaks reaching, in extreme cases, as high as 350 percent.

In the EU, in the agriculture and fishery product group, 1,273 products have tariff peaks as follows: 572 products in the 12–19 percent range, 334 products in the 20–29 percent range, 334 products in the 30–99 percent range,

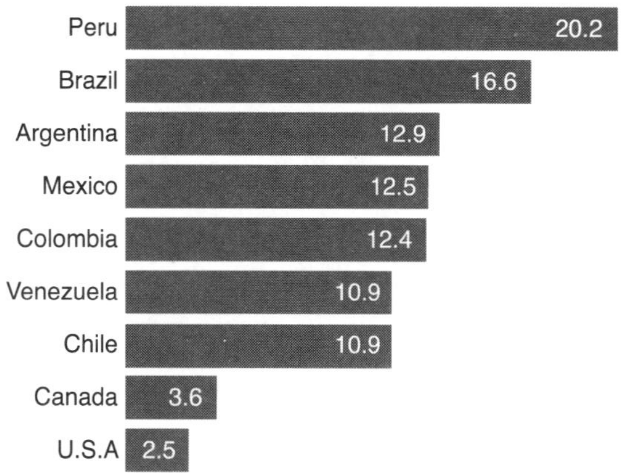

FIGURE 5.4 Average import tariff rates (percent) (J. P. Morgan Chase, US Commerce Department)

31 products in the 100–299 percent range and two products in the above 300 percent range.

In industrial products as a whole tariff peaks are as follows: 27 products are in the 12–19 percent range, seven products in the 20–29 percent range, and eight products in the 30–99 percent range. Motor vehicles, of which there are 184 products, account for 15 percent of tariff peaks, and chemicals, plastics and rubber products, of which there are 1,596 products, account for 21 peaks. Of the 967 products in textiles, three products are in the 12–19 percent range.

Optimal tariff

The *optimal tariff theory* assumes that by imposing a tariff on foreign pro-ducts sold locally, governments can capture a significant portion of the manufacturer's profit margin, without affecting the price of the products for domestic customers.

Thus, optimal tariff theory assumes that the exporter can absorb the lower prices and will not simply shift its efforts into other national markets. The theory also does not consider the fact that high tariffs might trigger smuggling, which eventually reduces government revenues. Such is the case for cigarettes and alcoholic beverages, traditionally high-tariff items, which are often smuggled across national borders.

Infant industries protection

Infant industry protection may justify tariffs. The reason is that an industry new to a country, especially a developing one, needs to be protected by tariffs; otherwise, it may be destroyed by global players before it is given a chance to grow and mature. The argument was vigorously raised by the USA, Japan, India, and Korea, since these countries wanted to encourage the development of their domestic industries at the expense of foreign manufacturers. Surely, the consumers paid higher prices locally and were compromised in the quality of the manufactured goods. A classic case was the US voluntary quotas set in the mid-1970s, which limited the number of Japanese cars sold in the USA and increased the price of cars locally. This protection was required since the Japanese cars were becoming extremely popular for their fuel efficiency and superior workmanship and quality. These voluntary quotas were against WTO politics and caused a major strife between the USA and WTO.

Import quotas

Import quotas are quantitative limitations on the amount of imports of goods in units (e.g., 5,000 PCs) or monetary value. Sometimes the quotas include a periodic increase or decrease.

The Global Economy and Free Trade

It seems that continued globalization – the relatively free movement of people, resources, and capital – is the key to helping the world out of its current economic crisis. Citing Tom Friedman, the noted author and expert on globalization in his article "The Open-Door Bailout" *New York Times*, February 10, 2009, the recovery from the global crisis is in further encouraging free trade and entrepreneurship.

> Leave it to a brainy Indian to come up with the cheapest and surest way to stimulate the US economy: immigration. "All you need to do is grant visas to two million Indians, Chinese, and Koreans," said Shekhar Gupta, editor of *The Indian Express* newspaper. "We will buy up all the subprime homes. We will work 18 hours a day to pay for them. We will immediately improve your savings rate – no Indian bank today has more than 2 percent nonperforming loans because not paying your mortgage is considered shameful in India. And we will start new companies to create our own jobs and jobs for more Americans." While his tongue was slightly in cheek, Gupta and many other Indian business people were trying to make a point that sometimes non-Americans can make best: "Dear America, please remember how you got to be the wealthiest country in history. It wasn't through protectionism, or state-owned banks or fearing free trade. No, the formula was very simple: build this really flexible, really open economy, tolerate creative destruction so dead capital is quickly redeployed to better ideas and companies, pour into it the most diverse, smart, and energetic immigrants from every corner of the world and continue doing so."

Friedman's comments are likely to cause howls of protest in some corners, but his basic arguments are sound. Recessions feed on themselves because businesses shed workers, creating fewer consumers, which cause greater concern, less demand, and more layoffs. The key to ending the current recession is job creation. Legislators around the globe who are considering stimulus packages should ask themselves the same question about every piece of legislation they see: will this help create jobs?

> While I think President Obama has been doing his best to keep the worst protectionist impulses in Congress out of his stimulus plan, the U.S. Senate unfortunately voted on

> Feb. 6 to restrict banks and other financial institutions that receive taxpayer bailout money from hiring high-skilled immigrants on temporary work permits known. However, in the age when attracting the first-round intellectual draft choices from around the world is *the* most important competitive advantage a knowledge economy can have, why would we add barriers against such brainpower – anywhere?

Up to now, China has been doing just the opposite. See yesterday's post Changing China. America has traditionally been the source of brain drains in other countries and, as Friedman noted, it has made America better, stronger, and more prosperous. Leaders in India, however, are applauding the move.

> "If you do this, it will be one of the best things for India and one of the worst for Americans, [because] Indians will be forced to innovate at home," said Subhash B. Dhar, a member of the executive council that runs Infosys, the well-known Indian technology company that sends Indian workers to the U.S. to support a wide range of firms. We protected our jobs for many years and look where it got us. Do you know that for an Indian company, it is still easier to do business with a company in the U.S. than it is to do business today with another Indian state?' Each Indian state tries to protect its little economy with its own rules. America should not be trying to copy that. "Your attitude," said Dhar, should be "whoever can make us competitive and dominant, let's bring them in." If there is one thing we know for absolute certain, it's this: Protectionism did not cause the Great Depression, but it sure helped to make it "Great." From 1929 to 1934, world trade plunged by more than 60 percent – and we were all worse off.

In the information age, one would think that the country that led the information revolution would be in the best position to leverage technologies to create jobs. That is what Friedman is hoping for:

> We live in a technological age where every study shows that the more knowledge you have as a worker and the more knowledge workers you have as an economy, the faster your incomes will grow. Therefore, the centerpiece of the economic stimulus, the core driving principle, should be to stimulate everything that makes the U.S. smarter and attracts more smart people to our shores. That is the best way to create good jobs. According to research by Vivek Wadhwa, a senior research associate at the Labor and Worklife Program at Harvard Law School, more than half of Silicon Valley start-ups were founded by immigrants over the last decade. These immigrant-founded tech companies employed 450,000 workers and had sales of $52 billion in 2005, said Wadhwa in an essay published this week on BusinessWeek.com. He also cited a recent study by William R. Kerr of Harvard Business School and William F. Lincoln of the University of Michigan that "found that in periods when H-1B visa numbers went down, so did patent applications filed by immigrants in the U.S. And when work visa numbers went up, patent applications followed suit."

You might wonder why patent applications are good indicators of economic health. Honestly, not all patent applications are born equally. Studies have shown, however, that some patents represent bellwether innovations that are repeatedly mentioned in other patent applications.

(*Continued*)

Companies that hold those types of patents have historically done much better financially than other companies – meaning they are more profitable, create more jobs, and have a more lasting impact on the economy. Friedman continues:

> The U.S. doesn't want to come out of this crisis with just inflation, a mountain of debt and more shovel-ready jobs. We want to – *we have to* – come out of it with a new Intel, Google, Microsoft, and Apple. The stimulus package should include a government-funded venture capital bank to help finance all the start-ups that are clearly not starting up today – in the clean-energy space they're dying like flies – because of a lack of liquidity from traditional lending sources. Newsweek had an essay this week that began: "Could Silicon Valley become another Detroit?" Well, yes, it could. When the best brains in the world are on sale, you don't shut them out. You open your doors wider. We need to attack this financial crisis with green cards not just greenbacks, and with start-ups not just bailouts.

Leaders in emerging market countries understand the importance of having in place a system that supports entrepreneurs. Entrepreneurs create jobs and stimulate the economy. They create value and they create wealth. America will eventually "work" its way out of the current recession, but creating the jobs for those that will do that "work" should be the single most important goal for Congress and the President. As Friedman notes, the jobs that are needed are not the kind created by Roosevelt's Civilian Conservation Corps. The jobs need to be created by entrepreneurs who are determined to build the future.

Source: DeAngelis, S. F., Hayes, B. C. (2009). Development and Global Stability, February 13, http://www.enterpriseresilienceblog.typepad.com/.

Import quotas may sometimes be set as an upper limit on market share of a specific imported product. Market share quotas are mostly used in the case of textile products or footware. Quotas may yield unintended consequences. For example, the voluntary quotas capping Japanese auto imports into the USA at roughly 1.8 million units, set in units rather than dollar value, encouraged Japanese manufacturers to develop, and export into the USA more expensive models so as to increase their dollar volume without violating the quotas. Furthermore, it encouraged the Japanese to establish manufacturing plants in the USA, circumventing the quotas altogether. Quotas do not have the potential to trigger the efficiencies that arise from the need to remain competitive with domestic producers. The unmet demand for Japanese cars in the USA was simply provided higher margins for the dealers.

Rules of origin

Rules of origin are the criteria used to determine the nationality of a product. Rules of origin were designed as an uncontroversial, neutral device essential to implementing discriminatory trade policies, compiling economic statistics, and marking a good. Once the origin of a good is known, the importing country can apply any country-specific or trade area-specific trade preferences or restrictions to the imported good, account for the good in its compilation of economic statistics on trade flows, and ensure that the good is clearly marked with its country of origin. Rules of origin remained an uncontroversial, neutral device as long as the parts of a product were manufactured and assembled primarily in one country. Rules of origin are an indispensable means of implementing discriminatory trade regimes and their importance has grown significantly as countries increasingly become part of a global trade and supply chain.

The rise of multinational corporations and the production of goods in multiple stages using parts produced in different places around the world has provided an opportunity to use rules of origin as an effective means of protection.

As an example, a BMW car that was manufactured in Germany and exported to England, and from there to the USA, will be considered a German car unless the product has undergone a major change in England. Rule of origin is often problematic, because the value added to the product in the transient country may be debatable.

To remedy the problem, the WTO issued an agreement on rules of origin. It requires that the rules of origin be transparent, that they be applied in a consistent and impartial manner and that they help support free trade.

Export controls and free trade

While free trade is supported by most forward-looking countries, many countries limit some types of products that can be exported to other countries. *Export controls* are typically set for products with a national security potential, such as arms, but also for "dual-use" products, such as computers and trucks, that may have both military and civilian uses. An example is the sale of aerospace equipment to China by McDonnell Douglas Corporation that was banned by the US government.

Export controls on trade are applied in emergency situations, in order to prevent the export of goods that are vital to domestic industry and armed forces, like steel and oil. Export controls are set by the exporting country rather than by the importing one. Thus, exporting companies often pressure their government to ease export controls, arguing that the importing country will get the products from a competitor whose country does not apply strict controls. Export controls have been applied in the USA and other Western countries regarding trade with Iraq, Iran, China, Syria, and North Korea.

Dumping and anti-dumping

Dumping is selling a product at an unfairly low price; the fair price is defined as the domestic price, relative to the production costs. Dumping interferes with free trade and undermines the principle of comparative advantage because it encourages the exporting country to specialize in a product or service in which it has no competitive advantage.

The WTO allows actions against dumping, including the application of extra duties that can bring the price back to a realistic level, restoring a level. However, anti-dumping duties end up protecting inefficient domestic producers.

China and European Union and dumping

Since dumping investigation compares domestic prices and costs of the accused dumping nation with prices and costs at the exporting country, China makes for an interesting case. If China is accused of dumping toys and textile goods, the basic approach is to consider the price of toys and textile goods in China against the price of Chinese toys and textile goods in, say, EU countries. But China does not have market economy status, so Chinese domestic prices cannot be used as the reference. Traditionally, the USA is used as a reference, or, analogue country, but so are Brazil and Mexico: that is, the price of toys and textile goods in these countries is regarded as a substitute for the price of toys and textile goods in China for a dumping ruling. The process of choosing an analogue market is subject to the influence of the complainant country, which has led to some criticism that there is an inherent bias in the process.

The Common Agricultural Policy (CAP) of the EU has often been accused of casing dumping, though significant reforms were made, including in the 2003 Luxembourg Agreement. The CAP tried to increase European agricultural production and provide support to European farmers through a process of market intervention, whereby a special fund – the European Agricultural Guidance and Guarantee Fund (EAGGF) – would buy up surplus agricultural produce if the price fell below a certain centrally determined level, the intervention level. Through this measure, European farmers were given a "guaranteed" price for their produce when sold in the European community. In addition to this internal measure, a system of export reimbursements ensured that European agricultural products sold outside of the European community would sell at or below world prices, with no financial consequences to the European producer.

The CAP measures were criticized as a dumping mechanism that distorted world trade and were replaced in the 1990s with direct payments to farmers, regardless of production. These payments encourage responsible, sustainable farming through animal welfare and environmental protection practices.

Nontariff Barriers

Nontariff barriers to trade are trade barriers that are not based on laws and official regulations and, thus, are not transparent. Since nontariff barriers are not transparent, it is impossible to fight them. Some barriers are especially difficult to detect and monitor, such as a change in domestic product technical standards that may take a long time to make adjustment for by the foreign manufacturer. When a developing country limits importing used cars, the official argument is safety, even though the imported cars may be safer than the cars used domestically. Nontariff barriers protect local manufacturers.

There are numerous nontariff barriers to trade that may be applied by countries, including import bans, general or product-specific quotas, rules of origin, quality conditions imposed by the importing country on the exporting country, sanitary conditions, packaging conditions, labeling conditions, product standards, complicated regulatory environment, determination of eligibility of an exporting country by the importing country, determination of eligibility of an exporting form of organization by the importing country, additional trade documents like Certificate of Origin or Certificate of Authenticity, occupational safety and health regulation, employment laws, import licenses, state subsidies, export subsidies, a fixed minimum import price, product classifications, quota shares, foreign exchange controls and multiplicity, inadequate infrastructure, "Buy national" policy, over-valued currency, intellectual property laws (patents, copyrights), restrictive licenses, seasonal import regimes, corrupt and/or lengthy customs procedures, bribery, and corruption. Some of these nontrade barriers are explored below.

Administrative barriers cause reduction in trade volumes

Governments may use an administrative measure to block the entry of products while not admitting to applying these measures. Extremely slow and inefficient custom offices may cause delays, for example. Most countries require product labels in the local language, a requirement that puts an additional burden on the small exporter, who may not find it economically feasible to do so.

Another example of an administrative barrier is banning the transport of exports on safety grounds. Even dealing inefficiently with disputes and complaints by the damaged party is a form of an administrative barrier.

Production subsidies are payments provided by governments to domestic companies in order to make them more competitive vis-à-vis foreign competitors.

Subsidies funnel resources away from their optimal deployment. However, subsidies do not affect consumer decisions, because they do not raise prices beyond their global level. Countervailing duties are set to counter and allow fair competition in a local market.

Emergency import protection protects against a *surge in imports*, a sudden and significant increase in imports that can cause damage to the domestic industry. The corrections are not targeted at a particular country. However, the connections establish a quota formula to allocate supply among different exporting countries. An example of emergency restrictions is the setting of quotas imposed by the US government to stop the Japanese auto imports in the 1980s and 1990s.

Emergency import protections help control free trade and achieve long-term stability in international trade. This intervention may be justified in light of the global economic crisis of 2010.

Foreign sales corporations are created in order to circumvent restrictions on trade set on an exporting country. Foreign sales corporations are founded off shore and may enjoy reduced tax rate that effectively reduces the product price.

Embargoes and boycotts interfere with the free flow of trade between countries by stopping trade that would otherwise take place. An *embargo* is the stopping of exports to a designated country: such is the case of the US embargo on Iraq and Iran. A *boycott* is the stopping of imports of all or some goods and services from a specific country. Boycotts often constitute nontariff barriers, as firms do not admit applying boycotts.

Boycotts are usually initiated by national governments. Examples are the US government embargo on Iran and North Korea. Nongovernmental organizations

(NGOs) such as business associations and consumer groups may initiate an embargo.

Buy local campaigns are initiatives to promote local products and services at the expense of all imported goods and services. These campaigns are a form of a nontariff barrier and interrupt the free flow.

Technical standards are rules and regulations sanctioned by government agencies regarding technical performance, safety, and the environment. Products sold in a destination country should comply with these rules and regulations. Technical standards are a form of trade barrier. This is true when standards differ from international norms, when restrictive standards are written to match the design features of domestic products and when there is a significant lack of transparency in the systems for developing technical regulations and assessing conformity of products to such regulations. An example of technical regulations that represent nontariff barriers are the EU bans on genetically modified agricultural goods produced in the USA. A further example of technical regulations is the US ban on toys imported from China that contain high quantities of lead.

We should note that the WTO agreement "encourages" countries to use international standards where appropriate, but does not obligate them to do so. The organization does, however, enforce import licensing procedures that require import licenses to be "simple, transparent and predictable". The goal is to ensure that the administrative process will not in itself restrict or distort imports. International trade is promoted by reducing the amount of bureaucracy involved in the issuing of import license. Thus, the WTO supports a clear and simple process regarding the conformance of importing goods to national technical standards.

Corruptions are practices that are mostly illegal and are used to delay or block imports unless certain favors are entertained by government officials in charge of the import process. These favors may be in the form of payments to these officials.

Although there are various free trade barriers, one should note a national vehicle to promote international free trade, termed A *Special Economic Zone* (*SEZ*), which is a geographical region that has economic laws that are more liberal than a country's typical economic laws.

The general category "SEZ" covers a broad range of specific zone types, including Free Trade Zones (FTZ), Export Processing Zones (EPZ), Free Zones (FZ), Industrial Estates (IE), Free Portsand, and Urban Enterprise Zones. Usually the goal of an SEZ definition in a specific country is to increase foreign investment and enhance international trade. One of the earliest and the most famous SEZs was founded by the government of the People's Republic of China in the early 1980s. The successful SEZ in China, Shenzhen, just north of Hong Kong, developed from a small village into a city with a population over 10 million within 20 years. SEZs have been established in other countries, including Brazil, India, Iran, Jordan, Kazakhstan, Pakistan, the Philippines, Poland, Russia, Peru, and Ukraine. A single SEZ can contain several specific zones within its boundaries, defined by the rules applied to each specific subzone. Subic Bay in the Philippines and the Aqaba Special Economic Zone in Jordan are examples of multilayered zones.

COUNTRY FOCUS

MEXICO

World Rank (EFI 2009): 49

Regional Rank (EFI 2009): 3

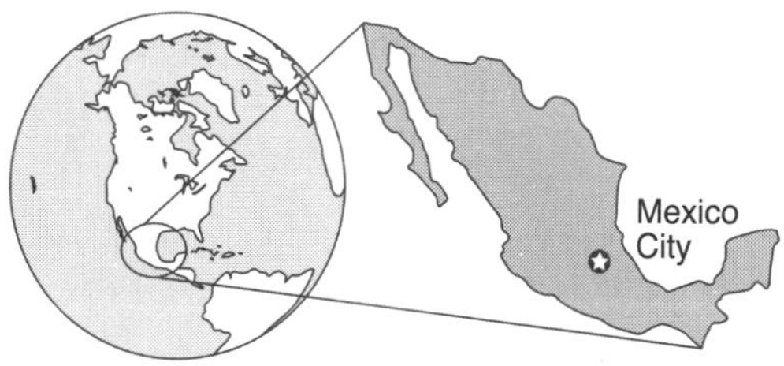

Quick facts

Population: 104.2 million

GDP (PPP): $1.3 trillion; 4.8 percent growth in 2006; 2.8 percent 5-year compound annual growth; $12,177 per capita

Unemployment: 3.7 percent

Inflation (CPI): 4.0 percent

FDI inflow: $19.0 billion

2006 data unless otherwise noted

Economic freedom score

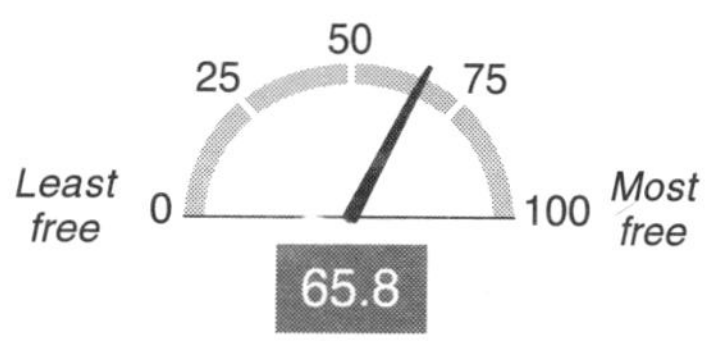

Mexico's economic freedom score is 65.8, making its economy the 49th freest in the 2009 Index. Mexico is ranked 3rd out of three countries in the North America region, but its score remains well above the world average and the third highest in Latin America.

Mexico scores above the world average in eight of the 10 economic freedoms. Commercial operations are becoming more streamlined, and business formation is efficient. Income and corporate tax rates are moderate, and the overall tax burden is low as a percentage of GDP. The government's reform agenda includes improving expenditure efficiency and accountability.

Freedom from corruption and labor freedom score below the world average. The government is working to make commercial regulations more investment-friendly, but foreign investment in many sectors is deterred by special licensing requirements. The judicial system is slow to resolve cases and is subject to corruption. The current government has vowed to continue to fight corruption at all levels.

Background

Mexico has been independent for almost 200 years and a democracy since 1917. It is a member of the North American Free Trade Agreement (NAFTA) with Canada and the USA and became the first Latin American member of the Organization for Economic Cooperation and Development (OECD) in 1994. The economy depends heavily on commercial relations

(Continued)

with the USA and remittances from migrant workers in the USA. Under the center-right National Action Party (PAN), President Vicente Fox (2000–2006), a divided Congress adopted some reforms after 71 years of rule by the center-left Institutional Revolutionary Party. The PAN's Felipe Calderon narrowly defeated populist Manuel Lopez Obrador in 2006 and has promised further liberalization, particularly in energy, but lacks a majority to legislate reforms. He also faces serious challenges fighting organized crime networks that traffic in illegal drugs.

Business freedom – 80.3

The overall freedom to conduct a business is protected under Mexico's regulatory environment. Starting a business takes an average of 28 days, compared to the world average of 38 days. Obtaining a business license requires less than the world average of 18 procedures and 225 days. Bankruptcy proceedings are relatively easy.

Trade freedom – 80.2

Mexico's weighted average tariff rate was 2.4 percent in 2006. Import restrictions, non-transparent tariff quota administration, import taxes and fees, services market access barriers, import licensing and registration, restrictive standards and labeling rules, burdensome sanitary and phytosanitary regulations, nontransparent and inconsistent customs administration and valuation, various export promotion programs, customs corruption, and weak enforcement of intellectual property rights add to the cost of trade. Fifteen points were deducted from Mexico's trade freedom score to account for nontariff barriers.

Fiscal freedom – 83.4

Mexico has moderate tax rates. Both the top income tax rate and the top corporate tax rate were cut to 28 percent in January 2007. A 16.5 percent flat-rate business tax (known as the IETU) replaced the asset tax as of January 2008 and now operates as an alternative to the corporate income tax for some companies. Other taxes include a value-added tax (VAT) and a property tax. In the most recent year, overall tax revenue as a percentage of GDP was 9.7 percent.

Government size – 81.8

Total government expenditures, including consumption and transfer payments, are low. In the most recent year, government spending equaled 24.6 percent of GDP. Privatization has progressed, but the energy and electricity industries remain government-controlled.

Monetary freedom – 77.5

Inflation is moderate, averaging 3.9 percent between 2005 and 2007. Although most prices are determined in the market, the government maintains suggested retail prices for medicines and influences prices through state-owned enterprises and utilities, including electricity and energy. Ten points were deducted from Mexico's monetary freedom score to account for policies that distort domestic prices.

Investment freedom – 50

Foreign and domestic capitals are not always treated equally. Foreign investors are barred from important sectors, such as petroleum and electricity, and restricted in others like telecommunications. About 95 percent of foreign investment does not require official approval. Bureaucracy can be burdensome and slow, and administration of the investment code is nontransparent. Residents and nonresidents may hold foreign exchange accounts. Most payments, transactions, and transfers are allowed. Some capital transactions are subject to government permission and controls. Foreign investment in real estate is somewhat restricted.

Financial freedom – 60

Mexico's financial sector has undergone a considerable transformation and has become more competitive. Government holdings in commercial banking are significantly reduced, and foreign participation has grown rapidly over the past decade. Banks offer a wide range of services. State-owned development banks provide financing to specific areas of the economy and influence credit. The government has adopted US accounting standards. The insurance sector is well developed, with five firms (three of which are foreign-owned) accounting for nearly 59 percent of policies. Although most large Mexican companies are traded on various stock exchanges, Mexico has the largest stock market in Latin America after Brazil.

Property rights – 50

The threat of expropriation is low. Contracts are generally upheld, but the courts are slow to resolve disputes and are allegedly subject to corruption. Despite a legal framework for the enforcement of intellectual property rights, the enforcement and prosecution of infringement cases are ineffective in practice. Foreign real estate investors have found it difficult to secure enforcement of their property interests in state-level courts.

Freedom from corruption – 35

Corruption is perceived as significant. Mexico ranks 72nd out of 179 countries in Transparency International's Corruption Perceptions Index for 2007. Corruption has been pervasive for many years, but President Calderon has committed his government to continue the fight against it at all levels of government-federal, state, and municipal. Local civil society organizations focused on fighting corruption are still developing.

Labor freedom – 59.8

Mexico's rigid labor regulations continue to hamper employment and productivity growth. Reform remains stalled. The nonsalary cost of employing a worker can be high, and the difficulty of laying off workers is a disincentive for additional hiring.

Source: Adapted from Terry Miller and Kim R. Holmes, *2009 Index of Economic Freedom* (Washington, DC: The Heritage Foundation and Dow Jones & Company, Inc., 2009), at www.heritage.org/index.

SUMMARY

International trade is the exchange of goods and services across borders. There are several theories explaining trade flows.

International trade has grown significantly during the 21st century, marked by a **global trade of services**, such as financial, trade and transportation services.

More **products and services** contain inputs that **originate in a variety of nations**, making it difficult to measure and analyze international trade in goods and services.

Theories explain the essentials of international trade, and **provide insights into why international trade occurs**.

(Continued)

Older theories such as the **mercantilist doctrine** and the **absolute advantage** theory, while accurate for their time, are inaccurate in today's world, due to drastic changes in technological diffusion, information exchange, and capital flow as well as the enhanced role of MNEs.

The **Heckscher–Ohlin theorem**, the most general explanation of the "old" trade, is not entirely obsolete. By integrating advanced technology and a skilled workforce into systems of comparative advantage between countries, modern international trade can be modeled relatively accurately by the theorem.

When a **new technology** is created, the innovating country has a massive trade advantage until the **imitation gap** is overcome.

The **new trade theory** explains intraindustry and intrafirm trade. Theories of international trade must be continually revised as new technology and new political and economic realities create a different global climate.

Trade in **labor-intensive and natural resources** are best explained by differences in **factor endowments** (Heckscher–Ohlin theory). Trade in technology-intensive products is best explained by **technological gap** and **product life-cycle** theories.

The **new international trade theories** should take into account free and fast flows of human, information, intellectual property, and technological resources across nations. Furthermore, a strong case can be made for the effect of openness of countries to free trade and country governance.

There are **tariff and nontariff barriers**. Tariff barriers include quotas, export controls and dumping regulations. Nontariff barriers include administrative barriers, technical standards, foreign sales corporations, and corruption. The WTO is creating mechanisms to remove both type of barriers and define a process of arbitration to settle disputes regarding barriers.

DISCUSSION QUESTIONS

1. How is the Internet changing international trade? Can you think of a possible change to trade theories as a result of major technological developments, such as Internet technology or mobile commerce (a combination of Internet and cellular technology)?
2. How does Internet-based market places, such as amazon.com and e-Bay, change international trade? Can you define new challenges to the legal settlement of disputes in light of these trade practices?
3. Assess the effect of international trade rules and regulations on the performance of global merchandisers such as Wal-Mart, Tesco, and Carrefour from the USA, the UK and France, respectively.

INTERNATIONAL MANAGEMENT INSIGHT

Global Sourcing and International Trade

Emerging economies vie to become part of the evolving global supply chain of various MNEs. This may be achieved through concerted efforts by governments and private sector initiatives in countries such as Ethiopia, Vietnam, and China.

In trying to make its country a sourcing hot-spot, the *Ethiopian government* has highlighted the textile and clothing supply chain as one of the country's key targets for growth, help, and investment over the next few years, and plans to raise the level of textile, knitwear, and clothing exports from US$11 million in 2005–06 to US$500 million by 2008–09.This industry focus is part of a major project to accelerate Ethiopia's industrialization, reduce its dependence on subsistence farming, generate foreign income through exports, increase employment and therefore, reduce poverty. The government has pledged as much assistance as possible to achieve its goal. Exports of knitted and woven clothing and home furnishings account for 45 percent of the government's overall export goal. However, existing factories either cater for the growing domestic market or export insignificant volumes relative to the program's targets.

The *Vietnamese* Thanh Cong Textile & Garment Joint Stock Co (TCM) has signed a contract to supply one million fashion items to US retail giant Wal-Mart Stores. The products are to be delivered in the third quarter of 2009. TCM, headquartered in Ho Chi Minh City, formerly in North Vietnam, has set itself a revenue target of US$85 million this year and a year-on-year increase of 33 percent.

China's largest cotton textile producer Weiqiao Textile Company Limited has posted a *35.7 percent* jump in full-year profit after increased marketing and better product quality generated higher sales for the yarn and denim fabric maker. Net profit for the year ended December 31, 2006 was CNY1.7 billion (US$218 million), on sales that rose *46 percent* to CNY19.8 billion compared with 2005. Ms Zhang Hongxia, chairman of Weiqiao Textile, said: "In 2006, the group worked to enhance its marketing effort. As a result, utilization rate of our production facilities was further improved. We also focused on continuously upgrading of our production facilities and technology in order to provide the markets with more high-end products." The company said the more stable trading environment following the implementation of safeguards on Chinese exports to the USA and Europe helped boost sales. But it said high energy and cotton prices, as well as the appreciation of the Renminbi, "continued to challenge to the group's efforts to control cost." Sales of gray fabric, cotton yarn, and denim, the group's core products, generated *49.5 percent*, *41.8 percent*, and *8.4 percent* of total revenues, respectively. In 2006, the group's production volume of cotton yarn, gray fabric, and denim were 882,000 tons, 1,634,000,000 meters, and 175,000,000 meters, respectively, increases of *33.8 percent*, *13.4 percent*, and *41.1 percent*, respectively, compared with 2005. Ms Zhang believes Weiqiao Textile will continue to see an increase in both domestic and international demand for its textiles – and that a move to more high-end products and technological upgrades will help maintain stable profit margins.

Questions

1 What are the main actions taken by managers in Ethiopia, Vietnam, and China in order to make their companies viable participants in international trade?
2 What are the actions taken by governments in Ethiopia, Vietnam, and China in order to make these corporations viable participants in international trade?
3 Can you describe the actions taken by both corporations and governments in these countries using international trade theories described in this chapter?

Bibliography

Abel, A. B., Bernanke, B. S. (1992). *Macroeconomics*. Boston, MA: Addison-Wesley, p. 30.

Bilkey, W. J. (1978). An attempted integration of the literature on the export behavior of firms. *Journal of International Business Studies*, Summer, 9, 33–46.

Cavusgil, S. T. (1980). On the internationalization process of firms, *European Research*, 8(6), 273–81.

Dakhli, M., De Clercq, D. (2004). Human capital, social capital, and innovation: a multi-country study, *Entrepreneurship and Regional Development*, 16(2), 107–128.

Dunning, J. (1988). The eclectic paradigm of international production: a restatement and some possible extensions. *Journal of International Business Studies*, 19, 1–32.

Freidman, T. (2005). *The World Is Flat: A Brief History of the Twenty-First Century*. New York: Farrar, Straus and Giroux.

Hymer, S. (1976). *The International Operations of National Firms*. Cambridge, MA: MIT Press.

International Finance Corporation (1995). *Privatization Principles and Practice*. Washington, DC: IFC.

Knight, G., Cavusgil, S. T. (1996). The born global firm: a challenge to traditional internationalization theory. In S. Cavusgil, T. Madsen (eds), *Advances in International Marketing*, Vol. 8. Greenwich, CT: JAI Press.

Knight, G. A., Cavusgil, T. S. (2004). Innovation, organizational capabilities, and the born-global firm. *Journal of International Business Studies*, 35(2), 12–41.

Kogut, B. (1988). Joint ventures: theoretical and empirical perspectives. *Strategic Management Journal*, 9, 319–32.

Lincoln, J., Ahmadjian, C., Mason, E. (1998). Organizational learning and purchase-supply relations in Japan. *California Management Review*, 40(3), 241–64.

Oviatt, B., McDougall, P. (1994). Toward a theory of international new ventures. *Journal of International Business Studies*, 25(1), 4–64.

Prestowitz, C. (1989). *Trading Places*. New York: Basic Books.

Porter, M. (1990). *The Competitive Advantage of Nations*. New York: Free Press.

Ricardo, D. (1911). *Principles of Political Economy and Taxation*. London: Everyman Edition.

Romalis, J. (2004). Factor proportions and structure of commodity trade. *American Economic Review*, 94(1), 6–97.

Rugman, A. (1980). A new theory of the multinational enterprise: internationalization versus internalization. *Columbia Journal of World Business*, 15(1), 23–4.

Thurow, L. (1992). *Head to Head: The Coming Economic Battle Among Japan, Europe, and America*. New York: William Morrow.

Todaro, M. P. (1996). *Economic Development*, 6th edn. Boston, MA: Addison-Wesley, p. 705.

UNCTAD (2008). *World Investment Report 2008*. New York: United Nations.

Vahlne, J. E. (1977). The internationalization process of the firm – a model of knowledge development and increasing foreign commitments. *Journal of International Business Studies*, Spring/Summer, 8, 2–32.

Varadarajan, P. R., Cunningham, M. H. (1995). Strategic alliances: a synthesis of conceptual foundations. *Journal of the Academy of Marketing Science*, 23, 28–296.

Vernon, R. (1996). International investment and international trade in the product cycle. *Quarterly Journal of Economics*, May, 80, 19–207.

PART 3

International Trade, Investment, and Regional Integration

6

Foreign Direct Investment

Learning Objectives

Following this chapter, the reader should be able to:

1. Recognize the growing importance and prevalence of foreign direct investment (FDI)
2. Describe the relationship between international trade and FDI
3. Describe the factors affecting FDI
4. Understand the role of entrepreneurs and small and medium-size businesses in FDI
5. Articulate management issues in FDI

Opening Case

FDI in Emerging Markets: The Case of the Chinese Electrical Car

Warren Buffett banks on an obscure Chinese electric car company and a Chinese CEO

Warren Buffett is famous for his rules of investing: first, when a management with a reputation for brilliance tackles a business with a reputation for bad economics, it is usually the reputation of the business that remains intact; second, you should invest in a business that even a fool can run, because someday a fool will; third, never invest in a business you cannot understand.

So when Buffett's friend and long-time partner in Berkshire Hathaway, Charlie Munger, suggested that they invest in BYD, an obscure Chinese battery, mobile phone (cell phone), and electric car company, one might have predicted Buffett would cite the rules above. He is, after all, a man who shunned the booming US tech industry during the 1990s.

In 2008 Berkshire Hathaway bought 10 percent of BYD for $230 million. The deal didn't get much notice at the time. It was announced in late September 2008, as the global financial markets were facing great uncertainlty. According to Berkshire Hathaway principals, Buffett, Munger, and Sokol, this foreign direct investment (FDI) is a very big deal. They think BYD may become the world's largest automaker, primarily by selling electric cars, as well as a leader in the fast-growing solar power industry.

Wang Chuan-Fu started BYD (the letters are the initials of the company's Chinese name) in 1995 in Shenzhen, China. A chemist and government researcher, Wang raised some $300,000 from relatives, rented about 2,000 square meters of space, and started to manufacture rechargeable batteries to compete with imports from Sony and Sanyo. By about 2000, BYD had become one of the world's largest manufacturers of cell phone batteries. The company went on to design and manufacture cell-phone handsets and parts for Motorola, Nokia, Sony Ericsson, and Samsung.

Wang entered the automobile business in 2003 by buying a Chinese state-owned car company that was all but defunct. He knew very little about making cars but proved to be a quick study. A BYD sedan called the F3, became the best-selling sedan in China, topping well-known brands like the Volkswagen Jetta and Toyota (TM) Corolla.

BYD has also begun selling a plug-in electric car with a backup gasoline engine, a move putting it ahead of GM, Nissan, and Toyota. BYD's plug-in, called the F3DM (for "dual mode"), goes farther on a single charge – 62 miles – than other electric vehicles and sells for about $22,000, less than the plug-in Prius and much-hyped Chevy Volt are expected to cost when they hit the market in late 2010. Put simply, this little-known upstart has accelerated ahead of its much bigger rivals in the race to build an affordable electric car. BYD employs 130,000 people in 11 factories – eight in China and one each in India, Hungary, and Romania.

Its US operations are small – about 20 people work in a sales and marketing outpost in Elk Grove Village, IL, near Motorola, and another 20 or so work in San Francisco, not far from Apple. BYD makes about 80 percent of Motorola's RAZR handsets, as well as batteries for iPods and iPhones and low-cost computers, including the model distributed by Nicholas Negroponte's One Laptop per Child nonprofit based in Cambridge, MA. Revenues, which have grown by about 45 percent annually in five years, reached $4 billion in 2008.

It should be noted that Berkshire Hathaway first tried to buy 25 percent of BYD, but Wang, the founder and owner, turned down the offer. He wanted to be in business with Buffett – to enhance his brand and open doors in the USA, he says – but he would not let go of more than 10 percent of BYD's stock. Warren Buffett, an exemplary investor, saw the fact that Wang did not want to sell the company as a good sign.

BYD in Shenzhen: entrepreneurship and strategy

Shenzhen is the manufacturing hub of the global electronics industry. It is the place from which your cell phone, digital camera, and laptop probably came from. Just across a river from Hong Kong, Shenzhen is the biggest and fastest-growing city in the world that most Americans cannot find on a map. It's also the Chinese city most like an American one, because people who live here have come from elsewhere in search of a better life.

When the Chinese designated Shenzhen as China's first "Special Economic Zone" in 1980, inviting capitalism to take root, it was a fishing village. Today, it's a sprawling megacity of 12–14 million people, most of them migrant workers who toil in vast factories like those run by BYD and earn about 1,300 renminbi, or US$ 190 per month.

In Shenzhen, BYD employs about 10,000 engineers who have graduated from the company's training programs – some 40 percent of those who enter either drop out or are dismissed – and another 7,000 new college graduates are being trained. Wang, BYD's founder, says that the engineers come from China's best schools: "They are the top of the top," he says "They are very hard-working, and they can compete with anyone." BYD can afford to hire lots of them because their salaries are only about $600–700 a month; they also get subsidized housing in company-owned apartment complexes and low-cost meals in BYD canteens. "They're basically breathing, eating, thinking, and working at the company 24/7," says a US executive who has studied BYD.

This attention to costs is one reason that BYD has made money consistently, even as it has expanded into new businesses. Each of BYD's business units – batteries, cell-phone components, and autos – was profitable in 2008, albeit on a small scale. Overall, net profits were around $187 million. BYD, which is traded on the Hong Kong exchange, has a market value of about $3.8 billion: that's less than Ford ($7 billion at the beginning of April), but more than General Motors ($1.3 billion).

BYD's electric car and solar energy ventures

To that end, the company has developed a nontoxic electrolyte fluid. With 100,000 employees, BYD has turned to the design and production of an electric car. Since it is assumed that energy companies will need to produce more energy while emitting less carbon dioxide, electric cars may be one answer. They generate fewer greenhouse gas emissions than cars that burn gasoline, and they have lower fuel costs, even when oil is cheap. That's because electric engines are more efficient than internal combustion engines, and because generating energy on a large scale (in coal or nuclear plants) is less wasteful than doing it on a small scale (by burning gasoline in an internal combustion engine).

The numbers look something like this: assume one drives 12,000 miles a year, gas costs $2 a gallon, and electricity is priced at 12¢ per kilowatt, about what most Americans pay. A gasoline-powered car that gets 20 miles to the gallon – say, a Chevy Impala or a BMW X3 – will have annual fuel costs of $1,200 and generate about 6.6 tons of carbon dioxide. Equip those cars with electric motors, and fuel costs drop to $400 a year and emissions are reduced to about 1.5 tons.

The big problem is that they are expensive to make, and the single largest cost is the battery. Manufacturing a safe, reliable, long-lasting, 100 percent recyclable, and fast-charging battery for a car is a complex and costly undertaking. BYD claims to have achieved a breakthrough with its lithium ion ferrous phosphate technology, but no one can be sure whether it will work as promised.

Even BYD's admirers say the fit and finish of the company's cars leave much to be desired. BYD currently exports gasoline-powered cars to Africa, South America, and the Middle East, but they compete on price, not quality.

BYD's first plug-in hybrid, called a dual-mode car, is designed to run primarily on electricity, with an internal combustion engine for backup. Two all-electric cars – the E3 and the E6 – will follow. Both will be sold first in China, primarily to fleet users: the government, post office, utilities, and taxi companies, all of which will build central fast-charging facilities. Europe, with its high gas prices, is the most promising export market for BYD's electric cars. BYD signed an agreement last year with Autobinck, a Dutch dealer group, to distribute BYD cars in the Netherlands and five Eastern European countries.

The company hasn't yet decided whether it will enter the US market, where the economics of electric cars are not as compelling. But it may become a battery supplier to global automakers.

Patterns of Foreign Direct Investment

The opening case calls for a reflection on a number of issues:

- What are the main reasons for the FDI by Warren Buffett and his partners in the Chinese BYD corporation?
- Why is Birkshire Hathaway ready to take a relatively smaller stake of 10 percent in BYD? What are the risks and what are the benefits of having a minority position in an overseas venture such as BYD?
- What is the business potential of BYDs' products, such as the electric car and the solar energy panels, on a global basis?
- How have entrepreneurs such as Mr Wang, the founder of BYD, contributed to the accelerated growth of the metropolis of Shenzen?
- What lessons can be drawn from the Chinese experience of Free Trade Zones?

These questions are indeed important for international business investment ventures and countries or regions that promote business and technological entrepreneurship funded by foreign funds.

The definition of a foreign direct investment is *a market entry strategy that involves establishing a subsidiary or acquiring a business in a target country*, like a manufacturing, R&D and distribution facilities.

A foreign direct investment takes various forms, which are discussed in the following sections, along with the reasons for the growth of FDI as well as target countries and sources of FDI.

Growth of Foreign Direct Investment

Foreign direct investment continues to expand rapidly. Despite the global economic crisis and the global economic slowdown of 2008 and 2009, FDI reached over $1.5 trillion.

The main reasons for the growth of FDI during the first decade of the 21st century are

1. Globalization.
2. Strategic alliances (SA) and mergers and acquisitions (M&A).

As explained earlier in the book, *globalization* has meant that more companies are trying to export their products to markets around the world. However, in order to circumvent international trade barriers, most companies have had to resort to investment in target countries. The value of FDI has grown in a very significant way between the years 2000 and 2007, as indicated in Figure 6.1.

Furthermore, companies realized that production may be executed in efficient and productive locations in target markets or exported to target markets from the most optimal subsidiary location. These locations are usually in developing countries, such as the Philippines or Zimbabwe. Table 6.1 lists the FDI investments by descending order of target countries.

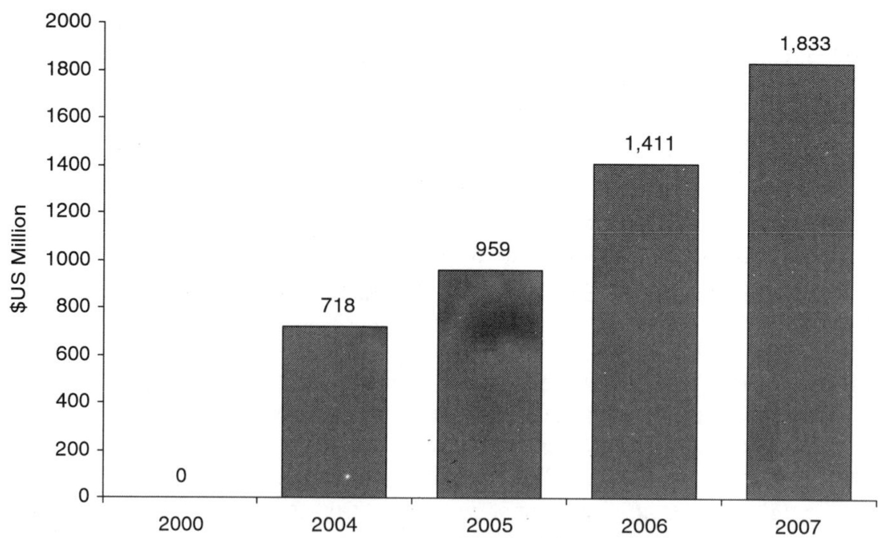

FIGURE 6.1 Value of Foreign Direct Investment 2000–2007 (US$ millions) (Based on Bureau of Economic Analysis, US Department of Commerce, US Government 2009)

TABLE 6.1 List of FDI Investments by Descending Order of Target Countries

Rank	*Country*	*FDI US$ millions*	*Rank*	*Country*	*FDI US$ millions*
1	United States	2,093,049	40	Nigeria	62,791
2	United Kingdom	1,347,688	41	British Virgin Islands	61,578
3	Hong Kong, China	1,184,471	42	Romania	60,921
4	France	1,026,081	43	Israel	59,952
5	Belgium	748,110	44	Indonesia	58,955
6	Netherlands	673,430	45	Colombia	56,189
7	Germany	629,711	46	United Arab Emirates	54,786
8	Spain	537,455	47	Greece	52,838
9	Canada	520,737	48	Egypt	50,503
10	Italy	364,839	49	Taiwan	48,640
11	Brazil	328,455	50	Croatia	44,630
12	China (PRC)	327,087	51	Venezuela	43,957
13	Russian Fed.	324,065	52	Kazakhstan	43,381
14	Australia	312,275	53	Slovakia	40,702
15	Switzerland	278,155	54	Vietnam	40,235
16	Mexico	265,736	55	Ukraine	38,059
17	Sweden	254,459	56	Bulgaria	36,508
18	Singapore	249,667	57	Morocco	32,516
19	Ireland	187,184	58	Luxembourg	30,176
20	Denmark	146,632	59	Tunisia	26,223
21	Turkey	145,556	60	Peru	24,744
22	Poland	142,110	61	Lebanon	21,121
23	Japan	132,851	62	Pakistan	20,086
24	Austria	126,895	63	Philippines	18,952
25	South Korea	119,630	64	Cyprus	18,414
26	Portugal	114,192	65	Estonia	16,594
27	Chile	105,558	66	Serbia and Montenegro	15,681
28	Czech Republic	101,074	67	Lithuania	14,679
29	Hungary	97,397	68	Panama	14,611
30	Norway	93,688	69	Jordan	14,549
31	South Africa	93,474	70	Sudan	13,828
32	Thailand	85,749	71	Trinidad and Tobago	13,475
33	Finland	85,237	72	Serbia	13,204
34	Malaysia	76,748	73	Bahrain	12,947
35	India	76,226	74	Iceland	12,269
36	Saudi Arabia	76,146	75	Angola	12,207
37	New Zealand	71,312	76	Algeria	11,815
38	Cayman Islands	69,784	77	Equatorial Guinea	10,745
39	Argentina	66,015	78	Latvia	10,493
79	Slovenia	10,350	116	Mozambique	3,216
80	Ecuador	10,310	117	Macedonia	3,084
81	Brunei Darussalam	10,045	118	Nicaragua	3,083
82	Syrian Arab Republic	9,684	119	Uganda	2,909
83	Costa Rica	8,803	123	Morocco	2,570

(Continued)

TABLE 6.1 Cont.

Rank	*Country*	*FDI US$ millions*	*Rank*	*Country*	*FDI US$ millions*
84	Macao	8,606	120	Montenegro	2,478
85	Jamaica	8,580	121	Armenia	2,448
86	Dominican Republic	8,269	122	Yemen	2,389
87	Bahamas	8,268	124	Liberia	2,278
88	Malta	7,457	125	Albania	2,264
89	Qatar	7,250	126	Paraguay	2,003
90	Azerbaijan	6,598	127	Antigua and Barbuda	1,986
91	Libya	6,575	128	Mauritania	1,905
92	Guatemala	6,506	129	Kenya	1,892
93	Bosnia and Herzegovina	5,990	130	Madagascar	1,830
94	Tanzania	5,942	131	Moldova	1,813
95	El Salvador	5,911	132	Saint Lucia	1,669
96	Oman	5,878	133	Uzbekistan	1,648
97	Cote d'Ivoire	5,702	134	Congo	1,512
98	Myanmar	5,433	135	Zimbabwe	1,492
99	Zambia	5,375	136	Fiji	1,464
100	Bolivia	5,323	137	Gibraltar	1,406
101	Iran	5,295	138	North Korea	1,378
102	Georgia	5,259	139	New Caledonia	1,360
103	Chad	5,085	140	Mongolia	1,326
104	Uruguay	5,069	141	Mali	1,326
105	Belarus	4,500	142	Botswana	1,300
106	Bangladesh	4,404	143	Bermuda	1,291
107	Honduras	4,328	144	Mauritius	1,249
108	Turkmenistan	3,928	145	Guyana	1,244
109	Namibia	3,822	146	Aruba	1,184
110	Cambodia	3,821	147	Laos	1,180
111	Congo	3,819	148	Iraq	1,162
112	Cameroon	3,796	149	Saint Kitts and Nevis	1,120
113	Ghana	3,634	150	Afghanistan	1,116
114	Ethiopia	3,620	151	Tajikistan	1,046
115	Sri Lanka	3,456			

Source: Adapted from 2007 Trade and Development Report, 2007, UNCTAD.

Even companies that have been founded in developing nations were using FDIs in order to exploit efficiencies of globally arranged value chains.

The growth of *strategic alliances* and of *mergers and acquisitions* and their deal values caused an increase in FDI. M&A activity has reached the $1 trillion mark, indicating large international investments. Some of the largest deals are shown in Table 6.2: note the large number of multinational enterprises (MNEs) in the areas of media (like Time Warner), pharmaceuticals, and telecommunications.

TABLE 6.2 Top M&A Deals Worldwide by Value (in $ billions) from 1990 to 2004

Year	*Purchaser*	*Purchased*	*Transaction value ($ billions)*
1999	Vodafone AirTouch PLC	Mannesmann	183
1999	Pfizer	Warner-Lambert	90
1998	Exxon	Mobil	77
1999	Citicorp	Travelers Group	73
1999	SBC Communications	Ameritech Corporation	63
1999	Vodafone Group	AirTouch Communications	60
1998	Bell Atlantic	GTE	53
1998	BP	Amoco	53
1999	Qwest Communications	US WEST	48
1997	Worldcom	MCI Communications	42
2000	Merger: America Online Inc. (AOL)	Time Warner	164
2000	Glaxo Wellcome plc	SmithKline Beecham plc	75
2004	Royal Dutch Petroleum Co.	Shell Transport & Trading Co.	74
2006	AT&T Inc.	BellSouth Corporation	72
2001	Comcast Corporation	AT&T Broadband & Internet Svcs	72
2004	Sanfoi-Synthelabo SA	Aventis SA	60
2000	Spin-off: Nortel Networks Corporation		59
2002	Pfizer Inc.	Pharmacia Corporation	59
2004	JP Morgan Chase & Co.	Bank One Corp.	58

Source: Based on Intralinks, www.intralinks.com, 2010.

Globalization has exponentially increased the market for cross-border M&A. This rapid increase has taken many MNEs firms by surprise because the majority of them never had to consider acquiring the capabilities or skills required to effectively handle this kind of transaction. In the past, the market's lack of significance and a more strictly national mindset prevented the vast majority of small and medium-sized enterprises from considering cross-border intermediation as an option, which left M&A firms inexperienced in this field. This same reason also prevented the development of any extensive academic works on the subject.

Due to the complicated nature of cross-border M&A, the vast majority of cross-border actions have been unsuccessful. Cross-border intermediation has many more levels of complexity to it than regular intermediation, seeing as corporate governance, the power of the average employee, company regulations, political factors, customer expectations, and countries' culture are all crucial factors that could spoil the transaction. However, with the weak dollar in the USA and the economic crisis of 2009–10 in most countries around the world, there is more cross-border bargain hunting as top companies seek to expand their global footprint and become more agile at creating high-performing businesses and cultures across national boundaries.

In general, cross-border M&A deals are driven by the need of local companies to get a foothold in a new geographic market, increase a firm's global competitiveness, fill gaps in companies' product lines in a global industry, and reduce costs in areas such as research and development, production, or distribution.

Side by side with the MNE's involvement with FDI, it is important to note the role played by international entrepreneurs and SMEs with FDI.

The role played by SMEs is enhanced since:

- financing is more easily available than in past.
- more small business people have international experience and are ready to exploit it.
- large MNEs are downsizing and outsourcing and provide business opportunities to international entrepreneurs.
- transportation, telecommunications, and information technology is available and economical for the smaller firms.
- the decision-making process in SMEs is faster than in large firms.

In most cases, entrepreneurs investing in other markets demonstrate initiative, resolution, and persistence that secures success in international ventures.

Foreign Direct Investment and Globalization

While developed countries remain the prime destination for FDI as cross-border M&As are attracting a growing amount of funding, developing countries in South East Asia, India, China, and the Philippines are also attractive to FDI. Almost US $2 trillion was involved in FDI in 2009 (compared to US $159 billion in 1991).

The USA remains the world's largest FDI recipient country, but with the global economic crisis of 2009, a reduction of global FDI flows is expected, including in countries in Central and Eastern Europe.

Foreign Direct Investment Theory

The theory of FDI must explain two interdependent decisions taken by executives of MNEs: namely, the best way to operate overseas and the best location for a overseas facility. There are several theories that explain why MNEs use FDI: international product life cycle, market internalization, eclectic theory, and market power. These are explained below.

International product life-cycle theory

The concept of international product life cycle helps explain both international trade and FDI. The theory of the international product life cycle is that a company will begin marketing a product through exports and later use FDI as a product moves through its life cycle. In the introductory product stage, it is produced in the home country because of uncertain domestic demand and to keep production close to the developing team in order to improve the product. In the growth product stage, the company directly invests in production facilities in countries where demand is large enough to warrant the ownership of production facilities. In the mature product stage, increased competition creates pressures to reduce production costs. In response, MNEs build production capacity in low-cost developing nations to serve its markets around the world competitively.

The international product life-cycle theory is limited in its power to explain why companies prefer FDI over other forms of selling overseas. A local firm in the target market could apply and pay for a license to use the special knowledge and assets needed to manufacture a particular product. This way, a company could avoid the additional risks associated with direct investments in the target market. The theory also fails to explain why firms choose FDI over exporting activities. It might be less expensive to serve a market abroad by increasing output at the home-country factory rather than by building additional capacity in the target market.

An alternative market implementation theory might explain better the use of FDI.

Market imperfections theory

Perfect markets are rarely, if ever, seen in business because of factors that cause a breakdown in the efficient operation of an industry – called market imperfections. Market imperfections theory states that when an imperfection in the market makes a transaction less efficient than it could be, a company will undertake FDI to internalize the transaction and thereby remove the imperfection. There are two market imperfections that are relevant to this theory: trade barriers and specialized knowledge.

Trade barriers

A common market imperfection in international business is trade barriers such as tariffs. Consequently, a large number of foreign manufacturers are opening facilities in Mexico or Canada and thereby enjoying the advantages of exporting within the North American Free Trade Agreement (NAFTA) region. In this way, the MNEs are able to avoid the North American tariffs that would have been levied if they were to export products from their home-based factories. In other words, the presence of a market imperfection, namely tariffs, caused MNEs to undertake FDI.

Specialized knowledge

At times, companies need an access to specialized knowledge that happens to be overseas, in a foreign country. One way to acquire this knowledge is to acquire the rights for a limited time or for a particular product. However, if this specialized knowledge is embedded in its employees, the best way to acquire it is through FDI.

ICQ is a specialised software that helps locate the presence of individuals on social networks. When AOL wanted to have this technology it has acquired Mirabilis, the developer of the ICQ software.

Eclectic theory

The eclectic theory states that MNEs undertake FDI when the features of a particular location combine with ownership and vertical integration advantages to make a location appealing for FDI. The advantages of locating a particular business activity in a specific location may be natural resources, such as oil or coal, but they may also be an educated, skillful workforce, brand recognition, technical knowledge, or management ability. A vertical integration advantage arises from making a business activity an integral part of the business rather than leaving it to a third party. The eclectic theory states that when all of the advantages are present in one form or another an MNE will undertake FDI.

Market power or dominance theory

The market or dominance power theory states that a firm tries to establish a dominant market presence in an industry by undertaking FDI. In this way, the firm is far better able to dictate the cost of its inputs and/or the price of its output.

As explained earlier, a vertical integration – the extension of company activities into stages of production that provide a firm's inputs or absorb its output – helps the company to achieve market dominance. This backward or forward integration may be done through FDI in target countries. Companies may also achieve market dominance by making investments in distribution channels in foreign markets in order to compete effectively with local or locally based corporations.

FDI Decisions and International Management

Decisions about whether to engage in FDI involve important issues regarding the management of the corporation and the environments in which it operates. Some of these issues are concerned with internal environment, such as the operation's control abroad or the corporation cost of production and labor. Other issues are related to the external environment, including government and public policy issues. Each of these issues is discussed below.

Internal environment

Acquire or build

One of the major decisions is to acquire an existing business or build a subsidiary abroad from the ground up – called a "Greenfield investment" – in a target country. An acquisition of an existing business usually provides the investor with an existing plant – equipment as well as personnel – in a target country.

Acquiring a local business helps the acquiring corporation benefit from the goodwill of the local company that was built up over the years as well as its brand recognition. However, factors that can reduce the appeal of an acquisition in a target country include obsolete equipment, poor relations with workers, an unsuitable location, and inadequate local management.

Teva, the world largest generic drug manufacturer, is a multinational company that has done very well in terms of sales and profits by buying inefficient plants around the world and improving manufacturing processes. The success of Teva in raising capital for acquisitions and streamlining production of facilities in both Europe and the USA is based mostly on acquiring existing businesses.

Greenfield FDIs may be the only way to enter a new market. However, greenfield investments may be difficult, owing to the need to obtain the necessary permits, financing, and hiring and training of local personnel.

Labor

In most FDIs the business engages the local workforce and middle management. As such, the acquiring corporations should study, explore, and adhere to local labor standards and practices.

Managers should not assume that policies used at home can simply be adopted in the local economy. These local policies abide by local regulations and laws. The local rules may dictate employment conditions and compensation rules that are gender- or age-based, different from the home-base rules.

Labor costs may vary from country to country owing to wage differences as well as mandatory or voluntary social benefits, health insurance, company-supplied clothing and meals, profit sharing, and dismissal policies. The costs of these programs may double employee wages. Violations of these regulations may result in government seizure of company property, assessment of large fines, and prosecution of executives. Unions differ from country to country. In other countries unions negotiate through national trade unions that meet with the national employers' association.

Production costs

Production costs affect MNE's profitability and competitiveness and are affected by many factors, such as hourly wages, benefits package, productivity levels, training expenses, and local taxes. These costs change over time. As a result, MNEs may change the locations of facilities.

Global supply chains, a worldwide network of facilities, all engaging in the manufacturing of parts of a particular product are based on location. This approach is termed a nationalized or agile production system. A television made in China may be produced from parts that are imported to China from all over the world. The risk of such an approach to production is that stoppage of imports from a certain country owing to labor unrest may cause an assembly line to cease production altogether.

Control

Most corporations that invest overseas are concerned about control of their operations. The need for control is obvious. Overseas operations need to be managed in a manner that conforms to the overall corporate strategy, including pricing, marketing, and human resources development. In order to assure control, corporations insist on 100 percent ownership, if possible by local laws. However, in some countries 100 percent ownership is not possible, and a partnership with local entities in the target country is required. Many governments, even in developing countries, lure FDIs by relaxing FDI regulations and cooperating with MNEs.

Governments of many developing countries acknowledge the benefits of investment by MNEs, including decreased unemployment, increased tax revenues, training of a skilled workforce, and the transfer of production and process technologies. Countries in central Europe and China welcome FDIs, while India practices a restrictive policy regarding FDI investments.

External environment

Customer behavior

FDI in a target country enhances the corporate understanding of local customer behavior and helps adjusting the product or service according to local preferences. Furthermore, an FDI in a facility is sometimes affected by customer perception. As an example, a manufacturer of textile fashion goods should be located in Italy, since Italy is noted for the quality of its fashion designers.

Supply chain considerations

Since many MNEs outsource components and subassemblies from various suppliers, an FDI by the MNE may necessitate the suppliers also, setting up shop in a foreign country through FDI. This proximity is required in order to maintain the MNE as a customer.

Competitors considerations

Competitor presence in a particular country may cause an MNE to initiate an FDI in that country. The rivalry between Pepsi and Coca-Cola caused the presence of both in many countries.

FDI and Regional Headquarters

A specific form of FDI is a regional headquarters (RHQ). Regional headquarters are established in order to control and coordinate MNE activities in various regions of the world. For example, the automotive manufacturer BMW's RHQ in China, the pharmaceutical corporation Pfizer RHQ in Nigeria, and the Hewlett Packard RHQ in Prague.

The roles of RHQ are many and include:

- identifying new business opportunities in the region;
- recruiting local talent in the region;
- assisting in communicating the corporate strategy to the local subsidiaries;
- assisting in planning and coordination of activities in the region;
- providing efficient customer service in the region;
- following closely competition activities in the region;
- providing a significant presence in the region.

Establishing an RHQ requires an FDI in a carefully selected location. The location decision is based on a variety of factors, including locational stability in a target country, appropriate infrastructure (telecommunications, transportation), appropriate regulatory system, access to local financial and commercial services, attractive tax rates, and availability of highly skilled workers.

Public Policies and Foreign Direct Investment

Public policies in various countries are designed to control the amount and intensity of FDI. This control is exercised in order to limit the influence of FDI on host country jobs, balance of payments, domestic corporations, and local culture.

One of the most important public policy issues is a country's balance of payment, which is a national accounting system that records all payments to organizations in other countries and all receipts coming into the nation. International transactions that result in payments (outflows) to organizations in other nations are balanced against receipts (inflows) from other nations and adequately recorded. Thus, when a German company buys 20 percent of the publicly traded stock of a Japanese company, the German balance of payments records the transaction as an outflow of capital.

Income from the sale (or purchase) of products and services abroad is recorded on the national balance of payments as a "current account." Funds from the sale (or acquisition) of assets such as manufacturing plants are recorded on the national balance of payments as a "capital account." Both of the accounts are guarded carefully by public policymakers and governments. All international investments affect the balance of payments of both the home and host countries.

Host country intervention

Many governments consider intervention in FDI transactions as the only way to keep the balance of payments under control. By encouraging FDI, the balance of payments improves at the host country due to cash inflows. In addition, by controlling the modus operandi of the invested organization, jobs may be maintained and expanded and export intensity by the invested organization may be managed to bring the desirable impact on the balance of payments of the host country.

Beyond balance of payments' reasons, public policymakers might intervene in an FDI for other reasons such as encouraging access to the technology used in products and production processes, acquiring management skills, and encouraging employment.

Home country intervention

Home countries from which MNEs launch their investments also seek to control outflows of FDI. These are several reasons to control outflows of FDI. First, investing in other nations sends resources out of the home country and fewer resources are used for development and economic growth at home. Second, outgoing FDI may ultimately damage a nation's balance of payments by taking the place of its exports. For example, if a US based facility that is producing cars for export purposes mainly is replaced by a comparable facility bought through an FDI in India, all income from exports is lost from the US balance of payments (from "current accounts"). Third, jobs resulting from outgoing investments may replace jobs at home. The relocation of production to a low-wage nation, such as India or China, can have a strong impact on the home country. Fourth, an outward FDI can increase long-term competitiveness by having MNEs conduct business in the most favorable locations anywhere in the world. As a result, MNEs continuously improve their performance relative to competitors, and derive technological advantages from alliances formed with other companies.

This is especially true for home countries who would like to get rid of sunset industries with outdated and obsolete technologies and employment of low-wage workers with few skills. By allowing the sunset industries' jobs to go abroad and retraining workers in higher-paying skilled work, they can upgrade their economies toward new industries such as biotechnology, nano technology, software development, and event-based telecommunications.

As stated in several chapters in the book, governments issue policies, laws and regulations that affect international business in general and FDIs in particular. Some of the ways in which governments may intervene in FDI appear in Table 6.3.

TABLE 6.3 Government Intervention and Foreign Direct Investment

	FDI promotion	*FDI restriction*
Host countries	Personal and corporate tax incentives Low-interest loans Infrastructure	Ownership restrictions Performance demands Environmental protection
Home countries	FDI insurance Loans Tax breaks Political pressure	Differential tax rates FDI sanctions

Source: Adapted from http://www.answers.com/topic/mergers-and-acquisitions.

COUNTRY FOCUS

CANADA

World Rank (EFI 2009): 7

Regional Rank (EFI 2009): 2

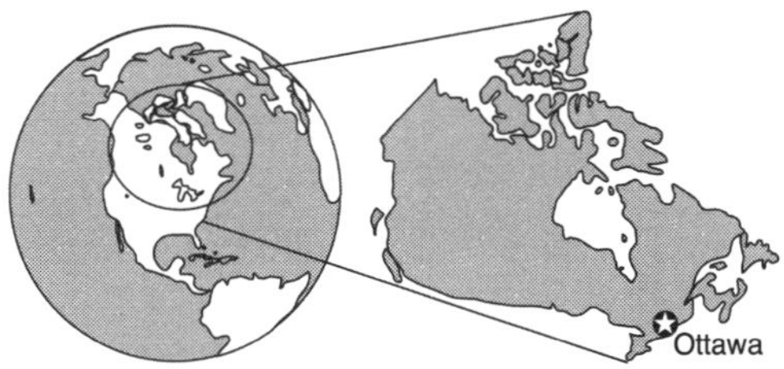

Quick facts

Population: 32.6 million

GDP (PPP): $1.2 trillion; 2.8 percent growth in 2006; 2.7 percent 5-year compound annual growth; $36,713 per capita

Unemployment: 6.0 percent

Inflation (CPI): 2.1 percent

FDI inflow: $69.0 billion

2006 data unless otherwise noted

Economic freedom score

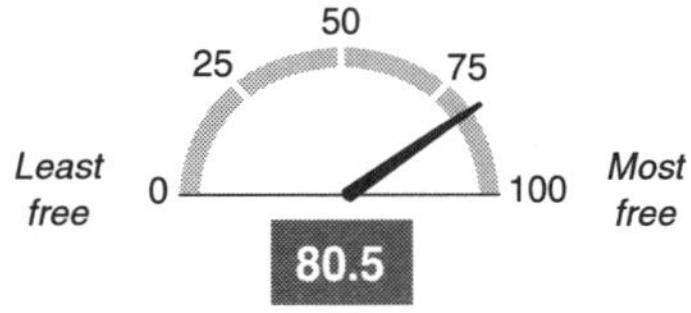

Canada's economic freedom score is 80.5, making its economy the 7th freest in the 2009 Index. Canada is ranked 2nd out of three countries in the North America region.

Canada scores very high in eight of the 10 economic freedoms, especially business freedom, property rights, and freedom from corruption. The process for conducting a business is straightforward and facilitates vibrant entrepreneurial activity. Overall regulation is thorough but essentially transparent. A strong rule of law ensures property rights and the transparent application of the commercial code.

Canada trails the world average only in size and expense of government. Like many European democracies, Canada has elaborate social and welfare state programs that raise government spending. However, it has been able to establish sound fiscal management and federal budget surpluses in recent years, providing a competitive edge.

Background

Canada is a multicultural society with a strong and stable democratic political system that has proven capable of handling ethnic tensions that have arisen from time to time. One of the world's leading free market economies, Canada is a major exporter of oil, minerals, automobiles, manufactured goods, and forest products. Over 75 percent of its exports are to the USA. Despite one of the Organization for Economic Cooperation and Development's (OECD's) most restrictive foreign ownership policies in telecommunications, publishing, broadcasting, aviation, mining, and fishing, macroeconomic fundamentals remain strong. In May and June of 2008, Canada strengthened its commitment to become a more active economic and social partner in the Americas by concluding free trade negotiations with Colombia and signing a similar agreement with Peru.

(Continued)

Business freedom – 96.5

The overall freedom to start, operate, and close a business is strongly protected under Canada's regulatory environment. Starting a business takes an average of five days, compared to the world average of 38 days. Obtaining a business license requires less than the world average of 18 procedures and 225 days.

Trade freedom – 88.2

Canada's weighted average tariff rate was 0.9 percent in 2006. Federal and provincial non-tariff barriers, restrictions on imports of domestic "supply managed" agricultural products, restricted access to telecommunications and media, export controls, import and export taxes, export-support programs for industry and agriculture producers, state trading boards for some agriculture products, and issues involving the protection of intellectual property rights add to the cost of trade. Ten points were deducted from Canada's trade freedom score to account for nontariff barriers.

Fiscal freedom – 76.6

Canada has moderate tax rates. The top federal income tax rate is 29 percent, and provincial rates range from 10 percent to 24 percent. The federal surtax has been eliminated, the general corporate tax rate reduced to 19.5 percent and the federal goods and services tax reduced to 5 percent. Other taxes include a value-added tax (VAT) and a property tax. In the most recent year, overall tax revenue as a percentage of GDP was 33.4 percent.

Government size – 53.7

Total government expenditures, including consumption and transfer payments, are high. In the most recent year, government spending equaled 39.3 percent of gross domestic product (GDP). Privatization is widespread, and the government encourages competition even in sectors formerly operated by government or privately owned monopolies.

Monetary freedom – 80.8

Inflation is low, averaging 2.1 percent between 2004 and 2006. The market determines most prices, but the government regulates the prices of some utilities, provides subsidies to industry and agriculture producers, controls prices for some agricultural products, and may influence prices through state-owned enterprises. Ten points were deducted from Canada's monetary freedom score to account for measures that distort domestic prices.

Investment freedom – 70

Canada treats foreign and domestic capital equally in almost all situations. A federal agency, Investment Canada, must approve FDIs, whether through new ventures or through acquisitions. Though investment is usually approved, Canada remains one of the few OECD countries to require approval. Restricted sectors include broadcasting and telecommunications, newspapers, energy monopolies, book publishing, filmmaking and distribution, retail banking and insurance, and air transport. There are no restrictions on current transfers, repatriation of profits, purchase of real estate, or access to foreign exchange.

Financial freedom – 80

Canada's financial system provides many options for businesses and a wide range of competitive services for investors. Credit is allocated on market terms without government interference. The "big six" domestic banks dominate the financial sector, and foreign banks, despite their recent growth, account for a small portion of total assets. The procedure for foreign banks' entry into the Canadian market has been simplified, and their overall regulatory burden has been reduced. Revisions of the Bank Act in 2007 focused on streamlining regulation and enhancing consumer protection. Mergers between large banks remain restricted, and large banks may not buy large insurance companies. The largest insurance companies are global and conduct more than half of their business overseas. Securities markets are well developed; the Montreal and Toronto exchanges merged in May 2008 while maintaining their areas of specialization.

Property rights – 90

Private property is well protected. The judiciary is independent, and judges and civil servants are generally honest. Foreign investors have full access to the legal system, and private property rights are limited only by the rights of governments to establish monopolies and to expropriate for public purposes. Canada has yet to ratify the World Intellectual Property Organization's Internet Treaties, which it signed in 1997. Some companies have complained that enforcement against counterfeiting and piracy is cumbersome and ineffective.

Freedom from corruption – 87

Corruption is perceived as minimal. Canada ranks 9th out of 179 countries in Transparency International's Corruption Perceptions Index for 2007. Bribery and other forms of corruption are rare. Canada has signed the UN Convention Against Corruption.

Labor freedom – 81.9

Flexible labor regulations enhance employment and productivity growth. The nonsalary cost of employing a worker is moderate, and dismissing a redundant employee is relatively inexpensive. Rules on expanding or contracting working hours are flexible.

Source: Adapted from Terry Miller and Kim R. Holmes, *2009 Index of Economic Freedom* (Washington, DC: The Heritage Foundation and Dow Jones & Company, Inc., 2009), at www.heritage.org/index.

SUMMARY

Foreign direct investment (FDI) continues to expand. Although the global economic slowdown in 2009 caused FDI to grow at a slower rate, it gets closer to $2 trillion and is an important part of both world production and trade.

Developed countries account for more than three-quarters of global FDI inflows, while developing countries' share of world FDI flows is about one-quarter.

Globalization and a growing number of mergers and acquisitions (M&A) account for the growth in FDI. This growth pattern and its causes are expected to continue well into the future, despite the global economic crisis of 2009.

The **international product life-cycle theory** states that an MNE will begin an international activity by exporting its product and later undertake FDI as a product moves through its life cycle. In the new product stage, a good is

(Continued)

produced in the home country. In the maturing product stage, the company directly invests in production facilities in the countries in which demand is high. In the final standardized product stage, a company builds production capacity in low-cost nations to serve its markets around the world.

The **market imperfections theory** states that when an imperfection in the market makes a transaction less efficient than it could be, a company will undertake FDI to internalize the transaction and thereby remove the imperfection. This may take the form of buying supplies or acquiring distribution channels.

The **eclectic theory** states that firms undertake FDI when all parameters of a particular location combine with ownership and internalization advantages to make a location appealing for investment.

The **market power theory** states that a firm tries to establish a dominant market presence in an industry by undertaking FDI. One way a company achieves market power is through backward or forward vertical integration

There are key management issues involved in FDI decisions. First, MNEs need to make decisions regarding control of activities in a host country. This control may take the form of hiring and compensation of employees, reporting standards and practices, etc. Second, MNEs make decisions to acquire an existing business or take the approach of "Greenfield investment." Third, the MNE has to decide on the best location to produce each one of the components, around the world – an approach termed "rationalized global supply chain." Fourth, MNEs make location decisions based on the need to be close to the customers and to the competitors.

Governments intervene in foreign direct investment for several reasons: to protect their balance of payments of host countries; to improve their balance of payments position from the exports of local production operations created by an FDI; to increase the productivity and competitiveness of the nation through local investment in technology. By encouraging FDI, nations can also bring in people with management skills who can train locals and thus improve the competitiveness of local companies. Furthermore, many local jobs are also created as a result of an incoming FDI. Home countries intervene in FDI in order to protect local jobs and maintain an acceptable balance of payments.

Governments use various tools to promote and restrict foreign direct investment, including ownership restrictions, tax incentives, loans, FDI insurance rates, and political pressure.

DISCUSSION QUESTIONS

1. What may be the reason for a US automotive manufacturer to set up plant in China? What FDI issues may this manufacturer face?
2. What changes to FDI do you observe as a result of the 2009 global economic crisis?
3. Describe the role of production costs in the FDI decision. How can rationalized production help in regard to the FDI decision?
4. How does the need for following customers and following competition impact the FDI decision?
5. For what reasons do host countries and home countries intervene in FDI?
6. In what ways do home and host countries promote and restrict FDI?
7. This chapter presents several theories that have been proposed to explain the flow of FDI. Which of these theories seems most appropriate to explain FDIs made by (a) pharmaceutical MNEs, (b) telecommunications MNEs, and (c) major accounting and consulting firms?

A Case

South Korea: Foreign Direct Investment in First Quarter of 2009 – Down 44 percent

On March 24, 2009 it was observed that inbound foreign investment to South Korea dropped 44 percent on a year-to-year basis in the first quarter. This plunge was attributed to the global economic slump that has sapped most business sectors.

In dollar terms the amount of FDI monies were down from $2.7 billion to around $1.5 billion, attributed to the lack of M&A deals and the fact that large investments were going to the USA.

Most funds that were to arrive during 2009 are follow-up investments for existing local operations, with very few new arrivals. It was pointed out that while bargain-hunting investments flowed into the country following the 1997–98 Asian financial crisis, global funds are currently seeking bargain purchases in the USA.

Business investment is important to South Korea because it fuels growth and creates more jobs. The country was expected to post –2 percent growth in 2009 compared with a 2.5 percent gain in 2008.

Questions

1 How can South Korea encourage the amount of FDI? What kind of public decisions should be made to make it happen?
2 How can South Korea benefit from FDI outflows (a) to industrialized countries and (b) to developing countries in the South East Asia region?

INTERNATIONAL MANAGEMENT INSIGHT

Procter & Gamble Foreign Direct Investment in Egypt

This decade marks a 25-year history of FDI in Egypt of one of the leading MNEs in consumer products. The development of Egypt's industrial sector and economy in the 1980s lured Procter & Gamble (P&G) to establish an Egyptian subsidiary, and a factory was built. The factory produced two brands of soaps – Camay and Crest® – and involved a modest capital of 12 million Egyptian pounds and a workforce of 50 people. During two decades, manufacturing facilities have grown and now generate more than 1.25 billion Egyptian pounds in revenues, placing P&G among the country's leading FDIs.

With this large expansion, P&G's Egypt's production level and development have been significant. In 1990, P&G Egypt constructed the biggest synthetic detergent tower of its kind in the Middle East to produce Ariel, the Company's well-known detergent, and other brands followed almost annually. Today, P&G Egypt manages a portfolio of 14 brands out of the nearly 300 P&G international brands. In the year 2000, P&G established a plan to make Egypt the main production center for Ariel for the whole Middle East region. Thus, the Egyptian facilities are becoming the main source of exporting detergents and paper products in the area.

Today, P&G Egypt is the country's biggest exporter of packaged goods, and one of the top 10 exporting companies, exporting to more than 34 countries in Africa, Asia, and Europe. The FDI has contributed to the advancement of local management talent skills in Egypt, as 700 employees are employed directly by P&G and thousands of others are employed indirectly, using the most advanced technologies and management practices.

P&G claims that it has seen its investments grow more than 100-fold, the workforce increase 15-fold, and exports grow by 85 times. At the end of 2006, in recognition of its outstanding performance and quality, P&G Egypt was honored with the National Award for Quality, awarded by Ministry of Trade and Industry's Industrial Modernization Center (IMC). As such, this FDI was beneficial to both P&G and the local Egyptian economy.

Bibliography

Bora, J. (ed.) (1998). *Foreign Direct Investment*. London: Routledge.

Cavusgil, S. T. (1998). International partnering: a systematic framework for collaborating with foreign business partners. *Journal of International Marketing*, 6, 91–107.

Chung, W., Alcacer, J. (2002). Knowledge seeking and location choice of foreign direct investment in the United States. *Management Science*, 48(12): 1534–54.

Contractor, F., and Lorange, P. (2002). *Cooperative Strategies and Alliances*. Oxford: Elsevier Science.

Davidson, W. H. (1982). *Global Strategic Management*. New York: Wiley.

Dunning, J. (1981). *International Production and the Multinational Enterprise*. London: Allen and Unwin.

Hamel, G., Doz, Y., Prahalad, C. K. (1989). Collaborate with your competitors – and win. *Harvard Business Review*, January–February, 67, 133–45.

Head, T. C., Sorensen, P. (2005). Attracting foreign direct investment: the potential role of national culture. *Journal of American Academy of Business*, 6, 305–9.

Javalgi, R., Griffith, D. A., Steven, D. (2003). An empirical examination of factors influencing the internalization of service firms. *Journal of Services Marketing*, 17, 185–201.

Katz, B., Owen, J. (2006). Should governments compete for foreign direct investment? *Journal of Economic Behavior & Organization*, 59, 230–48.

Kearny, A. T. Inc. (2004). *FDI Confidence Index*. Alexandria, VA: Global Business Policy Council.

Lotsson, A. (2005). Tomorrow: a sneak preview. *Business 2.0*, August, 77–84.

Nachum, L., Wymbs, C. (2005). Product differentiation, external economies and MNE location choices: M&As in global cities. *Journal of International Business Studies*, 36, 415–34.

Townsend, J. (2003). Understanding Alliances: A Review of International Aspects in Strategic Marketing. *Marketing Intelligence & Planning*, 21(3): 58–143.

UNCTAD (2008). *World Investment Report 2008*. New York: United Nations Conference on Trade and Development.

7

International Trade, Investment, and Regional Integration

Learning Objectives

Following this chapter, the reader should be able to:

1. Understand regional economic integration
2. Define the benefits of regional integration
3. Identify regional blocks in various parts of the world
4. Understand management and entrepreneurial implications of regional integration

Opening Case

Advancing e-Commerce in the Asia-Pacific Economic Cooperation (APEC) Region

APEC is a group of countries in the Asia-Pacific region that subscribe to economic cooperation. During the past decade, governments and private organizations in the region of APEC have had to deal with the issue of e-commerce, as it has become a growing domestic, regional, and international marketplace and trading mechanism. There are many examples of e-commerce, including the popular eBay internet trading marketplace as well as Amazon.com, supporting both customer-to-customer (C to C) and business-to-customer (B to C) transactions.

Over the past decade, APEC has created an Electronic Commerce Steering Group and the APEC Telecommunications and Information Working Group, and has made advances in areas such as cyber security, data privacy, and consumer protection. The main goal of these initiatives is to develop practical policy solutions to help the region deal with cross-border issues associated with the growth of electronic commerce.

The APEC region has experienced tremendous growth since its formation in 1989. APEC members account for half of world trade, 41 percent of the world's population and 57 percent of world gross domestic product (GDP). Per capita GDP has increased by 26 percent compared with 8 percent for non-APEC economies. Tariffs in APEC economies have decreased from 17 percent in 1988 to below 5 percent in 2008. Furthermore, more efficient customs procedures, progress towards paperless trading, and other trade facilitation measures were introduced to save businesses millions of dollars each year. Thus, the APEC region is a dynamic and important market, with enormous potential for e-commerce development.

In achieving its status as the pre-eminent organization promoting economic growth in the Asia-Pacific region, APEC has developed some unique ways of conducting its business. Unlike negotiating bodies such as the World Trade Organization (WTO), APEC works on the basis of voluntarism, consensus, and concerted unilateralism, and provides a forum for discussing best-practice advice and guidelines on a wide range of governance and technical issues.

Senior public decision leaders and decision makers meet to harmonize economies, standards, and practices. This forum is called The Leaders' Meeting. At this meeting the leaders set the priorities for APEC and make the key decisions that are then implemented by ministers and officials from each economy.

APEC solidifies its relationship with the private sector through the APEC Business Advisory Council, or ABAC, which consists of three business representatives appointed by each member economy. Its members meet annually with the public decision makers each year to provide recommendations on issues that are of importance to business in the region.

APEC deals with several issues that are related to commerce and e-commerce, as follows. First, APEC promotes a multilateral trading system and investment liberalization with the goal of free and open trade in developed economies by 2010 and in developing economies by 2020. It should be noted that, for APEC economies, the WTO remains the primary mechanism by which APEC countries aim to achieve free and open trade. Second, APEC is committed to ensuring the energy needs of the economies of the region while, at the same time, addressing the issue of environmental quality and contributing to the reduction of greenhouse gas emissions. Third, APEC is actively looking for new ways to promote regional economic integration, including a free trade area of the Asia Pacific as a long-term prospect. Fourth, APEC makes doing business easier by implementing structural reforms within domestic APEC economies and making them more transparent and efficient and less bureaucratic, costly, and burdensome for business. It has been estimated by the World Bank that these changes could be worth in the range of $100–150 billion annually in new trade and investment for APEC economies.

APEC has implemented a number of e-commerce initiatives as it recognizes the enormous potential of electronic commerce to facilitate trade, expand business opportunities, reduce costs, increase efficiency, and facilitate the greater participation of small businesses in global commerce. However, these e-commerce initiatives involve complex and highly advanced technologies. Thus, given the highly diverse group of countries within APEC, when it comes to designing effective strategies and action plans for e-commerce, it is essential for APEC to take into account the different stages of development of member economies, and the varied regulatory, social, economic, and cultural frameworks in the region.

APEC has defined a road map of strategies and action plans. First, following the 1998 Blueprint for Action on e-commerce which was designed to consolidate and reinforce the various APEC initiatives related to e-commerce, the Electronic Commerce Steering Group (ECSG) was established. The first action was the promotion of the e-commerce Readiness Initiative through a private sector-driven project. This project was designed to assess the status of the e-commerce environment in each individual member economy so that concrete steps could be taken to address national-level issues, thereby facilitating the acceleration of e-commerce at a regional level. Second, a project was initiated under the title of Paperless Trading Initiative. APEC member economies have agreed to "reduce or eliminate the requirement for paper documents needed for customs and other cross-border trade administration" during the first decade of the 21st century, setting target dates dependent on the level of economic development of member economies. Progress made is tracked via each economy's Paperless Trading Individual Action Plan. Third, APEC has initiated work to enable the electronic transmission of trade-related information across the region by 2020. Fourth, a large majority of economies have started to develop and implement information and communications technologies (ICT) or e-commerce strategies. However, these strategies are at very different stages of development. Whereas developed economies are focused on issues such as broadband access, or the building of regional networks, developing countries focus on key elements such as human capacity building, basic access to ICT, and low-cost hardware and software to list a few. Fifth, access to new technologies and the Internet is considered a key element of e-commerce strategies and a prerequisite for enhancing the participation of businesses and consumers in e-commerce and the digital economy. Thus, APEC economies are reducing telecommunications trade barriers, resulting in increased accessibility and the long-term affordability of telecommunications access in the region, particularly for people in developing countries. Internet access in the APEC region has more than doubled since the year 2000 and some economies have more than tripled their Internet access. Sixth, the digital divide in the Asia-Pacific region, as is the case in other parts of the world, is not only between developed and developing economies but also between urban and rural populations, between more- and less-educated people and between women and men. Thus, the Digital Divide Blueprint for Action and the e-APEC Strategy aim to transform the digital divide so that APEC economies will benefit from the opportunities presented by a networked environment of the new digital economy.

In all of the above initiatives, the most important prerequisite is that businesses and consumers are educated about the opportunities and benefits offered by ICT, and people are trained to use the Internet.

Without confident e-consumers, there would be no e-commerce. It is imperative to ensure consumer protection and to ensure that online traders observe specific rules and guidelines to diffuse the fears of consumers and promote ethical online transactions. In order to build trust in e-commerce, work has been undertaken to help economies implement APEC's voluntary consumer protection guidelines for the online environment. These cover international cooperation, education and awareness, private sector leadership, online advertising and marketing, and the resolution of consumer disputes. Furthermore, the APEC countries have to deal with the issues of security and privacy. With regard to security, APEC member economies have combined their efforts to combat threats under the APEC cyber security strategy, which includes a package of measures to protect business and consumers from cyber crime and to strengthen consumer trust in the use of e-commerce. Practical tools to protect small and medium-sized enterprises (SMEs) as well as home users, from attacks and spreading viruses have also been developed. These include advice on how to use the Internet securely, safety issues relating to wireless technologies, and safe e-mail exchanges.

APEC is a regional group of countries that is working to facilitate and enhance e-commerce. However, in order for the regional effort to be successful on security and safety issues, a global approach is needed to combat cyber crime. To that end, APEC is cooperating with the International Telecommunication Union (ITU) and the Association of Southeast Asian Nations (ASEAN) on cyber security and network security and with the Organization for Economic Cooperation and Development (OECD) on the preparation of action plans against malicious software. Recent initiatives adopted to promote consumer trust and business confidence in cross-border data flows include the APEC privacy framework and the APEC data privacy framework.

APEC recognizes that the business sector plays a leading role in developing electronic commerce technology, applications, practices, and services. Thus, a public–private collaboration is required in order to develop and implement joint initiatives for the fast development and use of electronic commerce in the region: hence the participation of business organizations, including the Global Business Dialogue on Electronic Commerce, the International Chamber of Commerce (ICC), and the Pan Asian Alliance on e-Commerce (PAA). Data privacy issues are dealt with by the OECD, and electronic standards for paperless trade are dealt with the United Nations Centre for Trade Facilitation and Electronic Business (UNCEFACT).

APEC member countries have concluded that in order to ensure the development of an efficient and productive global e-commerce working environment all relevant stakeholders must work together, including the private sector and governments.

Introduction – Think Global, Act Regional

Business activities around the world are affected when several countries decide to create a trading region. Multinational enterprises (MNEs) operating within a trading region have to abide by national as well as regional business standards and practices, including, for example, environmental and labor laws.

Regional trade agreements lower trade barriers and open up new markets for goods and services. As trade agreements allow domestic companies to seek new markets abroad, they also let competitors from other nations enter the domestic market. Such openness increases global competition in all market that are part of the regional trade agreement.

Trade agreements are being structured in all continents. Nations in the Americas are working to create a free trade area from North America to South America. This trading region is called Free Trade Area of the Americas (FTAA).

The FTAA is expected to create a huge marketplace, without tariffs and equipped with regional mechanisms to control the orderly production of goods and services and the provision of goods and services. The APEC trading region described in the opening case consists of economies in South East Asia. In the opening case, it becomes clear how e-commerce initiatives in the region are helped by regional cooperation in infrastructure and operating standards development for e-commerce.

In Part Two of the book we describe the advantages of specialization and trade. Further advantages are a result of eliminating trade barriers on a regional basis and encouraging intra-region investments. This chapter begins by defining regional economic integration and integration levels. This is followed by a list of benefits and drawbacks of regional trade agreements. The chapter further describes several long-established and emerging regional trade agreements.

Defining Regional Economic Integration

Regional economic integration is a process whereby countries in a geographic region enter into an agreement to reduce or eliminate barriers to the international flow of products, people, or capital.

This agreement includes the creation of regional institutions and rules. Its objectives could range from economic to political. Sometimes it is the means to achieve broader socio-political and security objectives. Past efforts at regional integration have been focused on removing barriers to free trade in the region, increasing the free movement of people, labor, goods, and capital across national borders, reducing the possibility of regional armed conflict and adopting a cohesive regional approach towards policy issues, such as the environment, climate change, and migration.

There have been several efforts at regional integration, including ASEAN, NAFTA (North American Free Trade Agreement) and MERCOSUR (Southern Common Market). The most well-known and developed regional integration initiative has been the European Union (EU), which, in some policy areas, has moved beyond an inter-governmental approach to decision making at a federal level.

Regional integration has been based on an association of states located in a given geographical area, whose terms are fixed by a treaty or other arrangements. Regional integration is the joining of individual countries within a region into a larger whole. The degree of integration depends upon the willingness and commitment of independent sovereign countries to share their sovereignty.

Regional integration initiatives fulfill at least eight important functions:

- the strengthening of trade integration in the region;
- the creation of an appropriate enabling environment for private sector development;
- the development of infrastructure programs in support of economic growth and regional integration;
- the development of strong public sector institutions and good governance;
- the reduction of social exclusion and the development of an inclusive civil society;
- contribution to peace and security in the region;
- the building of environment programs at the regional level;
- the strengthening of the region's interaction with other regions of the world.

A group of nations in a geographic region undergoing economic integration is called a regional trading bloc.

The goal of countries undergoing economic integration is not only to increase cross-border trade and investment but also to raise living standards for their people. We saw in Chapter 5, for instance, how specialization and trade create real gains in terms of greater choice, lower prices, and increased productivity. Regional trade agreements are designed to help countries accomplish these objectives. Regional economic integration sometimes has additional goals, such as protection of intellectual property rights or the environment.

Levels of regional integration

Various theories have demonstrated the potential gains available through international trade. Based on these theories, nations have developed national policies and practices to reap these benefits in a variety of ways. Figure 7.1 shows six potential levels of economic and political integration in creating regional trading blocs. An economic and trade cooperation is the lowest form of regional integration. Each level of integration incorporates the properties, rules, and regulations of the levels that precede it.

Economic and trade cooperation

An economic and trade cooperation is the lowest form of regional integration. At this initiation level, countries create committees and task forces on trade and investment liberalization, business facilitation, economic and technical cooperation, counter terrorism, human security, climate change, emergency preparedness, energy security, clean environment, and the global financial crisis. The latter cooperation effort is a result of the financial crisis of 2008–10. An example of this type of regional arrangement is APEC, the Asia-Pacific Economic Cooperation initiative, where a coordinated effort by nations, regionally and

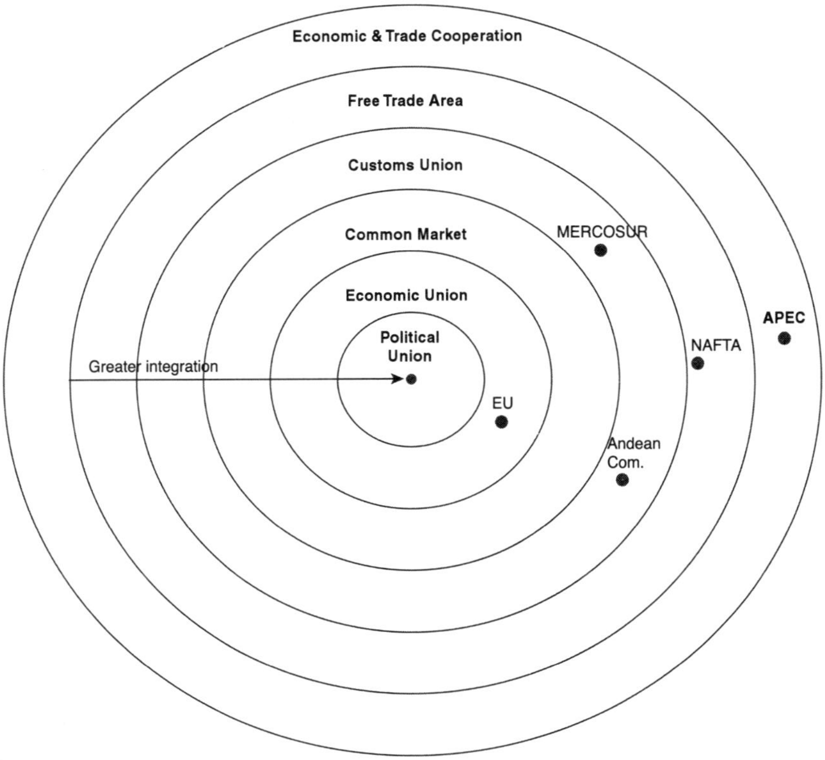

FIGURE 7.1 Levels of regional integration

around the world, seem to have contained the collapse of world economies and financial markets.

Free trade area

A free trade area is an economic integration whereby countries remove all barriers to trade between themselves, but each country determines its own barriers against nonmembers.

Countries belonging to the free trade area remove all tariffs and nontariff barriers, such as quotas and subsidies, on international trade in goods and services. Countries belonging to a free trade area establish a process by which trade disputes are resolved.

Customs union

A customs union is an economic integration whereby countries remove all barriers to trade among themselves and establish a common trade policy against nonmembers. Countries belonging to a customs union might also negotiate as a single entity with other regions and international organizations like the WTO.

Common market

A common market is an economic integration whereby countries remove all barriers to trade and the movement of labor and capital between themselves but establish a common trade policy against nonmembers. A common market integrates the elements of free trade areas and customs unions and adds the free movement of important factors of production, such as workers, and free cross-border investment. This movement of production factors requires a major political commitment and may drain a particular member country of factors of production, labor, and capital.

Economic union

An economic union is an economic integration whereby countries remove barriers to trade and the movement of labor and capital, establish a common trade policy against nonmembers, and coordinate their economic policies. An economic union goes beyond the demands of a common market by requiring that member nations harmonize their tax, monetary, and fiscal policies and that they create a common currency.

Political union

A political union is an economic and political integration whereby countries coordinate aspects of their economic and political systems. A political union requires member countries to accept a common approach towards economic and political policies regarding nonmember nations. A group of countries currently taking steps in this direction is the European Union, which has founded pan-European political governing bodies.

Effects of Regional Economic Integration

Regional trade agreements have a major impact on jobs, companies, cultures, and living standards. There are several arguments for and against regional trade agreements. However, on balance, there are more initiatives to create regional trading blocs, reflecting the overall positive impact of same.

Aside from the economic effects of regional integration, there is the cultural aspect of such agreements. Some people are concerned about the loss of cultural identity if the nation cooperates too much with other nations. As explained in Chapter 3, culture does matter in international business. The following paragraphs list the main benefits and drawbacks of regional integration.

Benefits of regional integration

Chapter 5 indicates that countries are focused on specialization and trade because of the accrued gains in output and consumption. Greater specialization, increased efficiency, greater consumption, and higher standards of living should all result from higher levels of trade between nations. The following paragraphs elaborate on these benefits.

Trade creation

Economic integration removes barriers to trade and investment for nations belonging to a trading bloc. The increase in the level of trade between nations that results from regional economic integration is called "trade creation," which presents consumers and industrial buyers in member nations with a wider selection of goods and services not available before. For example, as a result of the NAFTA, between Canada, the USA and Mexico, many Canadian goods are offered in US shops and supermarkets. Another result of "trade creation" is that buyers can acquire goods and services at lower cost since tariffs are lowered.

Greater consensus

While the WTO tries to lower barriers on a global scale by gaining consensus from 144 member countries, a smaller number of countries that belong to a specific region may reach consensus more easily.

Political cooperation

With regional economic integration, a group of nations may negotiate more effectively than single nations vis-à-vis the WTO. In addition, regional political cooperation may reduce the potential for an armed conflict between nations.

Employment opportunities

Regional integration improves employment opportunities by enabling people to move from one country to another to find work. The establishment of a European Passport for residents of EU countries, as well as the granting of pan-European academic degrees, facilities the migration of skilled blue collar workers and educated professionals to gain employment anywhere within the European common market. In this way the quality of life and the living standards of the residents of all members countries in the region are improved.

Negative effects of regional integration

Regional integration may have negative effects as follows.

Protecting less-efficient economies

Regional integration can result in increased trade with a less-efficient producer within the trading bloc and reduced trade with a more-efficient nonmember producer. As a result, buyers will likely pay more for goods and services due to the inefficient production methods of the less-efficient member nation.

As an example, before the UK joined the EU, most lamb imports came from New Zealand, as it was the least expensive lamb producer. After the UK joined the EU, the external tariff applied by the EU on products from nonmember countries made it more expensive to import lamb. Thus, France became the source for lamb, even though it was not the least expensive source of livestock product.

Shifts in employment

The formation of trading blocs significantly reduces barriers to trade among member nations. Thus, companies requiring mostly unskilled labor will tend to shift production to low-wage nations within a trading bloc.

Countries protecting low-wage domestic industries from competition will see these jobs move to the country where wages are lower. The net effect of regional trading blocs on employment is not easily calculated and is a contentious issue among trading bloc member nations. This was a main concern when former communist countries joined the EU.

Loss of national sovereignty

As in the case of EU, a political union requires nations to give up a high degree of sovereignty in foreign policy. It has been argued that Belgium, totally committed to the EU, has lost its sovereignty as well as its cultural identity and heritage.

The following paragraphs describe regional integrations in Europe, the Americas, Asia, the Middle East, and Africa.

Regional integration in Europe

Following the Second World War, several Western European countries initiated regional integration, which led eventually to a political union. This initiative seems to be the most advanced example of regional integration.

The European Union

The European Union began as a free trade agreement with the goal to become a customs union and to integrate in other ways. The formation of the European Parliament and the establishment of a common currency, the euro, make the EU the leader of all the regional trade groups.

EU History

Table 7.1 lists the key events in the evolution of the EU.

The Birth of the EU

The destruction in Europe caused by the Second World War was the main impetus for the cooperation among the European countries of Belgium, France, West Germany, Italy, Luxembourg, and the Netherlands. These countries signed the Treaty of Paris in 1951, creating the European Coal and Steel Community, removing barriers to trade in coal, iron, and steel, and controlling the postwar arms industry.

The same country members signed the Treaty of Rome in 1957, creating the European Economic Community (EEC). The Treaty of Rome outlined a future common market for member countries. It also aimed at establishing common

TABLE 7.1 Key Events in the Evolution of the European Union

Year	Event
1957	The Six founding countries sign the Treaty of Rome establishing the European Economic Community (EEC) and the European Atomic Energy Community (EAEC).
1959	The first steps are taken in the progressive abolition of customs duties and quotas within the EEC.
1960	The Stockholm Convention establishes the European Free Trade Association (EFTA) among seven European countries (Austria, Denmark, Norway, Portugal, Sweden, Switzerland, the United Kingdom). The Organization for Economic Cooperation and Development (OECD) is formed.
1961	The first regulation on free movement of workers within the EEC is enacted.
1962	The Common Agricultural Policy is adopted.
1966	Agreement is reached on a value-added tax (VAT) system; a treaty merging the Executives of the European Communities comes into force; and the EEC changes its name to European Community (EC).
1967	All remaining internal tariffs are eliminated, and a common external tariff is imposed.
1972	The Six agree to limit currency fluctuations between their currencies to 2.25 percent.
1973	Denmark, Ireland, and the United Kingdom become members of the EC.
1979	European Monetary System comes into effect; European Parliament is elected.
1980	Greece becomes the tenth member of the EC.
1985	Commission sends the Council a White Paper on completion of internal market by 1992.
1986	Spain and Portugal become the eleventh and twelfth members of the EC. Single European Act (SEA) is signed, improving decision-making procedures, and increasing the role of the European Parliament; comes into effect on July 1, 1987.
1989	Collapse of the Berlin Wall; German Democratic Republic opens its borders.
1990	The first phase of European Monetary Union (EMU) comes into effect. Unification of East and West Germany.
1992	European Union signed in the Maastricht Treaty, adopted by member countries on November 1, 1993.
1993	The Single European Market comes into force. Council concludes agreement creating European Economic Area, effective January 1, 1994.
1995	Austria, Finland, and Sweden become the thirteenth, fourteenth, and fifteenth members of the EU.
1996	An EU summit names the 11 countries that will join the European single currency, with all EU countries joining but Britain, Sweden, Denmark (by their choice), and Greece (not ready).
1999	The euro, the single European currency, comes into effect (January 1, 1999).
2001	Greece becomes the twelfth country to adopt the euro (January 1, 2001).
2002	The euro coins and notes enter circulation (January 1, 2002). The EU announces 10 new countries to join the EU in May 2004 (October 2002). All the EU member states ratify the Kyoto Protocol.
2004	Admission of Cyprus, the Czech Republic, Estonia, Hungary, Latvia, Lithuania, Malta, Poland, Slovakia, Slovenia, bringing number of member states to 25.
2007	Bulgaria and Romania join, bringing number of member states to 27. Candidate countries are Croatia, Former Yugoslav Republic of Macedonia, and Turkey.

Source: Adapted from European Union, "The History of the European Union," at http://europe.eu.int (accessed July 2007). ©European Communities. 1995–2007. Reprinted with permission.

transportation and agricultural policies among members, and included additional industries, such as atomic energy. The European Community (EC) was expanded during the period 1973–1995. By 1994, the EC name changed to the European Union (EU). The 15-member EU had a population of about 400 million people and a GDP of over US$6 trillion.

Single European Act

By the mid-1980s, EU member nations faced the need to harmonize laws and policies and remove trade barriers to form a common market. The removal of barriers and harmonizing taxation and legal systems led to the enactment of the Single European Act (SEA), in 1987. This act caused a significant growth of mergers and acquisitions of corporations across Europe. MNEs in Europe took advantage of economies of scale. SMEs were engaged in networking with one another in order to protect their interests and market share, improving their competitiveness.

The Maastricht Treaty

In 1992, a summit meeting of EU member nations took place in Maastricht, the Netherlands, resulting in the Maastricht Treaty, which went into effect in 1993.

The Maastricht Treaty had several aims:

1. It initiated the call for a single currency, the euro, starting in 2002, abolishing the expensive mechanism of exchange rate and freeing more capital investments. This single currency reduced the risks associated with extreme rate fluctuations.
2. The Maastricht Treaty set up monetary and fiscal targets for countries that are part of the monetary union.
3. The treaty called for political union of the member nations including the development of a common foreign and defense policy and common citizenship.

Table 7.2 lists the key features of the EU member countries.

European Union enlargement

The EU allows for more countries to join, conditional upon meeting the Copenhagen Criteria. Namely, the candidate country:

1. Has stable institutions, which guarantee democracy, the rule of law, human rights, and respect for and protection of minorities.
2. Has a functioning market economy.
3. Subscribes to the aims of economic, monetary, and political union.
4. Has the ability to adopt the rules and regulations of the Community, including the European Court of Justice and the various treaties.

EU institutions

Five EU institutions monitor and govern EU economic and political integration, as shown in Figure 7.2, and as explained below.

The European Parliament

The European Parliament has 600 members elected by popular vote within each member nation every five years. The European Parliament debates and constructs

TABLE 7.2 Key Features of the European Union Member Countries

Members	*Population (millions)*	*GDP (US$, billions; PPP terms)*	*GDP per capita (US$; PPP terms)*	*Exports (as a percentage of GDP)*
Austria	8	299	36,189	29
Belgium	10	353	33,908	52
Bulgaria	8	83	10,844	16
Cyprus	1	20	23,419	7
Czech Republic	10	210	20,539	44
Denmark	5	204	37,398	26
Estonia	1	26	19,243	36
Finland	5	179	34,162	29
France	63	1,988	31,377	17
Germany	83	2,699	32,684	26
Greece	11	274	24,733	3
Hungary	10	190	18,922	42
Ireland	4	192	45,135	53
Italy	59	1,791	30,383	17
Latvia	2	34	15,062	21
Lithuania	3	57	16,756	36
Luxembourg	0.5	35	76,025	28
Malta	0.4	8	21,081	44
The Netherlands	17	550	33,079	44
Poland	38	557	14,609	24
Portugal	11	218	20,673	18
Romania	22	219	10,152	51
Slovakia	5	101	18,705	67
Slovenia	2	49	24,459	38
Spain	42	1,203	28,810	16
Sweden	9	297	32,548	30
United Kingdom	61	2,004	32,949	14
Total	491	13,840		

GDP, gross domestic product; PPP, purchasing power parity.
Source: International Monetary Fund at www.imf.org.

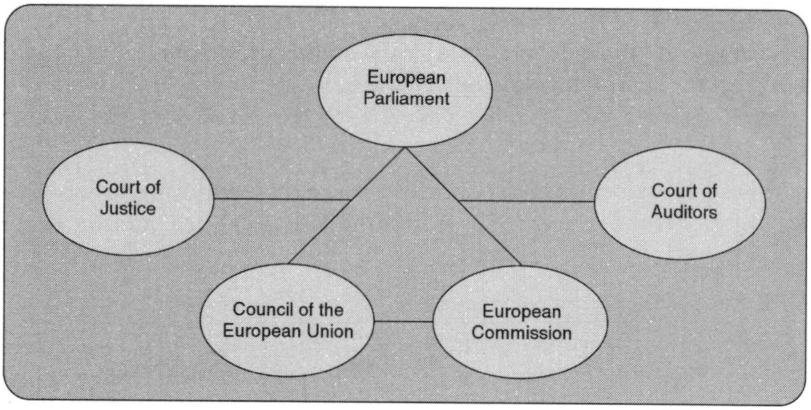

FIGURE 7.2 Institutions of the European Union

legislation proposed by the European Commission. It exercises political supervision over all EU institutions. The Parliament conducts its activities in Brussels (Belgium), in Strasbourg (France), and in Luxembourg.

Council of the European Union

The Council, based in Brussels, is the legislative body of the EU. All proposed legislation regarding the EU is brought before the Council. The Council also negotiates and approves, on behalf of the EU, international agreements with other nations or international organizations.

European Commission

The Commission, based in Brussels, is the executive body of the EU. It comprises commissioners appointed by each member country: larger nations get two commissioners; smaller countries get one. It drafts legislation, is responsible for managing and implementing policy, and monitors member nations' implementation of and compliance with EU law. Commissioners are expected to behave in the best interest of the EU as a whole, not in the interest of their own country.

Court of Justice

The Court of Justice, located in Luxembourg, is the court of appeals of the EU and is composed of one justice from each member country. Justices are required to act in the interest of the EU as a whole, not in the interest of their own countries.

Court of Auditors

The Court of Auditors, located in Luxembourg, is composed of members from each member nation, appointed for a six-year term. The Court audits the EU accounts and implements its budget. It also aims to improve financial management in the EU and reports to member nations' citizens on the use of public funds. The Court of Auditors has 250 auditors.

European Free Trade Association (EFTA)

Some European nations shied away from the EU goals and limited their interests to simply forming a free trade region. These nations formed the European Free Trade Association (EFTA) to focus on trade in industrial, not consumer, goods. Currently, the group consists of Iceland, Liechtenstein, Norway, and Switzerland. The EFTA is small relative to the EU. However, member nations remain committed to free trade principles and raising standards of living for their people. The EFTA and the EU created the European Economic Area (EEA) to cooperate on matters such as the free movement of goods, persons, services, and capital. Both EFTA and EU member nations cooperate on the environment, social policy, and education issues.

Central European Free Trade Area (CEFTA)

The EU encourages candidate countries to establish their own free trade area. Thus, the Central European Free Trade Area (CEFTA) was formed. Among other goals, CEFTA aims is to remove customs duties and other barriers to trade in industrial products and agriculture.

Bilateral agreements

In addition to the reduction of trade barriers for member countries, the EU has signed bilateral free trade agreements with other countries outside of the European region. In 2007, the EU announced a proposal for a strategic partnership with Brazil. Similar partnerships and free trade agreements have been signed with other countries.

EU and corporate strategy

The EU is a globally significant market in terms of both population and income, and so it is one that MNEs cannot ignore. Doing business in the EU can influence corporate strategy, especially for non-EU MNEs. The following is a list of strategic issues pertaining to the EU:

1. Determination of location of European operations. A possible strategy is to produce products in a central location in Europe to minimize transportation costs and the time it takes to move products from one country to another. However, the highest production costs are in central Europe, limiting the possible economic attractiveness of such a location.
2. Determination of growth strategy. MNEs may expand into Europe through new investments, through expanding existing investments, or through joint ventures and mergers. Most experts feel that mergers and acquisitions may be the preferred way of MNEs into Europe, as US companies are buying European companies to gain a market presence.
3. Consider national differences. National differences occur in the EU, mostly a result of language and history but also because of different growth rates of the many smaller nations such as Ireland and Belgium. This has increased the

smaller nations' attractiveness for foreign direct investment (FDI), due to favorable infrastructure and government support. It should be noted that as a result of the global economic crisis and major financial markets' corrections, some smaller European countries have become less attractive to MNEs: for example, Ireland and Iceland.

Regional Integration in the Americas

The *North American Free Trade Agreement (NAFTA)*, which comprises Canada, Mexico, and the USA, went into effect in 1994. The USA and Canada signed the Canada–US Free Trade Agreement, effective January I, 1989, which eliminated all tariffs on bilateral trade by January 1, 1998. In February 1991, Mexico approached the USA to establish a free trade agreement. The formal negotiations that began in June 1991 included Canada. The resulting North American Free Trade Agreement became effective on January 1, 1994.

The North American Free Trade Agreement Rationale

NAFTA has a logical rationale, in terms of both geographic location and trading importance. The two-way trading relationship between the USA and Canada is the largest in the world. NAFTA is a powerful trading bloc with a combined population greater than the EU. What is significant in NAFTA and affects its development is the tremendous size of the US economy in comparison with those of Canada and Mexico. In addition, it should be noted that Canada has a much richer economy than that of Mexico, even though its population is about a third that of Mexico.

Even though NAFTA is a free trade agreement instead of a customs union or a common market, its cooperation extends far beyond reductions in tariff and non-tariff barriers and includes provisions for services, investment, intellectual property, and a dispute resolution process.

As a result of NAFTA, most tariffs on originating goods traded between Mexico and Canada were eliminated immediately or phased in over a 10-year period that ended on December 31, 2003. Tariffs between the USA and Mexico were, in general, either eliminated immediately or over a 5- or 10-year period that ended on December 31, 2003.

As a result of NAFTA, Canadian, and US consumers benefit from lower-cost agricultural products from Mexico. US producers also benefit from the large and growing Mexican market, which prefers US-made products.

Many US and Canadian companies have established manufacturing facilities in Asia to take advantage of cheap labor. Now, US and Canadian companies can establish manufacturing facilities in Mexico rather than in Asian countries to take advantage of relatively cheap labor.

Clothing stores, like Gap Inc., are increasingly buying garments of good quality from Mexican contractors, who can offer faster delivery than Asian contractors. Table 7.3 lists the key features of Canada, Mexico, and the USA, the member countries of NAFTA.

TABLE 7.3 North American Free Trade Agreement (NAFTA)

Members	*Population (millions)*	*GDP (US$ billions; PPP terms)*	*CDP per capita (US$; PPP terms)*	*Exports (as a percentage of GDP)*
Canada	33	1,225	37,321	29
Mexico	108	1,192	10,993	18
United States	302	13,678	45,257	6
Total	443	16,095		

GDP, gross domestic product; PPP, purchasing power parity.
Source: International Monetary Fund at www.imf.org.

Local content requirements and rules of origin

Manufacturers and distributors are finding that although NAFTA encourages free trade between Canada, Mexico, and the United States, local content requirements and rules of origin are among the agreement's most complex criteria, and make trade more difficult. These rules create special problems for producers and distributors. Although manufacturers and distributors rarely know the precise origin of every part or component in a piece of industrial equipment, they are responsible for determining whether a product has sufficient North American content to qualify for NAFTA tariff-free status. The producer or distributor must also provide a NAFTA "certificate of origin" to an importer to claim an exemption from tariffs. Four criteria determine whether a good meets NAFTA rules of origin:

1 Goods wholly produced or obtained in the NAFTA region.
2 Goods containing nonoriginating inputs but meeting certain origin input rules.
3 Goods produced in the NAFTA region wholly from originating materials.
4 Unassembled goods and goods classified in the same harmonized system category, but have sufficient North American regional value content.

Effects of NAFTA

Between 1993 and 2008, trade among the three nations – the USA, Canada, and Mexico – increased markedly, with the greatest gains occurring between Mexico and the USA. As a matter of fact, the USA exports more to Mexico than it does to Britain, France, Germany, and Italy combined. In the first 17 years of NAFTA, Mexico's exports to the USA grew by an average annual rate of 35 percent. However, it seems that there is a possible net loss of jobs in the USA because of NAFTA. Some US companies headed for Mexico after NAFTA came into being, thus reducing employment opportunities in the USA.

In addition to claims of job losses, opponents claim that NAFTA has damaged the environment, particularly along the USA–Mexico border. Although the agreement included provisions for environmental protection, Mexico is finding it difficult to deal with the environmental impact of the greater economic activity, and had to develop its own waste reduction and recycling systems.

NAFTA expansion

Chile is a leading candidate to join NAFTA next. In spite of the fact that it has small population of 14 million people, it is a model for economic reform of South American nations, and is open to trade and investment.

It is expected that future integration will occur among nations in the Americas. It is possible that the North American economies will one day adopt a single currency, like the EU.

Regional trade within the Andean Community

The first try at regionalization in Latin America, the Latin American Free Trade Association (LAFTA), was made in 1961. However, because of the debt crisis in South America and concerns about economic sovereignty, the agreement was curtailed. The demise of LAFTA led to the creation of two regional trading blocs – the Andean Community (AC) and the Latin American Integration Association (ALADI).

Formed in 1969, the Andean Community (AC) today includes five South American countries located in the Andes mountain range – Bolivia, Colombia, Ecuador, Peru, and Venezuela. The AC represents a market of about 110 million consumers and a total GDP of about $500 billion. The main objectives of the group are tariff reduction for trade among member nations, a common external tariff, and common policies in both transportation and certain economic sectors. But political ideology is generally against free markets and encourages government involvement in business.

Uneven prospects for economic growth in Venezuela and political unrest in Colombia indicate that a common market is difficult to implement within the framework of the Andean Community. Typically, each country has been given exceptions in the tariff structure that they have in place for trade with nonmember nations. In addition, countries continue to sign agreements with just one or two countries outside the Andean Community framework. These arrangements hurt the credibility of the Andean Community vis-à-vis the rest of the world and reduce the effectiveness of regional integration.

Latin American Integration Association (ALADI)

The Latin American Integration Association (ALADI) was formed in 1980. The objectives of ALADI are limited in scope and call for preferential tariff agreements to be made between pairs of member nations, termed bilateral agreements, that reflect the economic development of each nation. The agreements did not accomplish a great deal of cross-border trade and caused certain South American nations to form a separate trading bloc called MERCOSUR.

Southern Common Market (MERCOSUR)

By 1996 the Southern Common Market (MERCOSUR), which was established in 1988, included Argentina, Brazil, Paraguay, and Uruguay, as well as Bolivia and Chile as associate members. Peru and Venezuela are possibly the next members to join MERCOSUR.

MERCOSUR is a customs union with more than 220 million consumers, nearly half of Latin America's total population. MERCOSUR makes progress on trade and investment liberalization and is emerging as the most powerful trading bloc in Latin America. MERCOSUR may incorporate all the countries of South America into a South American Free Trade Agreement (SAFTA), after which it would join NAFTA to form a Free Trade Area of the Americas.

Latin America's large consumer base and its potential as a low-cost production platform for worldwide export appeal to both the EU and the USA, and many MNEs have opened up facilities in South America.

Central America and the Caribbean

There have also been experiments of economic integration in Central American countries and throughout the Caribbean.

Caribbean Community and Common Market (CARICOM)

The Caribbean Community and Common Market (CARICOM) trading bloc was formed in 1973, and consists of 15 countries, including the Bahamas, Grenada, Guyana, Haiti, and Trinidad and Tobago. Although the Bahamas is a member of the Community, it does not belong to the Common Market. CARICOM has a GDP of about $30 billion and a market of about 6 million people.

In early 2000, CARICOM created a Single Market, with free movement of products, services, capital, and labor. The main difficulty in this regional arrangement is that CARICOM members trade more with nonmembers than they do with each other.

Central American Common Market (CACM)

The Central American Common Market (CACM) is a common market between Costa Rica, El Salvador, Guatemala, Honduras, and Nicaragua. The members of CACM comprise a market of 33 million consumers and have a combined GDP of about $120 billion. However, the war between El Salvador and Honduras and guerrilla conflicts in several countries prevents the CACM from appropriate launching and operating. In addition, the CACM group has not yet created a customs union, a required step of regional integration.

Free Trade Area of the Americas (FTAA)

The Free Trade Area of the Americas (FTAA) is an ambitious regional integration proposed agreement to eliminate or reduce the trade barriers among all countries in the Americas (North, Central, South), excluding Cuba. It should be noted that in the 1960s there were several modest attempts at regional integration in South

America, Central America, and the Caribbean. The approach of these regional initiatives was to lower tariffs internally while maintaining high trade barriers against nonmembers. Regional initiatives included the 1960 Latin American Free Trade Association (LAFTA), the 1960 Central American Common Market (CACM), the 1965 Caribbean Free Trade Association (CARIFTA), and the 1969 Andean Pact.

The FTAA initiative includes 34 nations with a total population of about 850 million consumers and a total GDP of about $13 trillion. In the latest round of negotiations, trade ministers from 34 nations met in Miami, Florida, in 2003 to discuss the proposed free trade area agreement. The last summit was held at Mar del Plata, Argentina, in November 2005, but no agreement on FTAA was reached. Of the 34 countries present at the negotiations, 26 countries pledged to meet again in 2006 to resume negotiations, but no such meeting took place. The proposed agreement is an extension of NAFTA. At that time, opposing this initiative were Cuba, Venezuela, Bolivia, Ecuador, Dominica, Nicaragua, and Honduras, which entered the Bolivarian Alternative for the Americas in response. Argentina, Chile, and Brazil were not opposing but also were not supporting the FTAA initiative.

Initiatives and impediments regarding the FTAA

In previous negotiations, the USA has proposed a single comprehensive agreement to reduce trade barriers for goods, while increasing intellectual property protection, including copyright protections, similar to the US–Australia Free Trade Agreement. Another protection would likely restrict the reimportation or cross-importation of pharmaceuticals, similar to the proposed agreement between the USA and Canada. Brazil has proposed a three-track approach that calls for a series of bilateral agreements to reduce specific tariffs on goods, a regional agreement on rules of origin, and a dispute resolution process. Brazil also seeks to let the WTO deal with the more controversial issues of the agreement.

The location of the FTAA Secretariat was to have been determined in 2005. However, as of 2007, only Miami (USA) and Port of Spain (Trinidad) are actively seeking to establish the FTAA Secretariat headquarters within their borders.

While there is a little chance for the FTAA vision materializing, the following countries have shown interest at some point in becoming members of the Free Trade Area of the Americas: Antigua and Barbuda, Argentina, Barbados, Belize, Brazil, Canada, Chile, Colombia, Costa Rica, Dominica, Dominican Republic, El Salvador, Grenada, Guatemala, Guyana, Haiti, Honduras, Jamaica, Mexico, Panama, Paraguay, Peru, St Kitts and Nevis, St Lucia, St Vincent and the Grenadines, Suriname, Trinidad and Tobago, USA, and Uruguay.

Major initiatives opposing the FTAA have evolved in the past, including initiatives by senior citizens, labor groups, environmentalists, human rights advocates, and peace advocates, as well as by concerned citizens. A major political opponent of the FTAA is Venezuelan president Hugo Chávez, who has described the FTAA as an annexation plan of Latin America by North America and as a tool of imperialism for the exploitation of Latin America. As a counterproposal to this initiative, Chávez has promoted the Bolivarian Alternative for the Americas, based on the model of the EU, emphasizing energy and infrastructure agreements that lead eventually to total economic, political, and military integration of the member countries. On the other hand, the presidents of Brazil, Luiz Inácio Lula da Silva, and Argentina, Cristina Fernandez de Kirchner, have stated that they do not oppose the FTAA but they do demand that the agreement provide for the elimination of US agriculture subsidies, the provision of effective access to foreign markets and further consideration towards the needs of its member countries.

One of the most contentious issues of the treaty proposed by the USA is with concerns with patents and copyrights. Critics claim that if the measures proposed by the USA were implemented and applied this would prevent scientific research in Latin America, causing, as a consequence, more inequalities and technological dependence from the developed countries. Some critics claim that the proposed patent and copyright proposals have gone far beyond their initial scope of protecting original inventions or cultural products and promote the rights of MNEs over the rights of local communities.

Corruption in various member countries is an area of contention for Canada and the USA, who fear that it may lead to piracy and loss of sales to counterfeit goods. Latin America has long been identified as a market for pirated merchandise, including music on digital media and computer software.

If the FTAA is going to be a success, corruption will have to be rooted out. Table 7.4 shows the results of a survey on corruption in almost 150 countries around the world. Note the higher corruption rates in FTAA countries. These corruption rates are a concern for MNEs conducting business in South American countries.

The EU–US Accord on Transatlantic Economic Partnership (TEP)

Since 1998, the EU and the USA have decided to enhance transatlantic economic partnership, contributing to stability, democracy, and FDI. Put together, the USA and the EU have a consumer base of about 700 million and account for about US$ 30,000,000 million, approximately half of the world's GDP, as of 2007.

It should be noted that these two economic regions are the most attractive source and destination for FDI. This economic partnership aims to:

- induce extensive economic collaboration between the EU and USA, creating a transatlantic market without barriers;
- promote common standards and practices for industrial companies and financial service providers;
- induce harmonization of accounting standards and practices, including balance sheet directives that are recognized by the USA and the EU as of 2008;
- promote harmonization of admission procedures in the pharmaceutical and chemical industries, as well as for the cosmetics sector and automobile parts;
- create a forum on energy technologies.

TABLE 7.4 The 2007 Corruption Perceptions Index (CPI)

Country	*2007 CPI Score*	*Country*	*2007 CPI Score*
Denmark	9.4	Montenegro	3.3
Finland	9.4	Swaziland	3.3
New Zealand	9.4	Thailand	3.3
Singapore	9.3	Madagascar	3.2
Sweden	9.3	Panama	3.2
Iceland	9.2	Sri Lanka	3.2
Netherlands	9.0	Tanzania	3.2
Switzerland	9.0	Vanuatu	3.1
Canada	8.7	Algeria	3.0
Norway	8.7	Armenia	3.0
Australia	8.6	Belize	3.0
Luxembourg	8.4	Dominican Republic	3.0
United Kingdom	8.4	Lebanon	3.0
Hong Kong	8.3	Mongolia	3.0
Austria	8.1	Albania	2.9
Germany	7.8	Argentina	2.9
Ireland	7.5	Bolivia	2.9
Japan	7.5	Burkina Faso	2.9
France	7.3	Djibouti	2.9
USA	7.2	Egypt	2.9
Belgium	7.1	Eritrea	2.8
Chile	7.0	Guatemala	2.8
Barbados	6.9	Moldova	2.8
St. Lucia	6.8	Mozambique	2.8
Spain	6.7	Rwanda	2.8
Uruguay	6.7	Solomon Islands	2.8
Slovenia	6.6	Uganda	2.8
Estonia	6.5	Benin	2.7
Portugal	6.5	Malawi	2.7
Israel	6.1	Mali	2.7
St. Vincent and the Grenadines	6.1	Sao Tome and Principe	2.7
Qatar	6.0	Ukraine	2.7
Malta	5.8	Comoros	2.6
Macao	5.7	Guyana	2.6
Taiwan	5.7	Mauritania	2.6
United Arab Emirates	5.7	Nicaragua	2.6
Dominica	5.6	Niger	2.6
Botswana	5.4	Timor-Leste	2.6
Cyprus	5.3	Vietnam	2.6
Hungary	5.3	Zambia	2.6

TABLE 7.4

Country	*2007 CPI Score*	*Country*	*2007 CPI Score*
Czech Republic	5.2	Burundi	2.5
Italy	5.2	Honduras	2.5
Malaysia	5.1	Iran	2.5
South Africa	5.1	Libya	2.5
South Korea	5.1	Nepal	2.5
Bahrain	5.0	Philippines	2.5
Bhutan	5.0	Yemen	2.5
Costa Rica	5.0	Cameroon	2.4
Cape Verde	4.9	Ethiopia	2.4
Slovakia	4.9	Pakistan	2.4
Latvia	4.8	Paraguay	2.4
Lithuania	4.8	Syria	2.4
Jordan	4.7	Gambia	2.3
Mauritius	4.7	Indonesia	2.3
Oman	4.7	Russia	2.3
Greece	4.6	Togo	2.3
Namibia	4.5	Angola	2.2
Samoa	4.5	Guinea-Bissau	2.2
Seychelles	4.5	Nigeria	2.2
Kuwait	4.3	Azerbaijan	2.1
Cuba	4.2	Belarus	2.1
Poland	4.2	Congo, Republic	2.1
Tunisia	4.2	Côte d´Ivoire	2.1
Bulgaria	4.1	Ecuador	2.1
Croatia	4.1	Kazakhstan	2.1
Turkey	4.1	Kenya	2.1
El Salvador	4.0	Kyrgyzstan	2.1
Colombia	3.8	Liberia	2.1
Ghana	3.7	Sierra Leone	2.1
Romania	3.7	Tajikistan	2.1
Senegal	3.6	Zimbabwe	2.1
Brazil	3.5	Bangladesh	2.0
China	3.5	Cambodia	2.0
India	3.5	Central African Republic	2.0
Mexico	3.5	Papua New Guinea	2.0
Morocco	3.5	Turkmenistan	2.0
Peru	3.5	Venezuela	2.0
Suriname	3.5	Congo, Democratic Republic of	1.9
Georgia	3.4	Equatorial Guinea	1.9
Grenada	3.4	Guinea	1.9

(Continued)

TABLE 7.4 Cont.

Country	*2007 CPI Score*	*Country*	*2007 CPI Score*
Saudi Arabia	3.4	Laos	1.9
Serbia	3.4	Afghanistan	1.8
Trinidad and Tobago	3.4	Chad	1.8
Bosnia and Herzegovina	3.3	Sudan	1.8
FYR Macedonia	3.3	Tonga	1.7
Gabon	3.3	Uzbekistan	1.7
Jamaica	3.3	Haiti	1.6
Kiribati	3.3	Iraq	1.5
Lesotho	3.3	Myanmar	1.4
Maldives	3.3	Somalia	1.4

Notes:

1 According to the annual survey by the Berlin-based organization Transparency International, Finland, Denmark, and New Zealand are perceived to be the world's least corrupt countries, and Somalia and Myanmar are perceived to be the most corrupt.

2 The index defines corruption as the abuse of public office for private gain and measures the degree to which corruption is perceived to exist among a country's public officials and politicians.

3 The scores range from 10 (no corruption) to 0 (very corrupt). A score of 5.0 is the number Transparency International considers the borderline figure, distinguishing countries that do and do not have a serious corruption problem.

Source: Transparency International, 2007. website: www.transparency.org.

Both the US administration and the European Commission are expected to create an administrative post to deal with transatlantic trade issues and develop administrative organizations to deal with the Transatlantic Economic Partnership, including the Transatlantic Economic Council (TEC).

Regional Integration in Asia

There are two important initiatives in Asia and among Pacific Rim nations – the Association of Southeast Asian Nations (ASEAN) and the organization for Asia-Pacific Economic Cooperation (APEC). Both are geared towards economic and political integration.

Association of Southeast Asian Nations (ASEAN)

The Association of Southeast Asian Nations, abbreviated ASEAN in English, the official language of the regional trading bloc, is a geopolitical and economic organization of 10 countries located in Southeast Asia, which was formed in 1967 by Indonesia, Malaysia, the Philippines, Singapore, and Thailand. Since then, membership has expanded to include Brunei, Burma (Myanmar), Cambodia, Laos, and Vietnam. Its goals are to accelerate economic growth, social progress, and cultural development among its country members, the protection of the peace and stability of the region, and the provision of opportunities for member countries to discuss differences peacefully. The ASEAN region had a combined nominal GDP of US$1.4 trillion in 2008 and a combined population of about 600 million consumers.

The evolution of ASEAN

ASEAN was preceded by an organization called the Association of Southeast Asia, commonly called ASA, an alliance consisting of the Philippines, Malaysia, and Thailand that was formed in 1961. The trading region bloc itself, however, was established on August 8, 1967, when foreign ministers of five countries – Indonesia, Malaysia, the Philippines, Singapore, and Thailand – met at the Thai Department of Foreign Affairs building in Bangkok and signed the ASEAN Declaration, more commonly known as the Bangkok Declaration.

The motivations for the birth of ASEAN were the desire for a stable external environment, the common fear of communism, reduced faith in the external powers in the 1960s, and the aspiration for national economic development. Furthermore, Indonesia wanted to become a regional center of power through regional cooperation and Malaysia and Singapore wanted to constrain Indonesia, and bring it into a more cooperative framework. Unlike the European Union, ASEAN was designed to serve nationalism.

In 1976, the Melanesian state of Papua New Guinea was accorded observer status, and Brunei Darussalam became the sixth member in 1984. In July 1995, Vietnam became the seventh member. Laos and Burma (Myanmar) joined two years later in 1997. Cambodia joined in 1999, following the stabilization of its government.

The main ASEAN initiatives

In 1992, the Common Effective Preferential Tariff (CEPT) scheme was signed as a schedule for phasing tariffs in order to increase the region's competitive advantage as a production base geared for world market. This scheme would act as the framework for the ASEAN Free Trade Area. After the East Asian Financial Crisis of 1997, ASEAN countries called for better integration between the economies of ASEAN and China, Japan, and South Korea.

Uniquely, the ASEAN countries made steps to promote peace and stability. In 1995, the Southeast Asian Nuclear Weapon Free Zone Treaty was signed with the intention of turning Southeast Asia into a Nuclear Weapon Free Zone. The treaty took effect in 1997, after all but one of the member countries ratified it. It became fully effective in 2001, after the Philippines ratified it, effectively banning all nuclear weapons in the region.

At the turn of the 21st century, issues shifted to involve a more environmental prospective. The ASEAN organization started to discuss environmental agreements. These included the signing of the ASEAN Agreement on Transboundary Haze Pollution in 2002 as an attempt to control haze pollution in Southeast Asia. Unfortunately, this was unsuccessful due to the outbreaks of the 2005 Malaysian haze and the 2006 Southeast Asian haze. Other environmental treaties introduced by the organization include the Cebu Declaration on East Asian Energy Security, the ASEAN-Wildlife Enforcement Network in 2005, and the Asia-Pacific Partnership on Clean Development and Climate, which are all responses to global warming and the negative effects of climate change.

Through the Bali Concord II in 2003, ASEAN has subscribed to the notion of democratic peace, which means all member countries believe democratic processes will promote regional peace and stability. The nondemocratic members have also all agreed that it was something all member states should aspire to.

In 2006, ASEAN was given observer status at the United Nations General Assembly. As a response, the organization was awarded the status of "dialogue partner" to the United Nations.

In 2007, ASEAN celebrated its 40th anniversary, and 30 years of diplomatic relations with the USA. In 2007, ASEAN stated that it aims to complete all its free trade agreements with China, Japan, South Korea, India, Australia, and New Zealand by 2013, leading the way to the establishment of the ASEAN Economic Community by 2015. In November 2007, the ASEAN members signed the ASEAN Charter, a constitution governing relations among the ASEAN members and establishing ASEAN itself as an international legal entity. On February 27, 2009 a Free Trade Agreement (FTA) with the ASEAN regional block of 10 countries and New Zealand and its close partner Australia was signed. It is estimated that this FTA would boost aggregate GDP across the 12 countries by more than US$48 billion over the period 2010–20. Table 7.5 lists the key features of the member nations of ASEAN, including population size, GDP, and exports as percent of GDP.

TABLE 7.5 Association of Southeast Asian Nations (ASEAN)

Members	*Population (millions)*	*GDP (US$ billions; PPP terms)*	*GDP per capita (US$; PPP terms)*	*Exports (as a percentage of GDP)*
Brunei	0.4	10	26,098	52
Cambodia	15	41	2,673	6
Indonesia	225	1,146	5,097	8
Laos	6	15	2,402	3
Malaysia	27	341	12,703	47
Myanmar (Burma)	58	105	1,814	3
Philippines	88	474	5,409	9
Singapore	5	140	31,165	130
Thailand	66	626	9,427	16
Vietnam	86	300	3,503	10
Total	576	3,198		

GDP, gross domestic product; PPP, purchasing power parity.
Source: International Monetary Fund at www.imf.org.

Integration in the Middle East and North Africa (MENA) and Africa

The Middle East and North Africa, or in short MENA, relates to a vast region, that extends from Morocco in northeast Africa to Iran in southwest Asia. It includes all of the Arab Middle East and North African countries, as well as Iran and Israel, but does not include Turkey. The World Bank defines the region in terms of the following countries: Algeria, Bahrain, Djibouti, Egypt, Iran, Iraq, Israel, Jordan, Kuwait, Lebanon, Libya, Morocco, Oman, Palestinian Territories (the West Bank and Gaza Strip), Qatar, Saudi Arabia, Syria, Tunisia, United Arab Emirates, and Yemen.

The population of the MENA region is composed of about 6 percent of the total world population, with approximately 410 million residents. For comparison purposes, the size of the MENA population is about the same as that of the EU, it is one-third of the population of the People's Republic of China and is about one-quarter bigger than the population size of the USA.

As of 2009, the MENA region had vast reserves of petroleum (70 percent of the global oil reserves) and natural gas (46 percent of the global gas reserves), which makes the MENA region a vital source of global economic stability and major impetus for limited regional cooperation. Security issues may be resolved through greater economic and trade cooperation.

Two important regional bodies are identified in the MENA and African countries: the Gulf Cooperation Council (GCC) and the Economic Community of West African States (ECOWAS). It should be noted that as of 2009, 8 of the 12 OPEC (Organization of the Petroleum Exporting Countries) countries were included in the MENA region.

Gulf Cooperation Council (GCC)

Bahrain, Kuwait, Oman, Qatar, Saudi Arabia, and the United Arab Emirates formed the Gulf Cooperation Council (GCC). The primary goal of the GCC was to cooperate with the emerging regional trading blocs in Europe, the EU. However, the GCC has become a political as well as an economic regional entity. The GCC allows citizens of member countries to travel freely in the GCC without visas, as well as to own land, assets, and businesses in any other member country as a sole owner.

Economic Community of West African States (ECOWAS)

In 1975 the Economic Community of West African States (ECOWAS) was formed. The goal of ECOWAS is the formation of a customs union, a common market, and a monetary union. Whereas the ECOWAS countries comprise a large portion of the economic activity in sub-Saharan Africa, progress on market integration is almost nonexistent. However, ECOWAS has made progress in allowing the free movement of people, creating a regional road infrastructure, and developing international telecommunication links. ECOWAS countries have encountered difficulties due to political instability, weak national economies, poor infrastructure, and poor economic policies.

To summarize the overview provided in this chapter of the regional integration phenomena, Table 7.6 lists the world's main regional trading blocs and indicates the member countries in each.

TABLE 7.6 The World's Main Regional Trading Blocs

EU	**European Union** Austria, Belgium, Britain, Denmark, Finland, France, Germany, Greece, Ireland, Italy, Luxembourg, Netherlands, Portugal, Spain, Sweden
EFTA	**European Free Trade Association** Iceland, Liechtenstein, Norway, Switzerland
NAFTA	**North American Free Trade Agreement** Canada, Mexico, USA
ANDEAN	**Andean Community** Bolivia, Colombia, Ecuador, Peru, Venezuela
ALADI	**Latín American Integration Association** Argentina, Bolivia, Brazil, Chile, Colombia, Ecuador, Mexico, Paraguay, Peru, Uruguay, Venezuela
MERCOSUR	**Southern Common Market** Argentina, Brazil, Paraguay, Uruguay (Bolivia and Chile are associate members)
CARICOM	**Caribbean Community and Common Market** Antigua and Barbuda, Bahamas, Barbados, Belize, Dominica, Grenada, Guyana, Haiti, Jamaica, Montserrat, St. Kitts and Nevis, St. Lucia, St. Vincent and the Grenadines, Suriname, Trinidad and Tobago
CACM	**Central American Common Market** Costa Rica, El Salvador, Guatemala, Honduras, Nicaragua
FTAA	**Free Trade Area of the Americas** Caribbean, Central America, North America, South America
TEP	**Transatlantic Economic Partnership** European Union (15 countries), USA
ASEAN	**Association of Southeast Asian Nations** Brunei, Cambodia, Indonesia, Laos, Malaysia, Myanmar, Philippines, Singapore, Thailand, Vietnam
APEC	**Asia-Pacific Economic Cooperation** Australia, Brunei, Canada, Chile, Hong Kong, Indonesia, Japan, South Korea, Malaysia, Mexico, New Zealand, Papua New Guinea, Peru, Philippines, Russia, Singapore, Taiwan, Thailand, USA, Vietnam
GCC	**Gulf Cooperation Council** Bahrain, Kuwait, Oman, Qatar, Saudi Arabia, United Arab Emirates
ECOWAS	**Economic Community of West African States** Benin, Burkina Faso, Cape Verde, Gambia, Ghana, Guinea, Guinea-Bissau, Ivory Coast, Liberia, Mali, Mauritania, Niger, Nigeria, Senegal, Sierra Leone, Togo

COUNTRY FOCUS

GERMANY

World Rank (EFI 2009): 25

Regional Rank (EFI 2009): 2

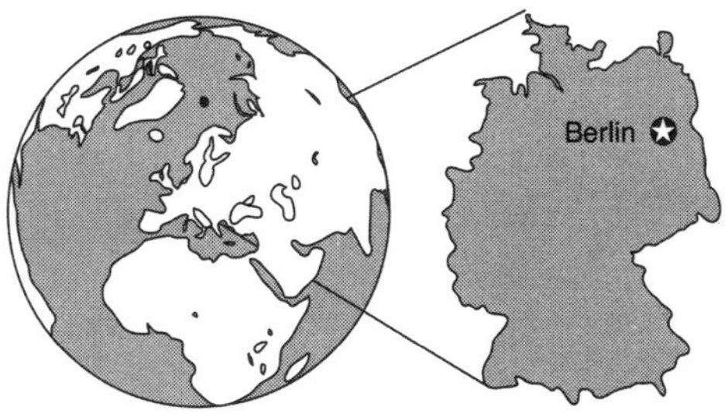

Quick facts

Population: 82.4 million

GDP (PPP): $2.7 trillion; 2.9 percent growth in 2006; 0.9 percent 5-year compound annual growth; $32,322 per capita

Unemployment: 8.4 percent

Inflation (CPI): 2.3 percent

FDI inflow: $42.9 billion

2006 data unless otherwise noted

Economic freedom score

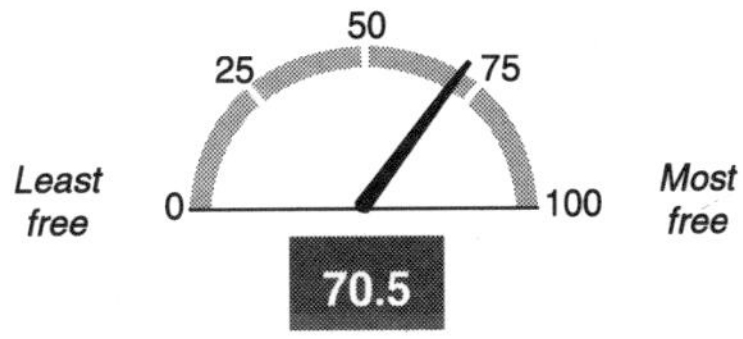

Germany's economic freedom score is 70.5, making its economy the 25th freest in the 2009 Index. Germany is ranked 2nd out of 43 countries in the Europe region, and its overall score is significantly higher than the world average.

The German economy has benefited from strong institutional capacity that facilitates economic freedom and vibrant entrepreneurial activity. Protection of property rights is exemplary. The judicial system is strong, professional, and independent of political influence. A lack of corruption underpins the security of economic activity. The German economy also enjoys strong business freedom and investment freedom. Foreign and national investors are treated equally under the law. Although investors continue to face some bureaucratic red tape, regulations are clear and evenly enforced.

As in many other European social democracies, government spending and tax rates remain high in support of an extensive welfare state. Despite a modest decrease in government expenditures, Germany's government size score is well below the world average. The labor market operates under restrictive conditions.

Background

Germany is the largest economy in Europe and the third largest in the world. A significant adjustment period followed reunification in 1990, and growth rates have been slow. Unemployment, particularly in the former East Germany, remains high. Measures aimed at rationalizing complex social welfare and labor regulations remain under active political debate. The fiscal budget deficit exceeds the European Union's Stability and Growth Pact standards. Nonetheless,

(Continued)

Germany is home to many world-class companies and has an enormous export industry and one of the world's highest incomes per capita. The election of conservative reformer Angela Merkel to the chancellorship in 2006 led to some economic reforms, but inclusion of the Social Democrats in a grand coalition continues to hamstring the government's ability to deal with structural challenges and ensure long-term sustainable economic development.

Business freedom – 90.3

The overall freedom to start, operate, and close a business is protected under Germany's regulatory environment. Starting a business takes an average of 18 days, compared to the world average of 38 days. Obtaining a business license requires less than the world average of 18 procedures and 225 days.

Trade freedom – 85.8

Germany's trade policy is the same as that of other members of the European Union. The common EU-weighted average tariff rate was 2.1 percent in 2005. Nontariff barriers reflected in EU policy include agricultural and manufacturing subsidies, import restrictions for some goods and services, market access restrictions in some services sectors, nontransparent and restrictive regulations and standards, and inconsistent customs administration across EU members. The burden of regulations and standards exceeds EU policy, and the enforcement of intellectual property rights is problematic. Consequently, 10 points were deducted from Germany's trade freedom score.

Fiscal freedom – 58.5

Germany has a high income tax rate and a burdensome corporate income tax rate. The top income tax rate is 47.5 percent (45 percent plus a 5.5 percent solidarity surcharge). The federal corporate tax rate is 15.8 percent (15 percent – down from 20 percent – plus a 5.5 percent solidarity tax), but a 7–17 percent trade tax raises the effective rate to roughly 33 percent. Other taxes include a value-added tax (VAT) and a flat tax of 25 percent on all investment income, including capital gains. In the most recent year, overall tax revenue as a percentage of GDP was 40.6 percent.

Government size – 38.2

Total government expenditures, including consumption and transfer payments, are very high. In the most recent year, government spending equaled 45.4 percent of GDP. Social welfare programs remain large and expensive.

Monetary freedom – 80.8

Germany is a member of the euro zone. Between 2005 and 2007, its weighted average annual rate of inflation was 2.1 percent. As a participant in the EU's Common Agricultural Policy, the government subsidizes agricultural production, distorting the prices of agricultural products. It also regulates prices for pharmaceuticals, electricity, telecommunications, and other public services. Ten points were deducted from Germany's monetary freedom score to adjust for measures that distort domestic prices.

Investment freedom – 80

Foreign and domestic investors are treated equally in accordance with EU standards. Some businesses, including certain financial institutions, passenger transport businesses, and real estate agencies, require licenses. There are no permanent currency controls on foreign investments and no serious limitations on new projects, except that the sale of defense companies to foreign investors requires permission. Foreign and domestic firms face the same barriers to investment, such as labor laws that impede hiring and dismissals. New rules have helped to cut red tape, but bureaucracy remains burdensome. There are no restrictions on capital transactions or current transfers, real estate purchases, repatriation of profits, or access to foreign exchange.

Financial freedom – 60

Germany's financial system is efficient, although bank consolidation has been slow and marginal because of political obstacles. Regulations are generally transparent and consistent with international norms. All types of capital are available to foreign and domestic businesses. Most of the roughly 2,000 banks are local savings banks and cooperative institutions. Private banks account for less than 30 percent of the market, and government-linked publicly owned banks account for nearly 50 percent; the rest are cooperative banks. Banks are competitive and offer a full range of financial services. Interest rates are market-determined, and foreign investors can access credit freely. The insurance sector and capital markets are open to foreign participation. The stock market is well developed.

Property rights – 90

All property, including intellectual property, is well protected. Contracts are secure, and the judiciary and civil service are highly professional. Separate supreme courts deal with commercial, tax, and constitutional cases.

Freedom from corruption – 78

Corruption is perceived as minimal. Germany ranks 16th out of 179 countries in Transparency International's Corruption Perceptions Index for 2007. Strict anti-corruption laws are enforced, and Germany has ratified the GECD Anti-Bribery Convention.

Labor freedom – 43.4

Restrictive labor regulations hinder employment and productivity growth. The nonsalary cost of employing a worker is high, and dismissing a redundant employee is costly. Wages and fringe benefits remain among the world's highest. The difficulty of laying off workers is a disincentive for additional hiring.

Source: Adapted from Terry Miller and Kim R. Holmes, *2009 Index of Economic Freedom* (Washington, DC: The Heritage Foundation and Dow Jones & Company, Inc., 2009), at www.heritage.org/index.

SUMMARY

Define regional economic integration, and identify its six levels. The process whereby countries in a geographic region cooperate with one another to reduce or eliminate barriers to the international flow of products, people, or capital is called regional economic integration. A group of nations in a geographic region undergoing economic integration is called a regional trading bloc. There are six potential levels (or degrees) of integration for regional trading blocs. Each level of integration incorporates the properties of those preceding it. (1) Economic and trade cooperation seeks to advance the intensity of trade among nation members. (2) A free trade area is an economic integration in which countries seek to remove all barriers to trade between themselves, but each country determines its own barriers against nonmembers. (3) A customs union is an economic integration in which countries remove all barriers to trade between themselves but erect a common trade policy against nonmembers. (4) A common market is an

(Continued)

economic integration in which countries remove all barriers to trade and to the movement of labor and capital between themselves but erect a common trade policy against nonmembers. (5) An economic union is an economic integration in which countries remove barriers to trade and to the movement of labor and capital, erect a common trade policy against nonmembers, and coordinate their economic policies. (6) A political union is an economic and political integration in which countries coordinate aspects of their economic and political systems.

Discuss the benefits and drawbacks associated with regional economic integration. The resulting increase in the level of trade between nations as a result of regional economic integration is called trade creation. One result of trade creation is that consumers in member nations are faced with a wider selection of goods and services that were not available before. Also, consumers can acquire goods and services at lower cost following the lowering of trade barriers such as tariffs. A political benefit is that a smaller, regional group of nations can find it easier to reduce trade barriers than can a larger group of nations. Nations can also reduce the potential for military conflict and expand employment opportunities.

The downside of trade creation is trade diversion, the diversion of trade away from nations not belonging to a trading bloc and towards member nations. Trade diversion can result in increased trade with a less-efficient producer within the trading bloc. Regional integration also forces some people out of work. In addition, political union requires nations to give up a high degree of sovereignty in foreign policy.

Describe regional integration in Europe and discuss its future enlargement. The European Coal and Steel Community was formed in 1951 to remove trade barriers for coal, iron, steel, and scrap metal among the member nations. Following several waves of expansion, broadenings of its scope, and some changes, the European Union (EU) was formed. Several nations from Central, Eastern, and Southern Europe are awaiting future EU expansion as soon as they meet the so-called Copenhagen Criteria that relate to their political, legal, and economic systems. The five institutions that form the main institutional framework of the EU are the European Parliament, European Commission, Council of the European Union, Court of Justice, and Court of Auditors.

Other European nations created the European Free Trade Association (EFTA) to focus on trade in industrial, not consumer, goods. Today EFTA has just four members. The EFTA and EU created the European Economic Area (EEA) to cooperate on trade matters. To prepare for eventual EU membership, candidate countries established the Central European Free Trade Area (CEFTA). The aim is to remove customs duties and other barriers to trade in industrial products and agriculture.

Discuss regional integration in the Americas and analyze its future prospects. The North American Free Trade Agreement (NAFTA) between Canada, Mexico, and the USA became effective in January 1994. As a free trade agreement, NAFTA seeks to eliminate most tariffs and nontariff trade barriers on most goods originating from within North America by 2008.

The Andean Community was formed in 1969 and calls for tariff reduction for trade among member nations, a common external tariff, and common policies in transportation and certain industries. The Latin American Integration Association (ALADI) formed in 1980 between Mexico and 10 South American nations has had little impact on cross-border trade. The Southern Common Market (MERCOSUR) was established in 1988. Today, MERCOSUR acts as a customs union and is emerging as the most powerful trading bloc in all of Latin America.

The Caribbean Community and Common Market (CARICOM) trading bloc was formed in 1973. The main difficulty CARICOM faces is that most members trade more with nonmembers than they do with each other. The Central

American Common Market (CACM) was formed in 1961 but conflicts have hampered progress for the CACM.

The objective of the Free Trade Area of the Americas (FTAA) is to create a trading bloc encompassing all of Central, North, and South America (excluding Cuba). The goal of the Transatlantic Economic Partnership (TEP) between the USA and the EU is to contribute to stability, democracy, and development worldwide, in addition to forging closer economic ties between the two economic regional trading blocs.

Characterize regional integration in Asia and discuss how it differs from integration elsewhere. The Association of Southeast Asian Nations (ASEAN) formed in 1967, and has three main objectives: (1) to promote economic, cultural, and social development in the region; (2) to safeguard the region's economic and political stability; and (3) to serve as a forum in which differences can be resolved fairly and peacefully. Today, ASEAN has 10 members but China, Japan, and South Korea may join in the future.

The organization for Asia-Pacific Economic Cooperation (APEC) was formed in 1989. Begun as an informal forum among 12 trading partners, APEC now has 21 members. Together, the APEC nations account for more than half of world trade and a combined GDP of more than $16 trillion.

The stated aim of APEC is not to build another trading bloc. Instead, it desires to strengthen the multilateral trading system and expand the global economy by simplifying and liberalizing trade and investment procedures among member nations. In the long term, APEC hopes to have free trade and investment throughout the region by 2010 for developed nations and 2020 for developing ones.

Describe regional integration in the Middle East and Africa and explain why progress there has been slow. Several Middle Eastern nations formed the Gulf Cooperation Council (GCC) in 1980. Members of the GCC are Bahrain, Kuwait, Oman, Qatar, Saudi Arabia, and the United Arab Emirates. The primary purpose of the GCC at its formation was to cooperate with the increasingly powerful trading blocs in Europe at the time – the EU and EFTA. Today, the main GCC thrust is to allow citizens of member countries to travel freely without visas and to permit citizens of member nations to own properties in another member nation without the need for local sponsors or partners.

The *Economic Community of West African States (ECOWAS)* was formed in 1975 but relaunched its efforts at economic integration in 1992 because of a lack of early progress. One of the most important goals of ECOWAS is the formation of a customs union and eventual common market. The group's lack of progress on economic integration largely reflects each nation's lack of economic development.

DISCUSSION QUESTIONS

1 What is the final goal of regional economic integration? List the levels of regional integration.
2 Identify potential benefits and problems of regional economic integration.
3 What is trade creation?
4 Identify the reasons for European nations to form a regional trading bloc.
5 What is the European Union (EU)? What is NAFTA?
6 Identify the main institutions of the European Union.
7 What is the European Free Trade Association (EFTA)?
8 What three countries belong to the North American Free Trade Agreement (NAFTA)?

(Continued)

9 What is the Andean Community? Give one reason why it is behind schedule in forming a free trade region.
10 Who are the members of the Southern Common Market (MERCOSUR) trading bloc?
11 What is the Free Trade Area of the Americas (FTAA)?
12 What are the main objectives of the Association of Southeast Asian Nations (ASEAN)?
13 How do the goals of the organization for Asia-Pacific Economic Cooperation (APEC) differ from those of other regional blocs?
14 What is the Gulf Cooperation Council?
15 What is the Economic Community of West African States (ECOWAS)?

ACTION ITEMS

1 At what point do you think the integration process of regional trading blocs will stop?
2 How do regional trading blocs impact free trade made possible by the World Trade Organization (WTO)? How can these initiatives complement each other?
3 The World Bank makes a distinction between resource-based, efficiency-based, and innovation-based countries/economies. How are integration arrangements among these types of countries affected?
4 Malaysia is an interesting case of national development in a regional context. Over the years the Malaysian economy has relied on foreign direct investment (FDI) as well as exports of goods manufactured locally. This is no longer the case. Malaysia is in transition, promoting developing domestic industries such as biotechnology and tourism, increasing regional trade through ASEAN, intensifying trade with emerging markets such as India and China, and supporting progressive liberalization, including services and market opening for agricultural and nonagricultural products. How can Malaysia pursue both ASEAN-oriented trade standards and practices alongside its bilateral agreements with Japan, China, and India? What are the probable problems in such a case? Can you identify other countries that are in the same predicament vis-á-vis its relevant region and, once such a country identified, what are the issues that should be addressed and how?

Bibliography

Aarts, P. (1999). The Middle East: a region without regionalism or the end of exceptioalism. *Third World Quarterly,* 20, 911–25.

Acharya, A. (1999). Realism, institutionalism, and the Asian economic crisis. *Contemporary Southeast Asia,* 21, 1–29.

Alagappa, M. (1993). Regionalism and the quest for security: ASEAN and the Cambodian Conflict. *Journal of International Affairs,* 46, 439–67.

Balassa, B. (1961). *The Theory of Economic Integration*. Homewood, IL: Irwin.

Bar-El, R., Benhayoun, G., Menipaz, E. (eds) (2000). *Regional Cooperation in Global Context*. Paris: L'Harmattan.

Benhayoun, G., Bar-El, R., Lheritien, M., Menipaz, E. (eds) (2001). *La Coopération Régionale Dans Le Bassin Méditerranéen,* (Vols. I & II).Paris: L'Harmattan.

Blatter, J. (2000). Emerging cross-border regions as a step towards sustainable development? *International Journal of Economic Development,* 2, 1–25.

Boas, M., Marchand, M., Shaw, T. (1999). Special issue: new regionalisms in the new millennium. *Third World Quarterly,* 20, 897–1070.

Booth, K., Wheeler, T. (1992). Contending philosophies about security in Europe. In Colin McInnes (ed.), *Security and Strategy in the New Europe*. London: Routledge, pp. 3–36.

Bowles, P. (1997). ASEAN, AFTA and the 'New Regionalism'. *Pacific Affairs,* 70, 219–34.

Briceno R. J. (2001). Strategic regionalism and the remaking of the triangular relation between the USA, the European Union and Latin America. *Journal of European Integration*, 23, 199–214.

Buckley, P. J., Clagg, J., Forsans, N., Reilly, K. T. (2001). Increasing the size of the 'country': regional economic integration and foreign direct investment in a globalised world economy. *Management International Review*, 41(3), 75–251.

Bull, H. (1995). *The Anarchical Society*, 2nd edn. New York: Columbia University Press.

Buzan B., Waever O., de Wilde J. (1998). *Security: A New Framework for Analysis*. London: Lynne Rienner Publishers.

Calley, S. C. (2000). Regional dynamics in the Mediterranean, in *Regionalism*, pp. 115–210. in Calley, S. (ed.), *The Post-Cold War World*, Ashgate Publishing, Surrey: UK.

Calley. A. (2000). *Regionalism in the Post-Cold War World*. Hampshire: Ashgate Publising.

Central Intelligence Agency (2008). *CIA World Fact Book*.

Charrier, P. (2001). ASEAN's inhertittance: the regionalization of Southeast Asia, 1941–61. *The Pacific Review*, 14, 313–38.

Cotton, J. (1999). The 'haze' over Southeast Asia: challenging the ASEAN mode of regional integration. *Pacific Affairs*, 72, 331–52.

Crawford, J., Fiorentino, R. (2005). *The Changing Landscape of Regional Trade Agreements*. Discussion Paper No. 8. Geneva, Switzerland: World Trade Organization.

De Blij H. J., Muller, P. O. (2002). *Geography. Realms, Regions, and Concepts*, 10th edn. New York: John Wiley and Sons.

De Vree, J. (1972). *Political Integration: the Formation of Theory and its Problems*. Paris: Mouton.

Dreuil, E., Anderson, J., Block, W., Saliba, M. (2003). The trade gap: the fallacy of anti world-trade sentiment. *Journal of Business Ethics*, 45(3), 78–269.

Echandi, R. (2001). Regional trade integration in the Americas during the 1990s: reflections of some trends and their implication for the multilateral trade system. *Journal of International Economic Law*, 367–410.

Eichengreen, B. (1996). On the links between monetary and political integration. Center for International and Development Economics Research (CIDER). Working Paper Series C96/077.

Etzioni, A. (1965). *Political Unification. A Comparative Study of Leaders and Forces*. New York: Holt, Rinehart and Winston.

European Union. (2008). Website of the European Union at http://europa.eu.int.

Fawcett, L., Hurrell, A. (1997). *Regionalism in World Politics*. New York: Oxford University Press.

Gallant N., Stubbs, R. (1997). APEC's dilemmas: institution-building around the Pacific Rim. *Pacific Affairs*, 70, 203–18.

Gamble, A., Payne, A. (1996). *Regionalism and World Order*. London: Macmillan Press.

Garman, G., Gillard, D. (1998). Economic Integration in the Americas: 1975–1992. *Journal of Applied Business Research*, 14(3), 1–12.

Garofano, J. (1999). Flexibility or irrelevance: ways forward for the ARF. *Contemporary Southeast Asia*, 21, 74–94.

Ghemawat, P. (2001). Distance still matters: the hard reality of global expansion. *Harvard Business Review*, September, 3–11.

Gilpin, R., Gilpin, J. M. (2001). *Global Political Economy: Understanding the International Economic Order*. Princeton, NJ: Princeton University Press.

Grugel, J., Hout, W. (1999). *Regionalism Across the North–South Divide*. London: Routledge.

Harvie, C. (1994). *The Rise of Regional Europe*. London: Routledge.

Hettne B., Inotai, A., Sunkel, O. (1999). *Globalism and the New Regionalism*. London: Macmillan Press.

Kaltenthaler K., Mora, F. O. (2002). Explaining Latin American economic integration: the case of Mercosur. *Review of International Political Economy*, 9, 72–97.

Kellstrup, M. (1992). European integration and political theory. In Morten Kellstrup (ed.), *European Integration and Denmark's Participation*. Copenhagen: Copenhagen Political Studies Press, pp. 13–58.

Kemp G., Harkaw, R. E. (1997). *Strategic Geography and the Changing Middle East*. Washington, DC: Brookings Institutions Press.

Knudsen, O. F. (1997). *Regionalism and Regional Cooperation*. Oslo: The Norwegian Institute of International Affairs.

Lim, R. (1998). The ASEAN regional forum: building on sand. *Contemporary Southeast Asia*, 20, 115–36.

Lindberg L. N., Scheingold S. A. (1970). *Regional Integration. Theory and Research*. London: Oxford University Press.

McInnes, C. (1992). *Security and Strategy in the New Europe*. London: Routledge.

Mansfield E. D., Milner H. V. (1997). *The Political Economy of Regionalism*. New York: Columbia University Press.

Mattli, W. (1999). *The Logic of Regional Integration. Europe and Beyond*. Cambridge: Cambridge University Press.

Muthiah, A. (1998). *Asian Security Practice. Material and Ideational Influences*. Stanford, CA: Stanford University Press.

OPEC (2003). *Annual Statistical Bulletin*.

Paasi, A. (2000). Europe as a social process and discourse: considerations of place, boundaries and identity. Proceedings of The Third European Urban and Regional Studies Conference, Voss, Norway, September 14–17 2000.

Pacific Economic Cooperation. (2003). At www.apecsec.org.sg.

Pelkmans, J. (2001). *European Integration. Methods and Economic Analysis*, 2nd edn. Essex: Pearson Education Limited.

Pinder, J. (2001). *The European Union. A Very Short Introduction*. Oxford: Oxford University Press.

Rosamond, B. (1995). Mapping the European condition: the theory of integration and the integration of theory. *European Journal of International Relations,* 1, 391–408.

Rosamand, B. (2000). *Theories of European Integration*. New York: Palgrave.

Rowntree, L., Lewis, M., Price, M., Wyckoff, W. (2000). *Diversity amid Globalization: World Regions, Environment, Development*. Upper Saddle River, NJ: Prentice Hall.

Rugman, A. (2001). *The End of Globalization: Why Global Strategy is a Myth and How to Profit from the Realities of Regional Markets*. New York: American Management Association.

Rugman, A., Verbeke, A. (2004). A perspective on regional and global strategies of multinational enterprises. *Journal of International Business Studies,* 35, 7.

Schulz, M., Söderbaum, F., Öjendal, J. (2001). *Regionalization in a Globalizing World*. London: Zed Books.

Skonieczny, A. (2001). Constructing NAFTA: myth, representation, and the discursive construction of U.S. foreign policy. *International Studies Quarterly,* 45, 433–54.

Stubbs R., Underhill, G. R. D. (1994). *Political Economy and the Changing Global Order*. London: Macmillan Press.

Taylor P. J., Flint, C. (2000). *Political Geography,* 4th edn. London: Prentice Hall.

Telò, M. (2001). *European Union and New Regionalism*. Burlington, VT: Ashgate Publishing Company.

Thomas, K. P., Tétreault, M. A. (1999). *Racing to Regionalize: Democracy, Capitalism, and Regional Political Economy*. London: Lynne Rienner Publishers.

Viotti, P. R., Kauppi, M. V. (1999). *International Relations Theory,* 3rd edn. Needham Heights, MA: Allyn & Bacon.

Waever, O., Lemaitre, P., Tromer, E. (1989). *European Polyphony: Perspectives Beyond East–West Confrontation*. London: Macmillan Press.

Webber, D. (2001). Two funerals and a wedding? The ups and downs of regionalism in East Asia and Asia-Pacific after the Asian crisis. *The Pacific Review* 14, 339–72.

Wivel, A. (1998). *Explaining European Integration*. Copenhagen: Copenhagen Political Studies Press.

World Trade Organization (2008). Statistics from the WTO website at www.wto.org.

Yamazawa, I. (2001). Whither East Asian regionalism. *Asia-Pacific Review,* 8, 18–27.

Yip Kia, W. (2001). Prospects for closer economic integration in East Asia. *Stanford Journal of East Asian Affairs,* 1, 106–11.

8

The Global Financial System

Learning Objectives

Following this chapter, the reader should be able to:

1. Recognize the main elements of national and global financial systems
2. Understand the role of international capital markets
3. Understand the concepts of foreign exchange markets and how they affect international business and management
4. Be familiar with the goals and policies of national currency restrictions

Opening Case
Exchange Rate Debate in New Zealand

The debate to de-float the New Zealand dollar has been heated, with the Alliance Party endorsing the call to introduce a managed exchange rate.

The so-called "kiwi dollar" is one of the top ten most traded currencies in the world, which has subjected it to unnecessary volatility. Exchange rate volatility hurts local exporters who economists believe will be the catalyst to lift the economy out of recession. But the recent rise in the dollar to almost US60c is seen as a stumbling block towards recovery. The currency's current volatility can be blamed partially on the fact that the market did not understand what was happening. Some have claimed that what is needed is an exchange rate target – with the associated policy mechanism and institution to ensure that the target is achievable.

This means using a Singaporean "managed exchange rate" model, allowing the market to influence the exchange rate, but having the Reserve Bank backstop any shifts outside target boundaries. "The New Zealand dollar is riding the economic rollercoaster, peaking, and plunging. It makes economic planning difficult and it costs New Zealanders jobs and financial stability," said Alliance economic development spokesperson Finlay.

BusinessDay blogger and Chairman of the Shareholders' Association, Bruce Sheppard, has called for the Reserve Bank to "print money" in an attempt to counter the effect of a migration of foreign capital overseas. He says foreign banks are slowly withdrawing funding to shore up their home markets, driving up the exchange rate. "The US is printing money and that is why the kiwi dollar jumped up from US51c to US59c in a week," said Sheppard. To counter this, the Reserve Bank should step in to provide low-cost business loans – in effect, print money. "There are some elements of deflationary pressure in the world economy, and trade is going to be constrained by a liquidity crisis. Fix it by printing money, advancing it to a commercial bank, lend it out," said Sheppard. As the economy recovers, withdraw the money and use money supply control to regulate inflation. As per Sheppard, "NZ needs to start doing things in the interests of our people and stop trying to be a goody two shoes on the international stage."

Source: Chang, A. (2009). "Exchange rate debate in New Zealand." *BusinessDay*, April 7, 2009. http://www.stuff.co.nz/business/2321346/Exchange-rate-debate-gathers-steam.

Introduction

As the opening case illustrates, national and international financial systems are totally dependent on one other. Thus, a well-developed international financial system is a key to an appropriate conduct of international business. International financial markets provide funds from institutions and national economies that have excess money to institutions and organizations that are short of funds and determine the exchange rates of converting one currency to another. Providing funds and determining exchange rates allow for appropriate investment capital and working capital that are required to start up businesses. These two types of capital facilitate international trade by multinational enterprises (MNEs). As an example, funds provided to initiate a business in New Zealand were withdrawn by banks as they tried to weather the global economic crisis of 2008–10. To ease up the credit crunch, the USA has increased its money supply and has reduced interest. Looking for funds, financial institutions and enterprises are shoring up demand for US funds, causing an increase of the "kiwi" dollar from US$0.51 to almost US$0.60. Generally, exchange rates are affected by the volume of trade, the demand and supply of the exchanged currencies, as well as the risk inherent in the currencies.

This chapter describes the global financial system, including international capital markets, which allow companies to borrow and lend money in order to finance growth and sustain operations worldwide. Capital markets raise capital by using various financial instruments, including bond and equity instruments. Exchange markets, in which currencies are exchanged at a particular rate, are also described. The chapter includes a discussion of how capital markets and exchange rates affect international business. It should be noted that a discussion of foreign exchange exposure is provided in Chapter 13, which deals with international financial management.

International capital market

A *capital market* is a system which allows for the allocation of capital resources in the form of debt and equity, according to their most efficient use. Its main function is to provide borrowers and investors with a marketplace in which money may be lent to borrowers and invested by investors. Individuals, MNEs, labor unions, pension funds, government and nongovernment organizations may participate in capital markets by lending and borrowing funds. A government may need the monies to build a water desalination installation, develop a fiberoptic telecommunication infrastructure or build a major toll-charging highway or bridge. An MNE may need the monies to construct a new manufacturing plant or build regional headquarters (RHQ) in China or the Philippines. In all of these cases capital markets provide the means to raise capital through various financial instruments, such as bonds, equity, or other financial derivatives.

National capital markets

Capital markets in national economies facilitate trade between lenders and borrowers. It helps individuals and organizations to borrow money obtained from individuals and organizations that have excess capital and would like to lend money. Commercial banks provide borrowers with capital obtained from investors' deposits. Investment banks act as agents, introducing clients to individuals or organizations that are interested in an investment or in borrowing money. Corporations may obtain financing using debt or equity financing through national capital markets, as explained below.

Debts investment in capital markets are loans that government and non-government organizations take in exchange for a commitment to pay the lenders an interest on the principal amount during the term of the loan. The borrowing organization issues bonds which specify the payments of both principal and interest. Bonds issued by local governments are called municipal bonds, whereas bonds issued by corporations are termed corporate bonds. If organizations do not live up to the payment commitments as specified in the debt instrument terms, the investors may force bankruptcy upon these organizations.

In *equity instrument* financing, the organization issues ownership rights to the investors, in exchange for a claim against future financial gains (or losses). The ownership is granted through the issue of shares of the organization. The investors are entitled to a share of the profits, termed dividends. Dividend payments are not guaranteed. The organization's board of directors may or may not authorize dividend payments. The stockholders may trade the stock in the stock market. The value of the stock is usually determined by the laws of supply and demand and reflects, the investors' sentiments regarding future prospects, future profits, inherent industry risk, and dividend policy.

Figure 8.1 lists the main international and national capital market institutions and systems, including three international organizations (the International Monetary Fund, the Bank for International Settlements, and the World Bank) and three types of national organizations (central banks and stock/bond markets). Together, these institutions constitute the global financial system.

International capital market

Multinational enterprises rely on large national and international financial institutions, such as investment and commercial banks. These large financial institutions assist MNEs by creating debt and equity instruments, as well as by managing assets and savings of individuals and organizations.

Large financial institutions are present in tens of countries around the world and have an asset base and lending capabilities of hundreds of billions of dollars. This international presence and size of financial resources contribute to the sustainable growth of MNEs. Most global financial services provide the following services:

1. *Private banking services*: investments, estate planning, treasury, foreign exchange, domestic and international securities.

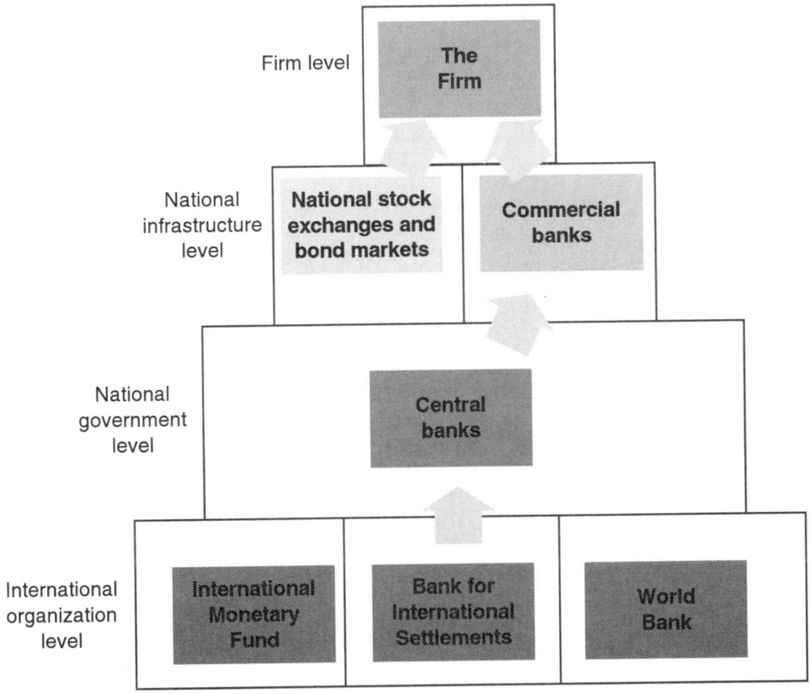

FIGURE 8.1 The hierarchies and main organizations in the global monetary and financial systems

2. *Corporate and institutional banking*: credit and trade services.
3. *Treasury and foreign exchange services*: spot, forwards, options, currency, and interest rate swap.
4. *Investment banking services*: securities-related services, such as advisory and execution services for securities, corporate finance, private placements, initial public offerings (IPOs), mergers and acquisitions, leveraged (M&A) finance, private equity, and debt instruments).
5. *Offshore banking services*: a dedicated manager and preferential interest rates on deposits, mortgages and lending. Accounts are available in most major currencies, and customer service is provided in several ways, including telephone and Internet.

International financial centers

The international capital market consists of financial institutions, such as banks, stock markets, MNEs, individuals, and government and nongovernment agencies, that invest and borrow monies, transcending international borders. In these markets, funds are collected, disseminated, and cleared. Monies become available through electronic means that are Internet-based. Various financial instruments are used by financial services providers in order to borrow, deposit, and invest funds around the world. The basic mechanisms that facilitate national capital markets are at work in the international capital market: namely, funds are collected in deposits by investors and are made available to borrowers around the world.

There are several reasons for the growth of the international capital market. First, the international capital market expands the money supply for borrowers, by making funds available from capital markets in developed and developing countries. MNEs that need financing for high-risk investments or governments that need financing for large-scale projects, such as regional development projects, rely on international capital markets to provide financing. Second, as most funds become available from around the world, the cost of monies for the borrower is reduced. The law of supply and demand dictates a lower price for funds as the international supply of funds is increased. The price of funds is the interest paid on borrowed funds. Alternatively, the price may be the dividend expected to be paid for equity issues. The lower price of funds makes for a lower threshold for rate of return on proposed ventures. Third, the international capital market helps reduce the risk inherent in lending monies, since investors may choose from a larger set of investment opportunities around the world, with lower rates of risk. Better yet, investors may make portfolio investments in international markets that are not affected the same way by economic changes: that is, as some markets go down, others may go up, reducing the overall risk involved in a particular portfolio.

The growth of international capital market is affected by several developments:

- *Developments in information technology (IT)*. Information is important for capital markets because investors need information about investment opportunities and their corresponding risk level. Large investments in information technology over the past decades have drastically reduced the cost, in both time and money, of communication around the world. Investors and borrowers can now respond in record time to breaking news in the international capital market.
- *Deregulation*. Deregulation of national capital markets has helped expand the international capital market. The need for deregulation became apparent when heavily regulated markets in the largest countries were facing competition from less regulated markets in smaller nations. Deregulation increased competition, lowered the cost of financial transactions and opened many national markets to global investing and borrowing.
- *Financial instruments*. Greater competition in the financial industry is creating the need to develop innovative financial instruments. It should be noted that several advanced financial instruments came under fire since an abundance of these instruments became insolvent and have contributed to the collapse of financial markets, which led to the 2008–10 global financial and economic crisis.

The Global Financial Crisis and the International Capital Market

It should be noted that as a result of the global economic crisis, countries around the world have taken measures that affect the international capital market. In particular, during the third quarter of 2008, the major instability in world financial markets caused various agencies and regulators, as well as public policymakers, to take comprehensive steps to handle the evolving crisis that started in the North America about a year earlier, following the collapse of the subprime mortgage market. As a result of the global crisis, various government agencies have committed to spend trillions of dollars in loans, asset purchases, guarantees and direct spending, affecting major changes to the national capital markets and the international capital market.

The changes took the form of monetary, fiscal, and regulatory measures, as follows. First, central national banks have expanded their lending and money supplies, to offset the decline in lending by private institutions and investors, increasing liquidity, or funds available for the respective national economies. Second, as some financial institutions were facing risks regarding their solvency, or ability to pay their obligations, alternative ways to maintain sustainability were offered, such as restructuring through bankruptcy, adjusting bond commitments, or government bailouts through nationalization, receivership or asset purchases. Third, governments devised and offered economic stimulus programs, including programs for increased spending and cutting taxes to offset declines in consumer spending and business investment. Fourth, various homeowner assistance programs were offered, such as, adjusting the terms of mortgage loans by banks to avoid foreclosure, with the goal of maximizing cash payments, offering of financial incentives by governments for lenders to assist borrowers and systematic refinancing of large numbers of mortgages. Fifth, new or reinstated regulatory rules were designed to help stabilize the financial system over the long-run to prevent future crises.

Global financial centers

The main facilitators of the international capital market are the major financial centers in, so-called global cities such as New York, London, Frankfurt, and Hong Kong. These global financial centers include the banks, the insurance companies, the stock exchanges, and other financial service organizations. The global financial centers carry out most of the international capital market activity and compete on the basis of regulations, fees, operating and reporting requirements, and a variety of financial derivatives and interest rates.

Offshore financial centers and services

Offshore financial services (OFSs) are provided by banks and other financial institutions in offshore locations to nonresidents, including the borrowing of money from nonresidents and lending of money to nonresidents. This includes lending to MNEs and to other financial institutions, as well as taking deposits from individuals and investing the proceeds in financial markets elsewhere in the world. As explained later, offshore centers are usually located in countries with very few regulations and low or no taxes on financial transactions. *Offshore financial centers (OFCs)* are defined as any financial center where offshore financial services take place, including all the major financial centers in the world. In such major international financial centers, there may be little distinction between onshore and offshore business. Both funds and loans may be generated and awarded, respectively, on- or offshore. Offshore financial centers are found in countries that have relatively large financial systems, with assets and liabilities out of proportion to the size of the local economy (such as Luxembourg and the Island of Jersey in the English Channel). In addition, offshore financial centers are found in countries with low or zero taxation, with moderate or no financial regulation, and with banking secrecy and anonymity practices, conditions that for many years, have been practiced by Swiss financial institutions. There are several types of offshore financial center:

- well-developed financial markets, such as Hong Kong and Singapore; where a considerable amount of value is added to transactions undertaken for non-residents;
- centers with smaller populations, where value added is limited to the provision of professional support or the mere registration of the financial transaction;
- offshore centers, where services provided include fund management, insurance, trust business, and tax planning.

Although accurate statistics are not readily available, it seems that there has been a growth in many offshore financial centers. Table 8.1 lists the countries and territories, by world region, with offshore financial centers.

The following are several tasks of OFCs.

Task 1: Offshore banking l icenses

A multinational corporation sets up an offshore bank to handle its foreign exchange operations or to facilitate financing of an international joint venture. An onshore bank establishes a wholly owned subsidiary in an OFC to provide offshore fund administration services (e.g., fully integrated global custody, fund accounting, fund administration, and transfer agent services). The attractions of the OFC may include no capital tax, no withholding tax on dividends or interest, no tax on transfers, no corporation tax, no capital gains tax, no exchange controls, light regulation and supervision, less stringent reporting requirements, and less stringent trading restrictions. As an example, the Royal Bank of Canada (RBC) has provided offshore banking services in the Cayman Islands since 1972. The Cayman Islands office has a team of professionals who provide access to a complete range of wealth management services through their global network of offices. These RBC offshore services include offshore trusts and fiduciary services, private banking and credit services, captive insurance banking, fund administration, and investment advisory and discretionary investment management.

TABLE 8.1 Countries and Territories With Offshore Financial Centers Around the World

Africa	*Asia and Pacific*	*Europe*	*Middle East*	*Western Hemisphere*
Djibouti	Cook Islands	Andorra	Bahrain	Anguilla
Liberia	Guam	Campione	Israel	Antigua
Mauritius	Hong Kong, SAR	Cyprus	Lebanon	Aruba
Seychelles	Japan	Dublin, Ireland		Bahamas
Tangier	Labuan, Malaysia	Gibraltar		Barbados
	Macao, SAR	Guernsey		Belize
	Marianas	Isle of Man		Bermuda
	Marshall Islands	Jersey		British Virgin Islands
	Micronesia	Liechtenstein		Cayman Islands
	Nauru	London, UK		Costa Rica
	Niue	Luxembourg		Dominica
	Philippines	Madeira		Grenada
	Singapore	Malta		Montserrat
	Tahiti	Monaco		Netherlands Antilles
	Thailand	Netherlands		Panama
	Vanuatu	Switzerland		Puerto Rico
	Western Samoa			St Kitts and Nevis
				St Lucia
				St Vincent and Grenadines
				Turks and Caicos Islands
				Uruguay
				USA
				West Indies

Task 2: Offshore corporations or international business corporations (IBCs)

IBCs are limited liability entities registered in an OFC. IBCs are a popular vehicle for managing investment funds. They may be used to own and operate businesses, and issue shares, bonds, or raise capital in other ways. They can be used to create sophisticated financial structures. IBCs may be set up with one director only, which is not common in most countries. In some cases, residents of the OFC host country may act as nominee directors to conceal the identity of the true company directors, required at times by the true owner for a variety of reasons. In OFCs, registered share certificates may be issued, but no public registry of shareholders is maintained. In many OFCs, the costs of setting up IBCs are minimal and they are generally exempt from all taxes.

Task 3: Insurance companies

A commercial corporation establishes a captive insurance company in an OFC to manage risk and minimize taxes. In this case, an onshore insurance company establishes a subsidiary in an OFC to reinsure certain risks underwritten by the parent company while reducing overall reserve and capital requirements. Sometimes, an onshore insurance company incorporates a subsidiary in an OFC to insure catastrophic risks. The attractions of an OFC in these circumstances include favorable income tax, withholding tax and capital tax requirements, and loosely enforced actuarial reserve requirements and capital standards.

Task 4: Special purpose vehicles

One of the most rapidly growing uses of OFCs is when an onshore corporation establishes an offshore IBC in order to engage in a special purpose vehicle (SPV) practiced in a more favorable tax environment. The issuance of asset-backed securities is the most frequently cited activity of SPVs. The onshore corporation may assign a set of assets to the offshore SPV (e.g., a portfolio of mortgages, loans, credit card receivables). The SPV then offers a variety of securities to investors based on the underlying assets. The SPV, and hence the onshore parent, benefits from the favorable tax treatment in the OFC.

Task 5: Tax planning

Wealthy individuals make use of favorable tax environments in, and tax treaties with, OFCs, often involving offshore companies, trusts, and foundations. MNEs route activities through low-tax OFCs to minimize their total tax bill through transfer pricing: that is, goods may be made onshore but invoices are issued offshore by an IBC owned by the multinational, moving onshore profits to low-tax regimes.

Task 6: Tax evasion

There are also individuals and enterprises who rely on banking secrecy to avoid declaring assets and income to the relevant tax authorities. Individuals moving money gained from illegal transactions also seek maximum secrecy from tax and criminal investigation. At times, money laundering is the reason for the use of an OFC.

Task 7: Asset management and protection

Wealthy individuals and enterprises in countries with weak economies and fragile banking systems may want to keep assets overseas to protect them against the collapse of their domestic currencies and domestic banks, and outside the reach of existing or potential exchange controls.

Investment banks

Investment banks are a major component of international capital markets. Investment banks issue financial instruments and locate investors that would like to participate in the international capital market. Among the main banks that participate in the international capital market are HSBC, Deutsche Bank, Citibank, JPMorgan, Barclays Capital, Morgan Stanley, and Credit Suisse. The global capital market is based on financial investments and derivatives such as international bonds, equity, and Eurocurrency.

International bonds markets

The *international bond market* consists of all bonds issued and traded by MNEs or governments outside their own countries. An increasing number of MNEs issue bonds and sell them internationally in order to raise capital. The buyers of international bonds are banks, retirement funds, mutual funds, and governments that need to invest their financial reserves for an appropriate return on investment on behalf of their constituents. Large international investment banks, such as the Rothschild Bank of Paris, manage the issuing, marketing and sales of new international bond issues for MNEs and government clients.

Types of international bonds

One type of financial instrument traded in the international capital market is the *eurobond*, which is issued outside the country in which it is denominated. A eurobond may be issued by Argentina, denominated in US dollars, and traded in the UK and France. In this case both the principal and the interest income associated with the eurobond are quoted and paid for by the Argentinean issuer of the bond in US dollars. Most international bonds are eurobonds and are popular since issuing countries (in this case Argentina) do not regulate the trade. This is preferable, since the associated risk is lower.

A second type of bonds is a *foreign bond*, which is denominated not in US dollars (like the eurobonds) but rather in the currency of the country in which it is sold. For instance, an Argentinean peso-denominated bond issued by the German carmaker BMW in Argentina's domestic bond market is a foreign bond. The foreign bonds are regulated by the countries in which they are traded (in this case, Argentina) and are subjected to all disclosure requirements as the locally issued bonds in Argentina.

Samurai bonds, Yankee bonds, Bulldog bonds, and Dragon bonds are foreign bonds issued and traded in Japan, USA, UK, and Asia (excluding Japan), respectively. All these foreign bonds are to meet local regulatory and disclosure requirements.

The growing volume of international bond issuance and trade is a result of two main developments: first, financial executives of corporations have become familiar with international bonds that help raise capital from sources other than local markets; second, current, local low interest rates have caused investors to look for higher returns on their capital through the purchase of international bonds. Developing nations are ready to pay higher returns on issued international bonds since their need for capital is increasing to support major infrastructure and industrial development projects, which makes international bonds issued by developing nations attractive.

Seeking funds through international bonds as opposed to local bonds instruments may be risky for countries with emerging markets, as the local currency may be devaluated considerably, which in turn makes interest payments to international bond holders extremely costly for the bond issuers.

The international equity market

The *international equity market* consists of all the government and corporate shares that are issued and traded outside of the issuing organization's home country. Individual investors, banks, insurance companies, retirement funds, and mutual funds participate in this marketplace and buy shares of foreign corporate and government organizations. The stock exchanges in the global cities of New York, London, and Frankfurt list most of the foreign shares. The growth in the international equity market is attributed to four reasons.

First, the *international trend towards privatization*: that is, the issuance of shares of formerly state-owned companies representing sizable capital. The shares are offered in international markets. Second, *emerging economies* require relatively larger amounts of funds to support infrastructure development and new investments; most of these funds are not available locally and thus require issuing shares on international equity. Third, *investment banks* are matching, between national corporate entities in need of cash and large international equity buyers who are located anywhere in the world. Thus, investment banks are contributing to the growth of the international equity market. Fourth, the development of markets with no physical trading, and thus no specific geographic location, which are open for trade over the Internet, 24 hours, seven days a week. The Internet-based capital market, termed the "cyber market," is dependent on a global network of high-speed data transfers, communication satellites, sophisticated support software, and personal computers. The cyber market requires specific electronic trading standards and practices. The growth of the cyber market contributes to the growth in the international capital market.

The eurocurrency market

Somewhat like the eurobonds describe earlier, the *eurocurrency market* encompasses all the world's currencies that are deposited outside their countries of origin. The eurobond market is a source of debt financing for MNEs that seek capital outside of their home market. A eurodollar is a certificate of deposit in US dollars in a bank outside of the United States. Thus, US dollars deposited in a bank in Hong Kong are called *eurodollars*. British pounds deposited elsewhere in the world are called *europounds*. Most eurodollar certificates of deposit (CD) are held in London, but they may be held anywhere outside of the USA. A major advantage of the Eurodollar is that it is not regulated by the government agencies, translating to lower interest and other fees involved in securing debt. Major sources of eurocurrencies are individuals who wish to hold dollars outside the USA, MNEs, and European banks with foreign currency in excess of immediate needs, international financial organizations and governments of countries that have a large balance of trade surplus.

The main importance of the eurocurrency market is the lack of regular banking regulations on the market and it is not required to be insured by a central bank: as a result, the risk involved is higher, but the deposits provide better profitability. The amount of interest on eurocurrency loans is in reference to the *interbank rate*, the rate that the largest banks charge one another for loans. The rate usually quoted on eurocurrency loans is the *London Interbank Offered Rate (LIBOR)*. The interest rate paid on eurocurrency deposits is the *London Interbank Bid Rate (LIBID)*. Both the LIBOR and the LIBID are used by financial institutions worldwide as a basis for financial transactions.

The eurocurrency market is significant in the context of international capital markets; it affects and is affected by the global economy. To wit, note, in Table 8.2, the gap of the LIBOR rates between December 2007 and March 2009, reflecting the global economic downturn. Assuming that the LIBOR rates reflect the demand for capital, the reduction in the LIBOR rates is caused by a shrinking global business activity.

The international loan market

The international loan market consists of financial institutions and banks that provide loans to MNEs overseas. Financial institutions use international lending as a way to expand their local markets overseas, as well as exploit the opportunities for better risk management. The markets for loans are globalized as a result of the harmonization of the Generally Accepted Auditing Standards (GAAS), Generally Accepted Accounting Principle (GAAP) and lending regulations. The harmonization of practices, standards, and regulations causes uniformity in the markets, which facilities a fair and adequate presentation of transactions in various countries and territories.

It should be noted that expanding markets and a variety of risk levels internationally are key to the success of international lending. However, as evidenced by the 2008–10 global economic crisis, at times, most markets present a higher degree of risk, provide no opportunities for risk reduction through an international portfolio and, thus, cause a significant reduction in global lending.

International lending

International lending also allows banks and other financial institutions to develop relationships with foreign firms, creating an opportunity for selling of other services. During the last decade there has been a major growth in *international mergers and acquisitions (M&As)*. This growth was particularly evidenced through the emergence and restructuring, internationally, of the biotechnology industry and the telecommunications industry. A large portion of international lending is to support international mergers & acquisitions in these industries and others. Commercial and investment banks serve as advisers and financial intermediaries, as they underwrite and place equity instruments, such as shares, bonds and loans,

TABLE 8.2 LIBOR Rate Information 2007–2009: A Reflection of a Global Economic Crisis

2007	*1-Month*	*12-Month*
January	5.3201	5.4414
February	5.3214	5.3328
March	5.3195	5.2009
April	5.3201	5.2976
May	5.321	5.3885
June	5.3195	5.4048
July	5.32	2.3832
August	5.4975	5.1860
September	5.4927	5.0618
October	4.9814	4.8771
November	4.7672	4.5219
December	5.0172	4.4227
2008		
January	3.9091	3.4415
February	3.1368	2.8046
March	2.8066	2.5133
April	2.7854	2.8288
May	2.5065	3.0306
June	2.4704	3.4176
July	2.46	3.2796
August	2.4682	3.2364
September	2.927	3.3709
October	3.8096	3.7893
November	1.621	2.8231
December	1.0826	2.3845
2009		
January	0.3834	1.9024
February	0.4628	2.0644
March	0.5325	2.1173

Source: Adapted from http://www.wsjprimerate.us/libor/libor_rates_history.htm.

to finance M&A. Loans are also provided, internationally, for financing *leveraged buyouts (LBOs)* by management. Since LBOs are financed mostly with debt, they result in a large demand for debt funds. As LBOs are supported by debt from an international consortium of banks, the risk from each loan to a particular bank involved is reduced. Furthermore, since LBOs are loaned to investor teams in a variety of countries and in various industries, representing various degrees of risk, a further reduction of risk is achieved.

Credit ranking

Credit ranking and monitoring is required of each country and MNE that are in the market for loans. The rankings are made for the purpose of determining the credit worthiness of countries and MNEs and are assessed by credit rating agencies such as Standard & Poor's and Moody's. This assessment is based on political risk and macroeconomic conditions. Rating is done on a scale. The Standard & Poor's system rates targeted countries and corporations, as indicated in Table 8.3.

TABLE 8.3 Bond Credit Rating by North American Agencies

Moody's	*Standard & Poor's*	*Credit worthiness*
Aaa	AAA	Credit risk almost zero
Aa1	AA+	Safe investment, low risk of failure
Aa2	AA	Safe investment, low risk of failure
Aa3	AA–	Safe investment, low risk of failure
A1	A+	Safe investment, unless unforeseen events should occur in the economy at large or in that particular economic sector
A2	A	Safe investment, unless unforeseen events should occur in the economy at large or in that particular economic sector
A3	A–	Safe investment, unless unforeseen events should occur in the economy at large or in that particular economic sector
Baa1	BBB+	Medium safe investment. Affected when economy is deteriorating. Problems may arise
Baa2	BBB	Medium safe investment. Affected when economy is deteriorating. Problems may arise
Baa3	BBB-	Medium safe investment. Affected when economy is deteriorating. Problems may arise
Ba1	BB+	Speculative investment. Occurs often in deteriorated circumstances, usually problematic to predict future development
Ba2	BB	Speculative investment. Occurs often in deteriorated circumstances, usually problematic to predict future development
Ba3	BB-	Speculative investment. Occurs often in deteriorated circumstances, usually problematic to predict future development
B1	B+	Speculative investment. Deteriorating situation expected
B2	B	Speculative investment. Deteriorating situation expected
B3	B-	Speculative investment. Deteriorating situation expected
Caa	CCC	High likelihood of bankruptcy
Ca	CC	High likelihood of bankruptcy
C	C	High likelihood of bankruptcy
	D	Bankruptcy. Continued inability to make payments most likely

Note: The North American Agency Moody's assigns bond credit ratings of Aaa, Aa, A, Baa, Ba, B, Caa, Ca, and C; Standard & Poor's and Fitch Agencies assign bond credit ratings of AAA, AA, A, BBB, BB, B, CCC, CC, C, and D, as well as intermediate ratings noted by + and – signs.

Source: Based on Moody's, www.Moodys.com; Standard & Poor's, www.Standardandpoors.com.

While the issue of foreign exchange is dealt with later in the book, as part of Chapter 13, a discussion of the foreign exchange market is provided in the following paragraphs for completeness.

Foreign Exchange Market

The international capital market as well as international business transactions mostly involve two nations with different currencies. The currencies are exchanged according to the rate determined by the *foreign exchange market*, which encompasses the purchase and sale of world currencies. The rate of exchange depends on the amount of currency being exchanged, government regulations, macroeconomic conditions, and the terms of the exchange. The laws of supply and demand apply in the foreign exchange market and the rates are determined as in any commodity which is traded internationally. The actual trading is done on the basis of bid quote and ask quote. As a financial institution may be the seller or the buyer of a foreign currency, it provides two quotes: the *bid quote* is the price at which the bank will buy the foreign currency; the *ask quote* is the price the bank is willing to sell the foreign currency. The difference between the two rates is the *bid–ask spread*. These rates are quoted in order to profit from the difference between the bid and the ask price.

The *foreign exchange market*, or the *currency exchange market*, is an *inter-bank market* that determines the basis for currency trade internationally.

The foreign exchange market is an over-the-counter (OTC) market, meaning that transactions are not done in a central, physical location between any two counter parties but rather via telephone or the Internet. Currency dealers often advertise their exchange rates using a distribution network that helps dealers agree to an exchange rate. The major dealing centers are London, New York, Tokyo, Zurich, Frankfurt, Hong Kong, Singapore, Paris, and Sydney.

The foreign exchange market is one of the world's largest and most liquid markets, with daily trading volumes in excess of US$1.5 trillion, larger than the bond or stock market. Because of the shear size of the foreign exchange market, it is impossible for any market participant to affect the exchange rates of the main traded currencies. The main traded currencies are the US dollar, Japanese yen, euro, Swiss franc, Canadian dollar, the British pound, and the Australian dollar. The value of these currencies in terms of US dollars is noted in Table 8.4.

The foreign exchange market operates 24 hours, 5 days a week. Trading begins Monday morning in Sydney, which corresponds to 3 pm EST in New York, Sunday, and moves around the globe until closing Friday evening at 4:30 pm EST in New York.

In the currency exchange market, most of the currencies are traded only against the US dollar. However, an exchange rate between two nondollar currencies is possible and is termed a cross rate. Trading between two nondollar currencies usually occurs by first trading one currency against the US dollar and then trading the US dollar against the second nondollar currency. Thus, the spread in the exchange rate between two nondollar currencies is often higher. Table 8.5 indicates the top 10 foreign currency traders in the world. Almost all of these institutions were affected by the global economic crisis of 2008–10. As an example, the most established and successful financial institution, Merrill Lynch, became insolvent.

TABLE 8.4 Rates of Exchange of Selected Currencies as Per the International Monetary Fund (May 8, 2009)

Currency	*Value in US dollars*
Euro	1.342500
Japanese yen	99.300000
UK pound sterling	1.504200
US dollar	1.000000
Argentine peso	–
Australian dollar	0.755600
Bahrain dinar	0.376000
Botswana pula	0.139500
Brazilian real	–
Brunei dollar	1.470100
Canadian dollar	1.158100
Chilean peso	564.440000
Chinese yuan	6.822100
Colombian peso	–
Cyprus pound	0.435958
Czech koruna	–
Danish krone	–
Hungarian forint	207.730000
Icelandic krona	125.380000
Indian rupee	49.250000
Indonesian rupiah	10,415.000000
Iranian rial	–
Israeli new sheqel	4.101000
Kazakhstani tenge	150.460000
Korean won	1,262.400000
Kuwaiti dinar	0.290900
Libyan dinar	1.932367
Malaysian ringgit	3.532500
Maltese lira	0.319777
Mauritian rupee	33.587500
Mexican peso	13.106700
Nepalese rupee	–
New Zealand dollar	0.594100
Norwegian krone	6.436900
Rial omani	0.384500
Pakistani rupee	80.424800

(Continued)

TABLE 8.4 Cont.

Currency	*Value in US dollars*
Polish zloty	3.241900
Qatar riyal	3.640000
Russian ruble	32.553400
Saudi Arabian riyal	3.750000
Singapore dollar	1.470100
South African rand	8.375000
Sri Lanka rupee	–
Swedish krona	7.835000
Swiss franc	1.129300
Thai baht	–
Trinidad and Tobago dollar	6.277200
UAE dirham	3.672500
Bolivar fuerte	2.144600

Source: Based on: The International Monetary Fund (IMF), http://www.imf.org/external/index.htm.

TABLE 8.5 The Top Ten Most Active Foreign Currency Traders

Top 10 currency traders rank	*Name*	*Percent of volume*
1	Deutsche Bank	19.26
2	UBS AG	11.86
3	Citigroup	10.39
4	Barclays Capital	6.61
5	Royal Bank of Scotland	6.43
6	Goldman Sachs	5.25
7	HSBC	5.04
8	Bank of America	3.97
9	JPMorgan Chase	3.89
10	Merrill Lynch	3.68

Source: Based on Euromoney, http://www.euromoney.com/.

Exchange rate systems

Countries manage exchange rates using various systems, with different levels of flexibility and volatility, such as the fixed peg system, crawling peg system, target-zone arrangement, managed float system, or independent float system.

Under the *fixed peg* system, practiced by North Korea and Cuba, the exchange rate is pegged at a particular level. As required by the fixed peg system, these countries maintain an exchange rate by increasing or decreasing their hard currency reserves such as euro or US dollars. When pegged rates become overvalued, countries use their foreign exchange reserves to defend the currency rate. The *crawling peg system*, practiced by Argentina, Iraq, Panama, Hong Kong, Cameroon, Chad,

Togo, Estonia, Libya, Bangladesh, Czech Republic, Kuwait, and Iceland, is based on measured change of the exchange rate over time. With a *floating rate system*, countries maintain their foreign reserves and do not deplete their hard currency reserves, maintaining a defense against financial crisis. *Target-zone arrangement* is a foreign exchange system arranged by a group of nations sharing some common goals. Under a target-zone arrangement, countries adjust their national economic policies to maintain their exchange rates within a specific margin around agreed-upon, fixed central exchange rates. This is practiced by the European Monetary Union. The target-zone arrangement minimizes exchange rate instability and enhances economic stability in the region. The *managed float system* is employed by governments to preserve an orderly pattern of exchange rate changes and is designed to eliminate excess volatility. Each central bank sets the nation's exchange rate against a predetermined goal, which is based on the country's balance-of-payments position, foreign exchange reserves, and rates quoted outside the official market. As an example, Brazil, China, Egypt, Hungary, Korea, Israel, Poland, Turkey, and Russia maintain a managed float system. Full flexibility is allowed through an *independent float* currency exchange system. Under this system, an exchange rate is allowed to adjust freely according to the supply and demand for a particular currency. This currency exchange system is practiced by both developed countries such as USA and developing countries such as Peru.

Foreign exchange market function

The foreign exchange market facilitates corporate financial activities investment venues and international transactions in various ways, as follows:

1. MNEs use the foreign exchange market to *convert one currency into another*. This currency conversion is required in order to facilitate the sale of products and services across international borders. In addition, the need for the foreign exchange market arises in cases of foreign direct investment (FDI). In this case an MNE that invests in a foreign country needs to convert the investment capital from its home currency to the target country currency.
2. The foreign exchange market is used for *currency hedging*, which is the practice of insuring against possible losses that result from adverse changes in exchange rates. Currency hedging is used to reduce investment risk using call options, put options, short-selling, or futures contracts. As many transactions of international business are time dependent, where there may be a time lag between billing and receipt of payment, currency hedging helps protect the value of the transaction.
3. The foreign exchange market is used for *currency arbitrage*, which is an instantaneous purchase and sale of a currency in different markets for profit. An Internet system, aided by an appropriate trading system, facilitates a quick profit to be made. This type of transaction mostly suits professional traders and financial institutions with large amounts of foreign currency.
4. Professional traders and corporations with large capital reserves may engage in *foreign currency interest arbitrage*. Foreign currency interest arbitrage

products, include government treasury bills and corporate and government bonds denominated in different currencies. This foreign currency interest arbitrage is used to exploit interest rates overseas that are better than the ones available locally.

5 Professional traders and financial institutions may be engaged in *currency speculation*, which is the purchase or sale of a currency in the expectation that its value will change up or down and will, thus, generate a profit.

As shown later in the book, (Chapter 13), foreign exchange in international business is of strategic importance. Thus, executives of MNEs should be familiar with issues regarding foreign exchange markets, such as currencies quoted in the foreign exchange market and government restrictions that may be imposed on the convertibility of currencies for profit repatriation.

Table 8.6 lists the 14 most traded currencies in the world, led by the US dollar, the euro, the Japanese yen, and the pound sterling.

Currency quotes

Exchange rate quotes are based on the quoted currency and the base currency. If an exchange rate quotes the number of euros needed to buy one Canadian dollar (euro/CAD$), the euro is the *quoted currency* and the Canadian dollar the

TABLE 8.6 Top Fourteen Foreign Currencies Traded by percent of Volume, August 2007

Rank	*Currency*	*Symbol*	*Percent daily share (April 2007)*
1	United States dollar	USD ($)	86.3
2	Euro	EUR (€)	37.0
3	Japanese yen	JPY (¥)	17.0
4	Pound sterling	GBP (£)	15.0
5	Swiss franc	CHF (Fr)	6.8
6	Australian dollar	AUD ($)	6.7
7	Canadian dollar	CAD ($)	4.2
8	Swedish krona	SEK (kr)	2.8
8	Hong Kong dollar	HKD ($)	2.8
10	Norwegian krone	NOK (kr)	2.2
11	New Zealand dollar	NZD ($)	1.9
12	Mexican peso	MXN ($)	1.3
13	Singapore dollar	SGD ($)	1.2
14	South Korean won	KRW (₩)	1.1
Other			14.5
Total			**200**

Source: Based on Euromoney, http://www.euromoney.com/.

base currency. The quoted currency is the numerator and the base currency the denominator. So that a euro/Canadian dollar exchange rate quote of 0.70 means that 0.70 euro are needed to buy 1 Canadian dollar. The numerator is 0.70, the quoted currency, and the denominator 1, the base currency. The same exchange rate may be denoted as euro 0.70/CAD$.

Direct and indirect rate

Since the eurodollar is the quoted currency, the *direct quote* is on the euro and the *indirect quote* is on the Canadian dollar. Whether one uses a direct or an indirect quote, it is easy to find the other by dividing the quote into the numeral 1. The following formula is used to derive a direct quote from an indirect quote:

$$\text{Direct quote} = \frac{1}{\text{Indirect quote}}$$

In addition,

$$\text{Indirect quote} = \frac{1}{\text{Direct quote}}$$

Foreign exchange risk

Currency exchange risk is the risk of adverse changes in the exchange rates that may affect negatively the profitability of international transactions. Executives of MNEs should guard against such risk by applying a financial instrument that will protect the profit from adverse change in the exchange rate. These instruments are used to hedge against possible changes in the exchange rate that may affect profitability.

Cross rates

In many international transactions, executives should find out an exchange rate which is calculated using two other exchange rates. This is done when there are international transactions involving two currencies other than US dollars. In these cases the currency conversion is done first against the dollar and then against the other currency involved in the transaction. To find the conversion rate using their respective exchange rates with the US dollar, one works out the *cross rate*, an exchange rate calculated using two other exchange rates.

Spot rates

Spot rates are used in large transactions between currency traders of international financial institutions. The spot market assists MNEs in converting income generated from sales in another country into the MNE's home country currency and converting funds into the currency of an international supplier for payment purposes. It may also be used for FDI purposes, allowing an MNE to invest in a target country.

Buy and sell rates

The spot rate is available only for large trades and is handled by professional traders. However, for regular bank customers and for a smaller amount of foreign currency, the spot rate is replaced with a *buy rate* (the exchange rate at which the bank buys a currency) and an *ask rate* (the rate at which it sells a currency to its customer). These rates correspond to the *bid* and *ask quotes* noted earlier. The bid and ask rates equal to the rates used by the large currency traders plus a certain profit margin. The buy and sell rates are published by all financial institutions, and are displayed in many foreign exchange locations, hotels, etc.

The Forward Market and Foreign Exchange Institutions

Forward rates

Forward rates reflect the expectations of the foreign market makers, such as currency traders and bankers, regarding a currency's future spot rate. A *forward rate* is an exchange rate at which two parties agree to exchange currencies on a specified future date. These forward rates are useful when a seller extends credit to the buyer for a period that is longer than the two days used for spot rates. Thus, forward rates are used when an MNE knows that it will need a certain amount of foreign currency on a certain future date. The *forward market* is the market for currency transactions at forward rates and handles most main world currencies.

Forward contracts

A *forward contract* is a contract that requires the exchange of an agreed-upon amount of a currency on an agreed-upon date at a specific exchange rate. Forward contracts are used to decrease an international business transaction exchange rate risk. A forward contract is commonly signed for 30, 90 and 180 days into the future.

The currency's forward exchange rate can be higher or lower than its current spot rate. If its forward rate is higher than its spot rate, the currency is trading at a *premium*. If its forward rate is lower, it is trading at a *discount*. If a forward contract involves the simultaneous purchase and sale of foreign exchange for two different dates, it is termed a *currency swap*.

Currency options and futures

A *currency option* is a right, or *option*, to exchange a specific amount of a currency on a specific date at a specific rate. In other words, while forward contracts require the parties to follow through with currency exchanges, currency options do not require same – it is just an option. Under currency options the MNE is not obliged to exercise the option, and may use the spot rate if it provides a better exchange rate at any given time. MNEs often use currency options to hedge against negative changes in the exchange rate.

A *currency futures contract* is a contract which requires the exchange of a specific amount of currency on a specific date at a specific exchange rate. However, all of these currency future contracts' terms and conditions are fixed and not changeable. A currency future is traded on an exchange and not OTC and is not "custom tailored" for the specific situation. In this case, MNEs work with exchange brokers when purchasing futures contracts that are marked for a specific amount and a specific maturity date.

Currency trading centers

The foreign exchange market is one of the largest and most liquid financial markets in the world and is based on an advanced electronic system that connects the world's major trading centers. The foreign exchange market handles about 4 trillion dollars a day, including currency swaps, spot contracts, and forward contracts and is involved in trading between large banks, central banks, currency speculators, corporations, governments, and other institutions. The purpose of trading centers is to facilitate trade and investment. The trade in currencies in all trading centers is characterized by large transaction volumes, high liquidity, geographic dispersion, long trading hours (24 hours a day except on weekends), a variety of factors that affect exchange rates and low profit margins compared to other capital markets.

There is no unified or centrally cleared market for the majority of foreign exchange trades and there is very little cross-border regulation. Of the total daily global turnover, trading in London accounts for around 34.1 percent of the total, making it by far the global center for foreign exchange. In second and third places, respectively, trading in New York accounts for 16.6 percent, and Tokyo accounts for 6.0 percent. While the main trading centers are in London, New York, and Tokyo, the centers in Hong Kong and Singapore are also important trading centers. Currency trading takes place continuously throughout the day: thus, as the Asian trading session ends, the European session begins, followed by the North American session, and then back to the Asian session, excluding weekends.

Foreign exchange and MNEs

There are several uses of foreign exchange for MNEs. First, MNEs use the foreign exchange market for import and export purposes. When the international retail chain Tesco of the UK buys products from Japan for the UK market, it needs to convert British pounds to Japanese yen in order to pay for the imported goods. Second, MNEs use foreign exchange to buy target country currency in order to pay the expenses that accrue to the executive relocated overseas. Third, MNEs use foreign exchange to secure the funds required for an FDI, a direct purchase of assets located in a target country, as well as to take out profits from a target country. Renault of France has built a facility in Mexico and has converted the required funds from euros to Mexican pesos. In addition, Renault has taken profits out of Mexico by converting the Mexican currency to euros. Fourth, MNEs use the foreign exchange market in order to make a profit through currency speculation and interest arbitrage.

Since MNEs have several ways of using foreign exchange in conducting their business, it is important for their executives to understand how exchange rates are determined and how exchange rates may be forecasted.

How foreign exchange rates are determined

The foreign exchange rates are either floating or fixed: in a fixed exchange rate system, the government decrees the exchange rate; however, under a floating exchange rate system, the rates are determined by a variety of factors. These factors are articulated by several theories, or models, as follows:

- *International parity conditions model.* Under this theory, exchange rates between two currencies reflect the purchasing power difference of the currencies in the two countries. The rates may also indicate the difference in the interest rates between the two countries. This theory has a weakness in that it is based on the assumption of free flow of goods, services and capital between countries, an assumption which may not be true.
- *Balance of payments model.* This model explains the currency value and, thus, the exchange rate by the value of tradable goods and services, ignoring the increasing role of global capital flows. However, the model fails to provide any explanation for continuous appreciation of currencies in face of growing current account deficits.
- *Asset market model.* This model views currencies as an asset class for constructing investment portfolios. Assets prices are influenced mostly by investors' willingness to hold the existing quantities of assets, which, in turn, depends on their expectations on the future worth of these assets. The asset market model of exchange rate assumes that the exchange rate between two currencies represents the price that balances the relative supplies of, and demand for, assets denominated in two currencies.

The above models demonstrate that several macroeconomic factors affect the exchange rates and are a result of the forces of demand and supply. Supply and demand for any given currency, and thus its value, are not influenced by any single element, but rather by several elements. These elements generally fall into three categories: economic factors, political conditions, and currency market psychology.

Economic factors

Economic factors include economic policy – affected by government agencies and central banks – such as government fiscal and monetary policies, and economic conditions:

- *Government budget deficits or surpluses.* The market usually reacts negatively to growing government budget deficits, and positively to decreasing budget deficits. The impact of budget deficits and surpluses is reflected in the value of a country's currency.

- *Balance of trade levels and trends.* The trade flow between countries reflects the demand for goods and services, which, in turn, determines demand for a country's currency used to conduct trade. Surpluses and deficits in trade of goods and services reflect the competitiveness of a nation's economy. Thus, trade deficits may have a negative impact on a nation's currency.
- *Inflation levels and trends.* A currency will lose value if there is a high or rising level of inflation in the country. This is because inflation reduces purchasing power and, thus, reduces demand for that particular currency. However, sometimes a currency may rise in value when inflation rises because of expectations that the central bank will raise short-term interest rates to combat rising inflation, causing an influx of foreign currency that increases the demand, and thus the value of the local currency.
- *Economic growth and health.* Generally, the more robust the economy of a country, the higher the value for its currency. Thus, positive reports on gross domestic product (GDP), employment levels, retail sales, and capacity utilization reflect positively on a country's economic growth and sustainability and may increase the value of its currency.

Political conditions

Exchange rates are susceptible to political instability and anticipations about political changes. National, regional, and international political conditions and events can have positive or negative effect on currency markets. The rise of a political regime that is perceived to be fiscally responsible can have a positive effect on the country's value of currency and vice versa.

Currency market psychology

Currency market psychology, including traders' perceptions, influences the foreign exchange market in a variety of ways: (1) international events, such as a threat of an imminent arms race, can lead investors to increase the demand for currencies perceived as stronger over relatively weaker currencies; (2) currency markets often change in long-term trends, which are noted and acted upon by currency analysts; (3) the currency market tends to price a currency that reflects the impact of a particular action before it occurs; (4) economic reports that forecast a particular currency value may be adopted as true, even if the economic fundamentals do not support them; (5) some analysts may use technical forecasting or trading techniques that indicate the next currency exchange rate, which is adopted by the currency market.

Institutions of the foreign exchange market

Foreign exchange market makers

Unlike other capital markets, the foreign exchange market is divided into various levels, based on accessibility and terms of the currency settlement. At the top is the inter-bank market, which is made up of the largest investment banking firms. At this level, spreads, which are, as explained earlier, the difference between the bid and ask prices, are small and usually unavailable to other market makers. Below is a short description of the main foreign exchange market makers.

Banks. The interbank market handles large amounts of currency trading every day both on behalf of the bank's customers and for the bank's own account. The interbank market constitutes the world's largest banks' exchange of currencies at spot and forward rates. Each bank satisfies client requests for exchange quotes by obtaining them from other banks in the interbank market. For transactions that involve commonly held currencies, the largest banks often have sufficient currency on hand. These days most interbank trading is made through efficient electronic systems and does not require brokers.

MNEs and local enterprises. A significant part of the foreign exchange market comes from the financial activities of enterprises seeking foreign exchange to pay for goods or services or for FDI. Usually, local enterprises and MNEs trade fairly small amounts of currencies compared to those of banks or speculators, and their trades often have little short-term impact on market rates. However, at times, MNEs may have a significant impact on the value of the currency when a very large amount of currency is exchanged to finance an FDI or some other major business transaction.

Central banks. National central banks play a significant role in the foreign exchange markets. The main goal of central banks is to control the money supply in order to manage inflation rates, and interest rates and to meet official or unofficial target exchange rates for their currencies. National central banks use their foreign exchange reserves to affect and stabilize the currency market. Nevertheless, at times, local and international factors may overwhelm central banks, leading to a currency collapse such as in Turkey in 2001 and in Southeast Asia in 1997.

Hedge funds. Hedge funds control billions of dollars of equity and may borrow heavily, and thus may overwhelm intervention by central banks, especially when economic conditions justify such speculation. Hedge funds engage mostly in speculative trades where the parties that bought or sold the currency have no plan to actually take delivery of the currency in the end.

Investment management firms. Investment management firms, who typically manage large accounts such as pension funds and endowments on behalf of customers, use the foreign exchange market to facilitate transactions in foreign securities. For example, an investment manager who manages an international equity portfolio may need to purchase or sell foreign currencies to pay for foreign securities purchases.

Retail foreign exchange brokers. Retail traders are individuals engaged in trading, usually in smaller amounts relative to the currency market, and may only participate indirectly through brokers or banks.

Money transfer companies. Money transfer companies perform high-volume low-value transfers generally by economic workers and migrants back to their home country. The four largest markets for these services correspond to the countries best known for economic migrant workers – India, China, Mexico, and the Philippines. They also provide money transfers for tourists at most international tourist destinations. The largest and best-known service provider is Western Union with hundreds of thousands of agents around the world.

The over-the-counter (OTC) market. The OTC is a foreign exchange market with no central trading location. It consists of a global computer network of foreign exchange traders and other market makers. All foreign exchange transactions can be performed in the OTC market. The main market makers are large financial institutions and investment banks.

Securities exchanges. Securities exchanges provide currency derivatives, such as foreign currency futures and options of financial instruments and transactions. The world's largest futures and options exchanges are the following: Chicago Board of Trade (CBOT) in the USA, with 3,600 members trading in various futures and options products; the Chicago Mercantile Exchange (CME) in the USA, with 2,725 members dealing in futures of most major currencies; the London International Financial Futures Exchange (LIFFE), which trades futures and options for major currencies; and the Philadelphia Stock Exchange (PHLX) in the USA, which deals in both standardized options and customized options with the resulting flexibility in the currency option contracts.

The interbank market. The interbank market constitutes the world's largest banks' exchange of currencies at spot and forward rates. Each bank satisfies client requests for exchange quotes by obtaining them from other banks in the interbank market. For transactions that involve commonly-held currencies, the largest banks often have sufficient currency on hand. As explained earlier, large banks in the interbank market may secure better currency exchange rate for large clients. However, often, SMEs deal with smaller amount of foreign currency and, thus, a smaller corporation may prefer to use a discount international payment service to provide it.

Internet currency traders. These traders offer Internet exchange trading and provide real-time, online, 24-hour trading facilitated by a network of similar operations internationally. Three of the biggest participants in the foreign exchange market – Deutsche Bank, Chase Manhattan, and Citigroup – teamed up with Reuters, an information company, to offer a range of foreign exchange services over the Internet. Banks have set up proprietary electronic systems, giving clients access to their research and prices. Citibank and Chase Manhattan both offer such systems, promising clients greater efficiency, saving them having to phone for prices, and offering an array of analytical tools. However, both banks admit that clients would prefer a multi-bank site, rather than having to log onto a dozen different websites to get a price.

An essential part of the of the international currency market is the process of international clearing. International clearing entails aggregating the currencies that one bank owes another and then carrying out that transaction. Traditionally, clearing was done once a day and involved the actual daily shipping of currencies from one bank to another. But nowadays clearing is performed very frequently and is executed through computerized clearing mechanisms. Clearing mechanisms are an important element of the interbank market, since banks continuously perform foreign exchange transactions with other banks but do not settle after each individual trade in a single currency.

We now demonstrate the importance and significance of a local currency value and an exchange rate system in the context of a country's competitiveness, in this case of the Ukraine.

Ukraine's Biggest Vulnerability: Soaring Inflation

The Ukrainian economy is enjoying strong growth of income, consumption and investments, without the severe external imbalances like most Baltic and Balkan countries seem to be facing. However, double-digit growth of household consumption, well above the productivity growth, may translate into a worsened external balance. The surplus of the balance of services, together with strong FDI inflows, have sufficiently covered trade deficit financing needs. The government has outlined an ambitious privatization plan, ensuring that strong FDI inflow should continue through 2008.

Inflation

Annual inflation hit 30 percent in April, threatening to undermine the entire national budget. The dollar peg not only causes Ukraine import inflation but also breeds additional inflation, which undermines the country's competitiveness. The dollar peg forces the National Bank of Ukraine (NBU, the central bank) to maintain a negative real interest rate and pursue an extremely loose monetary policy – Ukraine's current discount rate is a paltry 10 percent a year. Each cut of the US federal funds rate has been accompanied by a tidal wave of dollars coming to the Ukraine, which the NBU buys with freshly printed hryvnias, leading to higher inflation, and soaring real estate prices and stock market indices.

Monetary policy

In its attempt to curb inflation, the NBU has been tightening monetary conditions by stepping up stabilization and broadening reserve requirements. A free float, a broader band or a simple strengthening in the hryvnia's exchange rate vs the dollar would help to suppress import price inflation. However, it would threaten competitiveness of the country's two main exporting industries, metallurgy and chemicals. The NBU is suspicious of a switch to inflation targeting for fear of being undercut by the government. Currently, every important interest rate in the country is negative in real terms; to make them positive would require increasing the differential between Ukrainian and US rates to such an extent that hot money flows would multiply to a dangerous degree. Because of the limits on monetary policy in the Ukraine, the NBU would have to rely on the government to pursue a responsible fiscal policy if the central bank were to have any realistic hope of meeting a respectable inflation target. Another reason arguing against hurrying to float the currency is the lack of political stability.

Interest rates are not seen as a very efficient monetary policy tool that could significantly help the central bank in its disinflationary effort, yet key interest rates were raised to 12 percent from 10 percent to tame the spiraling inflation. During the period of low liquidity, banks had to sell their dollar resources to increase their hryvnia (UAH) liquidity, pushing the US$/UAH exchange rate to the stronger end of the band.

Fiscal policy

Over the past years the Ukrainian fiscal policy has been characterized as pro-cyclical, yet the burden of controlling demand and inflation must fall on fiscal policy, because limits to exchange rate flexibility preclude sufficiently effective monetary policy action. The government expects the state budget deficit for 2008 to reach 2.0 percent of GDP or US$ 3.4 billion. Social spending has played an important role in the state budget of Prime Minister Tymoshenko. On average, social spending will increase by 30 percent in 2008. Another big government bill is related to compensation for savers at Oschadbank, who suffered from devaluation of the currency after the collapse of communism, for which the government earmarked UAH 20 billion (US$3.96 billion) in the 2008 budget. However, the restitution of lost savings should be spread over a number of years or offset by spending cuts elsewhere. Given the positive dynamic of state revenue collection and the prospects of strong privatization, the state budget deficit of 2 percent of GDP should be met in 2008.

WTO accession

The Ukraine recently joined the World Trade Organization (WTO); associated policy changes are expected to raise the GDP and bring additional billions in foreign investment, better living standards, higher wages, and improved social standards and economic life. Ukrainian FDI is expected to reach US$11.5 billion (6.7 percent of GDP) in 2008, exerting appreciation pressure on the local currency. The current account deficit will continue to widen in 2008, driven by cheaper imports and skyrocketing domestic consumption. Fiscal problems due to WTO accession are unlikely. Some export and import tariff rates are being drastically reduced, which will lead to somewhat lower fiscal receipts. The tariff reduction would potentially lead to only US$0.3 billion of a shortfall in budget revenues, which is likely to be covered by additional income from higher volumes of imports and a decreasing share of "shadow imports."

Source: RGE Analysts' EconoMoni, May 27, 2008.

As can be observed from the information on Ukraine, both fiscal and monetary policies have affected Ukrainian competitiveness. In addition, a fixed exchange rate, pegged to the US dollar, may have contributed to inflation and adversely affected the Ukrainian economy.

Global Management Perspective

1 A manager of an MNE should become familiar with opportunities to use the international financial system. In particularly, the MNE manager should be familiar with the various financial instruments and the terms and conditions entailed in securing funds through various instruments in various markets around the world.

2 Of particular interest are financial instruments that are available through financial markets in emerging economies, which is also an effective way of exposing these emerging markets to products and services sold by the MNE.

3 Raising capital in a foreign country may be easier to do than in one's own country. This is particularly true for MNEs or governments of developing countries in which national capital markets are small or nonexisting. These are *emerging stock markets*.

4 The international capital market helps reduce the risk inherent in lending monies. In essence, investors may choose from an international set of investment opportunities around the world, with various rates of risk.

5 Information technology and telecommunications may be used to search for the best financial institution and financial instrument or derivative to use.

7 Trade with major financial institutions in the foreign exchange market, by consolidating all foreign exchange transactions.

SME's Perspective

1 *Microcredit option*. SMEs in developing countries should take advantage of the microcredit option in which small amount of money is made available without the need for collateral. In many cases this kind of loans is provided to women entrepreneurs in developing countries.

2 *Government institutions and banks support SMEs' quest for international business*. Government and financial institutions may serve as advisor and underwriter of a bond or a share issue, as well as provider of a loan to the aspiring SME.

COUNTRY FOCUS

JAPAN

World Rank (EFI 2009): 19

Regional Rank (EFI 2009): 5

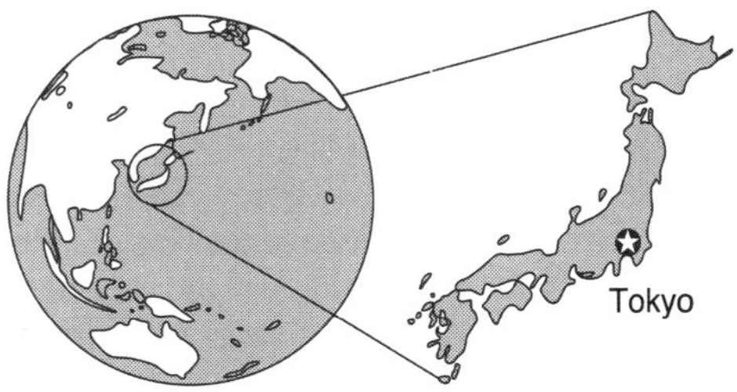

Quick facts

Population: 127.8 million

GDP (PPP): $4.1 trillion; 2.4 percent growth in 2006; 1.8 percent 5-year compound annual growth; $31,947 per capita

Unemployment: 3.9 percent

Inflation (CPI): 0.0 percent

FDI inflow: $6.5 billion

2006 data unless otherwise noted

Economic freedom score

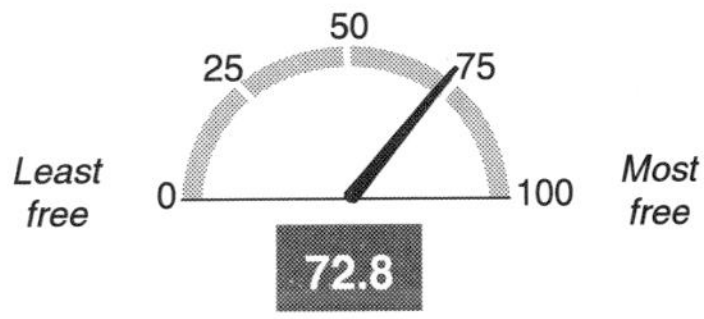

Japan's economic freedom score is 72.8, making its economy the 19th freest in the 2009 Index. Japan is ranked 5th out of 41 countries in the Asia-Pacific region.

The Japanese economy has long benefited from international commerce, although its non-tariff barriers linger, hurting its overall trade freedom. Achieving an average economic growth rate of close to 2 percent over the past five years, Japan has gradually been overcoming sluggishness that lasted for more than a decade. The economy scores above the world average in many of the 10 economic freedoms, including business freedom, monetary freedom, trade freedom, property rights, freedom from corruption, and labor freedom. The regulatory environment is efficient and facilitates overall entrepreneurial activity. Property rights are generally well respected, and corruption is perceived as minimal.

Japan has relatively weak scores in fiscal freedom, government size, and financial freedom. Total government spending equals more than a third of GDP. The financial sector is modern and well developed, but it remains subject to government influence and a host of restrictions. Taxation is fairly burdensome, and Japan's corporate tax rate is becoming increasingly uncompetitive.

Background

Japan is an established democracy and the world's second-largest economy. Its "lost decade" of the 1990s was followed by a strong recovery under former Prime Minister Junichiro Koizumi, who cleaned up the banking sector, started the privatization of the mammoth postal system, and tried to reform the dominant Liberal

(Continued)

Democratic Party. His successors, however, have backtracked on economic reform. Japan's economy remains heavily protected in some sectors, such as agriculture, and foreign investment is subject to often opaque regulatory barriers.

Business freedom – 85.8

The overall freedom to conduct a business is strongly protected under Japan's regulatory environment. Starting a business takes 23 days, compared to the world average of 38 days. Obtaining a business license takes less than the world average of 18 procedures and 225 days. Bankruptcy proceedings are easy and straightforward.

Trade freedom – 82

Japan's weighted average tariff rate was 1.5 percent in 2006. Import and export bans and restrictions, import quotas, services market access barriers, nontransparent and burdensome regulations and standards, restrictive sanitary and phytosanitary rules, state trade in some goods, subsidies, and inefficient customs administration add to the cost of trade. Fifteen points were deducted from Japan's trade freedom score to account for nontariff barriers.

Fiscal Freedom – 67.5

Japan has a high income tax rate and a burdensome corporate tax rate. The top income tax rate is 40 percent, which local taxes can raise to almost 50 percent. The standard corporate tax rate is 30 percent, which local taxes can raise to around 41 percent. Other taxes include a value-added tax (VAT), a tax on interest and an estate tax. In the most recent year, overall tax revenue as a percentage of GDP was 27.4 percent.

Government size – 61.1

Total government expenditures, including consumption and transfer payments, are high. In the most recent year, government spending equaled 36.0 percent of GDP. Efforts to reinvigorate the economy and the rising cost of social welfare for the aging have put government spending on an upward trend.

Monetary freedom – 93.6

Inflation is imperceptible, averaging 0.01 percent between 2005 and 2007. Formal price controls apply to rice, but major producers, backed by regulators, are able to dictate retail and wholesale prices. Five points were deducted from Japan's monetary freedom score to account for policies that distort domestic prices.

Investment freedom – 60

Foreign investment is officially welcomed and inward direct investment is subject to few restrictions, but foreign acquisition of Japanese firms is inhibited by insufficient financial disclosure and cross-holding of shares among companies in the same business grouping (*keiretsu*). Further deterrents include public resistance to foreign acquisitions, overregulation, and a slow court system. Government approval is needed for investments in agriculture, forestry, petroleum, electricity, gas, water, aerospace, telecommunications, and leather manufacturing. There are no controls on the holding of foreign exchange accounts or on transactions, current transfers, repatriation of profits, or real estate transactions by residents or nonresidents.

Financial freedom – 50

Japan's modern financial system remains subject to government influence. Overall transparency is still weak despite gradual improvement. Deregulation and competition have led to consolidation in an effort to create banks large enough to be major players abroad. Japanese corporations and banks maintain tight relationships, and banks often hold shares in companies with which they conduct business, giving them access to cheap credit, and lessening accountability. The government supports bank mergers to speed up the transformation of the financial sector and continues to update laws and regulations to facilitate them. Credit is available at market rates. State-run institutions affect the supply of credit. The government-owned postal savings system, the world's largest single pool of savings, is Japan's biggest financial institution by assets. In October 2007, under a 10-year privatization plan, the Japanese post office was divided into four commercial entities – a bank, an insurance company, a mail delivery service, and a branch-management entity. Capital markets are relatively well developed.

Property rights – 70

Real and intellectual property rights are generally secure, but obtaining and protecting patents and trademarks can be time-consuming and costly. The courts do not discriminate against foreign investors but are not well suited to litigation of investment and business disputes. Businesses tend to write their contracts in general terms, but contracts are highly respected.

Freedom from corruption – 75

Corruption is perceived as minimal. Japan ranks 17th out of 179 countries in Transparency International's Corruption Perceptions Index for 2007. Foreign investors complain of close relationships among companies, politicians, government organizations, and universities that can be difficult to penetrate.

Labor freedom – 82.5

Japan's relatively flexible labor regulations could be further improved to enhance employment opportunities and productivity growth. The nonsalary cost of employing a worker is moderate, and dismissing a redundant employee is not costly. Regulations on the number of work hours remain rigid.

Source: Adapted from Terry Miller and Kim R. Holmes, *2009 Index of Economic Freedom* (Washington, DC: The Heritage Foundation and Dow Jones & Company, Inc., 2009), at www.heritage.org/index.

SUMMARY

The international capital market has three purposes. First, it provides an expanded supply of capital for borrowers because it joins together borrowers and lenders across different nations. Second, it lowers the cost of money for borrowers because a greater supply of money lowers the cost of borrowing (interest rates). Third, it lowers risk for lenders because it makes available a greater number of investments.

The growth in the international capital market is due mainly to three factors. First, advances in *information technology*, which allow borrowers and lenders to do business more quickly and cheaply. Second, the *deregulation* of capital markets is opening the international capital market to increased competition. Third, new and creative *financial instruments*

(Continued)

are increasing the appeal of the international capital market.

The most important financial centers are located in London, New York, and Tokyo. These cities conduct a large number of financial transactions daily. Other locations, called *offshore financial centers*, handle less business but they do have their appeal as these places have few regulations and few, if any, taxes.

Three of the main financial markets are the international bond market, the international equity market, and the eurocurrency market. The *international bond market* consists of all bonds sold by issuers outside their own countries. It is experiencing growth primarily because investors in developed markets are searching for higher rates from borrowers in emerging markets and vice versa. The *international equity market* consists of all stocks bought and sold outside the home country of the issuing company. The four factors primarily responsible for the growth in international equity are *privatization*, greater issuance of stock by *companies in newly industrialized and developing nations*, greater *international reach of investment banks*, and *global electronic trading*. The *eurocurrency market* consists of all the world's currencies that are banked outside their countries of origin. The appeal of the eurocurrency market is its lack of government regulation and, therefore, lower cost of borrowing.

The foreign exchange market is the market in which currencies are bought and sold and in which currency prices are determined. It has four primary functions. First, individuals, companies, and governments use it, directly or indirectly, to convert one currency into another. Second, it offers tools with which investors can *insure against adverse changes in exchange rates*. Third, it is used to earn a profit from *arbitrage* – the purchase and sale of a currency, or other interest-paying security, in different markets. Fourth, the foreign exchange market is also used to *speculate about a change in the value of a currency*.

A currency quote is a main activity in the foreign exchange market. An *exchange rate quote* between currency A and currency B (A/B) of 5/1 means that it takes 5 units of currency A to buy 1 unit of currency B. This example reflects a *direct quote* of currency A and an *indirect quote* of currency B. A *cross rate* is when the exchange rate is calculated between two currencies by using their respective exchange rates with yet another common currency.

There are several rates customarily used for foreign exchange. A *spot rate* is an exchange rate that requires delivery of the traded currency within two business days. This rate is normally obtainable only by large banks and foreign exchange brokers. The *forward rate* is the rate at which two parties agree to exchange currencies on a specified future date.

Several main institutions are active in the foreign exchange market. The world's largest banks exchange currencies in the *interbank market*. *Securities exchanges* are physical locations where currency futures and options are bought and sold, in smaller amounts than those traded in the interbank market. The *over-the-counter (OTC)* market is an exchange that exists as a global computer network linking traders to one another.

Governments restrict currency convertibility for a number of reasons. First, a government may be attempting to *preserve the country's hard currency reserves* for repaying debts owed to other nations. Second, convertibility might be restricted to *preserve hard currency to pay for needed imports or to finance a trade deficit*. Third, restrictions might be used to *protect a currency from speculators*. Finally, such restrictions can be an *attempt to keep badly needed currency from being invested abroad*. Policies used to enforce currency restrictions include government approval for currency exchange, imposed import licenses, a system of multiple exchange rates, and imposed quantity restrictions.

DISCUSSION QUESTIONS

1 Define and give an example of the various institutions that are part of the international financial system.
2 Identify the main benefits of the international capital market.
3 Describe the contributors to the growth in the international capital market.
4 Define the role of offshore financial centers.
5 What is the eurocurrency market? Explain how it functions.
6 Discuss the main functions of the foreign exchange market? Describe the currency and interest arbitrage mechanisms.
7 Distinguish between spot rate and forward rate and between direct quote and indirect quote. Define currency swaps, currency options, and currency futures.
8 Identify the reasons and policies used by governments to restrict currency convertibility.
9 Regional or worldwide harmonization (or appropriate coordination) of interest rates, currencies and capital markets' regulations advances the cause of a global capital market. How close is the world to realizing that cause?
10 How does a regional currency help in supporting international business? Is a global currency a possibility? Would it help support and advance international business?
11 How do offshore financial centers help to promote international business?
12 How do advances in information technology, telecommunications, the Internet, and cellular technology affect the international capital market and the international capital system?

ACTION ITEMS

1 Check, using the Internet, and note, the spot exchange rates between the four most commonly traded world currencies.
2 Initiate a conversation with a main trader in town and find out what is the business model used by traders as well as what are the main financial instruments they use to participate in the international capital market.
3 The Chinese economy has enjoyed an unparalleled annual growth during the last several years. To support its economic expansion, it needs hard currency reserves. How can China secure those currency reserves?
4 What are the main business strategies that may be used by MNEs to protect against changes in currency values when operating in emerging economies?

Bibliography

Ajayi, R. A., Mougoue, M. (1996). On the dynamic relation between stock prices and exchange rates. *Journal of Financial Research*, 19, 193–207.

Aybar, C. B., Milman, C. (1999). Globalization, emerging market economics and currency crisis in Asia. *Multinational Business Review*, 7, 37–44.

Bank for International Settlements (2001). Consultative document: the new Basel capital accord. Retrieved from www.bis.org.

Barda, J., Kutan, A., Zhou, S. (1997). The exchange rate and the balance of trade: the Turkish experience. *Journal of Development Studies*, 33, 675–92.

Bartlett, C. A., Ghoshal, S. (1989). *Managing Across Borders: The Transnational Solution*. Cambridge, MA: Harvard Business School Press.

Beshouri, C. (2006). A grassroots approach to emerging-market-consumers. *The McKinset Quarterly No. 4*. Retrieved from www.mckinseyquarterly.com

Braithwaite, J., Drahos, P. (2000). *Global Business Regulation*. Cambridge, UK: Cambridge University Press.

Coninx, R. G. F. (1986). *Foreign Exchange Dealer's Handbook*. Homewood, IL: Dow Jones-Irwin.

Cooper, R. N. (1987). *The International Monetary System: Essays in World Economics*. Cambridge, MA: MIT Press.

Doz, Y. L. (1980). How MNEs cope with host government intervention. *Harvard Business Review*, March–April, 149–57.

Eitman, D., Stonehill, A., Moffett, M. (2006). *Multinational Business Finance*, 11th international edn. London: Pearson.

Elegant, S. (1998). Comeback kid. *Far Eastern Economic Review*, September 3, 10–14.

Ellis, H., Metzler, L. (eds). (1949). *Readings in the Theory of International Trade*. Homewood, IL: Irwin.

Federal Reserve Bulletin (various years). Retrieved from www.federalreserve.com

Garten, J. (1997). *The Big Ten: The Big Emerging Markets and How They Will Change Our Lives*. New York: Basic Books.

Gitman, L. (2005). *Principles of Managerial Finance + FinanceWorks*, 11th international edn. New York: Addison-Wesley.

Greenspan, A. (1997). The globalization of finance. *The Cato Journal, 17*.

Gruber, W. H., Metha, D., Vernon R. (1967). The R&D factor in international trade and international investment of United States industries. *Journal of Political Economy*, February, 20–37.

Helms, B. (2006). *Access For All: Building Inclusive Financial Systems*. Washington, DC: The World Bank.

Helpman, E. (1981). International trade in the presence of product differentiation, economies of scale, and monopolistic competition: a Chamberlinian–Heckscher–Ohlin approach. *Journal of International Economics*, 11, 305–40.

International Labor Office (2005). *Yearbook of Labor Statistics*, Geneva, Switzerland.

International Monetary Fund (1998). *World Economic Outlook*, Washington, DC: IMF.

International Monetary Fund (2004). Global financial stability report. Retrieved from www.imf.org.

International Monetary Fund (2008). Effects of financial globalization on developing countries: some empirical evidence. International Monetary Fund. Retrieved from www.imf.org.

Kim, D., Kandemir, D., Cavusgil. S. T. (2004). The role of family conglomerates in emerging markets: what Western companies should know. *Thunderbird International Business Review*, 46, 13–20.

Kolodko, G. (ed.) (2003). *Emerging Market Economics: Globalization and Development*. Aldershot, UK: Ashgate.

Krugman, P. (1981). Intra industry specialization and the gains from trade. *Journal of Political Economy*, 89, 959–73.

Ohlin, B. (1967). *International and Interregional Trade*. rev. edn. Cambridge, MA: Harvard Economic Studies.

Panni, A. (1994). Sweden's mobile leader. *International Management*, 49, 24–9.

Posner, M. (1961). International trade and technical change. *Oxford Economic Papers*, 13, October, 323–41.

Prahalad, C. K. (2005). *The Fortune at the Bottom of the Pyramid: Eradicating Poverty Through Profits*. Philadelphia, PA: Wharton School Books.

Ricardo, D. (1948). *On the Principles of Political Economy and Taxation*. New York: Dutton.

Smith, A. (1869). *An Inquiry into the Nature and Causes of the Wealth of Nations*. Oxford: Clarendon Press.

Sukar, A. H., Hassan, S. (2001). US exports and time-varying volatility of real exchange rate. *Global Financial Journal*, 12, 14–109.

World Trade Organization (2005). *International Trade Statistics*.

PART 4

International Business Strategy

9

International and Global Strategy

Learning Objectives

Following this chapter, the reader should be able to:

1. Define key terms such as strategy, external environment, and internal environment
2. List the major steps involved in strategy formulation of MNEs
3. Define the five forces involved in industry competitiveness
4. Define the main issues involved in internal environment assessment
5. Identify value chains of MNEs
6. Describe how MNEs control and assess their strategy

Opening Case

Intel's Global Corporate, Business Unit, and Functional Strategies

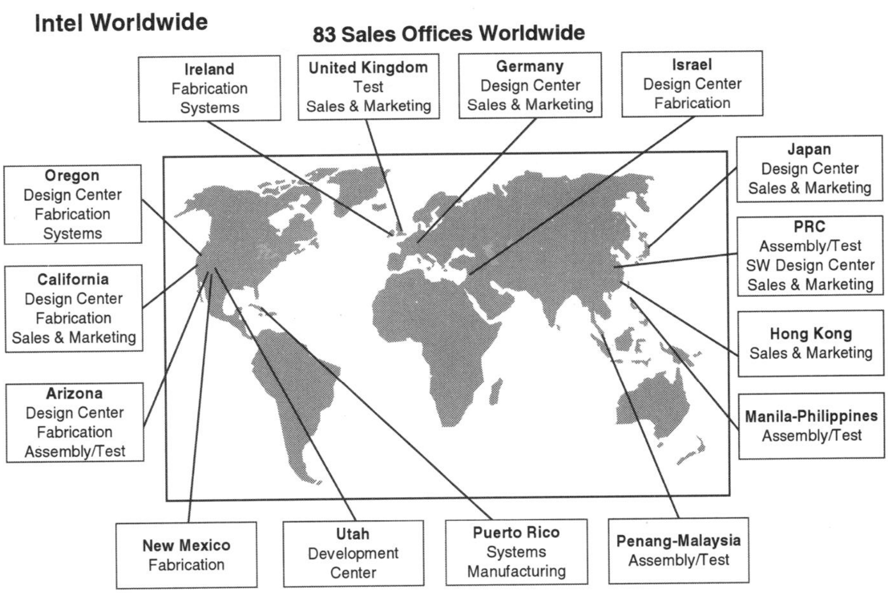

Intel is a global company with 80 percent of its business outside of the USA. Intel relies on an extensive array of highly qualified product, operations, logistics, distribution, and service personnel and is based on exploiting a global supply chain. Intel's facilities and regional headquarters are based in almost all continents. Intel's corporate strategy is focused on differentiation as well as on exploiting economies of scale and learning curve effects. Operationally, Intel relies heavily on a global supply chain, moving raw materials and semi-processed products from one location to another, and performing various value-added manufacturing tasks. istorically, Intel has focused most of its attention and resources on microprocessors used for personal computers (PCs). The company invested its considerable cash resources into designing new generations of powerful microprocessors fabricated in internationally based, large-scale, highly invested facilities, exploiting economies of scale, and perfecting production processes. owever, Intel's strategy of staying as one, single, business was forced to change. At the beginning of the 21st century, the PC industry reached almost saturation as the growth in the demand for PC slowed down.

Furthermore, an accelerated growth in the communications industry was evident. Thus, Intel decided that the way to improve its return on invested capital was to invest in product development and production technology focused on designing and producing the fastest communication chip. The strategy adopted was that in order to enter the communication chip industry expeditiously, Intel had to acquire the technology, the manufacturing plants, and the distribution channels currently catering to the telecommunication chip industry. The idea was that following the acquisition, Intel could improve the acquired businesses by transferring its competencies to the acquired companies. As a result of Intel's 2001 global strategy, it had invested US 8 billion in acquiring 18 companies in the communication chip business. Intel became the fourth largest in that business, behind Lucent, Motorola, and Texas Instruments. owever, there were two ma or setbacks to Intel's global strategy first, the slump in the global demand in the telecommunication equipment market for telecommunication chips second, while Intel was focused on designing and producing the fastest communication chip, the customers preferred a communication chip that could support high bandwidth and process larger amounts of information for high-quality music, high-definition movie and T viewing, and videoconferencing. Competing products, such as Advanced Micro Devices, were introduced successfully into the market. As of 2006, conceding its earlier poor competing advantage, Intel introduced new dual-core and quad-core chips that helped it regain its competitive advantage. To wit, as of the summer of 2009, Intel had finalized an agreement with China ailways. The Chinese Ministry of ailways has partnered with Intel to develop the *data network* for controlling a new railway with over 40,000 km (24,854 miles) of high-speed track. The pro ect is to be launched in 2012, with a completion date pro ected for 2020.

Another successful functional strategy of Intel was the single global sourcing strategy it adopted across its entire indirect materials budget. The strategy entails an internally developed five-step process emphasizing the use of source teams, which are made up of representatives of the company's various global business units. Within the five steps are such activities as a documented sourcing plan, Internet negotiations and e-catalogs, and formal supplier business reviews. In two years, the global indirect materials organization (IDM) has used the five-step process to source 95 percent of the company's indirect goods and services budget, which has helped to reduce costs by 10 percent, and accelerated global sourcing of indirect materials. Intel's indirect budget consists of spending for construction, travel, professional services, marketing services, logistics, IT, and facilities services, and makes up 60 percent of the company's annual procurement budget. Until 2002, Intel had been mainly sourcing indirect goods and services by region. Purchasing professionals in three regions – USA, Europe, and Asia – did not work closely with their internal customers in the business units or exchange best practices. It was clear, the IDM organization was not fully leveraging the company's global buying power.

At the same time, Intel was becoming more global. More of the company's revenues were starting to come from regions other than the USA and the separate business units were becoming increasingly global in nature. Spending on indirect goods and services was growing faster than spending on direct materials – 25 percent faster from 1997 to 2002 – and the off-contract budget was growing in tandem.

The IDM organization conducted some extensive benchmarking activities and learned that more world-class sourcing organizations were working hand in hand with their internal customers at company business units, aggregating volumes worldwide, consolidating purchasing activities, and documenting global strategy.

To reach world class, the IDM organization first had to overcome several ma or challenges. First, the company's organizational structure (solution while a sourcing specialist for IT in Europe now reports to European management, his or her functional responsibilities align to a global IT sourcing team). Second, minimal indirect costs data (solution Intel has one E P (enterprise resource planning) system that tracks more than 90 percent of the indirect expenses worldwide). Third, the business units viewed the IDM organization as a resource and not a business partner (solution Intel implemented formal business partnering training). ow, through its e-procurement sourcing program, for each commodity, Intel has one global source strategy that clearly states how purchasing function operated in the Americas, Europe, and Asia.

The opening case demonstrates several aspects of Intel's corporate, business units, and functional strategy. Specifically, one can clearly observe that at each strategic level – corporate level, strategic business unit (SBU) level, and functional level – Intel's strategy transcends international boundaries. This chapter covers the essential elements of corporate strategy in the global context.

Going Global as a Business Strategy

Many executives are convinced that going global is an imperative in today's business environment. More firms are pursuing global operations to take advantage of national differences in the cost and quality of labor, talent, energy, facilities, and capital. All these resources are combined to increase the productivity of the multinational enterprise (MNE). Thus, it is becoming less and less meaningful to talk of "American products," "Italian products," or "Japanese products."

The seven most common reasons that a domestic business – be it a manufacturer or service provider – decides to enter into some form of international operation are as follows:

1. Reduce costs.
2. Reduce risks.
3. Improve the supply chain.
4. Provide better goods and services.
5. Attract new markets.
6. Attract, retain and deploy global knowledge.
7. Attract and retain global talent.

The catalyst for global business operations typically come from one of two sources: either the domestic or local company *chooses to compete* in markets abroad due to some realization of a competitive advantage vis-à-vis their global competitors or *global competition is forced* upon a company with the market entry of foreign competitors to the domestic companies' local customer base.

The following section provides a review of a number of ways to build a global strategy in order to increase competitiveness and secure sustainability of MNEs.

MNE's Orientation and Strategy

While there are many issues that determine the nature of the strategic plan, the one overwhelming issue is the MNE's orientation. An MNE with a *polycentric predisposition* tailors its strategic plan to meet the needs of the local culture. If the firm is doing business in more than one culture, the overall plan is adapted to reflect these individual location needs. The basic mission of a polycentric MNE is to be accepted by the local culture and to blend into the country. Each local subsidiary decides on the objectives it pursues, based on local needs. Profits will be put back into the country in the form of expansion and growth.

An MNE with a polycentric predisposition is interested in obtaining both profit and public acceptance and uses a strategy that allows it to address both local and regional needs. The company is less focused on a particular country than on a geographic region. For example, an MNE doing business in the European Union (EU) will be interested in all the member nations of the EU as they are all in the European region.

An MNE with a *geocentric predisposition* views operations on a global basis. The large international corporations often use this approach. They produce global products with local variations and staff their offices with the best people they can find, regardless of country or origin. Multinationals, in the true meaning of the word, have a geocentric predisposition. However, it is sometimes possible for an MNE to have a polycentric or geocentric predisposition if the company is moderately small or limits operations to specific cultures or geographic regions.

The predisposition of an MNE greatly influences not only the nature of the strategic plan but also its strategic planning process. For example, some MNEs, as they are developing a comprehensive corporate strategy, may be more interested in large-scale manufacturing that will allow them to exploit economies of scale and compete on a price basis across the country or region, and less interested in developing a high degree of responsiveness to local demand and tailoring a product to specific market niches. Other MNEs may prefer to sell in countries where the cultures are similar to their own so that the same basic marketing orientation can be used in several countries or regions. Thus, the MNEs' predispositions are reflected in the strategic planning process and greatly influence their strategies.

Strategy Formulation

Strategy formulation is the process that involves evaluating the MNE's external environment and its internal environment. The process begins with consideration of the external environment, since the MNE is first and foremost interested in opportunities that can be exploited and seeks to hedge against identified threats. The process continues with an assessment of the internal environment and the resources the organization has available, or can develop, to take advantage of these opportunities. At the same time the organization might like to identify its weaknesses and plan accordingly.

External environmental assessment

The analysis of the external environment entails two activities: information gathering and information assessment. These steps help to answer two key questions: What is going on in the external environment? How will these external developments affect the MNE? One of the most common ways in which this is done is through *competitive intelligence*: namely, the use of systematic techniques for obtaining and analyzing public information about the MNE's competitors. This data is particularly useful in keeping MNEs alert to likely moves by their competition.

Information gathering and environmental assessment

Information gathering is an important phase of international strategic planning.

There are four ways that MNEs conduct environmental information gathering and then forecast the future:

- asking industry experts to discuss industry trends and to make projections into the future
- using historical industry trends to forecast future developments
- asking knowledgeable executives to write scenarios describing what they foresee for the industry over the next two to three years
- using computers to simulate the industry environment and to generate likely future developments.

Of these methods, the first option, expert opinion, is the most commonly used. Large Japanese trading firms require their branch managers to send back information on market developments and changing consumer behavior. These data are then analyzed and used to help formulate future strategies for the firms. Sometimes the same information is gathered by independent agents.

This information helps MNEs to identify competitor strengths and weakness and to target new and required initiatives. Careful and detailed information gathering is particularly important when a company is delivering a product or service for many market niches around the world that are too small to be individually profitable. In such situations, the MNE has to identify a series of different niches and attempt to market successfully in each of these geographic areas, balancing business risks and profits. A careful information gathering is also critical to those firms that might be impacted by unexpected local or regional events such as a global economic crisis or the breakout of a major epidemic such as the Swine Flu pandemic that affected countries around the globe in 2009. For example, during the global financial crisis of 2009–10 many MNEs were suddenly unable to finance ongoing operations through credit instruments, as the amounts of credit provided by the banks shrunk significantly, or stopped all together. These changes affected various markets, countries, and regions in different ways, as each adopted various strategies to cope with the crisis, including changes in budget allocations, operations, risk policies, and personnel.

Information assessment

After the information on the companies and the industry is gathered, MNEs evaluate the data. One of the most common approaches is to make an overall assessment based on the six forces that determine industry competitiveness – buyers, suppliers, potential new entrants to the industry, the availability of substitute goods and services, rivalry among the competitors, and availability of complementing products and services. Figure 9.1 shows the relationship among these forces.

Bargaining power of buyers

MNEs examine the power of their buyers because they want to predict the likelihood of maintaining these customers. If the firm believes buyers may be moving their business to competitors, the MNE will want to formulate a strategy for countering this move. For example, the company may offer a lower price or increase the amount of service it provides.

Bargaining power of suppliers

An MNE looks at the power of the industry's suppliers to see if it can gain a competitive advantage here. For example, if there are a number of suppliers in the industry, the MNE may attempt to play them off against each other in an effort to

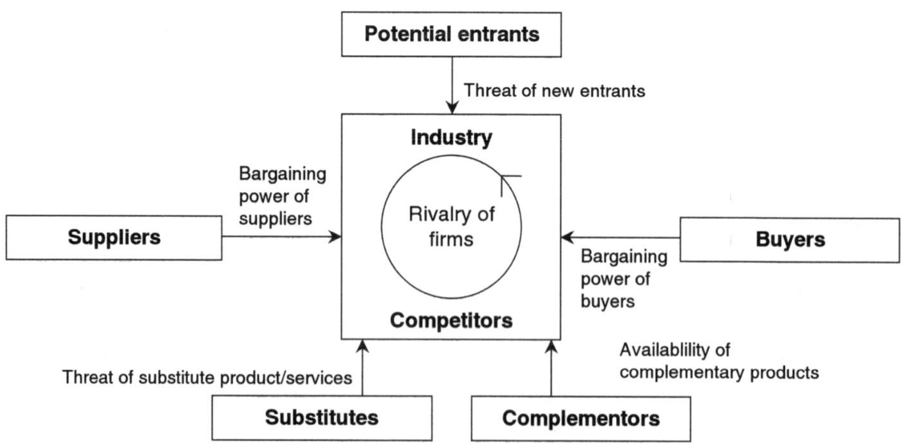

FIGURE 9.1 The six forces of industry competitivenes

get a lower price. As an alternative, MNEs may move to eliminate any threat from the suppliers by acquiring one of them, and thus guaranteeing itself a ready source of inputs.

New entrants

An MNE examines the likelihood of new firms entering the industry and tries to determine the impact they might have on itself. Two typical ways that international MNEs attempt to reduce the threat of new entrants are by (1) keeping costs low and consumer loyalty high and (2) encouraging the government to limit foreign business activity through regulations such as duties, tariffs, quotas, and other protective measures.

Threat of substitutes

MNEs look at the availability of substitute goods and services and try to anticipate when such offerings may reach the market. There are a number of steps that the company may take to offset this competitive force, including (1) lowering prices, (2) offering similar products, and (3) increasing services to the customer.

Rivalry

An MNE examines the rivalry that exists between itself and the competition and seeks to anticipate future changes in these rivalries. Common strategies for maintaining and/or increasing market strength include (1) offering new goods and services, (2) increasing productivity and thus reducing overall costs, (3) accentuating differentiation between current goods and services from those of the competition, (4) increasing the overall quality of goods and services, and (5) targeting specific niches with a well-designed market strategy.

Complementing products

Any accessories or additional services that are created around a base product can increase barriers for competitors. For example, Apple has successfully developed an entire ecosystem around the iPod mp3 player with hundreds of lifestyle accessories (e.g. headphones, cases) and the iTunes music store service, making it hard for competing mp3 players that lack such rich complementing products.

As MNEs examine each of these six forces, they decide on the attractiveness and unattractiveness of each of them. This helps the MNE decide how and where to make strategic changes. Figure 9.2 shows the six forces model applied to the cellular phone (cell phone or mobile phone) industry.

The suppliers noted in the cellular phone industry (in Figure 9.2) were not very powerful, which is an attractive force for the cellular phone manufactures. Buyers have many substitute products from which to choose, and there was some backward integration. Overall, the attractiveness of buyer power was low. The third force, entry barriers, was quite attractive because of the high costs of getting into the industry and the short product life cycles that existed there. It is very difficult for a company to enter this market. The fourth force, substitutes, was unattractive because new products were being developed continually and customer loyalty was somewhat low.

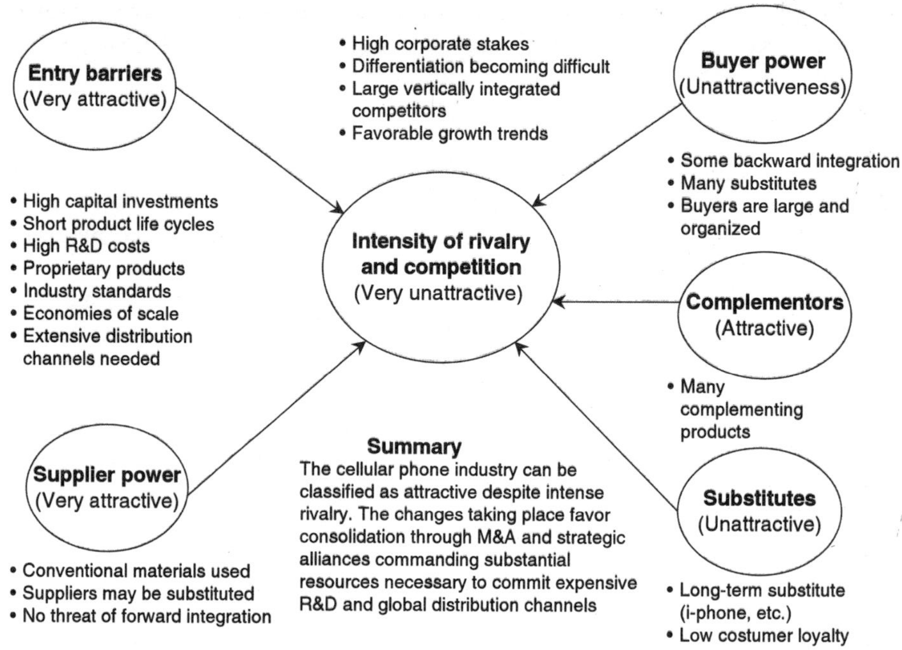

FIGURE 9.2 The six forces model applied to the cellular phone industry

The fifth force, industry rivalry, was also unattractive because of the high cost of doing business, the cyclical nature of sales, and the difficulty of differentiating one's products from those of the competition. The sixth force of complementing products was attractive, as many hardware and software producers caused increasing demands for more options and features, thus justifying consumer upgrades and investment in research and development (R&D).

On an overall basis, however, the industry was classified as attractive. It also appeared that the industry would see more consolidation of firms that would have greater resources to commit to R&D.

MNEs operating in the cellular phone industry may use this analysis to help them increase the attractiveness of those forces that currently are not highly attractive: for example, they could work to develop a state-of-the-art cellular phone that might be substituted for the competition's products. In summary, environmental assessment, such as that provided by an analysis of competitive forces, is used to determine MNE opportunities and threats in an industry or region and to help identify strategies for improving market position and profitability.

Internal Environmental Assessment

The internal environmental assessment helps to pinpoint MNE strengths and weaknesses. There are two areas that an MNE examines in this assessment: (1) physical resources and personnel competencies, and (2) alternative ways to build profitable synergies based on the resources and competencies identified.

Physical resources and personnel competencies

Physical resources are the assets that the MNEs use to implement the strategic plan. Many of these are reported on the balance sheets as reflected by the firm's cash, inventory, machinery, and equipment accounts. The strategic impact of these resources is based on the way the resources are deployed, including both location and disposition. For example, an MNE with manufacturing plants in China and the Philippines may be in a much better position to compete worldwide than a competitor whose plants are all located in the USA. Of strategic importance is also the degree of integration that exists within the various operating units of the MNE. Large companies, in particular, tend to be divided into *strategic business units (SBUs)*. These are operating units with their own strategic space, value added, and profit accountability. An SBU produces and sells goods and services to a defined market segment and has a well-defined set of competitors.

Some large MNEs use *vertical integration*, which is the ownership of all assets needed to produce the goods and services delivered to the costumer. The objectives of vertical integration are to obtain control and be accountable for the supply chain and to ensure that the materials or goods are delivered as needed. Vertical integration may reduce costs in some instances, but it can be an ineffective strategy in other cases. In particular, one of the major problems with vertical integration is defending oneself from competitors who are less vertically integrated and are able to achieve cost efficiencies by changing suppliers flexibly to optimize for new features or cost. This focused approach to successful and sustainable competitiveness relies heavily on outsourcers and employs *virtual integration*, which is the ownership of core technologies and manufacturing capabilities needed to produce outputs, while depending on outsourcing services to provide all other needed inputs. Virtual integration allows an MNE to operate as if it were vertically integrated, through commercial agreements, but it does not require the company to own all of the factors of production, as is the case with vertically integrated firms.

Personnel competencies refer to the skills and abilities of the MNE's workforce. An MNE needs to examine these because they reflect many of the company's strengths and weaknesses. For example, an MNE with an outstanding purchasing department may be able to find low-cost suppliers of high quality, leading to lower prices, which can help the MNE to enter new international markets with a competitive advantage. A company with no sales and distribution unit will sell the products to a firm that will handle the international marketing and distribution functions more efficiently. A pharmaceutical MNE with no R&D capabilities, but well-developed manufacturing abilities, may simply wait for the expiry of a patent on a selected drug and then start producing generic versions of the drug at lower cost in order to dominate the world market.

An understanding of what an MNE does well may help it decide whether the best strategy is to lead or to follow close behind and copy an industry leader. Not every

MNE has the personnel competencies to be the first in the field, and many are content to reduce the investment risk, and potential profit, by following the leader.

Value chain analysis

An alternative approach to an internal environment assessment is to examine the firm's value chain. A *value chain* is the way in which primary and support activities are combined to provide products and services to increase profit margins and add value to the goods or services. Figure 9.3 provides a generic presentation of a value chain. The primary activities in this chain include (1) inbound logistics (receiving, storing, materials handling, and warehouse activities); (2) operations in which inputs are put into final product form by performing value-added activities (machining, assembling, testing, and packaging); (3) outbound logistics, which involves distributing the finished product to the customer; (4) marketing and sales; and (5) service provided after the sale of the product (repair, product adjustment, training, and parts supply). The support activities in the value chain comprises (1) the MNE's infrastructure, including general management, planning, finance, accounting, legal, government affairs, and quality management areas; (2) human resource management, including the selection, placement, appraisal, promotion, training and development of the MNE's personnel; (3) technology, including knowledge, R&D, and procedures that can result in improved goods and services; and (4) procurement, which involves the purchasing of raw materials, suppliers, and other goods.

MNEs can use these primary and support activities to increase the value of the goods and services they provide. As such, all primary and support activities form a value chain.

Analysis of the value chain can also help an MNE determine the type of strategy that will be most effective. There are three generic strategies an MNE can take: cost, differentiation, and focus:

1 **Cost strategy** relies on creating efficient facilities, cost and overhead reductions, and cost minimization in areas like R&D, sales, services, and advertising.

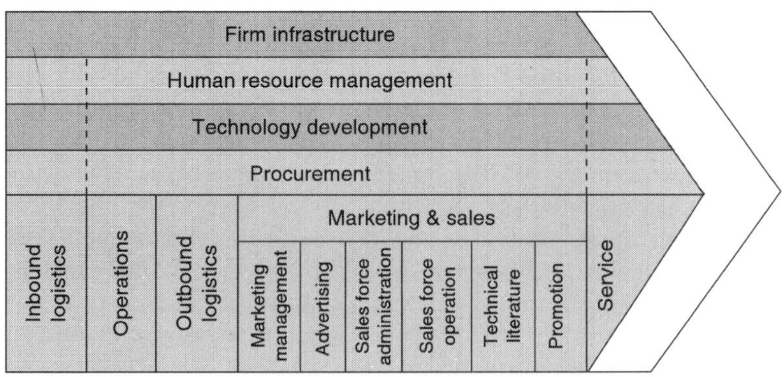

FIGURE 9.3 A generic value chain (Based on Buzzle.com)

2. **Differentiation strategy** is focused on creating a product or service that is perceived as being unique. Approaches to differentiation include the creation of a design or brand image, improved features, and increased dealer networks or after-sales service and support.
3. **Focus strategy** involves focusing on a particular buyer group and segmenting that niche based on a product line or geographic market.

The value chain can help an MNE create synergies within the organization's activities. In this case the overall success is the ability to manage the introduction of new products, without spending money on excessive investment. By analyzing the ways of combining their primary and support activities, some MNEs have been able to create a strategy that allows them to draw heavily on their strengths while minimizing the effect of weaknesses.

Goal determination

MNEs use the external and internal environmental analyses to provide the information needed for setting goals. Some of these goals are determined during the external analysis, as the company identifies opportunities that it wants to exploit. Others will be finalized after the value chain analysis is complete. In all cases, the outcomes of the environment and value chain analysis result in the identification of strategic goals.

There are two options for examining the goals of international business operations. One option is to review them on the basis of functional areas. Table 9.1 lists some of the major goals and measures that are related to profitability, marketing, manufacturing and operations, finance, human resources, and R&D. A second option is to examine these goals by geographic area or on an SBU basis. In either case, once profitability goals are determined for each SBU, functional goals and measures are defined for marketing, production, human resources, finance, and R&D. Each SBU of the MNE develops its list of goals for each geographic area. A possible list of goals and measures by function is shown in Table 9.1.

The strategic planning process is a cascading process. The MNE might start out by setting a profitability goal for the MNE as a whole. Each geographic area or SBU will then be assigned a profitability goal, which matches and support the MNE's profitability goal as a whole. The same approach is used in order to develop functional strategies, such as marketing, production, and finance. Within each SBU these goals are further divided and are assured to support and complement the goals at all levels of the organization.

Strategy implementation

Strategy implementation is the process of working towards strategic goals by using the organizational structure to execute the agreed-upon strategy. There are many decisions that are made in the process, including location, ownership decisions, and functional area implementation.

TABLE 9.1 Goals and Measures of an MNE

Profitability	*Marketing*	*Manufacturing and operations*	*Finance*	*Human resources management*	*Research & development*
• Profit level	• Total domestic and international sales	• Ratio of foreign to local production volumes • Worldwide logistics costs	• Financing of foreign subsidiaries through retained earnings and locally raised capital • Minimizing the world-wide taxation burden	• Development of managers with global orientation • Training of host country managers	• Develop and exploit worldwide knowledge internally • Acquire/retain external/outsourced knowledge and intellectual property
• Return on assets • Return on invested capital (ROIC) • Return on equity • Return on sales • Profit growth per year	• Worldwide market share • Regional market share • Domestic market share • Sales growth per quarter/year • Sales volume	• Economies of scale via international production integration • Learning curve effect through international production integration • Quality and cost reduction and control	• Optimum ratio between equity and debt • Minimum cost of capital	• Development of worldwide harmonized local compensation packages	• Steady flow of new products and services introductions • Appropriate ratio of funds invested in R&D vs funds invested in new country entry campaigns
• Price/earnings ratio • Corporate valuation • Share value growth	• Integration of country distribution channels for cost reduction and better service levels efficiency	• Introduction of efficient manufacturing and service methods	• Optimal and flexible foreign exchange management – minimizing losses from foreign currency exchange rate fluctuations	• Maintaining appropriate ratio of core corporate employees to temporary employees outsourced	• Benchmark R&D investment against the competitors

Location Considerations

Many governments help local business fashion a strategy to enter new markets. Take for example, an Australian Government agency, Austrade. Austrade helps corporate strategists with a decision regarding a location for new ventures around the world. Specifically, the agency provides key issues to be considered when selecting a country for a new venture, such as:

- *cultural distance* – language, ethnicity, religion
- *administrative distance* – institutional weaknesses, government policies, political hostility
- *geographic distance* – lack of common border, physical remoteness, size of country
- *economic distance* – differences in consumer incomes, cost differences

The agency further suggests that the main factor quoted by Australian firms as influencing their location decision is the *size of the market*. Other reasons determined as important to the location decision include:

- *political stability* – political history, fiscal, and monetary policy
- *economic stability* – growth rates, incomes, costs, resources, interest rates, and inflation
- *geographic borders* – remoteness, size of country, population, and climate
- *infrastructure* for transportation and communication
- *business ethics* – language, ethnicity, and culture
- *competitors* and industry structure
- *tax* policy, tariffs and other trade barriers, incentives offered by government
- *labor costs*
- quality of potential *local partners*
- availability of *local suppliers*

Using such a strategic approach to the selection of location, the two possible locations considered by Austrade were the Netherlands and Fiji.

Case study: Why choose the Netherlands?

- Highly productive and qualified workforce
- Innovative R&D
- Geographic location
- Infrastructure
- Social, economic, and political stability
- Regulatory environment
- Base for sales to other EU markets
- Government support, including subsidies, tax, and incentives

Case study: Why choose Fiji?

- Geographic closeness to Australia
- Tax climate and incentives

- Government support, including subsidies
- Favorable labor costs
- Similar legal system
- Good starting point for moving into Asia-Pacific markets
- Preferential access to Australian markets
- Australian financial services established

Source: Adapted from Government of Australia site: http://www.austrade.gov.au/Market-entry-strategies/.

The location decision is a strategic decision. Namely, it has a long term impact and involves a significant capital commitment. The boxed item below (Location consideration) is an example of how governments may assist with the location decision.

Side by side with the location decision, the ownership of international operations has become an important issue in recent years. Countries that want to remain economically strong make efforts to attract foreign investors who will provide jobs and allow their workers to increase their skills and build products that are demanded internationally. In order to accomplish this, MNEs use various forms of ownership arrangements. In particular, MNEs use both international joint ventures and strategic alliances.

Ownership Arrangements

International joint ventures

An *international joint venture (IJV)* is an agreement between two or more corporate entities to own and control an overseas business. IJV take a number of different forms and provide many business opportunities, which explains their rise in popularity in recent years. Among the reasons for the increase in IJVs are: first, government encouragement and legislation that are designed to make it attractive for foreign investors to join with local partners; second, the growing need for partners who know the local economy, the culture, and the political system; third, the desire by outside investors to find local partners with whom they can team up effectively.

It should be noted that in many cases IJVs have not fulfilled their potential. The high rate of failure of IJVs is a result of the desire by MNEs to control the operation, which leads to poor decision making and conflicts with the local partners. In general, international, as well as local, joint ventures are difficult to manage and are frequently unstable. Thus, many MNEs have turned to alternative forms to outright ownership, such as the use of strategic alliances and partnerships. While strategic alliances and joint ventures are dealt with in Chapter 10, a short discussion is provided here in the context of international and global strategy.

Strategic alliance

A *strategic alliance or partnership* is an agreement between two or more competitive MNEs for the purpose of serving a global market. In contrast to a joint venture, where the partners may be from a separate business entity, strategic partnerships are almost always formed by firms in the same line of business. In recent years these partnerships have become increasingly popular. A recent example of a strategic partnership is that of Sony of Japan, teaming with Ericsson to design, produce, and market the Sony-Ericsson cellular telephone. In the past both firms have developed their own products, but the strategic partnership allowed for a technological and commercial success on a global basis.

Strategic alliances illustrate the growing popularity of international business ownership arrangements that are not based on 100 percent ownership. Rather, they use IJVs, strategic partnerships, and other business arrangements to reduce the risk involved in operating globally and increase the odds of making a profit.

Functional Strategies

Once an overall strategy for the MNE or SBU is determined, functional strategies are used to coordinate operations and to ensure that the plan is carried out properly. Whereas the specific functions that are critical to the success of the MNE will vary, depending on the type of business, they fall into several major areas: marketing, after-sales service and support, manufacturing, finance, procurement, technology, and human resources. Some of these strategies are discussed below.

The marketing strategy is designed to identify consumer needs and to formulate a plan of action for selling the desired goods and services to these customers. Most marketing strategies are built around what is commonly known as the "four Ps" of marketing: product, price, promotion, and place.

Table 9.2 indicates the main assessment areas and tasks in global market opportunity assessments, including the identification of tasks, objectives, outcomes, and selection criteria.

The issue of after-sales service and support, especially in the case of global distribution of products, is a key to commercial success. For example, while software by Microsoft can be supported over the Internet, white goods (e.g., microwaves, toaster-ovens) and cars must be serviced through local representatives.

The manufacturing strategy is designed to match the marketing plan and to ensure that the right products are built and delivered in time for sale and distribution. Manufacturing should align its strategy with the procurement and technology units, so as to ensure that the desired materials are available on time and with quality. If the MNE is producing goods in more than one country, it will give attention to coordinate these activities as needed. For example, as shown in the Intel case, it manufactures goods in various countries and then sells them in other geographic regions. Such global production and assembly operations have to be coordinated carefully in order to assure efficiency and profitability.

Financial strategies are usually formulated and controlled out of the home office. However, in recent years, MNEs have learned that this approach may be inefficient

TABLE 9.2 Main Assessment Areas and Tasks in Global Market Opportunity Assessment

Assessment areas and tasks	*Objective*	*Outcomes*	*Criteria*
Is the organization ready to internationalize?	An assessment of the corporation readiness to engage in international business activities	A strategic assessment of the corporate strengths and weaknesses re international operations and a plan to exploit strengths and eliminate weaknesses	Evaluate factors required for international business success, including financial and tangible resources, relevant skills, and competencies, management commitment, and motivation
Are the products and services suitable for foreign markets?	An assessment of the suitability and compatibility of the corporate products and services for international customers	Identification of product and service adaptations required for initial and ongoing market entry	Assess products and services regarding foreign market customer requirements, government regulations, required distribution channels changes, competing products and services in target markets
Screen countries to identify possible target markets	Identifying an initial set of countries that require in-depth investigation re market entry	Identification of a few high-potential country markets	Assess candidate countries regarding market size, market expected growth rate, country's receptivity to imports, country's ease of doing business, degree of economic freedom and corruption perceptions, and political and business risk
Assess foreign market potential	Estimate the market share in each foreign market	Identify sales volumes several years down the road in each foreign market and develop a plan to remove market barriers	Assess market potential in the foreign market by considering market size, growth rate, local competitive intensity, tariff barriers, nontariff trade barriers, regulations, distribution channels, customer requirements and preferences
Identify qualified business partners in the foreign market for merger, acquisition, joint venture, and strategic alliance	To decide on the type of business partner, decide on the entry strategy	Determination of the value-adding activities to be executed by the foreign partner and characterizing the partner	Select partners based on manufacturing, marketing and service expertise, expertise in international ventures, distribution channels, financial strength, technical and management proficiency, and required infrastructure

and, because of fluctuating currency prices, may be both costly and more risky. Thus, currently, overseas units of an MNE may have more control over their finances than before, but the units' budgets are streamlined and conform to the overall strategic plan of that MNE. Each of the overseas units of the MNE is held accountable for financial performance in the form of value-added return on investment, profit margin, capital budgeting, debt financing, and working capital management.

Control and Evaluation

Following the strategy formulation and the initiation of the strategy implementation processes, MNEs should establish control and evaluation processes. The control and evaluation process involves an examination of the MNE's performance for the purpose of determining how well the MNE as a whole or the SBU in particular has done and what actions should be taken in light of this performance. The control and evaluation process is tied directly to the overall strategy in that the strategic objectives serve as the basis for comparison and evaluation, as well as consideration for possible changes.

If the comparison and evaluation show that the SBU or overseas operation is performing according to expectations, then no change will be initiated. On the other hand, if gaps between objectives and performance are identified, the MNE will want to identify the causes for these gaps and decide to eliminate or minimize them. In making these decisions, the MNE may use a variety of measures. Some measures will be highly quantitative and depend on financial and productivity performance; others will be more qualitative. The common methods of measurement for control and evaluation purposes are sales growth, market share, new products introduction, financial performance, operational performance, and management performance. Management performance includes an assessment of government relations with the local subsidiary and management relations with the home office.

Balanced Scorecard and Strategy

The balanced scorecard (Figure 9.4) is a strategic planning and management system that is used extensively in business and industry, government, and nonprofit organizations worldwide to align business activities to the vision and strategy of the organization, improve internal and external communications, and monitor organization performance against strategic goals. It was originated by Drs Robert Kaplan (Harvard Business School) and David Norton as a performance measurement framework that added strategic nonfinancial performance measures to traditional financial metrics to give managers and executives a more "balanced" view of organizational performance.

The balanced scorecard has evolved from its early use as a simple performance measurement framework to a full strategic planning and management system. It provides a framework that not only provides performance measurements but also helps planners identify what should be done and measured. It enables executives to truly execute their strategies.

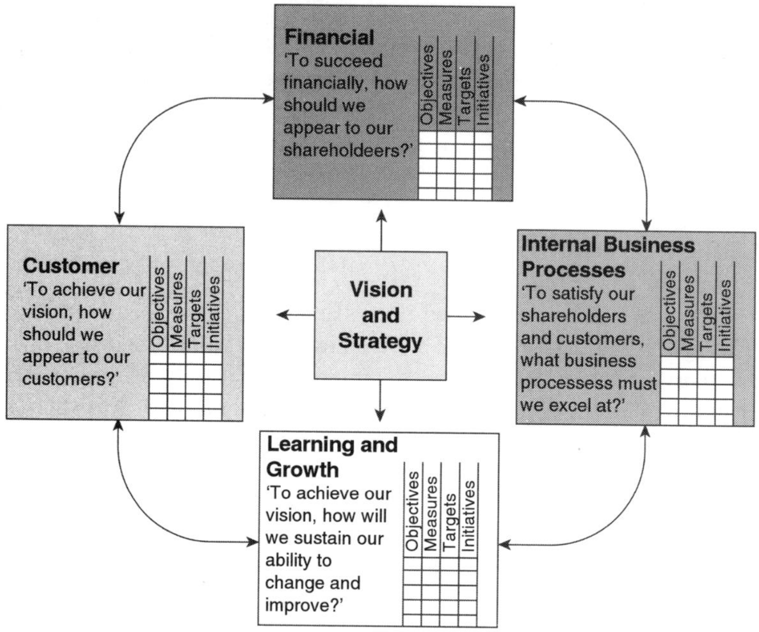

FIGURE 9.4 Strategy evaluation: balanced score card. (Adapted from ©1998–2009 Balanced Scorecard Institute, a Strategy Management Group company: http://www.balancedscorecard.org.)

Kaplan and Norton describe the innovation of the balanced scorecard as follows:

> The balanced scorecard retains traditional financial measures. But financial measures tell the story of past events, an adequate story for industrial age companies for which investments in long-term capabilities and customer relationships were not critical for success. These financial measures are inadequate, however, for guiding and evaluating the journey that information age companies must make to create future value through investment in customers, suppliers, employees, processes, technology, and innovation.

All of these measurements are used in arriving at an overall assessment of the SBU's performance. Based on the results, the MNE will then set new goals, make adjustments or start a new international strategic planning process.

International Location Selection

As noted in the opening case of Intel, multiple locations are key to global operations. The location decision is made concurrently with international entry strategies.

In particular, entry strategies entail considerations regarding time of entry and the mode of entry to a new geographic area. These decisions affect the investment environment, operational arrangements, and resource commitment.

International location selection usually involves selection of a continent for possible location, followed by country selection, and then selection of a region within the chosen country. The country selection determines the macroenvironment for operations at a specific site. To select an appropriate country and a region within that country, international managers should first appraise locational determinants that are likely to influence future operations and expected returns.

Location characteristics

Location characteristics can be categorized into the following groups of variables or factors: (1) cost/tax factors; (2) demand factors; (3) strategic factors; (4) regulatory/economic factors; and (5) sociopolitical factors. The importance of each of these factors to a specific MNE depends on the MNE's objectives and the business nature of the foreign direct investment (FDI) venture. For instance, a high-tech FDI, such as Intel, may depend more on strategic factors, whereas labor-intensive ventures, such as in the textile industry, may be more dependent on cost/tax factors. Local market-focused investments may rely more on demand factors, whereas export market-focused investments may be impacted more by cost/tax conditions. The location for SKYPE's headquarters – a software VOIP (voice over Internet protocol) communications company – is Luxembourg, Europe, chosen for its favorable regulatory environment and industrial policies with respect to the telecommunications industry. The following is a short discussion of each of the main location factors.

Cost/tax factors

1. *Transportation costs.* For country selection, MNEs should consider the costs incurred in transporting materials from a home country to a host country or transporting products from a host country to a home market. For site selection, MNEs need to consider the costs of the various transportation channels (air, sea, railway, and highway) from the site considered for location to destinations of major local, and foreign customers. For example, Hewlett-Packard (HP) has decided that choosing Singapore as a manufacturing base provides it with the least expensive hub from which to distribute its printers to countries located in South-East Asia and elsewhere.
2. *Wage rate.* Labor costs constitute a substantial proportion of total production costs. Foreign production is more likely to occur when production costs are lower abroad than at home. Labor costs affect investment location decisions in a significant way, particularly for firms in labor-intensive industries. The decision by Delta Textile Corporation to locate in Cairo, Egypt, was partially based on lower wage rates available in Egypt, compared to wage rates in Israel.
3. *Availability and costs of land.* Availability of suitable plant sites, the cost of land, space for expansion, and local government policy on renting or purchasing land have been recognized by international managers as critical factors in the early stages of venture development and late stages of venture startup and operation.

4 *Construction costs.* These costs account for a substantial part of the capital investment. Different sites vary in the cost of construction materials, labor, land, equipment rental, and quality of construction.

5 *Costs of raw materials and resources.* Strategically, MNEs are increasing the percentage of local outsourcing in the total production. This localization reduces foreign exchange risks from devalued currencies and improves relationships with local governments and local firms. Obviously the lower costs of local materials and resources needed in production affect the MNE's gross profit margin.

6 *Financing costs.* The cost and availability of local capital through a local stock exchange or a local bank are a major concern for MNEs. The reason is that local financing provides much of the capital needed in creating mass production facilities. Financing by local banks and financial institutions also helps an MNE hedge against possible financial risks arising from fluctuations in foreign exchange rates and uncertain foreign exchange policies, as well as hedge against political risk in a host country.

7 *Tax rates.* Both nominal and effective tax rates influence a firm's profitability. The *nominal tax* rate determines the corporate tax burden. The *effective tax rate* on corporate income is the nominal corporate tax rate adjusted for all other taxes and subsidies affecting an MNE's taxable income, which in turn determines the MNE's net return from its revenues.

8 *Investment incentives.* Many countries, especially developing countries, compete to attract FDI to enhance their domestic economies. In so doing, they often offer preferential incentives to foreign investors. Although these are country-specific, various investment incentives that attract FDI include (see also Chapter 6):

- tax breaks on corporate income taxe;
- financial assistance, such as preferential terms of financing, wage subsidies, investment grants, or low-interest loans;
- tariff concessions, including exemption from duties on imports, or additional duties on imports;
- business assistance, such as employee training, R&D support, land grants, site improvements, and site selection assistance;
- other incentives, such as infrastructure development, legal services, business consultation, and partner selection assistance.

9 *Profit repatriation.* Repatriation restrictions have a negative impact on the net income or dividends remitted to overseas-based headquarters. Restrictions can involve a remittance tax on the cash repatriated to a home country or a cap on the cash amount that may be repatriated. Approval may be required from the local central bank or foreign exchange administration department to repatriate dividends. Restrictions on foreign exchange flows are still practiced in China and India, affecting MNEs operating in these countries.

Demand factors

1. *Market size and growth.* Different MNEs consider local consumers in assessing market size and growth. At the national level, the size and growth rate of markets indicate market opportunities and potential. At the regional level, per capita consumption and the growth rate of consumption in respective regions (state, province, city) may be used to measure market size and growth.
2. *Presence of customers.* MNEs may find it desirable to locate their manufacturing sites in the area where they have a proven and sustainable group of customers. The closer operations are to major buyers, the better the cost efficiency and marketing effectiveness.
3. *Local competition.* The intensity of competition in a host country or specific region is important because it directly impacts a firm's market position and gross profit margin from local sales. In general, MNEs are located in sites where competition is relatively low unless they have sufficient advantages to ensure their competitive edge in the market.

Strategic factors

1. *Investment infrastructure.* MNEs attach great importance to infrastructure conditions. This is especially true for companies investing in knowledge-or technology-intensive projects. Singapore attracted many of those MNEs mainly because of its ideal infrastructure. Major infrastructure variables include transportation (highways, ports, airports, and railroads), telecommunications, utilities, capital markets, and governmental efficiency.
2. *Manufacturing concentration.* One of the major factors of location selection is the strength of existing manufacturing activities. Cost savings can result from manufacturers locating in close proximity, all sharing an adequate labor pool and supply network supporting production or operations, for particular types of industries.
3. *Industrial linkages.* The nature and quality of complementary industries and special services (distribution, consulting, auditing, banking, insurance, marketing services, etc.) are also important as MNE operations interact actively with these sectors in a host country.
4. *Workforce productivity.* As a result of increasing technological change and process innovation, international production requires high workforce productivity and superior labor skills. The labor requirements of new systems and techniques are driving the need for a better-educated direct-labor workforce. The availability of a skilled managerial, marketing, and technical workforce is also crucial, because it helps gain competitive advantages in the market.
5. *Inbound and outbound logistics.* Inbound logistics include proximity to suppliers and sources of raw materials and inputs. Since MNEs have a tendency to rely on local input sources, this type of logistics should be among the critical considerations for international managers. Outbound logistics are based largely on proximity to major markets, buyers and end consumers. This factor can heavily influence the effectiveness of customer responsiveness.

A main reason why Procter & Gamble chose Egypt as its major production base for the Middle East and North America is the effective inbound and outbound logistics.

Regulatory/economic factors

1 *Industrial policies.* In many countries, industrial policies are used to control new entrants, net profit margins, degree of competition, structural concentration, social benefits, anti-trust rules, and project approval and registration. In selecting a location, MNEs need to make sure that the candidate country or region allows foreign business entry and that industrial policies are reasonably favorable.

2 *FDI policies.* In determining a foreign location, MNEs need to learn how the local FDI policies may impact business plans and payoffs. First, they should know what entry modes are allowed, in specific industries or regions, or for specific ownership sharing (such as minority joint ventures). MNEs should check content localization requirements. A foreign company is often required to purchase and use local materials, parts, semi-products, or other supplies made by local firms for the production of its final outputs. MNEs must also appraise foreign exchange control measures in a host country. Figure 9.5 demonstrates the FDI Confidence Index, which may be used to evaluate, compare,

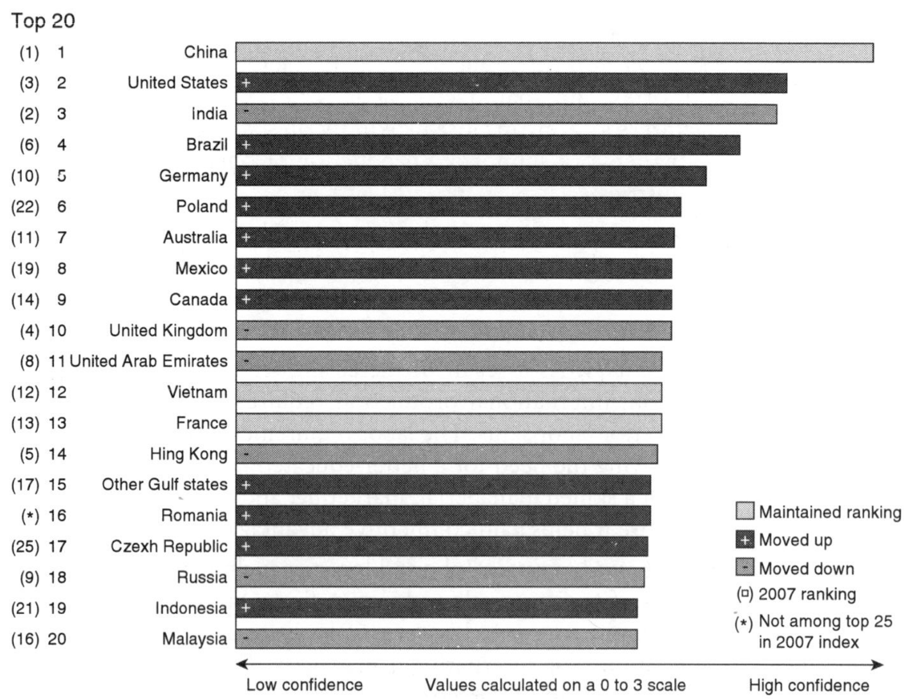

FIGURE 9.5 A. T. Kearney 2010 FDI Confidence Index®. (Adapted from http://www.atkearney.com.)

and contrast various FDI destinations. The confidence index may be based on key measures, such as a country's financial structure, its business environment, and its people with the necessary technical and managerial skills.

In light of the global economic crisis of 2008–10, as well as the European economic crisis of 2010, it is clear that these indices should be updated continuously, allowing for an up-to-date assessment of entry destinations and entry modes.

Furthermore, as shown in Tables 9.3 and 9.4, a different assessment may be used for emerging markets such as China or Hungary.

TABLE 9.3 Application of Indexing and Ranking Methodology: Emerging Market Potential Indicators, 2007

Country	*Market size*		*Market growth rate*		*Market intensity*		*Market consumption capacity*	
	Rank	*Index*	*Rank*	*Index*	*Rank*	*Index*	*Rank*	*Index*
China	1	100	1	100	25	23	12	59
Hong Kong	24	1	20	23	1	100	13	54
Singapore	27	1	18	27	9	59	11	62
Taiwan	12	5	6	57	11	57	–	–
Israel	25	1	12	45	2	79	4	82
South Korea	7	12	16	30	5	63	2	99
Czech Rep.	23	2	9	48	13	55	3	97
Hungary	26	1	24	14	3	76	1	100
India	2	44	3	63	22	37	7	77
Poland	14	5	27	1	10	58	6	80

Note: Only the top 10 countries are provided here; consult www.globaledge.msu.edu for the complete list.
Source: GlobolEDGE™ (www.globaledge.msu.edu/ibrd/morketpot.asp).

Country	*Commercial infrastructure*		*Economic freedom*		*Market receptivity*		*Country risk*		*Overall index*	
	Rank	*Index*	*Rank*	*Index*	*Rank*	*Index*	*Rank*	*Index*	*Rank*	*Index*
China	16	45	27	1	22	3	13	49	1	100
Hong Kong	2	97	6	79	2	75	2	90	2	96
Singapore	6	83	10	71	1	100	1	100	3	93
Taiwan	1	100	8	76	5	23	3	87	4	79
Israel	3	94	3	86	4	26	5	63	5	78
South Korea	5	90	7	78	10	13	4	65	6	75
Czech Rep.	4	91	2	93	9	15	6	63	7	73
Hungary	7	78	4	83	8	16	8	62	8	64
India	25	17	17	44	27	1	16	39	9	55
Poland	8	71	5	82	14	7	9	58	10	46

Note: Only the top 10 countries are provided here; consult www.globaledge.msu.edu for the complete list.
Source: GlobalEDGE™ (www.globaledge.msu.edu/resourcedesk/mpi).

TABLE 9.4 Variables Used for Country Screening in the Emerging Market Potential (EMP) Index

Variable	*Definition*	*Weight (out of 100)*	*Example measurement indicators*
Market size	Proportion of the country's population in urban areas	20	• Urban population
Market growth rate	Pace of industrialization and economic development	12	• Annual growth rate of commercial energy use • Real GDP growth rate
Market intensity	Buying power of the country's residents	14	• Per-capita gross national income, based on purchasing power parity • Private consumption as a percentage of GDP
Market consumption capacity	Size and growth rate of the country's middle class	10	• Percentage share of middle-class income and consumption
Commercial infrastructure	Ease of access to marketing, distribution and communication channels	14	• Telephone mainlines (per 100 in habitants) • Cellular mobile subscribers per 100 inhabitants • Paved road density • Internet hosts per million people • Population per retail outlet • Television sets per capita
Economic freedom	Degree to which the country has liberalized its economy	10	• Trade and tax policies • Monetary and banking policies • Government consumption of economic output • Capital flows and foreign investment • Property rights • Extent of black market activity
Market receptivity to imports	Extent to which the country is open to imports	12	• Per-capita imports • Trade as percentage of GDP
Country risk	Level of political risk	8	• Country risk rating
Total		**100**	

Source: Market Potential Index for Emerging Markets (http://globaledge.msu.edu/resourcedesk/mpi).

3 *Availability of special economic zones.* One way many countries (especially in the developing world) attempt to attract FDI is through the establishment of special zones such as Free Trade Zones (FTZs), Special Economic Zones (SEZs), Economic and Technological Development Zones (ETDZs), High-Tech Development Zones (HTDZs), open economic regions (OERs), bonded areas, and so on. In general, these zones provide preferential treatment to MNEs in terms of taxation, import duties, land use, infrastructure access, and governmental assistance.

Sociopolitical factors

1 *Political instability.* This factor reflects uncertainty over the continuation of present political and social conditions and government policies that are critical to the survival and profitability of an MNE's operations in the host country. Changes in government policies may create problems related to repatriation of earnings, or, in extreme cases, expropriation of assets.

2 *Cultural barriers.* A possible trigger of uncertainty surrounds the differences in culture between the home and host countries. These factors determine an MNE's receptivity and adaptability to the social context of a host country. Language barriers are also an important consideration underlying location selection, affecting communication with head office.

3 *Local business practices.* Culture-specific business practices often constitute key forms of knowledge that MNEs must acquire. A common reason behind formation of international cooperative ventures with developing country enterprises is to gain such country-specific knowledge.

4 *Government efficiency and corruption.* Efficient and less corrupt governments are more responsive to an MNE's requests or complaints, take shorter time periods to approve ventures and provide superior assistance and support.

5 *Attitudes toward foreign business.* Social and governmental attitudes toward foreign businesses often have influences on MNE operations and management. If the society and government of a host country are friendly to foreign business, MNEs will benefit from a supportive environment.

6 *Community characteristics.* Site selection must include considerations of community environment aspects such as community size, educational facilities, housing facilities, police and fire protection, climate, suitability for expatriates and their families, facilities for children, the social environment for spouses, hotel accommodations, crime level, and other quality of life issues. All these characteristics define the attractiveness of the site for foreign expatriates.

7 *Pollution control.* Environmental protection laws and regulations in the target location influence the choice and cost of investments. Before making a location decision, an MNE should appraise these laws and regulations, assess whether the MNE is able to comply with them, and evaluate whether it is financially feasible to invest in pollution control.

Table 9.5 summarizes the major location factors explained above. Overall, site selection should be based on both micro-context and macro-context factors.

Decision framework

The preceding section presented factors that must be assessed in choosing a location. They constitute the framework of a location decision-making process. Side by side with this framework, MNEs also need to take into account their strategic objectives, global integration considerations, and market orientation.

TABLE 9.5 Location Factors

Micro-context factors	*Macro-context factors*
Cost/tax factors	*Regulatory factors*
Transportation costs	Industrial policies
Wage rate	Foreign direct investment (FDI) regulations
Land availability and costs	Availability of special duty free and tax free zones
Construction costs	
Costs of raw materials and resources	*Sociopolitical factors*
Financing costs	Political instability
Tax rates	Cultural barriers
Investment incentives	Local business practices
Profit repatriation	Government efficiency and corruption
	Attitudes towards foreign business and personnel
Demand factors	Community characteristics
Market size and growth	Sustainable development, recycling regulations and pollution control
Customer presence	
Local competition	
Strategic factors	
Accessibility to capital	
Manufacturing clusters	
Workforce productivity	
Inbound and outbound logistics	

Location and strategic objectives

If an MNE wishes to pursue market growth and a competitive position in a host country, demand factors and strategic objectives appear to be its most critical considerations. Because these factors generally concern long-term investments and long-term commitment, macroeconomic and sociopolitical factors have an impact on location selection. If an MNE seeks short-term profitability, it should attach more value to cost and taxation factors. The costs of production factors and operational expenses will determine the profit margin, whereas income tax rates and profit repatriation rules will affect the net return to the MNE.

If an MNE states strategic objectives that diversify risks or stresses the importance of operating in a stable environment, sociopolitical factors become fundamental to the location decision. Since macroeconomic factors, such as exchange rate and the inflation rate, are related to environmental uncertainty, they should also be included in the decision framework. Finally, if an MNE states as an objective to secure innovation and learning from international expansion, strategic factors that help promote innovation and learning often outweigh other groups of factors in affecting location choice.

Location and global integration

The location decision should be framed within the design for global integration and global supply chain. As the world economy becomes increasingly regionalized (see Chapter 7), MNEs may first decide which trading region they should enter, followed by a country selection and specific site selection. In considering trading region selection, managers may want to review the characteristics at the trading region level, such as the EU vs NAFTA (USA, Canada, and Mexico) and find out how the removal of inter-country barriers within the blocs have reduced cost and tax burdens and improved the regulatory and economic environments. Today, MNEs use host country sites to achieve global or regional integration. They tend to locate labor-intensive processes in sites that are relatively well endowed with labor or locate an R&D facility in an area where abundant technological capabilities exist. As an example, Google, e-Bay, Microsoft, Motorola, and Intel have all located R&D subsidiaries in Israel, as the number of engineers and technical experts is relatively high in that country, and since Israel is in close proximity to the EU and has bilateral trade agreements with most Western and emerging economies.

Location and market orientation

Market orientation is concerned mainly with whether an MNE primarily targets a host country market, export market, or both. Naturally, different market orientations vary in their relationship with location determinants. Local market-oriented ventures are highly sensitive to demand and strategic factors in the local environment. Some regulatory and economic factors are also relevant because they affect an MNE's stability and the exposure of its operations to environmental risks. Certain sociopolitical variables, including cultural distance, government efficiency or corruption, and political stability, are likely to have a stronger effect on a local market orientation than on an export orientation. Production facilities for an export market can be located with little regard to domestic demand. Therefore, cost and tax factors, together with strategic factors such as investment incentives, input logistics, labor productivity, and infrastructure, are important microeconomic factors underlying this location strategy. For example, many US companies relocate their production facilities just south of the USA–Mexico border. These production facilities, called maquiladoras, assemble imported, duty-free components into finished goods, most of which are then reexported to the USA. In addition to benefiting from lower labor costs, these companies enjoy reduced transportation costs, eliminated tariff burdens, and logistics convenience.

Currently, approximately 4,000 maquiladoras with over 1.2 million employees operate along the border zone, accounting for nearly one-third of Mexico's industrial jobs and 45 percent of its total exports.

Timing of Entry

Timing of entry involves the sequence of an MNE's entry into a foreign market vis-á-vis other MNEs (i.e., first mover, early follower, and late mover). Timing of entry is important because it determines the risks, environments, and opportunities the MNE may confront. In today's increasingly integrated global marketplace, where demand level, consumption sophistication, and rivalry intensity are all changing rapidly, the decision on when to embark on international expansion is critical for transnational operations. Transnational investors are likely to have more investment opportunities in foreign markets than in their home markets.

This is largely because of the different market and industry structures between home and host economies. By investing in a foreign market, a later mover in the home country may become an early mover in the host country.

Early-mover advantages

When entering a foreign market, first mover, or entrant, MNEs generally have advantages – such as greater market power, more opportunities, and more strategic options – over late entrants. These advantages might be ultimately reflected in higher economic returns compared with later movers or later entrants. There are several reasons for this phenomenon. First, pioneering MNEs tend to outperform later entrants in acquiring market power. Second, early movers gain from preemptive opportunities and benefit from many strategic options. Pioneer investors often have more strategic options in selecting industries, locations, and market orientations. In addition, early movers are often given priority access to natural resources, scarce materials, distribution channels, promotional arrangements, and infrastructure and may enjoy a support from the local governments.

Early-mover disadvantages

However, early movers also suffer from some disadvantages compared to late entrants. Pioneer investors may be confronted with greater environmental uncertainty and operational risks. Environmental uncertainty generally comes from (1) underdeveloped FDI laws and regulations in a host country, (2) the host government's lack of experience in dealing with MNEs, and (3) infant or embryonic stages of the industry or market in a host country. Operational risks of an early mover originate from (1) a possible shortage of qualified supply sources and other production inputs such as qualified managers and R&D workforce; (2) underdeveloped support services such as local financing, foreign exchange facilities, arbitration organs, consulting firms, and marketing advisory services; (3) poor infrastructure in transportation, utilities, and communications; and (4) an unstable market structure in which market demand and supply are misaligned and local governments often interfere with MNE operations.

In contrast with early movers, *late investors* do not suffer, or suffer less, from the preceding uncertainties and risks. When late movers arrive, the host country environment is usually more stable, regulatory conditions are more favorable, and the market infrastructure is already developed.

Early movers also tend to pay higher costs in learning and adapting to local environments. Many early movers are forced to invest more in building industrial infrastructure (e.g., supply bases and distribution networks) and technological or service standards. Conversely, later movers who use a wait-and-see strategy gain from lessons from early movers.

Finally, early movers may have to spend money to fight followers who imitate their strategies or innovations, counterfeit their products, or infringe on their trademark, brand or intellectual property rights. This cost is especially high when early movers invest in a country with underdeveloped and underenforced legal systems in protecting these rights, such as was the case in the People's Republic of China. When followers infringe on a first-mover's property rights, the latter has to spend on litigation, investigation, lobbying, or arbitration. In addition to direct costs of anti-imitation, early movers have to pay higher switching and start-up costs.

Table 9.6 summarizes the advantages and disadvantages of being an early mover. It should be noted that virtually all advantages of an early mover are the disadvantages of the late mover.

Entry Mode Selection

Entry mode choices

Entry modes are specific forms or ways of entering a target country to achieve strategic goals. An MNE seeking to enter a foreign market must make an important strategic decision concerning which entry mode to use. The choice falls into three categories: international trade-related, transfer-related, and FDI-related entry modes. The levels of resource commitment, organizational control, involved risks, and expected returns all increase from the least commitment at the trade-related entry mode category to the most commitment at the FDI-related entry mode.

International trade-related entry modes

International trade-related entry modes include exporting, subcontracting, and countertrade.

Exporting

Most MNEs get started in international expansion through exporting, in which the firm maintains its production facilities at home and sells its products abroad. In exporting, the MNE gains valuable expertise about operating internationally

TABLE 9.6 Advantages and Disadvantages of Early Movers

Advantages	*Disadvantages*
Barriers to potential competitors	Nonexisting laws and regulations
Technical standards determination	Start up industrial sector
Customer loyalty	Lack of supporting services
Flexibility in determining product positioning	Underdeveloped sources of supply and raw materials
Brand recognition	Nonexisting infrastructure
Flexibility of facilities location	Local workforce training costs
Access to infrastructure	Franchise protection costs

as well as specific knowledge concerning the individual countries in which it operates.

An MNE can either export goods directly to foreign customers or buyers or through export intermediaries. *Export intermediaries* are third parties that specialize in facilitating imports and exports. These intermediaries may offer limited services, such as handling only transportation, documentation, and customs claims, or they may perform more extensive services, including taking ownership of foreign-bound goods and assuming total responsibility for marketing and financing exports. Typical export intermediaries are export management companies. An *export management company* (EMC) is an intermediary that acts as its client's export department. Small firms may use an EMC to handle their foreign shipments, prepare export documents, and deal with customs offices, insurance companies, and commodity inspection agencies.

Managers involved in exporting must be familiar with the various *terms of sale*, which are conditions stipulating the rights or responsibilities and the costs or risks borne by the exporter and the importer. These terms have been harmonized and defined by the International Chamber of Commerce as standard practices, and, thus, are widely used in export transactions. Major terms include:

- FOB (free on board): a term of sale in which the seller covers all costs and risks up to the point whereby the goods are delivered on board the ship in a designated export port, and the buyer bears all costs and risks from that point on.
- FAS (free alongside ship): a term of sale in which the seller covers all costs and risks up to the side of the ship in a designated export port. The buyer bears all costs and risks thereafter.
- CIF (cost, insurance, and freight): a term of sale in which the seller covers cost of the goods, insurance, and all transportation and miscellaneous charges to the named foreign port in the country of final destination.
- C&F (cost and freight): similar to CIF, except that the buyer purchases and bears the insurance costs.

Export managers should also be familiar with key documentation in exporting. A letter of credit (L/C) is a contract between an importer and a bank that transfers liability for paying the exporter from the importer to the importer's bank. A bill of lading (B/L) is the document issued by a shipping company or its agent as evidence of a contract for shipping the merchandise and as a claim to ownership of the goods.

International outsourcing

Outsourcing has been used extensively by MNEs seeking low labor costs in a host country. Generally, outsourcing is the process in which a foreign company provides a local manufacturer with raw materials, semi-finished products, sophisticated components, or technology for producing final goods that will be bought back by the foreign company.

Many MNEs producing technologically advanced products reduce their manufacturing function by using the *original equipment manufacturing (OEM)* approach.

OEM is one specific form of international outsourcing, in which a foreign firm (i.e., original equipment manufacturer) supplies a local company with the technology and sophisticated components so that the latter can manufacture goods that the foreign firm will market under its own brand in international markets.

Countertrade

Countertrade is a form of trade in which a seller and a buyer from different countries exchange merchandise with little or no cash changing hands. Because of the nature of this trade, it is also viewed as a form of flexible financing or payment in international trade. Countertrade, which accounts for approximately 20 percent of world trade, has evolved into a diverse set of activities that can be categorized as four distinct types of trading arrangements: barter, counter purchase, offset, and buyback (or compensation)

Barter is the direct and simultaneous exchange of goods between two parties without a cash transaction. Barter trade occurs between individuals, between governments, between firms, or between a government and a firm, all from two different countries.

A *counter purchase* is a reciprocal buying agreement whereby one firm sells its products to another at one point in time and is compensated in the form of the other's products at some future time. Counter purchase is more flexible than barter in facilitating many transactions because the volume of trade does not have to be equal: that is, the dollar amount of goods exported need not be equal to the dollar amount of goods taken back.

An *offset trade* arrangement is an agreement whereby one party agrees to purchase goods and services with a specified percentage of its proceeds from an original sale. Unlike counter purchase, whereby exchanged products are normally unrelated, products taken back in an offset trade are often the outputs processed by this party in the original contract.

A *buyback* arrangement occurs when a firm provides a local company with inputs for manufacturing products to be sold in international markets, and agrees to take a certain percentage of the output produced by the local firm as partial payment.

Transfer-related entry modes

Transfer-related entry modes are those associated with transfer of ownership or utilization of specified property, such as technology or assets, from one party to the other in exchange for royalty fees. These modes differ from trade-related entry modes in that the user in a transfer-related mode assumes certain rights of transacted property, like the use of technology, from the owner.

Transfer-related entry modes include the following: international leasing, international licensing, international franchising and build–operate–transfer (BOT).

International leasing

International leasing is an entry mode in which the foreign firm (lessor) leases out its new or used machines or equipment to the local company (often in a developing country). International leasing arises largely because a developing country's manufacturers do not have the financial capability or lack the foreign currency to pay for the equipment.

International licensing

International licensing is an entry mode in which a foreign licensor grants specified intangible property rights to the local licensee for a specified period of time in exchange for royalties paid by lump-sum payment, or downpayment plus periodic payments. Property rights may include patents, trademarks, technology, managerial skills, and so on. They allow the licensee to produce and market a product similar to the one the licensor has already been producing in its home country without requiring the licensor to actually create a new operation abroad.

International franchising

International franchising is an entry mode in which the foreign franchisor grants specified intangible property rights (e.g., trademark or brand name) to the local franchisee, which must adhere to strict rules as to how it does business.

Compared to licensing, franchising involves longer commitments, offers greater control over overseas operations to the franchisor, and includes a more intensive and detailed package of rights and resources. Production equipment, managerial systems, point-of-sale equipment and systems, operating procedures, access to advertising and promotional materials, and loans and financing may all be part of a franchise. Needless to say, the economic benefits to the franchisee should be considered and negotiated carefully as the terms of the franchising may limit these benefits.

The main advantages of international franchising to the franchisor include little political risk, low costs, and fast and easy avenues for leveraging assets such as a trademark or brand name.

Build–operate–transfer

Build–operate–transfer is an arrangement whereby a foreign investor assumes responsibility for the design and construction of an entire operation, and, upon completion of the project, turns the project over to the purchaser and hands over management to local personnel whom it has trained. In return for completing the project, the investor receives periodic payments that are normally guaranteed. BOT is especially useful for very large-scale, expensive, long-term infrastructure projects such as power-generation, or water-desalination facilities, airports, dams, highways, and chemical plants. Managing such complex projects requires special expertise and most of these projects are administered by large construction firms, such as Bechtel (USA), Veolia (France), Hyundai (Korea), or Friedrich Krupp (Germany).

The BOT approach requires complex, government-backed or international consortium support for financing and equity arrangements. MNEs may set up BOT project firms by means of either equity or cooperative joint ventures with local partners.

FDI-related entry modes

FDI-related entry modes involve ownership of property, assets, projects, and businesses invested in a host country. This commitment is more significant than the one required by the international trade-related or the transfer-related entry modes. MNEs undertaking FDI have complete control of the overseas operations and the economic activities. FDI-related entry modes are more sophisticated than trade-related modes, demand more management commitment, involve higher risk, and require longer-term contribution than both trade- and transfer-related choices. FDI-related modes reflect the firm's long-term strategic goals of an international supply chain. FDI-related entry modes include branch office, cooperative joint venture, equity joint venture, wholly-owned subsidiary, and umbrella holding company.

Branch office

A branch office is a foreign entity in a host country in which it is not incorporated but exists as an extension of the parent company and is legally registered as a branch.

Corporate law in many countries allows foreign companies to open branches that engage in production and operating activities. Unlike representative offices, which by law are prohibited from engaging in direct, profit-making business activities, branch offices are entitled to run businesses within a specified scope or location. Some may even serve as a regional headquarters, overseeing operations in a particular trade region.

Cooperative joint venture

A cooperative joint venture is a collaborative agreement whereby profits and other responsibilities are assigned to each party according to a contract. Each party cooperates as a separate legal entity and bears its own liabilities. Most cooperative joint ventures do not involve constructing and building a new legally and physically independent entity. As such, cooperative joint ventures normally take the form of a legal document, such as a cooperative agreement, whereas equity joint ventures take the form of a new entity.

Equity joint venture

In an equity joint venture, MNEs establish a new entity that is jointly owned and managed by two or more parent firms in different countries. To set up an equity joint venture, each partner contributes cash, facilities, equipment, materials, intellectual property rights, labor, or land-use rights. According to joint venture laws in most countries, a foreign investor's share must exceed a certain percentage ownership of the total equity.

Generally speaking, cooperative joint ventures and equity joint ventures are together termed global strategic alliances (GSAs). The proliferation of such alliances among MNEs from different countries is transforming the global business environment. These alliances are gaining importance worldwide as global competition intensifies for access to markets, products, and technologies. A separate discussion of strategic alliances is provided in Chapter 10.

Example: Disney plans a channel for Russian TV

The Walt Disney Company announced a joint venture to unlock the doors to one of the world's last untapped media megamarkets, Russia.

Disney would introduce a broadcast version of the Disney Channel in Russia, a market the company has identified as part of its growth strategy and one that Western entertainment companies have been trying to enter for a decade with little success.

The initiation of the 24-hour branded channel will immediately give Disney a bigger entertainment foothold in Russia than any of its rivals. The closest is Viacom, which licenses certain MTV content to a broadcast channel owned by a Russian media company. Other channels, like VH1, appear on cable and satellite, but those delivery routes reach only about 5 percent of the country.

Disney plans to introduce its channel by working with Media-One Holdings Limited, a Russian broadcaster that operates 30 television stations that reach 75 percent of the country and the bulk of its population. Disney and Media-One will operate the channel via a newly created joint venture company. In return for a 49 percent stake in the company, Disney will invest cash and provide programming and marketing.

The channel, which has preliminary support from regulators and has to obtain final approval from the Russian government, will include Disney programming like "Mickey Mouse Clubhouse" and "Hannah Montana," as well as Russian programming.

Disney's TV channel has long been crucial to its global strategy. Typically, the company seeks to introduce the Disney Channel to a new market so it can deliver its brand directly into people's homes. Executives, in turn, use that foothold to foster interest in Disney theme parks and consumer products. The Disney Channel is available in 22 languages across 135 countries.

But Russia has proved difficult for Disney to navigate because of bureaucratic hurdles and restrictions on foreign media. Disney programming only gained access on free television in 2007. In particularly, in December 2007, the state broadcaster Channel One agreed to show "The Wonderful World of Disney" once a month, and in April 2008, an independent local broadcaster agreed to show films like "The Incredibles."

Wholly-owned subsidiary

A wholly-owned subsidiary is an entry mode in which the investing firm owns 100 percent of the new entity in a host country. This new entity may be built from scratch by the investing firm – otherwise termed a greenfield investment – or may take the form of an acquisition of a local business – otherwise termed a cross-border acquisition. This mode offers foreign investors increased flexibility and control. It allows international managers to make their own decisions with no local resistance. Wholly-owned subsidiaries also allow foreign investors to set up and protect their own processes and procedures, which leads to more careful strategic and operational control. During the 1980s, Japan's KAO Corporation established a number of wholly-owned manufacturing and marketing subsidiaries overseas. For example, it established a wholly-owned subsidiary in Arnprior, Canada, for the following reasons:

- KAO wanted to establish its presence in North America, specifically in the high-technology industry.

- A wholly-owned subsidiary gave KAO the tight control over its operations which was necessary for global integration and contributed to a greater global value.
- A wholly-owned subsidiary reduced the risk of losing control of KAO's technological expertise. It should be noted that KAO has used its proprietary expertise in surface technology in order to enter the computer memory devices market in North America and Europe.

Wholly-owned subsidiaries have traditionally been viewed by many host country governments, particularly those of developing economies, as offering little in the way of technology transfer or other benefits to local economies. Recently, this entry mode has become more attractive to them. It should be noted that when domestic credit is tight, this entry mode provides host countries with a means of attracting foreign investment and infusing capital that contributes to the growth of the local economy.

International holding company

An international holding company is an investment company that unites the firm's existing international investments such as branch offices, joint ventures, and wholly-owned subsidiaries under one holding company so as to combine sales, procurement, manufacturing, training, and maintenance within the host country. Many foreign companies are now seeking better integration of these functions for a broad range of products and services within a single but important country. Such coordination becomes necessary as each production division sets up its own foreign subunits separated from other divisions' foreign subunits in the same host country.

An MNE may consider establishing an international holding enterprise to achieve the following objectives: (1) getting a commitment of the executives to the holding company unit; (2) investment in subsidiary projects; (3) facilitation of cash flow or foreign exchange balance for all local activities; (4) centralized purchase of production materials for subsidiary projects; (5) provision of product maintenance services and technical support; (6) training of subsidiary project personnel and end users of products; (7) coordination and consolidation of project management; and (8) marketing of subsidiary products.

Greenfield investment, acquisitions, and mergers

As noted earlier, an MNE can set up a wholly-owned subsidiary, through either greenfield investment or international acquisition. A greenfield investment is an initial establishment of fully-owned new facilities and operations undertaken by the company alone. An international acquisition is an international transaction in which an MNE acquires an established local firm and makes the acquired local firm a subsidiary business within the MNE. International acquisition of a local firm or another foreign company with local ventures is the quickest way to expand the MNE's investment in the target country. An acquisition is particularly useful for entering economic sectors formerly held by state-owned enterprises.

Moreover, cash flow may be generated in a shorter time than in the case of greenfield investment, since the acquired firm, by definition, does not have to be built from scratch.

An international merger is the same as an equity joint venture; however, it is an international transaction in which two firms from different countries agree to integrate their operations on a relatively co-equal basis because they have resources and capabilities that together may create a stronger competitive advantage in the global marketplace. Like joint ventures, international mergers can generate many positive outcomes, such as:

- learning and resource sharing by the partners, improving economies of scale or scope
- reducing costs by eliminating expenditures for redundant resources
- capturing greater market share by providing more comprehensive offerings increasing revenue by cross-selling products to cross-border customers.

The major difference between equity joint ventures and mergers is that the former involves formation of a third entity (equity joint venture) which may last for a limited time, whereas the latter does not form any third party or specify any duration.

International mergers and acquisitions inevitably confront many challenges, especially during early operations. About 80 percent of mergers and acquisitions do not fully achieve their revenue and profit potential. The fundamental challenges are often rooted in cross-national differences in culture, managerial styles, and corporate values. To overcome these challenges, international managers should develop a new corporate mission, vision, and strategic objectives. It is also imperative to insist on an appropriate post-acquisition and merger integration, including the alignment of operations, communications, and human resources of the merged entities.

In many circumstances, an international entry is not a one-step action but rather an evolutionary process involving a series of incremental decisions during which firms increase their commitment to the target market by shifting from low- to high-commitment entry modes. Although some firms may bypass some steps or speed up the entire process, many MNEs follow the learning curve of accumulating competence, knowledge, and confidence in the international entry process. They move sequentially from no international involvement to export, to overseas assembly or sales subsidiaries, to overseas production via contractual or equity joint ventures, and, ultimately, to overseas penetration and complete integration through wholly-owned subsidiaries or international holding companies.

Large and experienced MNEs may combine several entry modes at the same time. For instance, selecting between an equity joint venture and a wholly-owned subsidiary is not necessarily an either–or decision. Sometimes a local partner has a strong distribution network or operates in a restricted sector that is attractive to a foreign investor. In such situations, foreign companies can, for instance, surround their wholly-owned subsidiary production operation with equity joint ventures that supply resources, or market and sell their products in the host market.

COUNTRY FOCUS

ROMANIA

Regional Rank (EFI 2009): 29

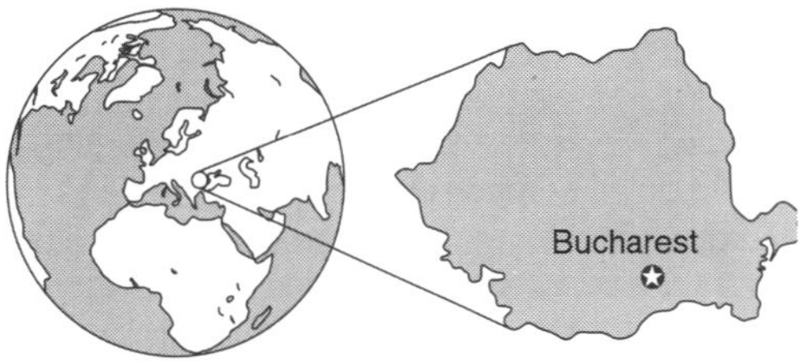

World Rank (EFI 2009): 65

Quick facts

Population: 21.6 million

GDP (PPP): $225.2 billion 7.9 percent growth in 2006; 6.1 percent 5-year compound annual growth; $10,432 per capita

Unemployment: 4.1 percent

Inflation (CPI): 4.8 percent

FDI inflow: $11.4 billion

2006 data unless otherwise noted

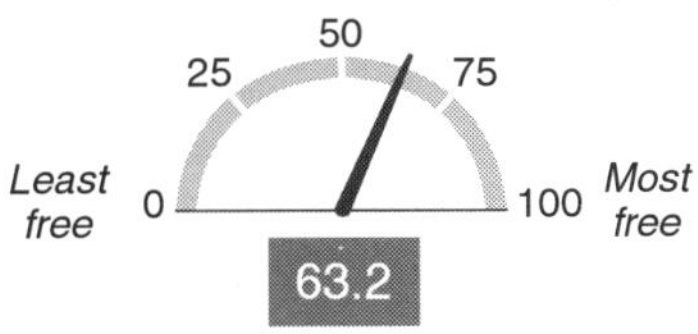

Romania's economic freedom score is 63.2, making its economy the 65th freest in the 2009 Index. Romania is ranked 29th out of 43 countries in the Europe region, and its overall score is higher than the world average.

Romania has steadily restructured its economy, improving economic freedom in many areas and achieving an average economic growth rate of approximately 6 percent over the past five years. The overall regulatory framework is streamlined and efficient. The top income and corporate tax rates are a flat 16 percent. The financial system is consistent with international standards and has been enhanced by a recent reform and privatization program that has privatized 39 of Romania's 41 banks.

There are several remaining institutional challenges to economic freedom. Labor freedom, property rights, and freedom from corruption lag behind other countries in the region. Although Romania has made some progress in the fight against corruption, the judiciary remains vulnerable to corruption and inefficiency.

Background

Romania is a fast-growing member of the European Union (EU) and North Atlantic Treaty Organization (NATO), and the government has been implementing economic reforms that are consistent with the Maastricht criteria. The minority government of the National Liberal Party and the Hungarian Democratic Union in Romania, led by Prime Minister Călin Popescu Tariceanu, remains dependent on the tacit support of the former communist Social Democratic Party. GDP (gross domestic product) growth rose during the first quarter of 2008 as a result of government spending, foreign investment and generous expansion of credit. Growth should level off following the 2009 parliamentary elections if, as expected,

(Continued)

government spending is reduced. Macroeconomic improvements have spurred the growth of the middle class and have helped to reduce poverty.

Business freedom – 74.9

The overall freedom to conduct a business is relatively well protected under Romania's regulatory environment. Starting a business takes only 10 days, compared to the world average of 38 days. Obtaining a business license takes about the same as the world average of 18 procedures and 225 days. Closing a business can be a lengthy process.

Trade freedom – 85.8

Romania's trade policy is the same as that of other members of the EU. The common EU-weighted average tariff rate was 2.1 percent in 2005. Nontariff barriers reflected in EU policy include agricultural and manufacturing subsidies, import restrictions for some goods and services, market access restrictions in some services sectors, nontransparent and restrictive regulations and standards, and inconsistent customs administration across EU members. Restrictions on biotechnology and sanitary and phytosanitary regulations exceed EU policy, and corruption and the enforcement of intellectual property rights are problematic. Ten points were deducted from Romania's trade freedom score to account for nontariff barriers.

Fiscal freedom – 87

Romania has low flat tax rates. Both the income tax rate and the corporate tax rate are a flat 16 percent. Other taxes include a value-added tax (VAT), a land tax, and a vehicle tax. In the most recent year, overall tax revenue as a percentage of GDP was 28.1 percent.

Government size – 70

Total government expenditures, including consumption and transfer payments, are moderate. In the most recent year, government spending equaled 31.6 percent of GDP. Most small and medium-size public enterprises have been privatized, but privatization of large-scale companies has been sluggish.

Monetary freedom – 75

Inflation is moderate, averaging 5.6 percent between 2005 and 2007. As a participant in the EU's Common Agricultural Policy, the government subsidizes agricultural production, distorting the prices of agricultural products. It also influences prices through regulation, subsidies, and state-owned enterprises and utilities. Ten points were deducted from Romania's monetary freedom score to account for policies that distort domestic prices.

Investment freedom – 60

Foreign and domestic investments receive equal treatment under the law. Deterrents to investment include judicial and legislative unpredictability and cumbersome and nontransparent bureaucratic procedures. Residents and nonresidents may hold foreign exchange accounts, subject to some restrictions. All payments and transfers must be documented. Most restrictions on capital transactions have been removed, but derivative-based transactions still require approval. EU citizens may own land in Romania, subject to reciprocity in their home countries, and foreign investors are allowed to acquire nonagricultural land for business use.

Financial freedom – 50

Romania's financial supervision and regulation are largely consistent with international standards. Significant reforms since the late 1990s include the privatization of many state-owned banks. Of Romania's 41 banks, 39 are in private hands, and foreign-owned banks account for close to 90 percent of banking-sector assets. The five largest commercial banks control 60 percent of total assets, and state-owned banks hold less than 6 percent, down from 75 percent in 1998. Privatization stalled in December 2006 when the state halted the sale of its majority stake in the State Savings Bank. There is no current timetable for reviving stalled privatization. Capital markets are underdeveloped compared to those of other Eastern European countries, and most trading involves government debt.

Property rights – 35

Investors have expressed concern about unpredictable changes in legislation and weak enforcement of contracts and laws. The judicial system suffers from corruption, inefficiency, and excessive workloads. Romania is a signatory to international conventions concerning intellectual property rights and has legislation protecting patents, trademarks, and copyrights, but enforcement is very weak.

Freedom from corruption – 37

Corruption is perceived as widespread. Romania ranks 69th out of 179 countries in Transparency International's Corruption Perceptions Index for 2007. The government's Anticorruption Strategy, which includes enforcement of laws and procedures to combat money laundering and tax evasion, has produced an improvement in Romania's ranking. Accession to the EU has also spurred gains against corruption.

Labor freedom – 57.1

Romania's rigid labor regulations hinder employment and productivity growth. The non-salary cost of employing a worker is very high, and the difficulty of firing a worker creates a disincentive for additional hiring. Regulations related to the number of work hours are not flexible.

Source: Adapted from Terry Miller and Kim R. Holmes, *2009 Index of Economic Freedom* (Washington, DC: The Heritage Foundation and Dow Jones & Company, Inc., 2009), at www.heritage.org/index.

Closing Case

Going to the Far East: Chinese Business Boost for UK Firm

We have another product line that has gained a China mining approval MA certificate and we regard this as a key achievement. This product has potential of £3–£5m per annum, this is serious money.

Throughout this process UK Trade & Investment has been paramount. They have helped with funding and given me advice and help with ideas at every step of the way, from one to one chats to joining the Passport to Export program. As the UK business has had to finance the China operation, it's been quite tough to get to this stage, as you really have to be patient to do business in China, particularly when you don't understand the

(Continued)

> Chinese language. Although our agent speaks reasonable English, we've had to sit through three-hour meetings not even understanding a word. But Chinese companies like dealing with Western companies, they know the products are good and there is also a certain credibility associated with it. The key to doing all of the business so far is having a good Chinese agent, without their assistance we would never have broken in to this market.

The executive of FA-ST Filtration Analysis continues

> I would encourage other companies across the East Midlands to go for it if they get the opportunity. Obviously winning this kind of business is great and we know there are lots more opportunities on the horizon, but the experiences as a whole have been incredible, from meeting so many welcoming and smiling people to seeing everyday life across China, visiting the mining town of Daliuta to learning about the culture and learning the language.

Mike Warriner, International Trade Advisor for UK Trade & Investment, said

> It's vital to remember though that although Andy's email was genuine and his business success has been immense it's important that companies check any emails they receive thoroughly as some companies in China are sending out multiple offers for large contracts as part of an elaborate scam. So far, we have been suspicious of business offers from companies in ainan, Guangdong, Guangxi and Yunnan Provinces.
>
> When entering a new overseas market UK companies should always ensure they use the appropriate support networks available such as UK Trade and Investment and the China–Britain Business Council (CBBC).

Questions

1 What type of entry ownership approach would you recommend for FA-ST Filtration Analysis services

2 ow could the East Midlands company use the four Ps of marketing to help enter China

If production must be globally coordinated, will FA-ST have a ma or problem Why or why not

Source Adapted from *Business of Language*, the free monthly magazine from UK Trade and etwork East Midlands. www.ukti.gov.uk/eastmidlands

SUMMARY

Strategy formulation is based on internal and international and external environment assessments. M Es use these assessments to pinpoint strengths and weaknesses, identify threats, and exploit opportunities.

International entry strategies are concerned with where, when, and how firms should enter in their international expansion. Location selection concerns not only country selection but also pro ect location within this country. Managers need to consider various locational characteristics such as cost/tax factors, demand factors, strategic factors (e.g., investment infrastructure, manufacturing concentration, industrial linkage, workforce productivity, and inbound and outbound logistics), regulatory and economic factors, and sociopolitical factors.

The decision on **location selection** is also contingent on the firm's strategic ob ectives of expansion, required global integration between this location, and the rest of the M E network, and the pro ect's market orientation (local market vs export market). The firm may also take into account its familiarity with the location, geographical market coverage, competitors' location pattern, and trading region characteristics such as member of the EU or AFTA.

Each **timing option**, whether early mover or late entrant, has distinct advantages and disadvantages. Entry occurs when the firm anticipates gains to exceed risks or costs. Early movers benefit from greater market power, such as barriers for followers, technological leadership, customer loyalty, and product positioning greater preemptive opportunities in marketing, resources, and branding and greater strategic options, such as site selection, infrastructure access, and low competition.

Early-mover disadvantages are late-mover advantages. Early movers tend to face greater uncertainty derived from variable regulations and rules and unstable industrial and market structures greater operational risks as a result of less-developed infrastructure, and a lack of supporting services and resources and greater operational costs arising from adaptation, training, learning, and anti-imitation.

Firms can enter a target country through several entry modes, ranging from international trade-related modes (export, subcontracting, and countertrade), to transfer-related modes (leasing, licensing, franchising, and BOT), to FDI-related modes (branch, cooperative oint venture, equity oint venture, wholly-owned subsidiary, and international holding company). Levels of risk, control, and commitment vary significantly across categories and across entry modes within each category.

Most international companies, whether large or small, still actively participate in import and export businesses. Export intermediaries specialize in import and export management. Managers should familiarize themselves with key concepts such as terms of price (e.g., FAS, CIF, C&F, and FOB) and key documents (e.g., L/C and B/L) involved in import and export processes.

Original equipment manufacturing (OEM) is an increasingly popular mode used by many large M Es looking for cheaper production overseas. Countertrade methods such as barter, counter purchase, offset, and buyback offer more flexibility than conventional import and export, since the former do not involve hard currency cash flows. Transfer-related entry modes are widely used in technological, intellectual, or industrial property right transfers or transactions.

Joint venture and wholly-owned subsidiary are the two major entry modes embedded in FDI. The oint venture enables the firm to share risks and costs with others, acquire new knowledge from others, bypass entry barriers in a host country, and capitalize on the partner's reputation, experience, networks, and marketing skills. The wholly-owned entry mode provides the firm with stronger organizational control and knowledge protection.

Bibliography

Agarwal, S., Ramaswami, S. N. (1992). Choice of foreign market entry mode: impact of ownership, location, and internalization factors. *Journal of International Business Studies*, 23 (1), 1–27.

Anderson, E., Gatignon, H. (Fall, 1986). Modes of foreign entry: a transaction cost analysis and propositions. *Journal of International Business Studies*, 17, 1–26.

Buckley, P. J., Casson, M. (1981). The optimal timing of a foreign direct investment. *Economic Journal*, 91, 75–87.

Chang, S. J. (1995). International expansion strategy of Japanese firms: capability building through sequential entry. *Academy of Management Journal*, 38, 383–407.

Culem, C. G. (1988). The locational determinants of foreign direct investments among industrial countries. *European Economic Review*, 32 (4), 885–94.

Davidson, W. H. (1980). The location of foreign direct investment activity: country characteristics and experience effects. *Journal of International Business Studies*, 11 (2), 9–22.

Dunning, J. H. (1993). *Multinational Enterprises and the Global Economy*. Reading, MA: Addison-Wesley.

Finger, S. (2008). Regional headquarters of multinational corporations: a structural modeling of regional strategy and determinants of location. Unpublished PhD dissertation, Ben Gurion University.

Finger, S., Menipaz, E. (2008). Regional headquarters of multinational corporations: Literature review and taxonomy, Menipaz, E., Ben Gal, I., *Logistics in a Flat World: Strategy, Operations and Management*, Proceedings of ICIL'08, Tel Aviv, Israel, March 10–15.

Friedman, J., Gerlowski, D. A., Silberman, J. (1992). What attracts foreign multinational corporations: evidence from branch plant location in the United States. *Journal of Regional Science*, 32 (4), 403–18.

Gomes-Casseres, B. (1990). Firm ownership presences and host government restrictions: an integrated approach. *Journal of International Business Studies,* 21 (1), 1–21.

Hennart, J. F., Park, Y. R. (1994). Location, governance, and strategic determinants of Japanese manufacturing investment in the United States. *Strategic Management Journal,* 15 (6), 419–36.

Hill, C. W. L., Hwang, P., Kim, W. C. (1990). An eclectic theory of the choice of international entry mode. *Strategic Management Journal,* 11, 117–28.

Johanson, J., Vahlne, J. E. (1977). The internationalization process of the firm: a model of knowledge development and increasing foreign market commitments. *Journal of International Business Studies,* 8 (1), 23–32.

Lambkin, M. (1988). Order of entry and performance in new markets. *Strategic Management Journal,* 9, 127–40.

Lieberman, M. B., Montgomery, D. B. (1988). First-mover advantages. *Strategic Management Journal,* 9, 41–58.

Luo, Y. (1988). Timing of investment and international expansion performance in China. *Journal of International Business Studies,* 29, 391–408.

Mascarenhas, B. (1992). Order of entry and performance in international markets. *Strategic Management Journal,* 13, 499–510.

Mitchell, W. (1989). Whether and when? Probability and timing of incumbents' entry into emerging industrial sub fields. *Administrative Science Quarterly*, 34, 208–30.

Porter, M. E. (1986). *Competition in Global Industries*. Boston, MA: Harvard Business School Press.

Root, F. R. (1994). *Entry Strategies for International Markets*. Washington, DC: Lexington Books.

West, D. (2001). Counter trade. *Business Credit,* 103 (4), 64–7.

10

Global Alliances: Joint Ventures and Merges and Acquisitions

Learning Objectives

Following this chapter, the reader should be able to:

1. Define the key terms of global strategic alliances (GSAs), joint ventures (JVs), and mergers and acquisitions (M&As)
2. Design GSAs, JVs, and M&As
3. Manage GSAs, JVs, and M&As
4. Identify the main forms of strategic arrangements of key industries

Global Alliances: Joint Ventures and Mergers and Acquisitions

Since the beginning of the century, activity in global alliances, joint ventures (JVs), and mergers and acquisitions (M&A) has been booming, partly despite and partly because of the global economic crisis of 2008–10. Globally, the number and size of deals and business arrangements of this nature is heading toward record levels. Of particular importance are cross-border deals and strategic business arrangements. As pointed out in Chapter 9, multinational enterprises (MNEs) take advantage of available financing to pursue their expansion strategies or, in light of the global economic crisis, use global alliances, JVs and M&As as the only way to rescue their business from complete demise, government takeover, or loss of ownership. However, while these strategic business arrangements become more prevalent, it should be noted that many MNEs fail to fully exploit the potential value from these arrangements. While this reality is not a new one, it is all the more striking in today's environment, where some deals require significant capital investment. In today's global environment, corporate strategy is focused firmly on M&A as a tool to foster future growth and create sustainable value worldwide. As a result, companies are aggressiveldddy seeking and buying compatible and synergistic businesses to enhance core strengths, and shelling noncore operations.

A survey conducted by Accenture and the Economist Intelligence Unit focused on companies based in certain wealthy Western nations in Europe and Scandinavia, along with US companies. The survey responses offer unique insights into recent and potential M&A activity, especially cross-border M&A, which has been a growing focus for MNEs in Western economies.

The following are the key observations from hundreds of senior executives who responded from companies headquartered in the USA, UK, Germany, Sweden, Norway, and Finland:

1. Most recent acquisitions have been cross-border (58 percent). Domestic acquisitions are easier to execute and present less risk, but globalization is a key driver. The trend toward international M&A is likely to continue.
2. Executives worldwide know that cross-border deals are essential. Fifty-five percent of companies are planning to acquire overseas interests in years to come to guarantee the profitability of the business, and thereby secure strategic sustainability.

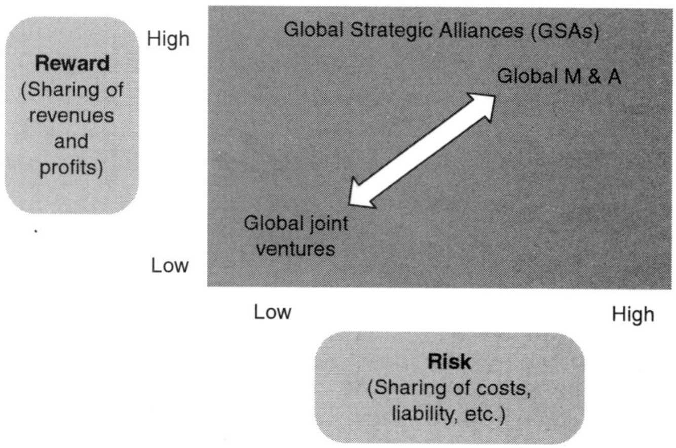

FIGURE 10.1 Risk/reward trade offs of an MNE's global expansion methods

Global strategic alliances (GSAs) entail both M&As and JVs. M&As were the more common method for international expansion historically; however, in recent years many other forms of strategic alliances have been used. Figure 10.1 illustrates the risk/reward tradeoffs of various forms of GSAs and their correlation to ownership or control of the foreign entity by the MNE.

Table 10.1 lists the key factors for international joint ventures and international M&As. It should be noted that the motives for international M&A include a significant component of technology and resource transfer to the foreign entity.

TABLE 10.1 Key Factors of GSAs

Key factors for international JVs	*Key factors for international M&As*
Sharing costs/risks	Synergy
Acquire knowledge	Technology transfer
Economies of scope	Economies of scale
Prevent/reduce competition	Increase market share
Increase local acceptance	–
Reduce entry barriers	Cross selling
Reduce taxation	Reduce taxation
Increase geographic diversification	Increase geographic diversification
–	Resource transfer
–	Vertical integration
–	Management hubris
–	Empire building
Acquiring local executive talent	Acquiring local executive talent

Opening Case

Global Strategic Alliance in the Automotive Industry: Chrysler–Fiat

The 2008–10 global economic crisis has caused ma or M Es to consider various ways to weather the difficult times ahead. During the month of anuary 2009, Chrysler announced that it, along with its ma ority owner Cerberus Capital Management, had signed a deal with Italy's automotive giant Fiat to establish what it termed a global strategic alliance.

Chrysler said the alliance is a key element of its viability plan that must be submitted to the American Congress by March 2009. Chrysler announced that the alliance would allow Fiat and Chrysler to take advantage of each other's distribution networks and optimize fully their respective manufacturing footprint and global supplier base.

Under the terms of the deal, Fiat takes an initial 5 percent equity interest in Chrysler, for which it will not pay cash or commit to future funding of Chrysler. Chrysler said Fiat would provide the automaker with access to competitive, fuel-efficient vehicle platforms, powertrain, and components to be produced at Chrysler's manufacturing sites. Fiat would also provide distribution capabilities in key growth markets, as well as substantial cost savings opportunities.

The deal includes

- product and platform sharing, including city and compact segment vehicles, to expand Chrysler's current product portfolio
- technology sharing, including fuel-efficient and environmentally friendly powertrain technologies, detailed by *Edmunds' Green Car Advisor*
- access to additional markets, including distribution for Chrysler vehicles in markets outside of orth America.

The Chrysler–Fiat alliance also gives Fiat access to the American market, from which it has long been absent. Fiat had plans to begin selling its Alfa- omeo line in the USA, but these were postponed or derailed by the 2008–10 economic crisis.

In the companies' statement, Fiat CEO Sergio Marchionne, who is credited with Fiat's recent financial turnaround and who has made it quite public that he wanted a strategic alliance, said

> This initiative represents a key milestone in the rapidly changing landscape of the automotive sector and confirms Fiat and Chrysler commitment and determination to continue to play a significant role in this global process.

e added

> The agreement will offer both companies opportunities to gain access to most relevant automotive markets with innovative and environmentally friendly product offering, a field in which Fiat is a recognized world leader while benefiting from additional cost synergies. The deal follows a number of targeted alliances and partnerships signed by the Fiat Group with leading carmakers and automotive suppliers over the last five years aimed at supporting the growth and volume aspirations of the partners involved.

Chrysler Chairman and CEO Bob ardelli, who also has been very public about the automaker seeking strategic alliances, said

> A Chrysler/Fiat partnership is a great fit as it creates the potential for a powerful, new global competitor, offering Chrysler a number of strategic benefits, including access to products that compliment our current portfolio a distribution network outside orth America and cost savings in design,

engineering, manufacturing, purchasing and sales and marketing.

e said the deal will enable Chrysler to offer a broader competitive lineup of vehicles for our dealers and customers that meet emissions and fuel-efficiency standards, while adhering to conditions of the Government Loan. e added

The partnership would also provide a return on investment for the American taxpayer by securing the long-term viability of Chrysler brands in the marketplace, sustaining future product and technology development for our country and building renewed consumer confidence, while preserving American obs.

United Auto Workers (UAW) President on Gettelfinger, who is negotiating new contract terms with Chrysler and General Motors as part of the federal loan agreement, praised the deal. "This is great news for the UAW Chrysler team and we look forward to supporting and working with them to ensure Chrysler's long-term viability," he said.

Source Adapted from Krebs, M. (2009). *Edmund's Car Advisor*, anuary 20.

The nature of the global strategic alliance between Chrysler and Fiat offers a technology exchange opportunity between the parties and also an access to the markets in Europe and North America. The fact that there is a capital investment by Fiat in Chrysler makes what appears on the surface to be a joint venture, to in fact take on characteristics of an M&A, by giving Fiat a higher degree of control in return for the added risk of their investment into Chrysler.

Global strategic alliances are exercised by MNEs in almost all traditional and emerging industries. Nestlé, the global leader for food and kindred products, is using GSAs (in particular M&As) to gain entry into foreign markets. For example, having decided to enter the Israeli market, Nestle chose to acquire a majority stake in Osem, the leading national food manufacturer and distributor in Israel. In this way, Nestlé could easily introduce their products to the local market, as well as their operational and financial management systems in return for their capital investment.

Defining Global Strategic Alliances

Types of GSAs

As the opening case illustrates, global strategic alliances have become a common venue for MNEs to expand globally and improve their global competitive advantage. Through strategic alliances Chrysler gains more than it would by itself, especially in light of the global economic crisis and the fact that the US government is committed to help save the US automotive industry. *Global strategic alliances* are cross-border ventures between two or more corporations from different countries attempting to pursue mutual interests through sharing of resources and capabilities. There are two types of GSAs: M&As, which represent an equity joint ventures, and JVs, which are based on some kind of contractual agreement.

It is estimated that the failure rate in terms of realizing the full potential of the strategic arrangements is 30–60 percent.

M&A is a legally defined entity created by two or more MNEs that together invest financial as well as other resources to pursue certain strategic common goals. In a global context, these MNEs are from different countries. To set up an M&A deal, each partner contributes capital, facilities, equipment, materials, intellectual property rights, labor, or land-use rights. An M&A can be structured on a 50–50 ownership or a majority–minority basis.

A *JV* is an agreement whereby profits and responsibilities are assigned to each party according to a contractual agreement. Although the two MNEs entering into a contractual partnership have the option of forming a limited liability entity with legal status, most cooperative ventures involve focused joint activities without the creation of a new corporate entity. JV partners have the freedom to structure assets, organize production processes, redefine distribution channels, and share management and control responsibilities. These arrangements are attractive for a foreign investor interested in property development, resource exploration, and other projects in which the foreign entity can be developed quickly to take advantage of short-term business opportunities, and then dissolved when its tasks are completed.

JVs have several forms, including joint exploration (such as offshore oil exploration consortia), research and development (R&D) entities (such as IBM global services, an R&D consortium with academic institutions in various countries), and co-production (such as is customary in the entertainment industry), all of which are typical forms of contractual partnerships. Other forms of JVs include joint marketing, long-term supply agreements, and joint management.

Of particular interest for JVs are *co-marketing arrangements* that provide access to a new customer base for all parties. As an illustration, consider the Star Alliance, a group of national airline carriers together under a common marketing agreement that has expanded the global offering for each airline to include services from all the others. For example, Air Canada has a strong distribution infrastructure in North America but is a minor player in the USA and Asia. United Airlines, in contrast, is strong in the USA and Asia and absent from the Europe, where Lufthansa is a major player and an allied member.

Another common JV is a *long-term supply agreement*, where the manufacturing buyer provides the supplier with updated free information on products, markets and technologies, which in turn helps ensure the input quality and supply sustainability. For example, Ceragon Networks Ltd (NASDAQ and TASE: CRNT), announced a long-term equipment supply agreement with Tata Teleservices Limited, a leading global communications provider and one of India's leading mobile operators. Ceragon provides Tata with its leading-edge FibeAir solution, along with installation services. Ceragon's market-leading solutions enable Tata to deliver both Ethernet and TOM traffic over their high-capacity wireless networks. Taking advantage of Ceragon's pay-as-you-go concept, Tata will be able upgrade its wireless backhaul capacity in the future and reach up to 500 Mbps per radio channel. Tata Teleservices has over 29 million customers in more than 6,600 towns across India and has a pan-India presence spread across 19 of the nation's 22 cellular service circles. Having pioneered the COMA 2000 1x technology in India, Tata Teleservices has established a robust, 3G ready telecom infrastructure that ensures the delivery of high-end quality services. The company also holds a leading position in India's fixed-wireless telephony market. Ceragon's microwave solution was selected to provide high-capacity backhaul for the COMA network. Once the solution has been deployed, Tata Teleservices was able to offer a wide range of data and multimedia applications on top of its voice centric package. Furthermore, as Tata advances towards Next Generation Network and 3G services, wireless solutions from Ceragon provide flexible and scalable answers for cost-effective, future-proof high-capacity backhaul connectivity. The long-term agreement with Ceragon enables Tata to roll out robust networks, and ensure customers the best-quality service.

At times, JVs are focused on a *co-management arrangement*, which is an alliance in which cross-national partners collaborate in training, production management, information systems development, and value-chain integration. Co-management arrangements occur because MNEs often realize that they lack the managerial skills necessary to run foreign operations. In addition, local corporations often find that they can benefit from foreign counterparts' international experience and organizational skills.

Benefits and challenges in building GSAs

Although GSAs may take different forms, they are created for similar reasons. MNEs team together seeking some synergy. *Strategic synergy* means additional economic benefits (financial, operational, or technological) arising from cooperation between two parties that provide each other with complementary resources or capabilities. In practice, these synergies and related economic benefits can be the result of pooling resources, risk reduction, knowledge acquisition, economies of scale and rationalization, competition reduction, improved local acceptance, and international market entry. The particular GSA benefits are:

1. A GSA allows an MNE to enter into activities that might be too costly and risky to pursue on its own. For example, if the business environment in a host country is highly uncertain or unfriendly to a foreign MNE, a GSA with a local firm may allow an MNE to share political risks and defuse hostile local reactions.
2. A GSA allows a firm to acquire partner knowledge or resources to build competitive strength. Since R&D expenses in all industries, including emerging industries like biotechnology or nanotechnology, are prohibitively high, access to a partner's technology enables an MNE to avoid rapidly escalating R&D costs.
3. A GSA allows a firm to enhance economies of scale or scope and to improve product offerings. Two international small and medium-sized Enterprises (SMEs) in an industry can form an alliance to achieve economies of scale similar to those that are enjoyed by their large MNE competitors. GSA partners may also cooperate to take advantage of pooled nonfinancial resources.

The joint use of complementary resources, competencies, and skills possessed by different organizations can create synergistic effects that none of the companies is able to achieve if acting alone.

4 A GSA allows an MNE to prevent or reduce competition, potential, or existing, with a major rival. For example, Nestlé SA is a publicly owned company, headquartered in Switzerland, with 406 subsidiaries in 104 countries. Many of these companies are operated in its own name, with exceptions such as the Israeli food company Osem. The joint ventures are intended to reduce competition with major local rivals. By recruiting Osem, the leading and continuously profitable local food processor, as Nestlé's strategic alliance partner, Nestlé has reduced national competition in the food market, for such items as soups, snack foods, and coffee.

5 GSAs can also be used to develop technological standards that help control the competition within an industry. For example, Tata of India, as described earlier, facilitated the adoption of the FibeAir solution as a standard system for 19 out of India's 22 cellular services circles. This innovation may bring Tata to a cellular market in India.

6 A GSA allows an MNE to boost local acceptance as perceived by foreign consumers. A foreign MNE can use a local partner to gain access to the local market, as was indicated by Nestlé Corporation earlier. The Nestlé GSA with Osem assisted Nestlé in understanding the consumer behavior, distribution network, and effective marketing and advertising strategies in Israel. The distinctive marketing and distribution practices in China encourage foreign companies to set up partnerships with Chinese organizations as the preferred means of getting into the Chinese market.

7 A GSA allows a firm to bypass entry barriers into a target foreign country. Many governments, particularly in emerging economies, expect MNEs to conduct foreign direct investment (FDI) in the form of M&As with local companies rather than wholly-owned subsidiaries. To the foreign MNE, an alliance with a local organization, either business or governmental, may be required in order to enter these countries. Entry into India is facilitated by GSA in order to bypass entry barriers. As an example, Teva Pharmaceutical of Israel, the world's largest generic drugs manufacturer invested over $1 billion in India to acquire Indian drug companies and set up greenfield manufacturing facilities. The investment included $250–$300 million for the construction of new manufacturing facilities and the remaining funds for joint ventures and acquisitions in India. Teva Pharmaceuticals has set up an active pharmaceutical ingredient (API) manufacturing facilities on 100 acres of land near Gwalior, Madhya Pradesh. The planned capacity of the manufacturing facility will match the production capacity of Indian generic major corporations, such as Ranbaxy, Cipla, Dr. Reddy's, Sun Pharma, and Wockhardt. Teva has been proposing to get into several joint ventures with drug majors like Aurobindo, Orchid, Cipla, and Matrix. It is also integrating Regent Drugs, now a 100 percent subsidiary of Teva, with its API business (TAPI), which it had acquired from JK Industries in 2003. Regent manufactures

some APIs that Teva requires for its global business and also sources APIs from many Indian companies. In addition, Teva started Teva India, an R&D center in New Delhi. Teva's plans coincide with plans of Japan's largest research-based player, Takeda, to set up its India operations. The company may put its plans in place in 2008. Takeda is following its peers, Daiichi Sankyo and Eisai, and plans to source raw materials from India. Both the generic major Teva and the Japanese research players are drawn to India by cheaper labor and material costs, besides a skilled talent pool. Needless to say, GSA with local partners contributes to Teva's market power, marketing channels, and strong ties with officials in India.

There are significant challenges involved in GSAs. According to a survey by McKinsey & Company and Coopers & Lybrand, about 70 percent of GSAs fall short of expectations. A very common challenge of a GSA formed by MNEs is the complexity involving multiple inter-organizational relationships. Each of these relationships can be extremely difficult to manage on an international basis. GSAs represent an inter-cultural and inter-organizational linkage between two separate MNEs that join forces with different strategic interests and objectives. The difficulties arise from cross-cultural differences and conflicting strategic expectations, which may lead to workforce and management instability as well as poor performance of the GSA alliance.

In almost all GSAs, the following challenges must be carefully managed:

1. Loss of autonomy and control, which may create inter-partner conflicts and alliance instability. Disagreements may involve conflicting long-term objectives, time horizons, operating styles, and expectations of the alliance.
2. The risk of possible leakage of critical technologies, which may be high and often difficult to avoid. Risks associated with limited protection of intellectual rights are particularly high in emerging economies and countries where intellectual property rights systems are not cognizant of the importance of intellectual property protection.
3. Inter-partner differences in strategic goals may lead to complex and convoluted decision-making processes, which may in turn cause strategic inflexibility. The MNE should maintain global integration of all parts of its network for strategic or financial purposes, but because of the inflexibility of the GSA, global optimization may not be possible for functional issues such as outsourcing, capital flows, tax reduction, transfer pricing, and rationalization of production and marketing.
4. Local partners may become global competitors in the future, after developing skills and technology via the GSA. Corporations in emerging economies may be interested to enter a GSA in order to become familiar with proven technologies and eventually strike out on their own.

As the earlier discussion indicates, there are both benefits and drawbacks to GSAs. Thus, before entering into a GSA, MNE executives must initiate an assessment process emphasizing the GSA's value creation. In particular, there must be appropriate consideration given to the risk reduction when entering a new market,

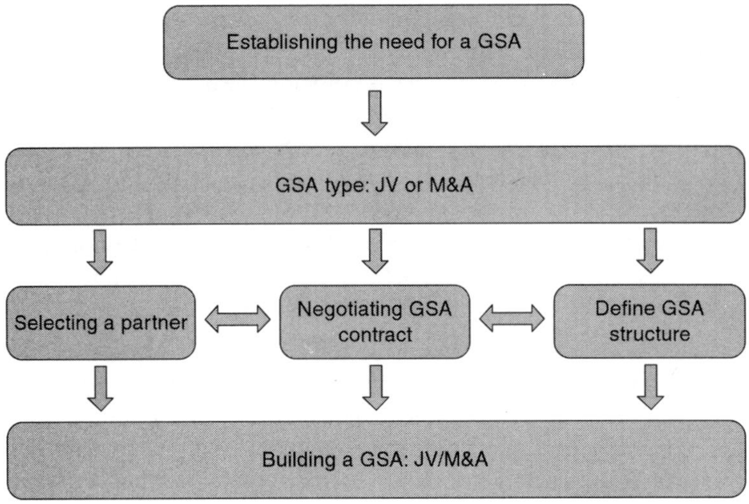

FIGURE 10.2 Main processes involved in building GSAs: JVs and M&As

adopting a new technology, etc. Creativity and ingenuity is required in order to deal with new and foreign corporations. The MNE should give due process to the GSA type, partner selection, GSA structure, and contract negotiation. All these elements are illustrated in Figure 10.2.

Building a Global Strategic Alliance: M&A and JV

The success of GSAs is highly dependent on the following: the selection of the appropriate partner; successful negotiation of an agreement; defining an appropriate GSA structure; and managing and controlling the resulting corporate entity.

Local partner selection

Partner selection determines the portfolio of skills, technical knowledge, management expertise, resources, operating policies, and processes. Since the partners to the alliance are foreign corporate entities, the selection criteria should be based on the relative importance of each of the following variables:

- partner commitment
- complementary resources
- cooperative culture
- goals compatibility
- partner capabilities

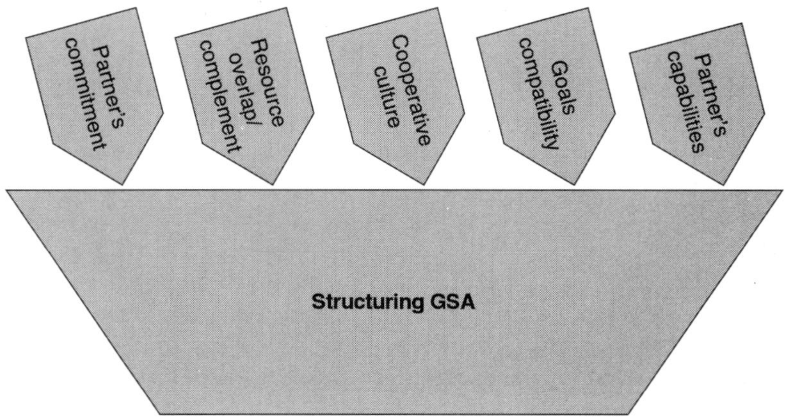

FIGURE 10.3 Partner selection considerations

Figure 10.3 highlights the considerations for selecting appropriate local partners.

Partner commitment

Partner commitment indicates the extent to which the partners continuously commit the resources and skills to the joint operations. This bilateral commitment assures the sustainability of the new corporate entity. The partner's commitment is reflected not only in the extent of contribution of resources and skills, but also in mutual trust and focused strategic intent. In light of economic crises and effects of changing global environmental conditions, the partner's commitment serves as a stabilizing force to offset risks and uncertainties. In almost all GSAs, one of the key elements announced publicly to key shareholders and the public at large is the commitment of both parties to the new corporate entity. As an example, when Merck & Co. (NYSE: MRK) and Schering-Plough (NYSE: SGP) announced a new merger in March 2009, both parties declared their long-term commitment to the new corporate entity. Specifically, in order to assure this commitment, a senior executive integration team was formed, headed by Mr Adam Schechter, President of Global Pharmaceuticals. A key priority for this team was to keep the best talent from both companies. Reflecting the long-term sustainable commitment to the new corporate entity was the fact that both parties instituted an immediate hire freeze in order to provide time to leverage the in-house talent in both companies appropriately. Without a sincere and long-term commitment, partnerships are unable to cope with the inevitable challenges and surprises that are faced over time – especially if the expected business results are not realized. For example, in 1998 DaimlerChrysler was founded through the merger of Mercedes-Benz (a German automotive manufacturer) with Chrysler Corporation (an America automotive manufacturer). By 2007, the merger was dissolved when Mercedes-Benz sold the Chrysler business to a private equity firm for restructuring and reverted back to the original Daimler AG company.

Complementary resources

Complementary resources lead to better synergies by both partners to the GSA. The greater the complementary resources between global partners, the greater the potential value of the GSA. Complementary resources lead to a reduction of coordination expenses and improve learning-curve effects. As the opening case of this chapter regarding Chrysler–Fiat GSA indicates, Fiat marketing presence in Europe complements the Chrysler customer base in the USA. In addition, Fiat's innovative and environment-friendly product offerings complemented the traditional product portfolio of Chrysler. As the Chrysler chairman and CEO indicated, the Chrysler–Fiat GSA offers Chrysler a number of strategic benefits, including access to products that complement Chrysler's current portfolio, the distribution network outside North America and cost savings in design, engineering, manufacturing, purchasing and sales and marketing.

Cooperative culture

Cooperative culture deals with the extent to which each partners' corporate culture is compatible and leads to a more cooperative working environment of the GSA. As was indicated in Chapter 3, maintaining a cooperative culture GSA consisting of partners from different nationalities is challenging. The difficulties that stem from the clash of two foreign cultures can be neutralized if both partners become more familiar with each other's business and national cultures. In the DaimlerChrysler example mentioned above, the clash of cultures, both corporate and national, was a major contributing factor leading to the failed partnership of the GSA.

An interesting case in point regarding cooperative culture is the contrast between the executive cultures in Western corporations vs Far Eastern corporations. Typically, negotiations between the two groups involve different attitudes towards risk, hierarchy, and communication styles, as well as the time horizon:

- Western executives tend to be more risk-seeking (seeing the potential in the deal first) than their Eastern counterparts (who first want to understand the risks involved).
- A Western senior executive tends to lead the conversations and delivery of the communication, whereas in Eastern corporate cultures the most senior leader tends to speak the least in a business meeting.
- Western executives tend to have a time horizon for decisions and planning that is measured in days, weeks or months (typically linked to quarterly reports), whereas their Eastern peers can evaluate a GSA relationship for months or years before making a binding decision.

To negotiate, structure, and implement a successful GSA, both teams will need to make efforts to understand each other's frame of reference and strive to build a common shared relationship based on aligned goals and demonstrated signs of commitment to the success of the partnership. To facilitate bridging these cultural gaps, international business executives with a deep understanding of both cultures are often used (whether they are part of the negotiation teams of either MNE or are hired as consultants or agents from a third-party entity).

Goal compatibility

Goal compatibility concerns the extent to which the goals of each of the partners of the GSA align. In particular, the alignment should exist at all levels of both organizations, including corporate goals, strategic business unit (profit center, subsidiaries) goals, and the functional goals (e.g., manufacturing, marketing, distribution, sales, etc.) of the partnership itself. Goal compatibility is essential to minimize managerial and organizational efforts regarding the attainment of these goals. Gaps in the various partners' goals should be identified early on and dealt with explicitly within the framework of the GSA agreement. Mechanisms should be put in place in order to escalate and resolve these gaps.

The degree of goal compatibility may change over time as a result of changing external conditions and/or changes in the internal capabilities of either partner. For instance, in 2006 Motorola Inc., a US-based telecom manufacturer, and Huawei Technologies Co., a Chinese-based telecom manufacturer, teamed up to develop UMTS technologies together in China. This partnership was meant to help both companies compete with Nokia, who achieved market leadership in this field. Although the goals were aligned at the outset of the GSA, the goals may diverge if Nokia drops its lead and both parties see an opportunity to grab the leadership role themselves or the relative strength of each company changes over time such that one is better positioned (either financially, operationally, technologically, etc.) to aggressively pursue market leadership on its own. It should be noted that while the GSA agreement between Motorola and Huawei has been signed in 2006, by 2010 Motorola is claiming that Chinese electronics giant Huawei Technologies has been stealing its trade secrets and is suing Huawei, following an earlier lawsuit originally filed back in 2008.

Partner's capabilities

Partner capabilities in the context of a GSA can be assessed at three different levels: strategic, organizational, and financial capabilities.

Strategic capabilities

Strategic capabilities mostly refer to the various business functions such as marketing and technology. In many GSAs the impetus for an alliance comes from the synergies in the marketing area, which contribute to a greater market presence, a larger portfolio of products and services, and economies of scale in marketing and distribution networks. For example, Pixar, the successful animation studio, entered into a GSA with the Disney Company for distribution and marketing of its films worldwide. Under the agreement Pixar was responsible for producing the content (e.g., films like Toy Story, Finding Nemo) and Disney was responsible for global marketing, distribution, and licensing. The creative and technological capabilities of Pixar, matched with Disney's global marketing reach and capabilities, created an incredibly powerful alliance that generated billions of dollars in revenues for both companies. In 2006, Disney acquired Pixar Studios and has since continued their string of successful animated films.

Organizational capabilities

Organizational capabilities of GSAs include prior international experience of workers and executives alike, experience with previous international collaboration and multicultural organizational skills. As indicated in Chapter 3, cultural differences, when dealt with effectively, may contribute to the success of the partners of GSAs. A lack of prior international experience may undermine the success of GSAs and may lead to the demise of the new corporate entity. In addition, previous international collaboration is of great help in achieving organizational goals, including the successful recruitment of qualified employees, establishing appropriate compensation schemes, and allowing for cross-border placement and promotion opportunities. Global MNEs, like Intel, Motorola, Citibank, and British Petroleum, all have extensive programs for relocation, cultural training, and career development paths of company managers in various capacities globally and all are meant to provide greater experience and talent to manage a distributed global business effectively.

Financial capabilities

Financial capabilities in the context of GSAs reflects the ability of the partners to obtain local capital, both in the form of equity and debt, conform successfully to local business rules and regulations, and deal successfully with vulnerability of exchange rates and currency fluctuations in the host country. Successful GSAs are often based on the partners' ability to deal with financial risks using an appropriate composition of international debt and equity instruments that minimize currency risks and financing costs. The results of robust financial capabilities of GSAs are better profitability, higher liquidity, favorable working capital, and strong cash positions. In industries where the development costs required to bring a new product to market are very high (e.g., due to regulation, complexity, and intensive experimentation), financial capabilities become a key success factor. For example, in the pharmaceutical industry, the cost of bringing a new drug to market can be hundreds of millions of dollars. Many small biotechnology companies are not able to raise such funds, and they do not have the operational reach and expertise to pass regulatory requirements in each and every market globally. Large pharmaceutical companies possess deep financial resources and strong operational capabilities, as well as the marketing and distribution reach required to bring the product to worldwide markets. The large pharmaceutical company gains new products for its pipeline, whereas the small biotechnology company gains the financial capital it needs to complete development, testing, and approval of the product.

Negotiating alliance contracts

Negotiating alliance contracts is an important part of forming a GSA for two reasons: first, the negotiating process itself is an opportunity for both partners to

TABLE 10.2 Alliance Contract Negotiations: Main Terms and Clauses

1. Joint venture name and its legal nature
2. Scope and scale of operations
3. Amount of capital investment and ownership distribution
4. Partners' forms of contribution
5. Each partner's responsibilities
6. Knowledge transfer
7. Marketing issues
8. Composition of the board of directors in the case of M&A
9. Senior executives' names, authority and responsibility
10. Joint venture project preparation and execution
11. Human resources issues
12. Accounting, finance, and tax issues
13. Termination conditions and exit terms of the alliance
14. Disposal of assets after termination
15. Amendments and alterations of the agreement
16. Liabilities for breach of contract of agreement
17. Handling of force majeure
18. Dispute settlement mechanisms
19. Launching date

build the rapport necessary in order to form a workable alliance; second, it determines the main terms of the GSA agreement. As a result, selecting the appropriate negotiating team members, as well as deciding on the general framework of the final agreement is significant. It is an advantage that the executives meant to run the GSA participate in the negotiations, so as to begin building a strong working relationship, which can provide continuity in the implementation of the GSA and joint ownership over the goals of the venture. The resulting GSA agreement would normally include the items listed in Table 10.2. Often negotiators spend most of their efforts on agreeing on the business scope and terms of the GSA. In practice the most heavily used clauses in such agreements are typically the termination or exit items. When the partnership is working well, no one refers to the contract; however, should the GSA struggle, one or both partners will look at the contract to understand the consequences of dissolving the partnership.

Ownership of global strategic alliances

The ownership structure of a GSA defines the percentage of equity ownership as well as the voting rights of each partner. The ownership structure is of particular importance for M&As, since the equity level is commensurate with the level of profit sharing, dividend distribution, and degree of control. In a JV, where no equity contribution is involved, the control of the new corporate entity is not determined by the amount of equity contributed by the parties but on a negotiated basis.

In an equity-based joint venture, such as a merger between two international partners, the correlation between invested equity and managerial control may not always be the same. It is possible for a partner to have a smaller equity investment but have the right to exercise a decisive controlling vote. This is often the case when the party contributing a smaller equity share has a greater bargaining power in the context of the GSA. Such is the case when government regulations in emerging markets may dictate a decisive control for the local partner vis-à-vis the foreign partner. Naturally, an equal ownership of the partners to GSAs ensures a fair split of profits and dividends, and also secures the full commitment of all partners to the goals of the new corporate entity.

A special case of nonequity GSA is a project-based international venture. These kinds of business deals involve partners to a project with a relatively narrow scope and well-defined timetable and do not involve the creation of a new legal entity. In a project-based, nonequity venture, the parties to the GSA combine personnel, resources, and capabilities and collaborate until the venture reaches a certain goal. In most cases, the partners to a project-based nonequity venture collaborate on joint development of new technologies, products or services, sharing their expertise. Project-based nonequity joint ventures are prevalent in technology-intensive industries such as telecommunications, biotechnology, and nanotechnology. It should noted that project-based collaborations differ from equity joint ventures in several ways. First, no new legal corporate entity is created, and the partners operate based on some agreement. Second, the partners do not seek ownership of a new corporate entity on a sustainable basis. Third, the joint venture has a well-defined exit date. Fourth, the collaboration has a focused scope typically involving a new product, development, manufacturing or distribution.

An extension of a project-based nonequity venture is a consortium. A consortium is a nonequity venture with multiple partners created for the purpose of carrying out a significantly large-scale project. For example, the Airbus–a British, French and German consortium – was formed to develop and manufacture the next generation of commercial airliners.

Successful IBM and Cognos Global Strategic Alliance Leads to Acquisition

It took 18 months for the global strategic alliance to transform to an acquisition of Cognos by IBM for $4.9 billion. In 2006, IBM and Cognos announced a strategic alliance to jointly develop, market, and sell integrated business intelligence solutions. In 31 January 2008, IBM acquired Cognos, signifying a major software industry change in distribution channels as well as in product design and offerings.

About the strategic alliance partners

Cognos, a world leader in business intelligence and corporate performance management, delivers software and services that help companies drive, monitor and understand corporate performance. Cognos delivers a competitive advantage tool, corporate performance management (CPM), achieved through the strategic application of business intelligence on an enterprise scale. The integrated CPM solution helps customers drive performance through planning; monitor performance through score carding and understand performance through business intelligence. Cognos serves more than 23,000 customers in over 135 countries. Cognos enterprise business intelligence and performance management solutions and services are available from more than 3,000 worldwide partners and resellers.

IBM (www.ibm.com) is the world's largest information technology company, with 80 years of technological and business leadership in helping organizations innovate. Drawing on resources from across IBM and key IBM business partners, IBM offers a wide range of services, solutions, and technologies that enable customers, large and small, to take full advantage of the new era of mass customization, just-in-time delivery, and on-demand business.

The strategic alliance

In 2006, Cognos and IBM announced an expansion of their relationship to help customers integrate their business processes across the enterprise and gain greater insight into business performance. The new strategic alliance agreement includes joint development, marketing, and sales of service-oriented architecture (SOA) based solutions to supply customers with an advanced corporate performance management tools.

As part of the agreement, IBM is committed to increase its Cognos consultant capabilities to support the activities and solutions. Cognos is committed to further enhance and optimize its business intelligence products for IBM hardware, software, and services. Cognos will also deliver IBM products, such as IBM's WebSphere and Information Management technologies, providing a complete business intelligence solution that covers reporting, analysis, score carding, dash boarding, and event management.

At the time of the strategic alliance announcement, it was predicted that the market opportunity for such products and services, including software, services and hardware, will reach $21 billion by 2007, as customers have the opportunity to easily overcome one of the key challenges of business infrastructure: managing, integrating, and unlocking value from their business information – an organization's most valuable asset.

The deal represents a significant commitment to providing clients with open standards-based business solutions that will allow them to leverage their existing information technology assets, lower costs, and provide flexibility regarding their choice of operating environments. Building on its existing successful relationship, the strategic alliance tightened the integration between Cognos and IBM across all areas of the organizations, including software, hardware, services, marketing, and joint product development.

Cognos and IBM were expected to develop and market new vertical offerings to help customers address their business challenges across industries such as insurance and the public sector.

The CEO of Cognos, as well as IBM's vice president for strategic alliances, was quoted as saying that they are satisfied with the strategic alliance, illustrating both companies' commitment to helping their clients deliver innovative solutions that solve their industry-specific business challenges.

The acquisition

In January 2008, the strategic alliance led to the acquisition of Cognos by IBM for $4.9 billion, ending the business intelligence as an add-on to current business software. Business intelligence,

(Continued)

along with business process management (BPM), is becoming integral to business solutions, as was also reflected in major vendor acquisitions during the same period, including that by Oracle Corporation, which acquired Hyperion Solutions Corporation, and SAP AG, which acquired Business Objects SA.

The acquisition of Cognos by IBM signified a major industry change, including distribution channels and product design and offerings.

Sources: http://www.cognos.com/news/releases/2006/0307.html (March 7, 2006), http://searchsoa.techtarget.com/news/article/0,289142,sid26_gci1281824.00.html.

Managing Global Strategic Alliances

While the phases of forming and negotiating a GSA are of critical importance to its success, the management of global alliances determines the sustainability of such a business arrangement. Figure 10.4 illustrate the various issues that are involved in managing a GSA, comprising managing learning, managerial control, cooperation and trust, and exit planning.

Managing learning

A GSA presents an opportunity for cross-learning among the GSA partners. The learning opportunities may be of an operational or managerial nature. Operational knowledge may refer to any functional area, including R&D, manufacturing, distribution, marketing and sales, or finance. Managerial learning includes the organizational frameworks, people management, reporting and

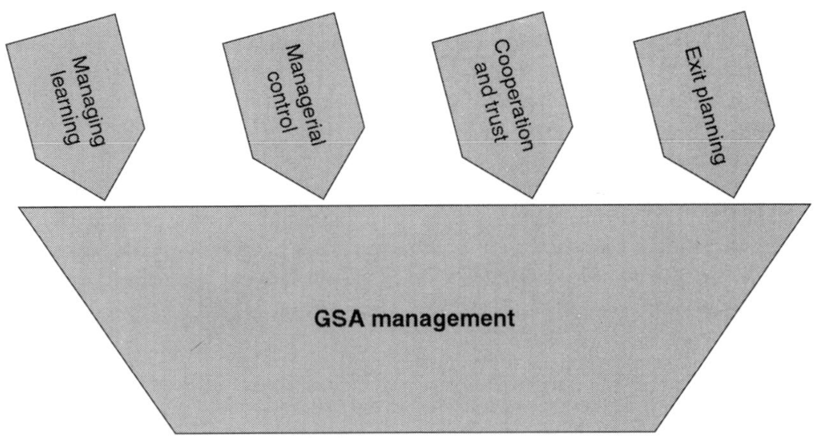

FIGURE 10.4 Managing GSAs: JVs and M&As

control methodologies, and methods for management of global teams across multiple sites. To acquire partner knowledge effectively and efficiently, a partner to a GSA must identify a knowledge gap and actively seek to fill this gap through transfer of knowledge from the other party. This works especially well when the two partners' skill sets complement one another, encouraging exchange of ideas. Cisco, a global supplier of networking equipment, has built a strong reputation for successful GSAs, in particular through acquisitions of smaller technology companies. Cisco gains knowledge of new technologies, products or services to add to its portfolio (i.e., R&D learning) while the smaller technology company gains access to world-class operational best practices that quickly grow the new product line globally (i.e., operational learning).

An essential part of learning within a GSA is based on an honest and open transfer of information regarding knowledge, procedures, and practices. At the same time safeguards must be built to hedge against an uncontrolled leakage of information among the GSA partners. These safeguards are of three types:

1. Keeping the most strategically sensitive business assets outside of the GSA agreement.
2. Contractual safeguards protecting the most strategically sensitive business assets from being shared outside of the GSA agreement.
3. Establishing cross-licensing agreements regarding specific skills and technologies to compensate either party for the value of the shared assets.

Managerial control

The partners in a GSA should exercise managerial control over the alliance in order to secure the protection of each party's interests. This control may involve the following:

1. Executive nomination and appointment – exercising managerial control through selection of key personnel to manage the new corporate entity.
2. Board of directors/decisions – exercising managerial control through determination of the Board's agenda, and committee structure.
3. Managerial policies and practices – exercising managerial control through adoption of specific managerial policies and practices.
4. Budget control – exercising managerial control through the allocation of financial resources.
5. Provision of partner services – exercising managerial control through the provision and administration of partner services to the shared entity.
6. Resource allocation – exercising managerial control through resource identification and appropriation.
7. Interpersonal relationships – exercising managerial control through relationships between key personnel of the new corporate entity with senior management of the partners in the GSA.

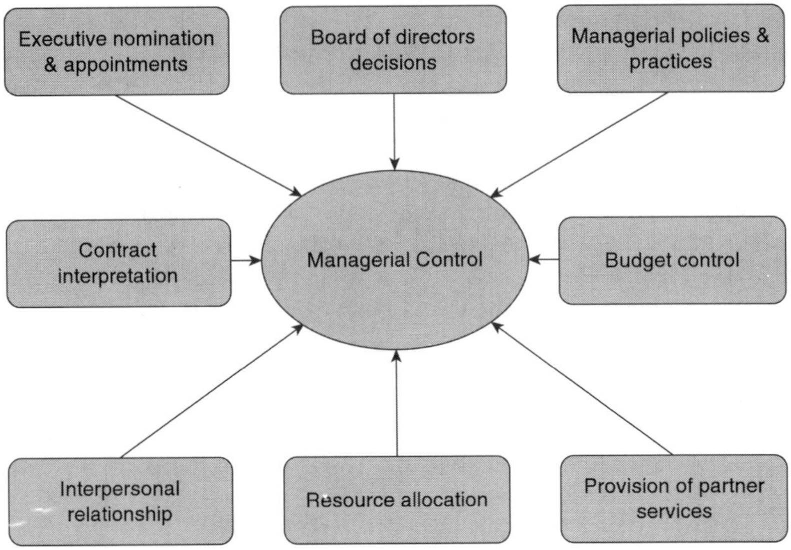

FIGURE 10.5 Maintaining managerial controls over GSA operations

8 Contract interpretation – exercising managerial control through application of the contractual obligations of the partners to the GSA.

These managerial control methods are outlined in Figure 10.5.

Cooperation and trust

Organizational commitment and *conflict avoidance* are key success factors for a sustainable and successful GSA. Organizational commitment to the alliance is beyond the contractual agreement terms of the GSA. It requires the nurturing of business and social relationships. Key executives should develop personal relationships that improve trust and contribute to alliance sustainability and counter pressures towards the dissolution of the GSA. The CEOs of the partners to the GSA should develop personal contacts and maintain and nurture these relationships through mutual visits that are carried out on a regular basis. Other executives, managers, and workers take note of the rapport of the CEOs and behave accordingly. Furthermore, it is very important to determine a longer term of service for executives involved with the GSA, allowing for longer-term relationships to evolve and develop. A longer time of service, say three years and more, allows the executives to learn a foreign language and become well versed with local business culture, standards, and practices. It should be noted that Japanese executives are usually assigned to GSAs for longer periods of time than Western executives.

GSAs provide ample opportunities for conflicts, which may be triggered by technological, financial or managerial issues and may be aggravated by cultural and interpersonal issues. To enhance conflict avoidance, it is important to address the following:

- Provide an opportunity for mutual study of the national and organizational cultures of the partners to the GSA.
- Structure intensive consultation bodies, task forces, and committees that meet regularly, set up strategic goals and manage expectations of all partners to the GSA.
- Personnel that are assigned to work in the new corporate entity, resulting from the GSA, must have the ability to work well with people from other national and organizational cultures in addition to possessing the appropriate technical abilities.
- The GSA agreement and modus operandi must allow the flexibility required in order to adapt to internal and external changes, such as those resulting from technological breakthroughs, market opportunities or macroeconomic downturns. Although GSA partnerships are meant to abide by strict guidelines imposed by the partners, the ability to reassess the agreement in the context of dramatic changes represents an important competitive success factor for a given GSA. Having built into the new corporate entity, the right balance of flexibility to adapt with the rules and guidelines to follow for efficiency can help conflict avoidance.
- Executives in charge of GSAs should be tuned to the concerns of the personnel engaged with the new corporate entity in order to identify potential conflicts up front and take measures to prevent them. This is a particular challenge, given the heterogeneity of the mix of national and corporate cultures existing in a given GSA.

Exit Planning

All GSAs are subject to a voluntary or nonvoluntary end of life, otherwise known as GSA exit or dissolution. The ending of a GSA may be done at a time when the GSA's strategic goals are met and the partners to the GSA have realized the potential of the partnership. Alternatively, an opportunity for exit may exist when the value of selling the asset exceeds the potential value of the GSA as a going concern. Finally, a GSA can be dissolved when one or both partners are dissatisfied with the results of the corporate entity. For example, in 2005, eBay Inc. (a global e-commerce company based in the USA) acquired Skype (an internet telephone company based in Luxembourg) with the intention of leveraging the Skype communication platform as another medium of communication between the buyers and sellers that transact on eBay. In 2009, eBay sold Skype to a private equity firm after acknowledging the lack of synergy with the e-commerce platform and realizing great value of the company as a standalone business.

A GSA termination may be affected through acquisition, dissolution, and reconfiguration of the GSA. The form of termination is determined by the partners to the GSA in an effort to minimize negative effects on the partners and maximize the value of the GSA's assets.

COUNTRY FOCUS

HUNGARY

World Rank (EFI 2009): 44

Quick facts

Population: 10.1 million

GDP (PPP): $184.0 billion; 3.9 percent growth in 2006; 4.3 percent 5-year compound annual growth; $18,277 per capita

Unemployment: 7.3 percent

Inflation (CPI): 7.9 percent

FDI inflow: $6.1 billion

2006 data unless otherwise noted

Regional Rank (EFI 2009): 22

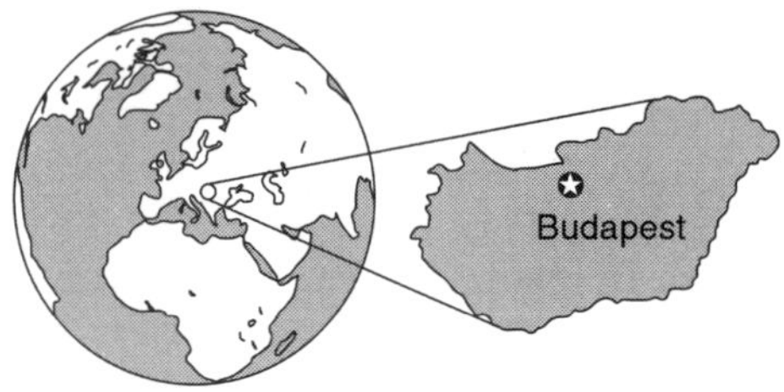

Economic freedom score

Hungary's economic freedom score is 66.8, making its economy the 44th freest in the 2009 Index. Hungary is ranked 22nd out of 43 countries in the Europe region, and its overall score is well above the world average.

Hungary has transformed its economy from a centrally planned system to a more market-oriented one, building a robust private sector, and attracting substantial foreign direct investment (FDI). With economic growth of slightly over 4 percent over the past five years, Hungary boasts strong trade freedom, business freedom, property rights, investment freedom, and financial freedom. Investing is easy, and foreign capital and domestic capital enjoy virtually the same protections and privileges. The rule of law is strong, and corruption is perceived as moderate.

Challenges include the need for fiscal consolidation and better management of public finance. The size of government is Hungary's biggest weakness, with its score far below the world average. The labor market also could be improved.

Background

Though the Hungarian Revolution of 1956 was brutally suppressed by Soviet troops, Hungary eventually emerged from 40 years of Communist rule more politically and economically open than its Eastern Bloc neighbors. Hungary held its first multi-party elections in 1990 and has transformed itself into a market economy. It joined the European Union (EU) in 2004. The ruling coalition of the Hungarian Socialist Party and the liberal Alliance of Free Democrats collapsed in April 2008 over disputes about reform measures, dismissal of the health minister, and a major defeat in a referendum organized by the opposition, and the Socialists now govern with a parliamentary minority. Despite progress in 2007, Hungary still has the EU's largest budget deficit: 5.5 percent of GDP. The opposition FIDESZ party is running on a populist platform.

Business freedom – 77.4

The overall freedom to start, operate, and close a business is relatively well protected under Hungary's regulatory environment. Starting a business takes much less than half of the world average of 38 days, but obtaining a business license requires more than the world average of 18 procedures. Closing a business is relatively easy and costless.

Trade freedom – 85.8

Hungary's trade policy is the same as that of other members of the EU. The common EU-weighted average tariff rate was 2.1 percent in 2005. Nontariff barriers reflected in EU policy include agricultural and manufacturing subsidies, import restrictions for some goods and services, market access restrictions in some service sectors, nontransparent and restrictive regulations and standards, and inconsistent customs administration across EU members. Food and feed products are subject to restrictive biotechnology regulations. Ten points were deducted from Hungary's trade freedom score to account for nontariff trade barriers.

Fiscal freedom – 70.6

Hungary has a high income tax rate but a low corporate tax rate. The top income tax rate is 36 percent, and the top corporate tax rate is 16 percent. Other taxes include a value-added tax (VAT), a property tax, and a community tax. In the most recent year, overall tax revenue as a percentage of gross domestic product (GDP) was 37.3 percent.

Government size – 19.2

Total government expenditures, including consumption and transfer payments, are extremely high. In the most recent year, government spending equaled 51.9 percent of GDP. The private sector has grown substantially, but the government remains directly involved in such sectors as agriculture, electric power, and transport (railways). The fiscal deficit is high, partly because of large expenditures on government wages and social transfers.

Monetary freedom – 73.8

Inflation is relatively high, averaging 6.5 percent between 2005 and 2007. As a participant in the EU's Common Agricultural Policy, the government subsidizes agricultural production, distorting the prices of agricultural products. It also regulates prices for energy, telecommunications services, and subsidized pharmaceutical products, among others. Ten points were deducted from Hungary's monetary freedom score to account for policies that distort domestic prices.

Investment freedom – 80

Foreign capital receives domestic legal treatment, and foreign companies account for a large share of manufacturing, telecommunications, and energy activity. The government allows 100 percent foreign ownership with the exception of some defense-related industries, some types of land, airlines, and broadcasting. Bureaucratic procedures can be lengthy, and the investment code can be nontransparent. Residents and nonresidents may hold foreign exchange accounts. There are no restrictions or controls on current transfers or repatriation of profits and no restrictions on issues or sales of capital market instruments, but there are some reporting requirements.

(Continued)

Financial freedom – 70

Hungary's financial institutions still do not offer a full range of services, but banking is increasingly competitive. As of February 2008, there were 31 commercial banks and eight special credit institutions. Banks provide over 70 percent of credit, and the 10 largest account for about 80 percent of total assets. The government has been withdrawing from banking. Most remaining state-owned assets were privatized in 2003 and 2004, and over two-thirds of the sector is now foreign-owned. In August 2007, the state became a minority shareholder of FHB Land Credit and Mortgage Bank by selling half of its remaining 54.11 percent stake. Capital markets are relatively well developed, and foreign investors participate freely. The Budapest Stock Exchange has low volumes of trading and lacks liquidity, with about 60 companies listed. Foreign investors held more than 70 percent of listed shares in 2007.

Property rights – 70

The judiciary is constitutionally independent, and the government respects this in practice. The threat of expropriation is low. The courts are slow and severely overburdened, and a final ruling on a contract dispute can take more than a year. Protection of intellectual property rights has improved, but more needs to be done.

Freedom from corruption – 53

Corruption is perceived as present. Hungary ranks 39th out of 179 countries in Transparency International's Corruption Perceptions Index for 2007. Despite anti-corruption laws, nontransparency leads to persistent rumors of corruption in government procurement.

Labor freedom – 68.4

Hungary's relatively flexible labor regulations enhance employment and productivity growth. The nonsalary cost of employing a worker is burdensome, and dismissing a redundant employee is relatively costly. Regulations on work hours are not flexible.

Source: Adapted from Terry Miller and Kim R. Holmes, *2009 Index of Economic Freedom* (Washington, DC: The Heritage Foundation and Dow Jones & Company, Inc., 2009), at www.heritage.org/index.

SUMMARY

GSAs are of two kinds: **mergers and acquisitions**, which involve equity sharing, and **joint ventures**, which do not. MNEs use GSAs in order to penetrate new foreign markets, expand their product portfolio, transfer or acquire knowledge, share business and project risks, and reduce international competition.

Contractual joint ventures include joint exploration, R&D consortium, co-production, co-marketing, joint management, long-term supply agreement, and so forth.

Major advantages of building **GSAs** include cost/risk sharing, knowledge acquisition, product rationalization, competition reduction, local acceptance, and market access.

GSAs should be based on a careful **assessment of potential local partners** that present a good fit with current capabilities, as well as **congruence of strategic goals.**

The **GSA agreements** should allow for a careful structure of procedures and rules to govern the management of the new corporate entity.

GSAs should be based on **mutual learning** by all partners to the new corporate entity, allowing for a **higher value added** of its business and operational activities.

GSAs are based on agreements that allow for **appropriate exit mechanisms,** sometimes detailed and sometimes ambiguous, based on the needs and wants of the partners involved.

DISCUSSION QUESTIONS

1 Identify the two types of global strategic alliances (GSA). Explain the differences between them.
2 Search the Internet for an MNE which has recently gone into a GSA and identify the benefits of the GSA from both partners' perspectives.
3 Explain how GSAs can be of benefit to emerging industries such as biotechnology and nanotechnology.

EXERCISES

1 Identify a recent GSA in a biotechnology industry and indicate the essential elements of the GSA agreement.
2 Identify a GSA in the retailing industry and point out the main advantages of such a GSA.
3 Identify a GSA in the consultancy field and point out the main advantages for such a GSA.
4 IBM Global Services is an entity that was created based on the merger of IBM with a prominent consulting house. Point out the main advantages for such a new corporate entity to IBM.

Bibliography

Beamish, P. W. (1995). The characteristics of joint ventures in developed and developing countries. *Columbia Journal of World Business*, 13–19.

Beamish, P. W. (1998). *Multinational Joint Ventures in Developing Countries*, New York: Routledge.

Bianchi, M. (1995). Markets and firms: transaction costs versus strategic innovation. *Journal of Economic Behavior and Organization*, 28, 183–202.

Blodgett, L. L. (1992). Factors in the instability of international joint ventures: an event history analysis. *Strategic Management Journal*, 13, 475–81.

Bureth, A., Wolff, S., Zanfei, A. (1997). The two faces of learning by cooperating: the evolution and stability of inter-firm agreements in the European electronics industry. *Journal of Economic Behavior and Organization*, 32, 519–37.

Doz, Y. L. (1996). The evolution of cooperation in strategic alliances: initial conditions or learning processes? *Strategic Management Journal*, 17, 55–85.

Doz, Y. L., Hamel, G. (1998). *Alliance Advantage*. Boston, MA: Harvard Business School Press.

Doz, Y. L., Hamel, G. (1998). *Alliance Advantage: The Art of Creating Value through Partnering*. Boston, MA: Harvard Business School Press.

Economist (2009). The world according to Chambers. August 27.

Hagedoorn, J. (1993). Understanding the rationale of strategic technology partnering: interorganizational modes of cooperation and sectoral differences. *Strategic Management Journal*, 14, 371–85.

Hamel, G. (1994). Competition for competence and interpartner learning within international strategic alliances. *Strategic Management Journal*, 12, Special Issue, 83–103.

Inkpen, A. C. (1995). *The Management of International Joint Ventures: And Organizational Learning Perspective*. London: Routledge.

Inkpen, A. C., Beamish, P. W. (1997). Knowledge, bargaining power, and the instability of international joint ventures. *Academy of Management Review*, 22 (1), 177–202.

Khanna, T., Gulati, R., Nohria, N. (1998). The dynamics of learning alliances: competition, cooperation, and relative scope. *Strategic Management Journal*, 19, 193–210.

Lai, D., Slocum, J. W., Pitts, R. A. (1997). Building cooperative advantage: managing strategic alliances to promote organizational learning. *Journal of World Business*, 32 (3), 203–23.

Lorange, P., Roos, J. (1992). *Strategic Alliances: Formation, Implementation, and Evolution*. Cambridge, MA: Blackwell.

Luo, Y. (1999). *Entry and Cooperative Strategies in International Business Expansion*. Westport, CT: Quorum Books.

Park, S. H. (1996). Managing an inter-organizational network control. *Organization Studies*, 17, 795–824.

Parkhe, A. (1993). Strategic alliance structuring: a game theoretic and transaction cost examination of interfirm cooperation. *Academy of Management Journal*, 36, 794–829.

Powell, W. W., Koput, K. W., Smith-Doerr, L. (1996). Interorganizational collaboration and the locus of innovation: networks of learning in biotechnology. *Administrative Science Quarterly*, 41, 116–45.

Teece, D. J. (1992). Competition, cooperation, and innovation: organizational arrangements for regimes of rapid technological progress. *Journal of Economic Behavior and Organization*, 18, 1–25.

Weber, Y., Menipaz, E. (2003). Measuring cultural fit in mergers and acquisitions. *International Journal of Business Performance Management*, 5 (1), 54–72.

Yan, A., Lou, Y. (2001). *International Joint Ventures: Theory and Practice*. Armonk, New York: M. E. Sharpe.

PART 5

International Business Management

11

Global Technology Management

Learning Objectives

Following this chapter, the reader should be able to:

1. Understand the various roles technology can play in international business and global competitiveness
2. Consider how to leverage technology in order to enhance products, services, or processes in both large and small enterprises
3. Understand how to plan, organize, operate, and control global R&D functions or projects
4. Appreciate the transformative role of the Internet and how it is being used globally to support e-commerce, cross border trade, and international business
5. Assess the readiness of any given country to leverage the Internet for both local and international business ventures

Opening Case

Otis Elevator

Source: http //www.otisworldwide.com/.

Founded in 185 , Otis Elevator – a wholly-owned subsidiary of United Technologies Corporation – is the world's number one manufacturer of elevators and escalators. With 1.2 million installations in more than 200 countries, Otis has a 22 percent share of the global elevator market. Based in Connecticut, nearly 80 percent of its sales are outside the USA as are 55,000 of the company's 6 ,000 employees.

Integration of computer technology at Otis began in 1979, with the installment of microprocessors in elevators to detect problems and improve maintenance. In 198 , Otis started OTISLI E®, a computerized dispatch service for orth American elevators. In 1988, EM® allowed the firm to monitor elevator performance from distant locations in orth America. Otis then extended those innovations globally. In 1999, Otis introduced E*Display, an Internet-based information display in an elevator car, E*Direct, which allows customers to order elevators online, and E*Service, an online customer service website.

By the summer of 2000, Otis was taking online orders in 49 countries in 29 languages. The company expects online business to account for 25– 0 percent of its growth between 2000 and 200 . In selected markets such as France, the Otis site permits architects to submit their building specifications and have Otis engineers determine the type of elevators required.

E-commerce – a primer

The Internet is a worldwide network of computer networks known, as the world wide web (www), which constitutes all the resources and users on the Internet that use hypertext transfer protocol (htp, or http). This system comprises a set of rules for exchanging text, graphic images, sound, video, and multimedia files on the world wide web.

Electronic commerce (e-commerce) is the conduct of transactions to buy, sell, distribute, or deliver goods and services over the Internet.

(Continued)

E-commerce transactions are business to business (B2B), business to consumer (B2C), or consumer to consumer (C2C). B2B, which currently drives 90 percent of the pro ected growth in global e-commerce, involves interfirm transactions, including government procurement. B2C transactions are between firms and individuals purchasing goods or services over the Internet. Ordering a book online from a vendor is an example of a B2C transaction. C2C transactions involve individual transactions e.g., via online auction. All three types of transaction now occur globally as well as domestically. *Global e-commerce* is the conduct of electronic commerce, whether B2B, B2C, or C2C across national boundaries (e.g., a US customer purchasing pharmaceuticals from a Canadian site).

The emergence of the Internet and e-commerce created initial expectations for exploding global trade, expectations that have since been scaled down. The assumption was that "a firm marketing its products or services through the Internet is, by definition, a global firm because consumers worldwide can access it." Others acknowledged that "the Internet won't magically ensure overseas success, but it can ease some of the pain of going global." The Otis case illustrates that point. The company, which has been in international markets for over a century, uses the Internet as a supplementary tool in its global sales and service. The technology has expedited the procurement process but has not come to substitute for its "bricks and mortar" business. For some small firms, the impact has been more pronounced. The aushad Trading Company of Mombassa, Kenya (www.ntclimited.com), which sells African handcraft products, attributes much of its rapid growth, from 10,000 to 2 million in sales within a few years, to the web.

As in domestic markets, the main growth of global e-commerce has been in the B2B segment. Examples are the global automobile industry exchange established by the Ford Motor Company, General Motors, and DaimlerChrysler (with Toyota possibly oining as well) and the alliance of IBM, ortel etworks, Toshiba and cell phone makers Motorola, okia, and LM Ericsson. The alliance will link billions of dollars in annual purchasing in what could be the biggest B2B Internet auction marketplace.

Technology as an Enabler for Globalization

Technology has become the great equalizer both between multinational enterprises (MNEs) and small and medium-sized enterprises (SMEs) internationally as well as across geographies, as technological advancements drive common opportunities, common standards, and a fertile foundation for more innovative and competitive business models. These advancements can be summarized in four primary areas: information technology, telecommunications, manufacturing, and transportation.

Information technology

The impact of technology on the information technology (IT) industry over the past few decades has driven dramatic changes in industries ranging from textile manufacturing, to automotive, to financial services, to tourism. There is almost no business, or aspect of a business, that has not been affected, gained from or changed as companies have pursued IT to gain a competitive advantage, defend their market share or expand their global reach to leverage different country/market opportunities.

Plantronics, the world leader in communication headsets, has been in business since the early 1960s. Since then, they have grown from an airline pilot's vision for a lightweight cockpit headset to a company with revenues of $560 million, selling into 70 countries. In 1972, Plantronics started manufacturing headsets in Mexico as part of the Maquiladora program. Today Plantronics has shifted much of its manufacturing to China and is building a design center and manufacturing in Suzhou. (*Source:* Tom Gill, CIO Plantronics, May 2005 presentation to USCS Engineering).

IT solutions have enabled growth at Plantronics through: advanced supply chain solutions (e.g., Oracle eBusiness Suite: finance, manufacturing, purchasing, HR, logistics, order management), portals/knowledge management (e.g., Microsoft intranet and SharePoint portals), information warehouse/business intelligence (e.g., Informatica/Business Objects Information Warehouse and Business Intelligence Suite), wireless solutions, workflow and approval applications (e.g., Saratoga Avenue CRM and ATG contact management), shorter cycle time, increased collaboration, and improved productivity, which have all reduced barriers of time and geography (e.g., single instance/multi-org, customization of reports, forms, and alerts).

Telecommunications

Advancements in telecommunications have been revolutionary over the past few decades, driving changes in behavior both by consumers and in business. From the development of radio, to television, to movies, to podcasting (i.e., broadcast communications) to the evolution from original postal letter, the telegraph, fixed telephony, mobile and satellite telephony, e-mail, SMS, chat, blogs, twitter, videoconferencing, and telepresence services (one-to-one or one-to-many conversations). The modes of communication (broadcast, asymmetrical, and real time) have all exploded, while their costs have dramatically reduced with each passing decade – the introduction of the Internet in the 1990s has only fueled this trend (see Figure 11.1).

The sophistication of consumers in the Internet age – e.g., using applications such as Skype for chat, voice and video calls both local and international – has driven the incredible growth in the volume of communications globally. The use of teleconferencing, videoconferencing, and telepresence suites has provided a means for businesses to increase collaboration and interaction without incurring commensurate travel costs. For example, SKG DreamWorks had Hewlett-Packard (HP) install a telepresence system in their various studios globally and thereby, reduced the need for international travel by two-thirds and national travel by 80 percent while increasing the time and frequency of collaborative meetings. Overall, the availability and low-cost options for communications have become one of the most important enablers of global business worldwide and a great equalizer between large multinationals and SMEs.

Manufacturing

New technologies applied to manufacturing include inventory management systems, Kanban and just-in-time (see Chapter 14) production, computer-aided design systems, rapid prototyping systems and tools, modular architecture and

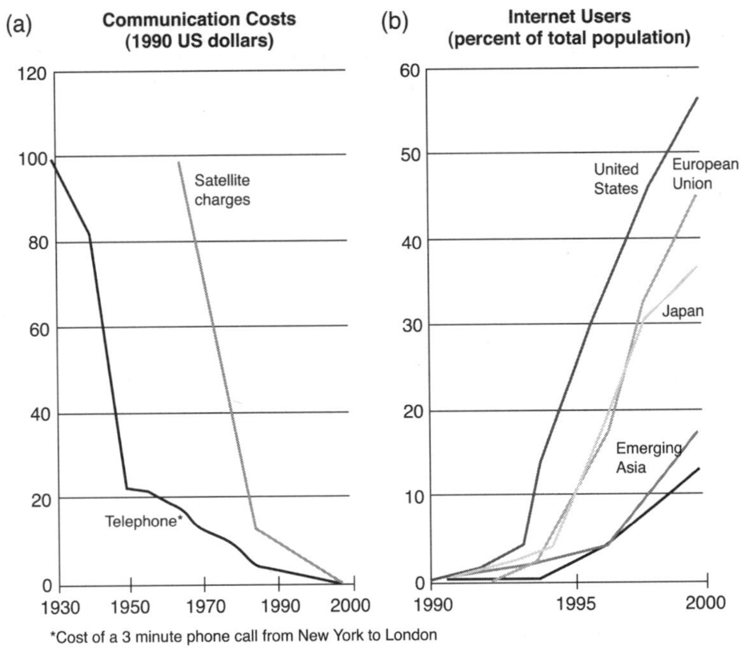

FIGURE 11.1 (a) Declining Costs for Communication, and (b) growing Number of Internet Users. (IMF (2005), World Economic Outlook. Washington, DC: International Monetary Fund)

flexible manufacturing systems, and sophisticated ERP (i.e., enterprise resource planning) systems that can link the supplier inputs with the final products and provide key information for after-sales service and support. The most far-reaching concept behind many of the great advancements in manufacturing over the past few decades involves the idea of "mass customization." For example, Dell computers allow consumers to configure the exact product they desire (online) and only then does Dell begin to manufacture the product through a tightly integrated supply chain: the product is made to order within days and shipped to the consumer. Dell gets paid at the time of the order, only buys relevant components from their suppliers and is left with no obsolete products in inventory, as anything ordered is immediately shipped upon completion. The fact that this is done for thousands of people every week through the same infrastructure shows the leverage it can bring.

Also, the developments of new materials have driven innovations in building planes (e.g., aluminum fiber alloy), making sports clothing (e.g., spandex), and the reliability and durability of end-user products.

Transportation

All innovations in the area of transportation ultimately drive speed, cost or security. The advancements in recent decades have spurred cross-border trade throughout the world. Major technology breakthroughs in advanced materials (used to build aircrafts and ships), advanced vehicle engines (powered by biofuels and hybrid engines), and advanced tracking systems, such as barcode scanners and radio frequency identification (RFID) tags, have all fueled unparalleled growth in the usage, security, and affordability of shipping products around the world. For example, the retailing industry has adopted the RFID technology to improve its supply chain and inventory systems. Wal-Mart is one of the major retailers in North America and elsewhere. It has about 15,000 suppliers that serve its stores, including the seven hundred Sam's Club mega discount stores, which contributed, as of 2007, US$42 billion in revenues to Wal-Mart's US$345 billion in revenues. As early as 2003, Wal-Mart publicly announced that it would ask its top suppliers to use RFID tags on pallets and cases. The new technology adopted by major retailers such as Wal-Mart, in North America and around the world, has marked a major change in the retail and consumer packaged goods industry. The logistics and inventory management system improved significantly at Wal-Mart's twenty two distribution centers when it adopted the RFID technology. However change was not easily. To induce the use of this technology, Wal-Mart charged suppliers a US$2 fee for each pallet without a RFID tag that is shipped to its Sam's Club distribution centers. One may question the way in which Wal-Mart has decided to introduce and enforce the RFID technology on its suppliers, but there is no doubt that the RFID technology has improved MNEs' global supply chains significantly. (*Source:* adapted from *News Report*, January 20, 2008, Paul Ma, http://blogs.techrepublic.com.com/tech-news/?p=1946 email sent 1/7/2010 question reference #100701-000051.)

To summarize, technology is a significant enabler for globalization. Advancements in IT and communications have driven unprecedented growth and innovation in enabling the successful expansion of global business, both large and small, empowering even the remotely located corporations and SMEs to become part of the global business arena. Furthermore, significant changes have been driven across all aspects of the global business: from the use of IT and communications to the introduction of entirely new methods and models of manufacturing and transportation. These, in turn, have given way to new business models – new ways of securing revenues from international business.

Technology as a Source of Competitive Advantage: Global Research and Development

Global markets, global resources, and global competition are also driving changes in the way companies are organizing themselves to leverage technology across their products, services, businesses, and organizations, both internally and/or with external partners. Over the past three decades there has been a clear trend toward greater global dispersion of research and development (R&D) activity. According to a 2005 study conducted jointly by INSEAD and Booz Allen Hamilton[1] on 186 companies, from 19 different countries, in 17 different economic sectors, with a combined R&D budget of $76 billion, the share of foreign R&D sites (i.e., dispersion of R&D) has increased from 45 percent to 66 percent over the past three decades, as noted in Figure 11.2.

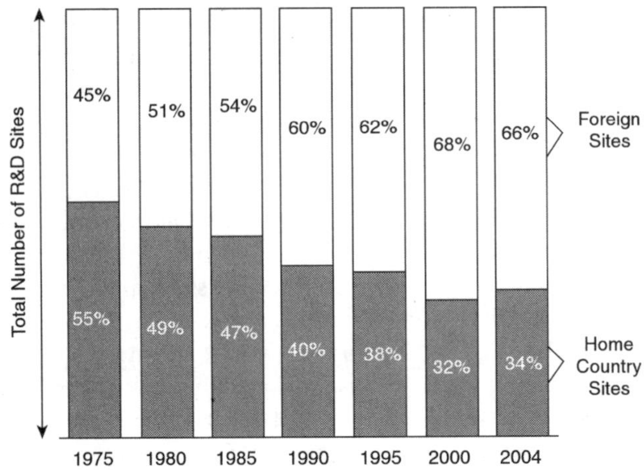

FIGURE 11.2 Growth in foreign research and development sites. (Adapted from Booz Allen Hamilton and INSEAD (2006). Fontainebleau, France: INSEAD, p. 2.)

Drivers for global research and development

The same INSEAD study investigated the main drivers cited for location decisions of future R&D sites by the participating companies, including:

- technology clusters or academic institutes
- qualified workers
- low-cost skill base
- markets or customers
- proximity to production facilities
- business environment/regulations

From the results displayed in Figure 11.3, it is clear that the biggest drivers differ by region, leading to a regional R&D dispersion that is structured around different global priorities, unique skills, and competitive advantages. For example, future R&D sites in regions such as Western Europe, the USA, and Japan are driven largely by the pursuit of "markets or customers" and/or "technology clusters", whereas in the developing world, such as China, India, and Eastern Europe, access to a "low-cost skills base" is very attractive. With respect to China, this trend is combined with the very attractive local market potential, which is another reason to drive significant foreign investment in R&D sites. As early as 2003, US-based Motorola announced plans to add seven more R&D units to the 18 R&D units it has operated in China. This included an investment of US$10 million of Motorola Global Software Group into expanding its software center in Nanjing, capital of east China's Jiangsu Province. All R&D units are expected to employ more local researchers and engineers, and generate more state-of-the-art technologies and software products. Other MNEs established R&D centers in mainland China.

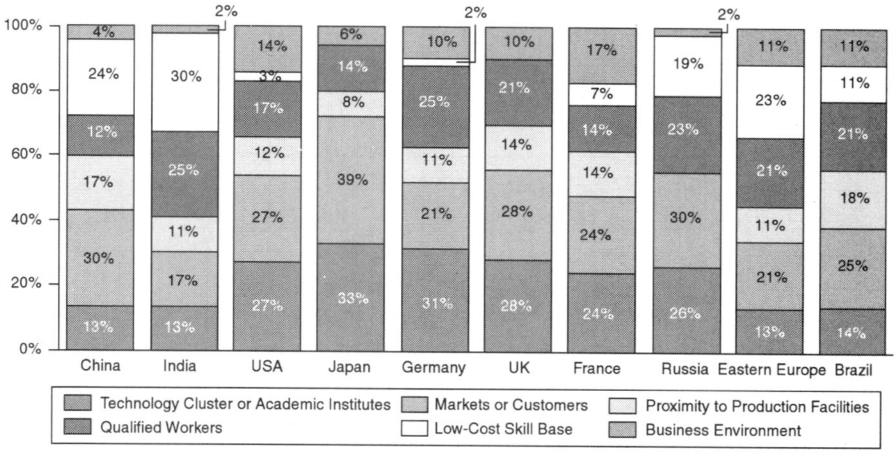

FIGURE 11.3 Drivers of future R&Ds sites. (Adapted from Booz Allen Hamilton and INSEAD (2006). Fontainebleau, France: INSEAD, p. 5.)

Honeywell moved its global R&D facility from northern Europe to Tianjin. Samsung of South Korea, which is the one of the largest MNEs, with a sales volume of over US$175 billion has established an R&D facility in China. Microsoft has invested more than US$130 million to establish R&D centers in Beijing, Shanghai, and Suzhou; General Electric has located its R&D center in Shanghai and Nokia has established its two global R&D centers in Beijing and Hangzhou.

In contrast, India and Eastern Europe benefit greatly from the perception of highly qualified staff, leading global companies to seek out new talent in these markets to augment their own resources in the home country. For example, The UK-based Concurrent Technologies of Colchester, Essex, has invested over £1 million to set up a base in Bangalore, India, where it hopes to recruit highly skilled specialist electronic design engineers, since India produces hundreds of thousands of very high-quality engineers each year. Concurrent Technologies is an MNE that designs, manufactures, and sells sophisticated computer equipment based on Intel CPU technology and has three offices in the USA and one in Beijing.

Role of foreign research and development sites

Although the dispersion of R&D facilities has been increasing, the division of work between the company's home office and the foreign R&D sites has generally kept most of the core technology and research at the central home site, with a greater emphasis on local customization and some specialized expertise at the foreign sites, as illustrated in Figure 11.4.

The role of a foreign R&D site can also evolve over time. Some may start as a site for adaptation of the home-based product to the local market and expand to add unique innovations to the products that are then taken up globally. Alternatively, some sites are initially set up as research facilities to seek out new technologies

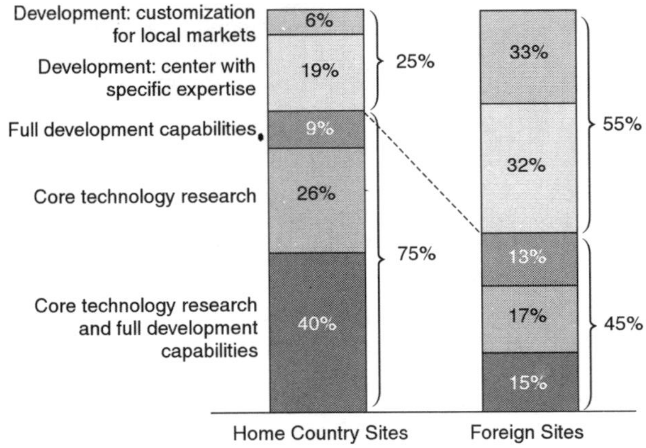

FIGURE 11.4 Activities of home-based and foreign R&Ds sites.(Adapted from Booz Allen Hamilton and INSEAD (2006). Fontainebleau, France: INSEAD, p. 6.)

from regions with competitive advantages (both academic and commercial) in the field in order to augment the home-based operations. Through acquisition or inspired innovation, these centers can move beyond knowledge transfer, to expanding their activities vertically, into developing complete products for the global company over time.

Organizational concepts for global research and development

Five organizational concepts for global R&D networks (Figure 11.5) have been identified through the research of Oliver Gassman.[2] Each concept is defined by the degree to which the individual sites differ in terms of their competency and/or knowledge base (i.e., expertise) and the degree to which they must cooperate in order to achieve the R&D goals of the global company.

The five organizational concepts are summarized briefly as follows:

1. *Ethnocentric (home-based) centralized R&D* – in this case all R&D activities are concentrated in the home country. It is assumed that the home country is technologically superior to its subsidiaries and partner companies in other countries, that decisions are taken by home office and that information sharing is asymmetrical. This is the 'think tank' approach where core technologies are closely guarded and the home office creates the new products, which are consequently manufactured and distributed worldwide. (For example, Apple is famous for its "top secret" design center in California, which created the Mac, iPod, and iPhone product lines; even employees working in the same campus but not part of the design teams are kept in the dark about new product development until the company, and Steve Jobs, decide the new products are ready to be unveiled.) The main weaknesses of such an approach are lack of awareness/sensitivity of foreign markets or

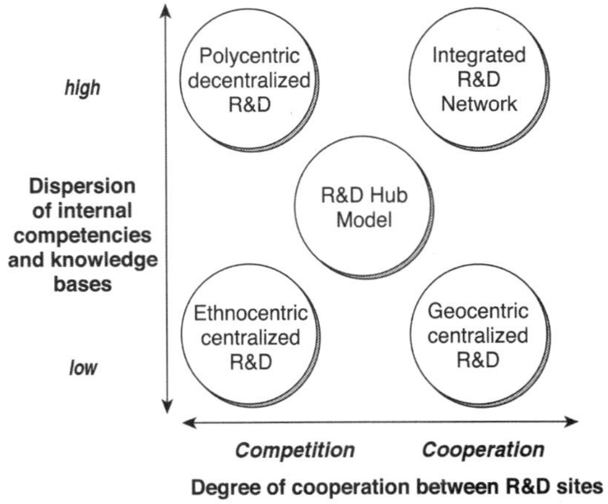

FIGURE 11.5 Five concepts of organizational design based on degree of cooperation vs competencies in R&D sites. (From Boutellier, R., Gassmann, O., von Zedtwitz, M. (2008). *Managing Global Innovation, Uncovering the Secrets of Future Competitiveness*, 3rd revised edn (2nd revised edn in 2000, 1st edn. in 1999). Berlin: Springer, p. 629.)

foreign technology trends, insufficient consideration of local market needs/adaptations, and a strong "not-invented-here" culture that is resistant to any ideas from outside the home site (whether internally or from other companies).

2 *Geocentric (foreign) centralized R&D* – when a company is dependent on foreign markets and local competencies, it becomes critical to incorporate that into the designs of products and services. The geocentric centralized model seeks to overcome the "home base" bias by combining the local market expertise from foreign sites with the efficiencies of a centralized R&D center. An example of this would be Nissan, who implemented this model in the 1990s to develop the Nissan Primera automobile for the European market. A core team of 100 engineers was created who had experienced European culture during numerous visits to the foreign markets working with the Nissan foreign marketing and technology liaison offices. The main weaknesses of this approach include strong dependencies on managers with strong intercultural experience and potentially less than complete coverage of local content restrictions and market specifications.

3 *Polycentric (multiple), decentralized R&D* – whereas the ethnocentric and geocentric centralized approaches may fail to sufficiently consider local requirements, the polycentric decentralized model ensures the most complete adaptations. This model has typically evolved from a foreign site that was originally set up to respond to customer product localization and manufacturing and expanded its activities. This can result in a federation of R&D sites, each reporting locally and working more or less independently of each other. The weaknesses in this approach include a lack of technology focus (as a company),

a lack of information sharing among sites, inefficiency and parallel developments, and problems creating critical mass around new ideas.

4 *R&D hub model* – this model seeks to combine tight central controls and resource allocation to avoid duplication of effort and ensure effective information sharing. eBay, Inc., has a centralized R&D home base in San Jose California as well as foreign R&D centers in India and China. In most cases R&D projects are assigned by San Jose to the various teams under very strict guidelines and control. This leverages the central coordination and ensures high reliability and integration of solutions for the global product, but limits greatly the local creativity and innovation. The weaknesses in this model include the high costs of coordination and time, and the danger of inhibiting creativity and flexibility in foreign sites through central directives.
5 *Integrated R&D network* – to fully exploit innovation and capabilities from around the globe, some companies are moving to an integrated R&D network model where different sites in the network are treated as leaders in a specific field, component or product, and apply their specialization to a globally coordinated set of strategic goals. The links in the network can change along with the projects, but, overall, the idea is to leverage local strengths across the global network. eBay, Inc., began applying this approach with an R&D center it acquired in Israel (part of Shopping.com, acquired in 2005) that specialized in machine learning and clustering technologies for structuring unstructured data. The weaknesses of this model include high coordination costs and potential complex decision processes and institutional rules to deal with the application and implementation of the solutions across the company (both technically and financially – as revenues and costs may no longer be accrued within the same country).

Although the five different organizational concepts have each been described separately, the reality is that the R&D organization of a given global company is often a function of historical growth of global footprint, the nature of the product or service (how global vs local it is) and the complexity of coordinaton (depending on the number of sites). There is often an evolution or mutation from one form to another, reflecting the changing needs, assets, and priorities of the global company. However, the chosen configuration should represent the optimal trade-off between tight control for global coordination vs the required flexibility to allow for local innovation and support for a given global corporate strategy.

Leading global R&D projects across multiple sites

The key issues to leveraging a global network of R&D centers in delivering a product roadmap can be grouped into two broad challenges: the global transfer of knowledge and global project coordination across multiple sites. When compared with working in a co-located domestic setting, complexities arise due to distance (e.g., difference in time zone limits overlapping workday), language and culture (e.g., both common language as well as a shared understanding of the company and function specific terminology), and the complexity of codifying much of the context and ideas.

One can imagine any global R&D project being broken down into three basic phases: pre-project, project execution, and market introduction. This idea is illustrated in Figure 11.6.

In the first phase, pre-project, teams are immersed in idea generation and knowledge sharing; this requires managing within a creative and unstructured environment. In this phase it is critical to create a shared understanding of the project by the global team while transforming ideas into explicit knowledge. The maximum amount of open and unstructured communication (face-to-face whenever possible) is most critical at this stage.

As the project becomes defined and moves towards execution, the need to provide more structure and control to the development process becomes critical to the successful implementation and launch of a given product or service. Milestones, costs, and more general project management methodologies are used to track progress and ensure delivery.

Finally, the market introduction of a global product to multiple markets requires the development teams to explain, motivate, and plan with multiple marketing and sales teams across different regions and coordinate successful plans for each market.

Companies use different management techniques and supporting infrastructure at each phase of the project, each of which can take place at a different geographical location in the network. These methods, along with the organizational concepts described above, define the form and function of the global R&D network of a given company.

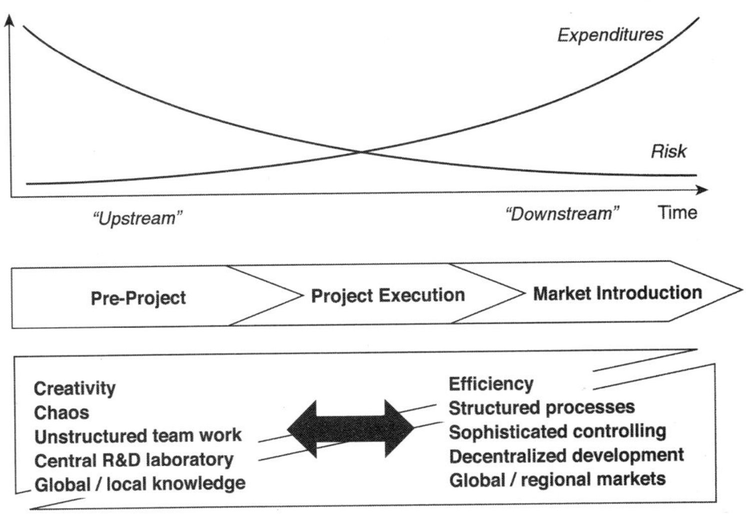

FIGURE 11.6 Management of three phases of R&D. (From Gassmann, O., von Zedtwitz, M. (1999). New Concepts and Trends in International R&D Organization. *Research Policy*, *28*, 231–50.)

To summarize, technology is a significant source of competitive advantage.

1 Managing knowledge-intensive enterprises and/or developing technology-intensive products and services on a global basis represents an increasingly complex set of challenges, raising strategic questions about the role of foreign vs home-based R&D, the organizational concepts for managing a network of R&D sites, and the challenges of executing a global product roadmap across multiple sites.
2 The global trend over the last three decades is towards increasing dispersion of R&D sites globally and over time an increasingly important role for the foreign sites in leading various parts of the global product roadmap.
3 There are five basic organizational concepts (ethnocentric, geocentric, polycentric, R&D hub, and integrated R&D network) that are based on the core competencies of each site and the extent to which more than one site needs to cooperate with another to deliver results. A given R&D network may evolve and change between these forms, depending on the optimal balance between centralized control and local freedoms required to cost-effectively achieve the desired innovation on a global scale.
4 Executing a global product roadmap among multiple sites requires a different set of management methods for each of three different generic phases of a global project: pre-project (idea generation), project execution, and market introduction. As the product goes from idea to end-user deliverable, the management environment must make the transition from one that encourages unstructured and continuous open communication to one with highly structured, time- and milestone-based methodologies, and systems in order to achieve successful market introduction.

Internet and E-Commerce Diffusion

In 2008, nearly a quarter of the world's population, about 1.5 billion users, used the Internet on a regular basis. By 2012, this number is expected to surpass 1.9 billion. Users accessed the Internet through more than 1.5 billion devices (e.g., PCs, mobile phones, online videogame consoles). This number is expected to double to over 3 billion devices by 2012.

The remainder of this chapter explores the spread and impact of the Internet and e-commerce around the globe.

Geographic dispersion of the Internet

Figure 11.7 lists the top 20 countries by number of Internet users. It shows the USA in second place after China. Together, these countries represent over three-quarters of the total global population "on the net." However, different countries are adopting and leveraging the Internet at different rates. For example, when comparing the penetration rates of the Internet by country (i.e., the percentage of the total population that is online) you find that the USA has a penetration rate of 72.5 percent,

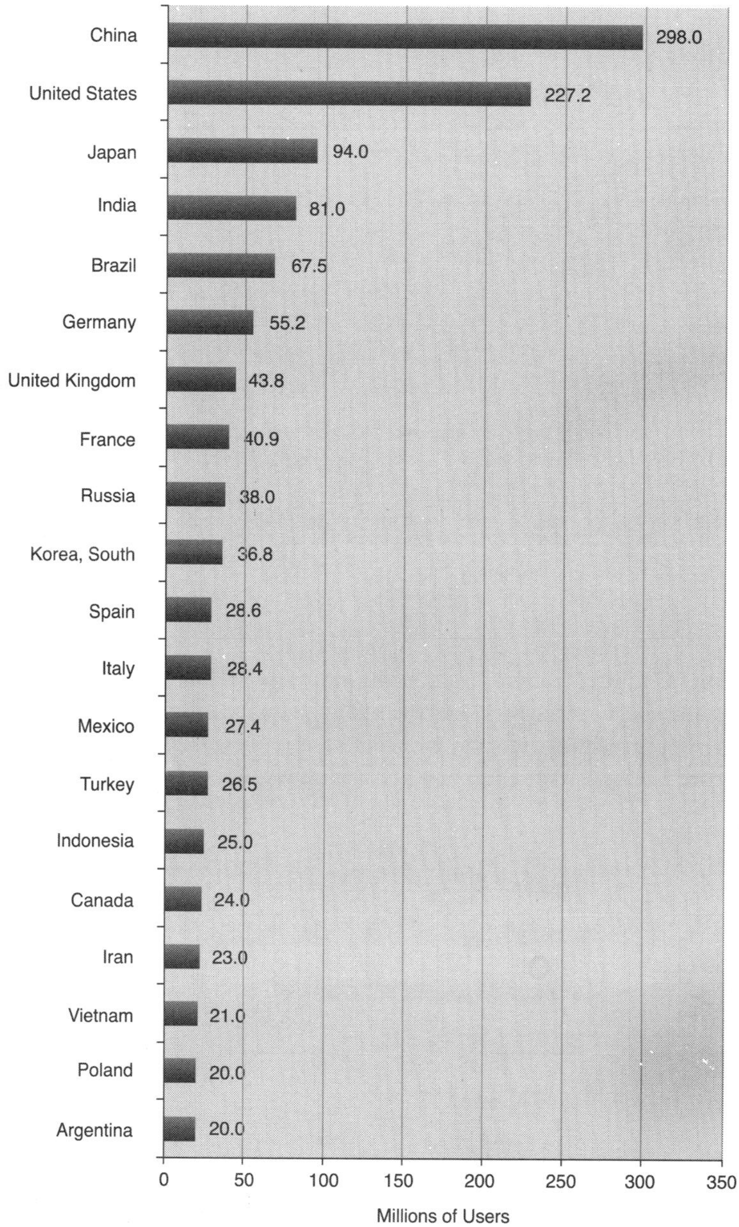

FIGURE 11.7 Internet top 20 countries by number of users (millions). (Internet World Stats – www.internetworldstats.com/top20.htm. 1,596,270,108 estimated world Internet users of March 31, 2009. Copyright © 2009, Miniwatts Marketing Group.)

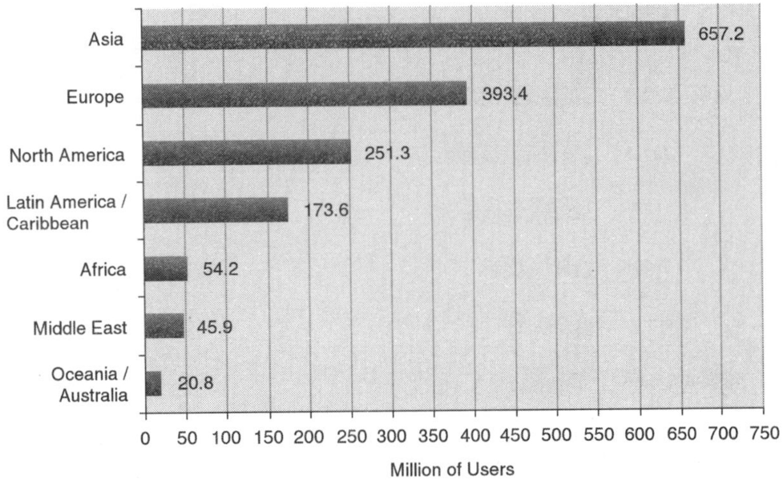

FIGURE 11.8 Number of internet users (millions) by geographic regions. (Internet World Stats – www.internetworldstats.com/stats.htm. Estimated Internet users 1,596,270,108 for March 31, 2009. Copyright © 2009, Miniwatts Marketing Group.)

(according to www.internetworldstats.com), which is significantly higher than the 19 percent for China (according to www.internetworldstats.com), even though by absolute numbers, China clearly has the higher number of Internet users.

Figure 11.8 presents the total number of users globally by geographic region, while Figure 11.9 presents their respective penetration rates by geographic region,

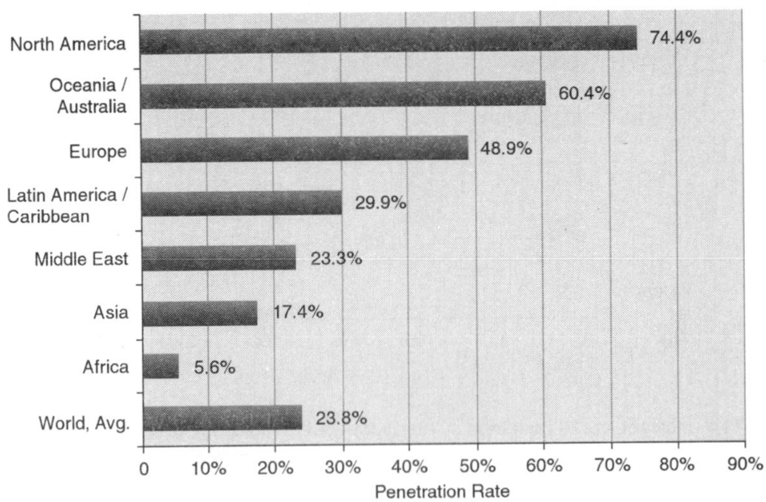

FIGURE 11.9 Internet penetration rates (percent) by geographic regions. (Internet World Stats – www.internetworldstats.com/stats.htm. Penetration rates are based on a world population of 6,710,029,070 and 1,596,270,108 estimated Internet users for March 31, 2009. Copyright © 2009, Miniwatts Marketing Group.)

TABLE 11.1 US and UK National Distribution of Internet Users by Gender, 2008–13

	US Internet users, by gender, 2008–13 (millions and % of total)					
	2008	*2009*	*2010*	*2011*	*2012*	*2013*
Male	19.5	20.1	20.7	21.2	21.7	22.1
% of total	51.1%	51.1%	51.0%	50.8%	50.6%	50.5%
Female	18.6	19.3	19.9	20.5	21.1	21.6
% of total	48.9%	48.9%	49.0%	49.2%	49.4%	49.5%
Total	38.1	39.4	40.6	41.7	42.8	43.7

Note: eMarketer defines an internet user as any person who accesses the internet from any location at least once per month.
Source: eMarketer, January 2009.

	UK Internet users, by gender, 2008–13 (millions and % of total)					
	2008	*2009*	*2010*	*2011*	*2012*	*2013*
Male	93.0	95.9	98.9	101.4	103.7	105.9
% total	48.2%	48.2%	48.2%	48.1%	48.0%	47.9%
Female	99.9	103.2	106.3	109.4	112.3	115.2
% total	51.8%	51.8%	51.8%	51.9%	52.0%	52.1%

Note: an internet user is anyone who accesses the Internet at least once per month from any location.
Source: eMarketer, January 2009: http://www.emarketer.com/Report.aspx?code=emarketer2000571emarketer, January–February 2009. http://www.emarketer.com/Report.aspx?code=emarketer 2000574.

as of March 2009. The differences in ranking across these two charts suggest a lot about the different stages of maturity, accessibility, and use of the Internet by region. We investigate this factor in more depth in the section on e-readiness.

Comparative Internet demographics: gender, race and age

User demographics within each country can also vary. Table 11.1 shows national distribution of Internet usage by gender in the UK and the USA. Note that female usage is higher in the USA both today and in the forecast through to 2013. The opposite is true for the UK. Most countries have a higher ratio of male usage to female usage.

Usage patterns can also vary by population group. Table 11.2 summarizes the results of a study in the USA by the Pew Internet and American Life Project that surveyed more than 20,000 men and women over five years. The survey highlights the most popular uses of the Internet by gender, race, and age.

The survey found that men use the Internet for solitary pursuits (e.g., news, content or transactional websites like stock or ticket sales), whereas women use it to enrich their relationships (e.g., through e-mail or support group websites). Both use the Internet for research but men target subjects like sports, politics, finance, and do-it-yourself information, whereas women are more interested in searches on health, medical, and religious information. Women are also more

TABLE 11.2 Internet Usage Differences by Gender, Race, and Age

	Percent	Percent
Men are more likely than women to do these activities online	*Online men*	*Online women*
Get news	77	66
Buy travel services or make reservations	60	51
Check sports scores and information	59	27
Get political news	57	42
Participate in online auction	28	18
Create content for the Internet	25	16
Download music files	18	11
Buy/sell stocks, bonds, mutual funds	16	9
Women are more likely than men to do these activities online	*Online women*	*Online men*
Get health information	85	75
Get spiritual and religious information	73	56
Use support-group websites	63	46
Online whites are more likely than minorities to do these activities	*Online whites*	*Online minorities*
Buy a product	63	53
Participate in online auction	24	16
African-Americans are more likely than whites to do these activities online	*Online blacks*	*Online whites*
Do research for school or job training	71	58
Look for information about a new job	61	38
Listen to music online	46	30
Download music files	25	13
Hispanics are more likely than nonHispanic whites to do these activities online	*Online Hispanics*	*Online whites*
Look for new job information	61	38
Listen to music online	46	30
Young internet users (ages 18–29) are more likely than others to do these activities online	*Young internet users*	*Those 30+*
Research for school or job training	76	48
Look for new job information	65	31
Use instant messaging	59	33
Listen to music online	53	27
Look up sports scores and information	51	37
Look for information about a place to live	43	27
Download music files	28	11
Share files from my computer	27	17
Log on using a wireless device	26	13
Using dating websites	16	5

TABLE 11.2 Cont.

	Percent	*Percent*
Online seniors (65+) are more likely than young internet users to do this online	*Online seniors*	*Those 18–29*
Use email	96	91
Online middle-aged (30–64) are more likely than the young or seniors to do this online	*Online middle-aged*	*Younger and older Internet users*
Research a product or service	81	71
Look for health and medical information	70	57
Do work-related research	56	38

Source: The Mainstreaming of Online Life. Pew Internet & American Life Project, 2005, http://pewresearch.org/assets/files/trends2005-internet.pdf, pg.5, accessed on June 7, 2009.

likely than men to go online to obtain maps and directions, which is remarkably similar to "offline" behavior. Men are also more likely to download new software and technologies and solve tech problems on their own.

Minorities (Blacks and Hispanics) were less likely to buy online than whites; however, they were more likely to do job searches, download music files, and other content from the Internet than whites were.

In terms of age differences, young Internet users (ages 18–29) were more likely to take advantage of almost every aspect of the Internet than older users (ages 30+), including researching online, downloading content, communicating (e.g., instant messaging), sharing files over the net, and even dating. For seniors, e-mail was by far the most common use of the Internet.

In addition, average weekly hours spent on the Internet differs by country. Table 11.3 lists the average weekly hours spent on various media by adults in selected countries. Note that regardless of the differences in weekly hours, in all cases the Internet has become the most popular media channel. In India, the

TABLE 11.3 Average Weekly Time Spent (hours) with Media in Selected Countries (2007)

	Internet	*TV/movies*	*Music*	*Games*	*Total*
Australia (n = 864)	22	14	8	3	46
France (n = 300)	18	12	8	3	40
Germany (n = 300)	21	11	10	2	44
Italy (n = 300)	23	10	8	3	44
New Zealand (n = 219)	22	14	10	2	48
Spain (n = 300)	19	10	8	3	41
UK (n = 300)	22	14	9	3	47
US (n = 1,085)	21	15	8	3	47

Note: ages 18+.
Source: Cisco Systems, The Connected Consumer – Australia and New Zealand, conducted by Illumines May 20 2008: http://www.emarketer.com/Article.aspx?R=1006541.

Internet has become a competitor to television for those families who can afford to have a computer and access at home.

E-commerce around the globe

According to IDC Digital Marketplace Model and Forecast report, June 2008, nearly half of all Internet users in 2008 would make online purchases, and by 2012 there would be more than 1 billion online buyers worldwide, making business-to-consumer (B2C) transactions worth $1.2 trillion. Business-to-business (B2B) e-commerce will be 10 times larger, totaling $12.4 trillion worldwide in 2012.

A global Internet shopping trends study by the Nielsen Company found that between 2006 and 2008 the percentage of the world's online population which had shopped online rose from 10 percent to more than 85 percent, as noted in Figure 11.10. Among the Internet users, the highest percentage of shopping online is found in South Korea, where 99 percent of those with Internet access have used it to shop, followed by the UK (97 percent), Germany (97 percent), Japan (97 percent), with the USA eighth at 94 percent. Globally, the most popular categories of products purchased over the Internet are Books, clothing/shoes/accessories, videos/DVDs/games, airline tickets, and electronic equipment, as noted in Figure 11.11 The most popular payment method online is the credit card, as shown Figure 11.12.

In the USA, e-commerce sales totaled $141 billion dollars in 2008, representing 5 percent of total retail sales (same as 2007); online sales are expected to grow faster than total retail sales, to represent 6 percent of total US retail sales in 2009 and 2010, 7 percent in 2011 and 8 percent in 2012 and 2013. Table 11.4 lists the top 10 US online retailers, as of October 2008.

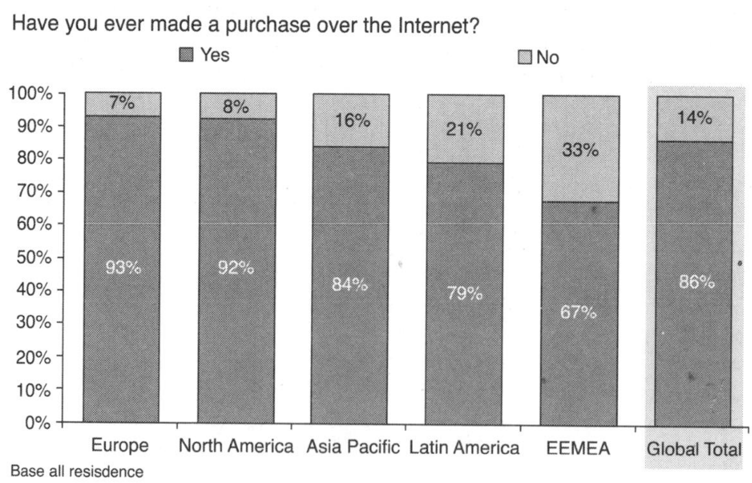

FIGURE 11.10 Internet users who have purchased online. (Nielsen (2008). *Trends in Online Shopping. A Nielson Global Consumes Report*: http://th.nielsen.com.)

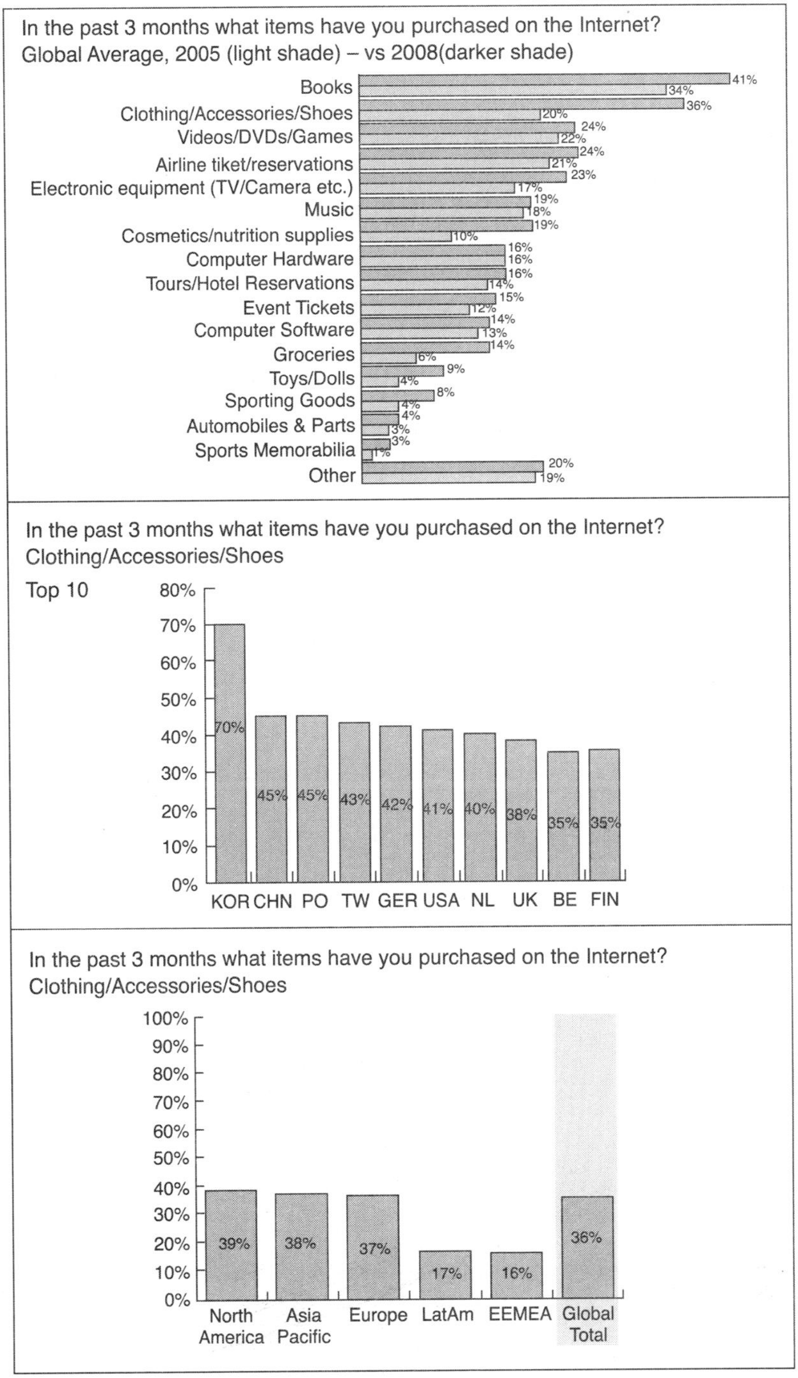

FIGURE 11.11 Items purchased online. (Nielsen (2008). *Trends in Online Shopping. A Nielson Global Consumes Report*: http://th.nielsen.com.)

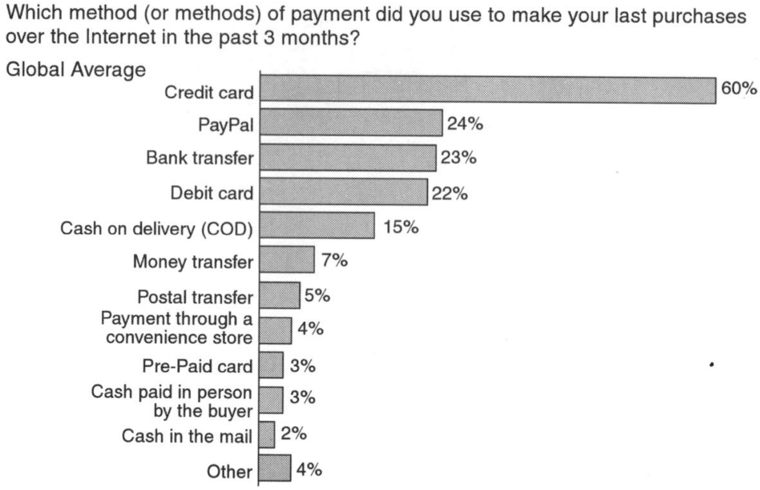

FIGURE 11.12 Method of payment online over past three months. (Nielsen (2008). Trends in Online Shopping. A Nielson Global Consumes Report: http://th.nielsen.com.)

Worldwide spending on Internet advertising in 2008 totaled $65 billion, which represents nearly 10 percent of all advertisement spending across all media. This share is expected to reach 13.6 percent by 2011 as Internet ad spending grows to $107 billion worldwide.

Table 11.5 illustrates some of the most relevant factors regarding demographic criteria that dictate the likelihood for a given consumer to click on online advertisements. Younger users are more likely to click on banner or video advertisements, whereas high-income earners are more likely to block advertisements through DVR, spam filters or other tools. Nearly two-thirds of users who are

TABLE 11.4 Top 10 US Online Retailers by Unique (Separate Individuals) Audience, October 2008

Brand	*Unique audience*	*Time per person*
eBay	49,213	1:47:26
Amazon	48,261	0:22:45
Wal-Mart Stores	25,312	0:13:55
Target	23,827	0:09:36
Netflix	14,284	0:34:58
Dell	14,272	0:14:13
Best Buy	12,446	0:10:57
Sears	11,752	0:07:33
The Home Depot	11,053	0:09:52
JCPenney	10,703	0:16:09

Unique audience in thousands; time per person in hours:minutes:seconds.

Source: Nielsen (2008). *Trends in Online Shopping.* A Nielsen Global Reoprt: http://th.nielsen.com.

TABLE 11.5 Demographic Profile of US Internet Users Who Are Likely to Click on Online Advertisements by Format, August 2008

	Text links	*Right banner*	*Top banner*	*Video ads*
Age				
<25	14%	14%	23%	31%
25–34	19%	19%	22%	21%
35–44	19%	22%	22%	14%
45–54	22%	22%	18%	16%
55–64	18%	16%	10%	13%
65+	7%	6%	4%	5%
Income				
<$50,000	36%	33%	39%	49%
$51,000–75,000	18%	20%	18%	18%
$76,000–100,000	15%	16%	11%	11%
$101,000–150,000	16%	15%	17%	10%
$151,000–250,000	10%	11%	9%	7%
$250,000+	5%	5%	6%	6%
*Frequency**				
First visit	17%	12%	14%	19%
Daily	29%	31%	36%	33%
Weekly	33%	34%	31%	31%
Monthly	15%	16%	14%	12%
Sporadic	7%	7%	5%	6%

Note: numbers may not add up to 100% due to rounding.

*Frequency of visiting the site on which the ad appears.

Source: iPerceptions Inc. survey provided to eMarketer, October 6, 2008: emarketer.com at http://www.emarketer.com/Article.aspx?R=I006648.

likely to click on an advertisement are a daily or a weekly visitor to the specific site, which suggests that frequency of visit is another relevant factor.

Impact on MNEs, SMEs, and intermediaries

The Internet can remove barriers to communication with customers and employees created by geography, time zones, and location. However, as may be seen in the final section of this chapter, physical barriers in the world can slow down or even stop progress in this area.

For MNEs, the Internet provides the opportunity to disseminate products globally, but it can also allow quicker imitation by competitors, downward pressure on price (as customers gain more selection and competition grows), and a significant challenge in managing various distribution channels.

For SMEs, the Internet provides a very inexpensive way to enter into international trade, both in developed and in developing countries. Small Latin American or Asian entrepreneurs are opening their own sites or leveraging platforms such as eBay or Amazon to sell their wares to developed countries. For example, eForcity started in 2001 by selling electronic accessories through eBay, grew by 2008 to a business selling over $40 million, working directly with over 100 Chinese manufacturers, and became the top-rated seller on eBay, by receiving over four million positive feedback scores from buyers on the site.[3]

A common belief, held early on, was that the Internet would eliminate all intermediaries, as it enables direct interaction between manufacturers and customers, home owners and buyers, musicians and their fans, and so forth. In fact, the impact of the Internet on intermediaries has been mixed. There have certainly been significant changes in the distribution of digitized products such as music (i.e., Apple's iTunes site), movies (i.e., Netflix), ringtones, software, etc. There have even been changes in service industries such as tax filing, brokerage, retail, and auction. However, a new breed of intermediaries grew whose primary value is not in the handling of physical distribution but in the aggregation, organization, interpretation, and dissemination of information. These "infomediaries" have become common throughout the Internet in areas such as Online Comparison Shopping sites (e.g., Shopping.com) that aggregate the best online offers from stores in order to help buyers make a better purchasing decision. Even Google can be thought of as a generalist infomediary of all the content on the web, which it monetizes by serving advertisements that are relevant to the searches of their users.

To summarize, the diffusion of the Internet and derivatives of the Internet, such as e-commerce and m-commerce (mobile e-commerce based on Internet and cellular technology), significantly affects international business:

1 Nearly a quarter of the world's population (1.5 billion) already uses the Internet, and this is expected to grow to close to 2 billion by 2012.
2 Although China leads the world in number of users, its penetration rate (19 percent) is very small compared to other countries. Penetration rates indicate the relative maturity, affordability, and accessibility of the Internet for the local population of a given country.
3 Usage patterns in a given country differ by gender, race, and age. Average time spent on the Internet vs other media differed between markets.
4 E-commerce activity around the globe has grown rapidly over the past few years for both B2B and B2C transactions. Online shopping has moved from a niche activity to a mainstream pursuit among Internet users and online sales represent a growing proportion (5 percent in 2008) of total retail sales. Online purchases are now spanning almost all categories of offline stores, as the online shopping population grows in confidence. The most popular payment method online is the credit card, followed by PayPal and bank transfers.
5 Internet advertising now represents about 10 percent of total advertising. People's propensity to click online advertisements differs by age, income bracket, and the frequency of visit to a given website.
6 For MNEs, the Internet represents both an opportunity (to expand geographically faster) and a threat (increased competitive pressures). For SMEs,

the Internet promises an economically viable mechanism for growth and a medium through which they can compete with larger companies. For intermediaries, the impact has been split between those who have been removed and those (i.e., the infomediaries) who have created a new business model on this medium.

E-Readiness

The Economist Intelligence Unit (EIU) has published an annual e-readiness ranking of the world's largest economies since 2000.[4] The model evaluates the economic, political, social, and technological assets of 69 different countries globally. In essence, it provides a snapshot of the state of a given country's information and communications technology (ICT) and the ability of its consumers, businesses, and government to leverage this ICT (including wireless connectivity) to their benefit. The premise is that a country that succeeds doing more online becomes more transparent and efficient and can support new business models and industries that can drive growth and innovation.

The rankings are a weighted collection of nearly 100 quantitative and qualitative criteria, grouped into six categories: connectivity and technology infrastructure; business environment; social and cultural environment; legal environment; government policy and vision; and consumer and business adoption.

Table 11.6 below lists the 69 countries rank ordered according to their overall e-readiness score. In the following section we will briefly define each of criteria used for this survey and discuss some of the interesting developments in some of the leading countries in each area.

Understanding a country's stage of development and forecasted growth in terms of e-readiness is useful both to provide a benchmark for governments to gauge the success of their technology initiatives against those of other countries, as well as providing companies that wish to invest in online operations with an overview of the world's most promising investment locations.

Connectivity and technology infrastructure

Ready access to voice and data communication networks is a critical foundation for enabling advanced digital services. A World Bank report highlighted the impact of broadband on growth in 120 countries from 1980 to 2006. Its analysis revealed that each 10 percentage points of broadband penetration results in a 1.21 percent increase in per capita GDP growth in developed countries, and a 1.38 percent increase in developing countries.[5] However, the demands on infrastructure have increased dramatically over the past few years. Regular telephone infrastructure – i.e., public switched telephone network (PSTN) – is no longer sufficient for Internet users. Broadband access – e.g., fiber, cable modems, – digital subscribe line (DSL), or wireless – have now become basic requirements for leveraging all the Internet can provide. Figure 11.13 lists the countries by region that scored highest in terms of availability of broadband infrastructure.

TABLE 11.6 Countries Ranked in Order for E-Readiness, 2007

Country	*Category scores by category weight (percent)*						
	Overall score	*Connectivity and technology infra-structure (20 percent)*	*Business enviroment (15 percent)*	*Social and cultural environment (15 percent)*	*Legal environment (10 percent)*	*Government policy and vision (15 percent)*	*Consumer and business adoption (25 percent)*
Denmark	8.88	8.40	8.65	8.60	8.50	9.85	9.15
USA	8.85	8.10	8.59	8.80	9.00	9.00	9.50
Sweden	8.85	8.60	8.40	8.20	8.50	9.70	9.35
Hong Kong	8.72	8.50	8.62	6.80	9.70	9.10	9.50
Switzerland	8.61	9.60	8.53	7.60	8.25	9.00	8.40
Singapore	8.60	8.10	8.67	7.00	8.55	9.40	9.45
UK	8.59	8.30	8.65	7.80	8.50	8.65	9.25
Netherlands	8.50	8.30	8.58	7.60	8.50	9.35	8.65
Australia	8.46	8.10	8.39	8.60	9.40	8.70	8.20
Finland	8.43	7.80	8.65	7.80	8.25	9.00	8.90
Austria	8.39	7.90	8.09	7.40	8.50	9.05	9.10
Norway	8.35	7.30	8.04	8.20	8.25	9.35	8.90
Canada	8.30	7.90	8.69	7.40	8.95	8.40	8.60
New Zealand	8.19	7.30	8.22	8.20	8.85	8.35	8.50
Bermuda	8.15	7.80	8.41	6.40	9.15	8.35	8.80
South Korea	8.08	7.10	7.47	8.20	7.80	8.75	8.85
Taiwan	8.05	8.00	7.96	8.00	7.80	8.15	8.20
Japan	8.01	7.50	7.16	8.00	8.00	9.05	8.30
Germany	8.00	7.10	8.25	8.20	8.25	7.85	8.45
Belgium	7.90	8.00	8.10	6.80	8.25	8.35	7.95
Ireland	7.86	6.80	8.59	7.80	8.50	7.50	8.25
France	7.77	6.90	7.97	7.40	8.25	8.15	8.15
Israel	7.58	8.00	7.61	7.20	7.00	7.05	8.00
Malta	7.56	6.65	7.76	6.60	8.00	8.25	8.15
Italy	7.45	6.90	6.85	7.40	8.50	7.90	7.60
Spain	7.29	6.70	7.84	7.00	8.00	7.25	7.35
Portugal	7.14	7.00	7.33	6.60	8.00	6.75	7.35
Estonia	6.84	6.00	7.78	6.00	7.35	6.25	7.60
Slovenia	6.66	6.40	7.21	6.60	6.50	5.75	7.20
Chile	6.47	4.60	7.99	6.20	8.00	6.80	6.40
Czech Rep.	6.32	5.45	7.44	6.00	7.05	5.55	6.70
Greece	6.31	4.70	6.68	6.60	7.95	6.90	6.20

UAE	6.22	5.20	7.54	6.00	5.55	6.45	6.50
Hungary	6.16	5.20	7.11	6.00	6.80	4.85	7.00
South Africa	6.10	4.30	6.84	5.00	6.60	7.05	7.00
Malaysia	5.97	5.30	7.38	4.60	5.55	6.45	6.35
Latvia	5.88	5.95	7.06	5.60	6.45	4.55	5.85
Mexico	5.86	3.55	7.06	5.20	7.40	6.80	6.20
Slovakia	5.84	4.50	7.48	6.00	6.50	4.55	6.35
Poland	5.80	5.10	7.18	5.60	7.05	4.70	5.80
Lithuania	5.78	4.80	6.93	5.60	6.50	4.70	6.35
Turkey	5.61	4.00	6.66	6.00	5.10	5.75	6.15
Brazil	5.45	3.10	6.88	5.60	7.40	6.10	5.20
Argentina	5.40	4.00	6.21	5.60	7.15	5.40	5.20
Romania	5.32	4.20	6.73	5.00	6.45	5.60	4.95
Jamaica	5.05	3.70	6.17	5.20	7.40	5.10	4.40
Saudi Arabia	5.05	3.80	6.37	4.80	4.80	6.05	4.90
Bulgaria	5.01	4.40	6.67	4.80	6.20	4.55	4.45
Thailand	4.91	3.10	6.97	4.40	5.65	5.40	4.85
Venezuela	4.89	3.75	4.57	4.60	6.60	5.75	4.95
Peru	4.83	2.70	6.20	5.00	7.40	5.10	4.40
Jordan	4.77	3.40	6.27	5.40	5.10	5.25	4.15
Colombia	4.69	3.60	6.27	4.40	6.30	5.40	3.70
India	4.66	2.90	6.25	5.20	5.50	4.60	4.50
Philippines	4.66	2.70	6.43	4.40	4.65	5.05	5.10
China	4.43	3.50	6.37	4.80	3.60	3.70	4.55
Russia	4.27	3.90	6.08	4.80	4.45	2.85	3.95
Egypt	4.26	2.75	6.04	5.00	4.00	5.10	3.55
Ecuador	4.12	2.85	5.04	4.20	6.05	4.25	3.70
Ukraine	4.02	2.95	5.27	4.60	4.45	2.85	4.30
Sri Lanka	3.93	1.80	5.90	4.40	5.40	3.75	3.70
Nigeria	3.92	2.00	5.08	4.40	5.15	4.40	3.70
Pakistan	3.79	2.90	5.34	3.00	4.65	3.90	3.65
Kazakhstan	3.78	2.40	5.93	4.20	3.40	2.85	4.05
Vietnam	3.73	2.25	5.98	3.60	4.05	4.25	3.20
Algeria	3.63	3.20	5.17	4.00	3.30	3.20	3.20
Indonesia	3.39	2.10	6.33	3.20	2.80	3.40	3.00
Azerbaijan	3.26	2.70	5.39	3.00	2.60	2.85	3.10
Iran	3.08	2.80	4.17	4.60	2.10	2.50	2.50

Source: The Economist Intelligence Unit (2007). *The 2007 E-Readiness Rankings*. London: The Economist.

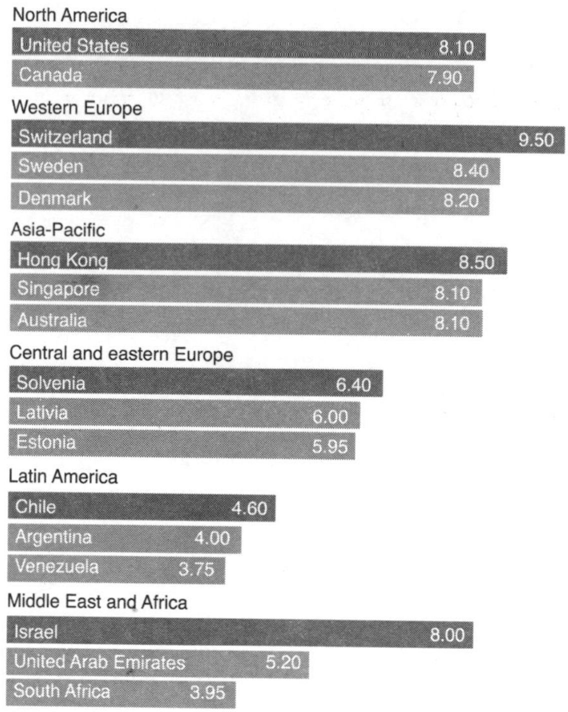

FIGURE 11.13 Connectivity and technology infrastructure: top scores by region. (The Economist Intelligence Unit (2007). *The 2007 E-Readiness Rankings.* London: The Economist.)

In addition to availability, affordability is another major factor when assessing the connectivity and technology infrastructure of a given country or region. The EIU report scored countries on a scale from 1 to 10, where 10 represented the highest level of affordability based on the cost of a monthly subscription as a percentage of median household income.

Figure 11.14 summarizes the findings by region. North America and Western Europe enjoy the most affordable broadband in the world (it should be noted that

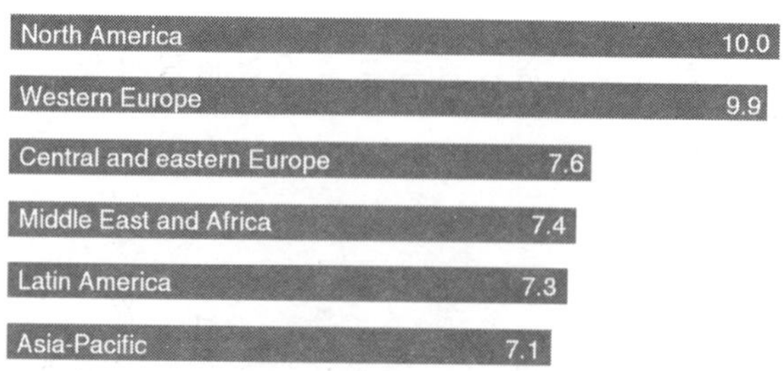

FIGURE 11.14 Average broadband affordability scores by region. (The Economist Intelligence Unit (2007). *The 2007 E-Readiness Rankings.* London: The Economist.)

in nearly every country in both regions, average broadband subscriptions represented less than 1 percent of median household monthly incomes). Across other regions the, costs represented 3–10 percent of household income, within range of a broad population of people.

Business environment

A business environment that consists of a stable government, a commitment to market competition, transparent taxation frameworks, and openness to borderless trade and investment is required to successfully leverage and nurture a digitized national economy. In North America, both Canada and the USA enjoy strong political stability, a positive foreign investment environment, and strong support for private enterprise and competition. In the 2007 report the USA dropped slightly, owing to a less stable political environment and concerns about macroeconomic growth prospects. In Western Europe, the most attractive business locations were Finland, Denmark, and the UK (Figure 11.15). The high ranking of the two Nordic countries is interesting, as they both have very high tax burdens but combine this with stable, transparent and effective institutions, competitive product markets, and a favorable official position on free trade. Eastern European

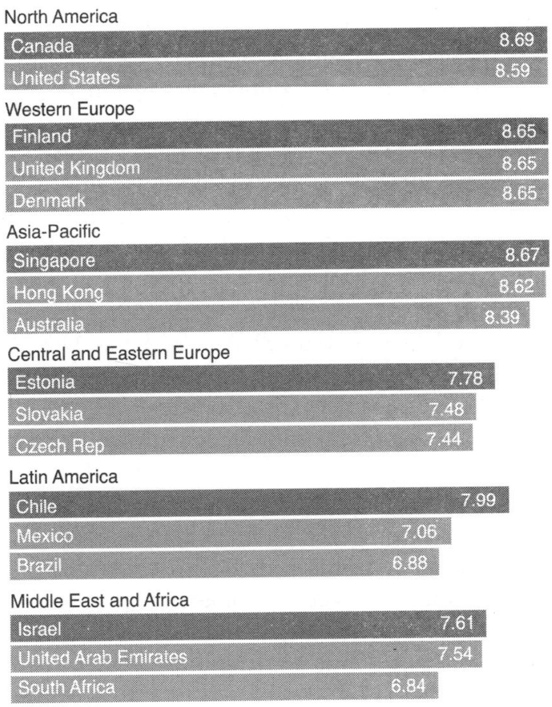

FIGURE 11.15 Business environment: top scores by region. (The Economist Intelligence Unit (2007). *The 2007 E-Readiness Rankings*. London: The Economist.)

countries have improved in recent years, in particular new members to the European Union (EU). In Asia, Singapore, and Hong Kong vie for the top spot; Singapore edging out primarily due to the China's increasing political influence over Hong Kong (China itself ranks low on business environment). In Latin America, Chile wins top spot thanks to its proven commitment to economic liberalization and structural reform since the 1970s. Mexico ranks second primarily due to the growing integration with the USA ever since the introduction of the North American Free Trade Agreement (NAFTA), which came into force in 1994. Israel enjoys the Middle East's top spot, notwithstanding the unclear political outlook and security situation. In Africa, South Africa represents the only country making significant progress both on political stability as well as improved foreign trade, tax policy, and in general a more open economy.

Social and cultural environment

Literacy and basic education are prerequisites to using the Internet and being able to access all the content and services available. In addition, this section measures the degree of experience and technical skills in the general population, as well as the level of entrepreneurship and innovation activity in the country and the degree to which governments support the training of these activities in education programs. In certain countries, governments are targeting special budgets and training programs to engage the elderly, disabled, and women online in order to provide them with access to all the services on offer online. For example, the government of Spain has made available $8 million in grants to organizations and projects aimed at familiarizing women and "vulnerable citizens" (elderly and disabled) with online services.

What role does language play in "Internet literacy"? Figure 11.16 highlights the top 10 languages on the Internet, as measured by number of users. In 2008, the top three (English, Chinese, and Spanish) accounted for over 50 percent of the total number of users online. To date, English is still the dominant international language; however, local services and, certainly, government use must be created in the local languages. According to the UN, the default language of the vast majority of websites in Central Asia and the Middle East is English; whereas the default for most sites in East Asia is the native language (i.e., Chinese, Japanese, or Korean). Increasingly, "native language" sites are serving not only the local population but also global diaspora populations living in other countries around the globe.

Mobile phones (cell phone) and social networks, each in their own way, contribute to e-literacy. The use of a mobile phone is simpler than a personal computer (PC), and the global use of text messaging (also known as SMS) has become a powerful tool for consumers to access commercial and public services, for businesses to advertise, and for governments to educate and inform, especially in developing countries where mobile phone penetration surpasses Internet-connected PC penetration by orders of magnitude. Social networks in developing countries are a very strong indicator of a vibrant online community that has begun to evolve and mature into networks of individuals beyond the intentions, guidance or control of

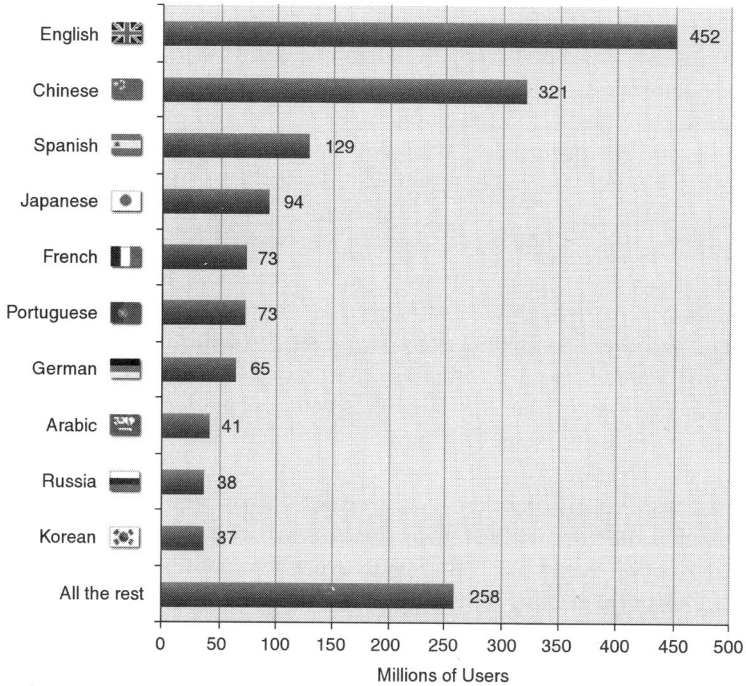

FIGURE 11.16 Top 10 Languages of the internet (millions of users). (Internet World Stats – www. internetworldstats.com/stats7.htm. Estimated Internet users is 1,581,571,589 for 2008. Copyright © 2009, Miniwatts Marketing Group.)

any formal entity. Examples of social networks include organizations like FaceBook and MySpace where people go to share their private data with others in their network or seek out new people in the network with common interests. These communities influence everything from communication patterns, to top music and movie choices, to purchasing decisions, and job searches.

Legal environment

E-business development depends on a country's overall legal framework and the specific laws governing the use of the Internet. For example, legal frameworks are needed to address online commerce, digital rights management, and intellectual property protection. Laws must protect consumer rights and intellectual property both online and offline and must foster development of digital security enablers such as authentication and certification of online transactions; they must allow new businesses to be registered quickly and easily and must not censor.

Top marks tend to go to North American or Asia Pacific countries; however, European organizations have led the development of relevant legislation for over a decade, with treaties on harmonizing approaches to cybercrime, digital data protection and privacy policies, and introduction of a framework for e-signature.

Government policy and vision

Governments can play a pivotal role in facilitating and even encouraging the adoption of the Internet and online services through clear and consistent policies on national investment in ICT infrastructure.

More directly, the government can adopt the use of the Internet and mandate it as the basis for transactions, communications, and interaction with citizens, suppliers and all other parties involved in providing or receiving services from public institutions. The buying power of a government is formidable enough to trigger significant online activity. For example, Chile introduced an online procurement and contract system through which the government processed more than $3 billion in 2005 and had over 164,000 registered suppliers (one-third of which were SMEs). Denmark mandated various transactions that must be completed online, including payments of taxes and other services. This was a strong catalyst for adoption of the Internet by many citizens. Denmark estimated to have saved over 100 million euros in administration costs after introducing the system.

The ultimate expression of citizen participation with the transparency and efficiency online is the potential for using the Internet for voting in elections. Various countries are in different stages of debate over the reliability and security of such a service. However, in 2007, Estonia – long in the forefront of using ICT in running the government and connecting it to the people – became the first country worldwide to introduce the Internet as an accepted voting channel.

Consumer and business adoption

Whereas the previous section considered government spending online, this section considers the consumer spending per capita, the level of online commerce and the availability and utilization of online public or private services for citizens and businesses. A 2007 IDC report estimated that B2B transaction volume in the USA would reach $650 billion by 2008, amounting to two-thirds of the world's $1 trillion B2B market at that time. Although the USA leads (by sheer volume) in this area, other countries have seen dramatic growth over this past decade and uniquely innovative services. Over 15 million businesses and consumers use Alibaba's online platform for buying and selling online in China. Although many of the services are free, over 100,000 businesses pay for advanced functionality. In Thailand, a number of mobile "loading" sites like Aryty enable the community of over 7 million Filipinos living and working abroad – who represent a major source of income for the relatives back home – to transfer funds directly to their mobile accounts. These portals have become a focal point for this community, as people rely on it for keeping in touch, and not simply for executing a transaction.

To summarize, since technology in general, and Internet technology in particular, are significant factors in international markets, "e-readiness" of countries and people should be examined. First, a country's "e-readiness" is a product of many factors: Internet connectivity and cost; the support and sophistication of the local business, social and cultural environments; the legal environments; the level of adoption by the government through various policies; and the level of of consumer and business adoption through availability and diversity of services. Second, National "e-readiness" varies greatly and offers guidance in terms of the future growth of e-commerce in a particular country or region. Studying the various factors provides important feedback about both the relative effectiveness of government policies as well as the relative potential of online services in each market.

Cross-Border E-Commerce

The 21st century ushered in an era of unprecedented growth in e-commerce which, in spite of the 2001–02 dot-com bubble bust (or perhaps because of it), created big expectations about the potential for cross-border e-commerce and trade. The promise of borderless, frictionless, and completely open transactions from one country to another over the Internet drove significant geographical expansion of MNEs (e.g., eBay, Yahoo, Amazon, ...) in the years following the dot-com bubble.

Despite the increasing popularity of online shopping within most markets around the world, cross-border trade through the Internet is growing more slowly. For example, a pan-European study[6] on e-commerce showed that the proportion of EU consumers buying at least one item over the Internet increased from an EU average of 27 percent to 33 percent between 2006 and 2008. These averages mask the huge popularity of online shopping in Nordic countries (over 90 percent) and in Western Europe's biggest markets in the UK, France, and Denmark (over 50 percent). In contrast, the growth in online purchasing between European countries has remained small, from 6 percent in 2006 to only 7 percent in 2008. What is holding back the cross-border trade?

Barriers to growth of cross-border E-commerce

Although most retailers already have websites that are visible to consumers everywhere, they still seem to operate along national borders; in practice, consumers are being refused or redirected back to their country of origin. Table 11.7 summarizes some of the main drivers behind this phenomenon.

Note, some of the issues are driven by "physical or real-world" constraints not immediately associated with Internet shopping, such as differences in technical standards outside of a home market (e.g., DVD players manufactured for Zone 1 work in the USA but not in Europe), cross-border payments, or shipping (e.g., a European customer order rejected because the customer could not fill in the "State" section in the US order form and the company was unable to calculate total delivery cost), and reverse logistics (e.g., handling returns outside of the home country).

Other issues are challenges unique to the Internet medium, such as the uses and limitations of search engines to drive traffic to a website outside of its home country or the legal restrictions regarding the sale or sharing of digital content or gambling services over the Internet.

E-commerce and taxation

E-commerce's impact extends to other realms. For example, it has made it more difficult to determine the origin of a product or a service, with concomitant implications

TABLE 11.7 Reasons That Could Discourage Businesses from Selling Across Borders

Language, cultural, and technical barriers	• Maintaining websites and customer support, complaint handling/dispute resolution in multiple languages • Different consumer preferences and technical standards translate into complex inventory management and website customization • Failure to understand customer demographics outside the home market
Cross-border logistics	• Lack of interoperability of postal systems and difficulty of managing the last mile to the consumer • "Border effect" increases cost of delivery • Difficult to set up reverse logistics to deal with returns
Cross-border payments	• Lack of interoperability of payment systems • Credit card fraud a real threat in cross-border transactions • Consumer reluctance concerning privacy/security
Administrative and regulatory barriers (*inter alia* VAT, national transposition of WEEE, copyright, consumer protection rules, selective distribution, sector-specific Rules)	• Uneven application at national level generates compliance costs that are prohibitive • Territorial nature of some rights may lead to market segmentation at retailer level • Retailers may refuse to serve some countries
Search and advertising	• Search engines might not naturally show cross-border offers, requiring more time and effort by consumers • Advertising is "geo-targeted" • Price comparison websites do not generally operate on a cross-border basis

VAT, value-added tax; WEEE, Waste Electrical and Electronics Equipment.
Source: Interviews with business stakeholders conducted between September and November 2008. European Union (2009). Report on Cross-Border E-Commerce in the EU. Brussels: EU.

for customs, tariffs, and taxation. This is because the server, the manufacturer, and the physical distributor may be located in different countries.

In the international arena, the implications of e-commerce taxation are more ominous. While cross-border catalog sales have existed for many years, they have not been substantial enough to generate a strong interest among governments. E-commerce has changed that. In the EU, value-added taxes (VAT) ranging from 15 to 25 percent – representing a key portion of government revenues – are at risk. In itself, a website is not considered a fixed place of business that would trigger taxation but it could be considered as such in conjunction with server location and other company operations in that country. However, web and server locations, as well as other components of e-commerce operations, are increasingly difficult to pinpoint. Furthermore, e-commerce makes it increasingly easy for MNEs to shift their domicile to low-tax locations and to offshore tax havens as it becomes difficult if not impossible for other nations to claim physical presence of the company in their territory. Problems such as transfer pricing become much more acute in this environment.

The Internet raises many other taxation issues. For instance, the traditional distinction between income and royalty taxation may be impossible to determine when a consumer downloads software from a vendor. Individual income tax may be largely avoided in countries with a territorial tax base, whereas the few countries with a global taxation base, such as the USA, may find it increasingly difficult to enforce their tax legislation. Certain states in the USA are seeking to claim tax revenues on Internet sales in spite of these challenges (See Box).

States Push to Collect Taxes on Internet Sales

New York – Shopping online can be a way to find bargains while steering clear of crowds and sales taxes. But those tax breaks are starting to erode. With the recession pummeling states' budgets, their governments increasingly want to fill the gaps by collecting taxes on Internet sales, which are growing even as the economy shudders.

And that is sparking conflict with companies that do business online only and have enjoyed being able to offer sales-tax free shopping.

One of the most aggressive states, New York, is being sued by Amazon.com Inc. over a new requirement that online companies must collect taxes on shipments to New York residents, even if the companies are located elsewhere. New York's governor also wants to tax *Taxman* covers and other songs downloaded from Internet services like iTunes.

The amount of money at stake nationwide is unclear; online sales were expected to make up about 8 percent of all retail sales in 2008 and total $204 billion, according to Forrester Research. This is up from $175 billion in 2007.

Based on that 2008 figure, Forrester analyst Sucharita Mulpuru says her rough estimate is that if web retailers had to collect taxes on all sales to consumers, it could generate $3 billion in new revenue for governments.

Source: *USA Today*, 1/12/2009, Rachel Metz, http://www.usatoday.com/tech/news/techpolicy/2009-01-12-online-sales-taxes_N.htm.

To the MNE as well as the SME, e-commerce taxation represents a significant challenge. Global e-commerce creates additional strategic opportunities, such as placing servers in low-tax jurisdictions. However, it also creates additional risks: for instance, most tax treaties do not refer to e-commerce activities, and they may be open to challenge.

The importance of tax revenues from national and international Internet-based deals becomes more important as more business activity goes online and as the economic crisis of 2008–10 reduces the tax revenues of each government.

Standardization versus localization

Standardization of online practices was the norm early on, but as e-commerce spreads across a broader population and users become ever-more demanding, localization is becoming a stronger requirement for successful global expansion.

In addition, the position of English as a lingua franca for international business has been considerably strengthened on the Internet, supported by the prevalence of English as a second language and by the dominance of US-hosted websites. Although less than a fifth of Internet users are native English speakers, the vast majority of e-commerce sites are in English (even in East Asia where Chinese, Japanese, and Korean are the primary languages, an estimated 91 percent of sites also support English versions to one degree or another). However, the dominance of English is being challenged: as you recall, earlier in the chapter it was noted that Chinese seems likely to surpass English as the dominant language online given the relative penetration and growth of each of the populations as noted in Table 11.8.

In addition to a "lingua franca," there have been other common assumptions behind the "cookie cutter" approach to online expansion that have undermined a "standardized" approach to global expansion. For example, eBay had to withdraw from the potentially lucrative Japanese market, admitting such missteps as emphasizing collectibles rather than new goods in the belief that the Japanese market would mirror the development of the US site. It did not. Still, eBay has been growing its international presence rapidly (outside of Japan), with 2001 revenues of $115 million, up from $34 million in 2000. In 2008, total global revenues had reached $8.5 billion, of which over 50 percent was generated outside of the USA.

A key response to localization pressures has been to establish local websites. It is here that Internet and e-commerce companies make a difference for MNEs: they need not establish physical premises in order to have local presence. As far back as 1997, Sony had 13 country-specific sites. UPS offers its services around the globe in multiple languages.

TABLE 11.8 Top Three Languages Used on the Web and Relative Growth

	Internet users by language	*Internet penetration by language*	*Language growth in Internet (2000–2008)*
English	463,790,410	37.2%	226.7%
Chinese	321,361,613	23.5%	894.8%
Spanish	121,993,069	32.0%	619.3%
Top three languages	915,927,167	30.3%	375.9%
Rest of languages	680,342,941	18.4%	303.7%
World total	1,596,270,108	23.8%	342.2%

Notes:

(1) Internet top three languages usage stats were updated for March 31, 2009.

(2) Internet penetration is the ratio between the sum of Internet users speaking a language and the total population estimate that speaks that specific language.

(3) The most recent Internet usage information comes from data published by Nielsen/NetRatings, International Telecommunications Union, and other reliable sources.

(4) World population information comes from the US Census Bureau.

(5) For definitions and navigation help in several languages, see the Site Surfing Guide.

(6) Stats may be cited, stating the source and establishing an active link back to Internet World Stats.

Source: Internet World Stats – www.internetworlstats.com/languages.htm. Based on 1,574,313,184 estimated internet users for December 2008. Copyright © Miniwatts Marketing Group.

The need for customization goes beyond language, however, to include local content, cultural awareness, and design. Some vendors have taken pains to localize their websites. IKEA, the Swedish furniture maker, designs its sites with an eye to national tastes and local events and "customer images." The sites in Saudi Arabia, Australia, and China all have a similar homepage layout, but each of the panels within is filled with local deals, events, and promotional advertisements.

To summarize:

1. Cross-border e-commerce is lagging behind the rapid growth of online shopping within markets due to "real-world" barriers, such as language, culture, logistics, payments, regulatory issues, and providing multilingual customer support. There are also barriers unique to the Internet medium, such as the use of search engines and the reach of Internet advertising across different markets.
2. Country-of-origin information is especially difficult to determine in global e-commerce transactions. Both MNEs and SMEs have to deal with the challenges and opportunities posed by this reality in taxation as well as in other realms.
3. The localization challenge in global e-commerce entails customization of websites, as well as of the supply chain and distribution network.

COUNTRY FOCUS

AUSTRALIA

World Rank (EFI 2010): 3

Quick Facts

Population: 21.0 million

GDP (PPP): $762.6 billion; 3.7 percent growth in 2008; 2.9 percent 5-year compound annual growth; $35,677 per capita

Unemployment: 4.2 percent

Inflation (CPI): 4.4 percent

FDI inflow: $46.8 billion

2010 Index of Economic Freedom

Regional Rank (EFI 2009, 2010): 3

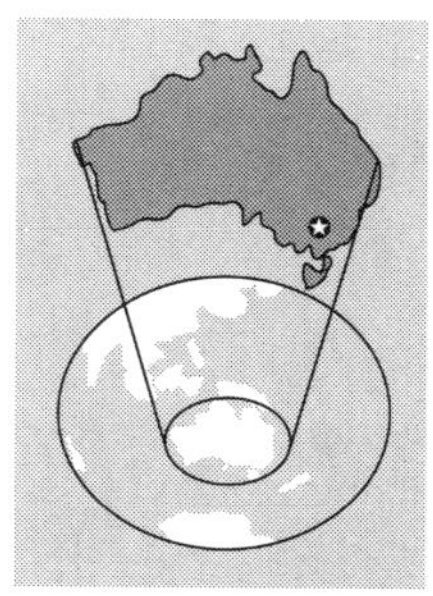

Economic freedom score

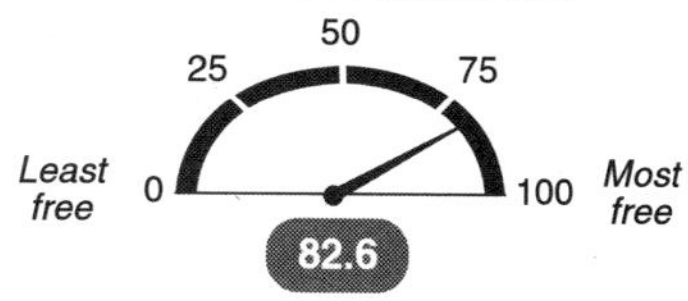

(Continued)

Australia's economic freedom score is 82.6, making its economy the 3rd freest in the 2010 Index. Its overall score is unchanged from last year. Australia is ranked 3rd out of 41 countries in the Asia-Pacific region, and its score is well above the regional and world averages.

Sound macroeconomic policies and well-implemented structural reforms have allowed the Australian economy to weather the recent global financial and economic crisis better than many other advanced economies. Facilitated by robust supervision and sound regulation, Australia's banks have coped well with the financial turmoil. Unemployment has been rising since the start of 2009, but remains well below the OECD (Organization for Economic Cooperation and Development) average. With growth recovering, the government's temporary stimulus measures are scheduled to phase out in 2010.

Overall, the Australian economy is well equipped in terms of its structural strength. Monetary stability and openness to global commerce continue to facilitate a competitive financial and investment environment based on market principles. A strong rule of law protects property rights, and corruption is perceived as minimal. Both foreign and domestically owned businesses enjoy considerable flexibility under licensing and regulatory schemes and in their employment practices. Measures to enhance public finance and maintain long-term fiscal sustainability are focused on achieving better efficiency and effectiveness.

Background

Australia is one of the Asia-Pacific's richest countries. Over a period of more than three decades, successive Labor and Liberal governments have deregulated financial and labor markets and reduced trade barriers. Now in its 18th year of uninterrupted economic expansion, Australia is an internationally competitive producer of services, technologies, and high-value-added manufactured goods. Its export sector remains heavily focused on mining and agriculture.

Business Freedom – 90.3

The overall freedom to start, operate, and close a business is strongly protected under Australia's regulatory environment. Starting a business takes two days, compared to the world average of 35 days. Obtaining a business license requires less than the global average of 18 procedures. Bankruptcy procedures are straightforward and not burdensome. The government generally follows a hands-off approach to sectors dominated by small businesses.

Trade freedom – 85.1

Australia's weighted average tariff rate was 2.5 percent in 2008. Import restrictions and bans, stringent sanitary and biotechnology measures, a quarantine regime, subsidies and other support programs for agriculture and manufacturing products, and barriers to trade in services raise the cost of trade. Exports of bulk wheat and containerized wheat have been liberalized, but bulk exports still require a license before shipment. Ten points were deducted from Australia's trade freedom score to account for nontariff barriers.

Fiscal freedom – 61.4

Australia has a high income tax rate and a moderately high corporate tax rate. The top income tax rate is 45 percent (plus a Medicare levy of 1.5 percent). The corporate tax rate is a flat 30 percent. Other taxes include a goods and services tax (GST) and a tax on the transfer of real property (applied at the state level). In the most recent year, overall tax revenue as a percentage of gross domestic product (GDP) was 30.6 percent.

Government size – 64.9

Total government expenditures, including consumption and transfer payments, are moderate. In the most recent year, government spending equaled 34.2 percent of GDP. A large stimulus package of transfers to households and increased infrastructure spending shifted the fiscal balance into deficit. State corporations increased public investment spending.

Monetary freedom – 82.7

Inflation has been moderate, averaging 3.8 percent between 2006 and 2008. The government can impose price controls, but competition reforms are reducing the range of goods subject to control. Retail gas and electricity prices are regulated, causing five points to be deducted from Australia's monetary freedom score.

Investment freedom – 80.0

Foreign and domestic investors receive equal treatment, but foreign investments may be screened. The government generally must be notified about proposals to start new businesses in sensitive sectors, acquisitions of substantial interests in existing businesses, plans to establish new businesses involving a total investment of A$10 million or more, significant portfolio investments and all nonportfolio investments in the media, takeovers of offshore companies with Australian subsidiaries valued at A$200 million or more, direct investments by foreign governments or their agencies, and certain acquisitions of interests in urban land. The government may reject proposals deemed inconsistent with the "national interest." Foreign investors may own land, subject to approval and a number of restrictions. Residents and nonresidents have access to foreign exchange and may conduct international payments and capital transactions. There are no controls on capital repatriation. Private property can be expropriated for public purposes in accordance with international law, and compensation is paid.

Financial freedom – 90.0

Australia's well-developed and highly competitive financial sector includes banking, insurance, and equity industries. All banks are privately owned. Government regulation is minimal, and foreign banks, licensed as branches or subsidiaries, offer a full range of services. As of June 2009, there were 58 licensed banks: 14 Australian-owned and 44 foreign-owned banks. The sector is dominated by four major Australian banks, which are not allowed to merge. Relatively low leverage and a high ratio of capital adequacy, coupled with banks' limited exposure to securitized assets, helped to avert a sharp credit contraction during the global financial crisis. Foreign insurance companies are permitted, and regulation is focused on capital adequacy, solvency, and prudential behavior.

Property rights – 90.0

Property rights are well protected. The rule of law is seen as fundamental, and enforcement is even-handed. The government respects the independence of the judiciary. Protection of intellectual property rights meets or exceeds world standards. Contracts are secure, and expropriation is highly unusual.

Freedom from corruption – 87.0

Corruption is perceived as minimal. Australia ranks 9th out of 179 countries in Transparency International's Corruption Perceptions Index for 2008, and the government actively promotes international efforts to curb the bribing of foreign officials.

Labor freedom – 94.9

Highly flexible employment regulations enhance employment and productivity growth. The nonsalary cost of employing a worker is moderate, and dismissing a redundant employee is costless.

Source: Adapted from Terry Miller and Kim R. Holmes, 2009 Index of Economic Freedom (Washington, DC: The Heritage Foundation and Dow Jones & Company, Inc., 2009), at www.heritage.org/index.

SUMMARY

Advancements in **IT and communications** technologies have driven unprecedented growth and innovation and enabled the successful expansion of global business, including new business models and business processes.

Managing knowledge-intensive enterprises and/or developing technology-intensive products and services on a global basis represents an increasingly complex set of challenges, including **foreign vs home-based R&D, the organizational concepts of managing a network of R&D sites and the challenges of executing a global product roadmap across multiple sites**.

The global trend over the last three decades is towards increasing **dispersion of R&D sites** globally while leading various parts of the global product roadmap.

As to global arrangements of R&D, there are five basic **organizational paradigms – ethnocentric, geocentric, polycentric, R&D hub, and integrated R&D network** –that are differentiated based on the core knowledge base of each site and the extent to which more than one site needs to cooperate with another to deliver results. A given R&D organization and management operations may evolve and change between these forms depending on the optimal balance between centralized control and local freedoms required to achieve the desired innovation on a global scale.

Executing a global product roadmap among multiple sites requires a different set of **management methods** for each of three different generic phases of a global project: **pre-project (idea generation), project execution, and market introduction**. As the product goes from idea to end-user deliverable, the **management environment must transform** from one that encourages **unstructured, continuous, and open communication** to **highly structured, time-constrained, and uncompromising milestones** in order to achieve successful market introduction.

Cross border **e-commerce is lagging behind the rapid growth of online shopping** within markets due to "real-world" barriers, such as language, culture, logistics, funds clearing and banking systems, regulatory environment, and the availability of multilingual customer support. There are also barriers to the Internet medium, such as the use of search engines and reach of Internet advertising across various markets.

A **country of origin** is especially difficult to determine in global e-commerce transactions. Both MNEs and SMEs have to deal with the challenges and opportunities including **taxation and intellectual property**, posed by this reality.

The **localization challenge** in global e-commerce entails customization of **websites** as well as localization of the **supply chains and distribution networks.**

DISCUSSION QUESTIONS

1 Read the following insert. Choose one of the companies mentioned and investigate how the company has organized its R&D facilities globally. What organizational concept does it apply? What is the role of R&D in its operations and/or product lines?

IS INNOVATION TOO COSTLY IN HARD TIMES?

BusinessWeek's list of the World's Most Innovative Companies Shows not All Are Reigning in R&D

Source: *Business Week*, Reena Jana, In Focus, April 9, 2009.

Not that long ago, innovation was a must-do priority for business. Now research and development (R&D) might seem more like vacation homes and new cars – luxuries that will have to wait for better times. "Innovation is an easy target," says Vijay Govindarajan, a professor at Dartmouth's Tuck School of Business. "R&D dollars by definition lead to uncertain outcomes. Companies don't want failure during difficult times."

In an annual survey of top executives by Boston Consulting Group (BCG), which provides the foundation of *BusinessWeek*'s 25 Most Innovative Companies list, more respondents said that innovation spending will be flat or down than since the ranking began in 2005. On the other hand, after focusing on shorter-term, lower-risk projects, a majority said they are satisfied with their returns on innovation investments.

But recession and market meltdown aside, many of the corporations in the 2009 ranking are finding ways to forge ahead. Some, such as Procter & Gamble (PG) (No. 12) and Vodafone (VOD) (No. 25), are teaming up with outsiders to share costs. Others, such as India's Tata Group (No. 13), are taking greater advantage of in-house experts. And a few, such as BlackBerry maker Research in Motion (RIMM) (No. 8), are even increasing their R&D staff.

IBM (IBM) (No. 6) illustrates yet another way. The information technology giant is shifting more jobs to low-cost places like India while broadening its services through acquisitions. "Some may be tempted to hunker down, to scale back their investment in innovation," says Chief Executive Samuel Palmisano. "While that might make sense during a cyclical downturn, it's a mistake when you're going through a major shift in the global economy."

But some previous winners clearly can't afford to spend on R&D for the long term now. General Motors (GM) ranked 18th in 2008. This year, as it struggles to survive, it didn't even make the Top 50.

Perennial top vote-getters shouldn't take their positions for granted either. Apple (AAPL), which has always held the survey's top position, had 33 percent fewer votes this year than in 2008, while Google (GOOG), consistently the list's No. 2, had 31 percent fewer. Why? Wrote one respondent of Apple: "Their products are improvements on previous technology. Their execution is flawless, but they are not necessarily innovative." Another respondent had the same criticism of Google: "Resting on past glory (search) and spending a lot on new things but no new breakthroughs."

In contrast, Jeffrey R. Immelt, CEO of recently battered General Electric (GE) (No. 17), nominates Southwest Airlines (LUV) (No. 45) as the most innovative company in the world. "They are always trying new ideas," he says. Risky? Of course. But success doesn't come any other way.

2 Describe the advantages and disadvantages of the R&D hub model and offer ways in which an organization may compensate and adjust for the noted weaknesses.
   - List the five basic organizational concepts that are used to manage R&D, based on the core competencies of each site and the extent to which each site needs to cooperate with another. Can you point to specific MNEs as an example for each?
   - In the chapter the main trends are identified regarding e-commerce around the world. An extension of e-commerce is mobile commerce, otherwise known as m-commerce. M-commerce requires the conversion of three technologies: the Internet technology; the cellular technology; and the payment, funds clearing system. Point out the countries in which these technologies are developed enough, in your opinion, to allow significant growth of m-commerce.

INTERNET EXERCISE

Online retailing is a growing and important economic phenomena and business activity around the world. Numerous large and small global ventures are making their mark using a plethora of approaches and methodologies. The ChannelAdvisor E-Commerce Framework provides a systematic and useful approach to online retailing, including strategy, positioning, and business model considerations.

(Continued)

Read and study the ChannelAdvisor E-Commerce Framework in the paragraphs below as well as the example contained in these paragraphs. Select another company and evaluate its business model using the ChannelAdvisor E-Commerce framework.

THE CHANNELADVISOR E-COMMERCE FRAMEWORK

Source: ChannelAdvisor Copyright February 2009. http://ebaystrategies.blogs.com/ebay_strategies/2009/02/episode-ii-introducing-the-channeladvisor-ecommerce-framework-cef.html.

ChannelAdvisor is a software company whose customers are online retailers of all sizes. We have over 6,000 customers and on a daily basis interact with literally hundreds of retailers from the big top 100 retailers all the way to very entrepreneurial businesses carving out their niche online.

Through the years you start to notice some trends (or patterns as we call them in the software world). What you start to notice is that retailers think about their strategies in different, yet in a way similar, ways. What products are you going to offer? What is your pricing strategy? What kind of buyers do you want to attract? Does your brand stand for great deals, great service?

There are five core areas of e-commerce that help think systematically about an e-commerce business as part of the ChannelAdvisor E-Commerce Framework (CEF). The CEF provides the ability to talk to customers and prospects in a coherent fashion and understand rapidly where they are today and what their goals are going forward.

THE CEF – FIVE PILLARS OF E-COMMERCE

When thinking about an online retailer's overall strategy, positioning, and business model (and thus their brand) there are five pillars of e-commerce that make up the CEF: selection, value, ease of use, trust, and merchandising.

It's important to note that not every retailer has to excel at all five dimensions to be successful, as you'll see in the case studies. However, it is observed that for a retailer of any size to be successful, they need to decide what their strategy is for each of these areas, stick to the strategy, and let buyers know what that strategy is. In many ways these decisions embody the retailers brand and how they are perceived by their customers.

First, the five parts of the framework are presented and then one specific case, that of the Zappos company, is studied in order to understand where various Internet retailers fit within the framework and how the CEF can guide how one analyzes Internet retailers.

Selection

First, and most importantly, consumers *love* selection. If they are going to spend their time looking for something online, they have an expectation they will find it. In itself, this seems simple. However, how many times have you driven to 2+ stores on a weekend looking for a product to not find it?

Bricks and mortar retailers are constrained by the physical shelf space which is extremely expensive and therefore has to hold "top sellers" to achieve the necessary monetization rates to support that expensive retail space. Online retailers move that physical aspect from an expensive store front to the substantially cheaper warehouse or distribution center (DC). Thus, online retailers are able to offer orders-of-magnitude broader selection. A very important concept called the "long-tail" comes into play. This concept, articulated by Chris Anderson, is an alternative way of thinking about the 80/20 rule: 20 percent of company's products will drive 80 percent of sales, but what about the other 80 percent of products? Offline, with the physical model, the focus is on the 20 percent, maybe even 15 percent because of the space constraint. But online, with virtual inventory nearly costless, one may consider approaching 100 percent selection and thus address that last 80 percent of long-tail products. In many markets, the 80 percent long-tail is big enough to be a multi-billion dollar opportunity.

Even with the Internet model, selection can get expensive on the DC side. For example, can a retailer afford to have something in the warehouse that may sell at the rate of one of a day? a week? a month? a year? As one goes down the "long-tail," the volume decreases and thus inventory "turns" decrease along with selection, and inventory costs and locked-up cash go up.

When discussing selection, most retailers think about the products on offer, or SKUs, which can include a variety of sizes, colors, and other attributes (styles). But it's important to note that selection can also mean different conditions (new, used, refurb) or even pricing models (auction, fixed price, negotiate/offer, mark-down). In today's world, consumers want options and that means not only product options but also "purchasing options."

For some products, "delivery method" can also be part of selection. For example, is the software/music/book/movie available via shipping, or download?

Value

The concept of value ties directly to an Internet retailer's business model. Does the retailer want to be a Nordstroms'-type department store (high service, with high gross margins without discounting) or does the retailer want to be Wal-Mart (the best prices, focusing on volume vs gross margins)?

In today's e-commerce world, consumers are very savvy: they know how to price shop; they know where to find coupons; they understand the implications of free shipping; and, yes, they are smart enough to add the core price and shipping price and compare that to other offers on the Internet.

Value is sometimes at odds with both selection and trust/customer service.

Ease of use

Ease of use is a broad category and for most e-commerce sites includes the following major subsystems:

- *On-site search* (one company calls it finding) – As a consumer, can I find what I'm looking for with one search and a couple of clicks or do I have to go through pages of items to find what I'm looking for?
- *Cart* – Does the system allow me to easily shop and keep track of what's in my cart, edit, etc.?
- *Checkout system* – Do I have to go through an hour-long process, or is it fast and easy? Do I have a number of shipping options to match my timing needs? Does the system correctly remember my settings from past transactions so I can minimize the data reentry?
- *Order tracking* – Once I've ordered with you, can I track my order, cancel, change? Can I look at what I ordered in June of 2006?
- *Returns processing* – After the purchase, how hard is it to return an item or get questions answered about the item?
- *Product descriptions* – Are the products available clearly described with all the relevant information you need.
- *Click and mortar* – For click-and-mortar companies (offline with online capabilities) – many consumers want to see some interaction between the two, such as online catalogs, circulars, in-store-pick up, shared registry, click-and-mortar royalty programs, etc.

Trust

Trust is hard to describe, because it's the culmination of many things that together give a consumer confidence to essentially turn over their credit card or other payment information. Some of the key elements that can build (or destroy) trust with an Internet retailer:

- *Customer service* – Does the company take care of you before and after the transaction? If you e-mail, do they respond quickly? If you call, does someone with product knowledge answer your question?
- *Security* – Does the site have good password security? Does the site use the latest and greatest technologies to protect your information?

(Continued)

- *Returns* – Unlike ease of use, the trust/returns category is more about policy. Does the site have a policy that makes it hard to return defective products?
- *Privacy* – Is the site trying to sell your information to others, or protect your information? Is the privacy policy clear and easy to read and understand?
- *Spam* – Does the site e-mail me incessantly or does it only e-mail me when needed. If the site has a newsletter, can I subscribe/unsubscribe easily?
- *Ads* – Is the site trying to throw irrelevant ads in your face so it makes money vs helping you find the products you are looking for?
- *Shipping and handling performance* – How quickly do your products get to you? Do you get exactly what you ordered, when they said you would get it?
- *Shenanigans* – Are there any shenanigans like forced up-selling ("Don't you want a filter kit with that camera?"), or anything that makes you feel uncomfortable?

Merchandising

The newest addition to the framework, merchandising, is related to the "ease of use" category, as something to keep an eye on. Since 2007, merchandising has become a "must have" that consumers are looking for. Actually, ChannelAdvisor acquired a firm in this field, named RichFX.

Examples of merchandising (the list is not comprehensive) are:

- *Advanced imaging* – for most product categories, consumers want to be able to rotate the product, see many images, zoom, pan, etc.
- *Recommendations* – technology has come along to the point where e-commerce sites can offer very rich and relevant recommendations that add a lot of value to the buying experience. This topic is worth of a series of blog posts, but suffice it to say that smart recommendations are (a) hard and (b) a "must have" now.
- *Product reviews* – there are many studies showing that one of the top considerations for someone buying something online (that most times they haven't seen or touched) is product reviews from peers.
- *On-site price/product comparisons* – advanced e-commerce sites are offering some really interesting ways to compare products, go through some guided selling utilities or even help you make sure you are getting the best price possible. This functionality substantially lowers shopping cart abandonment rates.
- *Wish/register lists* – for many categories, consumers may want to save an item for later in a wish list, or provide it externally via a registry.
- *Social features* – share a product, recommend to a friend, or find out who else is buying this.

At the end of the day, one of the most important metrics for an Internet retailer is conversion rate – the percentage of visitors that turn into buyers. Merchandising is one of the single best ways to move the needle on conversions and also helps increase average order value (AOV).

Now follows a case study that demonstrates how the framework may help assess online retailing.

Case Study

Zappos – "Powered by Service"

Zappos, an online shoe retailer, stresses great selection and great service, as these seem to be most important in the shoe retailing business. Specifically, if a shoe doesn't fit or match something, one is able tc return it hassle free – actually, with less effort than an offline store.

Zappos seem to be so different and it appears to be working. The visions of the chief executive officer (CEO), Tony Hsieh, and the chief operating officer (COO), Andrew Lin, appear in a blog and through YouTube. Zappos started in one of the toughest retailing categories, shoes, and has generated these results: revenues of around $ 1billion in 2008, 9.7 million purchasing customers, 75 percent recurring customer rate and repeat customers orders multiplied by two and a half times in the last 12 months.

Here's the real proof of Zappos online retailing success. About two years ago, Amazon realized the Zappos' threat and launched a direct attack at them via a microsite called *endless*. That effort hasn't seemed to put a dent in Zappos' accelerated and significant growth. *Here's a company that is going toe to toe with juggernaut Amazon, and winning – how do they do that?*

The following paragraphs analyze Zappos through the to figure out the secret of its success.

Zappos and the CEF

1 *Selection – excels*
Zappos started out in the shoe category and is rapidly expanding to other categories, such as apparel, handbags, and electronics. For shoes, Zappos has 1,200 brands, 200,000 types of shoes and when you look at the size/color/style matrix they have over 3,000,000 unique Universal Product Codes (UPCs). Amazon has 190,000 shoes by comparison, which probably represents 1,000,000 UPCs. eBay has about 524,000 UPCs. Zappos clearly gets the "long-tail" for shoes.

For selection, it seems Zappos has decided they want to win the shoe selection game. Focusing on one product, allows them to go deeper than a multi-product player like Amazon.

2 *Value – not a focus*
While Zappos provides free shipping and frequently upgrades the shipping from "standard" to "expedited" at no additional cost, Zappos is not always the lowest price on the Internet and has even stated, specifically, that it is not their goal. In fact, they rarely do mark downs or clearance and have acquired a business, 6pm.com, that has a different brand, where they do that kind of activity as-needed.

3 *Ease of use – excels*
Within the shoe category, Zappos is extremely easy to use. For some of their core customer sets they even have micro sites that cater the experience to that buyer type's needs (e.g., couture, running, rideshop). The Zappos search engine is very tailored to shoes – you can search by any combination of brand, size, color, width, gender, and price with an easy-to-use filtering system. A graphical experience is given to the user, who can quickly see if the result set is getting close to what he is looking for.

Zappos pioneered the return process of Internet retail and made it extremely easy to do. In fact, every package comes with easy-to-follow instructions and a return label. Zappos almost encourages returns and in fact charges zero for shipping. More on this issue under "Trust".

4 *Trust – innovates*
Zappos is a model citizen when it comes to trust. Their customer service is second to none and is clearly where they are investing to differentiate. In fact Tony Hsieh and Andrew Lin, describe the company as: "a service company that happens to be in the business of e-commerce." This is a clever way to signal to internal and external stakeholders just how important they view customer service to be. The company takes pride that their customer service representatives are not compensated on sales nor do they have any scripts or time limits. The goal is for them to answer every customer's questions regardless of time and not to pressure the customer into buying something.

When asked about abuse of the return policy at a recent shop.org event, Andrew Lin answered that they don't worry about it because they've found that it is their top repeat buyers that return products, so they actually view returns and the Zappo's return policies as an asset and not a liability, as many other retailers do. In other words, each return they take in, they believe extends the loyalty of the customer dramatically more than the cost of that return.

When it comes to shipping and handling, Zappos works 24 × 7 to ship out orders within four hours. They do this via an advanced robotic warehouse system powered by Kiva Systems.

5 *Merchandising – excels*
Zappos does an excellent work on merchandising. Specifically:

- Product reviews – they ask customers to review the fit, comfort, etc.
- Views – each product has 4–7 "views" and zoom capability, including various views of heels, with three-dimensional views, rotation and zoom.
- Wishlist – each product has a wishlist capability.
- Social network – it allows the customer to tell a friend and share the product. The customer may put the product out to his/hers favorite social network, Facebook, etc., for commentary/ reviews.
- Glossary – Zappos provides a comprehensive glossary of all shoe terms for neophytes.
- Recommendations – Zappos does a great job at learning about the kinds of shoes the customer browses/buys and then frequently serves up a value added product recommendation.

Zappos – conclusion

Zappos excels at four of the five pillars – all but value. In fact, Zappos' acknowledgment that a company can't have both the best customer service *and* the lowest prices *and* the best selection defines the Zappos brand. Zappos has clearly chosen customer service and selection to the detriment of value, and it works. Many retailers assume that consumers won't pay for service, but the Zappos case study proves that wrong.

Notes

1 Booz Allen Hamilton, INSEAD (2006). *Innovation: Is Global the Way Forward?* Fontainebleau, France: INSEAD.
2 Boutellier, R., Gassman, O., von Zedtwitz, M (2005). *Managing Global Innovation.* Berlin, Germany: Springer.
3 For a complete description of eForcity's success, the reader can visit the following webpage: http://ebayinkblog.com/2008/11/13/congratulations-to-jack-sheng/
4 The Economist Intelligence Unit (2007). The 2007 E-Readiness Rankings. London: The Economist.
5 The World Bank (2006). The World Bank Report. Washington, DC: World Bank.
6 European Community (2009). Report on Cross-Border E-commerce in the EU. Brussels: EU.

Bibliography

Booz Allen Hamilton, INSEAD (2006). *Innovation: Is Global the Way Forward?* Fontainebleau, France: INSEAD.

Boutellier, R., Gassman, O., von Zedtwitz, M (2005). *Managing Global Innovation.* Berlin, Germany: Springer.

Burk, R. R. (1997). Do you see what I see? The future of Virtual shopping. *Journal of the Academy of Marketing Science,* 25 (4), 352–60.

Dorenberg, R., Hinnekens, L. (1999). *Electronic Commerce and International Taxation.* The Hague: Kluwer Law International.

Economist Intelligence Unit (2007). *The 2007 e-Readiness Rankings.* London: The Economist.

European Community (2009). *Report on Cross-Border E-Commerce in the EU.* Brussels: EU.

Forrester Research (2000). Sizing global online exports. Boston, MA: Forrester Research. November.

Koth, S., Rindova, V. R., Rothaermel, F. T. (2001). Assets and actions: firm-specific factors in the internationalization of U.S. Internet firms. *Journal of International Business Studies,* 32 (4), 769–91.

Quelch, J. A., Klein, L. R. (1996). The internet and international marketing. *Sloan Management Review,* Spring, 60–75.

Rasmusson, E. (1999). E-commerce around the world. *Sales & Marketing Management,* 94.

Rasmusson, E. (2000). Targeting global E-customers. *Sales & Marketing Management,* 78.

Reychav, I., Menipaz, E. (2007). M-commerce technology perceptions on technology adoptions. In D. Taniar, (ed.), *Encyclopedia of Mobile Computing and Commerce.* Hershey, PA: Idea Group, pp. 413–18.

UNCTAD (2000). *Building Confidence: Electronic Commerce and Development,* UNCTAD.

World Bank (2006). The World Bank Report. Washington, DC: The World Bank.

12

Global Human Resources Management

Learning Objectives

Following this chapter, the reader should be able to understand:

1 The strategic importance of global human resources management (HRM)
2 The added complexity of global HRM as compared to its domestic equivalent
3 International staffing, recruiting, and selection policies for international assignments
4 Training and development for international assignments
5 International employee performance appraisal
6 Global employee compensation
7 Labor–management relations

Opening Case
Global HR Challenges at eBay

SAN JOSE, eBay, Inc. (www.ebay.com) was founded in 1995 as an online auction site where anyone could buy and sell anything at anytime. With a presence in 39 markets, including the USA, and approximately 84 million active users worldwide, eBay has changed the face of Internet commerce. In 2007, the total value of sold items on eBay's trading platforms was nearly $60 billion. This means that eBay users worldwide trade more than $1,900 worth of goods on the site every second.

A global multinational enterprise (MNE) such as eBay, which has 15,000 employees worldwide, must deal with many issues when managing its employees. Naturally, with offices in over 40 countries (including market sites and development centers), eBay must select people who will manage each local office by answering several key questions. Can a qualified manager be found locally? What will it pay a manager hired locally? Or, will it send in a manager from the USA or from an office in another nation? If it sends someone in, what will be his or her pay? Because of different practices around the world, eBay's compensation and benefits packages vary greatly from one country to another – while at the same time every effort is made to ensure that performance appraisal is consistent across the various sites, businesses, and functions.

Then there is the issue of culture. A manager hired locally understands the national culture, but what if a manager is brought into the local market? A manager sent from the US head office understands the MNE culture, but may have little understanding of the national culture. No matter the functional role of the manager, to be successful he must be able to bridge both cultures effectively, which requires training in one or both.

As you read this chapter, think of all the human resource issues that arise when international MNEs manage their employees around the world.

Complexity of Global vs Local Human Resource Management

In general, the most important resources of any successful business are the people who comprise it. If an MNE gives its human resource management (HRM) practices the importance they deserve, it can have a profound impact on performance. Highly trained and productive employees who are proficient in their duties allow an MNE to achieve its business goals both domestically and internationally. *HRM* is the process of staffing an MNE and ensuring that employees are as productive as possible. It requires managers to be effective in recruiting, selecting, training, developing, evaluating, and compensating employees and in forming good relations with them.

International HRM differs considerably from HRM in a domestic setting because of differences in national business environments. For one thing, there is the issue of *expatriates* – citizens of one country who are living and working in another. MNEs must deal with many issues when they have expatriate employees on job assignments that could last several years. Some of these issues are related to the inconvenience and stress of living in an unfamiliar culture. Since the mid-1980s Intel has provided various training programs for their employees to help prepare them both for their work experiences abroad, as well as helping them and their families readjust upon their return (see Figure 12.1, which is a screen capture from the Intel website on training for international assignments).

Likewise, training and development programs must often be tailored to local practices. Some countries, such as Germany,[1] have extensive vocational training schools that turn out graduates who are quite well prepared to perform their jobs proficiently. Finding well-qualified nonmanagerial workers in those markets is relatively easy. In contrast, developing a production facility in many emerging markets requires far more basic training of workers. For example, workers in China work hard and tend to be well educated. But because China lacks a vocational training system like those in Germany and Japan, Chinese workers tend to require more intensive on-the-job training. Also, recruitment and selection practices must often be adapted to the host nation's hiring laws. Hiring practices regarding nondiscrimination among job candidates must be carefully monitored so that the MNE does not violate such laws.

Other factors that are unique to global HRM vs its domestic equivalent include:

- *New Human Resources (HR) issues*: Issues related to taxation, relocation, orientation, and support services for expatriates and for host government relations. For example, an Israeli national posted to France as an expatriate may be subjected to taxation by both governments and can incur double

Jobs and Diversity

Training and development

Intel offers a variety of training and development opportunities including management and leadership development, employee development and education, online training courses, and classes taught through Intel University.

Intel University, Intel's worldwide internal training organization, offers more than 7,000 professional and personal growth courses in topics ranging from career and skills development to diversity and cultural training.
Intercultural initiatives
Since the mid-1980s, Intel has offered intercultural programs to help our employees perform more effectively in a global business environment. Learning opportunities include:

- Culture-specific courses
- Language courses including English as a Second Language (ESL)
- Expatriate pre-departure training
- Inpatriate adjustment training
- Cross-cultural team training
- Online learning tools

FIGURE 12.1 Intel training programs for international assignments (http://www.intel.com/intel/diversity/divjobs.htm)

taxation; therefore, the global HRM must ensure there is no tax disincentive associated with any particular assignment through some form of tax equalization.

- *Crafting broad and fair compensation scales internationally*: Many MNEs go abroad in the first place to take advantage of a lower pay scale in another country. Then they adjust their pay scales and advancement criteria to suit local customs. Union Bank of Switzerland in Zurich publishes an annual survey of earnings around the world. This survey has an interesting twist: it ranks earnings in terms of how long the average wage earner must work to be able to afford a Big Mac at McDonald's (www.mcdonalds.com). According to the survey of Big Mac buying power (see Table 12.1), employees in Chicago, Houston, Tokyo, Los Angeles, and Hong Kong enjoy the highest take-home pay. Workers in Nairobi, Caracas, Moscow, Jakarta, and Budapest rank at the bottom.
- *Greater involvement in the employees personal lives*: The HR manager often needs to support the expatriates and their families with regards to housing, health care, education for children, safety, and other cost of living adjustments where relevant.
- *Managing the mix of expatriate vs local staff*: Given the high cost of expatriate packages, an MNE needs to find the right mix of staffing based on the availability of relevant local knowledge and experience, the cost of living in the foreign location, and the international experience of the MNE and its managers.

TABLE 12.1 The Amount of time It Takes to Earn a Big Mac

Longest time		*Shortest time*	
City	Minutes	City	Minutes
Nairobi	193	Chicago, Houston, Tokyo	9
Caracas	117	Los Angeles	10
Moscow	104	Hong Kong	11
Jakarta	103	Toronto, New York	12
Budapest	91	Luxembourg	13
Bombay	85	Montreal, Sydney, Zurich	14
Manila	77	Athens, Geneva	15
Shanghai	75	Frankfurt	16
Mexico City	71	Vienna	17
Prague	56	Berlin	18

- *Greater exposure to risk*: International assignments can carry increased political or security risk that would require additional arrangements in any package to ensure the safety and security of the employee and their family.
- *External influences of the government and national culture*: Understanding the broader context of the host country environment can be critically important both in selecting appropriate candidates and preparing them effectively, as well as for providing appropriate HR guidelines evaluation and compensation of local staff. The degree to which labor is unionized and how unions are treated in a host country can make for very different labor–management relations (e.g., in Germany, union representatives are generally made part of the management of the firm). In some countries employees may officially work no more than a set number of hours per week (e.g., France established the 35-hour work week).

An overview of the global HRM activities is provided in Table 12.2. The chapter begins by reviewing international HRM staffing policies and the important factors that affect recruitment and selection. This is followed by a discussion on the different types of training and development programs MNEs use to improve the effectiveness of their employees. We will also examine the implications of an international workforce on performance appraisal and compensation programs. In closing we will cover international labor relations issues (Table 12.2).

International Staffing Policy

The guidelines and principles according to which international MNEs staff their global offices represent its *international staffing policy*. There are three broad

TABLE 12.2 Global HRM Activities

Activity	*Strategic goals*	*Illustration of challenges*
International staffing policy	• Decide between home, host, and third-country nationals • Recruit and select expatriates • Develop global managers	• Avoid country bias, nepotism or unwanted local practices • Cultivate a global mindset
Preparation and training of employees	• Increase effectiveness of international employees, leading to increased MNE performance • Train employees: regional studies, practical information, and cross-cultural awareness	• Minimize culture shock and occurrence of early departure by expatriates • Maximize chance and speed of success in cross-cultural situations
International performance appraisal	• Assess, over time, how effectively managers and other employees perform their jobs abroad	• Establish uniform organization-wide performance benchmarks while remaining sensitive to local practices
Compensation of employees	• Develop guidelines and administer compensation, e.g., base salary, benefits, allowances, and incentives	• Avoid double taxation of employees
International labor relations	• Manage and interact with labor unions, collective bargaining, handling strikes and other labor disputes, wage rates, and workforce reduction	• Reduce absenteeism, workplace injuries due to negligence, labor strikes, etc.

Source: Adapted from Cavusgil, S.T., Knight, G., Riesenberger, J.R. (2008). *International Business: Strategy, Management and the New Realities*. Saddle Creek River, NJ: Prentice Hall, p. 552.

approaches for staffing global sites (see Table 12.3 for a summary of when each is appropriate) – parent country nationals (PCNs), host country nationals (HCNs), and third country nationals (TCNs). Of course it is also possible to combine these approaches in different ways across the international MNE. For example, an MNE may choose to team a PCN with an HCN in order to benefit from the parent MNE control and knowledge transfer, but mitigate cross-cultural risks by pairing the PCN with a local HCN who can help bridge the cultural gaps and successfully adapt the concepts for the local teams, customers or market.

Parent country national (PCN) staffing

In *PCN staffing*, individuals from the home *or* parent country manage operations abroad. This policy tends to appeal to MNEs that want to maintain tight control over decision making in branch offices abroad. Accordingly, those MNEs work to formulate policies designed to work in every country in which they operate. However, firms generally pursue this policy only for the top managerial posts in their international operations. Implementing it at lower levels is typically impractical.

TABLE 12.3 Global Staffing Approaches

Staff with PCNs when...	*Staff with HCNs when...*	*Staff with TCNs when...*
Headquarters wants to maintain strong control over its foreign operations	The country is distant in terms of culture or language (such as Japan), or when local operations emphasize downstream-value chain activities such as marketing and sales, as HCNs usually understand the local business environment best	Top management wants to create a global culture among the firm's operations worldwide
Headquarters wants to maintain control over valuable intellectual property that is easily dissipated when accessible by HCNs or TCNs	Local connections and relations are critical to operational success (such as the governments in China or many South African countries)	Top management seeks unique perspectives for managing host country operations
Knowledge sharing is desirable among headquarters and the subsidiaries, particularly for developing local managers or the host country organization	The local government requires the MNE to employ the minimum proportion of local personnel, or tough immigration requirements prevent the long-term employment of expatriates	Headquarters wants to transfer knowledge and technology from third countries to host country operations
Foreign operations emphasize R&D and manufacturing, because PCNs are usually more knowledgeable about such upstream-value chain activities	Cost is an important consideration; salaries of PCNs, especially those with families, can be up to four times those of HCNs	The firm cannot afford to pay the expensive compensation typical of PCNs

PCNs, parent country national; HCNs, host country nationals; TCNs, third country nationals.

Source: Adapted from Cavusgil, S.T., Knight, G., Riesenberger, J.R. (2008). *International Business: Strategy, Management and the New Realities*. Saddle Creek River, NJ: Prentice Hall, p. 553.

Advantages of PCN staffing

- *Lack of local skills*: Locally qualified people are not always available.
- *Aligning corporate culture and promoting a common language across sites*: MNEs use PCN staffing to recreate local operations in the image of home country operations. Expatriate managers can infuse branch offices with the corporate culture. In addition, a system of shared values is important when an MNE's international units are highly interdependent. For instance, fashioning branch operations in the image of home office operations can also ease the transfer of best practices or specialized knowledge between home and country operations.

- *Home office oversight*: Some MNEs feel that managers sent from the home country will look out for the MNE's interests more earnestly than will host country natives. Japanese MNEs are notorious for their reluctance to place non-Japanese managers at the helm of international offices and, when they do, they often place a Japanese manager in the office to monitor important decisions and report back to the home office.

Disadvantages of PCN staffing

- *High cost*: Relocating managers from the home country is expensive. The bonuses that managers often receive for relocating, plus relocation expenses for entire families, can increase the cost of a manager several times over. Likewise, the pressure of cultural differences and long periods away from relatives and friends can contribute to the failure of managers on international assignments.
- *National culture clash can impede corporate goals*: A PCN policy can create barriers for the host country office. The presence of home country managers in the host country might encourage a "foreign" image of the business. Lower-level employees might feel that managers do not really understand their needs because they come from another culture. Occasionally they are right: expatriate managers sometimes fail to integrate themselves into the local culture. As they fail to overcome cultural barriers, they fail to understand the needs not only of their local employees but also those of their local customers.

Host country national (HCN) staffing

In *HCN staffing*, individuals from the host country manage operations abroad. MNEs may implement an HCN approach for top and mid-level managers, for lower-level staff, or for nonmanagerial workers. It is well suited to MNEs who want to give national units a degree of autonomy in decision making. Of course, this policy does not mean that host country managers are left to run operations in any way they see fit. Large international MNEs usually conduct extensive training programs in which host country managers visit home offices for extended periods. In this way they are exposed to the MNE's culture and specific business practices. Small and medium-sized enterprises (SMEs) can find this policy expensive, but being able to depend on local managers who fully understand what is expected of them can far outweigh any costs.

Advantages of HCN staffing

- *Managerial responsibility*: HCN staffing places managerial responsibility in the hands of people intimately familiar with the local business environment and national culture. Managers with deep cultural understanding of the local market are familiar with local business practices and can read the subtle cues of both verbal and nonverbal language. They need not overcome any cultural barriers created by an image of being an outsider, and they tend to have a better feel for the needs of employees, customers, and suppliers.

- *Lower cost than PCN*: Another important advantage of HCN staffing is the elimination of the high cost of relocating expatriate managers and families. This advantage can be extremely helpful for SMEs that cannot afford the expenses associated with expatriate employees.

Disadvantage of HCN staffing

- *Loss of control by parent MNE*: The major drawback of polycentric staffing is the potential for losing control of the host country operation. When an MNE employs natives of each country to manage local operations, it runs the risk of becoming a collection of discrete national businesses. This situation might not be a problem when a firm's strategy calls for treating each national market differently. It is not a good policy, however, for MNEs that are following global strategies. If these MNEs lack integration, knowledge sharing and a common image, performance will surely suffer.

Third country national (TCN) staffing

In *TCN staffing*, the best-qualified individuals, regardless of nationality, manage the operations abroad. The local operation may choose managers from the host country, from the parent country, or from a third country. The choice depends on the operation's specific needs. This policy is typically reserved for top-level managers.

For example, in early 2008, Disney, the leading MNE in family entertainment, relocated a managing director and VP of their Disney Channel Australia and New Zealand Division to the UK to take over as VP and general manager of Disney Channels UK and Ireland. This move was made in order to leverage this employee's deep experience and success in other markets in order to further develop their European markets.

Advantage of TCN staffing

- TCN staffing helps MNEs develop global managers who can adjust easily to any business environment, including to national cultural differences. This advantage is especially useful for global MNEs trying to break down nationalistic barriers, whether between managers in a single office or between different offices. One hope of MNEs using this policy is that a global perspective among its managers will help them seize opportunities that may otherwise be overlooked.

Disadvantage of TCN staffing

- The downside of TCN staffing is the expense. Understandably, top managers who are capable both of fitting into different cultures and being effective at their jobs are highly prized among international MNEs. The combination of high demand for their skills and their short supply inflates their salaries. Moreover, there is the expense of relocating managers and their families, sometimes every year or two.

Recruiting and Selecting Human Resources

Naturally, MNEs try to recruit and select qualified managers and nonmanagerial workers who are well suited to their tasks and responsibilities. But how does an MNE know the number of managers and workers it needs? How does it recruit the best-available individuals? How does it select from the pool of available candidates? In this section, we explore some answers to these and other important questions about recruiting and selecting employees.

Human resource planning

Recruiting and selecting managers and workers requires *human resource planning* – the process of forecasting both an MNE's human resource needs and supply. Based on the analysis between the MNE's needs and its supply of talent, the MNE must develop an appropriate plan to bridge any gaps that exist.

Collecting data

The first phase of International Human Resource planning (IHR) planning involves taking an inventory of the MNE's current human resources: that is, collecting data on every employee, including educational background, special job skills, previous jobs, language skills, and experience living abroad.

Assessing the gap

The second phase of IHR planning is estimating the MNE's future HR needs. For example, consider a firm that plans to sell its products directly to buyers in a new market abroad. Will it create a new operation abroad and staff it with managers from the home office, or will it train local managers? Will it hire its own local sales force, or will it retain a distributor? Likewise, manufacturing or assembling products in an international market requires factory workers. An MNE must decide whether to hire these people itself or to subcontract production to other producers, thus eliminating the need for it to hire factory workers.

Bridging the gap (recruitment/decruitment)

In the third phase of IHR planning, managers develop a plan for recruiting and selecting people to fill vacant and anticipated new positions, both managerial and nonmanagerial. Having understood the requirements for each role in terms of desired skills, behaviors and experience, the MNE must now plan how to fill each post either from its existing supply of talent or through acquiring talent from outside the MNE. Sometimes, a firm must also make plans for reducing its workforce, a process called *decruitment*, when current HR levels are greater than anticipated needs. Planning for decruitment normally occurs when an MNE decides to discontinue manufacturing, selling or any other business activity in a particular market. The decision by global MNEs to shift the location of manufacturing from one country to another can also result in lost jobs. Let's now take a closer look at the recruitment and selection processes.

Recruiting human resources

The process of identifying and attracting a qualified pool of applicants for vacant positions is called *recruitment*. MNEs can recruit internally from among their current employees or look to external sources. Nurturing a strong pool of talent, both within and from outside the MNE, has become a competitive advantage for many global MNEs.

Current employees

Finding an international manager among current employees is easiest for a large MNE with an abundance of internal managers. Many successful global MNEs have sophisticated programs for developing their top talent and building a strong internal pool of future global managers by providing their high-potential employees with opportunities to gain broader experience through international assignments with various functions around the business. For any given project, likely candidates within the MNE could be managers who were involved in previous stages of an international project: say, in *identifying* the new production site or potential market. It is likely that these individuals have already made important contacts inside the host country and they have already been exposed to its culture. However, not all personnel are well suited for an international assignment. Some prefer to remain at home (for personal reasons); others may be sent abroad only to discover that they are not (or their family is not) well suited for international work. Given the importance of such posts and the costs of sending staff on international assignments, it is especially important to select carefully from the talent pool those people who are best suited for the unique challenges of an international assignment. There are several characteristics shared by employees who tend to be more successful at international assignments.

- *Technical/functional competence*: The manager must have sufficiently strong managerial and technical capabilities to gain local credibility, direct local resources effectively, and fulfill the MNE's goals and objectives.
- *Self-reliance*: Having an entrepreneurial orientation, proactive mindset, and a strong sense of self-confidence is important because expatriate managers must often function with considerable independence abroad, but with limited support from headquarters.
- *Adaptability*: The candidate should possess an ability to adjust well to foreign cultures and new experiences. Important character traits are cultural empathy and curiosity, flexibility, diplomacy, and a positive attitude and tolerance about uncertainty and unexpected (foreign) situations.

- *Interpersonal skills*: Successful candidates are able to get along well with others; building and maintaining good relationships is key to being able to influence, and learn from local peers, employees, partners and government officials.
- *Leadership ability*: The most successful managers view change positively and proactively manage threats and opportunities confronting the MNE. They are able to provide clarity, motivation, and guidance to their teams. They are able to effectively leverage and collaborate with their employees to implement strategies and facilitate changes successfully.
- *Physical and emotional health*: Living abroad can be stressful and in some cases involve difficult adaptations to local climate, maladies, and conditions. Many expatriates experience culture shock and other traumas, and medical care may also be lacking. Thus, excellent physical and mental health is critical.
- *Spouse and/or dependents prepared to live abroad*: Should the candidate have a family or other dependents, their ability and interest in coping with new environments can become a critical factor in the success or failure of the manager during his international assignment.

Recent college graduates

MNEs also recruit from among recent college graduates who have come from other countries to attend college in the firm's home country (common in the USA) or some of its key markets (common in Europe or Asia). A particularly common practice among global MNEs is to provide talented graduates with a 6–18-month program that includes general and specialized training in their functional domain and experience in various international sites. They are then given positions in their native countries or can pursue their international career in other markets.

Local managerial talent

MNEs can also recruit local managerial talent. Hiring local managers is common when cultural understanding is a key job requirement or advantage. Hiring local managers with government contacts can speed the process of getting approvals for local operations. In some cases, governments force MNEs to recruit local managers so that they can develop their own internal pools of managerial talent. Also, governments sometimes restrict the number of international managers that can work in the host country.

Nonmanagerial workers

MNEs typically recruit locally for nonmanagerial positions because there is often little need for highly specialized skills or training. However, a specialist from the home country is typically brought in to train people chosen for more demanding positions.

Firms also turn to the local labor market when governments restrict the number of people allowed into the host country for work purposes. Such efforts are usually designed to reduce unemployment among the local population.

On the other hand, countries sometimes permit the importation of nonmanagerial workers for jobs that are not wanted by the native population. For example, the USA provides H-2 visas to foreign workers who come to work for employers who demonstrate that they could not find a US citizen to do the job. In 2008, US employers brought in 282,000 foreign workers to work in industries such as agriculture, construction and food processing.[2]

Selecting human resources for international assignments

The process of screening, evaluating, and hiring the best-qualified applicants with the greatest performance potential is called *selection*. The process for international assignments includes measuring a person's ability to bridge cultural differences. Expatriate managers must be able to adapt to a new way of life in the host country. Conversely, native host country managers must be able to work effectively with superiors who have different cultural backgrounds.

In the case of expatriate managers, cultural differences between home country and host country are important factors in their potential success. Culturally sensitive or curious managers increase the likelihood that an MNE will achieve its international business goals. Recruiters can assess cultural sensitivity by asking candidates questions about their receptiveness to new ways of doing things and questions about racial and ethnic issues.

It is also important to examine the cultural sensitivity of each family member who will be going to the host country. The inability of a family member (particularly a spouse) to adapt to a new culture is the most common reason for the failure of expatriate managers. In fact, in one recent survey of Canadian and US MNEs, nearly 20 percent cited "lack of adaptability by the employee's spouse" as the No. 1 cause of failed relocation.

Culture shock

Successful international managers typically do not mind, and often enjoy, living and working outside their native lands. In extreme cases, they might even be required to relocate every year or so. These individuals are capable of adapting quickly to local conditions and business practices. Such managers are becoming increasingly valuable with the emergence of markets in Asia, Central and Eastern Europe, and Latin America. They are also helping to create a global pool of managers who are ready and willing to go practically anywhere on short notice. However, the size of this pool remains limited because of the difficulties that many people experience in relocating to unfamiliar cultures.

Living in another culture can be a stressful experience. Therefore, selecting managers who are comfortable traveling to and living in unfamiliar cultures is an extremely important factor in recruitment for international posts. Set down in the midst of new cultures, many expatriates experience *culture shock*, a psychological process affecting people living abroad that is characterized by homesickness, irritability, confusion, aggravation, and depression. In other words, they have trouble adjusting to the new environment in which they find themselves. *Expatriate failure* – the early return by an employee from an international assignment because of inadequate job performance – often results from cultural stress. The high cost of expatriate failure is convincing many MNEs to invest in culture-training programs for employees sent abroad.

Culture shock generally affects an individual or family during stays of a few months or longer. Typically, an individual will experience four different stages of adaptation to the new cultural environment (though not everyone necessarily passes through all stages). The four stages of culture shock are summarized as follows.

Stage 1 – Honeymoon

This stage typically lasts a few days or weeks during which the individual experiences the new culture from the perspective of a tourist. Fascinated by the differences in the local culture, traditions, and habits and feeling confident about the new career opportunity the individual is filled with excitement and anticipation. However, at this stage the individual has not truly interacted directly with the new culture.

Stage 2 – Frustration

This stage can last from a few weeks to a few months and in some cases individuals never evolve beyond this stage. During this stage the individual finds some if not all the local customs and habits frustrating, silly or incomprehensible. They begin to mock the local norms and compare the "inferior" local customs with their native homeland. Relationships with colleagues and family may suffer as depression sets in.

Stage 3 – Adaptation

At this point the individual has reached their lowest point and they begin to work their way towards finding a way to accommodate the local customs within their own frame of reference. They begin to understand the customs and are able to either adopt or at least respect them while finding a way to assimilate their own work and personal habits into the local culture.

Stage 4 – Actualization

The individual in this stage has reached a point where they not only understand but also can appreciate many aspects of the local culture. An expatriate who has successfully reached this stage is very likely to succeed in their international assignment as they and their family will feel happy and secure in the new culture.

Reverse culture shock

Ironically, expatriates who successfully adapt to new cultures (i.e., achieve stage 4 – Actualization) often undergo an experience called *reverse culture shock*, the psychological process of readapting to one's home culture. Because values and behavior that once seemed so natural now seem so strange, reverse culture shock may be even more disturbing than culture shock. In addition, returning managers often find that either no position or merely a "standby" position awaits them in the home office. Often, MNEs do not know how to take full advantage of the cross-cultural abilities developed by managers who have spent several potentially valuable years abroad. In fact, expatriates commonly leave their MNEs within a year of returning home because of difficulty blending back into the MNE culture.

Moreover, spouses and children often have difficulty leaving the adopted culture and returning home. For many Saudi Arabian employees and their families, reentry into Saudi Arabian culture after a work assignment in the USA can be particularly difficult. The fast pace of business and social life in western countries, plus the relatively high degree of freedom and independence for women, contrasts sharply with conditions in Saudi Arabia. Returning Saudi expatriates can find it difficult to adjust back to life in Saudi Arabia after years of living in the western countries.

The effects of reverse culture shock can be reduced. Home-culture reorientation programs and career-counseling sessions for returning managers and their families can be highly effective. For example, the employer might bring the entire family home for a short stay several weeks before the official return. This kind of trip allows returnees to prepare for at least some of the reverse culture shock that may await them.

Likewise, good career development programs can help MNEs retain valuable managers. Ideally, the career development plan was worked out before the employee went abroad and revised before his or her return. Some MNEs work with employees before they go abroad to plan career paths of up to 20 years within the MNE. Mentors, managers who have previously gone abroad and had to adjust upon returning home, can also be assigned to returning managers. The mentor becomes a confidant with whom the expatriate manager can discuss particular problems related to work, family, and readjusting to the home culture.

Training and Development

After an MNE recruits and selects its managers and other employees, it normally identifies the skills and knowledge that employees have and those that they need to perform their duties. Employees who lack the necessary skills or knowledge can then be directed into specific training or development programs. For international business assignments these programs go beyond the functional and technical requirements of the job itself to include training about the environment, cultural awareness, language training, and other regional briefings about the host country.

According to the National Foreign Trade Council (www.nftc.org), 250,000 US citizens live outside the USA on international assignments, in addition to hundreds of thousands more who travel abroad on business for stays of up to several weeks. Some of the many costs of relocating an employee for a long-term international assignment include moving expenses and ongoing costs for things such as housing, education, and cost-of-living adjustments. That is why many MNEs realize the need for in-depth training and development programs if they are to get the maximum productivity from managers posted abroad.

Methods of cultural training

Ideally, everyone involved in business should be culturally literate and prepared to go anywhere in the world at a moment's notice. Realistically, many employees and many MNEs do not need or cannot afford to be entirely literate in another culture. The extent of a MNE's international involvement demands a corresponding level of cultural knowledge from its employees. MNEs whose activities are highly international need employees with language fluency and in-depth experience in other countries. Meanwhile, small MNEs or those new to international business can begin with some basic cultural training. As an MNE increases its international involvement and cross-cultural contact, employees' cultural knowledge must keep pace.

As one can see from Figure 12.2, MNEs use many methods to prepare managers for an international assignment. These methods tend to reflect a manager's level of international involvement. The goal is to create informed, open-minded, flexible managers with a level of cultural training appropriate to the duties required of them.

Environmental briefings and cultural orientations

Environmental (area) briefings constitute the most basic level of training, often the starting point for studying other cultures. Briefings include information on local housing, health care, transportation, schools, and climate. Such knowledge is normally obtained from books, films, and lectures. *Cultural orientations* offer insight into social, political, legal, and economic institutions. Their purpose is to add depth and substance to environmental briefings.

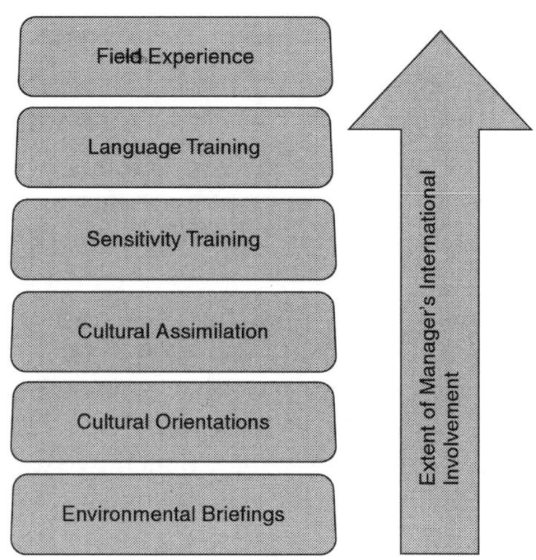

FIGURE 12.2 International assignment preparation methods

Cultural assimilation and sensitivity training

Cultural assimilation teaches the culture's values, attitudes, manners, and customs. So-called guerrilla linguistics, which involves learning some phrases in the local language, is often used at this stage. It also typically includes role playing: the trainee responds to a specific situation in order to be evaluated by a team of judges. This method is often used when someone is given little notice of a short stay abroad and wishes to take a crash course in social and business etiquette and communication. *Sensitivity training* teaches people to be considerate and understanding of other people's feelings and emotions: it gets the trainee "under the skin" of the local people.

Language training

The need for more thorough cultural preparedness brings us to intensive *language training*. This level of training entails more than memorizing phrases for ordering dinner or asking directions. It gets a trainee "into the mind" of local people. The trainee learns more about why local people behave as they do. This is perhaps the most critical part of cultural training for long-term assignments.

A survey of top executives found that foreign-language skills topped the list of skills needed to maintain a competitive edge. According to the survey, 31 percent of male employees and 27 percent of female employees lacked foreign-language skills. To remedy this situation, many MNEs either employ outside agencies that specialize in language training or develop their own programs. Employees at 3M Corporation (www.3m.com) developed a third way. They created an all-volunteer Language Society composed of current and retired employees and family members. About 1,000 people are members, and the group offers classes in 17 languages taught by 70 volunteer employee teachers. The society meets 45 minutes per week and charges a nominal membership fee of $5. Officials at 3M say that the society nicely complements the MNE's formal language education program.

Field experience

Field experience means visiting the culture, walking the streets of its cities and villages, and becoming absorbed by it for a short time. The trainee gets to enjoy some of the unique cultural traits and feel some of the stresses inherent in living in the culture.

Finally, spouses and children also need cultural training. Training for them is a good investment because the alternatives – an international "commuter marriage" or expatriate failure – are both psychologically and financially expensive options.

Compiling a cultural profile

Cultural profiles can be quite helpful in deciding whether to accept an international assignment. The following are some excellent sources for constructing a cultural profile:

- *Culture Grams*: Published by the David M. Kennedy Center for International Studies at Brigham Young University (www.kennedy.byu.edu, http://www.culturegrams. com/), this guide can be found in the reference section of many libraries. Frequent updates make *Culture Grams* a timely source of information. Individual sections profile each culture's background and its people, customs and courtesies, lifestyle, and society. A section entitled "For the Traveler" covers details such as required entry visas and vaccinations.

- *Country Studies Area Handbooks*: This series explains how politics, economics, society, and national security issues are related to one another and shaped by culture in more than 70 countries. Handbooks tend to be politically oriented because they are designed for US military personnel. The Country Studies Area Handbooks are available on the web at (http://rs6.loc.gov/frd/cs/).
- *Background Notes*: These notes contain much relevant factual information on human rights and related issues in various countries. However, because they are published by the US Department of State (http://www.state.gov/r/pa/ei/bgn/), they take a US political perspective.

Information can also be obtained by contacting the embassies of other countries in your home nation. People with first-hand knowledge and specific books and films are also good sources of information. Once inside a country, the home country's embassy is a good source of further cultural advice. Embassies maintain networks of home-nation professionals who work in the local culture, some with many years of experience upon which you can draw.

Nonmanagerial worker training

Nonmanagerial workers also have training and development needs. This is especially true in some developing and newly industrialized countries where people have not even completed primary school. Even if the workforce is fairly well-educated, workers may lack experience working in industry. In such cases, MNEs that do business abroad can train local workers in how to work on an assembly line or cultivate business leads to make sales. The need for such basic skills training continues to grow as MNEs increasingly explore opportunities in emerging markets.

In many countries, national governments cooperate with businesses to train nonmanagerial workers. Japan and Germany lead the world in vocational training and apprenticeship programs for nonmanagerial workers. Students who are unable or unwilling to enter college can enter programs paid for by the government and private industry. They undergo extensive practical training that exposes them to the cutting-edge technologies employed by the country's leading MNEs.

Another example can be found in Israel. The Israeli Defense Forces serve a similar vocational training ground, especially in the areas of information technology, software and communications, where thousands of young adults who serve in various divisions receive the opportunity to work on leading-edge technologies and on enterprise-class problems at a very young age. This, in part, explains the extraordinary global success of Israeli hi-tech MNEs in these fields.

International Performance Appraisal

The formal process of evaluating the effectiveness of employees in their jobs is known as performance appraisal. Performance appraisals are most obviously linked to assessments that determine an employee's compensation and bonuses on the basis of the results achieved. However, when conducted correctly by the manager, this formal process serves a more important long-term goal for the MNE. Ongoing performance appraisals are an important means for a manager to understand and give feedback on the strengths and weaknesses of his staff, to understand the gaps in performance, knowledge or skill sets that must be addressed and to identify the potential talents on the team that can be nurtured to increase their contribution to the MNE either through their domain expertise and thought leadership, their capacity for leading and managing people or a combination of both.

Elements of a comprehensive appraisal system

A comprehensive appraisal system should include the following elements.

1. Clarity on goals and measures of performance: Upfront, both the employees and the managers must be clear on the objectives for the period or appraisal, how it fits with the MNE goals, and how the results will be measured (quantifiable wherever possible).
2. Ongoing feedback, communication, and support between appraisals: Managers should ensure they are aware of their employees' progress during (not just after) the period and provide open and candid feedback, ensuring the appropriate cultural sensitivities regarding the form and content of the communications. If done correctly, employees should not be greatly surprised by their performance appraisal when the time comes.
3. Collection of all inputs for appraisal: Comparing the "actual vs targeted" quantitative results is generally straightforward and easily done. However, collecting feedback on the employees from peers, subordinates, customers, suppliers, and other managers provides for a stronger, richer assessment, more constructive feedback and a more effective mechanism for career-path discussions with employees on the basis of their interests and capabilities.
4. Evaluation framework: There are two broad approaches to evaluation of staff – on absolute or relative terms. Applying a performance appraisal system based on absolute measures of performance assumes the employee is being evaluated primarily on the basis of his results in accomplishing the goals set for him at the beginning of the period (regardless of the performance of his peers). A relative system (e.g., forced ranking of all staff in a department, from best to worst) involves assessing an individual performance against other peers and determining a score based primarily on his relative contribution to the business (i.e., even if he fulfilled all his duties, a colleague who was faster, more supportive or more effective at doing the same work would get a better rating).

5 Consistency and clarity of communication: Applying the performance appraisal system consistently across a global organization requires significant investments in training evaluators (e.g., managers), calibrating their efforts across relevant organizations (by function and/or by geography) and ensuring that the communication right down to the individual level is consistent with the goals of the firm.

Factors to consider for global operations

When managing foreign operations, MNEs give PCNs, HCNs, and TCNs organizational objectives to achieve that vary from site to site. A marketing and sales office may be charged with developing and executing against a sales plan to penetrate a new market and secure key customer accounts. A manufacturing site may be charged with achieving certain productivity, quality, and cost objectives in building the product. There may also be different challenges, depending on how new the operation is, whether or not it has undergone some recent changes in leadership or role in the global MNE and whether or not it is functioning well or poorly, wherein the role of the global manager is to investigate the root causes and get the operation back on track.

Where the manager identifies gaps in the team or in specific individuals, he is expected to develop plans to either overcome the gaps (e.g., training, additional resources, relocation of staff for cross-pollination of skills, and knowledge transfer), or to terminate staff that consistently underperform.

Factors that make performance evaluations more complicated when applying them internationally include:

- *Noncomparable outcomes*: differences in economic, political, legal, and cultural variables between markets can make direct comparisons difficult, and at times unfair. Different local accounting rules may make business results appear better or worse than those evaluated at home (under different rules). Expectations of a subsidiary manager of an operation in Mexico or Bangalore must take into account the local worker conditions and other local factors that affect worker productivity – often these are accepted in order to pursue cost savings in such regions. Finally, a foreign subsidiary may have a unique skill set (e.g., a development operation) that has no other comparison across the MNE and requires it to be evaluated against its past performance or future commitments rather than in comparison with another division or site in the MNE.
- *Incomplete information*: due to the separation in both distance and time, superiors at headquarters may not have many opportunities to directly observe employees working in foreign operations. MNEs try to mitigate this issue either by visiting operations abroad to meet the staff and observe local conditions, have constant weekly communications with foreign staff (where they learn about local challenges and get a sense of how the employees are performing on an ongoing basis) or have global staff evaluated

both by local managers and headquarters staff to get a more complete evaluation.

- *Maturity of the operation*: performance expectations of a given location must consider the maturity of the site in order to establish realistic and achievable objectives that can drive and grow the capabilities of the employees without demoralizing them.
- *Consistency of application*: to the extent that the MNE is seeking to nurture a global culture and consistent performance appraisal and career development systems, the need for alignment on the framework and groups, calibration of the staff against their peers worldwide and training of the global and local managers both in appraising and communication is critical.

Management must take into account these factors when assessing foreign operations, partners, and staff or it risks arriving at inaccurate or biased assessments.

Employee Compensation

Essential to good international HRM is a fair and effective compensation (reward) system. Such a system is designed to attract and retain the best and brightest employees and to reward them for their performance. Because a country's compensation practices are rooted in its culture and legal and economic systems, determining compensation can be complicated. For example, base pay accounts for nearly all employee compensation in some countries. In others, bonuses and fringe benefits account for more than half.

Managerial employees

Naturally, compensation packages for managers differ from MNE to MNE and from country to country. Good packages are fairly complicated to design for several reasons. Consider, for example, the effect of *cost of living*, which includes factors such as the cost of groceries, dining out, clothing, housing, schooling, heath care, transportation, and utilities.

Quite simply, it costs more to live in some countries than in others (Figure 12.3). Moreover, within a given country, the cost of living typically varies from large cities to rural towns and villages. Most MNEs add a certain amount to an expatriate manager's pay to cover greater cost-of-living expenses. On the other hand, managers who are relocating to lower cost-of-living countries are typically paid the same amount that they were receiving at the home office. Otherwise, they would be financially penalized for accepting an international job assignment.

Even when the cost of living abroad is lower than at home, MNEs may need to cover other costs incurred by expatriate managers. One important concern for relocating managers is the quality of local education. In many cases, children cannot immediately enter local classes because they do not speak the local language. In such instances, most MNEs pay for private school education.

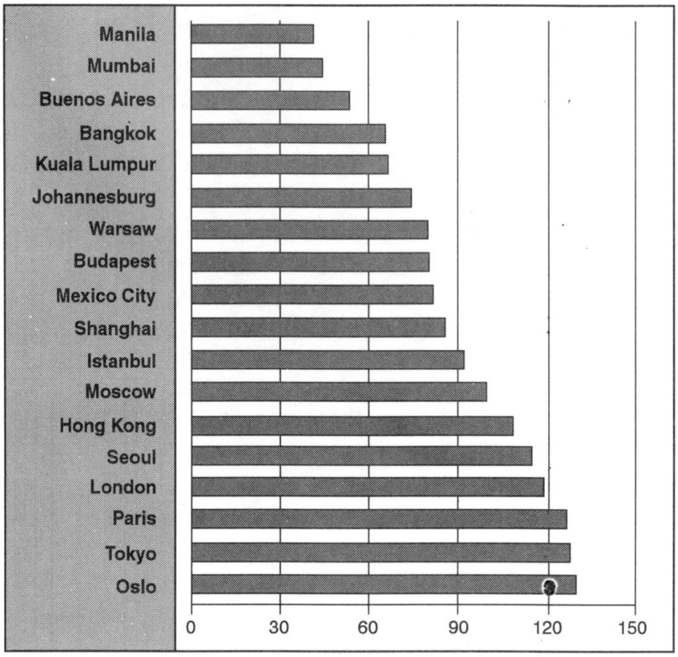

FIGURE 12.3 Cost of living in selected cities, 2006 (New York = 100) (© The Economist Newspaper Limited, London (2006))

Bonus and tax incentives

MNEs commonly offer managers inducements to accept international postings. The most common is a financial bonus. This bonus can be in the form of a one-time payment or an add-on to regular pay, generally 15–20 percent. Bonuses for managers who are asked to go into a particularly unstable country or one with a very low standard of living often receive *hardship* or *combat pay*.

Managers can also be attracted by another income-related factor. For example, the US government permits citizens working abroad to exclude "foreign-earned income from their taxable income in the USA, even if it was earned in a country with no income tax."

Cultural and social contributors to cost

Culture also plays an important role in the compensation of expatriate managers. Some nations offer more paid holidays than others. Many offer free medical care to everyone living and working there. Granted, the quality of locally available medical care is not always good. Therefore, many MNEs have plans for taking seriously ill expatriates and family members home or to nearby countries where medical care is equal to that available in the home country.

MNEs that hire managers in the local market might encounter additional costs engendered by social attitudes. For instance, in some countries employers are

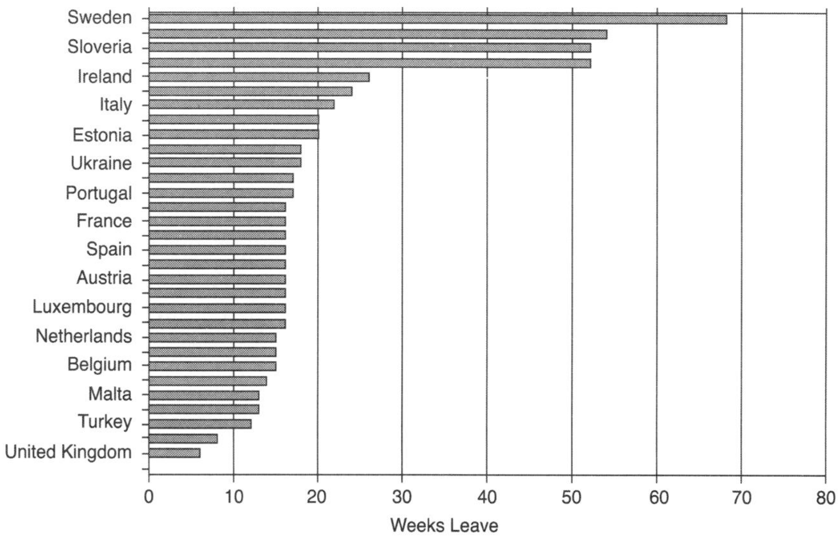

FIGURE 12.4 Maternity leave in Europe (Based on http://unstats.un.org/unsd/demographic/products/indwm/ww2005/tab5c.htm)

expected to provide free or subsidized housing. In others, the government obliges employers to provide paid maternity leaves of up to 1½ years. Figure 12.4 presents government-mandated maternity leaves for European countries. Although MNEs need not absorb all maternity leave-related costs, they tend to be reflected in a generally higher cost of doing business in a given country.

Managers recruited from within the host country generally receive the same pay as managers who work for local MNEs. However, they often receive perks not offered by local firms. For example, some are required to visit the home office two or three times per year. If time allows, many managers will make these into short vacations by taking along their families and adding a few extra days onto the length of the trip.

Nonmanagerial workers

Two main factors influence the wages of nonmanagerial workers.

First, their compensation is strongly influenced by increased cross-border business investment. Employers can relocate fairly easily to nations where wages are lower. Meanwhile, in the home country, workers must often accept lower wages when an employer gives them a choice of accepting the reduction or watching their jobs move abroad. One result of this situation is a trend toward greater equality in workers' pay around the world. In turn, this equalizing effect encourages economic development and improvement in workers' lives in some countries at the expense of those in others. Recall, Table 12.1 at the beginning of the chapter, which compares the average earning power across various countries by calculating the time that it would take an average worker to earn enough to buy a Big Mac. However, the freedom with which an employer can relocate differs from country to country. Although firms in some countries are allowed to move with little notice, in others they are highly restricted. In fact, some countries force MNEs to compensate workers who lose their jobs because of relocation. This policy is common in European countries that have erected extensive social safety nets for unemployed workers.

Second, the fact that labor is more mobile today than ever before also affects wages. Although labor laws in Europe are still more stringent than in the USA, the countries of the European Union (EU) are abolishing the requirement that workers from one EU nation must obtain visas to work in another. If workers in Spain cannot find work at home, or if they feel that their current pay is inadequate, they are free to move to another EU country where unemployment is lower (say the UK).

Labor–Management Relations

The relationship between an MNE's management and its workers (labor) is referred to as *labor–management relations*. Cooperative relations between labor and management can give a firm a tremendous competitive advantage. When management and workers realize they depend on one another, the MNE is often better prepared to meet its goals and surmount unexpected obstacles that inevitably arise.

Giving workers a greater stake in the MNE – say, through profit-sharing plans (e.g., options, restricted stock units, shares) – is one way to align shared goals, increase morale, and generate commitment to lower costs, improved quality, and better customer service.

Because relations between laborers and managers are human relations, they are rooted in culture and are often affected by political movements in a market or at head office. Large international MNEs tend to make high-level labor decisions at the home office because it gives them greater control over their network of production operations around the world and allows them to make decisions taking into account the whole of their global operations.

However, lower-level decisions are often left to managers in each country. In effect, this policy places decisions that have a direct impact on workers' lives in the hands of experts in the local market. Such decisions might include the number of annual paid holidays, the length of maternity leave, and the provision of day-care facilities. Localizing such management decisions tends to contribute to better labor-management relations because managers familiar with local practices are better equipped to handle matters that affect workers personally.

Labor unions: global trends

Table 12.4 provides a common reference for comparing the strength of labor unions across different countries since 1970. Union density measures the number of union members against the total number of wage earners in a given market. Union density rates in 2002 or 2003 are lower than in 1970 for all but four EU markets (Finland, Sweden, Denmark, and Belgium). These four markets are the only ones in which unions are involved in the administration and execution of unemployment insurance. In most cases membership dropped consistently across the time period, and even for exceptions during the 1990s in Ireland and the Netherlands, where there was rapid employment growth, the total growth of wage earners far outstripped the growth in union members. In other EU countries traditionally dominated by unions (e.g., France and Germany) one can see union density consistently falling in spite of extremely slow employment growth in those markets during the 1990s.

Table 12.4 shows a large variation in union density rates across various countries: very low rates in the USA, Republic of Korea, Poland, and Spain compared to high rates in Finland, Sweden, and Denmark. In general, union density is twice as high in Europe as it is in the USA, but in all cases trends are falling.

There are a number of factors contributing to this decline in union membership globally:[3]

- *International competition*: Global MNEs are competing across national borders with one another and this drives negotiations on costs, benefits, and worker rights towards the lowest common denominator globally.
- *Privatization*: Traditionally the public sector makes up one of the biggest member groups in any national union membership; as sectors are privatized, unions lose their influence in general.
- *Transition from industrial to service economies*: The other major contributor to union ranks historically has been workers from the manufacturing sector; in developing countries, outsourcing, offshoring and downsizing of these industries and the move towards and growth of the service sector has further contributed to losses in union members.
- *Higher long-term unemployment rates*: This is specific to Europe, but union membership has declined over the years as many union members have joined the ranks of the unemployed.
- *Flexible employment contracts*: The rise in temporary/part-time workers as well as the introduction of telecommuting and other forms of nontraditional work arrangements are typically not relevant to union groups.

As union density in national markets declines and global MNEs proliferate, national unions have begun to seek global alliances with unions in other markets and to lobby supranational organizations such as the International Labor Office (a UN agency) to require MNEs to comply with labor standards and practices worldwide. There are also unions that have successfully created global agreements that affect all the subsidiaries of an MNE by working through organizations such as Union Network International (UNI), formed in 2000, which represents 20 million workers in 900 unions worldwide. MNEs that have signed global agreements with the UNI include Allianz, Carrefour, H&M, Manpower, and Telefonica.

TABLE 12.4 Union Density in 24 countries and the EU, Adjusted Data for 1970-2003

Year	United States	Canada	Australia	New Zealand	Japan	Republic of Korea	European Union	Germany	France	Italy	United Kingdom	Ireland
1970	[1]23.5	31.6	[9]50.2	[14]55.2	35.1	12.6	37.8	32.0	21.7	37.0	44.8	53.2
1960	[2]19.5	[6]34.7	[10]49.5	69.1	31.1	14.7	39.7	34.9	18.3	49.6	50.7	57.1
1990	15.5	32.9	40.5	51.0	25.4	17.6	33.1	31.2	10.1	38.8	39.3	51.1
1991	15.5	—	—	44.4	24.8	16.1	34.1	36.0	9.9	38.7	38.5	50.2
1992	15.1	33.1	39.6	37.1	24.5	15.1	33.4	33.9	9.9	38.9	37.2	49.8
1993	15.1	32.8	37.6	34.5	24.3	14.5	32.7	31.8	9.6	39.2	36.1	47.7
1994	14.9	—	35.0	30.2	24.3	13.4	31.7	30.4	9.2	38.7	34.2	462
1995	14.3	—	32.7	27.6	24.0	12.9	30.4	29.2	9.0	38.1	32.6	45.8
1996	14.0	—	31.1	24.9	23.4	12.2	29.5	27.8	8.3	37.4	31.7	45.5
1997	13.6	28.8	30.3	23.6	22.8	11.9	28.8	27.0	8.2	36.2	30.6	43.5
1998	13.4	28.5	28.1	22.3	22.5	12.1	28.2	25.9	8.0	35.7	30.1	41.5
1999	13.4	27.9	25.7	21.9	22.2	11.1	27.8	25.6	8.1	36.1	29.8	—
2000	12.8	28.1	24.7	22.7	21.5	11.1	27.3	25.0	8.2	34.9	29.7	—
2001	12.8	28.2	24.5	22.6	20.9	11.2	26.6	23.5	8.1	34.8	29.3	36.6
2002	12.6	28.2	23.1	22.1	20.3	11.1	26.3	23.2	8.3	34.0	29.2	36.3
2003	12.4	28.4	22.9	—	19.7	11.2	—	22.6	8.3	33.7	29.3	35.3
Absolute change												
1970–1980	[3]–2.5	3.3	[11]–7	[15]13.9	–4.0	2.0	1.9	2.9	–3.4	12.6	5.9	3.9
1980–1990	[4]–4.0	[7]1.8	[12]–9.0	–18.1	–5.8	3.0	–6.7	–3.7	–8.1	–10.8	–11.4	–6.1
1990–2003	–3.1	–4.7	–17.6	–28.9	–5.6	–6.5	–6.7	–8.6	–1.9	–5.1	–10.0	–5.8
1970-2003	[5]–11.1	[8]–6.5	[13]–27.6	[16]–33.1	–15.4	–1.5	[17]–11.5	–9.5	–13.4	–3.3	–15.5	–17.9

Notes: [1]1973; [2]1983; [3]1973–1981; [4]1983–1990; [5]1983–2003; [6]1984; [7]1984–1990; [8]1984–2003; [9]1976; [10]1982; [11]1976–1982; [12]1982–1990; [13]1976–2003; [14]1971; [15]1971–1980; [16]1990–2002; [17]1970–2002.

	Finland	Sweden	Norway	Denmark	Netherlands	Belgium	Spain	Switzerland	Austria	Hungary	Czech Republic	Slovak Republic	Poland
1970	51.3	67.7	56.8	60.3	36.5	42.1	—	28.9	62.8	—	—	—	—
1980	69.4	78.0	58.3	78.6	34.8	54.1	12.9	31.1	56.7	—	—	—	—
1990	72.5	80.8	58.5	75.3	24.3	53.9	12.5	24.3	46.9	—	78.8	78.7	[5]53.1
1991	75.4	80.6	58.1	75.8	24.1	54.3	14.7	22.7	45.5	—	—	—	—
1992	78.4	83.3	58.1	75.8	25.2	54.3	16.5	23.0	44.3	—	—	—	—
1993	80.7	83.9	58.0	77.3	25.9	55.0	18.0	22.8	43.2	—	—	—	—
1994	80.3	83.8	57.8	77.5	25.6	54.7	17.6	23.3	41.4	—	—	—	—
1995	80.4	83.1	57.3	77.0	25.7	55.7	16.3	22.8	41.1	63.4	46.3	57.3	32.9
1996	80.4	82.7	56.3	77.1	25.1	55.9	16.1	22.9	40.1	—	—	—	—
1997	79.5	82.2	55.5	75.3	25.1	56.0	15.7	22.6	38.9	—	—	—	—
1998	78.0	81.3	55.5	75.6	24.5	55.4	16.4	21.7	38.4	32.8	—	—	24.2
1999	76.3	80.6	54.5	74.1	24.6	55.1	16.2	21.0	37.4	—	—	—	—
2000	75.0	79.1	53.7	73.3	23.1	55.6	16.1	19.4	36.5	—	—	—	14.7
2001	74.5	78.0	52.8	72.5	22.5	—	16.1	17.8	35.7	19.9	27.0	36.1	—
2002	74.8	78.0	53.0	—	22.4	55.4	16.2	—	35.4	—	—	—	—
2003	74.1	78.0	53.3	70.4	22.3	—	16.3	—	—	—	—	—	—
Absolute change													
1970–1980	18.1	10.3	1.5	18.3	−1.7	12.0	—	2.2	−6.0	—	—	—	—
1980–1990	2.9	2.8	.2	−3.3	−10.4	−2	−.3	−6.8	[4]−9.8	—	—	—	—
1990–2003	1.6	−2.8	−5.2	−4.9	−2.0	11.4	3.7	[4]−6.5	[1]−11.5	[7]−43.6	[7]−19.3	[7]−21.2	[7]−16.2
1970–2003	22.8	10.3	−3.2	10.1	−14.2	213.3	33.4	[5]−11.2	[2]−27.3	—	—	—	—

Notes: [1]1990–2002; [2]1970–2002; [3]1980–2003; [4]1990–2001; [5]1970–2001; [6]1989, [7]1995–2001.

Percent of union members out of total employed salary earners in a given country.

Source: Visser, J., (2006). Union membership statistics in 24 countries. *Monthly Labor Review*, January, p 45.

COUNTRY FOCUS

THAILAND

World Rank (EFI 2009): 67

Regional Rank (EFI 2009): 10

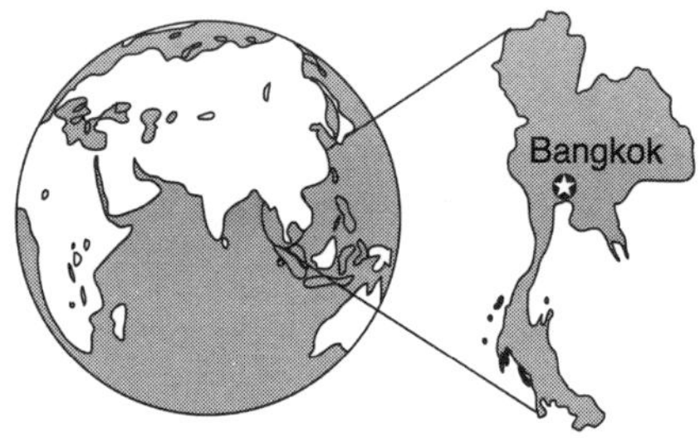

Economic freedom score

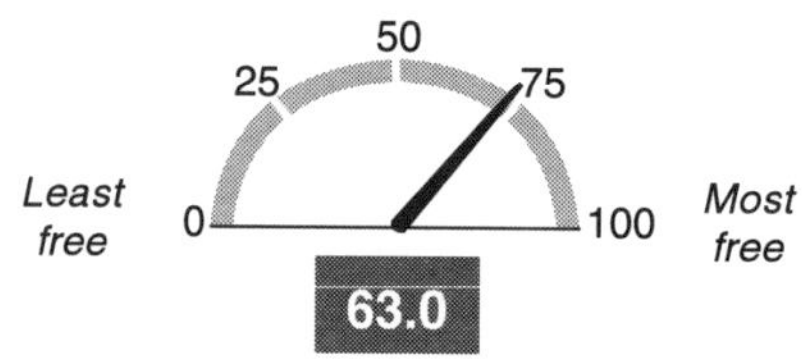

Quick facts

Population: 63.4 million

GDP (PPP): $482.1 billion; 5.1 percent growth in 2006; 5.7 percent 5-year compound annual growth; $7,599 per capita

Unemployment: 1.4 percent

Inflation (CPI): 2.2 percent

FDI inflow: $9.8 billion

2006 data unless otherwise noted

Thailand's economic freedom score is 63.0, making its economy the 67th freest in the 2009 Index. Thailand is ranked 10th out of 41 countries in the Asia-Pacific region, and its overall score is higher than the world average.

Showing a moderate degree of resilience, Thailand has continued its steady economic growth in recent years. The regulatory environment has become more efficient and streamlined. Opening a business takes less time than the world average, and overall licensing procedures are simple and transparent. The financial sector continues to be strengthened and is more open to competition. Private property is generally protected, although the judiciary is subject to inefficiency and corruption.

Thailand scores less well in monetary freedom, investment freedom and freedom from corruption. Though inflation is moderate, the government directly subsidizes the prices of a number of staple goods. Foreign investment is subject to a variety of serious restrictions that are not enforced uniformly. Corruption is significant, although not as extensive as in many neighboring countries.

Background

Thailand is a constitutional monarchy with a turbulent political history. Since 1932, the country has experienced more than five coups. In December 2007, a civilian government was elected and started the process of unwinding the former military government's protectionist economic policies, which included capital controls and restrictions on foreign investment. Thailand's economy is dependent on agricultural exports, particularly exports of shrimp and rice, and much of its population remains employed in the agricultural sector.

Business freedom – 71.1

The overall freedom to start, operate, and close a business is relatively well protected under Thailand's regulatory environment. Starting a business takes an average of 33 days, compared to the world average of 38 days. Obtaining a business license takes less than the world average of 18 procedures and 225 days. Bankruptcy proceedings are fairly easy and straightforward.

Trade freedom – 75.6

Thailand's weighted average tariff rate was 4.7 percent in 2006. Import bans and restrictions, services market access barriers, import taxes and fees, prohibitive tariffs, burdensome standards and import licensing requirements, restrictive sanitary and phytosanitary rules, nontransparent government procurement, nontransparent and inefficient customs implementation, export subsidies, and weak enforcement of intellectual property rights add to the cost of trade. Fifteen points were deducted from Thailand's trade freedom score to account for nontariff barriers.

Fiscal freedom – 74.4

Thailand has burdensome tax rates. The top income tax rate is 37 percent, and the top corporate tax rate is 30 percent. Other taxes include a value-added tax (VAT) and a property tax. In the most recent year, overall tax revenue as a percentage of gross domestic product (GDP) was 17.0 percent.

Government size – 90.6

Total government expenditures, including consumption and transfer payments, are low. In the most recent year, government spending equaled 17.7 percent of GDP. Government intervention persists, and privatization has suffered several setbacks that are due in part to political instability.

Monetary freedom – 69

Inflation is low, averaging 3.0 percent between 2005 and 2007. The government controls the prices of more than 200 products; it can set price ceilings for basic goods and services, and influences prices through regulation, subsidies, and state-owned utilities. Twenty points were deducted from Thailand's monetary freedom score to account for policies that distort domestic prices.

Investment freedom – 30

With few exceptions, the government prohibits majority foreign ownership in most sectors and reserves certain professions for Thai nationals. Investment regulations are burdensome and nontransparent, and bureaucracy is cumbersome. Residents and nonresidents may hold foreign exchange accounts, subject to approval in some cases. Foreign exchange transactions, repatriation, some outward direct investments, and transactions involving capital market securities, bonds, debt securities, money market instruments, real estate, and short-term securities are regulated and usually require government approval. In general, non-Thai businesses and citizens may own land only on government-approved industrial estates.

Financial freedom – 60

The government has made financial regulation and supervision more efficient and adheres to international best practices. The Financial Institutions Businesses Act empowers the Bank of Thailand (BOT) and the Finance Ministry to ease restrictions on foreign ownership and the number of foreign directors in commercial banks. The BOT's Financial Sector Master Plan Phase II focuses on increasing competition through a more flexible regulatory framework. Credit is generally allocated on market terms. As of March 2008, there were 17 domestic banks and 17 foreign banks. The government

(Continued)

still owns more than 40 percent of Krung Thai Bank, Siam City Bank, and BankThai, which are among the 10 largest domestic institutions. Roughly 100 insurance companies are registered, including many foreign firms, and capital markets are relatively well developed. The stock exchange is active and open to foreign investors.

Property rights – 50

Private property is generally protected, but the legal process is slow, and litigants, vested interests, or third parties can affect judgments through extra legal means. Despite a Central Intellectual Property and International Trade Court, piracy (especially of optical media) continues. The government can disclose trade secrets to protect any "public interest" not having commercial objectives, and there are concerns that approval-related data might not be protected against unfair commercial use.

Freedom from corruption – 33

Corruption is perceived as significant. Thailand ranks 84th out of 179 countries in Transparency International's Corruption Perceptions Index for 2007, a steep drop from 2006. Allegations of customs irregularities continue. The lack of administrative transparency is attributable to Thailand's complex hierarchical system of laws and regulations. The government is trying to make the evaluation of bids and awarding of contracts more transparent. Convictions of public officials on corruption-related charges are rare.

Labor freedom – 76.5

Thailand's relatively flexible labor regulations enhance overall employment and productivity growth. The nonsalary cost of employing a worker is low, and dismissing a redundant employee is not burdensome. Regulations related to the number of work hours are quite flexible.

Source: Adapted from The Heritage Foundation (2009). *2009 Index of Economic Freedom*. (Washington, DC: The Heritage Foundation and Dow Jones & Company, Inc., 2009), at www.heritage.org/index.

SUMMARY

Global human resource management (HRM) introduces more complexity to the domestic HR function through the need of the HR manager to deal with:

Expatriates' personal issues – for employees moved away from their native country to reside in another country to further the interests of a business, this involves developing expertise and policies around double taxation, relocation packages, cultural training, orientation and local support, and considering and providing for the family members of the expatriates in areas such as education, security, and lodgings.

- **Managing the mix of local versus global staff** – deciding on the right staffing policy in each business situation and for each market.
- **External influences** – understanding and considering the different government and cultural influences in different countries.
- **Having a global perspective** – considering recruiting, training, appraisal, and compensation policies across the global MNE.

There are five key tasks for the Global HRM:

- **International staffing policy** – choosing between PCN, HCN, and TCN solutions depending on the role, the market, and the objectives of headquarters for the foreign subsidiary. Recruiting and selecting appropriate staff for international assignments. Dealing with culture shock and reverse culture shock of the employee and their families.
- **Training and development** – in addition to professional training, cultural training is required to help prepare the employee (and their families) to adapt to the new personal and professional challenges.
- **International performance appraisal** – to develop and apply a fair appraisal system across the global MNE, an understanding of the various cultures and local market issues along with an understanding of the limitations of global managers to assess their local teams without extra efforts to overcome distance, time, and cultural gaps.
- **Employee compensation** – must take into account local cost of living, local norms, and local regulations alongside the guidelines and policies of the global MNE.
- **Labor management relations** – understanding the role and strength of the union groups in a given market is critical to understanding the resulting costs, challenges, and opportunities for staffing and managing in that market.

Ultimately, the challenge of the global HRM is to balance between a very broad understanding of the global objectives of the firm while leveraging advantages of various foreign markets through the right mix of local expertise and corporate experience.

DISCUSSION QUESTIONS

1. Compare and contrast international HRM to domestic HRM.
2. Describe the various types of international staffing policies employed by MNEs.
3. Explain culture shock and reverse culture shock.
4. Compensation for managerial and nonmanagerial workers is based on several main considerations. List and explain each of these considerations.
5. Identify a country where a particular approach for international staffing policy is dominant, and explain why.

EXERCISE

Why Skilled Immigrants Are Leaving the USA

As the debate over H-1B workers and skilled immigrants intensifies, we are losing sight of one important fact: the USA is no longer the only land of opportunity. If we don't want the immigrants who have fueled our innovation and economic growth, they now have options elsewhere. Immigrants are returning home in greater numbers. And new research shows they are returning to enjoy a better quality of life, better career prospects, and the comfort of being close to family and friends.

Earlier research by my team suggested that a crisis was brewing because of a burgeoning immigration backlog. At the end of 2006, more than 1 million skilled professionals (engineers, scientists, doctors, researchers) and their families were in line for a yearly allotment of only 120,000 permanent resident visas. The wait time for some people ran longer than a decade. In the meantime, these workers were trapped in "immigration limbo." If they changed jobs or even took a promotion, they risked being pushed to the back of the permanent residency queue. We predicted that skilled foreign workers would increasingly get fed up and return to

(Continued)

countries like India and China where the economies were booming.

Why should we care? Because immigrants are critical to the country's long-term economic health. Despite the fact that they constitute only 12 percent of the US population, immigrants have started 52 percent of Silicon Valley's technology MNEs, and contributed to more than 25 percent of our global patents. They make up 24 percent of the US science and engineering workforce holding bachelor's degrees and 47 percent of science and engineering workers who have PhDs. Immigrants have co-founded firms such as Google (NasdaqGS:GOOG – News), Intel (NasdaqGS:INTC – News), eBay (NasdaqGS:EBAY – News), and Yahoo! (NasdaqGS:YHOO – News).

Who are they? Young and well-educated

We tried to find hard data on how many immigrants had returned to India and China. No government authority seems to track these numbers. But human resources directors in India and China told us that what was a trickle of returnees a decade ago had become a flood. Job applications from the USA had increased tenfold over the last few years, they said. To get an understanding of how the returnees had fared and why they left the USA, my team at Duke, along with AnnaLee Saxenian of the University of California at Berkeley, and Richard Freeman of Harvard University, conducted a survey. Through professional networking site LinkedIn, we tracked down 1,203 Indian and Chinese immigrants who had worked or received education in the USA and had returned to their home countries. This research was funded by the Kauffman Foundation.

Our new paper, "America's Loss Is the World's Gain," finds that the vast majority of these returnees were relatively young. The average age was 30 for Indian returnees, and 33 for Chinese. They were highly educated, with degrees in management, technology, or science. Fifty-one percent of the Chinese held master's degrees and 41 percent had PhDs. Sixty-six percent of the Indians held a master's and 12.1 percent had PhDs. They were at the very top of the educational distribution for these highly educated immigrant groups – precisely the kind of people who make the greatest contribution to the US economy and to business and jo growth.

Nearly a third of the Chinese returnees and a fift of the Indians came to the USA on student visas A fifth of the Chinese and nearly half of the Indian entered on temporary work visas (such as the H-1B) The strongest factor that brought them to the US was professional and educational developmen opportunities.

What they miss: family and friends

They found life in the USA had many drawbacks Returnees cited language barriers, missing thei family and friends at home, difficulty with cultura assimilation, and care of parents and children as ke issues. About a third of the Indians and a fifth of th Chinese said that visas were a strong factor in thei decision to return home, but others left for opportu nities and to be close to family and friends. And i wasn't just new immigrants who were returning. I fact, 30 percent of respondents held permanent res ident status or were US citizens.

Eighty-seven percent of Chinese and 79 percen of Indians said a strong factor in their original deci sion to return home was the growing demand fo their skills in their home countries. Their instincts generally proved right. Significant numbers movec up the organization chart. Among Indians, the per centage of respondents holding senior managemen positions increased from 10 percent in the USA tc 44 percent in India, and among Chinese it increasec from 9 percent in the USA to 36 percent in China. Eighty-seven percent of Chinese and 62 percent o Indians said they had better opportunities for longer-term professional growth in their home countries than in the USA. Additionally, nearly half were considering launching businesses and said entrepreneurial opportunities were better in their home countries than in the USA.

Friends and family played an equally strong role for 88 percent of Indians and 77 percent of Chinese. Care for aging parents was considered by 89 percent of Indians and 79 percent of Chinese to be much better in their home countries. Nearly 80 percent of Indians and 67 percent of Chinese said family values were better in their home countries.

More options back home

Immigrants who arrived at America's shores have always felt lonely and homesick. They made big personal sacrifices to provide their children with better opportunities than they had. But they never had the option to return home. Now they do, and they are leaving.

It isn't all rosy back home. Indians complained of traffic and congestion, lack of infrastructure, excessive bureaucracy, and pollution. Chinese complained of pollution, reverse culture shock, inferior education for children, frustration with government bureaucracy, and the quality of health care. Returnees said they were generally making less money in absolute terms, but they also said they enjoyed a higher quality of life.

We may not need all these workers in the USA during the deepening recession, but we will need them to help us recover from it. Right now, they are taking their skills and ideas back to their home countries and are unlikely to return, barring an extraordinary recruitment effort, and major changes to immigration policy. That hardly seems likely, given the current political climate. The policy focus now seems to be on doing whatever it takes to retain existing American jobs – even if it comes at the cost of building a workforce for the future of America.

Source: Bloomberg Businessweek, March 2, 2009. http://www.businessweek.com

Discussion Question

The 2008 economic crisis affected more than just financial regulations; it spread to changes in immigration decision as well. Consider what would be the best human resource strategy from three perspectives: the government, a global corporation, and a local business.

Notes

1 Gordeeva, T. (2009). Vocational Education and Training, *German Culture Site,* available at: http://www.germanculture.com.ua/library/facts/bl_vocational_education.htm.
2 For detailed data see: http://www.globalworkers.org/migrationdata_us.html.
3 Visser, J. (2006). Union membership statistics in 24 countries, Monthly Labor Review, January, pp. 38–49.

Bibliography

Ang, S., Van Dyne, L., Koh, C. K. S. (2006). Personality correlates of the four factor model of cultural intelligence. *Group and Organization Management*, 31, 100–23.

Bain, G. S., Price, R. (1980). *Profiles of Union Growth: A Statistical Portrait of Eight Countries*. Oxford: Basil Blackwell.

Boeri, T., Brugiavini, A. Calmfors, L. (eds) (2001). *The Role of the Unions in the Twenty First Century*. Oxford: Oxford University Press.

Chang, C., Sorrentino, C. (1991). Union membership statistics in 12 countries. *Monthly Labor Review*, 46–53.

Dowling, P., Festing, M., Engle, A. (2008). *International HRM: Managing People in a Multinational Context,* 5th edn. London: Thomson Learning.

Dubofsky, M., Dulles, F. R. (2004). *Labor in America: a History*, 7th edn. Wheeling, IL: Harlan Davidson.

Harzing, A. (2001). Who's in charge? an empirical study of executive staffing practices in foreign subsidiaries. *Human Resource Management*, 40 (2), 139–45.

Harzing, A. (2001). Of bears, bumble-bees and spiders: the role of expatriates in controlling subsidiaries. *Journal of World Business*, 36 (4), 366–79.

Kedia, B. L., Mukherji, A. (1999). Global managers: developing a mindset for global competitiveness. *Journal of World Business*, 34 (3), 330–51.

Levy, O., Beechler, S., Taylor, S., and Boyacigiller, N.A. (2007). Managerial cognition in multinational corporations, 2007. *Journal of International Business Studies*, 38 (2), 231–58.

Mendenhall, M., Dunbar, E., Oddou, G. (1987). Expatriate selection, training and career pathing: a review and critique. *Human Resources Management*, 26, 331–45.

Moran, R. T. Harris, P. R., Moran, S. V. (2007). *Managing Cultural Differences: Global Leadership Strategies for the 21st Century*, 7th edn. Oxford: Elsevier.

Neelankavil, J., Mathur, A., Zhang, Y. (2000). Determinants of managerial performance: a cross-cultural comparison of the perceptions of middle level managers of four countries. *Journal of International Business Studies*, 31 (1), 121–41.

13

International Financial Management

Learning Objectives

Following this chapter, the reader should be able to:

1. Explain the ways in which financial management influences the global success of MNEs
2. Identify the major financial management issues that are essential for global operations, distinguish between *foreign exchange risk* and *foreign exchange exposure* and devise ways to reduce or eliminate both risks in international finance
3. Use international cash flow management and international trade financing techniques
4. Differentiate between domestic and international transactions payment methods and identify the means by which global payments are conducted
5. Define sources of financing for global business and export projects and follow the main steps and procedures involved in listing an MNE on the stock market
6. Indicate the steps that MNEs take to reduce risk from foreign exchange fluctuations, and distinguish between them

Opening Case
A Delicate Balancing Act

The chief financial officer (CFO) of MachineTech AG, a multinational German industrial machinery company, is considering various tax management, currency management, and funds flow management options to achieve a proper balance between three primary financial objectives: namely, to

- minimize the overall tax burden for the multinational enterprise (MNE);
- minimize the MNE's overall exposure to exchange rate fluctuations;
- ensure the correct positioning, or retain flexibility in transferring funds to where they best serve the global corporation's interests.

These goals are often incompatible, given that pursuing one goal could result in the failure of one of the others. Ultimately, the CFO must make decisions about the right trade-offs between these competing goals.

Figure 13.1 illustrates both the relationships between the German parent company and its three wholly-owned subsidiaries, in Brazil, China, and Japan, as well as summarizing some of the differences between the financial regulations in those countries.

In addition to manufacturing and selling in its local market in Germany, the German facility also sells its products regionally in Europe (to other European countries using the euro currency). All three foreign subsidiaries, in Brazil, China, and Japan, acquire sub-assemblies from the parent company, under agreed-on intercompany transfer pricing policies. Each one then adds value to the sub-assemblies, through local customization,

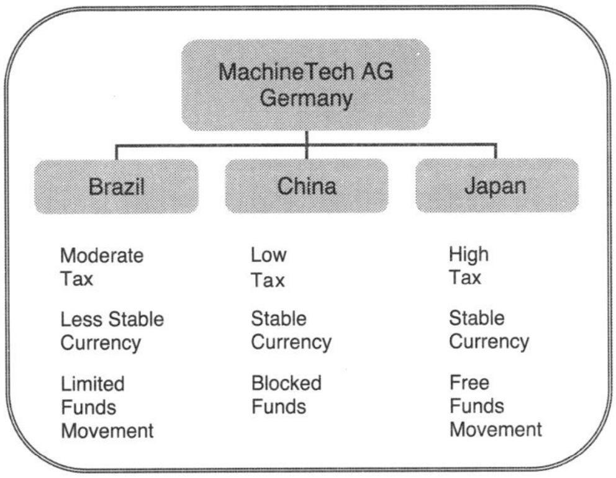

FIGURE 13.1 Corporate chart for MachineTech AG and Subsidiaries

marketing, sales and after-sales service, and support, to their local markets.

Each country where MachineTech AG has incorporated a local subsidiary, poses widely differing challenges for the company's financial management. Let us consider each issue that the CFO is facing to see how the country's specific regulatory differences might influence the CFO's decisions:

Currency management. The ability of each country's currency to maintain its value vs the euro (the reporting currency of the parent corporation) is critical to ensure that the consolidated financial statements are not adversely impacted by exchange rate fluctuations. In 2001, the euro replaced the German mark and 11 other European currencies. Since then, the euro has become one of the world's primary and most stable currencies. In comparison, the Brazilian real has been known to fall dramatically, wiping out all profits generated in Brazil when converted back to other currencies, although in recent years it has been relatively stable by world standards. The Chinese renminbi (RMB or yuan as it is known locally) is not freely convertible to other currencies without government approval and its value is therefore highly controlled and maintained, suggesting long-term stability. Finally, the Japanese yen, which is traded freely on capital markets, is also considered to be a primary currency worldwide and over the past five years has remained very stable vis-à-vis the euro. In terms of proper currency management policies, the CFO would like to reorganize the corporate profits as much as possible away from the Brazilian real and into any of the other currencies the corporation does business in.

Tax management. An obvious goal for the CFO is to strive to minimize the overall tax payments of the MNE worldwide. As Figure 13.1 shows, the statutory corporate income tax rates in Brazil and China (according to the CD Howe Institute, September 2005) are low to moderate compared to the high tax rate in Japan. This suggests that the CFO would be best served by somehow diverting profits away from the Japanese market in order to minimize the corporation's effective tax burden.

Funds flow management. The ability to move funds easily and quickly in an MNE is extremely important. In this case, although Brazil maintains a number of bureaucratic requirements for justifying the movement of funds in and out of the country, it is still relatively open to transferring funds across borders. However, in China the government makes it almost impossible for foreign corporations to transfer funds out of China (i.e., repatriation of profits) with any frequency, although bringing capital into China is not usually a problem. The Japanese subsidiary would have no problem with transferring funds both in and out of the country. Obviously, the CFO would prefer to avoid having funds blocked in China or slowed in Brazil and hence would seek to divert the subsidiaries' profits and cash flows through the Japanese subsidiary or the parent company in Germany.

To summarize, the challenge for the CFO of MachineTech AG is to judge what are the right trade-offs between the competing objectives cited above, in order to create the optimal results for the corporation.

The following chapter provides the various tools that assist the CFO of an MNE to deal with capital budgeting, capital structure, fund raising, cash flow management, and currency risk management. The complexity and interdependency of these tasks is amplified in light of the global economic crisis.

Introduction: The Goal of International Financial Management

As the opening case demonstrates, the international financial manager needs to clearly understand the differences across each geographic and trade region in order to decide how best to arrange the corporate assets, cash flows, and profits to optimize the financial results of the MNE. In other words, the goal of the international financial manager is to *maximize the consolidated after-tax profits* of the MNE. To do so, the international financial manager must deal with the same basic activities that a local financial manager regularly addresses: namely,

- *Capital budgeting and economic analysis*: The process of evaluating the financial viability of an individual investment opportunity for the MNE, whether it is an investment in a development project, real estate, stock, or in some joint venture in a foreign market.
- *Capital structure*: Determining the proportion of equity capital and debt capital which would provide the most appropriate form of financing for the investment.
- *Cash flow management and working capital*: Managing the operating and financing inflows and outflows of cash in a particular investment, and across the enterprise.

However, for the international financial manager, these basic activities are complicated by the differences in markets (such as growth rates, inflation rates, and business cycles), local and international rules and laws (such as regulations, standards, and openness to foreign investment), and currencies (such as exchange rate fluctuations) across countries and regions. Therefore, international financial managers of MNEs must take these other variables into account in their analysis, planning, and decision making. The complexity of the MNE's financial management is demonstrated in Figure 13.2.

Some MNEs might intentionally borrow foreign currencies, use forward contracts or price products or source inputs differently in different markets in an effort to manage the company's exposure to interest and exchange rate fluctuations. On the positive side, international financial managers can take advantage of the international markets for sourcing cheaper financing alternatives to those commonly available at their local banks.

Thus, international financial managers have higher levels of risk, opportunity, and complexity as compared to their domestic counterparts.

This chapter deals with an overview of the risks and complexities unique to international financial managers, followed by a description of the various tools,

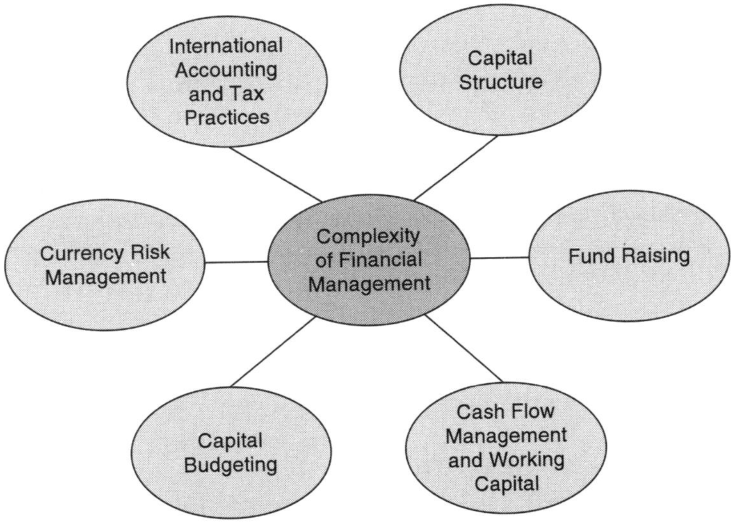

FIGURE 13.2 International financial management complexity

methods, and techniques the CFO uses to manage these risks, to exploit opportunities and to ensure the maximum consolidated after-tax profits for the MNE.

Exposure to Risk in International Finance

Managing foreign exchange exposure

MNEs as well as local enterprises which conduct business internationally are aware of the significant risks to asset values and annual earnings that interest and exchange rates can inflict on the enterprise. International financial managers, treasurers, and financial officers at every level of the enterprise are expected to protect it from, or at least limit its exposure to, these risks.

There are three categories of foreign currency exposure:

1 *Translation exposure* arises from the legal and accounting requirements for MNEs to report consolidated balance sheet and income statements of all their worldwide operations in their home currency. However, any enterprise with operations outside its home country will be earning revenue in a foreign currency and its assets will be valued in a foreign currency. To report the consolidated financial statements, an MNE or the local enterprise must convert all foreign currency values to its home currency equivalent (at least on paper, even if the tangible funds or assets remain at the foreign location), leaving it exposed (for better or for worse) to any fluctuations in the exchange rate between the two currencies.

2 *Transaction exposure* is associated with contractual commitments to pay or receive a payment in a foreign currency for products, services or even

investments outside the home country. For example, a British machine factory buying electronic components from a Hong Kong supplier may be required, in the contract, to pay the supplier in Hong Kong dollars within 90 days. Any changes in the exchange rate between the British pound and the Hong Kong dollar over those 90 days will affect the affect the payment to the British machine factory as well as the profit associated with it.

3 *Economic exposure* is a risk related to how an MNE's long-term cash flows are affected, positively or negatively, by any unexpected changes in exchange rates. Even enterprises that consider themselves purely domestic usually have some economic exposure, whether or not they are aware of it, even if it is indirectly through suppliers. For example, although the local bus company in a North American city like Chicago purchases all its vehicles and services locally as well as receiving all its revenues (from passengers, that is) and financing locally, it may still face exposure on replacement parts that need to be purchased from Canada. The cost of the parts might rise in line with the strengthening of the Canadian dollar vis-à-vis the US dollar.

Translation exposure

Translation exposure, sometimes called accounting exposure, is not a real exposure in the financial sense. There is no impact on the firm's value or cash flows over time due to this phenomenon. It is an impact on the financial statements due to accounting practices that guide the consolidation of an MNE's subsidiaries' financial statements under the parent corporation's control for reporting purposes.

However, there are ways in which translation exposure can have a very real impact on the corporation's value and operations. For example:

- Managers, analysts, and investors need some idea about the performance of the foreign business in terms they can relate to and compare across the MNE as a whole. Translated accounting data can give an approximation for this.
- Performance measurement for bonus plans, hiring, firing, and promotion decisions are often directly affected by translation accounting. As an example, if the foreign currency drops significantly in value against the parent company's reporting currency it could wipe out most or all of the gains of a subsidiary, even if in real terms locally it has outperformed on its business targets.
- Translated accounts serve as a baseline for evaluating discounted cash flows and comparing them across other alternatives for the MNE in other regions.
- In most countries there is a legal requirement to reflect one's subsidiaries in the consolidated financial statements through translated accounting numbers.

To illustrate how translation exposure can affect the reporting of the parent corporation's financial statements, consider the example shown in Figure 13.3.

	Unit (currency)	Profit (Millions)	Income Tax Rate	Tax Payment	Net Profit after Tax (Millions)	Exchange Rate (currency/ Euro)	Profit in Euros (Millions)
Parent	Germany (Euro)	5.00	38%	1.90	3.1	1	3.10 €
Subsidiary	Brazil (Real)	15.00	24%	3.60	11.4	0.33	3.76 €
						Subtotal	6.86 €
						Total Shares	10000000
						EPS	0.69 €

	Unit (currency)	Profit (Millions)	Income Tax Rate	Tax Payment	Net Profit after Tax (Millions)	Exchange Rate (currency/ Euro)	Profit in Euros (Millions)
Parent	Germany (Euro)	5.00	38%	1.90	3.1	1	3.10 €
Subsidiary	Brazil (Real)	15.00	24%	3.60	11.4	0.15	1.71 €
						Subtotal	4.81 €
						Total Shares	10000000
						EPS	0.48 €

FIGURE 13.3 Translation exposure at MachineTech AG

In Figure 13.3, the 2009 results for multinational MachineTech's parent company (Germany) and its wholly-owned subsidiary in Brazil show a profit contribution of five million euros from the parent company, and a 15 million in Brazilian real profit contribution from the Brazilian subsidiary. Under the current tax rates and average exchange rates for 2009, the results ultimately translate to earnings per share (EPS) of 0.69 euros/share. However, imagine that the Brazilian real's value had fallen by about 50 percent against the euro, so the Brazilian subsidiary's effective contribution in euros is halved, thus reducing the company's overall EPS from 0.69 euros/share to 0.48 euros/share. The impact on the company's consolidated profit statement, and the EPS, is significant. However, it does not necessarily have a true cash flow effect unless the German parent repatriates all the cash from the Brazilian subsidiary and converts it to euros. In this scenario, the Brazilian subsidiary may have performed above expectations, but due to the rules governing reporting of consolidated financial statements, the subsidiary appears to have performed only half as well.

MNEs often note such details in the financial statements, but it requires extra effort on the part of a stockholder to distinguish between the underlying numbers of the business and the translated baseline to the parent's local currency for reporting purposes. Hence the stock market may sometimes "punish or reward" MNEs for missing EPS targets, even though the difference can be explained due to translation exposure rather than any real gain or loss of cash, profits or the underlying value of the assets. An example of how translation exposure can also appear to benefit an MNE is seen in the article in the Box.

Newsflash: Weaker Yen Narrows Mitsubishi Motors Loss

Tokyo: Mitsubishi Motors, the only unprofitable Japanese automaker, said Wednesday that its first-quarter loss narrowed by 30 percent as a weaker yen inflated the value of overseas sales. The company's net loss shrank to ¥15.1 billion, or $US 132 million, in the three months ended June 30, from ¥21.6 billion a year earlier. Sales fell 0.4 percent to ¥483.9 billion.

President Osamu Masuko is trying to return Mitsubishi Motors to profitability for the first time in four years with new models including the i minicar and Outlander sport utility vehicle in Japan. A weaker yen against the dollar and the euro lifted the value of sales in the United States and Europe. "The automaker needs to sell more of those new models," said Ichiro Takamatsu, chief investment officer at Alphex Investments in Tokyo. "Mitsubishi Motors and other automakers are direct beneficiaries of a weaker yen."

The weaker yen narrowed the company's operating loss by ¥3.2 billion, Mitsubishi Motors said. The company's shares fell 1 percent to ¥202 in Tokyo. The stock has dropped 18 percent this year.

Source: Adapted from Fuji12mura, Naoka (2006). *International Herald Tribune*, Thursday August 3, p. 16, Marketplace Section.

Transaction exposure

In contrast to translation exposure, transaction exposure represents a real potential threat to an MNE's cash flow over time. Transaction exposure exists whenever an MNE enters any agreement where a cash flow is denominated in a foreign currency and that cash flow is expected to occur at some future date. Transactions that give rise to foreign exchange exposure include:

- purchasing or selling on credit, products and services whose prices are stated in foreign currencies, such as accounts payables or accounts receivables
- borrowing or depositing funds denominated in foreign currencies, including foreign debt or credit
- any other contractual commitments regarding transactions that are denominated in foreign currencies.

For example, suppose that a Chinese manufacturer of Bluetooth headsets signs a contract to purchase chipsets for £100,000 from a UK-based supplier. The payment will be due in 30 days upon delivery. This 30-day account payable represents a transaction exposure for the Chinese firm. If the spot exchange rate on the day the contract is signed is 14.845 RMB/£ (the source of the spot rate: www.oanda.com, August 1, 2006), the Chinese manufacturer would expect to pay £100,000 × 14.845 RMB/£ = 1,484,500 RMB.

However, the company is not certain what the exchange rate between the Chinese renminbi (RMB) and the British pound (£) will be in 30 days. If the spot rate at the end of 30 days is 10 RMB/£, the company will pay less for its supply of chipsets (i.e., 1,000,000 RMB instead of 1,484,500 RMB). However, if the RMB weakens against the British pound and the spot rate at the end of 30 days is 20 RMB/£, the company will end up paying much more for its supply of chipsets (2,000,000 RMB vs 1,484,500 RMB), which could easily wipe out all profit margins related to this batch of Bluetooth headsets. Clearly, this type of transaction exposure represents a very real problem for the international financial manager.

Managing transaction exposure

Managing transaction exposure is typically accomplished through various forms of hedging. A hedge is a term used to describe a limit or protection against potential financial losses due to any kind of transaction exposure. As indicated in Figure 13.4, there are two broad categories of hedging that an international financial manager may use to manage the MNE's transaction exposure: *commercial hedging* and *financial hedging*.

Commercial hedging. This involves incorporating safeguards directly into the terms of the commercial agreement or contract which limit the MNE's exposure to exchange rate fluctuations in some predetermined way. The parties should agree on these mechanisms while negotiating the agreement or contract. Some common examples are as follows:

- *Home currency invoicing*: When an MNE can invoice a specific transaction in its own home currency, or the currency of a third, very stable country acceptable to all parties in the agreement, it avoids any exchange rate risk. In case the parties to the agreement use a third country currency, the exchange rate risk is greatly limited. Naturally, this results in transaction exposure for the party that has to accept these terms, and is typically a function of the bargaining power between the two parties. In the example above, this would happen if the CFO of the Chinese manufacturer of Bluetooth headsets insists on paying the UK supplier of headsets in Chinese currency (RMB) instead of

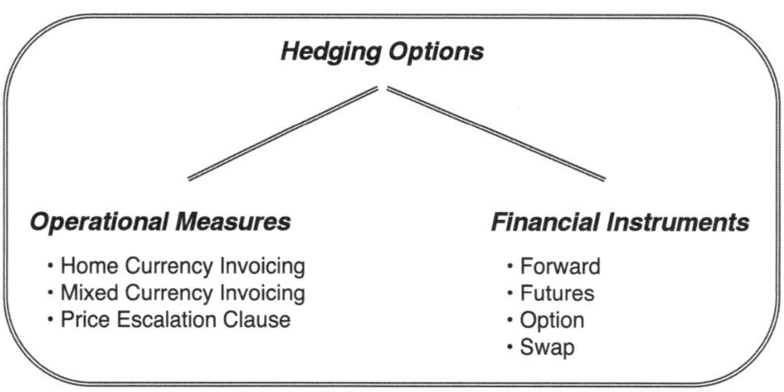

FIGURE 13.4 Tools for managing transaction exposure

British pounds. In effect, the CFO is transferring the transaction exposure in the agreement to his supplier. Why would the supplier agree to these terms? Perhaps the Chinese manufacturer is his biggest customer and accounts for a majority of his annual sales volume and the UK supplier does not want to lose the deal to a competitor.

- *Mixed currency invoicing*: Similar to home currency invoicing, but here the two parties agree to share the risk by splitting the payment into two parts: one part is to be paid in the home currency (in the above example, in RMB); the other part is to be paid in the foreign currency (in the above example, in British pounds).
- *Price escalation clause*: In this case, both parties agree to adjust the payment in full or in a certain proportion to the fluctuations of the invoice currency. If the weak currency defined in the contract depreciates by 1 percent, for example, the payment will automatically increase by 1 percent, or by some other percentage agreed on by both parties. In some cases another variation of this clause is when the two parties agree on some range for the spot rate at the time of settlement within which the payment will automatically be adjusted, but beyond which the two parties agree on some risk-sharing formula.

Financial instrument hedging. This involves entering into a financial agreement in tandem with any commercial contract between two MNEs directly participating in the business activity. This agreement represents financial assets, such as currency, or positions – such as obligation to buy or sell currency at a certain spot rate – that move in an equal but opposite direction to the exposure, and are used to limit or protect against the exchange rate fluctuations of a commitment to pay a certain sum of money in the future.

Some of the common examples for financial hedging are:

- *Forward contracts*: Forward markets are available in most of the world's major currencies. The time frame of a forward contract can extend over a number of years. A forward contract represents an obligation to pay a specific sum of money at a pre-agreed exchange rate on a specific future date. For example, a French exporter selling a shipment of champagne worth €500,000 to a UK retailer may choose to hedge that accounts-receivable entry by using a forward contract. It would therefore commit to a contract with a bank handling foreign exchange transactions to sell €500,000 in a forward contract at an expected three-month spot rate of €1.5/£. Built into the agreement would be a certain margin to the bank covering the transaction cost and whatever risk premium the bank deems relevant in the specific case and with the specific company. Once agreed upon, the forward contract is fixed and must be executed as agreed, on the specified date. The French exporter sells the forward contract on the assumption that the British pound will depreciate or the euro will appreciate around the settlement date. If the realized spot rate actually moves in the opposite direction, the exporter will lose foreign exchange gains that it would otherwise have obtained.

- *Futures (future contracts)*: These contracts are basically the same as a forward contract. The main difference is that in a forward contract all payments are made at the end, whereas in the futures market some of the payment is made through a margin account before the end of the period. In general, these adjustments, such as additions or subtractions to the margin account – vis-à-vis the difference between the agreed-upon spot rate in the futures contract and the actual spot rate – are done on a daily basis, called *marking to market*. At the end of the period the exporter receives both the principal amount (based on that day's spot rate) plus whatever sum has accumulated in the margin account. This should typically be almost equal to the original sum (as it would have been paid out under a forward contract) less some minor differences due to different pricing of this financial mechanism and the impact of interest rates over the three-month period. There is another difference between future and forward contracts, which is that future contracts are exchange traded and have standardized terms, whereas forward contracts are traded over the counter and are customized, involving a nonexchange counter party.
- *Options*: In the options market, a call option is used to purchase a stated number of units of a specific foreign currency at a specific price per unit during a specific period of time. A put option is to sell a stated number of units of a specific foreign currency at a specific period of time. The *strike* or *exercise* price represents the price at which the option holder has the right to purchase or sell the foreign currency. If the strike price of a call option is below the current spot price of the specified foreign currency (meaning that the owner of the option can purchase the currency at lower than the current spot rate) or the strike price of a put option is above the current spot price of the specified currency (the owner of the option can sell the currency at higher than the current spot rate), it is termed *in the money*. An international financial manager can secure an option to buy or sell a specific sum of a currency committed to in a commercial contract, at some future date, at a fixed rate in order to guard against unfavorable fluctuations in the exchange rates. If the exchange rates move favorably, the financial manager will not need to exercise the options, and will ultimately choose to do whatever creates the greatest cash inflow, or smallest cash outflow of home currency.
- *Swaps*: These agreements involve the exchange of interest or foreign currency exposures, or a combination of both, between borrowers. It is a transformation of one stream of future cash flows into another stream of future cash flows with different features. For example, if an international financial manager would like to hedge accounts payable using the swaps mechanism, he would do the following: (1) borrow the required sum, in home currency; (2) buy the foreign currency in exchange at the current spot rate; (3) invest the foreign currency in the foreign exchange until the date of payment; (4) when the payment date arrives, payment can be made directly using the foreign currency available; and (5) the domestic debt currency is repaid using home currency funds. This way, the MNE is not exposed to exchange

rate fluctuations on a specific transaction since the foreign currency has already been set aside at the beginning and whatever happens by the payment date won't affect the amount of home currency that would need to be used.

Transaction exposure obviously represents a very real and serious threat to the expected cash flows relating to any specific transaction. All the various methods and instruments used to mitigate these risks also come with a price – both administrative and financial – for the various parties involved.

However, the international financial manager must be vigilant, first understanding the extent of the exposure in a given transaction, and then deciding on the appropriate method to minimize the potential downside. The international financial manager must consider the size of the transaction, the relative power of the negotiating parties, and the established systems and procedures available in the market and for the MNE.

Economic exposure

Economic exposure, like transaction exposure, represents a real risk to the expected cash flows of an MNE. The difference being that typically economic exposure deals with the longer term and situations where exposure is recurrent and is not limited to a single or a small number of limited transactions.

Other than exchange rate fluctuations and general macroeconomic trends, there are a number of other factors that could affect the long-term value of cash flows from a particular country. These include changes in regulatory requirements, tax laws, and political risk that may put at risk cash flows generated in a specific country by an MNE.

Figure 13.5 summarizes a set of tools an MNE can use to help protect or at least limit the firm's economic exposure. The tools are grouped in two categories: intercompany financial programs/policies and production or corporate structuring programs.

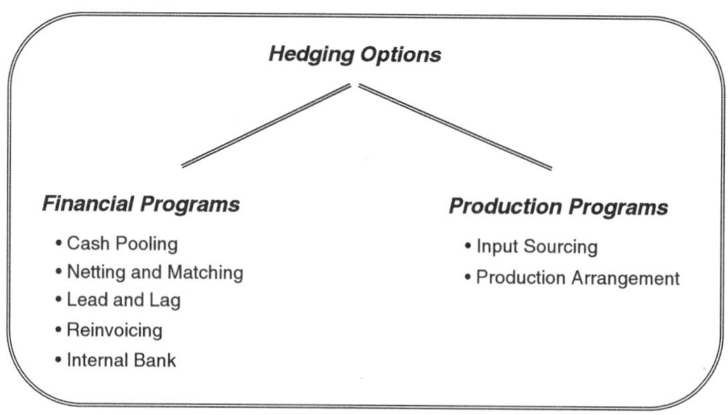

FIGURE 13.5 Tools for managing economic exposure

The first set of tools, *intercompany financial programs*, cover various methods for the MNE to coordinate its inter-corporate payments and financial commitments so as to offset adverse exchange rate changes affecting various country subsidiaries. These methods include *leading and lagging, netting and matching,* and *intra-company invoicing*. These tools are also used to minimize administration costs, tax exposure, and to provide optimal cash management. They tend to require a more centralized organizational structure to properly coordinate the activities. The various methods are discussed in greater detail in the next section on international cash flow management.

The second set of tools deals directly with the long-term planning of the MNE and represent methods that can be used to try and balance the cash inflows and cash outflows in any currency the MNE must do business in. This way, economic exposure is limited solely to those cash flows which are not offset by matching counter flows.

The two most common methods for long-term planning of economic exposure comprise:

- *Input sourcing*: In cases where a production facility in a foreign country accumulates accounts receivable, that is sales revenue, through selling locally, yet accumulates most of its accounts payable, that is cost of inputs for production, in the home currency (because it buys components from the parent company and localizes them) or another foreign currency (it uses third-party suppliers for various components, parts or services) there is significant exchange rate exposure to the subsidiary. One way to restrict this exposure is, wherever possible, to replace foreign suppliers with local ones, thus matching the currencies in which the subsidiary is accumulating both accounts payable and accounts receivable. Any changes in the local exchange rate will then have a very limited effect on the subsidiary's overall cash inflows and outflows.
- *Production arrangement*: An MNE that has production facilities in various countries worldwide (or plans to increase its production capacity by adding more facilities internationally) can use the diverse locations to offset, or even take advantage of, changing macroeconomic and exchange rate changes by adjusting the production quotas in different facilities in the most advantageous way to protect cash flows. The MNE may increase production volume of its products in a country where the currency has been devalued, or limit production activities in a country where the currency has increased in value, relative to the other currencies the MNE is dealing with.

International Cash-Flow Management

Ideally, an MNE would prefer to have one global treasury that acts as a single finance entity for the whole company. This single treasury would instantly collect all financial reserves worldwide and distribute them effectively, while minimizing risk and transaction costs. However, the complexity of managing an MNE exposed to various currency fluctuations, exchange controls, and tax jurisdictions makes this a very complex and dynamic challenge.

Typically, the international financial manager can apply three categories of cash management policies: *home country policies, host country policies*, and *cross-border policies*. These policies need to take into account the expected interactions between the MNE's subsidiaries and their local buyers and suppliers, their foreign buyers and suppliers, and the cash flow interactions within the various MNE entities themselves.

The uses and needs of cash flow between buyers and suppliers, whether local or foreign, are quite straightforward. However, before reviewing the various international cash management methods, it is essential to first understand the underlying elements of intra-company cash flows.

Intra-company cash flows

Cash flows between an MNE's parent company and its subsidiaries worldwide are particularly vulnerable to the impact of currency fluctuations, exchange controls, and multiple tax jurisdictions.

In addition, every transaction initiated by the MNE to manage the flows within a country and across various countries can incur administrative costs from the banks or other financial institutions that facilitate the financial transactions.

Broadly speaking, there are two types of cash flows a firm must manage – *operating cash flows* and *financing cash flows*.

Operating cash flows: transfer pricing, licensing fees, and overhead expenses

Transfer pricing One of the most difficult decisions for the financial manager is to decide on the pricing for goods and services that the MNE sells to its own subsidiaries or affiliates. This price is known as the transfer price. Although, in theory, the *transfer price* of a specific product or service is meant to be set by the open market (i.e., a subsidiary would not spend any more or less money acquiring the same, specific, product or service from a competing firm), in practice it is not always clear. This may be because the specific product is unique to the company (e.g., a proprietary component part in a larger product) and no benchmark pricing is available.

So the price is often set internally. This has a direct impact on the buying subsidiary's profitability and the resulting tax obligations in its host country. If the host government feels that the transfer price is too far from a "fair market price" (in other words, the company is exaggerating the price to avoid paying local taxes), it may step in to force the MNE to adopt different transfer pricing policies.

Licensing fees A foreign subsidiary may also be using technology, equipment or processes that are owned or patented by the parent entity or by a third-party provider who has signed a global agreement with the parent entity. In this case, license fees or royalty payments may have to be paid by the subsidiary.

Overhead expenses The parent entity often provides various administrative services to the subsidiaries around the world (such as centralized treasury services). Often these administrative management and overhead expenses are allocated across the various subsidiaries, who each contribute to paying the parent entity their respective share.

Financing cash flows: loans and dividends

Loans A subsidiary may be partially financed by loans provided by the parent company. In this case the subsidiary is expected to make regular payments to the parent entity. Moreover, various other forms of financing (through equity or debt) could be arranged by the parent entity as a cheaper source of funding than the local options. In this case there could also be financing flows that must be paid out on a regular basis.

Dividends If the subsidiary's operations are successful and generate profits, dividends can be paid back to the parent entity.

Having gained a thorough understanding of the various types of cash flows between MNE entities, their markets and their internal affiliates, one can consider the various techniques at the international financial manager's disposal, in order to collect and disburse financial reserves worldwide with the absolute minimum risk and transaction costs.

Techniques for international cash-flow management

Over the past decade, the trend has been towards centralizing many of the financial and treasury operations. This often provides significant economies of scale, more services, and greater expertise to the various units of the MNE worldwide than they could normally have accessed on their own.

To illustrate various international cash management structures and mechanisms, one should refer to the example in Figure 13.6. The example illustrates some of the cash flow relationships between a Japan-based MNE and its subsidiaries in Italy and Germany.

Cash pooling

An MNE with a number of units operating both within an individual country and across several countries may be able to economize on the amount of financial assets required to support a particular region if one central pool of money is used for *cash pooling*. With one pool of capital and up-to-date information on the committed cash inflows and outflows of the various units, the MNE can spend less on foregone interest on cash balances that are held in safekeeping to guard against unexpected needs; transactions costs can then be lowered thanks to economies of scale, and exchange rate exposure and conversion costs can be minimized.

In the example in Figure 13.6, the parent entity based in Japan could consolidate all cash management and resources in one place: for example, in Japan, the

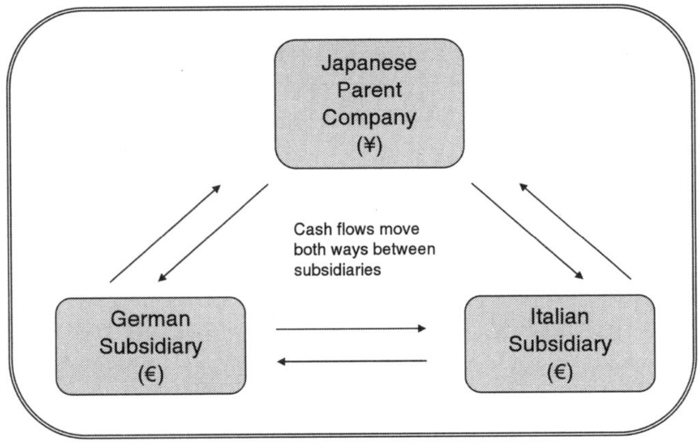

FIGURE 13.6 MNE illustration for cash pooling, netting, and matching

parent company's local headquarters. One manager responsible for cash flow management for the entire MNE is better positioned than each individual unit to plan intercompany payments, negotiate better rates with the banks, and exercise stronger control over currency exposures.

Alternatively, if the amount of activity in Europe requires more direct control and responsiveness due to time-zone differences and physical proximity, it could make sense to create a single cash pool to run both the European subsidiaries from one of the two sites. This would provide similar benefits to having one central pool (although obviously on a smaller scale) and would certainly help in significantly reducing currency exposure.

Netting and matching

Whenever there are two-way cash flows between subsidiaries, or between a subsidiary and the parent entity, there are opportunities to take advantage of *netting*. Given careful coordination, planning, and budgeting, two-way flows can be "netted" against one another with only one smaller cash flow eventually being sent, as opposed to having both cash flows transacted in full. It is particularly useful when the two-way flow of funds involves different currencies, as each would suffer currency exchange charges for intra-company transfers.

Imagine, for example, that the Italian subsidiary of the Japan-based MNE acquires components from the parent company in Japan but also sells finished goods to the parent company for the Asian market. At any point in time during the fiscal year, each party would owe money to the other. Were they to simply to "pay their bills," two cash flows would result. One from the subsidiary to the parent company (e.g., ¥10,000), and one in the opposite direction (e.g., ¥25,000). Each flow would incur administrative costs and require a currency exchange. Instead of sending ¥25,000 one way and ¥10,000 in the other, the MNE can simply "net" the two transactions and have the parent company (which owes the greater sum) send ¥15,000 to the subsidiary.

This is a single transaction which covers both obligations. It saves transaction costs both in terms of administrative costs as well as in currency exchange (from euros to yen in this example).

Matching refers to an activity similar to netting, but between more than two participants (all of whom owe money to one another, but not in the form of two-way flows). For example, imagine that the parent company in Japan owes money to its Italian subsidiary, which in turn owes money to the German subsidiary, which in turn owes money to the parent company. Instead of requiring three cash flows among the three units, a central cash manager could net certain payments between two units with certain payments between the others, in an effort to achieve the same end result for the participants in fewer transactions.

Lead and lag

The timing of payments between subsidiaries of the same MNE, or between the subsidiaries and the parent company, can be more flexible. This allows the financial manager to *lead* (pay early) or *lag* (pay later) on payments in such a way as to position cash flows where they are most needed and/or to limit or take advantage of exchange rate fluctuations.

For example, if the financial manager at the Italian subsidiary (from Figure 13.6) expects the euro (€) to lose value against the Japanese yen (¥) in the coming months, he may choose to lead (pay early) with certain payments while the value of the currency is still high.

Reinvoicing

MNEs with several manufacturing and distribution subsidiaries located over a number of countries in a given region may find it more cost-effective to have one office or a subsidiary assume ownership for all the invoices and payments between the subsidiaries.

For example, in Figure 13.7 a *reinvoicing* center is added to the original example in Figure 13.6. The reinvoicing center is located in Luxembourg (a country known to have low taxes and few restrictions on income earned from international business operations). In this case, while the physical products are sent directly from one (German) subsidiary to another (Italian), the Luxembourg subsidiary would be responsible for buying these products from the supplying unit (German subsidiary) and selling it to the buying unit (Italian subsidiary).

Once ownership is assumed by the Luxembourg subsidiary, the sale can be exchanged into another currency, netted or matched against other payments, hedged against specific currency exposures or repriced, bearing in mind the potential tax benefits of the reinvoicing center's host country, in this case Luxembourg.

Internal bank

Some MNEs with significant financial resources and needs that have grown either too large or too sophisticated for local financial institutions to cope with, have established their own *internal bank* within the firm. The internal bank actually buys and sells payables and receivables from the various subsidiaries, freeing their

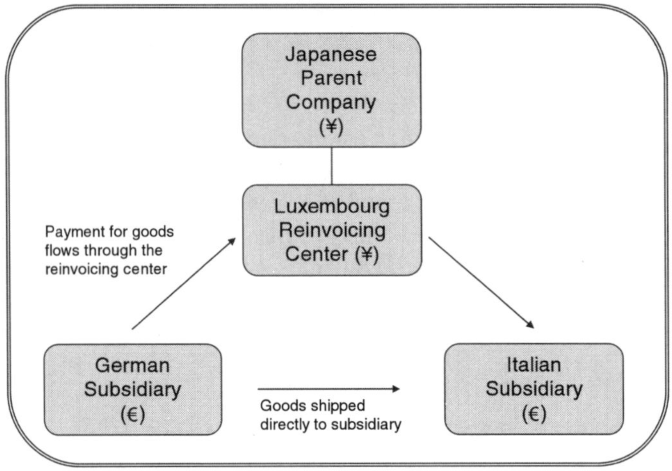

FIGURE 13.7 Re-invoicing center

management teams from dealing with working capital financing, and leaving them to focus on the core business activities.

Many of these structures and mechanisms can be combined and used in ways that best fit the needs of a specific MNE, given the constraints of the various countries where it is active. Many governments have laws and regulations that encourage or prohibit certain international cash-flow management techniques. For example, there are countries that severely limit the ability to lead and lag payments. International cash-flow management requires both a strong grasp of the tools and local regulations, alongside a significant amount of flexibility and creative thinking in seeking the optimal structure, and techniques to ensure the highest possible financial contribution worldwide, at the lowest cost and exposure to risk.

International Trade Financing

International business transactions generally involve greater challenges and risks than similar domestic transactions. This is because the two parties to the international transaction often do not know each other, the lead-times for shipping the product can be much longer, and the local business may not be as familiar with the foreign business norms and practices as the foreign agencies. For example, there are credit agencies that do background checks of suppliers or buyers in the foreign market to support financial transactions. In addition, there is also the ever-present exposure to currency fluctuations, given that the two parties are likely to be located in different countries which use different currencies.

For example, consider an Italian supplier of designer clothing that typically sells its branded products in specialty boutiques around Milan and Rome. In general,

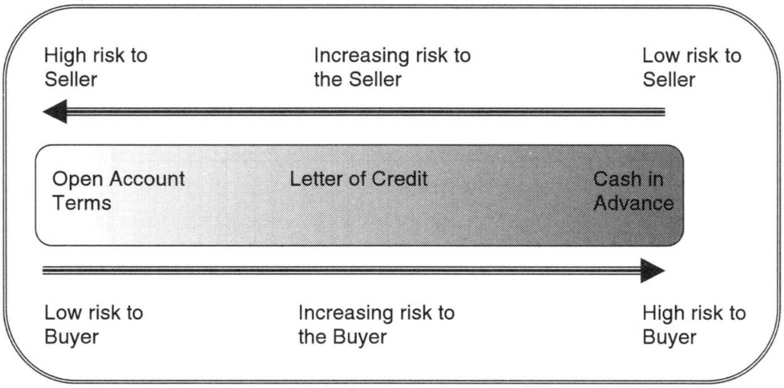

FIGURE 13.8 Spectrum of risk to suppliers/buyers

the clothing is shipped out to the stores upon receipt of the order, and payment is expected in 30 or 60 days, depending on the different stores. This represents a transaction on an "open account" basis. The supplier has placed his trust in the buyer's honoring its undertaking to pay for the products it has received. Open account terms are typically used in domestic business as the two parties have a long-standing relationship, or the seller is confident in his ability to judge a new buyer's creditworthiness, given his familiarity with the local market and perhaps use of some local credit agencies.

Should, however, the Italian supplier receives an order from a specialty boutique in Bangalore, India, extending the same level of financial trust is more of a problem. The degree of credit risk, the risk of not being paid after the product has been shipped, may be higher than the supplier is prepared to incur, and a guarantee of some kind is required in order to facilitate such a transaction.

The most extreme case of a guarantee for payment of goods is simply to request the cash in advance, before shipment. A first-time transaction between a buyer and seller often begins at this stage (especially if the buyer is relatively small or has limited buying power). In this case, the supplier avoids both the credit risk and the currency exposure on the transaction. However, buyers in most countries typically loath to pay upfront for any product or service, if they can avoid it.

On the spectrum shown in Figure 13.8, midway between total financial trust (open account terms) and complete financial distrust (cash in advance) lies the letter of credit (L/C) mechanism, which provides a guarantee of payment under certain conditions, through a sequence of documents and the involvement of one or two other parties (normally banks) in the transactions.

Trade financing using letter of credit

To illustrate how the L/C mechanism works, consider the following example. CSR, a semiconductor supplier based in the UK, receives a large order from HHR, a consumer electronics manufacturer in China. The UK supplier has never worked with this buyer before and therefore seeks some guarantee of payment before agreeing to ship the product. The Chinese buyer refuses to pay cash in advance, as this is a very large order, which will tie up a significant amount of working capital (working capital is defined as the difference between current assets and current liabilities) for six months (one month to deliver, one month to manufacture the product, one month to deliver to retailers worldwide under three-month payment terms). A letter of credit mechanism is therefore proposed.

Figure 13.9 illustrates the sequence of events used to complete the transaction with a letter of credit:

1 HHR requests a letter of credit (L/C) to be issued by its bank, the Bank of China (BoC).
2 BoC then determines whether HHR is creditworthy and has the financial resources to make the payments for the agreed-upon business transaction. Note that this is a critical step for BoC. In effect it is being asked to substitute its own creditworthiness (which is internationally recognized) for HHR. However, its intention is only to guarantee the payment, not to actually pay it, and hence it must be sure HHR has the funds available.
3 BoC, once it is satisfied with HHR's application, issues an L/C to a representative in the UK or to the supplier's bank, Citibank. The L/C guarantees payment for the products if they are shipped as listed in the accompanying documents. Generally, such documents will include a commercial invoice, customs clearance and invoice, packing list, certification of insurance, and a bill of lading.

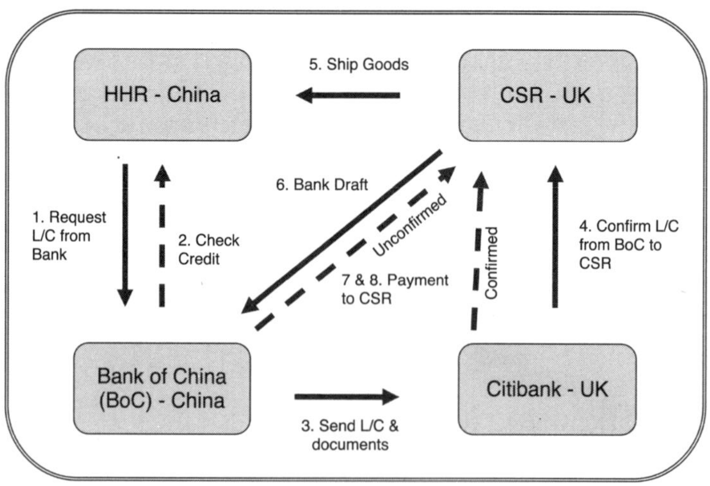

FIGURE 13.9 Example of letter of credit (L/C) process

4 Citibank assures CSR that the payment will be made after it has reviewed the L/C received from BoC. At this point, the credit standing of BoC has in effect been substituted for that of HHR.

5 When the product order is ready (a shipment of short-range wireless chips), it is loaded on board the carrier (the logistics provider). When the supplier signs a contract with a carrier, the signed contract serves as the receipt that the carrier has received the goods. This is called the *bill of lading*.

6 CSR draws a draft against BoC for payment. The draft is the document used in international trade to effect payment and explicitly requests payment for the product, which is now shown to be shipped and insured in compliance with the requirements of the L/C. If the draft is issued to the importer, HHR, it is a *trade draft*; if it is issued to the bank issuing the L/C, BoC, it is a *bank draft*. The draft, L/C, and all relevant documents are presented to Citibank for payment.

7 If Citibank has confirmed the L/C from BoC, it would immediately pay CSR for the product and then collect from the issuing bank, BoC. If not, it would simply pass the documents to BoC for payment (directly to CSR). Clearly, in the latter case the payment takes longer.

8 The final settlement between the buyer/importer, HHR, and its bank, BoC, depends on whatever agreements exist prior to the transaction. Either the money is taken out of an account registered with BoC or HHR transfers the sum to BoC upon receipt of all the appropriate documentation.

If the trade relationship continues over time, it is likely that both parties will build up reciprocal trust. As financial trust accumulates, the relationship can gradually shift towards a more open account relationship, with more generous payment terms.

Multinational Investing and Financing

Any type of investment in a foreign country must be financially justified by calculating the present value of the expected cash flows over the life of the investment. This is true for any investment activity, from buying stocks, to building a manufacturing facility, to acquiring a local company. The project can only be financially justified if the net present value of the project over its lifetime is shown to be positive.

The following section first reviews briefly how to construct a capital budget in order to evaluate a particular international project. Next, the various sources of financing that an international financial manager can draw upon in order to pursue shortlisted projects are reviewed.

Capital budget components and project evaluation

The difference between a good and bad capital budget is the quality of revenue and cost assumptions. Anticipating these realistically and accurately is critical to a proper analysis of a project and a true understanding of its potential contribution to the MNE over the life of the project.

In general, any capital budget includes three basic components:

1. *Initial cash flows*: These are the funds required to set up, enter or initiate the project and are typically the largest capital outlay of any project. Given that the cash outflow is done upfront, it has a significant impact on the present value of the project. For example, the upfront costs of construction for a new manufacturing plant affect significantly the present value of the project.
2. *Operating cash flows*: These are the anticipated cash inflows and outflows over the course of the life of the project, once the project has become operational. Typically, one would expect the inflows to exceed the outflows in order to generate a net positive contribution to the MNE – for example, once the plant has gone into production.
3. *Terminal cash flows*: These are the cash flows incurred at the end of a project. They may include cash outflows for shutting down a project and cash inflows from the sale of whatever residual assets there are. For example, the plant is shut down, staff is laid off (severance packages must be paid) and/or assets are sold (such as land, equipment, inventory and so on).

Of course, these capital budget components can exist in different forms in any project: for example, the acquisition of a foreign business, real estate, or stocks. The key question is whether the net present value of all the cash flows is positive or negative. The net cash flows over the project's lifetime are discounted by the MNE's average cost of capital, in order to reflect the fact that the MNE has financed the project at a certain cost of capital. If the project cannot show a financial return more than the cost, it is certainly not worth pursuing. However, even if it does prove to be an acceptable investment (if the net present value is positive and/or exceeds a certain minimum corporate contribution limit), it will then need to compete for financing with all the other possible project opportunities available to the MNE.

The added complexity that the international financial manager must deal with when evaluating capital budgets includes *currency fluctuations*, *market differences*, and *changing regulations* that could affect the net present value of the cash flows from the project. They too, must be taken into account and somehow be reflected in the calculations. This is why international investments are considered considerably riskier than domestic ones.

Consider the following example. A Spanish appliance manufacturer is considering opening a manufacturing facility in Russia, and its CFO is asked to evaluate the project. The CFO collects all the data about the expected revenues (such as expected sales revenues per year) and costs (build and set-up costs, costs of production, overhead expenses, depreciation of equipment, local tax rate on corporate income, for example) from the MNE's operations managers and various subcontractors.

The CFO also consults with various banks and other advisors (including the head of the Russian sales office) about expected exchange rate fluctuations and regulatory trends in Russia over the next few years. This is a critical step, unique to international projects. The shareholders of the parent company are ultimately interested in euros, not Russian rubles, and therefore would only approve a project shown to make a positive contribution to the MNE in euros.

The life of this project is expected to be four years. The CFO must forecast the exchange rate fluctuations of the Russian ruble (RUB) vis-à-vis the euro (€) over this period. On Thursday, August 24, 2006, the spot rate of the ruble to the euro was 34.27 RUB/ € (according to www.oanda.com). The CFO estimates that inflation in Russia is likely to grow at the rate of 4 percent per year. This means that every year it should take 4 percent more euros to buy one ruble. Based on this assumption, the CFO adjusts the yearly exchange rate.

Once the CFO has collected the data, the net present value (NPV) for the life of the proposed project is calculated, the results of which are summarized in Table 13.1.

Line 1 from Table 13.1 represents the expected cash flows in the local Russian currency, the ruble (RUB). Line 3 converts these cash flows to their equivalent value in the parent company's currency, the euro (€), using the expected exchange rate forecasted for each year (in Line 2). The present value factor takes into account the average cost of capital of the MNE and is used to calculate the NPV of the project (in both currencies). Although in Line 8 the NPV is positive (close to half a million rubles in total), when taking into account the expected exchange rates and converting back to euros, the present value of the project to the parent company (Line 6) turns out to be negative (by about 26,000 euros). So, although

TABLE 13.1 MNE's Capital Budget for a Russian Manufacturing Facility

	2008	*2009*	*2010*	*2011*
1 Net cash flow in (RUB)	(15,000,000.00)	3,000,000.00	7,000,000.00	14,000,000.00
2 Exchange rate (RUB/€)	34.27	35.64	37.07	38.55
3 Net cash flow (€)	(437,703.55)	84,173.76	188,851.38	363,175.74
4 Present value factor	1.00	0.83	0.69	0.58
5 Present value (€)	(437,703.55)	70,144.80	131,146.79	210,171.14
6 NPV in (€)	(26,240.81)			
7 Net Present Value (RUB)	(15,000,000.00)	2,500,000.00	4,861,111.11	8,101,851.85
8 NPV in (RUB)	462,962.96			

RUB, Russian ruble, €, euro, NPV, net present value; paraenthese, negative values.

Notes:

a) the spot exchange rate or 34.2 RUB/€ is assumed to change by 4 percent per year: ex. 34.27 × 1.04) = 35.64

b) the present value factor assumes a weighted average cost of capital (WACC) at a discount rate of 20 percent; thus present value factor = $1/(1+0.2)^t$, where t is the number of years in the future (1, 2, or 3) it seems a worthwhile project from the perspective of the Russian subsidiary, it is unacceptable from the parent company's perspective. This illustrates yet another issue that is unique to international investing: when compared to domestic investing, the perspectives of the parent, and the project/subsidiary are not always aligned.

In summary, international investing tends to be riskier. In addition to the anticipated project risk, international financial managers must take into account currency fluctuations, changing foreign market regulatory requirements, and tax regimes. Furthermore, they must keep in mind that a project with a favorable NPV locally may not meet the requirements of the parent company.

Sources of finance for an approved project

Assume that the international financial manager has shortlisted a project that, after careful analysis, has been proven to provide an acceptable return to the parent company and the management team has decided to push ahead. The international financial manager must now consider the most appropriate method of financing the project.

Four primary sources of international finance are available to the international financial manager (as listed in Figure 13.10): *intercompany, equity, debt,* and *local currency financing.*

The following section briefly defines each of them.

Intercompany financing

A common source of financing for international investments is from the parent company or sister subsidiaries. This can be done in different ways:

- Receiving financing from the parent company in the form of equity, loans, trade credit (i.e., deferring accounts payable), or borrowing with a parent

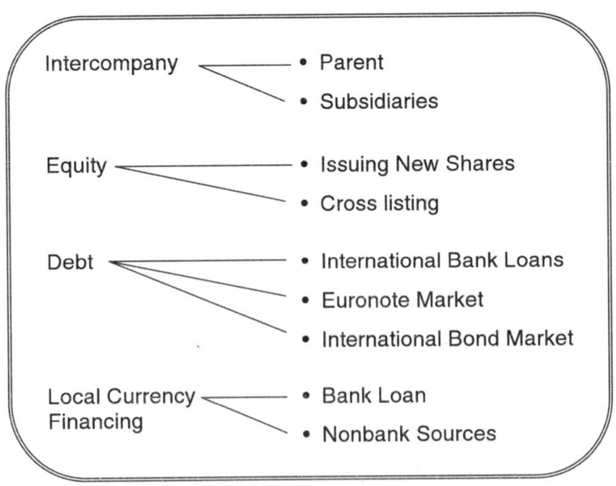

FIGURE 13.10 Sources of international financing

guarantee (which has access to more money or better rates than the subsidiary could have secured alone). This is especially common when setting up in a new market, before the subsidiary begins to generate any revenue and therefore has far less options to choose from.

- Arranging trade credit from other subsidiaries or affiliates of the parent company. This is relevant if the subsidiary buys from the other subsidiaries in order to produce, supply or service its local customers.
- The parent company can allow the subsidiary to retain a higher level of its local profits in order to invest in new projects that have been approved by the parent company.

For several reasons, MNEs often prefer parent loans to parent equity financing for international investments. Intercompany loan payments can be more easily repatriated than future dividends (due to local regulations and capital controls) and the interest expense on loans is often tax deductible, thus lowering the taxable income the subsidiary must pay locally.

Equity financing

Financing using the equity markets can be done in the parent company's home country, a foreign subsidiary's host country, and/or a third country altogether. Typically, equity financing would take the form of either selling new shares to foreign investors or cross listing the company's shares abroad at a foreign stock exchange.

Cross listing a company's shares on foreign stock exchanges can bring a number of benefits (beyond money). It can:

- increase the local awareness and acceptance of the company vis-à-vis its local customers, suppliers, creditors, and host governments;
- improve the liquidity of existing shares by making it easier for foreign shareholders to trade the shares in their home markets and home currencies;
- create a secondary market for shares that can be used to compensate local management and employees in foreign subsidiaries.

Cross listing on a foreign exchange market requires the company to commit to full disclosure of operating results and balance sheets, and it must comply with all the relevant minimum requirements of the foreign market.

Another alternative for equity financing is to issue equity by the local subsidiary in the host country – this is also an attractive means of accessing a new financial market, assuming the subsidiary is in a sophisticated equity market like the USA. There may be local restrictions or conditions on required levels of minority or majority ownership by local nationals, which is the case in China. In some cases, an MNE may prefer to "go-it-alone" in order to avoid any loss of control of the local subsidiary. On the other hand, a strong local partner with a stake in making the local subsidiary successful can often bring with it benefits from local relationships with customers, suppliers, and government officials.

Debt financing

Debt financing is a major source of financing for international investments. This can be done through international bank loans, the euronote market, and the international bond market.

International bank loans are often sourced in the eurocurrency markets. In other words, in countries not using the denomination currency (e.g., an Indian firm obtaining rupee loans from banks in the USA or Europe). These international bank loans are often called eurocredits. Lending banks typically form a syndicate in order to diversify the risk for these types of loans due to their size. The borrowing interest rate for a eurocurrency loan is usually tied to the London Interbank Offered Rate (LIBOR), which is the deposit rate applicable to interbank loans within London.

The euronote market is the collective term used to describe short- to medium-term debt instruments sourced in the eurocurrency markets. The euronote is a less expensive source of short-term funds than syndicated loans because the notes are placed directly with the investor public. Euronotes can be underwritten (i.e., one to three banks organize the others to share the total loan and are committed to buy any of the borrower's notes that could not be placed successfully in the market at the promised rates) or nonunderwritten. The nonunderwritten euronotes include Euro Commercial Paper (ECP) and Euro Medium Term Notes (EMTNs). ECP is a short-term debt obligation of a corporation or bank. Maturity is usually one, three or six months, while the EMTN's typical maturity ranges from as short as nine months to a maximum of 10 years.

The international bond market is composed of eurobonds and foreign bonds. A eurobond is underwritten by an international syndicate of banks and other securities firms, and is sold exclusively in countries other than the country in whose currency the issue is denominated (e.g., a bond issued by a company headquartered in Thailand, denominated in Thai bhat, but sold to investors in the USA or Europe). Most eurobonds use the straight fixed rate, with a fixed coupon, a set maturity date, and a full principal repayment upon final maturity. However, there are also convertible eurobonds which resemble the more common bonds in terms of price and payment characteristics but have the added feature that prior to maturity they are convertible to stock at a specified price per share. A foreign bond is underwritten by a syndicate composed of members from a single country, sold principally within that country, and denominated in its currency (e.g., a Japanese company issuing corporate bonds in Swiss francs and selling it to Swiss investors by Swiss banks).

Local currency financing

The three financing sources described above relate primarily to corporate-level financing options. However, the foreign subsidiary should also consider local options for financing its local investment requirements as a possible way of lowering the overall cost of capital and reducing financial risk. Local financing in a host country has two sources – bank loans and nonbank sources.

Bank loans include overdrafts, discounting, and term. Outside of the USA, banks tend to lend through overdrafts. An *overdraft* is a line of credit against which drafts (checks) can be drawn (written) up to a specified maximum amount.

Discounting is a short-term financing technique by which a local bank discounts a company's trade bills (e.g., a distributor has accounts receivable invoices in hand worth $100,000 that are set to be paid in 30 days; the bank may agree to lend the company $0.2 for every dollar owed immediately for repayment in 30 days, plus interest).

Loans can be either term loans or a line of credit. A term loan is a straight loan that is made for a fixed period of time and repaid in a single lump sum. For frequent borrowers, term loans can be relatively expensive and they may seek a line of credit instead. A line of credit, which is usually good for one year with renewals renegotiated every year, allows the company to borrow up to a stated maximum amount from the bank. Naturally, the company must pay interest on the amount borrowed.

Nonbank sources of funds include commercial paper, factoring (which is the sale of a company's accounts receivable to a financial institution known as a factor: in the USA it is known as a forfeiter), local bond or equity markets, and parallel or back-to-back loans with a foreign company (e.g., a loan involving the exchange of funds between companies in different countries with the exchange reversed at a later date: a Chinese company whose subsidiary needs US dollars might lend an equivalent amount of renminbi to the US company's subsidiary in China).

Financing decisions

Several considerations affect the financing decisions and choices taken by an MNE. Among them are minimizing taxes, managing currency risk, managing political risk, and exploiting financial market distortions, in order to raise money at below market rates.

Financing strategies for minimizing corporate taxes are usually concerned with choosing the tax-minimizing jurisdiction, currency, and corporate vehicle for a financing issue and selecting the tax-minimizing mode of internal transfer of currency and/or profit from the subsidiary back to the parent company. For example, many MNEs prefer parent loans rather than parent investment for funding subsidiaries, because interest payments on debt are tax-deductible but dividends are not. However, the debt/equity ratio of subsidiaries must be maintained within a reasonable limit. This is necessary both to fulfill operating needs as well as local government requirements in certain countries.

Dealing with currency risks due to regulations limiting convertibility of currency can be managed using different forms of intersubsidiary financing, arranging parent investment through debt (loans) rather than equity and/or using as much local financing as possible.

To mitigate political risk, a local subsidiary can seek financing from the host country, other interested governments, international development agencies, or overseas banks. In this way, the MNE not only shares the financial risks but also develops a network of political contacts that could be helpful in managing relations with the host country's government officials.

As a rule, an MNE is well-advised to avoid being dependent on only one source of international financing. This is both to minimize exposure to uncertain and at times volatile international financial markets as well as to exploit differences in the cost of borrowing across different countries and capital markets.

COUNTRY FOCUS

HONG KONG

World Rank (EFI 2009): 1

Regional Rank (EFI 2009): 1

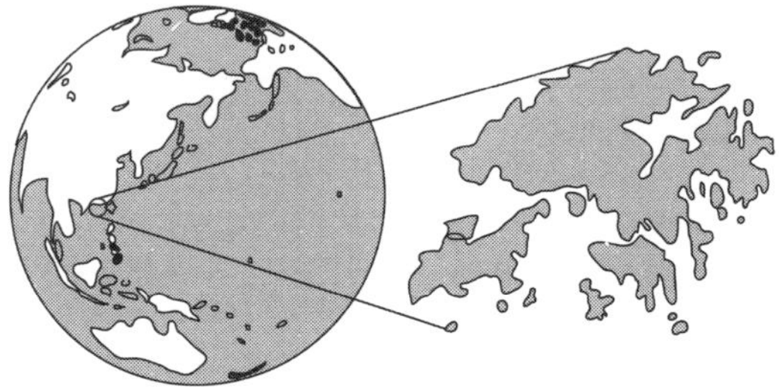

Quick facts

Population: 6.9 million

GDP (PPP): $267.8 billion; 7.0 percent growth in 2006; 5.5 percent 5-year compound annual growth; $39,062 per capita

Unemployment: 4.1 percent

Inflation (CPI): 2.0 percent

FDI inflow: $42.9 billion

2006 data unless otherwise noted

Economic freedom score

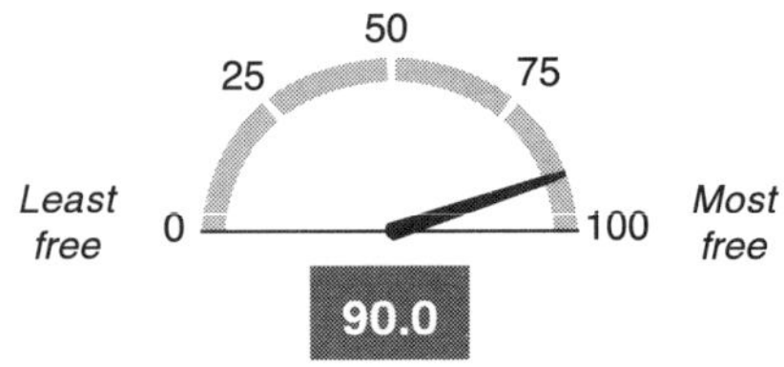

Hong Kong has an impressive record of openness to global trade and investment. Despite a lack of natural resources, the economy's institutional strengths have allowed it to achieve high levels of prosperity reinforced by vibrant entrepreneurial activity. The small island is one of the world's leading financial centers, and regulation of banking and financial services is transparent and efficient. Income and corporate tax rates are very competitive, and overall taxation is relatively small as a percentage of gross domestic product (GDP). Business regulation is straightforward, and the labor market is flexible. Property rights are well protected by an independent and corruption-free judiciary.

In the second half of 2008, the Hong Kong government began public consultation on government proposals for a new competition law. In addition, while the government has resisted any comprehensive minimum wage legislation, renewed debates on imposing a general minimum wage have begun. The outcome of these two political discussions will likely indicate the overall direction of Hong Kong's future economic policies and determine whether its extraordinary commitment to economic freedom will endure.

Background

The Special Administrative Region of Hong Kong is part of the People's Republic of China but governs its own affairs and enjoys a wide range of freedoms under the territory's mini-constitution, the Basic Law. Pledges to advance universal suffrage have stalled. Hong Kong boasts one of the world's most prosperous economies, thanks to its small government, low taxes, and light regulation. Major industries include financial services, shipping, and services, but manufacturing has migrated largely to mainland China.

Business freedom – 92.7

The overall freedom to conduct a business is well protected under Hong Kong's regulatory environment. Starting a business takes less than half the world average of 38 days, and obtaining necessary licenses takes less than the world average of 225 days. Bankruptcy proceedings are very easy and involve only modest costs.

Trade freedom – 95

Hong Kong's weighted average tariff rate was 0 percent in 2006. Restrictive pharmaceuticals regulation, market access restrictions for some services, limited import licensing, and issues involving the enforcement of intellectual property rights add to the cost of trade. Five points were deducted from Hong Kong's trade freedom score to account for nontariff barriers.

Fiscal freedom – 93.4

Hong Kong's tax rates are among the lowest in the world, and both the top corporate tax rate and top income tax rate were reduced by one percentage point as of July 2008. Individuals are taxed either progressively, between 2 percent and 17 percent on income adjusted for deductions and allowances, or at a flat rate of 15 percent on gross income, depending on which liability is lower. The top corporate income tax rate is 16.5 percent. In the most recent year, overall tax revenue as a percentage of GDP was 12.8 percent.

Government size – 93.1

Total government expenditures, including consumption and transfer payments, are fairly low. In the most recent year, government spending equaled 15.2 percent of GDP. The government has made efforts to maintain a balanced budget.

Monetary freedom – 86.2

Inflation is low, averaging 1.9 percent between 2005 and 2007. The government regulates the prices of public transport and electricity and some residential rents. Five points were deducted from Hong Kong's monetary freedom score to adjust for measures that distort domestic prices.

Investment freedom – 90

Foreign capital receives domestic treatment, and foreign investment is strongly encouraged. There are no limits on foreign ownership and no screening or special approval procedures to set up a foreign firm except in broadcasting, where foreign entities may own no more than 49 percent of the local stations, and certain legal services. There are no controls or requirements on current transfers, purchase of real estate, access to foreign exchange, or repatriation of profits. The government of Hong Kong owns all land, granting long-term leases to domestic and foreign interests equally.

Financial freedom – 90

Hong Kong is a global financial center with a regulatory and legal environment focused on enforcing prudent minimum standards and transparency. As of mid-2009, Hong Kong had a total of 202 banking institutions, of which 134 were incorporated outside of Hong Kong. Banks are overseen by the independent Hong Kong Monetary Authority. Credit is allocated on market terms. There are no restrictions on foreign banks, which are treated the same as domestic institutions. The Hong Kong Stock Exchange (HKSE) is one of the 10 most capitalized in the world, but its regulation and transparency

(Continued)

have been criticized in the past. Several mainland Chinese firms made a number of successful initial public offerings in 2007 and now account for more than half of the HKSE's market capitalization.

Property rights – 90

Contracts are strongly protected. Hong Kong's legal system is transparent and based on common law, and its constitution strongly supports private property and freedom of exchange. Despite government public awareness campaigns to protect intellectual property rights, pirated and counterfeit products such as CDs, DVDs, software, and designer apparel are sold openly. The government controls all land and, through public auctions, grants renewable leases that are valid up to 2047.

Freedom from corruption – 83

Corruption is perceived as minimal. Hong Kong ranks 14th out of 179 countries in Transparency International's Corruption Perceptions Index for 2007, and foreign firms do not see corruption as an obstacle to investment. Giving or accepting a bribe is a criminal act.

Labor freedom – 86.3

Hong Kong's flexible labor regulations enhance employment and productivity growth. The labor code is strictly enforced but not burdensome. The nonsalary cost of employing a worker is low, but dismissing a redundant employee can be relatively costly. Regulations on the number of working hours are flexible.

Source: Adapted from Terry Miller and Kim R. Holmes (2009). *2009 Index of Economic Freedom* (Washington, DC: The Heritage Foundation and Dow Jones & Company, Inc., 2009), at www.heritage.org/index.

SUMMARY

The **main goal** of all international financial managers is to maximize the consolidated after-tax profits of the MNE. To do this, they must manage various trade-offs to balance currency risks, minimize taxes, ensure that funds are positioned when and where most needed by the company and that profits can be repatriated or reinvested in the most effective manner. Traditional capital budgeting, structuring, and cash flow management all become more complex when taking into account the differences among markets, currencies, and regulations.

Managing Risk is a major component of international financial management. There are three categories of risk – translation exposure, transaction exposure, and economic exposure. Translation exposure, although not a true risk in the financial sense, can still impact the real business of an MNE by influencing how the market values the MNE or how the foreign management teams get evaluated. Transaction and economic exposure represent genuine financial risk for the MNE's future cash flows and must be considered and mitigated whenever possible. Tools for managing transaction exposure include commercial hedging (e.g., home currency invoicing, mixed currency invoicing or price escalation clauses) and financial hedging (forward contracts, future contracts, options, and swaps). Dealing with economic exposure can be done through intercompany financial programs, such as various international cash-flow management tools, or production-related programs (input sourcing or production arrangement).

International cash-flow management is significantly more challenging than the domestic form. Variations in currency fluctuations, exchange controls, and tax jurisdictions all need to be estimated and considered. Furthermore, in order to minimize administrative, transactional and tax costs, an appropriate set of international cash management policies must be put into place to support all the businesses worldwide. Apart from the intercompany cash flows, the international financial manager is also responsible for intra-company cash flows; that is, operating cash flows and financing cash flows. Methods commonly used by international financial managers include cash pooling, netting and matching, lead and lag, reinvoicing, and internal banking.

International trade financing requires a certain level of trust between local buyers/suppliers and their foreign counterparts. In the absence of trust, there exist several financial mechanisms that provide support for international business transactions between a buyer and seller, with the help of certain financial institutions. Payment agreements between two companies in different countries can range from "cash in advance" (least risk to supplier, most risk to buyer) to open account terms (most risk to supplier, least risk to buyer). Alternatively, the two sides can share the risk of the transaction through the payment mechanism known as a letter of credit (L/C). Here, international banks essentially guarantee payment on the condition that the order was fulfilled as agreed by all parties.

Multinational investing involves first building a capital budget and shortlisting acceptable projects. The evaluation of potential projects must take into account currency fluctuations and the budget targets of the corporate group in order to be considered acceptable to the MNE. Some projects may seem profitable at the local level, but when translated to the corporate currency may prove to be less so. The second part of multinational investing involves sourcing finance for the approved projects. This can be done via a range of sources: intercompany financing (receiving equity, loans or credit from the parent or subsidiary company), equity financing (through issuing new shares or cross listing the company), debt financing (securing international bank loans, or raising funds through the euronote market or the international bond market), and/or local currency financing (local bank loans or other nonbank sources). Financing strategies should seek to involve more than one source and take into account tax implications, political risk, and currency exposure.

DISCUSSION QUESTIONS

1 What are the main tools at the disposal of an MNE's international financial manager that may be used to maximize the consolidated after-tax profits? Consider the implications of currency risks, corporate taxes, funds' availability, and profit repatriation.
2 How can a CFO ensure that profits are repatriated or reinvested in the most effective way? Which changes are required, in traditional capital budgeting, structuring, and cash flow management, in order to account for differences between markets, currencies, and regulations?
3 Discuss the various risk management components: namely, translation exposure, transaction exposure, and economic exposure. What kind of impact does each of the identified risk components have on an MNE's profitability?

EXERCISES

1 Initiate a meeting with the CFO of a corporation that does business internationally. During your meeting, try to identify the corporate approach towards international cash-flow management.
2 Find the homepages of the three largest global retail stores – Wal-Mart, Carrefour, and Tesco – and identify the various international locations of each.
3 Pick one of the global retailers listed in Exercise 2, identify its various store locations and assess the effect of these locations on Wal Marts's bottom-line? Consider currency fluctuations, exchange controls, and tax jurisdictions. What impact could cash pooling, netting and matching, lead and lag, reinvoicing and internal banking have on the bottom line?
4 For the same retail stores, consider the various payment agreements that may be used to settle transaction. Discuss, for example, "cash in advance" (least risk to supplier, most risk to buyer) to open account terms (most risk to supplier, least risk to buyer) and consider the role of letters of credit (L/C).

Bibliography

Ahearne, A., Griever, W., Warnock, F. (2004). Information costs and home bias: an analysis of U.S. holdings of foreign equity. *Journal of International Economics*, 62, 313–36.

Albuquerque, R., Loayza, N., Servén, L. (2005). World market integration through the lens of foreign direct investors. *Journal of International Economics*, 66, 267–95.

Bacchetta, P., Wincoop, E. van (2003). Can information heterogeneity explain the exchange rate determination puzzle? *NBER Working Paper 9498*, February 3.

Blanchard, O., Giavazzi, F. (2002). Current account deficits in the euro area. The end of the Feldstein Horioka puzzle? *Brookings Papers on Economic Activity*, Fall.

Brandt, M., Cochrane, J., Santa Clara, P. (2004). International risk sharing is better than you think (or exchange rates are much too smooth). *NBER Working Paper 8404*.

Calderón, C., Loayza, N., Servén, L. (2003). Do capital flows respond to risk and return? *World Bank Policy Research Working Paper 3059*.

Calvo, G., Mishkin, R. (2003). The mirage of exchange rate regimes for emerging market countries. *Journal of Economic Perspectives*, 17, 99–118.

Calvo, G., Reinhard, C. (2002). Fear of floating. *Quarterly Journal of Economics*, 117 (2), 379–407.

Chari, V. V., Kehoe, P. (2003). Hot money. *Journal of Political Economy*, 111, 1262–92.

Cole H., Kehoe, T. (2000). Self fulfilling debt crises. *Review of Economic Studies*. 67 (1), January, pp. 91–116.

Edison, H., Klein, M., Ricci, L., Sloek, T. (2002). Capital account liberalization and economic performance: survey and synthesis. *NBER Working Paper 9100*, August.

Eiteman, D. K., Stonehill, A. I., Moffett, M. H. (2003). *Multinational Business Finance*. New York: Addison-Wesley.

Engel C. (1999). Accounting for US real exchange rate changes. *Journal of Political Economy*, 107 (3), June, pp. 507–38.

Ernst & Young (2006). *Globalisation Act II: Team Europe Defends Its Goals*. Paris: Ernst & Young.

Eun, C. S., Resnick, B. G. (1999). *International Financial Management*, 3rd edn. New York: McGraw-Hill.

Evans M., Lyons, R. (2001). Order flow and exchange rate dynamics. *NBER Working Paper 7317*.

Forbes, K. (2005). The microeconomic evidence on capital controls: no free Lunch. *NBER Working Paper 11372*.

Hausmann, R., Gavin, M., Pages, C., Stein, E. (1999). Financial turmoil and the choice of exchange rate regime. *Inter-American Development Bank, Research Department Working Paper No. 400*.

International Monetary Fund (2009). *World Economic Outlook*. Washington, DC: World Monetary Fund.

Kaminsky, G., Reinhart C. (1999). The twin crises: the causes of banking and balance of payments problems. *American Economic Review*, 89 (4), 473–500.

Keown, A. J., Martin, J. D., Petty, W., Scott, D. F. Jr (2005). *Financial Management*, 10th edn. Upper Saddle River, NJ: Pearson/Prentice Hall.

Kletzer K., Wright, B. (2000). Sovereign debt as intertemporal barter. *American Economic Review*, 90, June.

Kraay, A., Loayza, N., Servén, L, Venture, J. (2005). Country portfolios. *Journal of the European Economic Association*, 3, 914–45.

Lewis K. (1999). International home bias in international finance and business cycles. *Journal of Economic Literature* 37, June, 571–608.

Obstfeld M., Rogoff, K. (2000). The six major puzzles in international macroeconomics: is there a common cause?. *NBER Macro Annual 2000*.

OECD (2008). *Institutional Investors: Statistical Yearbook*. Paris: OECD.

Oxelheim, L. (1991). Managing foreign exchange exposure. *Journal of Applied Corporate Finance*, 3 (4), 73–82.

Oxelheim, L. (1997). *Managing in the Turbulent World: Economy-Corporate Performance and Risk Exposure*. New York: Wiley.

Pesenti, P., van Wincoop, E. (2002). Can nontradables generate substantial home bias?. *Journal of Money, Credit and Banking*, 34 (1), 25–50.

Prasad, E., Rogoff, K., Wei, S., Kose, M. (2004). Financial globalization, growth and volatility in developing countries. *NBER Working Paper 10942*.

Portes, R., Rey, H. (2005). The determinants of cross-border equity flows. *Journal of International Economics*, 65, 269–96.

Williamson, J. (2000) *Exchange Rate Regimes for Emerging Markets: Reviving the Intermediate Option*. Washington, DC: Institute for International Economics.

Van Wincoop, E. (1999). How big are potential gains from international risk sharing?. *Journal of International Economics*, 47, 109–35.

14

Global Operations and Supply Chain Management

Learning Objectives

Following this chapter, the reader should be able to:

1. Define key terms of operations management, goods and services, and productivity in a global context
2. List the major trends affecting global business and the main motivations for pursuing global operations
3. Describe the strategic relevance of global operations management to MNE
4. Understand the six main interdependent issues of planning and resources management
5. Analyze the six key activities in the global value chain: research and development; production systems; quality and excellence; inventory management; distribution systems; and after-sales service and support

Opening Case
Ford's Global Operations Management

Ford Motor Company, founded by Henry Ford in 1903, is an American multinational enterprise (MNE) and the world's third largest car company. It has been for many years the owner of many global brands associated with national markets, including Lincoln and Mercury of the USA, Jaguar, Aston Martin and Land Rover of Great Britain, Volvo of Sweden, as well as one-third ownership of Mazda of Japan.

Ford has been a leader in operations management since its inception, matching its operations management strategy and practices with the evolution of its North American and global markets. Among other innovations in operations management, Ford introduced methods for large-scale manufacturing of cars and large-scale management of an industrial workforce. In particular, it introduced engineered manufacturing sequences typified by moving assembly lines, and an operations management strategy based on a combination of highly-efficient factories, highly-paid workers, and relatively low car prices.

Initially, Ford models that were sold outside the USA were essentially versions of those sold on the home market, with no adaptations. Subsequently, models specific to Europe were developed, manufactured, sold, and serviced in Europe. Attempts to globalize the model line have largely failed. For example, Europe's Ford Mondeo was selling poorly in the USA, while US models, such as the Ford Taurus, were selling poorly in Japan and Australia, even when produced in right-hand drive mode. The small European model, the Ford Ka, which has sold well in Europe, has not been successful in Japan since it was not available as an automatic car. In Australia, the Ford Mondeo car was dropped, because the segment of the market in which it competes has been in steady decline, with buyers preferring the larger local model, the Ford Falcon. One recent exception is the Ford Focus – the European model has sold strongly on both sides of the Atlantic, and thus it is considered more of a global car, requiring relatively minor adaptations to the local markets.

(Continued)

Global operations management entailed, in the case of Ford, engineering changes, and manufacturing practices that were introduced in order to adapt the products to the various global markets. Ford in Germany and the UK built different models from one another until the late 1960s, with the Ford Escort and then the Ford Capri being common to both companies. Later on, the Ford Taurus and Ford Cortina became one, produced in left-hand drive and right-hand drive versions, respectively. Further economies of production were achieved through rationalization of model ranges. This meant that production of many models in the UK switched to locations in Europe, including Belgium and Spain as well as Germany.

Increasingly, Ford Motor Company has looked to Ford of Europe for its global cars that would be fit for use and appeal to all world markets. Examples of these "global cars" are the Mondeo, Focus, and Fiesta. However, these expectations have not been fully realized. Sales of European-sourced Fords in the USA have been disappointing and in Asia, models from Europe are not as competitively priced as Japanese-built rivals, nor are they perceived as reliable. The Focus has been one exception to this, and has become America's best-selling compact car since its launch in 2000.

In 2001, Ford ended car production in the UK. It was the first time in more than 80 years that Ford cars had not been made in Britain, although production of the Transit van continues at the company's Southampton facility, engines at Bridgend and Dagenham, and transmissions at Halewood. Development of European Ford is broadly split between Dunton in Essex (powertrain, Fiesta/Ka, and commercial vehicles) and Cologne (body, chassis, electrical, Focus, Mondeo) in Germany. Ford owns the Jaguar, Land Rover, and Aston Martin car plants in Britain, which are still operational and Ford's Halewood assembly plant was converted to Jaguar production.

The global network of facilities of Ford allows for the deployment of a global operations management strategy, including achieving economies of scale, as well as proximity to markets. In continental Europe, Ford assembles the Mondeo range in Genk (Belgium), Fiesta in Valencia (Spain) and Cologne (Germany), Ka in Valencia, and Focus in Valencia, Saarlouis (Germany), and Vsevolozhsk (Russia). Transit production is in Kocaeli (Turkey), and Southampton (UK), and Transit Connect is in Kocaeli. Ford also owns a joint-venture production plant in Turkey. Ford-Otosan, established in Turkey in the 1970s, manufactures the Transit Connect compact panel. This new production facility was set up near Kocaeli in 2002, and its opening marked the end of Transit assembly in Genk. Another joint-venture plant near Setubal in Portugal, set up in collaboration with Volkswagen, assembles the Galaxy people carrier as well as its sister ship, the VW Sharan.

In Australia and New Zealand, the popular Ford Falcon is considered the typical family car, though it is considerably larger than the Mondeo sold in Europe. Between 1960 and 1972, the Falcon was based on a US Ford of that name, but since then has been entirely designed and manufactured locally. In Australia, the Commodore and Falcon outsell all other cars and comprise over 20 percent of the new car market. In New Zealand, Ford was second in market share in the first eight months of 2006, with 14.4 percent.

Ford's presence in Asia has traditionally been much smaller. However, with the acquisition of a stake in Japanese manufacturer Mazda in 1979, Ford began selling Mazda's Familia and Capella, also known as the Mazda 323 and Mazda 626, as the Ford Laser and Telstar. Ford also acquired a stake in South Korean manufacturer Kia, which later built the Ford Aspire for export to the USA, but later sold the company to Hyundai. Ford also has a joint venture with Lio Ho in Taiwan, which has assembled Ford models locally since the 1970s. Ford came to India in 1998 with its Ford Escort model, which was later replaced by the locally produced Ford Ikon in 2001. It has since added Fusion, Fiesta, Mondeo, and Endeavour to its product line.

In South America, Ford has had to face protectionist government measures in each country, with the result that it has built different models in different countries, without particular regard to the rationalization or economy of scale inherent in producing and sharing similar vehicles between the nations. In many cases, new vehicles in a country were based on those of the other manufacturers it had entered into production agreements with, or whose factories it had acquired. For example, the Corcel and Del Rey in Brazil were originally based on Renault vehicles. In 1987, Ford merged its operations in Brazil and Argentina with those of Volkswagen to form a company called Autolatina, with which it shared models. Sales figures and profitability were disappointing, and Autolatina was dissolved in 1995. With the advent of MERCOSUR, the regional common market, Ford was finally able to rationalize its product line-ups in those countries. Consequently, the Ford Fiesta and Ford EcoSport are only built in Brazil, and the Ford Focus only built in Argentina, with each plant exporting in large volumes to the neighboring countries. Models like the Ford Mondeo from Europe could now be imported completely built up. Ford of Brazil produces a pick-up truck version of the Fiesta, the Courier, which is also produced in South Africa as the Ford Bantam in right-hand drive versions.

In Africa and the Middle East, Ford's market presence has traditionally been strongest in South Africa and neighboring countries, with only trucks being sold elsewhere on the continent. Ford in South Africa began by importing kits from Canada to be assembled at its Port Elizabeth facility. Following international condemnation of apartheid, Ford divested from South Africa in 1988, and sold its stake in Samcor, although it licensed the use of its brand name to the company. Ford bought a 45 percent stake in Samcor following the ending of apartheid in 1994, and this later became, once again, a wholly-owned subsidiary, the Ford Motor Company of Southern Africa.

Ford's market presence in the Middle East has traditionally been even smaller, partly due to previous Arab boycotts of companies dealing with Israel. Ford and Lincoln vehicles are currently marketed in 10 countries in the region. Saudi Arabia, Kuwait, and the United Arab Emirates (UAE) are the biggest markets. In 2004, Ford sold 30,000 units in the region, falling far short of General Motors' 88,852 units, and Nissan Motors' 75,000 units.

New government regulations and market expectations brought Ford to be the third to the automotive market with a hybrid electric vehicle, the Ford Escape Hybrid, which was also the first hybrid electric vehicle with a flexible fuel capability to run on E85 (85 percent ethanol, 15 percent gasoline). Other Ford hybrid electric vehicles are Mercury Mariner, Ford Fusion, and Lincoln. The company had made plans to manufacture up to 250,000 hybrids a year by 2010, but was confronted with excessively high development and manufacturing costs, lack of sufficient supplies of the hybrid electric batteries and shortage of drivetrain system components. Ford has replaced these plans with a commitment to accelerate the development of next-generation hybrid electric power plants in Britain, in collaboration with Volvo, Jaguar, and Land Rover. This engineering study is expected to yield more than 100 new hybrid electric vehicle models and derivatives.

Sources: Adapted from http://en.wikipedia.org/wiki/Ford, http://www.focusfanatics.com/, http://auto.consumerguide.com/Articles/index.

Introduction

As is evidenced from the opening case, Ford has to constantly match its product designs to market expectations, and employ a worldwide management strategy that determines manufacturing locations and manufacturing practices. Translating the strategic vision and business mission of a multinational enterprise (MNE) to its operational imperatives is a critical task for the global operations manager. This managerial function helps to crystallize the precise contribution of operations management to meeting the strategic business objectives of the enterprise. MNEs must acquire various resources internationally before starting up a manufacturing or a service facility. Deciding on a location for the MNEs' regional headquarters

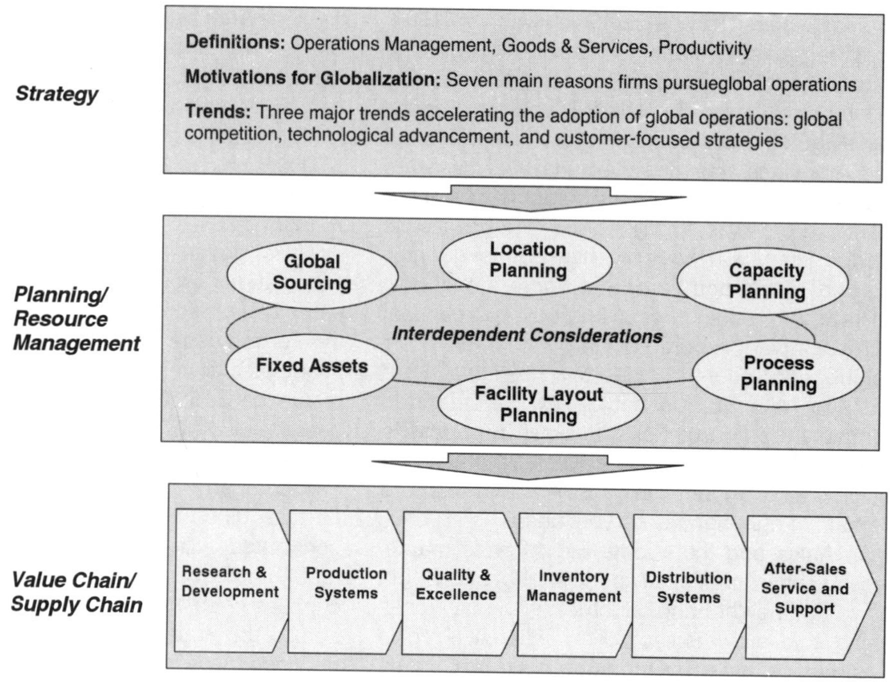

FIGURE 14.1 Chapter overview – global operations management

and facilities, identifying sources of raw material, determining manufacturing plant or service center capacities and assessing the trade-offs in satisfying the expected market demand, are all crucial decisions made by the MNEs' executives. The decisions are complex and are dependent on numerous considerations and constraints.

This chapter is organized in three parts, as can be seen in Figure 14.1.

The first part provides a definition of global operations management for goods and services and outlines the most common motivations for pursuing global initiatives from an operational perspective. It also reviews the major trends affecting global businesses today and concludes with the strategic importance of operations to an MNE's success.

The second part reviews the six main interdependent areas for planning and resource management of global operations: location planning; capacity planning; process planning; facility layout planning; fixed assets; and global sourcing. Each of these concepts is defined and a brief summary of the key decisions and variables is covered.

The third part addresses the key value chain activities impacted by global operation decisions: research and development (R&D); production systems; quality and excellence; inventory management; distribution systems; and after-sales service and support. Each area includes a brief introduction explaining the most recent trends that impact the area in question, and how these trends are addressed with some specific methods, tools, and concepts.

Strategic Overview

Definition of operations management

Operations management deals with the set of activities required to create goods and services through the transformation of inputs to outputs.

In manufacturing firms these activities can be identified readily in the creation of tangible products such as a Dell laptop computer or a Nike tennis shoe. In organizations that do not create physical products, the production function may be less obvious, as is the case with the transfer of funds at Citibank, the delivery of babies at the Mount Sinai Hospital ward or the development of a promotional campaign by the BBDO advertising agency.

The term "operations manager" is seldom used to label the operations management function. Instead, this function is often labeled by making reference to the operations process itself. For example, the operations manager at a company like Dell, which assembles computers on a customized basis, may be referred to as a production manager, whereas the operations manager at a company like Pixar, which produces full-length animated movies, would be referred to as a creative director.

Whether the end product is a good or service, the set of managed activities responsible for the transformation of inputs to outputs in an organization is referred to as "operations management." When performed by a global organization across various countries, this set of managed activities is referred to as *global operations management*.

Distinction between goods and services

In general, it is commonly accepted that *goods* constitute tangible products whereas *services* consist of mainly intangible products. However, in reality, many end products that are consumed in the economy include an element of both, as seen in Figure 14.2. For example, tangible products such as computers often include service components such as financing, transportation or after-sales service, and support.

Although there is no one definition of services, a common description of the services sector is that it comprises those economic activities that typically produce intangible products such as education, entertainment, government, lodging, financial, and health services. This part of the economy has been growing most rapidly over the past decades.

The main characteristics that distinguish services from goods are the following:

- Services are usually *intangible*, for example, when you purchase counseling from a psychiatrist.
- Services are often *produced and consumed simultaneously* and there is no stored inventory, for example, a hairdresser in a beauty salon cannot store a "haircut".
- Services are often *unique*, for example, the mix of financial instruments that are used to finance a home may differ from one individual to another.

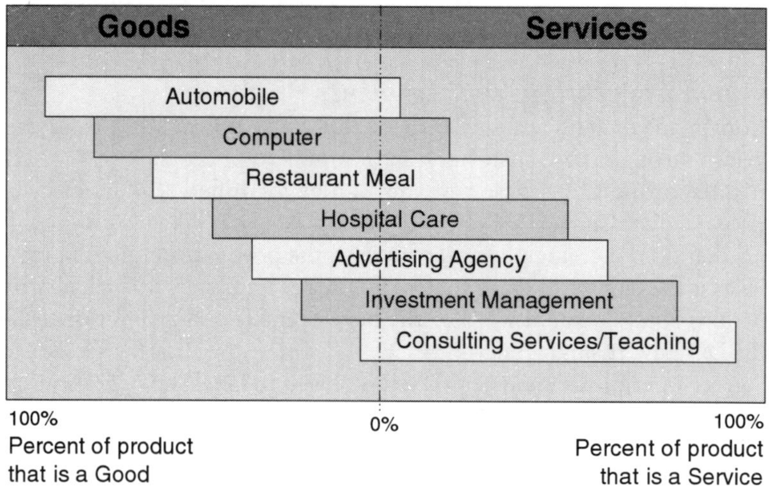

FIGURE 14.2 Goods and services continuum

- Services have *high customer interaction*, the interaction with the client often limits or precludes efforts of standardization which make it necessary to design the product and deliver the services accordingly.
- Services have inconsistent *product definition*; there may be rigorous definitions (e.g., life insurance) but the adaptation necessary to the specific case of the individual makes each application unique.
- Services are often *knowledge-based*, as in the case of education or legal assistance.
- Services are frequently *dispersed*; need for frequent and close interaction with the customer drives the need for the provider to be located locally, even in a global setting.

Many of the MNEs that are manufacturers also provide services such as after-sale service and support. At the same time, there are many global service organizations that may or may not produce physical products. Examples of the latter are eBay, which provides a global marketplace, or amazon.com, a merchandising global dealer that provides a service as well as delivers actual shipments. Other pure service organizations that operate globally are the major accounting and consulting firms such as McKinsey & Company, Deloitte, or IBM Global Services (IGS). Several global service MNEs typically employ thousands of individuals and make use of technology systems in order to provide customized local services while still exploiting economies of scale. For example, IGS, the world's largest information technology services and consulting provider, employs 190,000 professionals in more than 160 countries and provides services to clients in the area of strategy, systems, and technology. All of these service organizations deal with operational issues of designing and operating systems that support their operations globally.

TABLE 14.1 Differences between Goods and Services

Attributes of goods (tangible product)	*Attributes of services (intangible product)*
• Product can be resold	• Reselling a service is unusual
• Product can be inventoried	• Many services cannot be inventoried
• Some aspects of quality are measurable	• Many aspects of quality are difficult to measure
• Selling is distinct from production	• Selling is often a part of the service
• Product is transportable	• Provider, not product, is often transportable
• Site of facility is important for cost	• Service is often difficult to automate
• Often easy to automate	• Revenue is generated primarily from the intangible services
• Revenue is generated primarily from the tangible product	

Thus, for all MNEs and other international organizations, operational considerations are relevant whether they produce goods (tangible products) or services (intangible products). However, there are a number of differences that are particularly relevant to an operations manager in each one of the various organizations. Table 14.1 summarizes some of these differences.

Striving for productivity

The ongoing challenge for MNE's operations managers, whether they are dealing with goods or services is to achieve the highest ratio of outputs (goods and services) to one or more inputs (labor, capital, and management). This ratio is a measure of *productivity*. Productivity measures are used for individuals, teams, companies, and even a country's ability to improve its own standard of living. Only through increased productivity can the standard of living in a country be expected to improve. Figure 14.3 illustrates the benefits that may be realized when productivity improves.

Improvements in productivity can be achieved either through a reduction in inputs, while outputs remains constant, or an increase in outputs while inputs remain constant. When productivity increases, costs decrease and wages may increase. In an economic sense, inputs are typically land, labor, capital, and management which, when combined, represent the operation system. It is management that

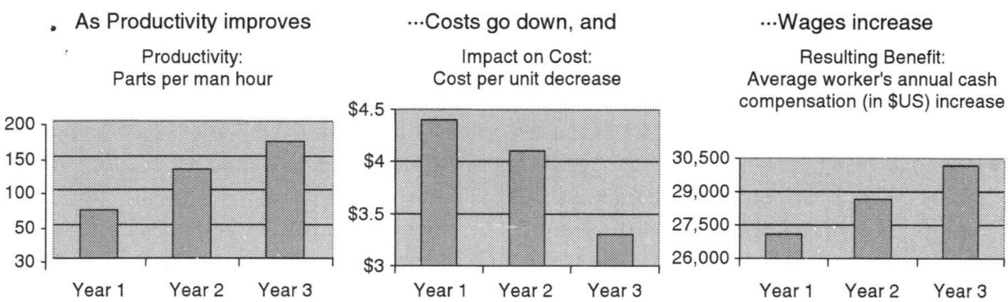

FIGURE 14.3 An illustration of the benefits from productivity improvements

TABLE 14.2 Global Distribution of Production Activities and Costs for the Pontiac Le Mans

Country	*Task, Part, and Assemblies*	*Costs ($)*
South Korea	Auto assembly	6,000
Japan	Engines, axles, and electronics	3,500
Germany	Design	1,500
Taiwan, Singapore, Japan	Smaller parts	800
England	Marketing	500
Ireland	Information technology	100
United States	General Motors, banking, insurance, legal services	7,600
	Total	20,000

creates this system for transforming inputs to outputs and, thus, determines the productivity of that system.

This chapter examines how to improve the productivity of an MNE through the global operations management function.

Rationale for global operations

More and more MNEs are pursuing global operations to take advantage of national differences in the cost and quality of labor, talent, energy, facilities, and capital. All these resources are combined to increase the MNE's productivity. Thus, it is becoming less and less meaningful to talk of "American" products, "Italian" products or "Japanese" products. For example, in Table 14.2, one can see that General Motors' Pontiac Le Mans, which is perceived to be an "American" car, has over half its production activities occurring outside of the USA. Most of the parts, assemblies, and production services come from South Korea, Japan, Germany, Taiwan, Singapore, England, and Ireland.

"Going global" in production and operations is not only practiced by traditional manufacturing industries such as automotive, telecommunications and the like but also by service industries. As the following insert indicates, even the animation production industry is incorporating global suppliers into its production process.

Global Production Sourcing in the America Industry

The rapid advancement of technology has made computer animation available to the masses and the animation industry is one of the fastest-growing sectors. The demand for animated entertainment has expanded with the increase in broadcasting hours by cable and satellite TV along with the growing popularity of the Internet. In the past, animation series were aimed at children aged nine and below. In recent years, however, TV stations have been producing animation series for teenagers, adults, and the whole family. Animation series like

The Simpsons and King of the Hill have been successfully aired on primetime TV. The major markets include the USA, Canada, Japan, France, Britain, and Germany. Licensing operations for T-shirts, caps, and other items have also been a major source of revenue for animation companies. In Japan, several successful computer games have crossed over and have become animated series like Pokemon, Monster Farm, Power Stone, and Detective Conan. More broadly speaking, animation is increasingly used in video games, and movies are also increasingly reliant on animation and computer graphic special effects.

A major trend witnessed in the animation industry has to do with the production function. The industry is outsourcing its animation content to Asia. This market is increasingly being tapped by North American film and television program producers. The major factor behind this shift of computer animation production to the Asia-Pacific region continues to be the availability of low-cost, powerful computer animation platforms, and much lower labor rates in the Asian and Pacific Rim countries compared to North America and Europe. The bulk of the outsourcing happens for 2D animation content with some amount of 3D content. Roughly 90 percent of American television cartoons are produced in Asia, with the Philippines leading the way. With their natural advantage of English and a strong familiarity with US culture, animation companies in Manila employ thousands of employees. Major studios such as Disney and Warner Brothers send cartoon action outlines, storyboards, and voice tracks to these offshore sites for production purposes. Thus, the studios can save up to 80 percent of production costs through global sourcing of production capabilities.

Source: Adapted from http://www.mindbranch.com, October 2006.

The seven most common reasons that a domestic business, be it a manufacturer or service provider, decide to enter into some form of international operation are as follows:

1. *Reduce costs*: Lower wage scales in foreign countries can help to lower direct and indirect labor costs. Less stringent government regulations on a wide variety of operation practices (e.g., environmental control, health and safety, etc.) can directly reduce the cost of operations in a foreign country. Opportunities to cut the cost of taxes and tariffs are also a reason to establish operations in foreign countries. In Mexico, the creation of *maquiladoras* (free trade zones) allows manufacturers to cut their costs of taxation by paying only on the value added by Mexican workers.

   If a US manufacturer, such as Hewlett-Packard (HP), brings an $800 laptop computer to a maquiladora operation for assembly work costing $50, tariff duties will be charged only on the $50 dollars of work performed in Mexico. Trade agreements have also helped reduce tariffs and thereby reduced the cost of operating facilities in foreign countries. The *General Agreement on Tariffs and Trade (GATT)* has helped reduce tariffs from 40 percent to 7 percent over a period of 50 years. Other international trade agreements including the *North American Free Trade Agreement (NAFTA)*, the *Mercosur*, the *ASEAN*

Free Trade Agreement (AFTA), the *EU Common Market* are described at length in Chapter 7.

2 *Reduce risks*: Going global has become easier and less risky for international operations because of international trade agreements. NAFTA, in addition to reducing tariffs, also seeks to promote conditions of fair competition and increased investment opportunities as well as provide for protection on certain intellectual property rights. For example, if an MNE wants to move a US production facility to Mexico, it could apply under NAFTA for protection of investment capital. This protection would obligate the US government to underwrite the risk of financial loss for the MNE's facility and help reduce the cost of capital by obtaining a lower interest rate on the loan to build it. Currently, the maquiladoras provide foreign operations a means of dispensing with much of the complicated legalities of operating a production facility in Mexico.

3 *Improve the supply chain*: The supply chain can often be improved by locating facilities in countries where unique resources are available. These resources may be expertise, labor, or raw materials. For example, computer chip manufacturers are locating many R&D facilities in Israel to take advantage of the technical workforce and expertise in advanced chip design technologies. Similarly, world athletic shoe production has migrated from South Korea to Guangzhou, China. These Chinese locations leverage the low-cost labor and production competence in a city where 40,000 people work making athletic shoes for the world.

4 *Provide better goods and services*: While the characteristics of goods and services can be objective and measurable, such as number of on-time deliveries, they can also be subjective and less measurable, such as sensitivity to culture. As an MNE enters new regional markets it needs an ever better understanding of the differences in culture and of the way business is handled in different countries. Improved understanding as the result of a local presence permits MNEs to customize products and services to meet unique cultural needs in foreign markets. Also, proximity to foreign customers improves responsiveness to customers' changing product and service requirements. Customers who purchase goods and services from US firms are increasingly located in foreign countries. Thus, locating a facility in a foreign country provides these customers with quick and adequate service.

5 *Attract new markets*: Because international operations require local interaction with foreign customers, suppliers, and other competitive businesses, international firms inevitably learn about unique opportunities for new products and services. Knowledge of these markets may not only help to increase sales but also permit organizations to diversify their customer bases and smoothen the business cycle. Global operations also add production flexibility, so that products and services can be switched between economies that are booming and those that are not. Another reason to establish a production facility in a foreign market is the opportunity to expand the *product life cycle* (a product life cycle, as explained in Chapter 6, comprises the stages a product goes

through from inception to obsolescence) of an existing product. While some products in the home territory of an MNE may be in a "mature" stage of their product life cycle, they may represent a state-of-the-art product in less-developed countries, thus providing a further market opportunity and extending the life of that product.

6 *Improve operations*: Jack Welch, the legendary CEO of General Electric once said: "Global companies must seek out the best ideas from *anywhere!*" Learning does not take place in a vacuum. Because the world is full of ideas, MNEs serve themselves and their customers well when they remain open to the free flow of ideas. For example, General Motors found that it could improve operations by jointly building and running, with the Japanese, an auto assembly plant in San Jose, California. This strategy allows General Motors to contribute its capital and knowledge of US labor and environmental laws while the Japanese contribute production and inventory ideas.

7 *Attract and retain global talent*: Global organizations can attract and retain better employees by offering more employment opportunities. They need people in all functional areas and in areas of expertise worldwide. For example, Sweden's leading pharmaceutical companies are building research and production facilities near American universities and pharmaceutical institutes so that they can better recruit and retain skilled researchers and technicians important to the development of new drugs. A new competing mobile operator in Italy located its network group in Rome in order to be able to "seduce" other technical staff from its entrenched competitors (all who have their network groups stationed in Rome).

These are some of the most common motivations for MNEs to seek competitive advantage through globalization of operations. The initiative for global operations typically comes from one of two sources: either the domestic or local company chooses to compete in markets abroad due to some realization of a competitive advantage vis-à-vis their global peers or global competition is forced upon a company with the market entry of foreign competitors to the domestic company's local customer base.

The following section provides a review of a number of trends that are accelerating competitiveness in the area of global operations and in many cases forcing even the most local of companies to consider certain aspects or impacts of global operations in order to remain competitive.

Impact of global trends

Historically, operations and logistics costs accounted for up to 25 percent of the total cost of goods sold. Clearly, any reductions in these costs can bring significant profits directly to the bottom line. In Europe, a study by A. T. Kearney showed a 50 percent reduction in logistics and freight cost averages (from 14 percent to 7 percent) over a period of 9 years. In addition, in recent years companies have begun to recognize operations as a significant competitive weapon for revenue generation and customer loyalty.

The renewed view of operations and logistics has been driven by three distinct global trends: increased global competition; the fast pace of technological development; and a new emphasis on customer-focused enterprises.

Increased global competition

As explained in Chapter 7, with the advent of the World Trade Organization (WTO), and regional free trade agreements (e.g., NAFTA, EFTA/EU Common Market, Asia, South America), local companies are suddenly finding themselves competing for customers in their home markets against foreign competitors in addition to their traditional adversaries. For example, GM is now competing not only with Ford and Chrysler but also with Japanese and European imports. In addition to the sheer number of new players, the rules that foreign competitors bring to the game can be very different. Foreign firms operate under different conditions than local firms and may face fewer limitations or have greater access to critical resources, giving them a distinct competitive edge over the domestic firm.

Fast pace of technological development

Another major factor shaping global operations is the increased pace of technological development. These changes impact the manufacturing environment through changes in both product as well as process design. An increasing rate of technological development leads to more frequent product introductions and in some cases the creation of whole new industry sectors. As described in Chapter 11, developments in computing and communications have significantly driven both new product development and manufacturing and distribution through increased automation, more powerful information systems, and the capabilities for online monitoring and control of global operations.

Customer focus – quality, speed, and flexibility

Traditionally, production, operations, and logistics were treated as cost centers that absorbed much of a firm's resources, a necessary evil. The focus was to meet schedules and produce and deliver the product or service at the lowest possible cost. When competition was primarily based on price, this was a consistent approach to viewing the operational functions. However, in today's global environment, increasing competition and the complexity of global operations are highlighting a number of ways that the operational functions can be used to provide a competitive advantage to the firm beyond simply minimizing cost. These advantages can be summarized as: quality, speed, and flexibility.

As Japan demonstrated so convincingly in the 1980s, quality has become a competitive weapon for both gaining market share and developing loyal customers to a particular product and brand. With product life cycles dropping and the global competition for innovation, time to market from concept to commercial realization has become one of the key differences between profitable initiatives and failures. Finally, as customers demand more and more personalized goods and services, the push towards mass customization and shorter life cycles requires manufacturing groups to adopt far more flexible practices. These practices strive to balance between efficient throughput and customizable products and services.

Strategic importance

The importance of operations and logistics for supporting world-class MNEs has been gaining more prominence as enterprises increasingly address both global supply opportunities as well as compete in a world market for their products and services. The global trends of increased globalization, rate of technological change, and customer-focused operational priorities are accelerating the need for both the understanding and tools necessary to manage global operations – for even the most traditionally domestic of companies.

In recent years the operations function in general has assumed increasing strategic importance as a competitive weapon. Nowhere has this been more acutely demonstrated than in the advent of e-commerce and the failure of most of the online businesses to survive due to a failure to meet customer expectations for quality, delivery and after-sales support. In spite of claims that the Internet is a medium for commerce and exchange that truly has no boundaries, many MNEs have learned the hard way that without dealing with the operational realities of providing both tangible and intangible products one can never succeed as a global organization.

Using a superior operational strategy and procedures, Amazon.com has become a global leader in its field. The following paragraphs explain the essential elements of the global operational strategy of the company. Amazon.com, Inc. (NASDAQ: AMZN), a Fortune 500 company based in Seattle, opened on the world wide web in July 1995 and today offers the world's largest selection of merchandise as a one-stop Internet shopping operation. Amazon.com seeks to be the world's most customer-centric company, where customers can find and discover anything they might want to buy online, and endeavors to offer its customers the lowest possible prices. Amazon.com and other sellers offer millions of unique new, refurbished, and used items in categories such as beauty, health and personal care, jewelry and watches, gourmet food, sports and outdoors, apparel and accessories, books, music, DVDs, electronics and office, toys and baby, and home and garden.

Amazon.com and its affiliates operate seven retail websites: www.amazon.com, www.amazon.co.uk, www.amazon.de, www.amazon.fr, www.amazon.co.jp, www.amazon.ca, and www.joyo.com.

Today, global operations is clearly recognized as a major competitive weapon to be leveraged not just with the objective of cost competition but also in the generation of a strong global brand and the generation of revenues through ever-greater responsiveness, quality, and personalized service.

In fact, a sound global operations strategy is critical to the successful execution of any of the classic competitive advantages of differentiation, cost leadership or quick response, as discussed in Chapter 9.

Planning and Resources Management

The following section reviews the main interdependent areas that an operations manager must plan carefully in order to successfully translate the MNE's vision and mission into an executable competitive advantage through global operations.

Appropriate planning and resources management worldwide is necessary to support the global value chain for the MNE and is a major factor in determining the costs, profit margins, and other operational metrics, such as worldwide and local productivity and quality levels.

Facility location planning

One of the most difficult planning decisions facing the global productions managers is the selection of facility locations for plants, subsidiaries, distribution outlets, and regional headquarters that support the global market. Generally, there are two broad approaches to selling products abroad: locating all operations in the home country and exporting to all markets, or locating certain operations in the host country.

The advantage of locating facilities and plants in the home country is that it is simpler to manage because the manufacturing firm does not have to face the challenges of overseas operations. In the initial stages of growth, when the size of the total market and the market share of the company are relatively small, such a strategy works well. However, as the company grows, it will need to develop an international operational and manufacturing base to compete with regional competitors, to comply with protectionist pressures or to better serve its global customers.

When considering locating a plant in a host country, the most common reasons for preferring one region over another are:

- access to low-cost production input factors
- proximity to the target market
- access to technological resources
- cost and availability of management
- access to better or cheaper raw materials, component parts, etc.
- more favorable energy policies, political environment, regulations, and bureaucracy
- strong economic development of a country
- fit with the local culture, local work, and business ethics

In addition, an MNE is often faced with the trade-off between centralizing all production globally in order to achieve economies of scale or decentralizing some facilities by market in order to pursue a differentiation strategy for delivering customized products through close interaction between the marketing, development, and manufacturing departments within a particular market.

MNE's often have many potential locations around the world from which to choose a site for a facility. One of the most common reasons to create an offshore facility is the need to reduce the cost structure of a selected product or service. However, this should be balanced against the potential lower-quality workmanship and lower productivity which may exist in some developing countries. In addition, the impact of offshore operations on the cost structure of an MNE is not straightforward. There is recent evidence that MNE's pay a wage premium that averages about 14 percent for high-paying occupations in emerging economies. Wages and salaries generally are closely correlated with the level of gross domestic product (GDP). However, the correlation is much weaker for managers' salaries. This means that labor markets are global but only for certain high-paying professions and for certain internationally-oriented countries. There is also a gap in minimum wages across countries that should be considered: for example, the minimum wage in Greece is about one-fourth of other, well-developed countries.

The location of service MNEs may also be dependent upon the type and quality level of service required, but, for manufacturing MNEs, supply issues are more important: the greater the distance between manufacturing facilities and target markets, the longer it takes for customers to receive shipments. Long supply periods – namely, long lead times – may mean delays that are compensated for by maintaining larger inventories in target markets with the resulting storage, handling and insurance costs. Transportation costs, which, on some merchandise types, may account for 10 percent of the value of the merchandise, are also positively related to the distance from main markets. The insert provides several examples of economic justifications for location decisions.

Examples of Economic Justifications for Location Decisions

Most location decision business cases are based on demonstrating the economic benefits of performing a particular business activity, or set of activities, in a different location. Of course, these benefits must outweigh the costs of having to manage a project or process multinationally.

To enjoy the economic benefits of different locations, an MNE can either undertake the specific activities in the location itself or outsource the specific activities to a local company while ensuring close monitoring, control, and interfaces with its own sites. Almost any activity undertaken by the business could be a candidate for this, including R&D, assembly and production, financial or advertising services or marketing and sales.

Below are three examples:

1 A company that designs precision ice hockey equipment chose to do the design in Sweden, the financing of the operation in Canada, assembling of the products in the USA (i.e., Cleveland, Ohio) and Denmark, while marketing it across North America and Europe. In addition, this equipment used alloys whose molecular structure was researched and patented in the USA (i.e., Delaware) and produced in Japan.

2 Boeing (www.boeing.com), an airplane manufacturer, designed one of its aircrafts in the USA (i.e., Seattle, Washington) and Japan, sourced the tail cones from Canada, tail sections from China and Italy and engines from Britain. The entire plane was finally assembled back in the USA (i.e. Seattle).

3 A company outsourced the development of their advertising campaign to a professional services firm that conceived the campaign in Britain, shot the footage in Canada, dubbed it back in Britain and sent it for final editing in New York.

(Continued)

In general, a major part of each of the decisions outlined in the examples above was the recognition that each activity done in a particular location was being done more productively. In general, the productivity of a particular location for any given activity is primarily a function of two factors – labor and capital. Of course, this extra productivity can often come with significant overheads (e.g., long-distance management can create communication and coordination challenges, local tax or labor law differences can make start-up or shut-down decisions unattractive, language differences can lead to translation needs, cultural differences can affect management practices, etc.) – that can overshadow the productivity gains. The challenge for the multinational manager is to investigate and consider all this before making a final decision.

One of the major worldwide industries is the automotive industry, which discovered early on the importance of global operations. In an effort to limit the impact of currency fluctuations on its business in the USA, Nissan located its manufacturing facilities closer to the market. Nissan set up a new location in Mississippi within the first few years of the new millennium that attracted clusters of suppliers, which in turn, attracted more car manufacturers to the same location. Specifically, Nissan received interest from over 2,200 suppliers, of which they accepted 1,300, to support the opening of their Canton, Mississippi assembly plant. Together, these suppliers invested over $100 million in building plants to support Nissan. On a longer-term basis, the supplier cluster enhanced the overall attractiveness of the area for other car manufacturers, which is also a goal of the local governments. Creating these clusters anew provided an opportunity to get the concession of the UAW (United Auto Workers) to adopt advanced manufacturing technologies as well as institute a modular and just-in-time assembly operations.

Perceptions and preferences

The location of the corporate headquarters is another location issue which executives of MNEs may be required to consider. Corporate headquarters tend to be found in cities that have excellent airline connections, an abundance of professional support services (such as legal, financial, and advertising), a diverse professional employee base, high-end hotels, restaurants, entertainment, cultural events, a good choice of office space or availability of land to build-to-suit, attractive housing for executives, affordable housing for managers, and support staff within reasonable commute, a strong educational system for employees' children, continuing adult education, and a high quality of life. Studies conducted on the issue of corporate headquarters indicate that the free flow of information is the most important factor, followed by, in order of importance, a low and simple tax system, a corruption-free government, and absence of exchange controls. A complete taxonomy of the factors that appear in the literature regarding MNEs' headquarters and regional headquarters are contained in Table 14.3.

TABLE 14.3 Headquarters and Regional Headquarters Locational Factors

	Location factor		*Location factor*
1	Political stability	27	Efficient capital and foreign exchange markets
2	High level of country security	28	Freedom to control domestic firms
3	Efficient government	29	Reliable protection mechanisms for foreign investors
4	Reliable justice system	30	Free movement of information
5	Transparent regulatory environment	31	Reliable protection of intellectual property rights
6	Low level of bureaucracy	32	Availability of highly-skilled staff
7	Ethical business environment (low level of corruption)	33	Competitively priced local staff
8	High-quality public infrastructure (utilities, roads, etc.)	34	Availability of English-speaking staff
9	Low operating costs	35	Availability of home-country language speaking staff (if not English)
10	Low office rent	36	Flexible employment contracts
11	Frequent and reliable international air flights	37	Low level of industrial/labor disputes
12	Low travel and transportation costs	38	Large local market
13	High-quality IT and telecommunication infrastructure	39	High market growth potential
14	Low telecommunication costs	40	Proximity to key clients
15	Stable economy	41	Proximity to key suppliers
16	Easy access to local financial and commercial services	42	Proximity to local supporting and related industries
17	Easy access to regional financial and commercial services	43	Availability of leading-edge suppliers
18	Free movement of capital and profits	44	Accessible central geographic location within region
19	Efficient banking systems	45	Convenient time zone location
20	Easy access to local capital markets	46	Proximity to marketing subsidiaries
21	Easy access to local venture capital	47	Proximity to R&D subsidiaries
22	Low cost of capital	48	Proximity to manufacturing subsidiaries
23	Attractive government investment and start-up incentives	49	Proximity to world-class universities and research institutions
24	Attractive government operating incentives	50	Favorable image of potential location for business activity
25	Attractive corporate tax rate and regulations (and incentives)	51	Proximity to surrounding markets
26	Attractive dividend withholding taxes	52	Adherence to international accounting and reporting standards
		53	High level of global economic integration

Source: Adapted from Finger, S. (2007). Unpublished PhD Dissertation.

While the actual data about country characteristics may be a key to the location decision by the executive of an MNE, the perception of a country and its global competitive characteristics has been found to significantly influence its attractiveness for foreign direct investment (FDI). In order to improve its competitive positioning, a country needs to alter those characteristics perceived as harmful to its positioning. It has been shown that there are four underlying factors against which a country's relative competitive positioning can be measured: physical environment of the country; government involvement and red tape; taxation and reporting; and ease of initiating operations in a new country. These underlying factors vary depending on the type of industry the MNE is operating in: for example, in the high-tech industry the underlying factors that mattered the most were the macroeconomic/physical environment, ease of financial operation in a country, government involvement, and ease of daily life.

Capacity planning

For any given network of facilities worldwide, the MNE must assess the company's capacity to serve each of its markets at any point in time. The analysis of the MNE's ability to produce enough output to fulfill the demand in a given market is called *capacity planning*. Companies must forecast as accurately as possible the global demand for its products and their regional distribution. If the capacity of its network of facilities exceeds the global demand from the market, production must be scaled back. If the gap is small, this could take the form of reducing work shifts in certain locations or repurposing certain resources to work on different products in the portfolio that may be in higher demand. If the gap is large, this could involve eliminating jobs, or in the worst cases shutting down certain facilities. Note, that different countries have different laws regulating the ability of employers to eliminate jobs. An MNE must take into account these differences in planning such decisions, both with regards to where to shut down and even more importantly how to do it correctly according to the local regulations and laws. If this is not managed correctly by the MNE, it can lead to ill will by the host country, bad publicity about the MNE, and additional unplanned costs, as illustrated in the insert for Hewlett-Packard in France.

HP Job Cuts: France wants its Subsidies back – Grenoble demands €1.2m

By John Oates
Published Tuesday September 27th, 2005, 11:32 Gmt

HP's job-cutting scheme has hit a snag – French politicians are claiming the firm owes mo than a million euros in subsidies. The company is looking to cut 6,000 jobs in Europe – ju under a thousand in the UK and 1,240 in France.

The mayor of Grenoble, where HP labs are based, flew to California to try and convince HP bigwigs to think again. If they do not he is calling for the return of €1.2m he claims was given to HP to help it set up in Grenoble in the first place.

But Patrick Starck, president of HP France, told *Le Figaro* newspaper that HP had never received any money from the French government, adding that the firm had paid €700m in taxes during the period.

French Prime Minister Dominque de Villepin said: "When there is public aid, it is normal that there is a minimum of return, of recognition." But Villepin said the intention was not to put up barriers to international investment and he hoped for constructive talks with HP, an indication that he is under pressure to cut French unemployment which is currently over 10 percent.

After a meeting with HP execs on Monday, French employment minister Gerard Larcher said the figure of 1,240 job cuts was not set in stone and could come down.

Source: adapted from http://www.theregister.co.uk/2005/09/27/hp_france_subsidies/.

By contract, should the market demand exceed the capacity of the MNE's facilities, management must determine which facilities to expand production or whether to add additional facilities, and if so, where (see Facility location planning section above). In cases where demand is high and the time lag for expanding production (e.g., setting up a new facility) is too long, an MNE may choose to subcontract another manufacturer to help meet the excess demand until the new facilities are operational.

Capacity planning is also critical for service companies. Telecommunication companies must plan their networks to be cost-efficient but also capable of handling peak call times. Hotels must forecast the number of guests for planning the rooms, the conference facilities, and even the number of staff needed to support the daily operations at different times of the year.

Process planning

In order to create and deliver a particular product or service, the MNE must develop a process that is consistent with its overall business strategy.

In general, MNEs pursuing a low-cost strategy will tend to favor processes that are very standardized in order to leverage economies of scale. In manufacturing, a company that mass produces bicycles will typically employ a highly automated production process, acquire the raw materials in bulk and spread the high cost of setting up the system over a large number of units produced. These operations tend to be large and centralized, supplying many parts, or all, of the MNE.

For an MNE pursuing a differentiation strategy, customization may take precedence over standardization. If we consider the example of a high-end racing bicycle producer, there would be many more unique features, materials, and specifications to tailor to the end-user's custom requests, which would require a much more flexible production process, ordering unique materials as needed, and justifying the significantly higher costs to the customer on the basis of the customizable features. These operations tend to be small and focused typically on serving a specific market or product/service niche.

Facilities layout planning

When manufacturing physical products, the spatial arrangement of production processes within a particular facility, or facility layout planning, is important and often greatly influenced by the region or country it is located in. For example, in countries such as Japan and Singapore space is a very scarce resource and facilities tend to be designed as compactly as possible, with minimal inventory space and maximum proximity of shared resources.

On the other hand, in countries such as Canada, China or the USA, the abundance of space both lowers the cost of building facilities in more than one location and allows more flexibility on the detailed designs.

Fixed assets

Many companies must acquire fixed assets such as production facilities, inventory warehouses, computer storage capacity, retail outlets or offices in a host country. An MNE may choose between acquiring and modifying existing facilities or building entirely new facilities.

Both options must take into account both the functional needs of the operations manager, any legal restrictions on the use of the premises (e.g., no polluting the local water supplies), public relations work with the local community and understanding how, if at all, the local cultures and values might influence or impact the site.

Global sourcing

The most common reason cited for pursuing *global sourcing* is cost. For example, when General Motors was faced with the fact that building cars in Detroit and shipping them to Europe made the cars' cost structure uncompetitive as compared to EU competitors, it began to source overseas suppliers and contract assembly plants to build much of what it sells in Europe.

However, there are many other reasons for MNEs to use *global sourcing.*

One reason is to strengthen the reliability of the supply network. If the company does not have two or three international sources of supply, it can face serious problems if the sole supplier fails to provide the needed materials or parts.

A second reason for global sourcing is that the MNE may be unable to get the needed materials from domestic sources. For example, most US products that use small motors are fitted with supplies from Asia because few other regions can produce small motors cost-effectively.

A third reason is quality. There are certain areas of the world where suppliers offer the highest-quality output. For example, Japan is well known for its robotics and Germany for its packaging machines. When MNEs need high-quality inputs, they are likely to source them internationally by purchasing from the highest-quality producer.

A fourth reason is to penetrate growth markets. A foothold in a promising new market can often be obtained by sourcing in that market. For example, Toyota sources from the Pacific Rim not just to achieve lower costs but also to enter markets with restrictive quotas by increasing the local component content of its cars. The various components of the Dell Inspiron Notebook are sourced around the world to create a competitively priced and high-quality product. Thus, the motherboard is sourced from a Korean-owned factory in China (Samsung), the memory may be sourced from a plant in Taiwan (Nanya), the Intel processor may come from Intel's plant in Malaysia, the keyboard comes from a Japanese plant in China (Alps), the LCD display comes from a plant in South Korea (LG), the battery comes from an American-owned plant in Malaysia (Motorola), the hard disk drive comes from an American plant in Singapore (Seagat), and the modem comes from a plant in China owned by a Taiwanese corporation (Liteon).

It should be noted that not all global sourcing is provided by outside suppliers. Some MNEs own their own source of supply or hold an equity position in a few important suppliers, otherwise known as *backwards integration*. The supplier must still compete with others on bidding for contracts; however, the supplier often has much closer ties with the MNE, in some case integrating enterprise resource planning (ERP) or ordering systems to support real-time management. The MNE, in turn, is provided with a strong supplier who adapts his operations to best suit the MNE's needs. In Japan, this concept has been very popular. In fact, most MNEs in Japan have each formed a *keiretsu*, or network of parts suppliers, subcontractors, and capital equipment suppliers (e.g., NEC). When the relationships are very close, suppliers often get involved in new product development as well.

When considering opportunities for global sourcing, there is typically a hierarchical order for decisions of *make* or *buy*. The company will give first preference to internal sources, such as having subassemblies produced by the manufacturing department or the subsidiary that specializes in this work. However, if a review of outside sources reveals that there is a sufficient cost/quality difference that would justify buying from an external supplier, this is what the company will do. In fact, sometimes an MNE will not attempt to make a particular part or product because it lacks the expertise to do so efficiently. The firm will simply solicit bids from outside suppliers and award the contract based on predetermined specifications (price, quality, delivery time, etc.). Over time, the MNE will learn which suppliers are best at providing certain goods and services and will turn to them immediately.

A successful global sourcing strategy depends on the implementation of a handful of important guidelines:

1. A commitment from top management to continually seek the best sources of supply, regardless of the geographic distance.
2. Not only examine the costs involved but also to weigh the quality of the supply source and the dependability of the supplier.
3. To develop the trust and respect of the supplier, and thus promote an ongoing, long-term relationship.

4 To use technologies that improve the ability to communicate with the supplier, to keep the individual apprised of company needs and to work with the supplier to ensure that there is mutual understanding.

5 To be prepared to accept the risk of global sourcing, including the impact of fluctuating foreign currencies and the possibility that political turmoil can result in the loss of a valuable supplier.

If the MNE can follow these guidelines, the company stands an excellent chance of developing an effective global sourcing strategy.

Value Chain and Supply Chain Considerations

Research and development

In recent years MNEs have been realizing more and more that controlling costs, accelerating time to market, and keeping pace with increasingly demanding consumers cannot be achieved through operational efficiencies alone. In fact, they have recognized the importance of considering operational issues when developing or redesigning new products. Often this multifunctional approach yields not only more profitable products but also some true innovations.

Trends in product innovation and product development

The number of new products or services introduced every year has been increasing rapidly, especially in certain economic sectors such as information technology (IT), telecommunications, the automotive industry, and life sciences. This has forced MNEs to (1) increase spending on R&D in order to keep pace with global competition and the battle for market share, (2) increasingly outsource R&D, and (3) form alliances or joint ventures to achieve accelerated product, process, and service innovation (see Chapter 10).

Certain MNEs in the most volatile industries, such as biotechnology, nanotechnology, and medical appliances, have begun to outsource their R&D. They do this through acquisitions of smaller early-stage companies that develop very specific advanced products to meet customer demands. A relevant example of R&D outsourcing is Cisco systems, which has grown into a giant sales and marketing organization that acquires and distributes new products and services under its global brand. This trend has also created a number of "IP houses" or technological labs that develop technologies with the purpose of licensing them to major manufacturers. For example, in semiconductors, these are referred to as "fabless chip companies" who develop chip designs for Bluetooth components or software designs for video streaming in handset processors. Similarly, third parties that receive royalties on each product sale develop many of Nintendo's video games.

In many cases MNEs are seeking alliances or joint ventures to achieve greater innovation by building on one another's strengths. For example, Ericsson joined forces with Sony Corporation in an effort to develop new mobile terminals by building on the wireless technology expertise of Ericsson and the consumer electronics experience of Sony.

Time to market and the development process

As product life cycles decrease, there is an ever-increasing competition for MNEs to get new products to market fast. Studies have shown that companies that get to market one month ahead of the competition can increase annual gross profit by $150,000 on a product that generates $25 million and $600,000 on a product that generates $100 million.

There are a number of methods MNEs have adopted to deliver products to market early. Sun Microsystems actually eliminated its New Products Group, which had centralized control for product development, and made the group a part of the manufacturing department. Now both groups work together. BMW has combined engineering, development, and production planning in bringing new cars to market in record time. Next, Inc. streamlined the relationship between design and production so that the plant can manufacture a totally new circuit board design in 20 minutes.

Much of the emphasis on new designs now focus on anticipating and reducing errors, bottlenecks and obstacles in the manufacturing process to ensure quality, performance, and quicker delivery. For example, the Ballistic Systems Division of Boeing Aerospace created a multifunctional product development team to speed development efforts and was able to cut design analysis from two weeks to 38 minutes and to reduce the average number of engineering changes per drawing from 20 down to one. A new concept known as *concurrent engineering* has been developed which involves design, engineering, and manufacturing people working together to create and build the product. This is useful for two reasons, as shown in Figure 14.4: (1) if the product is carefully designed, there are fewer changes needed later and (2) the good designs can be swiftly launched into market.

The costs associated with changes increase, as the product gets closer to completion. In most cases, it is almost twice as expensive to correct a problem during the production phase as it is during product design phase. Thus, it is best to figure out how to minimize costs and increase quality and productivity using the target cost approach instead of using the traditional design approach. In the

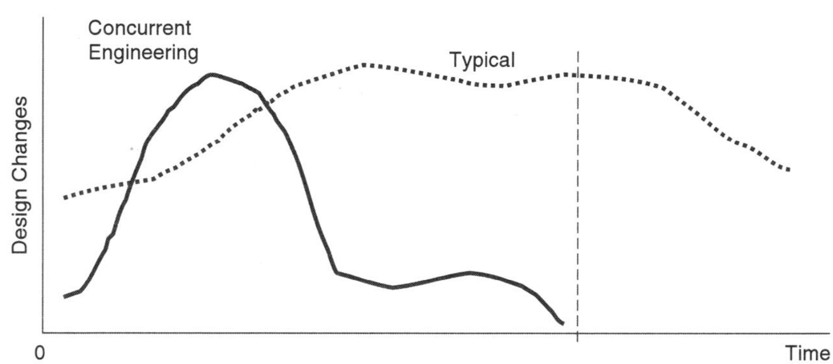

FIGURE 14.4 Design changes with concurrent engineering vs traditional approach

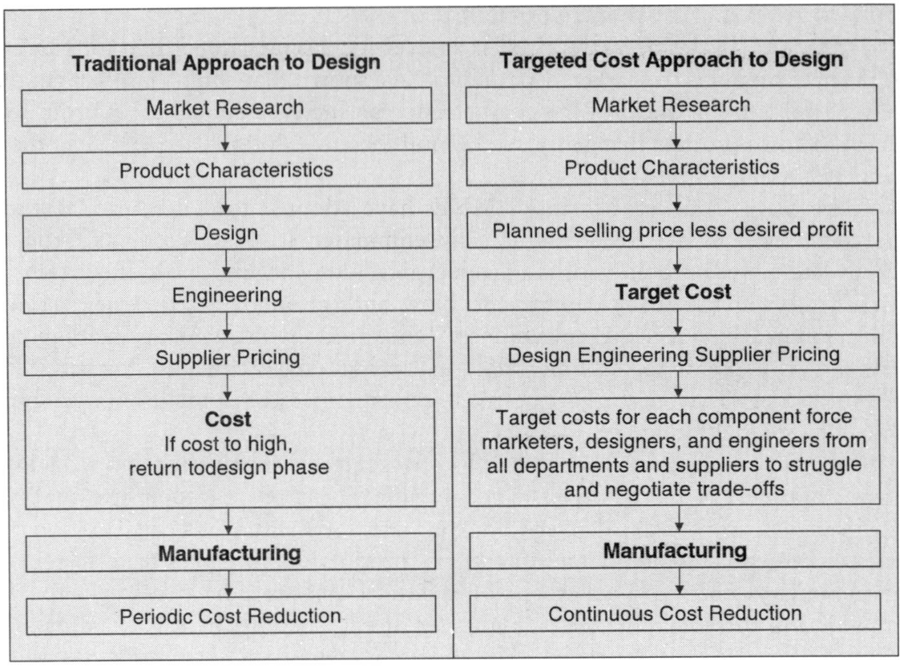

FIGURE 14.5 Target cost approach vs. traditional approach to design

target cost approach, introduced first in Japan, cost minimization and quality and productivity maximization are often considered during the design stage. This is in contrast to the traditional design approach, which is essentially sequential. Figure 14.5 compares the target cost approach to design with the traditional approach to design and maps out the implementation process. As an example, the modestly priced house furnishing MNE IKEA Corporation uses the targeted cost approach in developing all their product lines.

Production and operations systems

As has been explained earlier, the value-added activities are production activities in the industrial sectors and operations activities in the service sectors which add value command cost and determine a profit margin of products and services. Value-added activities must meet the multiple goals of capacity, quality, lead time, and customer service.

Selection of equipment

The decision about a particular process requires decisions about equipment and technology. These decisions may be complex, since alternative methods of production are present in virtually all operational functions. The particular equipment chosen should be selected considering cost, quality level, capacity, and flexibility.

The selection of the equipment should provide a sustainable competitive advantage. Unique equipment, with unique features, such as lower use of energy, may help the MNE sustain lower production costs, thus lowering product cost, which can be passed on to the customer. Advanced technology also allows operations managers to enlarge the processes' scope and provide for greater operational flexibility. In other words, with appropriate equipment, the MNE is able to respond to competitive pressures with lower costs and minimum customer service disruption.

Production technology

Technology advancements happen in a variety of ways, such as machine technology, automatic identification system (AIS), process control, vision system, robots, automated storage and retrieval systems (ASRS), automated guided vehicles (AGV), flexible manufacturing systems (FMS), computer-aided design (CAD), and computer-integrated manufacturing (CIM). All these technologies aim at replacing manual labor with automated systems, where processes that are repetitive and error-prone can benefit from automation to increase productivity, quality, and reduce variability of processes. Studies have shown that for a given process that is performed both manually and automatically with the same average performance time, the reduction in variability due to the automation results in a reduction of processing time by as much as 50 percent.

Quality and excellence

There are two main reasons for pursuing quality improvement in a company: customer value and cost.

The first reason is that clearly, customers respond positively to good-quality products and services. A good customer experience can lead to repeat sales, brand loyalty, word-of-mouth marketing, positive industry reviews, and ultimately, more revenue. Even companies that pursue low-cost strategies must meet minimum quality standards set by regulators and expected by their target customer base.

The second reason is to reduce the cost of waste in the system through running a quality operation and producing good-quality products: less rework, less-damaged inventory, less defective products, and so forth. That is why some quality experts claim that "Quality is Free" because the increased costs needed to measure and improve quality over time are often covered by the savings realized from "doing the job right the first time."

There are two management methods that are popular with MNEs that are trying to achieve quality excellence: Total Quality Management (TQM) and International Standards Organization (ISO) 9000 certification.

The *TQM* philosophy expects each individual in the MNE to take responsibility for quality, regardless of their position in the organization. Each individual is expected to focus on the quality of his or her own output, whether they are on the production floor, in administration or in the executive suite. Furthermore, TQM assumes that quality is achieved through continuous measurement and improvement – a never-ending process which drives better quality and reduces waste relentlessly out of every part of the business. This approach was first adopted in

Japan in the 1950's, and later introduced to the Western world by an American statistician called Dr W. Edwards Deming.

ISO 9000 is an internationally recognized certification that an MNE receives when it can demonstrate that it meets the highest-quality standards in its industry. European companies were the first to adopt such a system, but today it is very common across the Americas and Southeast Asia and China. Often MNEs pursue ISO certification as an internationally recognized accreditation to present to any prospective customers, especially foreign ones, which would treat this as an assurance of quality. To merit such certification, an MNE must demonstrate the reliability and soundness of all the business processes that affect the quality of their products. There are similar ISO certifications for service, for environmental processes, and so forth.

In practice, the TQM and ISO 9000 methodologies are complementary. When doing business internationally, ISO 9000 certification is becoming increasingly important. However, the ISO 9000 standards do not specify how a company should develop its quality processes. Rather, ISO requires each company to define and document its own quality processes and show evidence of implementing them. The following paragraphs describe how TQM and ISO 9000 principles can be linked to enhance a company's capability for delivering quality products or services. The main principles of TQM include:

- *Delight the customer*: Companies must strive to be the best at what customers consider most important. This can change over time, so business owners must be in close touch with customers.
- *Use people-based management*: Systems, standards, and technology cannot, in and of themselves, guarantee quality. The key is to provide employees with the knowledge of what to do and how to do it and to provide feedback on performance.
- *Continuous improvement*: TQM is not a short-term quick fix. Major breakthroughs are less important than incremental improvement.
- *Management by fact*: Quality management and improvement requires that managers clearly understand how consumers perceive the performance of an MNE's goods and services. Rather than trusting "gut feelings" it is critical to obtain factual information and share it with all employees.

MNEs can link these TQM principles to ISO 9000 standards in three ways:

- *Process definition*: The existing business process must be defined. Once defined, it must be satisfying to key stakeholders and it must "delight the customer."
- *Process improvement*: Everyone within the organization must use the defined process properly. If this is not the case, then an MNE must improve the management of its human resources.
- *Process management*: Management and employees must possess factual knowledge about process details in order to manage them properly.

Inventory management

Inventory ties up cash that an MNE can generally put to better and more profitable use elsewhere in the business. For this reason, operation managers strive to minimize inventory in the system through various techniques. A popular production technique for minimizing work-in-process inventory (the inventory needed to keep the production lines working) is called *just-in-time (JIT)* manufacturing. It was originally developed in Japan but has since spread to all parts of the globe. This technique requires that inventory be kept to a minimum and that inputs to a production process arrive exactly when they are needed to be worked on – and not stockpiled in advance. This technique drastically reduces the costs associated with large inventories and helps reduce wasteful expenses because of defective materials or components that were sometimes only discovered after assembling the final product.

Distribution systems

The purpose of distribution management and logistics is to obtain efficiency of operations through the integration of all material acquisition, movement, and storage activities. Firms recognize that as much as 25 percent of the costs of products are the costs associated with distribution activities.

The issue of distribution systems is of critical importance in the context of global MNEs. As shown in Figure 14.6, one way to look into distribution systems is by mapping the components of these systems along the dimensions of service level and product type.

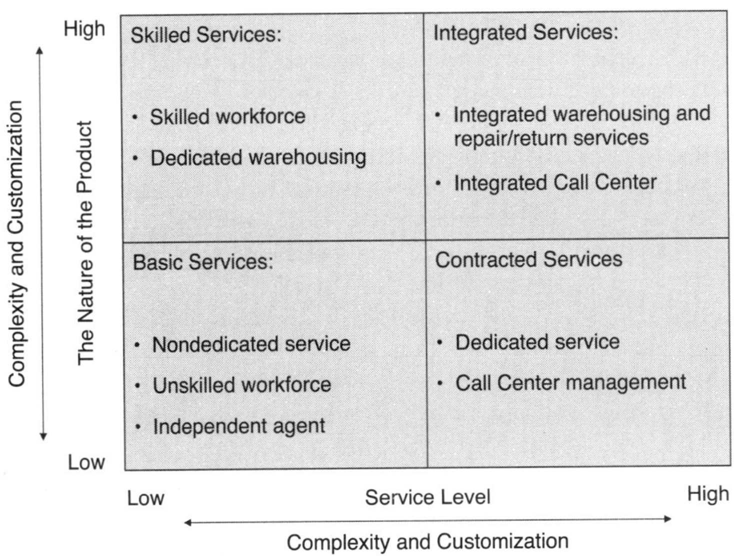

FIGURE 14.6 Taxonomy of logistics systems based on service level and product type

Basic services distribution system: for products that are simple and standardized and the service level expected by the customer is low, the distribution system can be provided by nondedicated distribution services executed by an unskilled workforce and based on independent agents. As an example, standard office supplies like pencils and scotch tape may be distributed through nonspecialized channels and sold across all forms of retail channels without need for special support or training.

Integrated services distribution system: products that are complex and customized require a carefully conceived integrated warehousing, repair and return services, and specialized call centers. As an example, personal computers, white goods, cars, and medical equipment (such as MRI machines) require integrated services distribution systems in order to provide the necessary set-up and after-sales service support.

Skilled services distribution system: when the product is complex and customized but requires a relatively low service level, the distribution systems should be based on dedicated warehousing and a skilled workforce but may forego call centers and dedicated service abilities. For example, the delivery and installation of a water treatment facility requires highly-trained personnel for set-up; however, the service level after set-up becomes routine and infrequent and thus does not require ongoing professional support through a call center (in some cases this may not even be possible).

Contracted services distribution systems: these systems which are characterized by standardized and noncustomized products that require high service levels, consist of dedicated call centers and dedicated services. For example, in the telecommunications sector supporting mobile phone subscribers requires specially trained service and support call center teams and ongoing availability.

Future trends in distribution systems

Future trends in the area of distribution systems, as seen in Figure 14.7, are using third-party logistics and service providers in order to leverage their focused expertise and economies of scale in delivering the appropriate levels of service at a reduced cost to their customers. As an example, MNEs use dedicated third-party carriers, call centers, spare parts providers, and repair management professionals. For the basic services distribution system, MNEs will likely use common carriers and public warehousing facilities. In this way the MNE is also able to focus more of its resources and attention on its core capabilities.

Figure 14.8 illustrates the evolution of distribution systems from disparate independent entities of plant, warehouse, and storage towards an integrated global system. Many MNEs vie to deploy integrated distribution systems in order to better monitor and control their operations systems worldwide from the production facility through to the point of sale. As an example, Benetton, a world leader in textile products, maintains its main production facility in Northern Italy but monitors on a real-time and continuous basis the point of sale performance of each product in stores globally. The Benetton distribution system allows for instantaneous replenishment of products, reflecting the in-store demand patterns, through a centrally controlled system.

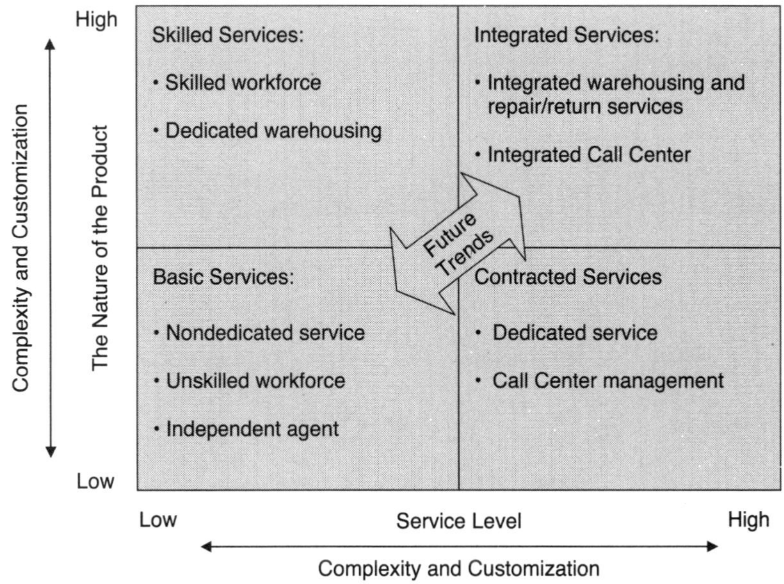

FIGURE 14.7 Future trends in the taxonomy of customization and management services

Another important trend noted for MNEs is the adoption of a consumer utility distribution model instead of the traditional functional distribution model. As seen in Figure 14.9, the functional distribution model was focused on minimizing costs for each intermediary in the supply chain with low regard to the consumer service level. The consumer utility distribution model provides equilibrium between consumer service level and resource allocation to achieve the optimal level of service at minimum cost.

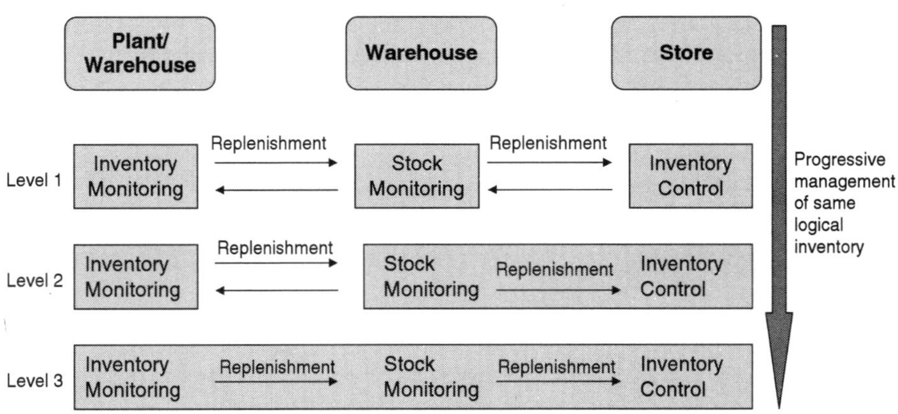

FIGURE 14.8 Towards an integrated distribution system

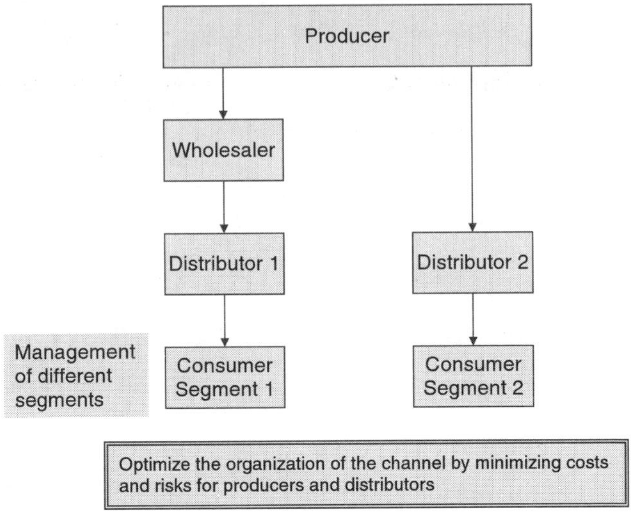

FIGURE 14.9 Functional vs consumer utility distribution model

After-sales services and support

After-sales services and support includes the following functions: installation, local customization and set-up support; maintenance, warranty, and return processes; upgrades and complementary product sales; and recycling and disposal.

After-sales services and support is a critical element of the value of the product. A positive experience reflects well on the product and builds customer loyalty to the brand. A poor experience can lead to the loss of a customer for life.

There are two essential elements of after-sales service and support. The first element involves the design of the product, which determines the ease of set-up and ongoing maintenance by the service provider. The second element is the delivery of the required service through professional, courteous, responsive, and effective people, processes, and systems.

There are various examples that demonstrate the value of products and services commanded by leading MNEs. Car manufacturers compete with one another not only on the basis of the product itself but also on the competing partners and systems in the market which provide after-sales services and support. Customers may prefer a product that they know comes with a very strong service system to one that they appreciate on the basis of its design but are unsure of local support.

An important component of after-sales services and support is the growing importance of customer relationship management (CRM) systems. Leading MNEs have recently created and enhanced divisions of CRM, which provide an infrastructure to maintain a close watch over customer needs, complaints, and expectations in order to introduce design changes, new product features, and new service capabilities. The location of CRM divisions is determined by the required mode of interaction with the customer, on the one hand, and the need to maintain costs, on the other. As a result, many CRMs are now located in remote locations such as

Eastern Canada (e.g., reservation systems for airline and travel systems) or India (e.g., support systems for software, billing, and telemarketing companies).

Another important element of after-sales services and support is the commitment of MNEs to the total cost of ownership, otherwise known as *lifelong costing* of the product. As an example, the Boeing Company maintains a large storage facility for obsolete aircrafts in the Mojave Desert where, at the company's expense, common carriers may dispose of obsolete aircrafts, thereby reducing the cost of disposing of their aircraft. The dry conditions of the desert also preserve the obsolete aircraft, which can then provide spare parts for servicing planes that are still being used.

COUNTRY FOCUS

UNITED ARAB EMIRATES

World Rank (EFI 2009): 54

Regional Rank (EFI 2009): 7

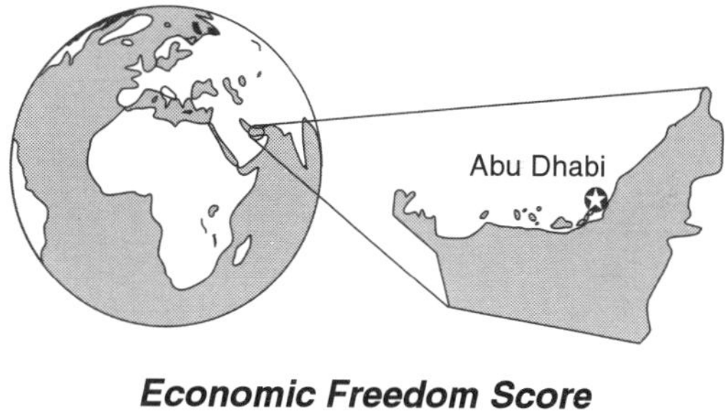

Quick facts

Population: 4.2 million

GDP (PPP): $151.7 billion; 9.4 percent growth in 2006; 8.3 percent 5-year compound annual growth; $35,882 per capita

Unemployment: 2.4 percent (2001)

Inflation (CPI): 11.0 percent

FDI inflow: $8.4 billion

2006 data unless otherwise noted

Economic Freedom Score

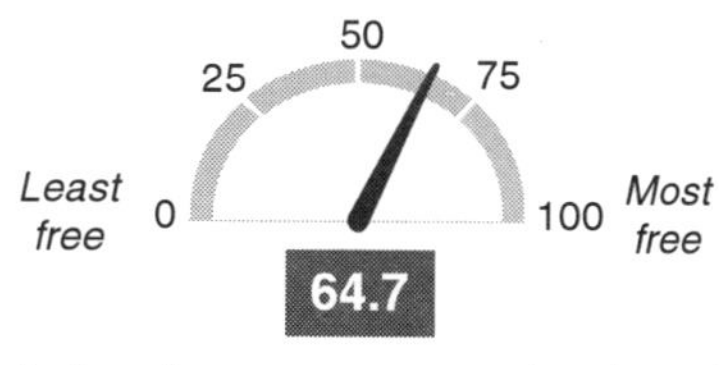

The United Arab Emirates' economic freedom score is 64.7, making its economy the 54th freest in the 2009 Index. The UAE is ranked 7th out of 17 countries in the Middle East/North Africa region, and its overall score is higher than the world average.

The UAE has achieved average annual economic growth of about 8 percent over the past five years and scores above the world average in fiscal freedom, government size, labor freedom, freedom from corruption, and trade freedom. The average tariff rate is not high, but nontariff barriers still limit overall trade freedom. There is no federal-level income or corporate taxes. The labor market is highly flexible. The level of corruption is low for a developing nation. The UAE aims to be a regional financial hub.

(Continued)

The UAE is weak in business freedom, investment freedom, and property rights. Foreign investment remains restricted, but lifting limits on foreign ownership in certain areas of the services sector is under consideration. The government has tried to streamline the regulatory process, but there is room for further improvement. The judiciary remains vulnerable to political influence.

Background

The United Arab Emirates is a federation of seven Arab monarchies (Abu Dhabi, Ajman, Dubai, Fujairah, Ras Al-Khaimah, Sharjah, and Umm al-Qaiwain). Abu Dhabi accounts for about 90 percent of UAE oil production and has taken a leading role in political and economic decision making, but many economic policy decisions are made by the rulers of the individual emirates. Dubai has developed into the UAE's foremost center of finance, commerce, transportation, and tourism. The establishment of free trade zones that offer opportunities for 100 percent foreign ownership with zero taxation has attracted substantial foreign investment. UAE nationals still rely heavily on the public sector for employment, subsidized services, and government handouts.

Business freedom – 57.4

The overall freedom to start, operate, and close a business is limited by the UAE's regulatory environment. Starting a business takes less than half the world average of 38 days, although the minimum capital requirement remains costly. Obtaining a business license takes less than the world average of 225 days. Bankruptcy proceedings are lengthy and cumbersome.

Trade freedom – 80.8

The UAE's weighted average tariff rate was 4.6 percent in 2006. Import restrictions, services market access barriers, nontransparent standards, sanitary and phytosanitary regulations, and inconsistent government procurement and customs valuation add to the cost of trade. Only firms with a trade license may engage in importation, and only majority-owned UAE firms may obtain such a license (except for goods imported into free zones). Ten points were deducted from the UAE's trade freedom score to account for nontariff barriers.

Fiscal freedom – 99.9

The UAE has no income tax and no federal-level corporate tax, but there are different corporate tax rates in some emirates (e.g., corporate tax rates of 55 percent for foreign oil companies and 20 percent for foreign banks). There is no general sales tax or value-added tax (VAT), but authorities are considering implementing the latter. Property transfers are subject to taxation. In the most recent year, overall tax revenue as a percentage of gross domestic product (GDP) was 1.4 percent.

Government size – 86.3

Total government expenditures, including consumption and transfer payments, are moderate. In the most recent year, government spending equaled 21.4 percent of GDP. The state remains significantly involved in the economy through regulation and state-owned enterprises.

Monetary freedom – 69.8

Inflation is high, averaging 10.2 percent between 2005 and 2007. The government influences prices through regulation, subsidies, and numerous state-owned enterprises and utilities, including oil, gas, electricity, and telecommunications. Ten points were deducted from the UAE's monetary freedom score to account for policies that distort domestic prices.

Investment freedom – 30

Foreign investors do not receive national treatment. Except for companies in the free zones, at least 51 percent of a business must be owned by a UAE national. Company bylaws often prohibit foreign ownership. Distribution of goods must be conducted through an Emirati partner, although "liberalized goods" may be imported without the agent's approval. There are no controls or requirements on current transfers, access to foreign exchange, or repatriation of profits.

Financial freedom – 50

The UAE's modern financial sector has become more efficient and competitive in recent years. Financial supervision has been strengthened. Domestic banks offer a full range of services. Islamic banking is increasingly prominent. Six major banks account for 70 percent of assets. The central bank has announced that it will issue licenses for new foreign bank branches. There are currently 23 local banks, 28 foreign banks (with more than 700 branches), over 60 investment companies, and other financial institutions. There is a 20 percent tax on foreign bank profits. The government has also announced that it will reopen the insurance sector. Capital markets are relatively developed, and the two stock markets have become more open to foreign investment.

Property rights – 40

The ruling families exercise considerable influence on the judiciary. Incompetence and corruption are rarely challenged. All land in Abu Dhabi, largest of the seven emirates, is government-owned (and, in some cases, government created by landfill in the Persian Gulf). Foreigners may buy and hold 99-year freehold interests in property in Dubai, and mortgages are available to them. The UAE leads the region in protecting intellectual property rights.

Freedom from corruption – 57

Corruption is perceived as present. The UAE ranks 34th out of 179 countries in Transparency International's Corruption Perceptions Index for 2007. A series of corruption scandals in early 2008 led to a broad campaign against corporate malfeasance and the arrest of many executives working for the huge government-owned property development companies. In a separate case, a federal minister of state was charged with breach of trust and fraud. A 2005 Abu Dhabi police study cited "rampant" bribery, nepotism, embezzlement, and abuse of power throughout local administrations.

Labor freedom – 76.2

The UAE's relatively flexible employment regulations facilitate overall employment and productivity growth. The nonsalary cost of employing a worker is moderate, but dismissing a redundant employee is relatively costly. Regulations related to the number of work hours are not rigid. There is no minimum wage.

Source: Adapted from Terry Miller and Kim R. Holmes, *2009 Index of Economic Freedom* (Washington, DC: The Heritage Foundation and Dow Jones & Company, Inc., 2009), at www.heritage.org/index.

SUMMARY

Global operations management deals with the set of activities required to create products and services through the transformation of inputs to outputs across national boundaries.

Goods constitute tangible products, whereas **services** consist of mainly intangible products. Operations management deals with both.

A **production system** consists of production inputs such as land, labor, capital, information, and management; a transformation function; and a set of outputs in the form of goods and services.

Global operations take advantage of national difference in the cost and quality of labor, talent, energy facilities, raw materials, and capital in order to enhance the productivity and cost structure of MNEs.

The **reasons** for entering some form of **international operations** are to reduce costs, reduce risks, improve the supply chain, provide better goods and services, improve operations, and attract and retain global talent.

The six main interdependent issues of **planning and resource management** are fixed assets, global sourcing, location planning, capacity planning, process planning, and facility layout planning.

Global trends in operations management are increased global competition, a faster pace of technological development, increased customer focus (quality, speed and flexibility), and the realization of the strategic importance of global operations management.

The global operations management **value chain** consists of research and development, production systems, quality and excellence, inventory management, distribution systems, and after-sales services and support. These activities add value in the eyes of the customer, command costs, and determine the profit margin for products and services delivered by the MNE.

DISCUSSION QUESTIONS

1 Recent years have seen an increase in the importance of global operations management. Select an MNE that provides global products and services and identify the main elements of its global operations.

2 Initiate a discussion with an executive of a local business. Discuss, document and rationalize the executive's decision process regarding international operations, if any? Are there any elements that can be improved or are missing in the delivery of products and services to customers?

3 Document the value chain activities of Amazon.com, which is described in this chapter, and determine the key success factors that make it a leading global MNE.

Bibliography

Alukal, G. (2003). Create a lean, mean machine, *Quality Progress*, 36 (4), 29–34.

Ashford, M. (1997). NIKE Europe. In D. Taylor (ed.), *Global Cases in Logistics and Supply Chain Management*. London: International Thomson Business Press.

Ashford, M., Naish, S. (1995). Nike's dream, *Logistics Europe*, 3 (1), 26–32.

Boeing (1996). *World Air Cargo Forecast 1996/1997*. Seattle, WA: Boeing Corp.

Buzby, C. M., Gerstenfeld, A., Voss, L. E., Zeng A. Z. (2002). Using lean principles to streamline the quotation process: a case study. *Industrial Management & Data Systems*, 102 (9), 513–20.

Christopher, M. (1998). *Logistics and Supply Chain Management*. London: Financial Times/ Pitman Publishing.

Duggan, K. J. (2002). *Creating Mixed Model Value Streams*. New York: Productivity Press.

Ferdows, K. (1997). Making the most of foreign factories. *Harvard Business Review*, March/ April, 74.

Finger, S. (2007). Regional headquarters of multinational corporations: an integrative framework for establishment and location. Unpublished PhD Dissertation, Ben Gurion University, Beer Sheva, Israel.

Friedman, T. (2005). *The World is Flat*. New York: Straus & Giraux.

Fung, P. (1999). Managing purchasing in a supply chain context: evolution and resolution. *Logistics Information Management*, 12 (5), 362–6.

Gregory, A. (2004). Running like clockwork. *Works Management*, 57 (2), 14–7.

Heizer, J., Render, B. (1999). *Operations Management*, 5th edn. Upper Saddle River, NJ: Prentice Hall.

Hines, P., Rich, N. (1997). The seven value stream mapping tools. *International Journal of Operations & Production Management*, 17 (1), 46.

Hines, P., Lamming, R., Jones, D., Cousins, P., Rich, N. (2000). *Value Stream Management*. Upper Saddle River, NJ: Pearson Education Limited.

Hyer, N. L., Wemmerlov, U. (2002). The office that lean built. *IIE Solutions*, 34 (10), 36–43.

Jared, L. (2001). Mapping the value stream, *IIE Solutions*, 33 (2), 26–33.

Jones, D., Hines, P., Rich, N. (1997). Lean logistics. *International Journal of Physical Distribution and Logistics Management*, 23, 73–153.

Kearney, A. T. Ltd (1999). *Survey of European Logistics 1998*. Brussels: European Logistics Association.

Khurana, A. (1999). Managing complex production processes. *Sloan Management Review*, 40 (2), 85–97.

Levy, D. L. (1997). Lean production in an international supply chain. *Sloan Management Review*, 38 (2), 94–102.

Lorge, S. (1998). Purchasing power. *Sales and Marketing Management*, 150 (6), 42–6.

Lovelle, J. (2001). Mapping the value stream. *IIE Solutions*, 33 (2), 26–33.

Lowengart, O., Menipaz, E. (2001). On the marketing of nations and multi-national corporations: a competitive positioning mapping. *Management Decision*, 39 (4), 302–8.

McGinnis, M. A., Vallopra, R. M. (1999). Purchasing and supplier involvement in process improvement: a source of competitive advantage. *Journal of Supply Chain Management*, 35 (4), 42–50.

Menipaz, E. (1984). *Essentials of Production and Operations Management*. Upper Saddle River, NJ: Prentice Hall.

Menipaz, E., Lowengart, O. (2002). On the marketing of nations: a gap analysis of managers' perceptions. *Journal of Global Marketing*, 15 (3/4), 65–94.

Menipaz, E., Ben-Yair, A. (2001). Reliability allocation models in system standards harmonization. *Communications in Dependability and Quality Management: an International Journal*, 4 (1), 58–67.

Michels, W. (2003). Extracting values from merged purchasing operations. *Mergers & Acquisitions*, 38 (8), 34–9.

Nigel, W. (2004). Lean thinking: what it is and what it isn't. *Management Service*, 48 (2), 8–10.

Pellew, M. (ed.) (1998). *Pan-European Logistics*. London: Financial Times.

Reddy, P. (1997). New trends in globalization of corporate R&D and implications for innovation capability in host countries: a survey from India. *World Development*, 25 (11), 1821–37.

Rodriguez, C. S., Lorente, A. R. M., Clavel, J. G. (2003). Benchmarking in the purchasing function and its impact on purchasing and business performance. *Benchmarking. An International Journal*, 10 (5), 457–71.

Ronald, M. B. (2001). Learning to think lean: lean manufacturing and the Toyota production system. *Automotive Production*, 113 (6), 64–5.

Rugman, A. M., Hodgetts, R. M. (2000). *International Business: A Strategic Management Approach*. Harlow, UK: Pearson Education.

Schary, P. B., Skjott-Larsen, T. (1995). *Managing the Global Supply Chain*. Copenhagen, Denmark: Munksgaard International Publishers.

Sobek, D. K., Ward, A. C., Liker J. K. (1999). Toyota's principles of set-based concurrent engineering. *Sloan Management Review*, 40 (2), 67–83.

Tapping, D., Shuker, T. (2003). *Value Stream Management for the Lean Office*. New York: Productivity Press.

Taylor, D. (1997). *Global Cases in Logistics and Supply Chain Management*. London: International Thomson Business Press.

Thompson, J. (1997). *The Lean Office*. Toronto: Productive Publications.

Vandermere, S. (1997). Increasing returns: competing for customers in the global market. *Journal of World Business*, 32 (4).

Voelkel, J. G., Chapman, C. (2003). Value stream mapping. *Quality Progress*, 25 (5), 65–8.

Warwick Manufacturing Group (1995). *Time Compression Self-Help Guide*. Warwick: University of Warwick.

Womack, J., Jones, D. (1996). *Lean Thinking*. New York: Simon & Schuster.

Wood, N. (2004). Learning to see: how does your supply chain function? *Management Services*, 48 (4), 16–20.

15

Global Marketing, Sales, and Support

Learning Objectives

Following this chapter, the reader should be able to:

1. Understand the essential elements of global marketing strategy, including screening issues and assessment of market potential
2. Understand global product strategy and its five essential elements
3. Understand global promotion and advertising, including push and pull strategies
4. Determine the key decisions for global distribution to a country and within it
5. Develop a global pricing strategy

Opening Case

Gillette: Global Strategy and Regional Derivatives

Preamble

Gillette, a world leader in consumer-packaged goods, exercises a global strategy approach, integrating all the aspects of its business: its suppliers, manufacturing sites, marketing, and after sale-services and support. As of the first decade of the 21st century, 70 percent of its sales, 72 percent of its profits, and 80 percent of its employees are outside the USA. Gillette assesses every product or service from the perspective of both domestic and international market standards. It had met world standards long before it entered world markets, and is a world class even in local markets. It understands local and cultural differences and adjusts products and service accordingly. True to the seminal approach of metanational corporations, proposed by INSEAD professor Yves Doz, Gillette listens to and learns from locations far from its home base. It searches globally for concepts as well as customers and suppliers, stimulating innovation and easing eventual entry into new markets. As part of its global strategy, it focuses on areas of excellence in the context of worldwide possibilities, determining the synergies that exist across markets, and alliance partners as well as necessary local adaptations. In its quest to adopt a global strategy, Gillette recognizes the need for strong local integration across functions and divisions in every place it operates, which affects its approach to the creation of regional headquarters and facilities.

A global leader in consumer goods

Gillette, one of the most successful global consumer-packaged goods companies, is well known for product innovation, aggressive acquisitions, and global strategies.

What are the keys to Gillette's global success? Take for example the Sensor shaving system (razor and blade). The Sensor shaving system is one of the enduring innovation successes of Gillette. Al Zein, who was the Chairman of Gillette in 1991 and headed the "Sensor" development project, directed his engineering head to first get the product in shape for testing and conduct a broad-scale user test. Only after it had past the large-scale user test did Gillette conceive a way to manufacture it. This was followed by an aggressive, well-thought-out global marketing campaign.

Gillette also has a unique product organization structure that has contributed to its global success. It has a program management system under which all technical activity, research and development (R&D), engineering and manufacturing is consolidated by product category. Such a program management system allowed Gillette to have a holistic approach to innovation in each category. Although this program faced initial resistance from employees, it was eventually well accepted.

Gillette insisted on high quality–high price positioning for the razor systems, which was proven right, in the face of the early tough competition from low-quality, largely disposable razor systems. Sensor far exceeded all its goals, as 24 million (vs the target of 18 million) razors sold and 300 million (vs a target of 200 million) blade cartridges sold in the first year of launch.

Gillette's strategies and operations in Latin America, Russia, China, Poland, and India led to its global success. By Gillette's own admission, it was operating more as a multinational company than as a truly global company prior to 1991. After 1991, its chairman, Al Zein, wanted Gillette to be like Coca-Cola and Johnson and Johnson's Band-Aid and insisted on product uniformity. His idea of a global mindset in marketing was that: first, Gillette should offer the same spectrum of products made to the same world standards under the same manufacturing processes; second, although Gillette may sell more of one product in Brazil and another in India, the product must be the same; third, Gillette should also have a global plan for launching new products – to wit, Sensor was simultaneously introduced in 19 countries; fourth, Gillette adopts an evolutionary approach towards the introduction of new products in new markets. As an example, in the razor market the evolution-oriented marketing strategy revolves around the principle that Gillette always offers double-edged blades that highlight Gillette's quality over those of the local products and upgrades customers to use higher-quality products over time. This strategy has relied on the existence of a sizeable affluent segment in every country that is an opinion leader and carries the bulk of the sales. In the context of vision, Gillette claims: "Our mission is to achieve or enhance clear leadership, worldwide, in the existing or new core consumer product categories in which we choose to compete." It should be noted that Gillette's mission is much more demanding than General Electric's, whose mission is to be number one or two in a given geographic market, but not necessarily worldwide. It is important to note other product categories. In the writing instruments category, Gillette has the Parker Pen brand in addition to the Paper Mate and Waterman brands, which were acquired earlier. It also acquired Duracell in a much-publicized takeover in 1996. It has the Oral-B toothbrush and other products in toiletries. What sets Gillette apart from most other companies that also have a continuous stream of new products is that Gillette seeks worldwide leadership for all its new products. Gillette's success in achieving its new product goals is reflected by the fact that about half of its sales come from products introduced in the past 5 years.

Asia-Pacific regional expansion of Gillette

In light of its global strategy, it is interesting to note the evolution of the regional site of Gillette Singapore (see "Country Focus" section at the end of this chapter). Gillette Singapore is the marketing and distribution arm for the Gillette Company in the small, Southeast Asian nation-state of Singapore. Gillette's Singapore, the most profitable market on a per capita basis in the Asia-Pacific region, started during the mid-1970s. Gillette-managed businesses (Shaving, Oral Care, and Personal Care) accounted for 57 percent, 31 percent, and less than 1 percent of profits, respectively. Non-Gillette-managed stationery accounted for 12 percent of earnings. Braun, another non-Gillette managed business, did not do business out of Gillette Singapore at the time. As the new, global, product-oriented organization structure of Gillette required, changes were introduced into the Singapore facilities and regional headquarters. Tapping the power of global brands and the economies of global production required greater integration across functions and divisions at the local level – and thus, strong local management. For example, the general manager (GM) of Shaving and Personal Care in Singapore had to assume the additional role of the local office head. In this capacity, he was responsible for overseeing all integration activities in Singapore and the region.

Even though Gillette was organized around worldwide or super-regional product groups and functional groups, managers on the ground in various countries did not report to international bosses outside of their local territory, thus losing touch with their local base. The vision of showing one face to the customer was the goal of the changes at the regional level. Without coordinated activities, the total effectiveness of Gillette's operations in Singapore would have been nothing more than the sum of its parts. Instead, the global synergies that Gillette sought were manifested through local relationships. In Singapore, Personal Care, Oral Care, and Duracell all benefited from the Shaving Department's relationships and clout with local distribution channels. The new Stationery sales force, responsible for both Parker and Waterman stocks, has also considerably enhanced leverage. It is noted elsewhere in this book that when operational synergies are the motivation for an acquisition, the need for links between the combining organizations is high. Housing all business units under one roof allows the relevant stakeholders, customers, suppliers, employees, and community members to view Gillette Singapore as one company with one vision and one way of operating. Employees are better able to understand, exchange ideas with, and transfer into other divisions. The strong operational integration required by the regional headquarters created a new and universally-accepted culture, one that can be consistently displayed to those outside the organization. Besides the obvious benefits of cost-cutting, the regional headquarters approach delivers bottom-line value by strengthening Gillette's brand identity in Singapore. Individual product lines are more easily associated with the Gillette name, thus elevating their perceived value in the marketplace. Like other successful integrators, Gillette understands that well-conceived acquisitions ensure that valuable customers win too. The emphasis on local integration in international markets is one reason the Gillette Company has developed such powerful global brands.

This case study reinforces the conclusion that the best definition of "global" is "integrated," not "international." As in the case of Gillette, companies with international activities have greater need for multiple forms of integration, but they do not always build the linkages across countries or products or functions, such as marketing and sales, that allow them to think about all of their resources simultaneously and therefore to tap the power of the whole. The key to success in the global economy is for companies to behave in a more integrated fashion – to tap the collaborative advantage that comes from being able to use all their resources and being able to work across boundaries. That means becoming knowledgeable about local needs, skillful at managing local changes, forging cross-boundary relationships, all that in many places at the same time, with a global, corporate, business unit, and functional strategy in mind.

Introduction

Throughout the book it becomes clear that international business is more complex to manage than a domestic business. The main reason for this complexity is that the supply chain that entails an international business transcends national borders and is exposed to a multiplicity of local cultures. All throughout the global supply chain, an appropriate consideration should be given to the various environments in which the business operates. These environments are affected, among other things, by national and business cultures, as has been explained earlier. This chapter discusses issues of global marketing strategy, including the extensions necessary in domestic marketing strategy in order to make it applicable in the international context.

As demonstrated in the opening case, Gillette was successful in managing a global strategy in product development (replacing price leadership with product differentiation through quality), a global strategy in new product introduction (launching products worldwide instead of a gradual introduction), and a global acquisition and operational integration strategy. The creation of the regional headquarters in Singapore, otherwise known in Gillette as a Singapore "campus" articulates the Gillette's global strategy. Needless to say, the main office in the USA, headquartered far away from Singapore, recognized the need to enhance marketing operations in the Far East and adopted a global marketing and sales strategy while considering local national and business cultures, local interactions, and local relationships. The acquisition of the Parker Corporation by Gillette, which was initiated and sealed in Europe, could be consummated in the marketing and sales divisions only after change in management practices was adjusted for the local customs and business culture in Singapore.

This chapter covers the essentials of global marketing strategy, including financial, economic, political, and legal screening of products and services.

1. Push and pull strategies as well as other distribution issues.
2. After-sale services and support, since it is a critical issue when products are sold and must be supported all over the world, across cultures, and time zones. There are several cases where early internationalized firms found themselves overextended and unable to live up to their after-sale services and support commitments.
3. Other global marketing strategies, such as pricing strategies.

Global Marketing Strategy

As the domestic market of a company becomes increasingly saturated or increasingly competitive, many companies look to new international markets as one strategy to grow the business. Whether or not to decide to market products or services to a foreign country, and if so, which one of those products and services to market overseas, are critical decisions for the international marketing manager. These decisions carry significant consequences to the company in terms of costs and management attention. Before taking such a critical decision, the company should make it a point to evaluate carefully the markets it intends to enter from a number of different, but interrelated, perspectives.

Need and potential screening

Assessing whether there is a need for the company's products or services in a target market is especially challenging for the international marketing manager, who should become familiar with an entirely new and perhaps significantly different marketplace. Identifying a need does not imply that the potential consumers in that market are necessarily aware of such a need. However, through a close analysis of the local alternatives to the company's products or services, their product or service characteristics, and the business models behind them, an understanding of the existing potential in the market can be developed.

If there is no competing product or service in the target market, that may not mean there is no potential for such a product or service. It simply requires a more indirect analysis to understand the local problems or local consumers' needs that the company's product or service could address, and to assess whether or not the local consumers share these issues and would understand the potential benefits.

Once the need has been clearly defined, the company can turn to assessing the market potential through country statistics. For example, a company that chooses to sell wireless routers for the home – used to connect one's personal computer (PC) to the Internet wirelessly – would be interested in collecting statistics on the size of the population and their growth (i.e., total market), the local average income in the country (i.e., Can they afford the product?), the penetration of PCs and Internet broadband connections in the market (i.e., what percentage of the total market represents an addressable market), consumer uses of the Internet (i.e., how aware are the consumers of the benefits of faster access to the Internet), and so forth.

For example, take the case of emerging economies' need and marketing potential assessment. Emerging economies comprise more than half of the world's population, account for a large share of world output and have very high growth rates, which means enormous market potential. They can be distinguished by the recent progress they have made in economic liberalization. Promising opportunities for trade are opening, as their need for capital equipment, machinery, power transmission equipment, transportation equipment, and high-technology products is substantial and is increasing rapidly. It may be clear that an appropriate marketing strategy should include moving into an emerging economy. The question is how to decide which emerging economy should be targeted first? Table 15.1 shows the ranking of emerging economies that may be used for prioritizing marketing decision purposes. Singapore, the country featured in the Gillette opening case, is at the top of the list. The ranking is based on an assessment of different market dimensions that allows ranking and matching marketing penetration priorities. The ranking in Table 15.1 is based on eight dimensions that are chosen to represent the market potential of a country over a scale of 1–100. The dimensions are: market size, market growth rate, market intensity, market consumption capacity, commercial infrastructure, economic freedom, market receptivity, and country risk. The dimensions are given weights that indicate their relevance to the overall market potential index. Table 15.1 contains the overall market potential index for each country.

For each industry the assessment might be different. Take, for example, the retailing industry. Retailers alluded to in the opening case of Chapter 1, may have benefited from the ranking compiled by A. T. Kearney and presented in Figure 15.1 in 2005. The findings by A. T. Kearney may explain why at least 15 retailers moved into new geographic markets, while more than 10 retailers left countries in which they were operating. Carrefour, alluded to in the opening case in Chapter 1, is withdrawing from several markets, Tesco holds the record for being the fastest-growing retailer outside its home market, while Wal-Mart has been busily opening new stores outside its home country every few days.

TABLE 15.1 Market Opportunities in Emerging Markets

Countries	*Overall market potential index*	
	Rank	*Index*
Hong Kong	1	100
Singapore	2	80
South Korea	3	74
China	4	73
Israel	5	69
Hungary	6	68
Czech Republic	7	67
India	8	60
Poland	9	50
Chile	10	45
Mexico	11	45
Russia	12	42
Thailand	13	42
Malaysia	14	40
Turkey	15	39
Egypt	16	35
Indonesia	17	33
Philippines	18	31
Argentina	19	29
Brazil	20	29
Peru	21	27
South Africa	22	22
Colombia	23	16
Venezuela	24	

Source: Adapted with permission from A.T. Kearney (2005) *Marketing Opportunities in Emerging Markets*. Chicago, Illinois: A.T. Kearney, Inc.

A mapping of the index, termed Global Retail Development Index (GRDI), against an economic and political stability dimension, demonstrates the dynamics of international business and the changing international business environment. This mapping, presented in Figure 15.2, reveals that in Europe, the most promising markets for retailers are moving further east.

As a matter of fact, more than half the markets that fall into the GRDI's attractive categories – "on the radar screen" and "to consider" – are from Eastern Europe. The Ukraine has climbed in a few years to reach third place; Macedonia and Bosnia-Herzegovina have entered the ranking for the first time. Russia, however, receded as retailers began to aggressively enter the market, thereby increasing the level of competition. The insight gained through the indexing and mapping helps in the need and potential assessment for the international retailers.

A.T. Kearney's 2005 Global Retail Development Index (top 30 emerging markets)

Rank/ Country	Region	Country risk	Market altractive-ness	Market saturation	Time pressure	
	Weight	25%	25%	30%	20%	Score
1 India	Asia	62	34	91	80	100
2 Russia	Eastern Europe	52	58	71	92	99
3 Ukraine	Eastern Europe	46	34	82	90	87
4 China	Asia	68	40	53	90	83
5 Slovenia	Eastern Europe	83	52	43	68	82
6 Latvia	Eastern Europe	67	49	51	79	81
7 Croatia	Eastern Europe	63	48	49	88	80
8 Vietnam	Asia	54	24	88	68	79
9 Turkey	Mediterranean	51	56	66	65	78
10 Slovakia	Eastern Europe	73	52	33	90	77
11 Chile	Latin America	73	56	60	44	76
12 Thailand	Asia	64	41	59	71	75
13 Bulgaria	Eastern Europe	48	39	73	68	73
14 South Korea	Asia	74	71	34	52	72
15 Tunisia	Mediterranean	66	38	84	28	71
16 Macedonia	Eastern Europe	31	31	86	75	70
17 Lithuania	Eastern Europe	67	50	51	55	68
18 Malaysia	Asia	70	49	58	40	67
19 Hungary	Eastern Europe	72	48	30	78	66
20 Bosnia-Herzegovina	Eastern Europe	36	18	79	85	64
21 Saudi Arabia	Asia	59	48	72	26	64
22 Romania	Eastern Europe	57	37	45	81	63
23 Morocco	Mediterranean	56	34	82	30	62
24 Mexico	Americas	61	65	49	35	61
25 Egypt	Mediterranean	51	35	85	30	60
26 Egypt	Asia	84	71	41	10	59
27 Philippiness	Asia	43	37	71	50	57
28 Indonesia	Asia	43	44	82	17	53
29 Brazil	Latin America	52	56	57	20	49
30 Pakistan	Asia	44	27	91	14	48

Key		Legend	Country risk	Market attractiveness	Market saturation	Time pressure
On the radar screen; To consider	Lower priority		0 = high risk 100 = low risk	0 = low attractiveness 100 = high attractiveness	0 = saturated 100 = not saturated	0 = no time pressure 100 = urgency to enter

Source: Euromoney database, World Bank reports and A.T. Kearney analysis

FIGURE 15.1 The 2005 Global Retail Development Markets (Adapted with permission from A. T. Kearney analysis (2005). *Emerging Market Priorities for Global Retailers.* Chicago, Illinois: A.T. Kearney, Inc)

The same analytical tools may be used by multinational enterprises (MNEs) from other industries, like automotive and electric appliances.

Once a promising market has been defined, the company is well advised to consider carefully what unique advantages it possesses over local competitors who are intimately familiar with the market, have strong relationships locally and may even be protected by certain government policies. At its most basic level, a company should be able to offer unique benefits to the local consumer (i.e., new features) or provide similar products or services at a much better price in order to expect to be successful. On rare occasions, companies may possess both unique benefits and be

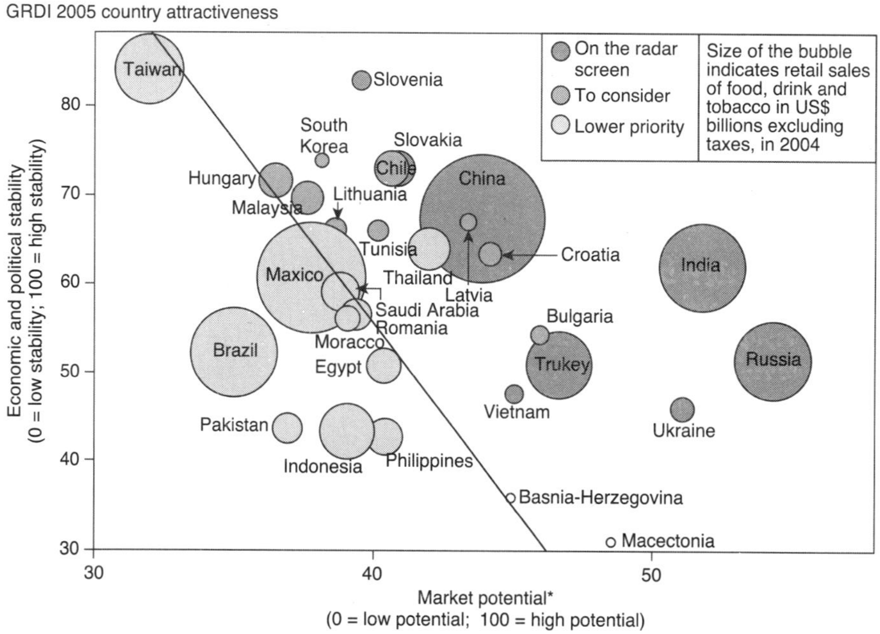

* Based on weighted score of market attractiveness, market saturation and time pressure socres

FIGURE 15.2 Global Retailing Development Index (GRDI) 2005, country attractiveness (Adapted with permission from A. T. Kearney (2005). *Emerging Market Priorities for Global Retailers*)

able to deliver them at lower costs. In any case, without a unique competitive advantage it is ill advised for a company to choose to enter a foreign market.

Financial and economic screening

Different regions and countries in the world are all at different stages of economic development and experiencing different economic conditions. The industrialized countries are characterized by high annual capita income, typically above US$20,000, and a higher, strong, and stable national infrastructure (i.e., telecommunications, transportation, regulatory bodies), and sophisticated financial and retail markets. The least-developed countries typically realize annual capita income of less than US$1,500, very little national infrastructure and very basic, if any, in the way of financial and retail markets. In these countries, trade is done by cash or barter, and credit arrangements by financial institutions is not readily available.

A common tool used to compare the relative buying power of consumers across countries for similar products or services is purchasing power parity (PPP). An often-cited example is the *Economist*'s monthly listing, called the Big Mac Index, where the different local prices of a Big Mac in different countries are converted to US dollars and can be compared. The index is presented in Figure 15.3. As an example, the Big Mac Index suggests that the euro is overvalued by 17 percent against the dollar. The following explains this gap. The euro is worth about

The hamburger standard

	Big Mac Price in dollars*	Implied PPP† of the dollar	Under (–)/ over (+) valuation against the dollar, %
United States‡	3.06	–	–
Argentina	1.64	1.55	–46
Australia	2.50	1.06	–18
Brazil	2.39	1.93	–22
Britain	3.44	1.63§	+12
Canada	2.63	1.07	–14
Chile	2.53	490	–17
China	1.27	3.43	–59
Czech Republic	2.30	18.4	–25
Denmark	4.58	9.07	+50
Egypt	1.55	2.94	–49
Euro area	3.58**	1.05††	+17
Hong Kong	1.54	3.92	–50
Hungary	2.60	173	–15
Indonesia	1.53	4.771	–50
Japan	2..34	81.7	–23
Malaysia	1.38	1.72	–55
Mexico	2.58	9.15	–16
New Zealand	3.17	1.45	+4
Peru	2.76	2.94	–10
Philippines	1.47	26.1	–52
Poland	1.96	2.12	–36
Russia	1.48	13.7	–52
Singapore	2.17	1.18	–29
South Africa	2.10	4.56	–31
South Korea	2.49	817	–19
Sweden	4.17	10.1	+36
Switzerland	5.05	2.06	+65
Taiwan	2.41	24.5	–21
Thailand	1.48	19.6	–52
Turkey	2.92	1.31	–5
Venezuela	2.13	1,830	–30

	Big Mac Price in dollars*	Implied PPP† of the dollar	Under (–)/ over (+) valuation against the dollar, %
Aruba	2.77	1.62	–10
Bulgaria	1.88	0.98	–39
Colombia	2.79	2124	–9
Costa Rica	2.38	369	–22
Croatia	2.50	4.87	–18
Dominican Rep	2.12	19.6	–31
Estonia	2.31	9.64	–24
Fiji	2.50	1.39	–18
Georgia	2.00	1.19	–34
Guatemala	2.20	5.47	–28
Honduras	1.91	11.7	–38
Iceland	6.67	143	+118
Jamaica	2.70	55.9	-12
Jordan	3.66	0.85	+19
Latvia	1.92	0.36	–37
Lebanon	2.85	1405	–7
Lithuania	2.31	2.12	–24
Macau	1.40	3.66	–54
Macedonia	1.90	31.0	–38
Moldova	1.84	7.52	–40
Morocco	2.73	8.02	–11
Nicaragua	2.11	11.3	–31
Norway	6.06	12.7	+98
Pakistan	2.18	42.5	–29
Paraguay	1.44	2941	–53
Qatar	0.68	0.81	–78
Saudi Arabia	2.40	2.94	–22
Serbia & Montenegro	2.08	45.8	–32
Slovakia	2.09	21.6	–32
Slovenia	2.56	163	–16
Sri Lanka	1.75	57.2	–43
Ukraine	1.43	2.37	–53
UAE	2.45	2.94	–20
Uruguay	1.82	14.4	–40

*At current exchange rates †Purchasing-power parity
‡Average of New York, Chicago, San Francisco and Atlanta
§Dollars per pound **Weighed average of member countries
Sources: McDonald's; *The Economist* ††Dollars per euro

FIGURE 15.3 Big Mac Index (© The Economist Newspaper Limited, London (2009))

$1.22 on the foreign-exchange markets. A Big Mac costs €2.92, on average, in the euro zone and $3.06 in the USA. The rate needed to equalize the burger's price in the two regions is just $1.05. Thus, to the customers of McDonald's, at least, the single currency is overpriced.

Ideally, the international marketing manager would want to identify a country with a large and growing population, high annual capita income, a strong national infrastructure, and well-developed financial and retail markets. However, in many cases the highest growth rates are typically found amongst developing countries (e.g., China and India) with lots of potential but immature national infrastructure.

The international marketing manager must screen out those regions or countries for which the products and services of the company may not be affordable or consistent with the local consumption patterns, or the current economic or regulatory environment in that country. Alternatively, a clear understanding of the differences and constraints in a developing country could suggest ways to adapt the product, or harvest older and hence cheaper versions of the product in such markets.

Political and legal forces screening

As already mentioned, the local political, legal, and regulatory environment could have serious consequences for a company's products and services. This could cause negative views of the company's products and brands due to political disputes between the local country and the company's domestic government. It could also reach outright embargoes, unfair tariffs or outright bans of such products or of all products from the producers of a specific country (e.g., the US embargo on Cuba).

In some cases political disputes between two countries might even impact a commercial agreement with a third country. For example, the USA has imposed export controls on sales to China of any equipment which could have military uses, not only military weapons but also any technology which could have a dual use as potential military equipment and, thus, could be considered a "strategic" technology. As an example, the article below illustrates how the USA pressured Israel to cancel orders of defense-related equipment and technological systems in order to protect the balance of power in the straits of Taiwan.

Israel Apologizes to U.S. Over China Arms Sale

Goldin, M. (2005). Israel apologizes to U.S. over China arms sale. *Reuters*, June 19. *URL Source*: http://reuters.myway.com/article/20050619/2005-06-19.

JERUSALEM (Reuters) – Israel publicly apologized to the United States on Sunday over arms exports to China that have drawn criticism from Washington and strained U.S.–Israeli security ties. "It is impossible to hide the crisis between Israel and the United States with regard

(Continued)

to the security industries. We are doing everything possible to put it behind us", Israeli Foreign Minister Silvan Shalom said on Israel Radio. The dispute centers on Israel's sale of Harpy attack drones and other advanced technology to China that the Pentagon fears could tilt the balance of power and make it difficult to defend Taiwan, which Beijing deems a renegade province.

"If things were done that were not acceptable to the Americans then we are sorry but these things were done with the utmost innocence", Shalom said in comments that coincided with a visit by Secretary of State Condoleezza Rice. "The United States is our biggest ally and none of the things that were done were done with the intention of harming U.S. interests", Shalom added. The dispute has strained security ties between Israel and the United States, its main ally and provider of about $2 billion in annual defense aid, at a time when it seeks U.S. assistance to help implement its planned withdrawal from Gaza. Commenting on the arms dispute ahead of her trip to Israel and the Palestinian territories, Rice said Israel should be "sensitive" to U.S. concerns on arms sales to China particularly given its close defense cooperation with Washington. "We have had some very difficult discussions with the Israelis about this. I think they understand now the seriousness of the matter and we'll continue to have those discussions", Rice said. An Israeli official is negotiating an agreement which would likely enable the United States to supervise Israeli arms sales to countries that Washington deems problematic, including China and India. Washington torpedoed Israel's multi-billion dollar sale of Phalcon strategic airborne radar systems to China in 2000, citing concerns it could upset the regional balance of power. U.S. displeasure over the Harpy deal played a role in a decision in April to suspend Israel from involvement in the F-35 Joint Strike Fighter project.

Socio-cultural forces

Chapter 3 covers a number of different elements of culture and considers some of the generalized differences among different nations and countries. Clearly different socio-cultural norms, perceptions, and traditions can have a significant impact on how a new product or foreign company will be perceived by the local population. Socio-cultural assessment is the most difficult assessment for an international marketing manager to make, as it is not a quantifiable data set that can be researched or analyzed as one might the financial or economic statistics of the target country. It requires a mix of historical and cultural awareness and understanding and often requires local expertise or, at the very least, a number of extensive visits by the international marketing manager to the target country.

The most important thing to keep in mind at all times is that people from different countries will tend to think and view things very differently from one's own home country. Understanding some of these differences and how they might impact the product proposition and company entry strategy is critical to the success of any marketing and sales strategy and program.

Global Product Strategy

There are a number of elements that can influence a global product strategy when seeking the right balance between global standardization (that brings economies of scale and minimizes duplication internally) and local customization (that can lead to greater competitive differentiation and local market acceptance).

In the following section, we will touch briefly on some of the major elements.

Laws and regulations

One of the most obvious needs for local adaptation comes from specific laws or regulations that are dictated by the local governments of the target markets. These requirements can range from specific labeling and packaging requirements to avoiding the use of banned substances in certain markets that are perfectly acceptable in one's own market – e.g., the ban in Europe on accepting any genetically modified (GM) foods – or adapting to local infrastructure requirements – for example, 110 V sockets in North America vs 220 V sockets in Europe.

An international marketing manager must be aware of any laws or regulations that could affect or even prevent the sale of the product in a target market. These regulations can range from environmental regulations, as demonstrated by the insert, local quotas, duties or tariffs or, in some cases, trade sanctions or embargoes due to political pressures. On the other hand, certain laws can be beneficial to the supplier, such as strict intellectual property rights (to help limit counterfeit products).

The insert describes a new set of environmentally driven directives that can require adaptation of a product. It describes a new set of directives, named RoHS (Restriction of certain Hazardous Substances), that consumer electronic and domestic appliance manufacturers from Asia would need to abide by in order to sell their products in the European Union (EU). The insert describes both a set of components that are to be banned starting from the summer of 2005 and lists a set of exceptions in the case of certain products. It further requires that for those products that contain banned substances, the product manufacturers or suppliers will be financially responsible for collecting and disposing of these items appropriately. If, for example, companies planning to introduce their company's refrigerators, PCs or new portable media players into a country belonging to the EU would need to ensure the products were consistent with these requirements and that after-sales services included collection and disposal of waste if required. Depending on the make-up of one's product and the potential in the market, this could drastically affect an MNE's decision to enter the market at all.

RoHS and WEEE Directives

(Based on directives of DTI – Dept. of Trade & Industry, UK)

What is RoHS?

RoHS is the Restriction of certain Hazardous Substances, a directive from the European Union (EU) for environment protection. This bans the use of certain substances in electrical and electronic equipment products after July 1, 2006.

What is WEEE?

Waste from Electrical and Electronic Equipment is the directive that deals with the recovery, sorting, and treatment of noncompliant products.

Who is affected?

Both directives (RoHS & WEEE) will affect:

- Manufactures and distributors selling electrical and electronic equipment within the specified categories.
- Companies selling equipment produced by other suppliers under their own brand.
- Companies importing (or exporting) affected equipment into European Union (EU) member states.

According to the directives, starting August 2005, such producers are responsible for financing the collection of waste electrical and electronic equipment from central points, specialist treatment, and meeting targets for re-use, recycling, and recovery. This directive covers the same scope as WEEE, except for medical devices and monitoring and control instruments. It also applies to electric light bulbs and light fittings in households.

What are the purposes of RoHS?

RoHS aims to:

- Protects human health and the environment by restricting the use of certain hazardous substances in new equipment; and
- Complement the WEEE Directive.

What are the substances?

There are six (6) substances that are banned under RoHS and must be replaced by other substances. The substances are:

1 Cadmium (Cd)
2 Mercury (Hg)
3 Hexavalent chromium (Cr (VI))
4 Polybrominated biphenyls (PBBs)
5 Polybrominated diphenyl ethers (PBDEs)
6 Lead (Pb)

Certain applications are exempt from the requirements of the Directive including:

- Mercury (in some lighting applications)
- Lead in the glass of cathode ray tubes, electronic components, and fluorescent tubes

- Lead in certain steel, aluminium, and copper alloys
- Lead in solders for servers, storage, and array systems (until 2010)
- Lead in certain high temperature solders
- Lead in solders for network infrastructure equipment
- Lead in electronic ceramic parts
- Cadmium plating
- Hexavalent chromium (in absorption refrigerators)
- Arms, munitions and war material

The exemptions are reviewed every four years

What countries are affected?

"Single market" Directives such as RoHS apply to all European Union (EU) member states and must be implemented in the same way to prevent differences in interpretation across the member states. The WEEE Directive is not a single market Directive; it sets minimum criteria for the collection of waste that member states may exceed if they wish.

What are the benefits of the RoHS?

The extraction of these raw materials and their eventual disposal can cause damage to both the environment in terms of pollution, as well as to human health from occupational exposure and exposure following disposal. The removal of these materials from production reduces the health risks of exposure, particularly for children, the elderly and pregnant women.

Timescale

The Government consultation paper of July 30, 2004 provides a detailed timetable to the development and implementation of the directives:

1. February 13, 2003 Directives published
2. March 31, 2003 First UK discussion paper issued
3. May 30, 2003 Closing date for replies to the above
4. August 1, 2003 Summary of all responses and initial Government views published
5. Early December 2003 Next detailed consultation paper planned
6. March 1, 2004 Deadline for responses to 2nd consultation
7. July 30, 2004 – October 29, 2004 Final consultation on draft regulations and nonstatutory guidance
8. Autumn 2004, Regulations laid
9. First quarter of 2005 Producers to commence registration
10. August 12, 2005 Producer responsibility for financing commences alongside retailer take-back
11. July 1, 2006 RoHS substance ban commences
12. December 31, 2006 Collection and recycling targets to be achieved

Cultural differences

Another element that can influence companies to adapt their products to different markets is cultural differences. These differences can represent different tastes or preferences. To wit, in Japan and Israel, McDonald's burgers are made spicier than in North America. In addition, different norms in the society may lead to the same product being perceived, and thus, positioned differently. As an example, a bicycle in China is considered a major mode of transportation whereas in the USA bicycles are sold mainly for recreation. In some cases a company may choose to adapt a product by incorporating local culture into the product in an effort to make it more appealing and successful with local consumers.

However, not all products require local adaptation. For example, Intel sells the same microprocessors to every market around the globe. In most cases products that are far removed from an individual consumer, such as industrial machines or electronic components, do not require much customization (with the possible exception of translation of labeling and documents) in order to cross cultural borders. Intel's microprocessors fall under the category of an original equipment manufacturer (OEM), that produces parts and assemblies that become part of a finished, assembled product. OEM products are sold as part of several leading brand name products.

Brand and product names

Brand and product naming is of great importance for marketing. It assumes even higher importance for international and global marketing. To understand the impact of brand and product naming, see Figure 15.4. Can you imagine a world without brand and product names? Imagine how you make your purchasing decisions today: Would it change if there are no brands and product names?

A MNE's brand name can be one of its most valuable assets if it successfully conveys certain desirable characteristics to a target buyer, such as quality, reliability, innovation, good value for money, fashionable or cool design. Similarly, the product name can provide similar information to the consumer. The company brand could be associated with the product (e.g., Starbuck's coffee or Coca Cola) or the product name could be a brand of its own (e.g., Kleenex tissue paper by Proctor & Gamble). Table 15.2 lists the top global brands by world regions. No doubt all of these brands are recognized. However, it should be noted that global brands are not readily associated with a particular country or region unless the MNE promotes it as part of its marketing strategy.

Brand names help suppliers differentiate their products, protect against copycats, and guard their margins. They also help protect consumers from cheap or defective copies of a particular product or service. Companies with valuable brands often spend a significant amount to protect their brands as well as ensure that consumers are not confused by similar-looking names or packaging.

There are many benefits in trying to build a global brand and maintaining consistency across markets, especially in today's world where more and more tourists and business people travel across the globe. However, there are also many examples of situations where the product name has to be localized, either to avoid

FIGURE 15.4 Global brands need names as well as identities

issues on how it would be received locally or in order to increase the chances for successful sales to the local population.

For example, a gaming keyboard developer, who was successfully selling in North America and Europe under the name Zboard, had to add an additional Chinese name when preparing to enter the Chinese market in mid-2005. It was clear to the local partner, the distributor, that the English name would be unfamiliar and hard to remember for Chinese consumers, but even more importantly it had no particular meaning. In China, names should and often have some deeper meaning. Clever use of this cultural norm is appreciated by the Chinese consumer. Therefore, a Chinese name was selected (pronounced "Chum Ba"), which meant

TABLE 15.2 Top Global Brands, By Region, 2007

Company	*Brand value (US$ billions)*	*Country of origin*	*Main product or service*
Asian brands			
Toyota	24.8	Japan	Cars
Honda	15.8	Japan	Cars
Samsung	15	South Korea	Consumer electronics
Sony	10.7	Japan	Consumer electronics
Canon	9	Japan	Copiers, cameras
European brands			
Nokia	26.5	Finland	Cell phones
Mercedes-Benz	20	Germany	Cars
BMW	17.1	Germany	Cars
Louis Vuitton	16.1	France	Fashion accessories
Nescafe	12.2	Switzerland	Coffee
US brands			
Coca Cola	67.5	United States	Soft drinks
Microsoft	59.9	United States	Software
IBM	53.4	United States	IT services and consulting
GE	47	United States	Appliances, jet engines
Intel	35.6	United States	Computer chips

Source: *Business Week* (www.businessweek.com/brand) *and Interbrand* (www.interbrand.com).

"King of the Competition," a very appropriate name for a gaming peripheral that was designed to help gamers win! The English name was also kept on the packaging, both to allow for the global brand to have a presence in China and because Western-sounding products are considered better quality and more innovative than current local versions. Thus, the company enjoyed the best of both worlds.

Nationality and product image

Another element that can influence consumers' view of a product relates to what country it appears to come from. In light of intense globalization, as has been explained in Chapter 1, different countries have different reputations with regards to quality, innovation, fashion and style, and so forth. For example, if you were invited to select a set of dress suits or evening gowns from various designers around the world – Would you have a preference for French- or Italian-based designers, over Russian or Ethiopian designers? On the other hand, Russian vodka is known worldwide as being among the best in the world and exudes the appropriate quality, fashion, and style.

Nationality can play another role in product adaptation for different markets. In many countries patriotism runs high and "buying local" campaigns can offer compelling motivations for choosing one product brand over another. For this reason some foreign companies try to stress local content in their products or, in extreme cases, try to pass the product off as part of the local culture.

However, there is an exception to every rule, and any country can – over time – change their image. As an example, during the 1960s, Japan used to be known for cheap and poor-quality electronic products. Today, the Japanese are known to supply among the highest-quality products in many categories. The same transformation has been currently noticed regarding China. It is important to be aware of, and sensitive to, the perceptions of any target market towards the nationality of the supplier of the product, as it can significantly impact the consumer's perception of the product and, in turn, affect sales.

Lifelong costing

The true cost to the consumer of a specific product is made up of more than just the acquisition price. It also includes maintenance and service, potential upgrades, and accessories as well as the cost for disposing of the product at the end of its useful life. The calculation of the total cost associated with all these steps is known as "lifelong costing."

Many information technology products (whether hardware or software) are sold with either mandatory or optional service agreements and upgrade packages. Printers require a continuous supply not just of paper but also of toner. As is evidenced through the RoHS and WEEE directives of the EU, disposing of an industrial chemicals mixer is not as easy as leaving it out for the garbage truck; it may have to be delivered to a hazardous waste site for treatment, depending on local or regional bylaws.

Depending on the distribution partners, retail sophistication, and consumer expectations, the product proposition may change for any given market. A simple example might be including batteries or a flash card when selling digital cameras in Western Europe, where the consumer expects the product to work out of the box, as opposed to Asia, where often consumers feel they don't want to be forced into paying for "extra" products they can get for cheaper on their own.

Global Promotion

A company's methods for targeting certain customer segments, informing and/or trying to influence their buying decisions and reaching them with their physical product, represent their *promotion mix*. The ultimate objective of these marketing activities is to create the right combination of product specifications, product

TABLE 15.3 The Largest Global Ad Agencies

Rank	*Agency*	*Headquarters*	*Parent company*
1	McCann Erickson Worldwide	USA	Interpublic Group, USA
2	Ogilvy & Mather	USA	WPP Group, UK
3	Grey Worldwide	USA	WPP Group, UK
4	Euro RSCG Worldwide	USA	Havas, France
5	Saatchi & Saatchi	USA	Publicis Group, France
6	BBDO Worldwide	USA	Ornnicom Group, USA
7	Publicis	France	Publicis Group, France
8	JWT	USA	WPP Group, UK
9	Y&R Advertising	USA	WPP Group, UK
10	Lowe Worldwide	UK	Interpublic Group, USA

Source: http://adage.com/datacenter/article.

availability, and product/value awareness that will drive market demand in the target country.

Global promotional campaigns are usually conceived by global advertising agencies, as noted in Table 15.3.

When developing a promotional campaign, an MNE must consider the promotion objectives carefully in order to tailor all aspects of the marketing communications plan accordingly. Generating sales or profits is too general an objective for a specific campaign to be measured effectively. Four common objectives that MNEs may have are:

1. *Awareness*: An MNE may be introducing a brand new product to a market or, in fact, introducing the company brand and values themselves to a new market, in which case the first step is to make customers aware of this. This is often done through advertising (on television, radio, or print media), sponsorship, and so forth.
2. *Trial*: Even when consumers know that a product exists and that it could satisfy some of their needs or desires, it may take time for them to make the effort necessary to try it, especially when there are so many other products in the market competing for their attention, and their money. So the next step for an MNE is often to get the consumer to try the product at least once, with the belief that they will become repeat purchasers, and if they are very pleased, act to promote the product through word of mouth.
3. *Attitude toward the product or brand*: Many people in North America are familiar with Tylenol headache medication, so awareness is not an issue. However, advertisements are often used in order to change people's view of the product by associating good things to it, about it or in reference to its competitors. Similarly, Shell Gas corporation, an MNE with a global presence, which most consumers know through their franchise gas stations,

may consider advertising Shell's activities in protecting the environment or providing aid in Africa (very worthwhile causes). The customers demonstrate their approval (whether consciously or subconsciously) by taking the extra effort to fill up at a Shell station.

4 *Temporary sales increase*: For mature products or brands, where even attitudes are fairly well established and not subject to a cost-effective change, an MNE may choose to run a limited promotional offer to generate a short-term spike in sales of the product (the effect of this typically ends when the incentives for buying, that is, the promotional offerings, are removed). The motivation for this may be to sell off oversupply of certain inventory, test new pricing policies against competitors, or drive increased traffic into the stores who may also buy other items. In developing countries this can also be used on new products to bring people in to try a product they are not familiar with and might otherwise not take the time to try.

Promotional campaigns should consider media characteristics in targeted regions and markets, including literacy rate, percentage of households with television, radio stations and newspaper readership, as noted in Table 15.4.

There are two general strategies that MNEs follow (both separately and in combination) when planning the global promotion strategy for each product and target market: *push strategies* and *pull strategies*. These general strategies may be deployed separately or in combination.

Push strategies

Push strategies are designed by MNEs to encourage or pressure distribution channel partners to both carry and promote the manufacturer's product to the

TABLE 15.4 Media Characteristics in Selected Countries

	Literacy rate (percentage of population)	*Percentage of households with televisions*	*Radio stations per one million people*	*Newspapers per one million people*
Argentina	97	97	6.5	2.7
Australia	99	96	30	2.4
China	91	91	0.5	0.7
India	60	37	0.2	4.8
Japan	99	99	9.2	0.9
Mexico	92	92	13	2.9
Netherlands	99	99	15.2	2.1
Nigeria	68	26	0.9	0.2
South Africa	86	54	13.7	0.4
United States	99	99	46.7	5

Source: *CIA World Factbook*, www.cia.gov; World Bank, www.worldbank.org.

end customers. The idea is to "push" the product through the channel to the buyer. These strategies are often used with consumer products sold in grocery stores and department stores where impulse buying or placement and discounts are most effective. Depending on the manufacturer's strength, like brand recognition and marketing budget, different incentives, such as higher distributor or retailer margins, or marketing contribution funds, provide "encouragement" in the form of a higher compensation to the channel partners. If the manufacturer is especially powerful or has a near monopoly on the desired product line, the manufacturer can also threaten – the stick – to stop supplying to a group of channel partners, thereby depriving them of many customers who may choose to go to competing stores in order to have access to his product. An example of this kind of situation would be Apple with their successful hit product the iPod and its derivatives or the royalty rates demanded by George Lucas from the film distributors for his final trilogy of Star Wars.

Manufacturing sales representatives spend a good portion of their time with the various channel partners, especially retailers, promoting the advantages of the product, trying to influence product placement and the labeling around it and trying to keep on top of any, in-store promotional tactics that could lead to higher run rates (e.g., number of units sold per week) that would motivate all the channel partners to spend more of their attention at pushing their product line over the competing or alternative ones.

Pull strategies

In contrast, pull strategies are targeted at the end customers themselves and are meant to create buyer demand, which will in turn encourage channel partners to stock an MNE's products, and place them more prominently in the store or in their promotional publications. The idea is to generate enough buyer demand that it will "pull" products through the distribution channels to the end customers. Pull strategies include all forms of direct marketing to consumers, such as distribution of free samples, coupons, direct mailing, telemarketing or online campaigns, endorsements by influential figures (e.g., a famous athlete, musician or scientist), sponsorship of events that are relevant to the targeted customer segment, and advertising (which will be discussed in more detail below).

Pull strategies are often used for children's toys. The strategy is that creating demand directly with the children will in turn translate to demand from the parents (the principal buyers), who, in turn, create demand at the retail level, all the way through the distribution channel and back to the manufacturer.

Push vs pull strategy

The decision to use one general strategy over the other is rarely an obvious one and, depending on the objectives of the promotion, appropriate elements of both push and pull strategies are often combined. However, there are a number of factors that can dictate the appropriateness of one strategy over the other.

Type of product

A pull strategy works best with products that have a high brand loyalty. Buyers who are brand loyal know what they want before they go to the store and, when they arrive to shop, they go looking for that product (ignoring perhaps better deals from competing alternatives). On the other hand, buyers of inexpensive consumer goods who are not brand loyal will go shopping for a product, probably not even knowing which is best and will simply end up selecting the one that seems best priced or most visible (related to push strategies). Push strategies are also most relevant when a product is complicated or the sales cycle is long (e.g., industrial equipment or home stereo system, where a direct sales approach is needed to explain everything to the potential buyer and build a trusting relationship). These deals also tend to be more expensive ones.

Local distribution channel structure

It can be difficult or prohibitively expensive to implement a push strategy if the distributors or retailers have significantly more power than the manufacturers. It can also be difficult in markets where there are many intermediaries in the channel to get to the end customer, which means the manufacturer must identify and convince/motivate many different groups in the channel to carry their product and promote it. In such cases it may be easier to try to drive that motivation by using a pull strategy.

Availability/access to mass media

In developed countries there are sometimes regulations against advertising certain products in traditional mediums. For example, in North America it is illegal to advertise tobacco or hard liquor products on television or radio. In developing countries there are often very few forms of mass media available for companies to use to create awareness of a product and generate demand. Where there are limited televisions or even daily/weekly/monthly publications available to the average citizen, companies may try to work through billboards, radio or more direct grassroots approaches in local communities.

Taking these factors, as well as the promotional objectives, into account will help the international marketing manager to create the most appropriate promotional mix for every product and each situation. Note that in new or emerging markets awareness and trial tend to be the focus, whereas in developed markets the focus tends to be more on influencing people's attitudes or perceptions around the product.

International advertising

International advertising is any paid form of nonpersonal presentation and promotion of ideas, goods and services through mass media such as newspapers, magazines, television or radio, by an MNE, which transcends international boundaries.

As challenging as it is to develop an effective communications strategy around a product or service in a company's domestic market, trying to do so internationally is even more complicated. In the case of international advertising, the international marketing manager has to consider the differences among the different regions and countries of the world and decide whether or not each new market can be approached with a similar advertisement, whether or not the advertisement must be adapted for the different markets, or in some cases scrapped for something more locally appropriate and/or effective.

A Hellish Controversy

Boeing and Bell Helicopter get into trouble with an ad

An advertisement for a revolutionary new helicopter has caused a row in America. A computer-generated picture shows an Osprey aircraft (which can fly like a plane and hover like a helicopter) above a mosque, with soldiers being lowered down on ropes onto the roof. The copy says "It descends from the heavens. Ironically it unleashes hell". It also says "Consider it a gift from above". The ad was intended to show off the ability of the aircraft to get soldiers into tight spots, such as areas where there is house-to-house fighting.

The offending picture first appeared in the *Armed Forces Journal*. When senior managers at Boeing and Bell saw what had been put together by their Texas advertising agency, they immediately withdrew it from the magazine and from a number of other publications where it had been booked to appear.

But last week it was republished, in error, by the *National Journal*, causing an outcry from the Council on American–Islamic Relations, an Islamic civil-liberties pressure group in Washington. Its fear was that the ad conveys an impression that the war on terror is in fact a war on Islam. Both Boeing and its joint-venture partner, Bell Helicopter, have said in statements that the ad was ill-conceived, offensive and should never have been published. It seems the Bell executive who cleared the ad for publication was not authorised to do so.

The companies have orders worth $19 billion for the aircraft, which has had a long and troubled development, with three fatal crashes of early models. Their prompt response may limit the damage to them, but it might not stop extremists using the whole episode as anti-American propaganda. For such purposes, it is indeed a gift.

The vast majority of advertising that occurs in any one country is produced solely for that domestic audience. However, companies that serve multiple markets have good reasons to try and standardize as many aspects of the campaign across different markets. Standardization can help to contain costs, ensure a consistent message and brand image across all markets, and can save time by avoiding the necessity to develop new material for every country campaign. MNEs pursue this consistency by standardizing the basic promotional message, the creative concepts, graphics, and/or information content.

Although there are obvious costs, management attention, and time benefits to using a standardized advertisement campaign across all geographical markets, there are a number of factors that force MNEs to adapt certain aspects of their campaigns or in some cases develop completely new ones for certain local markets. First, *language barriers* force MNEs to ensure that translation of marketing communication is not only into the specific language category but also to the specific version spoken in the region. Second, *cultural barriers,* which are local biases, filter the information provided as part of a marketing campaign through a set of local beliefs, norms, and values. These subtle cultural differences can make an advertisement that tested well in one country unsuitable in another. Third, *local attitudes towards advertising* differ across regions and cultures, as observed by the degree of acceptance and openness to different frequency, intensity, and ubiquity of advertising across all mediums. Fourth, *advertising regulations* vary from one country to another both in terms of content and delivery: for example, some countries ban advertising for tobacco or alcohol on television.

1. *Local attitudes towards advertising*: People in different countries have different attitudes towards advertising in general. Americans are very accepting of commercials; in fact, every year many tune in to watch the Super Bowl half-time show just to watch the commercials (even if they are not fans of football). On the other hand, some Europeans can find advertising to be too crass or commercial. In many countries cable TV is not well developed and so other mediums (such as print media or radio) are the main channel for advertising.
2. *Advertising regulations:* Most countries have various rules and regulations on what types of products and services can or cannot be advertised, in what form, and in some cases at what times. For example, advertisements for cigarettes or hard liquor are banned on television in the USA, whereas in the UK advertising of alcoholic beverages on TV is allowed, but only after 9pm, based on the assumption that younger children will not be exposed to this.

Other promotional tools for international marketing

There are other promotional tools that may be considered which effectively overcome the challenge of promoting successfully in a market outside the MNE's home market.

Licensing or cross promotion

In order to position a new product in a new market in the right way, it can be useful to cross-promote it with a complementary product or with a product that addresses the same target demographic, has positive characteristics that can be associated with the new product, and leverages the perception and awareness of the local brand or product to introduce the new product. For example, one Chinese digital radio manufacturer introduced their product to the UK market by licensing a new digital radio station, branding the product, and cross-promoting it alongside the new station and its content, which was targeted at the same demographic as the product.

Online promotional tools

Online marketing can involve more than just setting up a website with company and product information. Targeted mailings, online advertisement, buying Google ad words and search engine optimization tools are all examples of tools MNEs can take advantage of to promote their products online to target markets outside their home territory. Of course, the success of such activities is still subject to the condition that the manager (and/or his advisors) is sufficiently familiar with the target market to understand how to adapt the message and the delivery medium (TV, radio, banners) to local market tastes, needs and wants.

One extremely innovative online promotional idea was used by the high-technology start-up company Mirabilis to promote their ICQ chat program online. The company sent out 1,000 e-mails to people with a message indicating that they had been randomly chosen to participate in a Beta testing of the new functions and features in the newest release of ICQ; they were further instructed to keep this test version strictly secret as part of their responsibilities as a selected reviewer. As expected by Mirabilis, many of the excited technology enthusiast's just had to share their "special status and beta product" with one or two close friends or associates. This quickly led to tens of thousands of downloads, broad acceptance and useful feedback, and ultimately to the development of the world's most widely used Instant Messaging service online, which was later acquired by AOL.

Global Distribution

Global distribution involves the planning, execution, and control of the physical flow of a product and/or service from the point of manufacture or supply right to the end customer, which transcends international boundaries. The physical path that the product follows is known as the *distribution channel*. Companies that work together to deliver goods to their buyers are known as *channel partners or intermediaries* (e.g., importers, agents, distributors, wholesalers, value-added resellers, retailers).

Global distribution decisions involve two levels of decisions that are interrelated with the overall product positioning decisions in the target country: (1) how to get the goods (or services) *into* the target country and (2) how to distribute the goods *within* the target country. The following provides a brief review of some important factors that influence the decisions raised by these two questions.

Distribution channels into a country

Two issues that can significantly influence the decision of how to get into a country are:

- product characteristics or product proposition;
- aligning the mode of transportation to the local product proposition in the foreign market.

Product characteristics

Clearly, shipping roses grown in Israel to the flower markets in the Netherlands is very different from shipping giant plush dolls from China to the Disney Theme

Park stores in the USA. In the first case, the shelf life of the flowers is very limited (even in a refrigerated compartment they begin to wilt within a week or two), making delivery into a country by ship questionable (depending on the distance between the two countries). Therefore, goods that are perishable, like food products, flowers, and alkaline batteries, dictate certain constraints regarding the physical deliver of the goods from one country into another.

On the other hand, a plush doll, not a very expensive item, doesn't wilt over time but does take up a lot of volume in a container, which makes it unlikely to be cost-effective to deliver by airfreight. A key measure that influences distribution decisions for getting a specific type of product into a country is the concept of the value density of a product. *Value density* refers to the value of a product relative to its volume and weight. Generally, the higher a product's value density the more likely it is that a central hub for global distribution can be considered. Most commodities, like cement and crude oil, have a low density ratio: i.e., they are heavy but not "valuable" if measured in shipping weight per cubic meter. Therefore, relative to their values, the cost of transporting these type of commodities is very high. Generally, these commodities are integrated into the manufacturing process as close as possible to the local market they are meant to be consumed in. Alternatively, very low-cost items like toothbrushes, gum or plastic bags may not be heavy but are so inexpensive per unit that shipping them by air would either price them out of the market or lead the supplier to sell at a loss. On the other hand, products such as diamonds or semiconductors have such a high value density that they are often produced in one central location that supplies globally.

Finally, in some cases it is possible to combine the two systems where there is a high value density item, such as a car, which is centrally manufactured as a baseline model and then customized locally with various options, such as a CD player, GPS system, auto-lock system or alarm system, at the dealer's facilities.

Aligning mode of transportation to product proposition

Two main criteria are used to evaluate different modes of transportation: cost and speed. For example, shipping something by air is very fast but also very costly. This can only be justified if the products are extremely time sensitive or very valuable, such that the transportation cost is relatively insignificant, or used as an exception. Shipping by air is important in order to get certain volumes of product to a market to support a promotion on short notice which the company believes may kick start a longer-term steady business to be supplied by cheaper methods. On the other hand, marine shipping does very well on the cost side but is very slow and exposes a company to issues such as large inventory buffer requirements and exchange rate risks. In extreme cases, inventory shipped by sea may become obsolete by the time it arrives. For example, in the textile fashion industry "fads" can last for only a few weeks or months. Of course, different modes of transportation may be combined: for example, marine shipping to a continent and land transportation using trucks for distribution over land.

To align the modes of transportation to the product proposition, especially when there is a service component involved, it is essential to choose the right combination of transportation modes. A consumer in Paris looking to purchase a computer may ask for a customized color for the case. This request can take eight weeks to deliver from China with one vendor, or 24 hours to assemble and deliver locally from a Paris-based distribution center with a different vendor. All other things being equal, the consumer will select either the lowest-priced Chinese product and wait, or be willing to pay a higher price for receiving the product within a day.

The final combination of modes of transportation that is selected to deliver a specific product to a specific location is ultimately made through an analysis of the product characteristics, the geographic location, the local infrastructure of the target country and, more recently, the MNE's selection of channel partners. For example, direct sales from a manufacturer to a retailer may involve the retailer taking possession of the goods at the factory and using its own logistics system to carry the product through to the consumer.

Distribution channels within a country

Once an international marketing manager decides on how the product will reach the target country, he must then consider how to distribute it within the country. There are two major considerations:

- the degree of coverage that the product needs in that market;
- the cost of distributing the product.

Degree of coverage

When promoting a product in a new market, international marketing managers must consider how broadly or narrowly they wish to cover the local market. The extent of the coverage is a function of the spread of demand in the market, that is, the extent to which the product appeals to all consumers across the country or only to a narrow niche in major cities; the maturity of the product in the market, that is, new product introduction vs a mature product; the degree of local adaptation or support that the product requires, such as, installation services for car hands-free telephone kits vs office supplies.

There are three different approaches to covering a particular market:

1. Exclusive coverage: This involves only one local intermediary or channel partner in the target market.
2. Selective coverage: This involves choosing a number of specific intermediaries or channel partners for different geographical areas or addressing different market segments.
3. Intensive coverage: This involves distributing the product through the largest number of different types of intermediaries or channel partners as possible.

Typically, exclusive coverage is used when introducing a new product to market or when the product requires a high degree of local support. This approach provides the most control of the distribution channel for the MNE and encourages the channel partner to commit more of their resources and money to develop the market for the product. As demand grows for the product, the distribution channels may expand to cover more of the target market segment or attempt to reach new segments across the market through selective and eventually even intensive coverage.

Selective coverage is often used for products that are typically sold through specialty stores and/or require a certain amount of support. For example, home stereo systems are often sold in specialty retail outlets where the sales staff provides expert advice and support.

For simple mass market products or ones that have matured in the market, such as chewing gum or paper towels, more intensive coverage approaches are typically taken in order to provide the broadest coverage possible of the target market. This generally results in longer supply chains, more intermediaries such as wholesalers or agents and less control over the local promotions since the intermediaries compete with one another.

Cost of distribution

The cost of distribution is typically a function of two factors: the channel length (i.e., the number of intermediaries in the channel) and the relative power of the MNE vis-à-vis its channel partners.

Channel length In a zero-level channel, also called direct marketing, the MNE sells direct to the consumer. An example of this would be PC sales by Dell online, which sells directly to the end consumer. A one-level channel places one intermediary (e.g., a retailer) between the MNE and the consumer. A two-level channel places two intermediaries (e.g., a wholesaler and a retailer), and so forth. The more intermediaries in the channel, the longer the channel, the more costly the channel becomes as everyone places a small charge or margin on the product for their services. For products that are very price sensitive, too long a channel can price the product right out of the market.

Relative power Beyond the charges or margins, intermediaries charge for their services, which are usually passed off to the consumer; there are other costs related to promotional activities that channel partners require of the MNE. For example, the distributor or retailer may request money to promote the product. Depending on the maturity of the product and the relative power of the MNE, channel partners usually demand significant participation in such costs. Of course, if the manufacturer is the sole supplier of the product or has a very strong brand, it can negotiate more effectively to push these costs back onto its channel partners. For example, if a grocery store believes that many people might choose to go to a competitor for their groceries if they could not find Heinz ketchup, the number one Ketchup brand in North America, the store may be more inclined to underwrite more of the promotion cost or conclude that it does not require it. Alternatively, if the MNE is planning an expensive marketing campaign around the product to consumers, the channel partners may often waive these requirements as they can see the money is being invested to generate awareness for both the product and their stores in another manner.

After-sales services and support

An integral part of the product proposition is the after-sales services and support that is available to a consumer who buys the product or service. In international marketing this is almost always something that needs to be provided locally and, therefore, often involves local intermediaries, agents, resellers, or distributors, unless the company has a local subsidiary. Some companies are more geared towards international marketing as well as after-sales services and support than others. Take, for example, Dell, which is considered to be a successful local leader in the North American computer market. As a result of its selling and after-sale services and support, Dell has managed to attract international customers, as can be seen from the insert.

Dell and The American University of Beirut (AUB)

(www1.us.dell.com)

The American University of Beirut (AUB) found that a time-consuming bidding procedure had a number of disadvantages, including delays in procurement cycles, limited configurations, and costly overheads, while buying PCs and servers from disparate vendors was resulting in ineffective after-sales services and costly support. AUB decided to move to direct purchasing with Dell. In doing so, it has improved the procurement processes for PCs and servers and delivered a computing environment that is highly available. Working closely with Dell's distributor in the Lebanon, Systems Equipment Telecommunication Services (SETS), the university has access to built-to-order products at competitive prices, while enjoying quality support and after-sales services.

After-sales services and support is today more relevant than ever before as producers plan for the complete "life cycle" of a product, owing to environmental regulations. In some products, after-sales services and support becomes a major revenue source for the MNE: for example, in cars or printers.

After sales services and support may include:

1 Installation, local customization, or set-up support.
2 Maintenance, warranty, and returns policies and processes.
3 Upgrades, cross-promotional sales, or up-selling of complimentary products and services.
4 After service recycling and disposal.

These issues are of particular importance for industrial sales and high-technology or sophisticated and expensive consumer items such as home networking products or cars. It can also be a source of competitive advantage. For example, many consumers may decide to stick with a particular brand of car on their next purchase as a result of the great service they have received from the local dealers and garages.

Customer relationship management (CRM)

Another aspect of after-sales services and support for existing and potential new customers involves the use of information technologies through call centers, customer service departments, and/or the company's website to track sales data, support issues and build more information on each of the respective customers of the product. These systems are meant to support the channel partners in the local country. In some cases these systems can serve the end customer directly, depending on the structure of the distribution channels, and the product proposition. As with the service element in general, after-sales services and support can be a source of competitive advantage both for the positioning of the product in overseas markets as well as for the coordination of the distribution channels interacting with the MNE.

Global Pricing Strategies

As with all other elements of the product proposition, the pricing strategy an MNE adopts for a specific product must be consistent with its overall international strategy. For example, if an MNE is pursuing a differentiation strategy, through innovation in their products or a strong brand, they could command a price premium in the markets they enter. However, if they are pursuing a low-cost strategy, commanding a premium will prove impossible as the product is unlikely to have any unique or outstanding features.

Worldwide vs dual pricing

A *worldwide pricing policy* establishes one price for all international markets, the worldwide price. In practice, this is a very difficult policy to pursue internationally for many reasons:

1 It is almost impossible to keep production costs consistent across the world for an MNE that manufactures in more than one country due to the local cost structure (e.g., wages or efficiency) and sourcing of inputs or local regulatory requirements (e.g., environmental protection rules or child labor laws). This has a direct impact on the selling price from various locations.

2 For MNEs that manufacture in only one location, allowing for consistency on production costs, variations in logistics, duty, and local distribution create a different cost structure for each market, making it difficult to decide on a best price for all markets that is both competitive and covers all the costs.

3 Local managers of subsidiaries may push to lower prices in their local markets in order to gain market share or adapt to local reference prices, expectations or regulatory requirements.

4 Fluctuations in currency rates can directly impact pricing by making product sold internationally more or less expensive as compared to the home country's cost, depending on whether the home currency increases in value as

compared to the target country's currency, making the price in the foreign market rise or drop, making the price in the foreign market also drop.

To address many of these issues, an approach known as dual pricing can be used. *Dual pricing* involves establishing a pricing policy that sets one price in the home market and another price for each target market.

To successfully apply a dual-pricing policy, an MNE must keep its domestic buyers, regional buyers, and international buyers separate. Otherwise, buyers from one market who discover that other buyers can get a cheaper price may cancel orders or undermine the pricing policy using *arbitrage* – buying a product from a market where it is priced low and selling it off in the countries where the product is selling for a higher price. For example, a Bluetooth headset intended for sale in China, surfaced in Europe when distributors found they could purchase the products in China and ship them to the UK at a lower price than buying them direct from the MNE that had a different pricing strategy for Europe. To avoid or discourage arbitrage, companies need to ensure that the price premium closely reflects the added costs required to serve that market and not leave too much room for buyers from other markets to profit from moving the products from another market to their own.

Although typically a product's price in a foreign market would be expected to be more expensive than in the local market, as a result of distribution costs and currency fluctuations, in some cases it could be priced cheaper in foreign markets. This occurs in the case where an MNE would consider foreign sales a "bonus" to the main business in the home country, where the product is priced in such a way as to cover the up-front investments in design and development, whereas the foreign pricing covers only the marginal costs for producing more product. These situations can often lead to accusations by local competitors of dumping (see below).

Pricing considerations

Many factors can influence a manager's pricing decisions, including transfer pricing, arm's length pricing, price controls, dumping, and parallel distribution.

Transfer pricing

Transfer pricing refers to the price charged for goods and services that are transferred among an MNE and its subsidiaries. It is common for the MNE and its subsidiaries to buy components, license technologies, or various finished products from one another. The subsidiaries can often enjoy lower prices than buying on the open market. This may be achieved by limiting the external suppliers that the MNE has to pay for.

At one time, when MNEs enjoyed a great deal of freedom setting transfer prices, they would often use this mechanism to optimize their overall tax burden. A subsidiary located in a country with a high corporate tax rate would charge a lower transfer price for its output to other subsidiaries, thereby reducing profits in that country and minimizing the tax burden for the group. Similar considerations were made regarding duties and tariffs for various products and services. Although this practice still exists today, it has been reduced significantly through increased international and government regulations.

Arm's length pricing

The manipulation of transfer prices for the benefit of maximizing the corporate profits of MNEs clearly has an adverse effect on the local economies that are being "cheated" of their tax revenue, which contributes to that local economy. This revenue is used to invest in the local infrastructure, build schools, telecommunication systems, and so forth – especially in developing countries, which are extremely dependent on this income. This has led many governments to begin regulating internal MNE pricing policies by assigning products approximate transfer prices based on their free market price. This is commonly referred to as the arm's length price – the price that unrelated parties charge one another for the specific product or service. For an MNE to apply a transfer price very different from this baseline requires the approval of the relevant government body.

Price controls

In addition to regulating transfer prices, governments in many countries use price controls to regulate certain types of products or services. Upper-limit price controls are typically designed to provide price stability in an inflationary economy, one in which prices are rising, or in some cases ensure certain products, like pharmaceutical drugs, are available to the broadest segments of the population. Companies with strong contacts or lobby groups in the government may argue for price control exemptions; others that do not have these advantages might focus on reducing costs in order to protect their profit margins.

Lower-limit price controls prohibit the sale of a specific product or service below a certain price. These controls are often used by governments to protect local competitors from less-expensive imports of international companies. Alternatively, such policies could be used to ward off price wars that could eliminate competition in a specific industry, such as telecommunications charges, leaving one MNE with a monopoly in a domestic market.

Dumping

In general, it is illegal to sell a product at less than the cost of producing it. Simply put, dumping occurs when the price of a product or service in an export market is lower than the price of the same product in the MNE's domestic market. As highlighted above in the description of dual pricing, export markets are sometimes considered as "bonus" markets for certain manufacturers and hence are priced to cover marginal costs and not the fully loaded costs of the product. In addition, certain companies, in an attempt to gain advantage vs the local competitors, may choose to aggressively undercut the price of their competitors even below cost, in some cases subsidizing this through their domestic sales, which are higher priced. In such cases, complaints by the local competitors can lead one country's government to charge another country's producers with dumping and impose anti-dumping tariffs on those products. Such tariffs are designed to punish the manufacturers of the offending nation by increasing the price of their products in the local market to a fairer level.

It is possible for an MNE to unintentionally be involved in dumping due to significant changes in exchange rates, which can lead to a situation where the products that are being sold in the foreign market are priced significantly less than in the domestic market even though the company has made no active decision to do so.

Parallel distribution

Another related issue for companies that sell in many different countries is the risk of parallel distribution, where a buyer sources product meant for one country into a different one to take advantage of the price differential. As already described, there are many reasons that the pricing for different countries could be different and parallel distribution poses a real problem for the international marketing manager, especially with the authorized distribution partners.

A few mechanisms can be performed to avoid or limit parallel distribution:

1. Create different packaging for the product in different markets.
2. Alternatively, every attempt should be made to maintain the price differentials and minimize the gaps in such a way as to make it less appealing for a parallel distributor to go to the extra effort necessary to bring an "unofficial" product into their market.
3. Limit the quantity that distributors in lower-priced markets can receive per order so as to limit the availability of the lower-priced products.

Such mechanisms should be used carefully as they can adversely affect market share and/or profitability in the "penalized" markets. One should ensure that the cure is not worse than the disease.

COUNTRY FOCUS

SINGAPORE

World Rank (EFI 2009): 2

Regional Rank (EFI 2009): 2

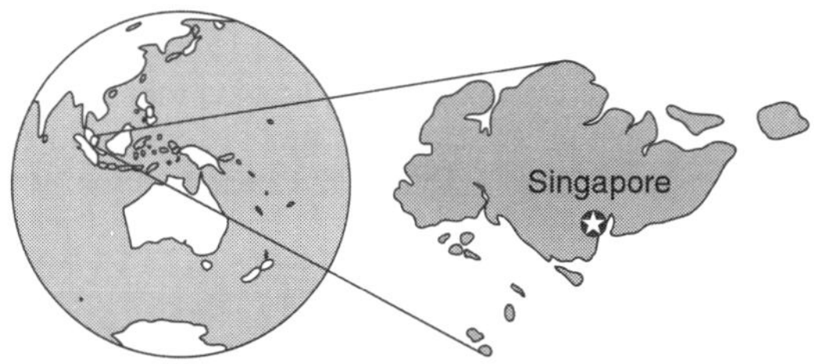

Quick facts

Population: 4.5 million

GDP (PPP): $200.5 billion; 8.2 percent growth in 2006; 6.4 percent 5-year compound annual growth; $44,708 per capita

Unemployment: 2.1 percent

Inflation (CPI): 2.1 percent

FDI inflow: $24.2 billion

2006 data unless otherwise noted

Economic Freedom Score

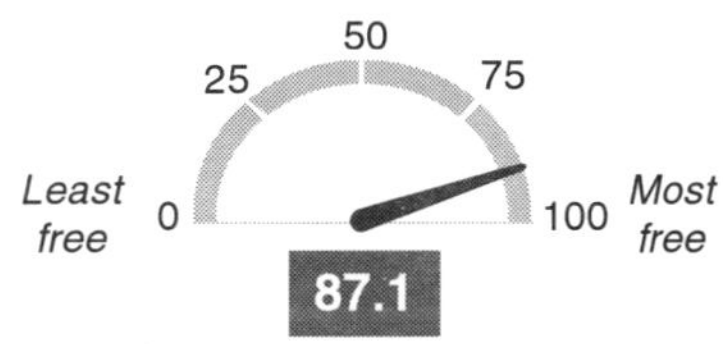

Singapore's economic freedom score is 87.1, making its economy the 2nd freest in the 2009 Index. Singapore is ranked 2nd out of 41 countries in the Asia-Pacific region, and its overall score is significantly higher than the world average.

Singapore's openness to global trade and investment has allowed its small economy to be one of the most competitive and flexible in the world. The Singaporean economy has shown a high degree of resilience, recording solid economic growth rates averaging over 6 percent in recent years. With an efficient business environment that is well maintained, Singapore has long benefited from vibrant entrepreneurial activity.

Singapore is a world leader in most facets of economic freedom. Regulations are straightforward, virtually all commercial operations are performed with transparency and speed and corruption is almost nonexistent. Both the income and corporate tax rates are competitive, and the overall tax burden is low. Foreign investment is welcome and given equal treatment. There are no tariffs, although nontariff barriers still limit overall trade freedom. Singapore's legal system is efficient and highly protective of private property. The labor market is highly flexible, facilitating employment, and productivity growth.

Background

Singapore is a nominally democratic state that has been ruled by the People's Action Party (PAP) since its founding in 1965. Certain rights, such as freedom of assembly and freedom of speech, remain restricted, but the PAP has also embraced economic liberalization and international trade. Singapore is one of the world's most prosperous nations. Its economy is dominated by its services sector, but the country is

(Continued)

also a major manufacturer of electronics and chemicals.

Business freedom – 98.3

The overall freedom to conduct a business is strongly protected under Singapore's regulatory environment. Starting a business takes four days, compared to the world average of 38 days. Obtaining a business license takes much less than the world average of 18 procedures and 225 days. Bankruptcy proceedings are easy and straightforward.

Trade freedom – 90

Singapore's weighted average tariff rate was 0 percent in 2006. Tariffs are generally low, but import restrictions, services market barriers, import taxes, import licensing, nontransparent regulations, burdensome sanitary and phytosanitary rules, weak enforcement of intellectual property rights, and export incentive programs add to the cost of trade. Ten points were deducted from Singapore's trade freedom score to account for nontariff barriers.

Fiscal freedom – 91.1

Singapore has low tax rates. The top income tax rate is 20 percent, and the top corporate tax rate is 18 percent, down from 20 percent. Other taxes include a value-added tax (VAT) and a property tax. In the most recent year, overall tax revenue as a percentage of gross domestic product (GDP) was 13.0 percent.

Government size – 93.8

Total government expenditures, including consumption and transfer payments, are low. In the most recent year, government spending equaled 14.4 percent of GDP. The state remains involved in the economy through Singapore's many government-linked companies. Plans to list state-owned energy and telecommunications enterprises have stalled in recent years.

Monetary freedom – 86.8

Inflation is low, averaging 1.7 percent between 2005 and 2007. The government influences prices through regulation and state-supported enterprises and can impose controls as it deems necessary. Five points were deducted from Singapore's monetary freedom score to account for policies that distort domestic prices.

Investment freedom – 80

Foreign and domestic businesses are treated equally, and nearly all sectors are open to 100 percent foreign ownership. Exceptions to Singapore's general openness to foreign investment exist in telecommunications, broadcasting, the domestic news media, financial services, legal and other professional services, and property ownership. The government screens investments for incentive eligibility. Government-linked corporations play a dominant role in the economy and may stifle investment. Residents and nonresidents may hold foreign exchange accounts. There are no controls or requirements on current transfers, payments, or repatriation of profits. Foreign ownership of certain landed properties is subject to approval, but there are no restrictions on foreign ownership of industrial and commercial real estate.

Financial freedom – 50

Singapore's financial sector is modern and competitive. Bank consolidations have left the country with three dominant banking groups. One of these three groups is the government-controlled Development Bank of Singapore, which is the largest and is publicly listed. The other two banking groups also have significant government-held minority shares. There were 113 commercial banks in mid-2008, 107 of them foreign. Foreign banks now have greater freedom to open branches and offer services, but the government seeks to maintain the domestic bank share of deposits above 50 percent, and the majority of domestic bank board members must be Singapore citizens and residents. License quotas for full-service foreign banks were eliminated in July 2005, and the quota for US wholesale banks was eliminated in January 2007. Foreign banks are allocated to three categories that specify the services they can provide: full service, wholesale, and offshore. Foreign firms compete aggressively in insurance, fund management, and venture capital. Capital markets are well developed, and the Singapore Exchange is increasing its ties with other Asian exchanges.

Property rights – 90

The court system is efficient and protects private property. There is no expropriation, and contracts are secure. Singapore has one of Asia's strongest intellectual property rights regimes, and foreign and local entities may establish, operate, and dispose of their own enterprises.

Freedom from corruption – 93

Corruption is perceived as almost nonexistent. Singapore ranks 4th out of 179 countries in Transparency International's Corruption Perceptions Index for 2007. The government enforces strong anti-corruption laws. It is a crime for a citizen to bribe a foreign official or any other person, whether within or outside of Singapore.

Labor freedom – 98.1

Singapore's highly flexible labor regulations enhance overall employment and productivity growth. The nonsalary cost of employing a worker is low, and dismissing a redundant employee is not burdensome. Regulations related to the number of work hours are very flexible.

Source: Adapted from Terry Miller and Kim R. Holmes, *2009 Index of Economic Freedom* (Washington, DC: The Heritage Foundation and Dow Jones & Company, Inc., 2009), at www.heritage.org/index.

SUMMARY

Global marketing strategy is an approach for answering the basic question about whether to market a product or service to foreign countries. In order to assess the attractiveness of a target market it is important to consider the market potential, financial and economic assessment and political and legal environment, and to understand the socio-cultural aspects of the market that may influence the positioning of the brand, product or service locally. An essential element of a global marketing strategy is the skillful, considered integration of the linkages across countries, products and functions that allow an MNE to tap the market potential worldwide.

Think local act local is the current evolution of the original adage "think global act local" and is based on the current experience of MNEs operating internationally. MNEs should

(Continued)

standardize their international marketing practices but they should adapt to local conditions. Sometimes the adaptations are just slightly modified promotional campaigns. However, at times, it may require the redesign of a new product altogether or opening up a brand new facility in the targeted locality, using local workers, as well as other adjustments.

Global product strategy deals with the issue of global standardization vs local customization. The strategy is based on the following elements: laws and regulations, cultural differences, brand and product names, nationality and product image, and lifelong costing.

Global branding involves the exploitation of global brands and the economies of global distribution across functions and divisions at the local level and a strong local management.

Global promotion deals with promotion mix, push and pull strategies, international advertising, and other promotional tools such as licensing or cross-promotion and online promotional tools.

Global distribution involves two major decisions: how to best transport the product to the target market and how to distribute the product locally within the target market. The second decision involves determining distribution channels within a country, degree of coverage, cost of distribution, after-sale services and support, and customer relationship management.

Global pricing strategies should be consistent with the overall international strategy, and may take the form of worldwide pricing or dual pricing. Issues considered include transfer pricing and arm's length pricing. Other localized requirements include price controls, dumping, and parallel distribution.

DISCUSSION QUESTIONS

1 What are the four issues that should be considered when devising a global marketing strategy?
2 What are the five issues that help in planning a global product strategy?
3 Explain the process of deciding on global distribution. Apply this decision process to a particular company you are familiar with.
4 What are the issues that are considered in global pricing?

EXERCISES

1 Identify two news articles from the *Wall Street Journal* (www.wsj.com), the *Financial Times* (www.ft.com), *Business Week* (www.businessweek.com), or *The Economist* (www.economist.com) and discuss how globalization affects the marketing decisions made by a well-known MNE. Repeat the above for a small and medium-sized enterprise (SME) or for a start-up venture.
2 Initiate a discussion with an executive of a local business. Discuss, internalize, and document the executive's decision process regarding international marketing, distribution, and after-sale services and support.
3 Choose an international company in the cell phone industry. Check its annual reports and find out what new cell phone models were introduced recently. Determine what international marketing issues are involved in this industry. In particular, identify what is involved in after-sale services and support on a global basis.

Bibliography

Batra, R. (1993). *The Myth of Free Trade*. New York: Charles Scribner's Sons.

Calantoni, R. J., Cavusgil, T., Schmidt, J. B., Shin, G.C. (2004). Internationalisation and the dynamics of product adaptation – an empirical investigation. *Journal of Product Innovation Management*, 21, 185–98.

Carvounis, C., Carvounis, B. Z. (1992). *United States Trade and Investment in Latin America: Opportunities for Business in the 1990s*. New York: Quorum Books.

Czinkota, M. R., Ronkainen, I. A., Tarrat, J. J. (1994). *The Global Marketing Imperative: Positioning Your Company for the New World of Business*. New York: NTC Publishing Group.

Dornier, P. P., Ernst, R., Fender, M., Kovvelis, P. (1998). *Global Operations and Logistics*. New York: Wiley.

Garber, P. M. (ed.) (1993). *The Mexico–U.S. Free Trade Agreement*. Cambridge, MA: The MIT Press.

Gregory, J., Wiechmann, J. (2002). *Branding Across Borders*. Chicago, IL: McGraw-Hill.

Gunter, B., Oates, C., Blades, M. et al. (2005). *Advertising to Children on TV: Content, Inputs, Regulations*. Augusta, GA: LEA Publishing Group.

Holt, D. B., Quelch, J. A., Taylor, E. (2004). How global brands compete. *Harvard Business Review*, September, 68–75.

Javalgi, R. G., Khare, V. P., Gross, A. C., Schever, R. F. (2005). An application of the consumer ethnocentrism model to French customers. *International Business Review*, 14, 325–44.

Kotler, P., Armstrong, G., Cunningham, P. H. (2005). *Principles of Marketing*, 6th edn. Upper Saddle River, NJ: Pearson Publishing.

Lustig, N., Bosworth, B. P., Lawrence, R. Z. (eds) (1992). *North American Free Trade: Assessing the Impact*. Washington, DC: the Brookings Institution.

Myers, M. B. (2004). Implications of pricing strategy – venture strategy congruence: an application using optimal models in an international context. *Journal of Business Research*, 57, 591–690.

Yip, G. (2003). *Total Global Strategy II*. Upper Saddle River, NJ: Prentice Hall.

Zou, S., Cavusgil, S. T. (2002). The GMS: a broad conceptualization of global marketing strategy and its effect on firm performance. *Journal of Marketing*, 66, 40–56.

Internet resources

www.export.gov/mrktresearch/index.asp – a US government export portal that includes country-specific market reports, industry sector analysis and marketing insights.

www.doingbusiness.org – a World Bank portal that provides snapshots of business climates in 145 countries, including investment regulations and policies and the ease of starting up and operating a business.

http://globaledge.msu.edu/resourcedesk/ – a resource desk at the Center for International Business Education and Research, Michigan State University that provides country insights and a directory of international business resources.

http://memory.loc.gov/frd/cs/list.html – the Library of Congress database presents information about more than 100 countries, including social, economic, political, national security systems and institutions.

https://www.cia.gov/library/publications/the-world-factbook/ – a CIA annual publication of country reports, including geography, people, government, economy, communication systems, military and transportation systems.

http://www.executiveplanet.com/index.php?title=Main_Page – the Executive Planet's International Business Culture and Etiquette guides that provide information about local customs in 49 countries.

16

International Accounting and Taxation

Learning Objectives

Following this chapter the reader will be able to understand:

1. The chronology of the accounting function around the world
2. The harmonization in accounting standards
3. The recording and translation in foreign currencies
4. Taxation systems around the world

Opening Case

FASB, Apple, and the Global Competitiveness of US Technology MNEs

New accounting rules put Apple and other US technology companies on equal footing with non-US peers

Regulators approved changes to accounting rules Wednesday that in the short term will make sales and profits seem higher at technology companies selling certain gadgets that blend hardware and software.

Under the old rules, companies like Apple Inc. had to spread revenue from the sale of an iPhone over two years, the estimated useful life of the device. That's because when Apple sells an iPhone, it agrees to provide software updates in the future.

Existing accounting rules require many software companies to divide up sales over the length of licensing contracts; until now, companies with hybrid hardware–software products were also guided by those standards.

The Financial Accounting Standards Board's (FASB's) latest changes mean that Apple, plus other smartphone makers, telecommunications equipment makers, semiconductor equipment manufacturers, and a host of others, will be subject to a less onerous accounting standard.

The new rules let Apple "unbundle" iPhone hardware from its software and report the hardware sales upfront. That makes it easier for investors to see how Apple did in any given period.

In the last quarter, for example, Apple said that if it were allowed to account for iPhone sales all at once, its sales would have been 17 percent higher and its profit would have been boosted by 58 percent.

"A lot of people really closely follow the reported revenues as the key measure of a company's performance. A company can provide disclosures, but people always go back to reported revenues," said Jay Howell, a partner at the accounting firm BDO Seidman LLP. Under the old rules, if the iPhone has an outstanding quarter – good or bad – investors might not be able to tell from the earnings report.

Howell said, "Apple will still have to account for software revenue over time, but that it makes up a small portion of the total sale."

The changes to the accounting rules go into effect in the middle of next year, though companies can put them into use immediately.

The FASB's decision also puts US companies on equal footing with overseas competitors, which already follow such accounting rules. With the old standards, a smartphone boom might seem to benefit a non-US company more in any given quarter because the US company could only record a fraction of its revenue.

Apple also used the drawn-out revenue recognition standard for Apple TV, a set-top box that delivers web content to televisions. But the

Cupertino, a California-based company recorded sales from Mac computers and iPods all at once, even though they, too, combine hardware and software.

"That was a business decision," Howell said. Because Apple sells support for Macs and iPods separately, it fits criteria for the all-at-once accounting. For the iPhone, because Apple didn't want to go back to buyers after a year and ask them to pay for support and upgrades, it was required to spread out the sales over time.

Source: Mintz, J. (2009). "New accounting rules mean boost to Apple, others." The Associated Press, Seattle. At http://www.thefreelibrary.com/.

Introduction

Multinational enterprises (MNEs) have long progressed beyond import–export types of transactions. Executives of MNEs are called to make decisions and/or report results based on reliable and timely information about accounting and taxation. In order to combine results from various sites around the globe, it is necessary to use a common methodology that considers each of the local accounting and taxation regulations, but still provides a global overview in a single currency.

Such analysis, regulation, and synthesis is critical to managing an MNE by allowing business results to be comparable and provide aggregate results to managers for decision making and to shareholders for assessing the health and potential of the company.

As indicated in Chapter 13, the actual flow of assets across national boundaries complicates the finance and accounting functions. In particular, the MNE must cope with differences in, among other things, inflation rates, currency controls, exchange rate fluctuations, custom duties, and corporate and individual taxation rates. One also needs to consider cultural issues. The financial executive has various traditional roles, including the measurement, the analysis and the communication of financial information used by top management. In addition, they are responsible for preparing the financial report for external stakeholders such as shareholders, regulatory bodies, and tax authorities. In an international context, the role of a financial executive is expanded beyond the traditional models. In particular, the international financial executive is required to evaluate potential acquisitions overseas, manage cash flow across international boundaries, hedge against currency, inflation and interest rate risks, and to seek new international sources of financing. Thus, the current-day international financial executive must have a broader perspective of international business than his domestic counterpart.

This chapter discusses some key accounting and taxation issues facing MNEs that conduct business overseas. In particular, the chapter describes different accounting standards and practices around the world and provides a way to harmonize them.

The Development of Accounting around the World

Challenges and evolution of international accounting

MNEs are challenged with various accounting standards and practices globally. Financial statements in various countries are different from one another. For example, it should be noted that North American- and European-based MNEs present two different formats for their balance sheet. On the one hand, the American-type balance sheet format carries the form of

$$\text{Assets} = \text{Liabilities} + \text{Shareholders' Equity}$$

On the other hand, the European format for a balance sheet looks like

$$\text{Capital and Reserves} = \text{Fixed Assets} + \text{Current Assets} - \text{Current Liabilities} - \text{Noncurrent Liabilities}$$

While the information transmitted in both formats is the same, the presentation is different in both cases.

Traditionally, accounting was defined as a service activity which provides quantitative information, primarily financial in nature, about economic entities helping with economic decision making. The accounting function was focused on identifying, recording, and interpreting economic events. The Financial Accounting Standards Board (FASB) is the private sector voluntary organization that determines accounting standards in the USA. The FASB requires that financial reporting provide information for the purposes of investment and credit decisions, assessment of cash flow projections, and evaluation of MNE resources.

The International Accounting Standards Committee (IASC), which is composed of professional accounting organizations, from over 100 countries, identifies the following main users of financial information: investors, employees, lenders, suppliers, customers, government organizations, and the general public. The identification of the main users of the financial information is important as it influences the type or format of the financial disclosure. As an example, Germany's main users of financial information have been the creditors: so the financial reporting was focused on the balance sheet, which details the MNE's assets. In the USA, the main users of financial information are investors: so financial information is focused mostly on the income or profit and loss statement. This heterogeneity amongst users of financial information across countries makes the development of a uniform set of accounting standards and practices challenging.

In Figure 16.1, the main factors affecting the development of international accounting standards and practices are listed. The relative importance of each one of these factors varies depending on the country and economic sector. These factors include:

- *Types of external users*: Creditors, investors, and security exchange officials can influence international accounting standards and practices followed by an MNE. For example, investors as well as creditors affect the development

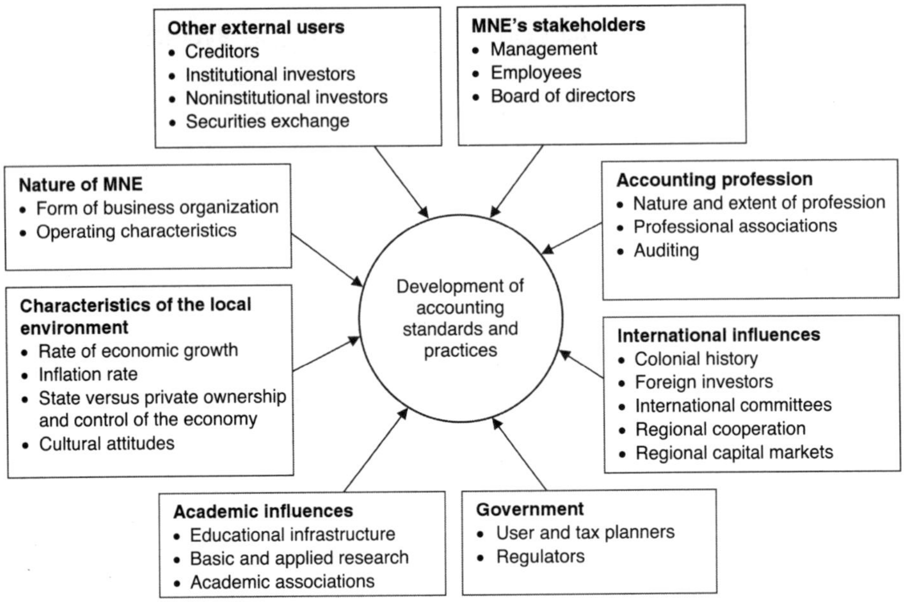

FIGURE 16.1 Factors affecting international accounting standards and practices

of accounting standards and practices. However, as suggested earlier, investors are much more influential in the USA and UK, while banks or creditors are more influential in Germany, Switzerland, and Japan.

- *The nature of the MNE*: This factor involves addressing questions such as how many operating units there are, in how many different countries or regions, the frequency at which transactions must be consolidated and reported, the location of the parent entity, and so forth.
- *Characteristics of the local environment*: This factor involves addressing questions such as what are the current and expected inflation rates, the relative importance of public vs private ownership in a given sector, the rate of economic growth, and local cultural attitudes.
- *Academic influences*: The involvement of academia in professional accounting bodies, the introduction and application of innovative reporting ratios, standards or harmonization techniques to promote better decision making, and transparency for shareholders.
- *Government*: Regulators and lawmakers affect accounting standards through legislation.
- *International influences*: Standards and practices that were instilled through the legacy of global empires. For example, accounting standards in India are greatly influenced by the legacy of the British Empire's rule over that region. In addition, this factor includes the development of regional financial information disclosure standards and practices that evolve over time.

- *Accounting profession*: The maturity of the profession in a given market dictates the amount of guidance and oversight of the profession and the development and sophistication of the standards and practices.
- *MNE stakeholders*: Managers, employees, and board members all contribute to the development of the company's standards and practices as they generate requirements for the purposes of reporting, control, and decision making.

Cultural differences in accounting

Culture affects accounting standards and practices. This is one reason for differences in accounting systems across countries. Financial reports provide information to businesses in a form unique to the local environment and thus the accounting system is environment-specific. There are five major environmental systems that influence cultural and social values, which in turn determine the form of financial information: the economic system, the political system, the legal system, the educational system, and the religious system (Figure 16.2).

The *economic system,* including the sophistication and level of technology in a given country, determines the complexity of its accounting system. For example, in an economically developed country intangible assets such as patents and copyrights have a greater value on the balance sheet than in countries where these types of assets either don't exist or are not respected. The intensity of ownership concentration of businesses in a country determines the extent of accounting and financial disclosure. For example, if ownership is concentrated within a few individuals or entities in a country, then there is no need for intensive disclosure across the wider public. If, however, ownership is distributed across a broad base of people, the need for intensive and broad disclosures is high. Furthermore, if a

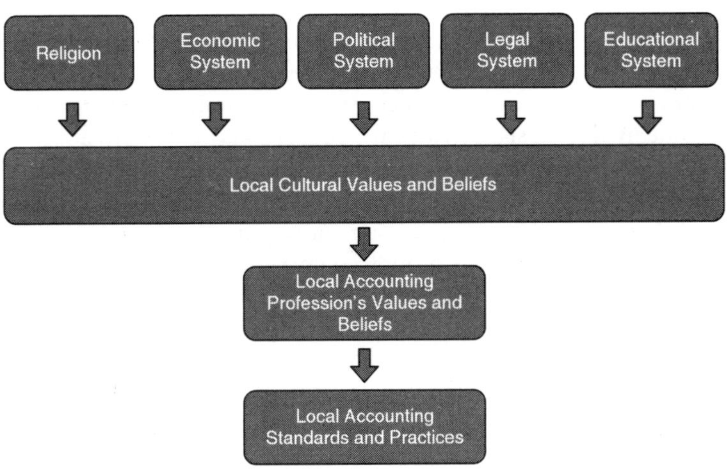

FIGURE 16.2 Environmental influences on accounting standards and practices

country has a high inflation rate, the accounting system should allow for inflation adjustments in reporting.

The *political system* of a country determines the broad economic policies and the business environment within which an MNE must interact. Different economic principles (e.g., emphasizing public over private industries or running a centrally planned vs a market-driven economy) can lead to different accounting standards and practices. Three common issues related to political systems that can impede the development of a robust accounting system and good business practices are political stability, heavy bureaucracy, and political corruption. The lack of political stability tends to carry over to a lack of economic stability, as the changing of governments or leadership each with its own agenda changes policy decisions, cancels previous agreements, and generally makes the process of decision making on local policies unclear. Another by-product of the political system can be excessively heavy or complex bureaucracies that create procedures and obligations that can delay the approval or implementation of large-scale projects by months or years, far beyond the capacity, patience or interest of an MNE. Finally, the issue of political corruption contributes to a situation where business interests are subject to the personal ambitions of political leaders whose motivations are less about the common good than their personal worth. Standard business practices and accounting reports become irrelevant in these situations and a robust and reliable set of accounting standards and practices is impossible.

The *legal system* in a country can have a direct impact on accounting standards and practices. In Western countries, accounting rules and regulations are part of legislation and governments take an active role in defining the requirements and enforcing them. In general, the concept of the "rule of law" in Western countries represents an ideology that is foreign to many Eastern countries (e.g., China), where the concept of written contracts is relatively new and contrasts with the traditional agreements based on personal relationships and understanding between individuals (generally considered too subtle and dynamic to be captured in a written document) as opposed to the written contracts which fundamentally represent a mistrust of individuals and governments and seeks to bind them to a static business agreement. As cross-border transactions and international business ventures grow, it becomes increasingly important to agree on a common understanding and commitment to written contracts which can accommodate the spirit of the agreement and abide by the legislative rules and regulations of Western countries. There are other ways in which the legal system can influence business practices in a given region. For example, in some Asian countries legal resolution of a case can take decades, which can greatly complicate agreements, resolution, and business activity. Finally, there is also the issue of judicial corruption in some countries, which, like political corruption, creates an environment that inhibits transparency, and fair business practices and within which comprehensive and reliable accounting standards and practices are unlikely to develop.

The *educational system* influences the development of accounting standards and practices as it dictates the level of literacy and capabilities of both the professionals who prepare the reports and the stakeholders who read and use them. Where the educational level is high, both groups are more sophisticated and professional with regards to the application of accounting standards and practices.

Religion can also affect basic accounting standards and practices. For example, in many Muslim countries the idea of interest on loans is considered unacceptable to Islam. Thus, different ways of presenting and communicating accounting information must be created when describing credit transactions.

These five local systems directly influence the accounting standards and practices by which an MNE performs its reporting and control. In some cases an MNE with operations in certain countries very different and unique from the common standards may choose to keep a second set of statements for the local stakeholders in addition to the primary statement for the use of the parent company and consolidated reporting.

One final note on cultural aspects in a particular region is that national boundaries and cultural boundaries may not always coincide and an MNE must be sensitive to how it chooses to address and integrate differences both globally and locally, where in some cases even the local culture may have a number of versions, depending on the specific location within the country.

Classification of accounting systems

One way to understand the accounting standards and practices in a given country is to study the evolution of its accounting system and the historical sources of influence. Figure 16.3 illustrates such a taxonomy.

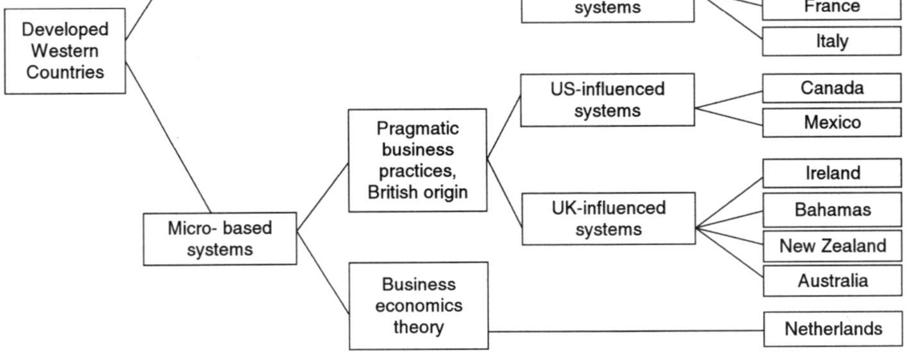

FIGURE 16.3 A taxonomy of accounting systems

Referring to most Western countries, the two main types of accounting systems are the macro-based and micro-based systems. The macro-based systems are shaped by governments more than the micro-based systems. The macro-based accounting systems are present in countries which have a robust legal system rooted in a systematic and codified legal system. These accounting systems also tend to be conservative and secretive about disclosure. As an example, Japan and Germany are law-based systems, while Spain and France are tax-based systems. Most of the centrally planned economies such as China belong to the macro-based category. Micro-based systems reflect pragmatic business practice and case law and are based on the British legal system. The USA is another example of a micro-based accounting system that is more transparent and relies less on legislated requirements than do the systems of Germany, France, and Japan. Canada and Mexico have a similar system to the USA. The British accounting system is also micro-based but it relies even less on legal influences than does the USA. Other countries that are similar to Britain are Australia, New Zealand, Ireland, and the Bahamas, all former Commonwealth members. It is interesting to note that Canada (another former Commonwealth member) has aligned with the US system more closely than with the British system.

The taxonomy makes it very clear that MNEs need to issue and consider the various accounting systems in the countries in which they operate, including the content and format of financial statements and accompanying footnotes to these statements. In most countries the four most common financial statements required are the income statement (otherwise known as a profit and loss statement), a balance sheet, a cash flow statement, and a statement of stockholder's equity. These four statements are usually required when an MNE lists its shares in any capital market. There are five ways in which financial statements differ from one country to another: language, currency, financial statement format, extent of footnote disclosures, and the type of financial statements. In most cases English is the language of choice for most MNEs vying to offer shares in capital markets overseas. As to the currency used in financial statements, the most common currencies used are euros and US dollars. However, other currencies may be used such as British pounds and Brazilian reals. It is highly recommended to have the financial statements use the currency of the parent entity for the benefit of the senior executives and the investors from the home market.

While Generally Accepted Auditing Standards (GAAS) are dictated and explicitly noted, the more problematic area is with the Generally Accepted Accounting Practices (GAAP). As an example, part of GAAP is the disclosure contained in the footnotes to financial statements. In MNEs with shares listed on US capital markets such as the NASDAQ (originally National Association of Securities Dealers Automated Quotations) or the NYSE (New York Stock Exchange), the greater transparency as compared to a country such as Germany, dictates more extensive footnote disclosures. MNEs should be intimately familiar with the local version of GAAP in whichever capital market they are listed in order to conform to these practices.

Harmonization in Accounting Standards

Several forces are at work that leads to the alignment of accounting standards in various countries. First, as MNEs work across multiple countries they need to make financial statements more compatible and comparable across markets. Second, regional trading blocs are making efforts to harmonize accounting standards as part of their political and economic integration.

The ambitious unification program of the European Union (EU) is reflected in its efforts to harmonize the accounting systems of all member countries. The European Commission (EC) has issued directives instructing member countries on the type and format of financial statements that European corporations must use. The directives also dictate the measurement basis on which the financial statements are based and stress the importance of consolidated financial statements. The EU's directives require that financial statements present a true and fair overview of corporate operations. The EU's influence goes beyond the European countries, as other countries in Europe (including former communist bloc countries) seek to adopt the EU's accounting directives in preparation for joining the EU.

International harmonization efforts are divided between organizations that represent governments and organizations that represent the accounting profession or other interest groups. In particular, one should note the work done by:

- The International Accounting Standards Committee (IASC), representing the accounting profession.
- The Organization for Economic Cooperation and Development (OECD), representing governments of member nations.
- The International Federation of Accountants (IAFC), which focuses on establishing international audit standards as well as dealing with education, ethics, and management accounting.

The IASC is the most active international body with the responsibility to create international accounting standards. The standards are intended to be applied in all economic sectors and all countries. The IASC has created processes to propose, assess, and issue such international standards. As of now, the membership approaches approximately 150 professional accounting organizations from over 100 countries. Officially, the IASC has adopted two main objectives:

- To formulate and publish accounting standards for use in the preparation and presentation of financial statements and to promote these standards globally; and
- To improve and harmonize accounting standards and procedures relating to the preparation and presentation of financial statements.

Figure 16.4 describes the development process of IASC international accounting standards, including the intensive consultative nature of the process. This consultative process aims to generate the voluntary acceptance of the developed standards.

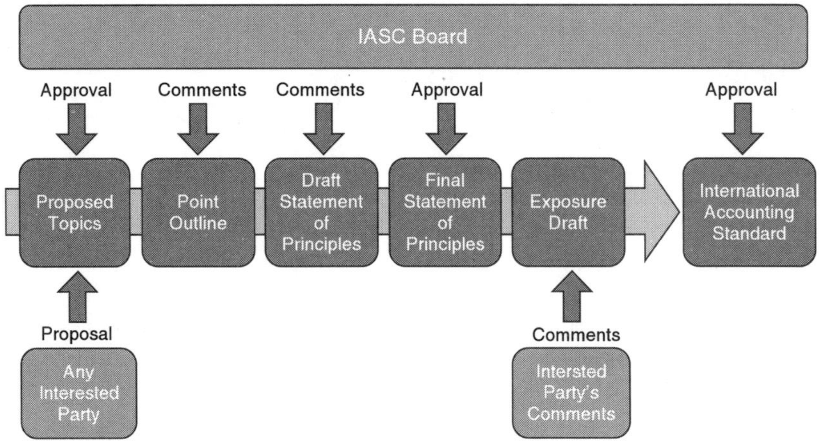

FIGURE 16.4 Development process of IASC international accounting standards

The OECD is a significant organization supporting the harmonization of accounting because most of the world's largest MNEs are based in OECD member countries. The OECD countries produce about two-thirds of the global economic output. The OECD's efforts to harmonize international accounting standards are part of the organization's focus on economic growth and development. Of particular value are the OECD's surveys of accounting practices in member countries and its assessment of conformity of such practices.

Of particular interest to the development of international accounting standards is the case of the USA. Since the US stock market is the largest stock market in the world, the US accounting standards dominate. Since international accounting standards – such as the ones issued by IASC – should be accepted globally, it is mandatory that the US Securities Exchange Commission (SEC) will accept these standards. However, there are still too many differences between the IASC GAAP and US GAAP and discussions continue.

One should note that in many countries around the world, apart from the USA, nations have adopted the international accounting standards and published them as their own national standards: such is the case for Singapore, Kuwait, Thailand, and Mexico. In other countries, national standards have been structured using the international accounting standards intensively: such is the case for Brazil, India, Portugal, and Taiwan.

Accounting and Financial Crisis

29 June 2009

Charlie McCreevy, the EU Commissioner for Internal Market and Services, spoke on issues relating to the economic and financial crisis before the Institute of Chartered Accountants in Ireland in Dublin on 26 June 2009. His comments on accounting included the following:

> As you all know, the role of accounting rules has become the subject of heated debate. But we remain convinced that the international standard-setting system is the best way forward. And this is not solely an EU view. It is also the view of the G-20. Accounting rules did not cause the crisis but it is fair to ask did they amplify it? We need to look at what has happened and see if the rules need to be adjusted so as to strengthen financial stability.

Source: http://www.iasplus.com/pastnews/2009jun.htm.

As the insert indicates, the role of the IASC and the need to harmonize accounting systems has not changed, even in light of the 2009 financial crisis.

Transactions and Translations in Foreign Currencies

For a complete treatment of foreign currency transactions and translations, the reader is referred to Chapter 13. As a matter of course, MNEs should record properly the value of assets, liabilities, revenues and expenses which are measured in foreign currencies.

National and international standards dictate the way in which foreign currency transactions are documented in the USA. Companies should follow the foreign currency transactions recording instructions of the Financial Accounting Standards Board. The FASB requires MNEs to record the initial transaction at the spot exchange rate that is in effect on the transaction date and record receivables and payables at subsequent balance sheet dates at the spot exchange rate on those dates. Any foreign exchange gains or losses that are a result of carrying receivables or payables due to exchange rate changes are recorded directly to the income statement. Other countries may recognize transaction losses but do not recognize gains in their profit and loss statements. Some other countries may allow a loss that occurs from a major devaluation to adjust the value of an asset rather than transfer the loss directly to the income statement.

The process of restating foreign currency financial statements into US dollars is termed translation. The aggregation of all translated financial statements into one statement is termed consolidation. Translation in the USA is done in two steps: first, MNEs format the foreign currency financial statements into statements that conform to US GAAP; second, MNEs translate all foreign currency amounts into

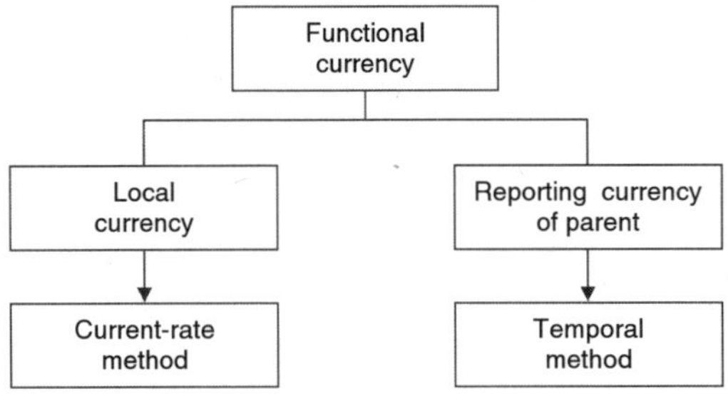

FIGURE 16.5 Translation methods according to FASB satement No. 52

US dollars. The particular rules regarding such a translation of foreign currency financial statements is contained in FASB Statement No. 52. As illustrated in Figure 16.5, FASB Statement No. 52 dictates two methods for translation of foreign currency financial statements into dollars: the current-rate method and the temporal method. The particular method used depends on the functional currency of the foreign operation. The functional currency is the currency of the primary economic environment in which the MNE's subsidiary operates. For example, if the largest MNE subsidiary operates in India, the primary economic environment of the Indian subsidiary is India and the functional currency is India's rupee. Factors that can help management determine the functional currency are stated by FASB and include cash flows, sales prices, expenses, financing, and transactions within the MNE. If the functional currency is that of the local operating environment, the MNE may use the current-rate method, which dictates that the MNE translates all assets and liabilities at the current exchange rate (the spot exchange rate on the date the balance sheet is published). All income statement items are translated at the average exchange rate over the reporting period.

If the functional currency is the MNE's parent currency, the temporal method should be used. The temporal method dictates that only monetary assets such as cash and receivables, and liabilities are translated at the current exchange rate. Inventory and property, plant and equipment should be recorded using the historical exchange rates: namely, the exchange rates that were in effect when the assets were acquired.

Other MNE Reports

As of late, innovative corporate reports have evolved to include environmental reports. Several stock exchanges dictate the filing of such a report. The environmental report is not part of the financial statements; however, it is considered to be an indication of good corporate citizenship to publish such reports. The report usually lists corporate-wide environmental programs and information about recycling and raw material and energy usage. While there is no mandatory environmental disclosure requirements such as the ones that exist for financial reporting purposes, several formats for environmental reports have evolved. These formats do not include quantitative information but do report on issues related to the environment, health, and safety. Triple bottom line reporting attempts to describe the social and environmental impact of MNEs' activities in a measurable way. There are currently few standards for measuring social and environmental impacts of an MNE. The phrase was coined by John Elkington, cofounder of the business consultancy SustainAbility. The Royal Dutch/Shell Group was one of the first MNEs to adopt the triple bottom line reporting scheme.

Taxation

MNEs are faced with the task of tax planning on an international basis since it may affect profitability and cash flow. Taxation is affected by some of the most strategic and significant MNE decisions, including:

- FDI location
- international operations such as export/import licensing agreement
- legal form of a new subsidiary
- method of financing, including debt or equity
- method of determining transfer prices

Taxation is highly dependent on the locality in which the MNE operates. In most cases it includes both corporate and individual taxation systems. In order to gain tax advantages of exporting, an MNE based in the USA may set up a foreign sales corporation (FSC) which engages in exporting of products and services. An FSC may be qualified as such if it maintains a foreign office, operates under foreign management, maintains a permanent set of books at the foreign subsidiary, conducts foreign economic processes, and is defined as a foreign corporation. In such a case, the foreign subsidiary, the FSC, is exempt from US corporate tax. A similar reduction in the tax rate is applied towards MNE dividends.

MNEs are using transfer prices in order to manage their tax rates effectively. A transfer price is a price on goods and services sold by one subsidiary of an MNE to another. Since the price between the two subsidiaries may be determined by head office, it can be set such that the difference between the selling and buying price is so small that it greatly reduces exposure to taxation. MNEs may also set arbitrary transfer prices for competitive reasons or because of restrictions on currency flows. If the MNE parent ships products at a low transfer price to a subsidiary, the subsidiary is able to sell the products to local customers for less, improving the competitiveness of its products in the local market. If a country in which an MNE's subsidiary resides has currency controls on dividends, the parent MNE may siphen off more hard currency by shipping in products at higher transfer prices. Needless to say, the transfer prices may be audited by the governments in these localities and the transfer price policy may be challenged.

Another taxation issue is the issue of double taxation. MNEs may have a problem when they earn income in a foreign country and are required to pay taxes in both the foreign country and the parent's home country. In many countries laws were put in place to allow for credit for income taxes paid to a foreign government. Such is the case for US-based MNEs. When a US parent entity realizes a foreign-generated source of income such as dividends, it may pay US tax on that income and the US internal revenue service allows the parent MNE to reduce its tax liability by the amount of foreign income tax already paid.

Tax planning

Since taxes affect both profits and cash flows, they should be considered as part of the strategy of the MNE. If a US-based MNE decides to export, it can set up an FSC, as explained earlier, to reduce its tax burden. When an MNE based in the USA decides to set up operations in a foreign country, it may do so through the creation of a foreign subsidiary. If the parent company expects the foreign-based operations to show a loss for several years, it should incorporate this subsidiary since the parent MNE can deduct the subsidiary's losses against its current year's income. An MNE's strategy may also lead to an investment decision that involves the allocation of appropriate financing, both debt and equity. It is clear that both debt and equity financing affect taxation. Funds invested in a subsidiary overseas should be defined as being debt- or equity-financed funds, which will determine the form of expatriation of the funds by way of dividends and interest payments to the parent entity. Obviously, the tax rate on dividends and interest payments may be different.

An MNE which tries to maximize its cash flow worldwide should record profits in tax-haven or low-tax countries. This may be done by carefully assessing and selecting a low-tax country or location for the initial investment, and setting up subsidiaries in tax-haven countries where it can receive dividends and manage its transfer pricing strategy carefully. For example, a parent company can shelter income from one jurisdiction where taxation rates are higher by using a tax-haven subsidiary located in a low-tax country, as illustrated in Figure 16.6. Common examples of tax havens are Luxembourg, the Channel Islands, and the Bahamas.

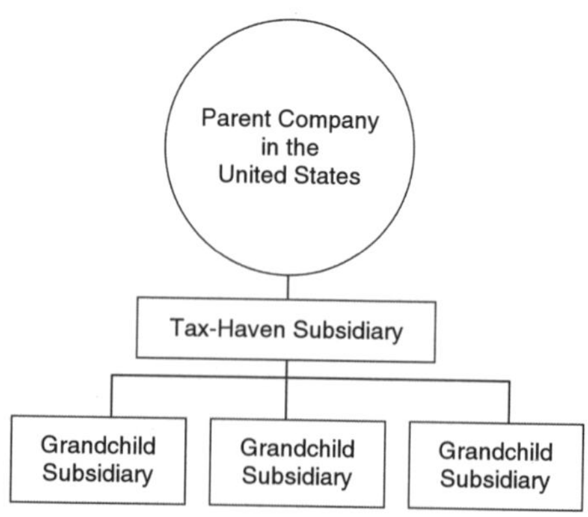

FIGURE 16.6 Tax sheltering methods

Knowledge of taxation rates and taxation systems may help MNEs' executives reduce the overall taxation bill. Countries may have unique systems for taxing earnings of foreign subsidiaries of their domestic MNEs: for example, France taxes only domestic source income, whereas other nations; such as Germany and the UK, tax the profits of foreign branches as well as the dividends received from foreign subsidiaries.

In various countries around the world and in most Western European countries a value-added tax (VAT) has been established. The VAT is a consumption-type tax, as it is dependent on the amount of purchases that a company or individual buys. The VAT is collected by the local corporate entities that sell goods and services in the local market. The funds collected by the corporate entities are then transferred to the local government taxation offices. MNEs may deduct the VAT paid to local suppliers from the VAT collected from its local customers. As the name implies a VAT means that each independent corporate entity is taxed only on the value it adds at each stage of the manufacturing process. Thus, for a company that is vertically integrated, the tax rate applies to its net sales since it owns the entire manufacturing process end to end.

The VAT rates vary from one country to another despite efforts to harmonize it.

COUNTRY FOCUS

CHILE

World Rank (EFI 2009): 10

Quick facts

Population: 16.8 million

GDP (PPP): $242.4 billion 3.2 percent growth in 2008 4.5 percent 5-year compound annual growth $14,465 per capita

Unemployment: 7.8 percent

Inflation (CPI): 8.7 percent

FDI inflow: $16.8 billion

2008 data unless otherwise noted
Data compiled as of September 2009

Regional Rank (EFI 2009): 1

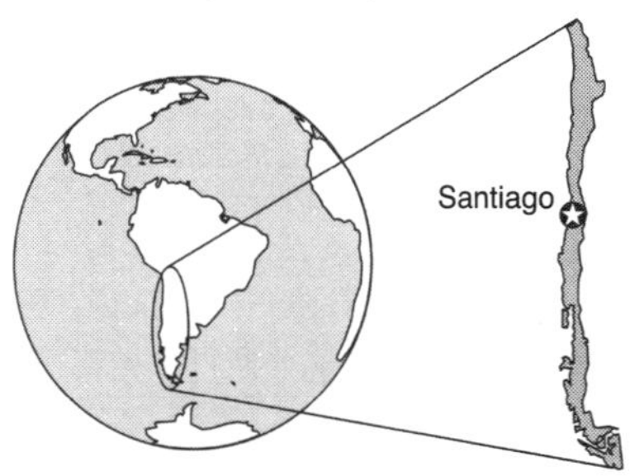

Economic Freedom Score

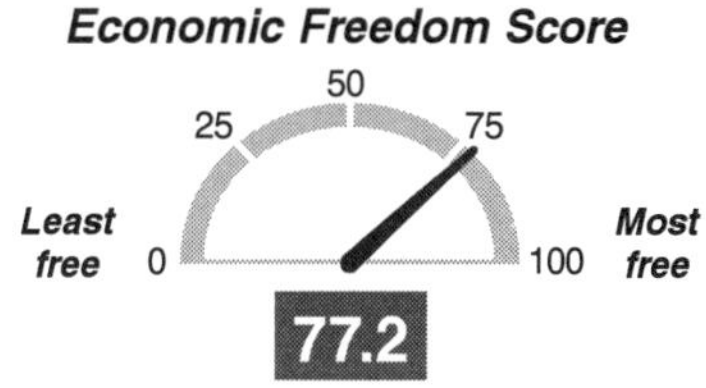

(Continued)

Chile's economic freedom score is 77.2, making its economy the 10th freest in the 2010 Index. Its overall score is 1.1 points lower than last year, reflecting small declines in six of the 10 economic freedoms. Chile enjoys the highest degree of economic freedom in the South and Central America/Caribbean region.

Openness to global trade and investment and a dynamic private sector have facilitated steady economic growth. Chile has pursued free trade agreements with countries around the world. The financial sector is diversified and stable compared to other regional economies, and prudent lending and regulations have allowed the banking sector to withstand the global financial crisis with little disruption. Other institutional strengths include transparent and stable public finance management and strong protection of property rights, although protection of intellectual property rights still needs to be strengthened.

Chile trails behind other comparable economies in business freedom, fiscal freedom, and labor freedom. Income taxes on individuals remain burdensome. Although overall regulatory licensing is easy, bankruptcy procedures remain cumbersome and costly.

Background

Since 1990, successive governments, though left-of-center, have largely maintained the market-based institutions and policies established under the 17-year rule of General Augusto Pinochet. Socialist President Michele Bachelet's coalition government has done so as well, although her rhetoric emphasizes income equality over freedom. Chile is the world's leading producer of copper, and exports of minerals, wood, fruit, seafood, and wine drive GDP growth. An Economic and Social Stabilization Fund manages taxes on copper revenues to maintain social spending during downturns. Chile belongs to the Asia–Pacific Economic Cooperation forum and has signed or is negotiating trade agreements with China and other Pacific Rim countries to supplement its agreement with the U.S. It also is on track to become the first South American country to join the Organisation for Economic Co-operation and Development.

Business freedom – 64.8

The overall freedom to establish and run a business is relatively well protected under Chile's regulatory environment. Starting a business takes an average of 27 days, compared to the world average of 35 days. Obtaining a business license takes the world average of 18 procedures and less than the world average of 218 days. Bankruptcy procedures can be burdensome and lengthy.

Trade freedom – 88

Chile's weighted average tariff rate was 1 percent in 2008. Chile is phasing out price bands for wheat, flour, and sugar, but approval requirements and stringent sanitary and phytosanitary regulations on imports of agricultural products and processed food, import bans, import taxes, export subsidies for some sectors, and issues related to the protection of intellectual property rights add to the cost of trade. Ten points were deducted from Chile's trade freedom score to account for nontariff barriers.

Fiscal freedom – 77.5

Chile's income tax rate is well above average, but its corporate tax rate is well below average. The top income tax rate is 40 percent, and the top standard corporate tax rate is 17 percent. Other taxes include a value-added tax (VAT) and a property tax. In the most recent year, overall tax revenue as a percentage of GDP was 18.9 percent.

Government spending – 89.6

Total government expenditures, including consumption and transfer payments, are low. In the most recent year, government spending equaled 18.6 percent of GDP.

Monetary freedom – 73

Inflation has been high, averaging 7.2 percent between 2006 and 2008. Many prices are determined in the market, but the government controls prices for utilities, and price bands for certain agricultural products remain in effect. Ten points were deducted from Chile's monetary freedom score to adjust for measures that distort domestic prices.

Investment freedom – 80

Foreign and domestic investments generally receive equal treatment. The Ministry of Economy reviews foreign investment and sets the terms and conditions for contracts involving foreign direct investment. Foreigners may invest in fishing companies and media only if their countries have reciprocity arrangements with Chile. Regulation tends to be transparent and efficient. Residents and nonresidents may hold foreign exchange accounts, and there are no restrictions on repatriation. There are few controls on current transfers and capital transactions. The government can expropriate property for public or national interests, on a nondiscriminatory basis and in accordance with the due process of law.

Financial freedom – 70

Chile's financial system is among the region's and the world's most stable and developed. Reforms that include capitalization requirements and shareholder obligations have increased competition and widened the range of operations. Twelve foreign banks and 13 domestic banks compete on an equal footing. The four largest banks control about 65 percent of total assets. The state-owned Banco Estado is Chile's third largest bank and accounts for about 15 percent of assets. Credit is issued on market terms. Domestic and foreign banking and insurance companies receive equal treatment. Chile's liberal capital market is the region's largest. Legislation to enhance access to financing for individuals and firms was passed in April 2009. The banking system has withstood the global financial turmoil well because of prudential lending and sound regulations.

Property rights – 85

Private property is well protected. Contracts are secure, and courts are transparent and efficient. Expropriation is rare, and owners receive compensation. Intellectual property rights laws and regulations are substantively deficient, and IPR enforcement is inadequate. Principal concerns involve protection of pharmaceutical patents and test data and copyright piracy of movies, music, and software. In 2008, the government created the National Industrial Property Institute to streamline IPR procedures.

Freedom from corruption – 69

Corruption is perceived as minimal. Chile ranks 23rd out of 179 countries in Transparency International's Corruption Perceptions Index for 2008. Contractual agreements are the most secure in Latin America, and local public administration is generally considered honest. Nevertheless, the ruling coalition is increasingly accused of corruption. Chile has ratified the Organization of American States Convention Against Corruption and the OECD Convention on Combating Bribery. Judicial corruption is rare.

Labor freedom – 75.4

The nonsalary cost of employing a worker is low, but dismissing a redundant employee is relatively costly. The labor market has become more rigid as regulations and minimum wage increases have exceeded overall productivity growth.

SUMMARY

Executives of MNEs need to make decisions and report financial results based on reliable and timely information in all geographical jurisdictions.

The international financial executive is charged with the same duties and responsibilities as a local financial executive but needs to also consider exchange rate fluctuations, expropriation risks, customs duties, tax rates and methods of determining taxable income, levels of sophistication of local accounting personnel, and local as well as home-country reporting requirements.

The actual flow of assets across national boundaries complicates the finance and accounting functions. In particular, knowledge of Generally Accepted Auditing Standards (GAAS) and Generally Accepted Accounting Practices (GAAP) should be adhered to in recording and reporting the economic transactions of the business in every jurisdiction.

North American- and European-based MNEs follow two different formats for reporting results: for example, the American format for balance sheet presentation is Assets = Liabilities + Shareholders' Equity, while the European format is Capital and Reserves = Fixed Assets + Current Assets – Current Liabilities – Noncurrent Liabilities.

The Financial Accounting Standards Board (FASB) is one of the organizations that determines accounting standards in North America. The International Accounting Standards Committee (IASC) helps to structure international accounting standards, with the aim of harmonizing the accounting systems globally.

Accounting standards are fashioned so as to provide the necessary information to financial information users: that is, investors, employees, lenders, suppliers, customers, government agencies, and the general public.

There are eight factors affecting the development of accounting standards and practices in a given country: external users of financial information, internal users, the accounting profession, international influences, government, academic influences, the local environment, and the nature of the MNE itself.

Germany's major u sers of financial information have historically been creditors, so that accounting has focused more on the balance sheet, which contains a description of the MNE's assets and liabilities. In North America, the major users of financial information are investors, so that accounting has focused more on the income statement, otherwise known as the profit and loss statement.

Culture is a major influencing factor on accounting standards and practices, including the measurement and disclosure rules. Disclosure defines what, and in what format, information will be provided in the annual and interim reports by MNEs to external users of financial information.

There are five environmental factors that define the culture of a given country and thus affect the nature of the national accounting standards and practices: religion, economic system, political system, legal system, and the educational system.

Optimism and conservatism in an accounting sense reflect the degree of caution MNEs exhibit in valuing assets and recognizing income. Countries that are more conservative, from an accounting point of view, tend to understate assets, and income.

There were efforts to classify accounting systems around the world. A possible taxonomy consists of four levels. The first level distinguishes between macro-based and micro-based systems. The macro-based systems lead either to law-based systems such as practiced in Japan and Germany or tax-based accounting systems such as can be found in Spain, Belgium, or France. The micro-based systems lead to either a UK- influenced accounting systems, such as those practiced by former Commonwealth countries, or to US-based systems, such as the one practiced by NAFTA members.

Since MNEs engage in international activity, they must deal with both recording transactions globally as well as translating these transactions in order to create consolidated reports. The two primary methods for translation are the current-rate method and the temporal method.

According to FASB Statement No. 52, the financial statements of foreign companies are translated into dollars by using the current-rate or temporal method. According to the current-rate method, all balance sheet accounts (except owners' equity) are translated into dollars at the current exchange rate in effect on the balance sheet date. All income statement accounts are translated at the average exchange rate in effect during the period.

Taxation rates for both individuals and corporations vary from jurisdiction to jurisdiction. MNEs must be familiar with these rates in order to plan their cash flows and investments in such a way as to minimize the tax burden on the MNE.

International tax planning has a strong impact on the choice of location for the initial investment, the legal form of the new enterprise, the method of financing, and the method of setting transfer prices.

MNEs may use a tax haven as a means to shelter income from its international subsidies so that the tax burden overall will be minimized.

DISCUSSION QUESTIONS

1 Venturing overseas requires the financial executive to start recording the transactions based on at least GAAS and GAAP in two jurisdictions. Discuss the organizational implications and operational implications of the same.
2 Compare and contrast the role of the various professional accounting organizations, such as the FASB, IASC, etc.
3 What are the main challenges facing the accounting profession regarding the harmonization of accounting standards and practices globally?
4 In what way did the world financial crisis affect international accounting standards and practices?

ACTION ITEMS

1 Select one EU-based MNE and a North American-based MNE. Compare and contrast the reporting of financial results in both their respective balance sheets and income statements.
2 Select a country and analyze the environmental factors that have influenced the development of the local accounting standards and practices.
3 Select an MNE based in a country whose currency experienced significant appreciation or depreciation of value during 2009. Assess in what way this volatility affected its financial results and how it reported the effect of the exchange rate fluctuations in the financial statements.
4 Assuming you are a financial executive in an MNE, how would you reconcile operating a global supply chain exploiting low-cost inputs with the various taxation rates across various jurisdictions? Consider the role of transfer pricing and the reporting jurisdiction of the financial results.

Bibliography

Alexander, D., Archer, S. (2009). *2009 International Accounting/Financial Reporting Standards Guide*. Boisbriand, Quebec: Coh Inc.

Antill, N., Lee, K. (2008). *Company Valuation under IFRS, Interpreting and Forecasting Accounts Using International Financial Reporting Standards*, 2nd edn. Petersfield, Hampshire, UK: Harriman House.

Bazley, J. S., Nikolai, L. A., Grove, H. B. (1995). *Financial Accounting: Concepts and Uses*. 3rd edn. Cincinnati, OH: South-Western College Publishers.

Caban-Garcia T. (2009). The impact of securities regulation on the earnings properties of European cross-listed firms. *International Journal of Accounting*, July 25.

Cairnes, D. (1999). *FT International Accounting Standards Survey*. London: Financial Times Business.

Chang, C., Huey-Lian S. (2009). Crossed-listed foreign firms' earnings informativeness, earnings management and disclosures of corporate governance information under SOX. *International Journal of Accounting*, 44 (2), June, 217–17.

Choi, F., Meeks, G. (2008). *International Accounting*, 2nd edn. Saddle Creek, NJ: Pearson.

Coke shuffles global management, but Ivester Mum on Successor (1999). *Wall Street Journal*, interactive ed., October 29.

Ernstberger, J., Vogler, O. (2008). Analyzing the German accounting triad – "Accounting Premium" for IAS/IFRS and U.S. GAAP vis-à-vis German GAAP? *International Journal of Accounting*, 43 (4), December, 339–86.

Frederick D., Choi, S., Meek, G. K. (eds) (2008). *International Accounting*, 6th edn. Upper Saddle River, NJ: Pearson Education.

Godfrey, J. M., Chalmers, K. (eds) (2007). *Globalization of Accounting Standards*. Cheltenham, UK: Edward Elgar.

Hodgdon, C., Tondkar, R. H., Adhikari, A., Harless, D. W. (2009). Compliance with International Financial Reporting Standards and auditor choice: new evidence on the importance of the statutory audit, *International Journal of Accounting*, 44 (1), March, 33–55.

Hoffman, W. H., Raabe, W. A., Smith, J. E., Maloney, D. M. (2000). *West Federal Taxation: Corporations, Partnerships, Estates, and Trusts*. Cincinnati, OH: South-Western.

International Accounting Standards Committee (1998). *International Accounting Standards*. London: IASC.

Kieso, D., Weygandt, J. (1998). *Intermediate Accounting*, 9th edn. New York: John Wiley & Sons.

Markarian G., Pozza L., Prencipe A. (2008). Capitalization of R&D costs and earnings management: evidence from Italian listed companies. *International Journal of Accounting*, 43 (3), September, 246–67.

Nobes, C. (2004). *Comparative International Accounting*. Upper Saddle River, NJ: Prentice Hall.

Radebaugh, L. H., Gray, S. J. (1997). *International Accounting and Multinational Enterprises*, 4th edn. New York: John Wiley & Sons.

Soltani, B. (2007). *Auditing: An International Approach*. Upper Saddle River, NJ: Prentice Hall/Pearson Education.

Stickney, C., Weil, R. (1997). *Financial Accounting: An Introduction to Concepts, Methods, and Uses*, 10th edn. Fort Worth, TX: The Dryden Press.

Tarantino, A. (ed.) (2008). *Governance, Risk, and Compliance Handbook: Technology, Finance, Environmental, and International Guidance and Best Practices*. Hoboken, NJ: Wiley.

US Tax Treaty Developments (1996). *Deloitte & Touche Review*, February 5.

Webb, K., Cahan, S., Sun, J. (2008). The effect of globalization and legal environment on voluntary disclosure. *International Journal of Accounting*, 43 (3), September, 219–45.

Williams, J., Haka, S., Bettner, M., Carcello, J. (2010). *Financial and Managerial Accounting: The Basis for Business Decisions*, 15th edn. New York: McGraw–Hill/Irwin.

GLOSSARY

Absolute advantage is the ability of a country or MNE to produce a particular good at a lower absolute cost than any other country or MNE.

Accounting is a process of communicating financial information by collecting, presenting, and analyzing financial data. The accounting information is used by management, investors, and other stakeholders to make appropriate business, operational, and investment decisions.

Accounting standards include the forms, conventions, and rules accountants follow in recording and summarizing transactions and in preparing financial statements, such as balance sheet and profit and loss statement.

Active or aggressive reciprocity occurs when a country applies retaliatory measures until the other country fulfills its obligations.

Antitrust regulations are designed to assure free market environment that provide a variety of products at a fair price by devising institutions and processes that prevent corporations from coordinating market sharing, fixing prices, and creating a monopoly over certain products or services.

Arbitrage is the purchase and sale of a currency, or other interest-paying security, in different international markets. It occurs whenever differences in price exist between markets for the exact same product, clever buyers leverage the differences to buy in one market in order to sell at higher margins in other markets.

Arm's length pricing is the manipulation of transfer prices for the benefit of maximizing the corporate profits of MNEs, which can also result in loss of tax revenue to a host country's economy.

ASEAN is a geo-political and economic organization whose aim it is to accelerate economic growth, social progress cultural development, and protect peace and stability in the region and amongst its member nations. It was formed in 1967 by Indonesia, Malaysia, the Philippines, Singapore, and Thailand. It has since expanded to include Brunei, Burma (Myanmar), Cambodia, Laos, and Vietnam.

Ask quote is the price the bank is willing to sell the foreign currency.

Ask rate is the exchange rate at which he bank sells a currency to its customer.

Asset market model suggests that a currency will be in more demand and hence will likely appreciate in value if the flow of funds into other financial market of the country, such as equities and bonds increases and vice versa.

Backwards integration involves a company acquiring control or a significant stake in one or more of their suppliers in order to increase productivity or lower costs for a given product or service by having deeper integration and/or more control over key suppliers.

Balance of payments explains the currency value and, thus, the exchange rate by the value of tradable goods and services, ignoring the increasing role of global capital flows.

Balance of trade is the difference between the value of exports and imports of goods and services.

Balance sheet is a summary of the financial condition of an enterprise and includes information regarding assets, liabilities, and ownership equity. The balance sheet may be compiled for the local subsidiaries as well as for the MNE as a whole, through a process of translation and consolidation.

Barter is the direct and simultaneous exchange of goods between two parties without a cash transaction and may occur between individuals, governments, firms, or between a government and a firm, all from two different countries.

Basic services distribution system can be used to supply simple and standardized products at low service levels through a nondedicated distribution system with an unskilled workforce.

Berne Convention of Literary and Artistic Work automatically extends protection of a copyright holder in one signatory country to all others, so that the copyright needs to be registered in only one office of a signatory country.

Bid-ask spread is the difference between the bid and ask price.

Bid quote is the price at which the bank will buy the foreign currency.

Blue Ocean Strategy is a business strategy developed by Kim and Mauborgne in 2005 and leads to MNE's high growth and profits by creating new demand in an uncontested, new, market space, as opposed to competing head-to-head with other suppliers for known customers in an existing industry.

Born global corporation are corporations that start out with a global focus.

Boycott is the stopping of imports of all or some goods and services from a specific country.

Buyback arrangement occurs when a firm provides a local company with inputs for manufacturing products to be sold in international markets, and agrees to take a certain percentage of the output produced by the local firm as partial payment.

Buy local campaigns are initiatives to promote local products and services at the expense of all imported goods and services.

Buy rate is the exchange rate at which the bank buys a currency.

Capacity planning is the process of analyzing and assessing the ability of a company or department to produce enough output (goods or services) to fulfill the demand of a given market.

Capital budget includes initial cash flows, operating cash flows, and terminal cash flows.

Capital budgeting is the process of evaluating the financial viability of an individual investment opportunity for the MNE, such as an investment in a development project, real estate, stock, or a joint venture in a foreign market.

Capital market is a system which allows for the allocation of capital resources in the form of debt and equity, according to their most efficient use by providing borrowers and investors with a marketplace in which money may be lent to borrowers and invested by investors.

Capital structure determines the proportion of equity capital and debt capital which would provide the most appropriate form of financing for the MNE.

Cash flow types are operating cash flows, including transfer pricing, licensing fees, overhead expenses, and financing cash flows, both loans and dividends.

Cash management policies include home country policies, host country policies, and cross-border policies and include the expected interactions between the MNE's subsidiaries and their local buyers and suppliers and the cash flow interactions within the various MNE entities themselves.

Cash pooling is using the cash reserves held by subsidiaries around the world in a centrally planned fashion to reduce interest charged on loans, use economies of scale, and exchange rate exposure.

Co-management arrangement is an alliance in which cross-national partners collaborate in training, production management, information systems development, and value-chain integration, complementing the MNE's managerial skills to run a foreign operation.

Co-marketing arrangements provide access to a new customer base for all parties to the arrangements.

Common market is an economic integration whereby countries remove all barriers to trade and the movement of labor and capital between themselves but establish a common trade policy against nonmembers.

Comparative advantage is the ability of a country or MNE to produce a particular good or service at a lower opportunity cost than any other country or MNE.

Comparative production cost is determined by the production process technology as well as the cost of the production factors, such as labor, land, capital, and natural resources.

Concurrent engineering is a work method that takes a cross functional team of designers, engineers, production staff, quality staff, and so forth and has them working closely together in an iterative manner from the initial design through to the launching of a new product to market. This contrasts with the traditional method of working, called "waterfall," wherein each step (i.e., design, engineering, production, quality) is done sequentially.

Consolidated financial statement is the result of first, restating foreign currency financial statements in one currency (e.g., US dollars) and, second, the combination of all the translated financial statements into one statement.

Contracted services distribution systems is required when providing a standardized product that requires a high level of service. In this case the distribution system can be fairly standard but to support the high service levels the distribution system would require a network of after sales service and repair centers and a dedicated and highly trained workforce for the call center (e.g., mobile phones).

Convertible eurobonds are eurobonds which may be convertible to stock at a specified price per share prior to maturity.

Corporate and individual property rules are of importance to MNEs, as they may limit 100 percent foreign ownership of assets. In the USA and other countries, a controlling majority of shares of airlines, radio, and television companies are not allowed because they are considered to be of strategic importance.

Cost strategy involves a set decision to create efficient facilities, cost and overhead reductions, and cost minimization in areas such as sales services, advertising, and R&D.

Counter purchase is a reciprocal buying agreement whereby one firm sells its products to another at one point in time and is compensated in the form of the other firm's products at some future time.

Countertrade is a form of trade in which a seller and a buyer from different countries exchange merchandise with little or no cash or cash equivalents changing hands. This is also viewed as a form of flexible financing or payment in international trade.

Crawling peg system is based on measured change of the exchange rate over time, practiced by Argentina, Hong Kong, Iceland, among others.

Cross listing of shares is issuing MNE's equity shares on one or more foreign stock exchanges in addition to its domestic exchange.

Cross rate is the currency exchange rate between two currencies, both of which are not the official currencies of the country in which the exchange rate quote is given in.

Cultural orientation is a component of the environmental briefing that focuses on social, political, legal, and economic topics.

Culture assimilation is training performed in order to introduce the expatriate to the values, attitudes, manners, and customs of the target country. Often used when someone is given little notice about a posting abroad.

Culture shock is a psychological process affecting executives, as well as other employees assigned overseas, that is characterized by homesickness, irritability, confusion, aggravation, and depression.

Culture shock, reverse, is the psychological process of readapting to the executive's home culture when returning from an assignment overseas.

Currency arbitrage is an instantaneous purchase and sale of a currency in different markets for profit.

Currency discount trading is if the forward rate of a currency is lower.

Currency futures contract is a contract which requires the exchange of a specific amount of money on a specific date at a specific exchange rate, where the terms and conditions are fixed and not changeable.

Currency option is a right to exchange a specific amount of a currency on a specific date at a specific rate.

Currency premium trading is if the forward rate of a currency is higher than its spot rate.

Currency speculation is the purchase or sale of a currency in the expectation that its value will change up or down and will, thus, generate a profit.

Currency swap is a foreign-exchange agreement between two parties to exchange aspects (namely the principal and/or interest payments) of a loan in one currency for equivalent aspects of an equal in net present value loan in another currency; see Foreign exchange derivative.

Current-rate method (or closing rate method, as termed by IASB) requires translating all assets and liabilities on the balance sheet at the current exchange rate, which is the spot exchange rate. Items of income, or profit and loss statement, are translated at the average exchange rate. The equity is translated at the rates in effect when the MNE issued capital stock and declared accumulated retained earnings.

Customer relationship management (CRM) systems provide an infrastructure that maintains close watch over customer needs, complaints, and expectations in order to introduce design changes, offer new product features, develop new service capabilities, and provide an effective operational support.

Customs union is an economic integration whereby countries remove all barriers to trade among themselves and establish a common trade policy against nonmembers.

Debt financing may be done through international bank loans, the euronote market, and the international bond market.

Debts investment in capital markets are loans that government and nongovernment organizations take in exchange for a commitment to pay the lenders an interest on the principal amount during the term of the loan.

Decruitment is a process of reducing an MNE's workforce.

Diamond model, developed by Michael E. Porter, explains why particular industries become competitive in particular locations based on six factors that interact with each other to create conditions where innovation and improved competitiveness occurs: factor conditions; demand conditions; related and supporting industries; firm strategy; structure and rivalry; government; and chance.

Differentiation strategy is focused on creating a product or service that is perceived as being unique, through the creation of design or brand image, improved features, increased dealer networks, and distinguished after-sale service and support.

Direct quote is a foreign exchange rate quoted as the domestic currency per unit of the foreign currency. In other words, it involves quoting in fixed units of foreign currency against variable amounts of the domestic currency.

Discounting is a short-term financing technique by which a local bank discounts a company's trade bills and provides a loan as a certain percentage of the total trade bills' value, considering time value of money.

Distribution channel is the physical path that the product follows. Companies that work together to deliver goods to the buyers are known as channel partners or intermediaries.

Dual pricing policy involves establishing a pricing policy that sets one price in the home market and another price for each target market. This can only be successful if the MNE can keep its domestic buyers separate from its international buyers otherwise the company risks arbitrage.

Dumping is selling a product at an unfairly low price which is defined as the domestic price relative to the production costs. It occurs when the price of a product or service in an export market is lower than the price of the same product in the MNE's domestic market. This can happen when an export market is treated by the MNE as a "bonus" market and the product is priced to cover only marginal cost, not the total cost for development that is used in the home market. This may also happen unintentionally due to a significant change in exchange rates.

Early movers are MNEs that enter a foreign market, in a significant way, first and, as a result, command greater market power, more opportunities, and more strategic options than late entrants.

e-Commerce is the conduct of transactions to buy, sell, distribute, or deliver goods and services over the internet. The e-commerce transactions are business to business (B2B), business to customer (B2C) or customer to customer (C2C).

e-Commerce localization entails the customization of websites to the country or region as well as the local adaptation of the supply chains and distribution networks involved in e-commerce.

Economic exposure is a risk related to how MNE's long-term cash flows are positively or negatively affected by any unexpected changes in exchange rates.

Economic union is an economic integration whereby countries remove barriers to trade and the movement of labor and capital, establish a common trade policy against nonmembers, and coordinate their economic policies.

Economy of scale is the reduction of manufacturing cost per unit as a result of increased production quantity during a given time period.

Educational system influences the development of accounting standards and practices as it dictates the level of literacy and capabilities of both the professionals who prepare the reports and the stakeholders who read and use them.

Embargo involves stopping of exports to a designated country.

Environmental briefings are used to inform expatriates about the local environment of their destination country prior to arrival. This may include information on local housing, healthcare, transportation, schooling, currency, and climate.

Equalizing effect of technology provides a leveled playing field for MNEs and SMEs internationally, as technological advancements drive common opportunities, common standards, and a robust foundation for more innovative and competitive business models.

Equity instrument is a form of financing where, the organization issues ownership rights to the investors, in the form of shares, in exchange for a claim against future financial gains (or losses) of the organization.

e-Readiness provides a snapshot of the state of a given country's information and communications technology (ICT) and the ability of its consumers, businesses, and the government to leverage ICT, including wireless connectivity, to their benefit.

EU common market, also known as the single market, describes the set of common economic policies that the 27 countries in the European Union countries share to promote the free circulation of goods, capital, people and services within the EU, as well as the customs and external tariffs union that is applied to any goods and services being imported into the

EU by the member countries. Note, not all EU countries have adopted all policies. However the long term objective is to work towards a larger common economic trading bloc.

Eurobonds are underwritten by an international syndicate of banks or securities firms, sold exclusively in countries other than the country in whose currency the issue is denominated, and carry straight fixed rate with a fixed coupon, a set maturity date, and a full principal repayment upon final maturity. Eurobond is issued outside the country in which it is denominated. A Eurobond may be issued by Argentina, denominated in US dollars and traded in the UK and France.

Eurobond market is a source of debt financing for MNEs that seek capital outside of their home market.

Euro-commercial paper (ECP) is a short-term debt obligation of an MNE where maturity is usually one, three or six months.

Eurocurrency market encompasses all the world's currencies that are deposited outside their countries of origin.

Eurodollars is a certificate of deposit in US dollars in a bank outside of the United States.

Euro-medium-term notes (EMTN) are short-term debt obligations of an MNE where maturity ranges from nine months to a maximum of ten years.

European Parliament, representing EU countries, consists of 600 members elected by popular vote within each member nation every five years and conducts its activities in Brussels, Belgium, in Strasbourg, France, and Luxembourg.

Europounds are British pounds deposited elsewhere in the world.

Exchange rate quote is based on the quoted currency and the base currency, where the quoted currency is the numerator and the base currency is the denominator.

Expatriate, also termed "expat," is an employee or an executive of an MNE sent to work in a country other than the country of his or her legal residence.

Expatriate, home-country national, is an expatriate who is a citizen of the country where the MNE is headquartered.

Expatriate, third-country national, is a citizen of a country other than where the MNE is headquartered or where the foreign subsidiary is located.

Export controls are set for products with a national security potential that may have both military and civilian use.

Export intermediaries are third parties that specialize in facilitating imports and exports, offering limited services, extensive services and/or assuming total responsibility for marketing, and financing exports.

Export management company (EMC) is an intermediary that acts as the corporates export department, usually engaged by SMEs to handle foreign shipments, prepare export documents, and deal with customs offices, insurance companies, and commodity inspection agencies.

Externality occurs when the actions of an organization, such as pollution or noise, directly affect the environment of another organization.

Factors affecting accounting standards are external users of financial information, internal users, the accounting profession, international influences, government, academic influences, the local environment, and the evolution of MNEs.

Factor-intensity reversal occurs when the relative prices of labor and capital change over time, which changes the relative mix of capital and labor in the production process of goods from being capital or labor intensive.

Factoring (or "forfeiter" in the USA) is the sale of a MNE's accounts receivable to a financial institution.

Field experience involves visiting the culture, walking the streets, and becoming absorbed by the target location. The idea is to expose the individual to the "daily life" in the target country.

Financial Accounting Standards Board (FASB) is a non-for-profit organization that the accounting profession in North America has created to disseminate the rules of GAAP reporting and to change the rules of GAAP reporting as required.

Financing strategies of MNEs are aimed at maximizing the consolidated after-tax profits of the MNE by choosing the tax-minimizing jurisdiction, selecting a corporate vehicle for a financing issue, and selecting tax-minimizing mode for profit transferred from the subsidiary back to the parent company.

Five forces model is a framework for industry analysis and business strategy developed by Michael E. Porter of Harvard Business School in 1979. It describes five forces that determine the competitive intensity, and therefore attractiveness or overall profitability, of a market.

Fixed peg system is when the exchange rate is pegged at a particular level, practiced by North Korea and Cuba.

Floating exchange rate system is where a currency's value is allowed to fluctuate according to the foreign exchange market.

Focus strategy involves focusing on a particular buyer group and segmenting that niche based on product line or geographic market.

Foreign bond is denominated not in US dollars, like the Euro bonds, but rather denominated in the currency of the country in which it is sold. Thus, an Argentinean peso denominated bond issued by the German car maker BMW in Argentina's domestic bond market is a foreign bond.

Foreign currency interest arbitrage is used to exploit interest rates overseas that are better than the ones available locally by trading financial products such as government treasury bills and corporate or government bonds denominated in different currencies.

Foreign exchange market consists of all transactions, worldwide, involved is the selling and buying of foreign currencies. It also consists of the interbank market, where the world's largest banks exchange currencies, the securities exchanges, which are physical locations where currency futures and options are bought and sold in smaller amounts than those traded in the interbank market and the over-the-counter (OTC) market, which is an exchange that exists as a global virtual network linking traders to one another.

Forms of regional integration include economic and trade cooperation, a free-trade area, a customs union, a common market, an economic union, and a political union.

Forward market is the over-the-counter financial market in contracts for future delivery, otherwise called forward contracts.

Forward rate is an exchange rate at which two parties agree to exchange on a specified future date.

Free trade area is an economic integration whereby countries remove all barriers to trade between themselves but each country determines its own barriers against nonmembers.

General Agreement on Tariffs and Trade (GATT) was a body formed in 1949 that governed rules and guidelines for the trade of goods between nations. In 1994, GATT was replaced with the World Trade Organization (WTO), an international institutional body that adopted the GATT mandate as well as enlarging the scope of its work to cover services and intellectual property.

Generally Accepted Accounting Principles (GAAP) is a standard framework of guidelines for accounting and includes the standards, conventions, and rules accountants follow in recording and summarizing transactions and in the preparation of financial statements. This term is used mainly in North America.

Global branding involves the exploitation of global brands and the economies of global distribution across functions and divisions at the local level.

Global distribution determines the best transportation mode of product to the foreign market as well as the best way to distribute the product locally within the target market. The process includes the identification of distribution channels within a country, degree of coverage, cost of distribution, after-sale services and support, and customer relationship management (CRM).

Global e-commerce is the conduct of electronic commerce, where B2B, B2C, C2C across national borders.

Global human resource management (HRM) entails the development of means and methods to build, develop, and retain executives and other personnel that enhance the MNE's global performance.

Global HRM challenge is to balance between a very broad understanding of the global objectives of the MNE while leveraging advantages of various foreign markets through the right mix of local expertise and corporate experience.

Global HRM complexity results from dealing with expatriates, deployment of the right mix of local, and global staff for each business situation and for each market, the need to consider the various government and cultural influences in different countries, and the need to have a global perspective when executing global HRM tasks.

Global HRM tasks are international staffing policy, training and development, international performance appraisal, employee compensation, and labor management relations.

Global marketing strategy of an MNE includes the assessment of target market attractiveness as well as the means and ways to integrate the linkages across countries, products and functions that exhaust market potential worldwide.

Global operations exploit national difference in the cost and quality of labor, talent, energy facilities, raw materials, and capital in order to enhance the productivity and cost structure of MNEs.

Global operations management is the set of activities required to create products and services through the transformation of inputs to outputs across international boundaries.

Global pricing strategies may take the form of worldwide pricing or dual pricing, and include transfer pricing, arm's length pricing, price controls, dumping, and parallel distribution.

Global product strategy deals with the issue of global standardization vs local customization and is based on the following elements: laws and regulations, cultural differences, brand and product names, nationality and product image, and lifelong costing.

Global promotion deals with promotion mix, push and pull strategies, international advertising, and other promotional tools, such as licensing or cross-promotion and online promotional tools.

Global sourcing describes the actions taken by a company to seek out and secure global suppliers in order to fulfill global demand for their product or service in the most cost effective and productive way.

Global strategic agreements include a structure of procedures and rules to govern the management of the new corporate entity; they allow for mutual learning, set the stage for higher value added and specify appropriate exit mechanisms.

Global strategic alliances (GSAs) are cross–border ventures between two or more corporations from different countries attempting to pursue mutual interests through sharing of resources and capabilities.

Global supply chain consists of a network of suppliers and corporate facilities that are dispersed across continents and deployed by most international industries.

Global value chain consists of R&D, operations system, distribution system, and after- sales services and support. These activities, along with supporting activities of information technology, human resource, quality and inventory management, add value to the product or service, command costs, and determine the profit margin and price flexibility for products and services delivered by the MNE.

Globalization entails the integration of markets for goods, services and capital, facilitated by multinational enterprises (MNEs) and global institutions, such as the International Monetary Fund (IMF), the World Trade Organization (WTO), the World Bank, and the United Nations.

Globalization awareness help executives to balance forces of standardization, coordination, and centralization against adherence to local adaptation and decentralization since globalization materializes in many ways and affects consumers, producers, managers, workers, and other participants in the world economy.

Globalization measurement is based on measuring economic integration, personal contact, technology connectivity, and political engagement.

Goods are tangible products (e.g., computer, chewing gum, cement truck).

Heckscher–Ohlin (HO) theorem explains the link between national factor endowments and comparative advantage of nations.

Host country national is an approach to staffing wherein individuals from the host country manage operations abroad.

Host country nationals (HCN) staffing is when individuals from the host country manage operations abroad. HCH staffing is well suited to MNEs and strives to give overseas subsidiaries a degree of autonomy in decision making.

Human resource management is the process of recruiting, selecting, training, developing, evaluating, and compensating employees.

Human resource planning is the process of forecasting and closing the gap between an MNE's human resource needs and human resource supply.

Human skills theory explains the source of a country's comparative advantage in terms of the comparative abundance of professional skills.

Hypertext transfer protocol (HTP) uses a set of rules for exchanging files such as text, graphic images, sound, video, and other multimedia files on the world wide web (www).

Independent float is a system where the exchange rate is allowed to adjust freely according to the supply and demand for a particular currency, used by both developed countries, such as USA as well as developing countries, such as Peru.

Indirect quote is a foreign exchange rate quoted as the foreign currency per unit of the domestic currency. In an indirect quote, the foreign currency is a variable amount and the domestic currency is fixed at one unit.

Infant industries protection may justify tariffs as the industry may be new to a country.

Initial cash flows are the funds required to set up, enter or initiate a project, and are typically the largest capital outlay of any project; they have a significant impact on the present value of the project.

Integrated services distribution system is required to supply complex and customized products that require high levels of service through customized integrated warehousing, repair, and return services and specialized call centers.

Interbank market is the most senior foreign exchange market where banks exchange different currencies.

Interbank rate is the rate that the largest banks charge one another for loans.

Intercompany financing is financing provided by the parent company in the form of equity, loans, trade credit, arranging trade credit from other subsidiaries or affiliates of the parent company or allowing the subsidiary to retain a higher level of its local profits.

Internal bank of an MNE buys and sells payables and receivables from the various subsidiaries, freeing their management teams from dealing with working capital financing, and lets them focus on the core business activities.

International Accounting Standards is gradually replacing Generally Accepted Accounting Principles (GAAP) as global business becomes more pervasive.

International Accounting Standards Board (IASB), or International Accounting Standards Committee (IASC), is an international organization that sets worldwide accounting recording and reporting standards, guidelines, and principles.

International bond market consists of all bonds issued and traded by MNEs or governments outside their own countries.

International business is all business activities, including the creation and transfer of resources, goods, services, know-how and intellectual property, skills and information, which transcend international boundaries.

International business corporate entities include multinational enterprises (MNEs), multi-domestic corporations (MDCs), transnational corporations (TNCs), early multinational corporations, born global corporations, international small and medium size enterprises (SMEs).

International capital markets provide an expanded supply of capital for borrowers by joining borrowers and lenders across different nations. It lowers the cost of money for borrowers by providing a greater supply of money and lowers the risk for lenders by providing a greater number of investments.

International cash-flow management includes cash pooling, netting and matching, lead and lag, reinvoicing, and internal banking.

International equity financing involves selling new shares to foreign investors or cross-listing the MNE's shares abroad at a foreign stock exchange.

International equity market consists of all the government and corporate shares that are issued and traded outside of the issuing organization's home country.

International Financial Reporting Standards (IFRS) is a single, harmonized, set of understandable, and enforceable global accounting standards used for financial reporting worldwide, while taking into account the special needs of small and medium-size enterprises (SMEs) and emerging economies. These standards were adopted by the International Accounting Standards Board (IASB).

International Organization of Securities Commissions (IOSCO) is an association of organizations that regulate the world's securities and futures markets, whose members are the Securities Commissions of 100 countries, with a secretariat in Madrid, Spain.

International outsourcing is the process by which a foreign company provides a local manufacturer with raw material, semi-finished products, sophisticated components, or technology for producing final goods that will be brought back by the foreign company.

International parity conditions model proposes that exchange rates between two currencies reflect the purchasing power difference of the currencies in the two countries.

International performance appraisal is the formal process of evaluating the effectiveness of executives and other employees in their jobs around the world.

International trade financing involves two parties to an international transaction which may not know each other, where the lead times for shipping the product is longer and the local business may not be familiar with the foreign business norms, practices, and local agencies.

Internet is a worldwide network of computer networks known as the world wide web (www).

Intracompany cash flows are cash flows between an MNE's parent company and its subsidiaries worldwide and are particularly vulnerable to the impact of currency fluctuations, exchange controls, and multiple tax jurisdictions.

Imitation lag is the inability of countries to immediately duplicate new products of an innovating country.

Import quotas are quantitative limitations on the amount of imports of goods in units or monetary value.

Investment banks are matching between national corporate entities in need of cash and large international equity buyers who are located anywhere in the world.

ISO 9000 is a family of worldwide proprietary and commercial standards related to quality management systems. An MNE can be certified that it meets the standards of their respective industry as defined by the International Organization for Standardization (ISO), a non-governmental organization with the ability to provide standards guidelines that often get adopted into law either through treaties or by the national standards bodies of participating countries.

Joint venture is an agreement whereby profits and responsibilities are assigned to each party according to a contractual agreement and, when its tasks are completed, it is terminated.

Just-in-time (JIT) operations require that inventory be kept to a minimum and that inputs to a production process arrive exactly when they are needed to be worked on and not stockpiled in advance. Thus, it reduces the costs associated with large inventories and helps reduce wasteful expenses because of defective materials or components that were sometimes only discovered after assembling the final product.

Just-in-time (JIT) manufacturing is a production technique for minimizing work-in-process inventory by ensuring that each piece arrives at the next step of the process when it is needed, rather than stockpiled in advance.

Keiretsu a term used in Japan that refers to a network of parts suppliers, subcontractors, and capital equipment suppliers that are tightly integrated and working very closely with the Japanese MNE to deliver a product or service. Typically all the companies that are part of a specific Keiretsu have interlocking business relationships and shareholdings that bind them together.

Labor management relations describe the relationship between an MNE's management and its workers.

Laissez-faire means freedom of enterprise and freedom of commerce.

Language training goes beyond a few phrases to instill a deeper understanding of the culture and thinking of the local culture through in depth study of their language and speaking norms.

Late movers are MNEs that enter a foreign market when market infrastructure is already developed, regulatory conditions are more favorable and the host country environment is more stable.

Lead and lag is making a payment between subsidiaries and the parent company earlier or later, respectively, in order to limit or take advantage of exchange rate fluctuations.

Lean manufacturing is an operations discipline that considers the tasks and expenditures of an MNE's value chain essential only if they create value to the customer. Otherwise, these tasks and expenditures should be eliminated.

Legal system of a country has a direct impact on accounting standards and practices.

Leontif paradox challenges the Heckscher-Ohlin theorem, showing that a country may not export goods that make intensive use of the country's abundant factor and do not import goods that make intensive use of the country's scarce factor.

Letter of credit is a document issued by a bank and provides an irrevocable payment for deals between a supplier in one country and a customer in another. The parties to a letter of credit are a beneficiary, who is to receive the money, the issuing bank of whom the applicant is a client, and the advising bank of whom the beneficiary is a client.

Leveraged buyouts (LBOs) are acquisitions of MNEs by management, financed mostly with debt underwritten by international consortium of banks.

Licensing fees is a charge, a fee or a royalty, applied by the parent company to a foreign subsidiary for the use of its own or third-party proprietary technology, equipment, or processes.

Local currency financing is initiated by a local subsidiary through bank sources (overdrafts, discounting, and loans) and nonbank sources to lower the MNE's overall cost of capital and capital financial risk.

London Interbank Bid Rate (LIBID) is the interest rate paid on Eurocurrency deposits. Used by financial institutions worldwide as a basis for financial transactions.

London Interbank Offered Rate (LIBOR) is the rate usually quoted on Eurocurrency loans. Used by financial institutions worldwide as a basis for financial transactions.

Long-term supply agreement is where the manufacturing buyer provides the supplier with updated free information on products, markets and technologies, which in turn help ensure the input quality and supply sustainability.

Maastricht Treaty was established in 1991 by EU member countries to launch a single currency, the euro, starting in 2002, to set up commonly defined monetary and fiscal targets for EU countries and to form a political union, including a common foreign and defense policy and common citizenship.

Main financial markets are the international bond market, international equity market, and the eurocurrency market.

Managed float system is a system of floating exchange rates with central bank intervention to reduce currency fluctuations.

Maquiladoras are free trade zones in Mexico that provide foreign companies who establish factories in the region to enjoy reduced taxes and tariffs.

Market economy is an economy based on the power of division of labor in which the price of goods and services are determined in a free price system set by supply and demand. As more countries change to market economy system, MNEs are seizing the opportunities to locate manufacturing plants in low wage and growth markets countries and make use of the grants, tax concessions, and other benefits provided by national, regional, local, and municipal governments.

Marketing, distribution, advertising, and promotion laws are based on moral principles, ethics, business practices, and social standards which regulate the design and operation of relevant MNEs' systems.

Matching is a netting process that involves netting with more than two parties.

Mercantilism, the first theory of international trade, proposes that the government has the ability to improve the well-being of its citizens using a system of centralized controls.

MERCOSUR was founded by Argentina, Brazil, Paraguay, and Uruguay to promote free trade and the free movement of goods, capital and people among the members. It has since expanded to a set of other associate members in South America including: Venezuela, Bolivia, Chile, Colombia, Ecuador, and Peru.

Mergers and acquisitions (M&A) is the buying, selling, and combining of different MNEs in order to grow rapidly an MNE in a given industry without having to create another business entity.

Mobile commerce (M-commerce) is the conduct of transactions to buy, sell, distribute or deliver goods and services over the Internet using cellular telecommunication technology, such as cell phones.

Multinational enterprise (MNE) is a large enterprise that engages in foreign direct investment and owns or controls value-adding activities in more than one country.

NAFTA is an agreement signed by the governments of United States, Canada and Mexico to reduce tariffs on trade and investment between the three countries. The trilateral agreement first took effect January 1, 1994.

National sovereignty is challenged if a shift in production to the most efficient location deprives a country of the base it needs to be a viable economic entity.

National culture and institutions may be threatened by free trade through adverse effects on a country's environment, safety, and workforce exploitation.

Net present value (NPV) is the net cash flows over the project's lifetime, discounted by the MNE's average cost of capital. The higher the NPV, the more attractive the project is.

Net present value for international investments should consider the NPV of the project, including currency fluctuations, foreign market differences, and changing regulations.

Netting is when two-way cash flows between subsidiaries, or between a subsidiary and the parent entity, are planned so that only one smaller cash flow is eventually sent, as opposed to having both cash flows transacted in full, reducing currency exchange charges for intra-MNE money transfers.

New trade theory proposes that countries do not necessarily specialize and trade just to take advantage of their differences in factors of production or technology but because economies of scale that causes increasing returns to a country.

Nonbank financing sources of funds include commercial paper, factoring, local bond, or equity markets, and parallel or back-to-back loans with a foreign company.

Nontariff barriers are indirect measures that discriminate against foreign manufacturers or service providers in the domestic market.

North American Free Trade Agreement (NAFTA) is an agreement signed by the governments of Canada, Mexico, and the United States, creating a trilateral trade bloc in North America. The agreement came into force on January 1, 1994 and is the largest in terms of combined purchasing power as of 2007.

Offset trade is an agreement whereby one party agrees to purchase goods and services with a specified percentage of its proceeds from an original sale.

Offshore financial centers (OFCs) provide offshore financial services and are usually found in countries that have relatively large financial organizations with assets and liabilities out of proportion to the size of the local economy.

Offshore financial services include off shore banking licenses, registration of offshore corporations or international business corporations (IBCs), incorporation of insurance companies in order to reduce actuarial reserve, locating special purpose investment vehicles to reduce tax burden, exploit opportunities of tax sheltering and tax evasion, reduce asset ownership risk, and protection.

Operating cash flows are the anticipated cash inflows and outflows over the course of the life of the project, once the project has become operational.

Operations management global trends include increased global competition, faster pace of technological development, increased customer focus (quality, speed, and flexibility), and the realization of the strategic importance of global operations management.

Optimal tariff theory proposes that by imposing a tariff on foreign product sold locally, governments can capture a significant portion of the manufacturer's profit margin, without affecting the price of the product for domestic customers.

Organizational commitment and **conflict avoidance** are key success factors for a sustainable and successful global strategic alliance (GSA).

Original equipment manufacturing (OEM) is a specific form of international outsourcing in which a foreign firm (i.e., original equipment manufacturer) supplies a local company with the technology and sophisticated components so that the latter can manufacture goods that the foreign firm will market under its own brand in international markets.

Overdraft is a line of credit against which drafts (checks) can be drawn (written) up to a specified maximum amount.

Overhead expenses are a charge applied by the parent company to the subsidiaries around the world for various administrative services, such as centralized treasury services or R&D support.

Parallel distribution happens when a buyer sources product meant for one country into a different one in order to take advantage of the price differential.

Parent country national (PCN) is an approach to staffing wherein individuals from the home country manage operations abroad.

Parent country nationals (PCN) staffing is when individuals from the home or parent country manage operations abroad.

Partner capability in the context of a global strategic alliance (GSA) may be assessed at three different levels: strategic, organizational, and financial.

Passive reciprocity occurs when a country refuses to lower its barriers to trade until the other country does the same.

Patent Cooperation Treaty allows for a single application for a patent that holds in all participating countries.

Political system of a country determines the broad economic policies and the business environment within which an MNE must interact.

Political union is an economic and political integration whereby countries coordinate aspects of their economic and political systems.

Preference similarity suggests that if two countries have the similar demand structures then their consumers and investors will demand the same goods with similar quality and sophistication.

Price controls governments in many countries regulate transfer prices for various products and services. Upper limit price controls are designed to provide price stability in an inflationary economy. Lower limit price controls prohibit the sale of a specific product or service below a certain price which is typically designed to protect local competition.

Process definition requires an MNE to define the business processes that they follow in providing the good or service to their customer.

Process improvement involves the continuous identification of bottlenecks or issues in a given process that can be improved to better service the customer.

Process management in order to best manage a given process, employees, and managers require factual data about the performance of each of the process tasks and the process as a whole. Should the company discovers gaps in expected performance, these must be addressed.

Productivity is the measure of throughput of a given individual, department, company or even country – the ratio between the outputs (goods and/or services) to inputs (labor, capital, and/or management). The greater the outputs per unit input, the greater the productivity.

Product life cycle includes all the stages a product goes through from idea through execution to obsolescence.

Product life cycle model proposes that changes occur in the input requirements of a new product as it becomes established in a market and standardized in production.

Product origin is determined based on the amount of the product value that was added domestically. It helps determine custom duties and tariffs as well as the degree of conformance to international trade laws and regulations.

Production factors consist mainly of labor, land, capital, and natural resources.

Production function expresses the amount of output that can be produced by using a given quantity of capital and labor.

Production subsidies are payments provided by governments to domestic companies in order to make them more competitive vis-à-vis foreign competitors.

Production system consists of production inputs such as land, labor, capital, information, and management, a transformation function and a set of outputs in the form of goods and services.

Promotion mix the portfolio of methods used by an MNE to target certain customer segments with different types and formats of information in order to influence their buying decision towards the physical product or service being offered. These methods include advertising, direct selling, promotions, press relations, and exhibitions.

Pull operations system reacts on time to market demand, as it is realized.

Pull strategies are a set of marketing strategies aimed at the end customer of the product in an effort to create large demand that will "encourage" channel partners to stock the product. Pull strategies include all forms of direct marketing to consumers such as: distribution of free samples, coupons, direct mailing, telemarketing or online campaigns, endorsements by influential people, sponsorship of events, and general advertising.

Push operations system builds inventories according to forecasted market demand.

Push strategies are a set of marketing strategies designed to incent or pressure the distribution channel in a given market to promote the MNE's product to the end customer. This is often done for consumer products and involves offering higher retail margins, marketing contribution funds or subsidizing "rebates." Depending on the strength of the MNE's brand a company could also threaten to cut distributors out of supply for popular products.

Recruitment is the process of identifying and attracting a qualified pool of applicants for vacant positions.

Regional economic integration is a process whereby countries in a geographic region cooperate with one another to reduce or eliminate barriers to the international flow of products, people, or capital.

Regional integration in Asia includes The Association of Southeast Asian Nations (ASEAN), established 1967, which includes 10 members (where China, Japan, and South Korea may join in the future) and The organization for Asia-Pacific Economic Cooperation (APEC), formed in 1989, which has 21 members. Together, the APEC nations account for more than half of world trade and a combined GDP of more than $16 trillion. APEC hopes to have free trade and investment throughout the region by 2010 for developed nations and 2020 for developing ones.

Regional integration in the Americas include the North American Free Trade Agreement (NAFTA) between Canada, Mexico, and the United States, established 1994; the Andean Community established in 1969; the Latin American Integration Association (ALADI), established in 1980; the Southern Common Market (MERCOSUR), established in 1988; the Caribbean Community and Common Market (CARICOM), established in 1973; the Central American Common Market (CACM), established in 1961; the Free Trade Area of the Americas (FTAA) encompassing all of Central, North, and South America (excluding Cuba); and the Transatlantic Economic Partnership (TEP) between the USA and the EU, designed to contribute to stability, democracy, and development worldwide.

Regional integration in the Middle East and Africa includes the Gulf Cooperation Council (GCC) of Bahrain, Kuwait, Oman, Qatar, Saudi Arabia, and the United Arab Emirates, formed in 1980; and the Economic Community of West African States (ECOWAS), formed in 1975 and relaunched in 1992.

Regional trading block is a group of nations in a geographic region undergoing economic integration.

Reinvoicing is when an MNE has one office or a subsidiary located in a low tax country, or a country with fewer restrictions on income assumes ownership for all the invoices and payments between the subsidiaries.

Repatriation is the process of integrating the expatriate into the MNE home country upon completion of an overseas assignment.

Reporting formats are standard forms of financial reporting, such as a balance sheet. The American format for balance sheet presentation is assets = liabilities + shareholder's equity. The European format is fixed assets + current assets – current liabilities – noncurrent liabilities = capital and reserves.

Research and Development, Ethnocentric (Home-Based) Centralized Model is when all research and development (R&D) activities are concentrated in the home country.

Research and Development, Geocentric (Foreign) Centralized Model combines the local market expertise from foreign sites while retaining the efficiencies of a centralized R&D center. This model is used when an MNE is dependent on foreign markets as well as local competencies.

Research and Development, Hub Model, seeks to combine tight central controls and resource allocation to avoid duplication of effort and ensure effective information sharing worldwide.

Research and Development, Integrated Network are where different sites around the world are treated as leaders in a specific field, component, or product and apply their specialization to a globally coordinated set of strategic goals.

Research and Development, Polycentric (Multiple), Decentralized Model evolves from a foreign site that was originally set up to respond to customer product localization and manufacturing and, following expansion of activities, results in a federation of R&D sites, each reporting locally and working more or less independently of the other.

Resource management planning involves the deployment of fixed assets, global sourcing, location planning, capacity planning, process planning, and facility layout planning.

Reverse culture shock a psychological process of readapting to one's home culture after an extended stay abroad.

Risk management of MNEs involves managing translation exposure, transaction exposure, and economic exposure by applying commercial hedging (home currency invoicing, mixed currency invoicing, or price escalation clauses), financial hedging (forward contracts, future contracts, options, and swaps), and intercompany financial programs, such as various international cash management tools or production-related programs (input sourcing, production arrangement).

Samurai bonds, Yankee bonds, Bulldog bonds, and **Dragon bonds** are foreign bonds issued and traded in Japan, the USA, the UK, and Asia (excluding Japan), respectively, and should meet local regulatory and disclosure requirements.

Selection is the process of screening, evaluating, and hiring the best qualified applicants with the greatest performance potential.

Sensitivity training teaches the expatriate to be considerate and understanding of the local peoples' feelings and emotions.

Services consist of mainly intangible products, including banking, consulting, and after-sale services and support.

Service trade includes the import and export of financial services, information services, education and training, transportation, tourism, entertainment, healthcare, accounting, and consulting services.

Six Sigma is an operational strategy that seeks to improve the quality of process outputs by identifying and removing the causes of defects and minimizing variability in manufacturing and business processes to the point where 99.99966 percent (3.4 defects per million) of the products manufactured or processes executed are free of defects.

Skilled services distribution system is required when supplying a complex and customized product that does not require a high level of service through dedicated warehousing and a skilled workforce to ensure setup, however after sales service and customer support may not be needed for these types of products.

Social commerce (s-commerce) is the conduct of transactions to buy, sell, distribute or deliver goods and services over the internet using social relationships drawn from digital social networks such as Facebook.

Special economic zone (SEZ) is a geographical region that has economic laws that are more liberal than a country's typical economic laws.

Spot rate is an exchange rate that requires delivery of the traded currency within two business days and is normally available only to large banks and foreign exchange brokers. These are used in large transactions between currency traders of international financial institutions.

Staffing policy entails three broad approaches: parent country national (PCN), host country national (HCN), and third country national (TCN).

Strategic business units (SBUs) are operating units with their own strategic space, value added, and profit accountability, producing goods and services to a defined market segment and a well-defined set of competitors.

Strategic synergy means additional economic benefits (financial, operational, or technological) arising from cooperation between two parties that provide each other with complementary resources or capabilities.

Strategy formulation is a process that involves evaluating the MNE's external environment and its internal environment resulting in a defined set of strategic directions.

Strategy implementation is the process of working towards strategic goals by using the organizational structure to execute the agreed upon strategy.

Subsidy is assistance provided to local businesses by the local government, giving a local company an unfair advantage over international competitors.

Supply chain management is the deployment of the network that links the various aspects of the value chain from product or service inception's activities to the final customer.

Target cost approach is an approach to product design wherein a target cost is given at the design stage as a further constraint to the design team ensuring cost minimization while optimizing for productivity and quality that would result in a product that can be launched at a price that positions it for business success.

Target zone system is applied when a group of countries share some common goals and adjust their national economic policies to maintain their exchange rates within a specific margin around agreed upon, fixed central exchange rates.

Tariff barriers are official constraints on importing of certain goods and services in the form of a total or a partial limitation or in the form of a special monetary levy.

Technical standards are rules and regulations sanctioned by government agencies regarding technical performance, safety, and the environment.

Technology gaps theory explains the source of a country's comparative advantage in terms of the comparative abundance of innovations and technology.

Temporal method requires that only monetary assets and liabilities (cash, receivables) are translated at the current exchange rate, while inventory, plants, and equipment are reported using historical exchange rates, that is, the rates that were in effect when the assets were acquired.

Terminal cash flows are the cash flows incurred at the end of a project and may include cash outflows involved in shutting down a project or cash inflows from the sale of whatever residual assets there are.

Terms of sale are conditions stipulating the rights or responsibilities and the costs or risks borne by the exporter and the importer as harmonized and defined by the International Chamber of Commerce.

Terms of trade is the relative price of exports, that is, the unit price of exports divided by the unit price of imports.

Third-country national is an approach to staffing where the best qualified individuals, regardless of nationality, manage the operations abroad.

Third country national (TCN) staffing is when the best-qualified individuals, regardless of nationality, manage the operations abroad. This policy is typically reserved for top-level executives.

Timing of entry involves the sequence of an MNE's entry into a foreign market vis-á-vis other MNEs (i.e., first mover, early follower, and late mover). Timing of entry is important because it determines the risks, environments, and opportunities the MNE may confront.

Total Quality Management (TQM) is a process that stresses customer satisfaction, continuous improvement and employee involvement, and strives to eliminate defects and to use best practices to reach a challenging benchmark.

Trade reciprocity occurs when countries open their borders on a bilateral basis for a free flow of goods and services.

Transfer pricing is the pricing for goods and services that the MNE sells to its own subsidiaries or affiliates. Set internally, transfer price has a direct impact on the buying of a subsidiary's profitability and the resulting tax obligations in its host country, and may be subjected to host-country scrutiny.

Transaction exposure is associated with contractual commitments to pay or receive a payment in a foreign currency for products, services, or even investments outside the home country.

Translation is the process of restating foreign currency financial statements into a single currency (such as US dollars or English pounds) for consolidated international financial reporting purposes. There are two methods of translation: current-rate method and temporal method.

United Nations organization was founded by member countries in order to foster peace and political stability around the world. It was founded after the Second World War and includes agencies that provide food and medical supplies, educational training, and financial resources to member countries.

Value chain is the way in which primary and support activities of an MNE are combined to provide products and services to increase profit margins and add value to the goods or services.

Value density refers to the value of a product relative to its volume and weight.

Vertical integration is the ownership of all assets needed to produce the goods and services delivered to the costumer, obtaining control of the supply chain, and ensuring that the materials or goods are delivered as needed.

Working capital management is managing the operating and financing inflows and outflows of cash in a particular investment and across the enterprise.

Worldwide pricing policy establishes one price for all international markets. In practice this is a very difficult policy to pursue for many reasons, such as the differences across markets with regards to distance to supply, local competition, and fluctuations in currency rates.

World wide web (www) constitutes all the resources and users on the Internet that use hypertext transfer protocol (HTP or HTTP).

INDEX

Figures in **bold**; Tables in *italics*